HERODOTUS AND THE QUESTION WHY

The Fordyce W. Mitchel Memorial Lecture Series, sponsored by the Department of History at the University of Missouri–Columbia, began in October 2000. Fordyce Mitchel was Professor of Greek History at the University of Missouri–Columbia until his death in 1986. In addition to his work on fourth-century Greek history and epigraphy, including his much-cited Lykourgan Athens: 338–322, Semple Lectures 2 (Cincinnati: 1970), Mitchel helped to elevate the ancient history program in the Department of History and to build the extensive library resources in that field. The lecture series was made possible by a generous endowment from his widow, Mrs. Marguerite Mitchel. It provides for a biennial series of lectures on original aspects of Greek history and society, given by a scholar of high international standing. The lectures are then revised and are currently published by the University of Texas Press.

PREVIOUS MITCHEL PUBLICATIONS:

Carol G. Thomas, *Finding People in Early Greece* (University of Missouri Press, 2005)
Mogens Herman Hansen, *The Shotgun Method: The Demography of the Ancient Greek City-State Culture* (University of Missouri Press, 2006)
Mark Golden, *Greek Sport and Social Status* (University of Texas Press, 2008)
Joseph Roisman, *Alexander's Veterans and the Early Wars of the Successors* (University of Texas Press, 2012)

HERODOTUS AND
THE QUESTION WHY

Christopher Pelling

UNIVERSITY OF TEXAS PRESS, AUSTIN

This book has been supported by an endowment dedicated to classics and the ancient world and funded by the Areté Foundation; the Gladys Krieble Delmas Foundation; the Dougherty Foundation; the James R. Dougherty, Jr. Foundation; the Rachael and Ben Vaughan Foundation; and the National Endowment for the Humanities.

Copyright © 2019 by the University of Texas Press
All rights reserved
Printed in the United States of America
First edition, 2019
First paperback printing, 2021

Requests for permission to reproduce material from this work should be sent to:
    Permissions
    University of Texas Press
    P.O. Box 7819
    Austin, TX 78713-7819
    utpress.utexas.edu/rp-form

♾ The paper used in this book meets the minimum requirements of ANSI/NISO Z39.48-1992 (R1997) (Permanence of Paper).

LIBRARY OF CONGRESS CATALOGING-IN-PUBLICATION DATA

Names: Pelling, C. B. R., author.
Title: Herodotus and the question why / Christopher Pelling.
Other titles: Fordyce W. Mitchel Memorial Lecture Series.
Description: First edition. | Austin : University of Texas Press, 2019. | Series: The Fordyce W. Mitchel memorial lecture series | Includes bibliographical references and index.
Identifiers: LCCN 2018044471
ISBN 978-1-4773-2425-7 (PAPERBACK)
ISBN 978-1-4773-1833-1 (library e-book)
ISBN 978-1-4773-1834-8 (nonlibrary e-book)
Subjects: LCSH: Herodotus—Criticism and interpretation. | History, Ancient—Historiography. | Greece—Historiography.
Classification: LCC PA4004 .P35 2019 | DDC 938.0072/02—dc23
LC record available at https://lccn.loc.gov/2018044471

doi:10.7560/318324

CONTENTS

Abbreviations ix

Preface xiii

CHAPTER 1 Why did it all happen?
(a) "Mother, what did they fight each other for?" *1*
(b) The words *5*
(c) Narrative: Show, not tell *11*
(d) Explanation: A game for two *13*
(e) Historical consciousness *15*
(f) Reconstructing mentalities *17*

CHAPTER 2 To blame and to explain: Narrative complications
(a) The proem *22*
(b) The exchange of abductions (1.1–5) *25*
(c) Payback and its complications *30*
(d) Whose fault is it anyway? *34*
(e) Them and us *38*

CHAPTER 3 How can you possibly know?
(a) Putting in the working *40*
(b) Scientific and historical explanation *46*
(c) Stories in cahoots *55*

CHAPTER 4 Adventures in prose
(a) Something different? *58*
(b) Hecataeus *62*
(c) Other peoples and their past *66*

(d) Rhetorical finger-pointing *68*

(e) Sameness and difference *75*

CHAPTER 5 Hippocratic affinities

(a) Medical science *80*

(b) Harmonious balancing *84*

(c) Corroboration and revision *88*

CHAPTER 6 Explanations in combination

(a) Hippocratics *94*

(b) Herodotus *101*

CHAPTER 7 Early moves

(a) Croesus and Candaules *106*

(b) Croesus: Pride, aggression, downfall *110*

CHAPTER 8 Empire

(a) Croesus again *114*

(b) From Cyrus to Xerxes *119*

(c) Blame? *123*

CHAPTER 9 Herodotus' Persian stories

(a) The world of the court *129*

(b) Biography? *133*

(c) Be careful what you say . . . *136*

(d) Overconfidence? *139*

(e) But are we so different? *142*

CHAPTER 10 The human and the divine

(a) Divine perspectives *146*

(b) Enigmatic divinity *149*

(c) Historical explanation? *156*

CHAPTER 11 Explaining victory *163*

CHAPTER 12 Freedom

(a) Inspiration *174*

(b) The unruly free *181*

(c) Freedom from and freedom to *184*

CHAPTER 13 Democracy
    (a) Democracy and freedom? *190*
    (b) Characterizing the *dēmos* *192*
    (c) Democracy in and out of focus *195*

CHAPTER 14 Individuals and collectives
    (a) Self-expression? *199*
    (b) Narrative shape *200*
    (c) Individuals and communities *201*
    (d) An Athenian virtue? *204*
    (e) National characteristics? *210*

CHAPTER 15 Then and now: Herodotus' own day
    (a) Shadows of the future *214*
    (b) Thinking backwards and forwards *223*
    (c) Back to the future *229*

CHAPTER 16 Why indeed? *232*

Notes *237*
Bibliography *301*
Passages in Herodotus *328*
Passages in Other Authors *337*
General Index *346*

ABBREVIATIONS

Abbreviations of authors and works normally follow the form in Liddell, Scott, and Jones (LSJ) and in the *Oxford Latin Dictionary*. An author's name in square brackets, e.g., [Aesch.] or [Longin.], indicates a work attributed to that author but unlikely to be his work.

All references to the Hippocratic Corpus give first the relevant Loeb volume and then the volume of Littré's ten-volume edition (Paris, 1839–1861).

BNJ	I. Worthington (ed.), *Brill's New Jacoby* (2006–): http://referenceworks.brillonline.com/browse/brill-s-new-jacoby.
DK	H. Diels and W. Kranz, *Fragmente der Vorsokratiker* (12th ed., Dublin and Zürich, 1966).
EGM	R. L. Fowler, *Early Greek Mythography* i–ii (Oxford, 2001–2013).
Fornara	C. Fornara, *Translated Documents of Greece & Rome* i: *Archaic Times to the End of the Peloponnesian War* (2nd ed., Cambridge, 1983).
FGrH	F. Jacoby et al., *Fragmente der griechischen Historiker* (Leiden, 1923–).
HCT	A. W. Gomme, A. Andrewes, and K. J. Dover, *A Historical Commentary on Thucydides* (Oxford, 1944–1981).
IG	*Inscriptiones Graecae* (Berlin, 1873–).
LSJ	H. Liddell and R. Scott, *Greek-English Lexicon* (9th ed., rev. H. Stuart-Jones, Oxford 1940; revised suppl. by P. G. W. Glare and others, Oxford, 1988).
ML	R. Meiggs and D. Lewis, *A Selection of Greek Historical Inscriptions to the End of the Fifth Century BC*, revised ed. (Oxford, 1988).
OCD[1]	S. Hornblower, A. Spawforth, and E. Eidinow (eds.), *Oxford Classical Dictionary* (4th ed., Oxford, 2012).

PMG D. L. Page, *Poetae Melici Graeci* (Oxford, 1962).
J. E. Powell, *Lexicon* J. E. Powell, *A Lexicon to Herodotus* (Cambridge, 1938; repr. Hildesheim, 1977).
POxy *Oxyrhynchus Papyri* (1898–).
R–E A. Pauly, G. Wissowa, and W. Kroll, *Real-Encyclopädie der klassischen Altertumswissenschaft* (Stuttgart, 1893–1980).
SVF H. von Arnim, *Stoicorum Veterum Fragmenta* (Leipzig, 1903–1924).
TGrF A. Nauck et al., *Tragicorum Graecorum Fragmenta* (Göttingen, 1889–).
Waterfield Translation in R. Waterfield and C. Dewald, *Herodotus: The Histories* (Oxford 1998).

ANCIENT AUTHORS AND WORKS

Abbreviated Author	Full Name of Author	Abbreviated Title of Work	Full Title of Work
Ael.	Aelian	NA	De natura animalium
		VA	Varia Historia
Aesch.	Aeschylus	Cho.	Choephori
		Pers.	Persians
Amm. Marc.	Ammianus Marcellinus		
Ar.	Aristophanes	Ach.	Acharnians
Arist.	Aristotle	NE	Nicomachean Ethics
		Phys.	Physics
		Poet.	Poetics
		Pol.	Politics
		Rhet.	Rhetoric
Cic.	Cicero	de Inv.	De Inventione
		de Or.	De Oratore
		Fin.	De Finibus
		Orat.	Orator ad M. Brutum
Clem. Al.	Clemens Alexandrinus	Strom.	Stromateis
Ctes.	Ctesias		
Dem.	Demosthenes		
Diod.	Diodorus Siculus		

ABBREVIATIONS

Abbreviated Author	Full Name of Author	Abbreviated Title of Work	Full Title of Work
Eur.	Euripides	Alex.	Alexander
		Hel.	Helen
		Hipp.	Hippolytus
		Or.	Orestes
		Phoen.	Phoenissae
		Suppl.	Suppliants
Galen		Comm. on	Commentary on
		Epid.	Epidemics
		Prorrhet.	Prorrhetikon
Gorg.	Gorgias		
Hdt.	Herodotus		
Hell. Oxy.			Hellenica Oxyrhynchia
Hes.	Hesiod	Theog.	Theogonia
Hymn. Hom.	Homeric Hymns	h.Ap.	Homeric Hymn to Apollo
Homer		Il.	Iliad
		Od.	Odyssey
Hyp.	Hypereides		
Isoc.	Isocrates	Busir.	Busiris
		Paneg.	Panegyricus
Luc.	Lucian		
Lyc.	Lysias	Alex.	Alexander
Nic. Dam.	Nicolaus Damascenus		
Paus.	Pausanias		
Phot.	Photius	bibl.	bibliotheca
Pind.	Pindar	P.	Pythian Odes
Pl.	Plato	Apol.	Apology
		Euthyd.	Euthydemus
		Gorg.	Gorgias
		Menex.	Menexenus
		Phd.	Phaedo
		Phaedr.	Phaedrus
		Prot.	Protagoras
		Rpb.	Republic
		Symp.	Symposium
		Tim.	Timaeus
Plb.	Polybius		
Plin.	Pliny (the Elder)	NH	Natural History

Abbreviated Author	Full Name of Author	Abbreviated Title of Work	Full Title of Work
Ptolemaios Chennos		*ap. Phot.*	As cited by Phot.
Plut.	Plutarch	*Apoph. Lac.*	*Apophthegmata Laconica*
		Arist.	*Aristeides*
		Cim.	*Cimon*
		Cor.	*Coriolanus*
		Them.	*Themistocles*
Ps.-Xen.	Pseudo-Xenophon	*Ath. Pol.*	*Athenaiōn Politeia*
Quint.	Quintilian		
Thuc.	Thucydides		
Xen.	Xenophon	*Anab.*	*Anabasis*
		Cyr.	*Cyropaedia*
		Hell.	*Hellenica*
		Mem.	*Memorabilia*

PREFACE

The origins of this book lie a long way in the past, in a two-year Leverhulme Fellowship that I gratefully held in the 1990s. Its theme was then envisaged rather differently, as "Character and Cause in the Greek Historians": that was prompted by an awareness that the historians had been neglected in a collected volume I had edited on characterization and individuality (Pelling 1990a). Those years allowed some first immersion in the Hippocratic corpus, and that in turn broadened the interest to historical explanation in general. I delivered some ruminations along those lines in the inaugural Christopher Roberts lecture that I had the honor of giving at Dickinson College in 1998, entitled "Causes, Scientific and Other: Hippocratics and Historians." As is the way with academic life (especially mine), other papers and projects and responsibilities then intervened, but at least—to use a distinction that will often figure in this book—there was by then a "disposition" to get a book written, and one that I hoped might be of interest not just to classicists but also to historiographic theorists and perhaps even to philosophers. That aspiration is still there. The "trigger" then came with the invitation to give the Fordyce Mitchel lectures at Columbia, Missouri, in October 2008. In a delightful week spent there, graciously hosted by Ian Worthington, I duly delivered three lectures under the title "How the Greek Historians Explained History," with one lecture each on Herodotus, Thucydides, and Polybius. A book with the same title was envisaged and contracted. I was even rash enough to promise it in print (2013b: 19).

That turned out to prefigure two other features discussed in this book: first, the way that a preparatory remark can often mislead the reader (and in this case the writer) about how long there will be to wait (p. 115) and second, the frequent need for "progressive correction" and "revision in stride" (chapter 5[c]). Distractions did not melt away with age; and it also became embarrassingly clear that a book covering all those authors would strain any reader's patience beyond endurance. A draft chapter on the Homeric background itself weighed in at more than 10,000 words. (It has been rescued from the cutting-room floor and rewritten as a sister paper, Pelling forthcoming [d].) I was most grateful for agreement with the University of Texas Press to recast the project to focus on Herodotus, though not on him alone: Thucydides and Polybius will appear from time to time as well, with some vestiges of those original Fordyce Mitchel lectures, and anyway it will be argued that we need to investigate more broadly the mindset that Herodotus could assume in his readers and hearers. What do they know of Herodotus who only Herodotus know?

Few of those distractions were unpleasant, and some were extremely helpful for this book, particularly my collaboration with Simon Hornblower on our green-and-yellow Cambridge commentary on book 6: I learned a great deal from my coauthor, and a commentator faces a salutary need to test grand generalizations against the awkward detail of the text itself. Some of my papers on Herodotus also developed ideas that surface again in various chapters here: the way in which East and West do and do not contrast, the role of the constitutions debate in its context, the intertextuality with Homer, the complexities of the Croesus-*logos*, and the interplay of speech and narrative (respectively Pelling 1997c, 2002b, 2006a, 2006b, and 2006c, the last bringing together points more fully argued in other papers). Some reflections on counterfactual history then came in Pelling 2013b.

As the book came closer to its final form, some sections were given airings more or less as they appear here. Thus a version of chapter 9 was delivered as the annual *Syllecta Classica* lecture in Iowa and has been published as Pelling 2016b, and some parts of chapters 5 and especially 6 have overlaps with Pelling 2018. The exceptionally curious would be able to run down echoes of shorter passages in others of my papers and books, including some not on Herodotus at all. In many cases these duplications have allowed an abbreviated or more sharply focused version here, but I still apologize. The cost in trees may be at least partly compensated by the convenience to readers, not all of whom will have access to a well-stocked library or a complete set of online subscriptions.

Parts have been shared with other audiences, too, in Charlottesville, Boulder, Leeds, Reading, London, Newcastle, Washington, Cambridge, and (several times) Oxford. I am most grateful to all those hearers and also to Emily Baragwanath, Simon Hornblower, Edith Foster, and Hans Kopp who read the entire manuscript; to Katherine Harloe, Charlie Kozeny-Pelling, Jessica Lightfoot, Judith Mossman, Robin Nicholas, and Rosalind Thomas for help on particular points and chapters; and to several Herodotean and historiographic friends whose conversations have over many years shaped the way I think about these authors: Carolyn Dewald, Michael Flower, John Marincola, Rosaria Munson, Philip Stadter, Tim Rood, Stephanie West, and many more. Another theme of the book is that blameworthiness is invariably a very complex matter; but after so much help and so much stimulating talk, the blame for remaining blemishes rests firmly with me.

All translations, unless otherwise stated, are my own.

Christopher Pelling
Oxford
April 2018

HERODOTUS AND THE QUESTION WHY

CHAPTER I

WHY DID IT ALL HAPPEN?

(A) "MOTHER, WHAT DID THEY FIGHT EACH OTHER FOR?"

On an autumn day in the year 480 b.c., watchmen on the peaks between Halicarnassus and Termera signalled the battle-fleet of Queen Artemisia returning from the west. As the ships rounded the point opposite Cos, and the Coan squadron veered southward, it was clear that there had been losses. When the flagship entered the bay south of the city it was seen that its prow was damaged; and when the fleet came to moorings the first call was for shore-boats to land the wounded. The face of the Queen-admiral was set and sad.

On the quay Rhoio, wife of Lyxes, her bright cheeks aglow with excitement—her name means "Pomegranate"—held fast her five-year-old "Gift from Hera," wide-eyed, alert, for ever asking questions and putting together answers. And, as they turned towards home there was one more question, never fully answered for him: Mother, what did they fight each other for?
(MYRES 1953: 1)

So began Sir John Myres' book *Herodotus, Father of History*. Whether or not Herodotus' interest in historical explanation really began at the age of five, it certainly preoccupied the man as an adult: "One thing we should not doubt is the seriousness of Herodotus' commitment to explain."[1] His very first sentence, amply sketching the vast range that the work will cover, comes down at the end to "including in particular why they came to war with one another." τά τε ἄλλα καὶ δι' ἣν αἰτίην ἐπολέμησαν ἀλλήλοισι (below, p. 22)—the phrase that inspired Myres' lovely vignette. One may suspect, too, that Myres was right in saying that the question was never fully answered for him. Any simple or single answer would never be enough.

Not that explanation is Herodotus' only concern. That phrase is literally "other things and" why they came to war—regular Greek idiom for "and especially" or "and in particular, but the "other things" are important too. The sentence has already promised what is "wonderful" or "marvelous," *thōmasta*, in human achievements (below, p. 24), and Herodotus' curiosity will indeed extend to much that is marvelous for its own sake, not for what it explains. Still, explanation will indeed be a central concern, and not just of the war, nor indeed just of human events and actions. Herodotus is interested in explaining phenomena of the physical world as well. Why does the Nile flood (2.20–27)? Why are Egyptian skulls so much tougher than Persian? Why are the most timid creatures the most prolific, and the most vicious the least (3.108–109)? Why are Libyans so healthy (4.187)? What explains the peculiar geography of Thessaly (7.129)? If no explanation is available, that can be a matter of comment—he cannot explain why there are no mules in Elis (4.30.1); and "I wonder what can be the explanation" (θωμάζω δὲ τὸ αἴτιον—"wonder," that distinctive Herodotean word)[2] why lions should have attacked camels one night but no other creatures, when they would never have seen any before (7.125).

Nor should we underrate the logic of his argumentation: that emerges clearly from Rosalind Thomas' outstanding book.[3] It cannot be the tradewinds that explain the Nile flood, for there are times when they have not blown and the Nile flooded anyway, and if that were the explanation, other rivers would show the same phenomenon to an even greater extent (2.20.2–3). The argument that then follows may be wrong, but it is based on sound empirical principles, drawing the inferences that best fitted the generalizations that the knowledge of the day would support:[4] to explain it in terms of melting snow would imply the presence of snow in a region that all the evidence suggested was hot and dry (2.22), and it was better to think in terms of the visible path of the sun, dipping lower in winter so that it draws the water to it by evaporation, then releasing the flow in summer (2.24–27). This is following the Presocratic principle that "the evident phenomena are a sight of what is unclear" (ὄψις ἀδήλων τὰ φαινόμενα, Anaxagoras DK 59 B 21a, cf. Democritus DK 68 A 111),[5] a phrase that Herodotus echoes a little later when discussing the symmetry of Nile and Danube (ὡς ἐγὼ συμβάλλομαι τοῖσι ἐμφανέσι τὰ μὴ γινωσκόμενα τεκμαιρόμενος, "so I conjecture, drawing conclusions from what is evident to what is not perceived," 2.33.2)[6] and a principle that we can see him applying elsewhere in his text.[7] Herodotus' predecessor Hecataeus could reasonably have claimed to be doing the same if he explained the Nile flood in terms of an encircling Ocean (p. 64), but for Herodotus "the man who spoke about Ocean"—Hecataeus is left unnamed—"refers the story to the realm of the nonevident, and offers no way of testing what he said (or 'refuting' it, οὐκ ἔχει ἔλεγχον)"; anyway "I know" no such stream as "Ocean," and that is likely to be pure invention by Homer or some earlier poet (2.23).[8] So "Ocean" cannot count among things that are evident or known after all, whatever "the man who spoke about it" may have thought: empirical knowledge ("I know"), and the possibility of rational testing and verifying or refuting are essential to claiming a causal explanation.

What, then, about the history of events? One of the questions for this book will be how far Herodotus approached historical explanation—not least "why they came to war with another"—in the same way and with the same techniques as scientific explanation. Is explaining why Xerxes invaded felt to be the same type of exercise as explaining why the Nile floods, or for that matter why a human body gets ill, or even why and how the *cosmos* came about? Evidently empirical testing is going to be hard to conduct in quite the same way, but it can immediately be seen that there are some analogies, ones that we will examine more closely in chapter 3.[9] Both with history and with science Herodotus can play with counterfactuals: what would happen if the Nile flowed into the Arabian gulf rather than the Mediterranean (2.11.4)? What would be the consequences for the Danube if the sun passed across the sky in the north rather than the south (2.26.2)? What would have happened if the Athenians had gone over to Xerxes (7.139)? What would the Phocians have done if the Thessalians had not Medized (8.30.2)? Scientific investigation involved a careful use of analogy to identify similarities and differences: how do other north-flowing rivers behave? How can Nile and Danube illuminate one another? How do we explain perceived similarities between Egyptian and Colchian (2.104)? Here too we may find some parallels in the way Herodotus guides his audience to reflect on events, both noticing analogies and differences between events within his own narrative—expansionist Persian kings who eventually stumble, or different freedom struggles with different outcomes—and linking his own narrative with others familiar to his audience from literature or from life (the Trojan War, the first phases of the Peloponnesian War). History, ethnography, geography—all come together not just as curiosities of the world that were all fascinating but also as phenomena that repaid investigation along similar lines.

When such audience familiarity is indeed based on life, it may even emerge as a parallel to "drawing conclusions from what is evident" for what happened in the past: when he notes that the Corinthians and Corcyreans "are at odds with one another and have been continually, kinsmen as they are, ever since they first colonized the island" (3.49.1), any audience that remembered the friction between the two in the late 430s would nod in agreement and be more ready to accept Herodotus' inferred explanation for Corinthian behavior several generations earlier (pp. 56, 226). And, if Herodotus' work reached its final form some time in the 420s (pp. 215–217), readers and hearers would also know the cataclysmic consequences that followed those later squabbles: such animosities, in that case as in others, can lead to very big and very bloody things indeed.

Philosophers and theorists of historiography still debate how far scientific and historical explanation can work in quite the same way:[10] more on that in chapter 3. But we should not find it surprising that in Herodotus' own day explanations of social and political phenomena, the historians' typical concern, do not seem to have been regarded as belonging in a separate category from everything else.[11] Heraclitus and Parmenides could talk of cosmic patterns as regulated by the principle of justice (or retaliation, *dikē*), a word naturally used of human and societal exchanges (DK 22 B 94, DK 28 A 37, DK B 8.14); Anaximander had done the same, combining the word with *tisis*, "payback" (DK 12 B 1). Alcmaeon of Croton, probably about the same time as Heraclitus or a little later, is said to have conceived the body as a sort of *isonomia* of powers that ran the risk of "monarchy" if any element came to dominate (DK 24 B 4, cited at p. 84)[12]—*isonomia*, an "equality of rights" or "assignment by equality," later became a catchword for democracy (p. 191). Democritus, if we can trust Aristotle's language, described the initial chaotic motion of atoms by the verb *stasiazein*—they were "in faction" with one another (DK 68 A 37 = Arist. fr. 208 Rose). The Hippocratic *Airs Waters Places* uses the same word *stasiazein* to describe different sorts of water fighting one another in the human body until one "prevails" ([*kratei*], 9 I p. 94 J = II p. 38 L), and speaks of the ideal climate being one in which an "equal portioning" (*isomoiriē*) of the elements "prevails" (*kratei* again, 12 I p. 106 J = II p. 54 L). Historians and dramatists naturally wrote about "diseased" states, and Plato often compared the role of the statesman to that of a physician; medical writers would talk of the brain as the "metropolis" of the body or of one element "playing the master" (*dunasteuon* or *dunastēs*).[13] Elsewhere we can trace a much more elaborate imaging of the universe in terms of a human body, most strikingly in the Hippocratic *On Regimen* I and *On Sevens*.[14]

We naturally talk of such language as "metaphors" or "analogies" drawn from one domain and applied to another:[15] this indeed is the way that Beer put it in her brilliant study of "Darwin's plots," for instance his use of metaphors such as life as a "tangled bank" or a "struggle for existence,"[16] and similar language is used by Lakoff and Johnson in their *Metaphors We Live By*.[17] That is doubtless right for the nineteenth century and the modern world, but not for the fifth century BCE.[18] Then it was more than that, reflecting an assumption (at least a provisional assumption, one we stick to until it has been proved wrong) that there is what we might call an "integrated universe," with similar clockwork making each part of it tick.[19] To talk of the human body in societal language or the other way round is not a fleeting, casual analogy,[20] any more than it was a casual analogy for Presocratic philosophers to figure the birth of the universe in terms of human or animal procreation;[21] it is more like a modern physician examining a bruised right wrist and looking at the left one to see how it ought to look. In its way, it is a further application of ὄψις ἀδήλων τὰ φαινόμενα, "the evident phenomena are a sight of what is unclear" (p. 2).

So historians' causal schemes ought not to be a law unto themselves; their cogency will indeed be enhanced by the way they fit into the manner in which readers and hearers are accustomed to think about other matters. It is also because of suspicion of "borrowing" language that I will speak more about "affinities" than "influences":[22] what I am concerned with are similarities of mindset and conceptualization. The question remains how deep those similarities can really go. In particular, Herodotus writes narrative (section (c) below): not always linear narrative, to be sure, and narrative with many loops and byways, but narrative all the same. From Homer on, narrators have their own ways of making intelligible the events they describe. Narrative insinuates more often than it argues. It often suggests perspectives that supplement Herodotus' explicit comments; it sometimes points in a quite different direction. For the moment, it is enough to note that the *Histories* are saturated in explanation, as Herodotus struggles not merely to describe the wondrous things of the world but also to understand them. Explanation is part of his "voiceprint."[23]

(B) THE WORDS

Herodotus would not have had a single word for "explanation." It is not a single thing, even if the question "why" may seem clear enough. Events and phenomena can be looked at, and can be found puzzling, in a number of ways, and different people—or the same person in a different mood or mindset—can put different questions to them. This book will interpret the word broadly as well. It is best to focus on what explanation may hope to achieve, and that is to make something more *understandable*. That something may be, and often is, a war's outbreak, or it may be its outcome, or it may be something entirely different: all will feature in later chapters. Explaining will often be a question of seeing what led to something, a matter of causation: it would not or might not have happened if some prior condition had not been fulfilled. But by the end of this chapter we shall begin to see that there are other ways too of rendering something more intelligible, by locating it in a framework of experience that can be acknowledged as familiar, as a phenomenon by which we need no longer be perplexed.

Let us look at causation first. Herodotus may not have had a single word for causal explanation, but he certainly has some of the verbal and conceptual tools for the job. Lexically, *aiti-* roots are a basic resource. The verb-form *aitiaomai* carries a strong sense of "blame," but that aspect is less felt in the neuter *to aition*, "what is responsible," and this is the form that, like the Hippocratics,[24] he tends to use when discussing physical causes or phenomena. We saw this in his "wondering what could be *to aition*" for the strangely selective lion attack on the camels (above, p. 2). Thus, the neuter is used also of the disingenuous physical explanation that the failed navigator gives when he did not complete his circumnavigation of Africa (4.43.6) and also for the reason for the withdrawal and then the sudden inrush of the waters to drown the Persian forces at Potidaea (8.129).[25] Similarly when the people of Apollonia send to ask the oracles what is the cause (*to aition*) of their present dearth (9.93.4), the answer will in fact point a blaming finger at human individuals, but they do not know this when they pose the question. But, again like the Hippocratics, even with physical phenomena he can use the *aitios* adjectival formation and make it grammatically agree with the presumed cause: that rejected explanation for the Nile flood held the tradewinds to be *aitious*, 2.20.2. If there is "blame" implied there, it is in an extended sense, as when we "blame the weather," or "bad luck" or even "life" for a setback: if we really meant that morally, we would have an odd moral sense (which does not mean that such cases cannot carry moral *implications*, as they can let other, more morally responsible agents off the hook). It is possible too, though rare, to use the neuter form even in cases where human or divine decisions will be in point, such as when the Spartans seem momentarily sanguine over the possibility of Athenian Medism at the beginning of book 9:

> I cannot give an explanation (οὐδ' ἔχω εἰπεῖν τὸ αἴτιον) for the way that the Spartans had exerted great effort to prevent Athenian Medism when Alexander of Macedon arrived at Athens [at the end of Book 8], but were now unconcerned—except for the fact that the Isthmus wall had now been built and they thought they had no more need of the Athenians, whereas at the time of Alexander's arrival in Attica the wall had not yet been built and they were working hard on it in fear of the Persians. (9.8.2)

Normally, though, with humans the adjective *aitios* is used of the person held responsible, and the element of moral blame is more strongly felt. Generally, though not quite always, it is strongly focalized: blame is in the eye of the beholder. The word is often found together with *adikiē*, the "injustice" that individuals are blamed for. In such cases not merely blame but also punishment is often in point, as it is when Cleomenes is determined to arrest the Aeginetans who are "most to blame," *aitiōtatous*, for the decision to offer Darius earth and water (6.50.1). That superlative implies that there can be degrees of blameworthiness, with others who were also *aitioi* but to a lesser degree. No surprise, then, that it can also become an issue how broadly the blame should spread: are, for instance, the ordinary people *metaition*, do they "share the blame," for a course of action initiated by their leaders? (See 4.200.1, where the answer is Yes, below, p. 127; 7.156.2, where it is No.)[26] So, as with other uses of that word *metaitios* (2.100.3, 4.202.1, 8.101.2, 9.88), blame can clearly be shared, just as later we will see Herodotus dealing comfortably with a confluence of several different causes (chapter 6[b]). That word *metaitios*, "sharing the blame," is another that is used by the Hippocratics (pp. 89, 100).

Blame too is generally in point with the abstract *aitiē* or its plural *aitiai*, for which the best translation can sometimes be "charge." It is used of the reason why Darius sets about punishing a corrupt judge (7.194.1) or why Xerxes is about to execute the navigator who has not completed his mission and hence has not atoned for an earlier rape (4.43.2), whereas Cambyses executes prominent Persians "on no *aitiē* that deserved such a response" (3.35.5). Even when it is not a question of punishing someone on a "charge," there is usually an element of "blame" or "grievance" or "criticism," deserved or undeserved. Ephialtes is in fact killed "on another *aitiē*," not for showing Xerxes the path around Thermopylae (7.213.3) but that clearly was the act of treachery that one might expect to be the reason, and "I put him down as *aitios* for that" (7.214.3). Within half a page of one another, there is *aitiē* that Cleomenes was having an affair with Isagoras' wife, and (twice) the Alcmaeonids incur *aitiē* for the death of Cylon and his followers (5.70.1, 5.70.2, 5.71.2).[27] A page later, the Athenian envoys incur "great *aitiai*" when they return from offering the Persian satrap earth and water, the symbols of submission (5.73.3). When some Egyptian soldiers desert on the *aitiē* that their guard duty has not been relieved for three years, they certainly have something to complain about (2.30.2–3).

As in that last case, too, we usually sense the importance of the act of blaming itself, with the resentment of the blamers being as important in explaining outcomes as the actions that they are blaming (chapter 2).[28] That can be much more important than any question about whether the blame is justified. This is why Periander launches a campaign against his father-in-law Procles, holding him "most *aitios*" for Periander's present troubles (3.52.7); Xerxes' wife Amestris terribly mutilates the wife of Masistes because she thinks her "to blame," *aitiēn*, for Xerxes' dalliance, whereas Xerxes himself knows she is *anaitiēn*, "blameless" (9.110.1, 3; p. 32).

Such *aitiai* are particularly aired when aggression is in point, with at least an affectation that this is a matter of payback and punishment.[29] Croesus attacks each of the Ionian and Aeolian peoples in turn, bringing different *aitiai* against different people, bigger ones when he could "come up with" any, but in some cases bringing trivial charges (1.26.3): that also shows that not all *aitiai* are justified ones, and even when they are they may not be the true reasons—"come up with" is Waterfield's felicitous translation of παρευρίσκειν, where the παρ- prefix suggests something devious and disingenuous about this ferreting even if there were genuinely things to be found.[30] Already, then, with that first aggression of this "first man to start unjust actions against the Greeks" (1.5.3), we see that surface explanations and blamings are not the whole story. So many other campaigns too will begin amid recrimination but also complexity, with genuine grievances jostling with dubious ones, and even genuine ones being only part of the answer. As so often, Croesus provides a vignette version of much of the human experience to come.

There is more, too, to *aitiē*. For one thing, payback can be for positive reasons as well as negative. When Darius takes Samos "because of an *aitiē* along the following lines," the story told of Syloson begins as one of gratitude for a favor years ago (3.139.1; p. 124). Like the neuter *aition*, the abstract noun *aitiē* can also extend to a broader "explanation," though this usually involves a sequence in which blameworthiness plays an important part: how important is not always clear, especially initially. As he introduces Cyrus, Herodotus promises that he will later give the *aitiē* for his destruction of Astyages (1.75.1), and when we get there the narrative itself gives a full account of Astyages' reprehensible conduct; but others, especially Harpagus, have even more reason to blame him than Cyrus does himself. We shall see in the next chapter that blame, and the payback that so often is the wished-for consequence of blame, can work in very complicated ways. But it is at least clear that it often plays a part and that human blaming, with all the passion and all the rhetoric involved when one can claim one has been wronged, cannot be removed from the causal process.

We also find the other explanation-words that will become familiar in later writers. *Prophasis* (plural: *prophaseis* or, in Herodotus, *prophasies*) seems to capture any explanatory claim or justification that is put forward, whether true or false.[31] *Prophasis*-language is particularly prominent in contexts of aggressive campaigning, where it is often tempting to translate by "pretext": when Darius leaves the least strong troops behind for the Scythians to catch, it was "because of their weakness, but on the *prophasis* that he would attack the Scythians with a force of uncompromised quality while they guarded the camp" (4.135.2); Megabates sails on the *prophasis* of going to the Hellespont, when in fact his target is Naxos (5.33.1); in a context when hostilities were looming, the Athenians "dragged out" *prophasies* when they did not want to give back to Aegina their "deposit" of rich exiles—effectively hostages (6.86.1).

Often, though, such language conveys something of the truth, even though it may not be the whole truth. Solon travels on the *prophasis* of reflective sightseeing (*theōriē*, 1.29.1),³² and this captures an explanation that is partly true; there is more to it, for he needs to be absent from Athens for ten years, but he arrives "for that reason *and* because of his theōriē . . ." (1.30.1). A *prophasis* can also trigger a development that has a deeper background. Cambyses admits that he has long been wanting a *prophasis* to lay hands on Croesus (3.36.3); the Samians are already feeling defeatist when they seize the *prophasis* of the Ionian refusal to train in the hot sun (6.13.1); Darius wants to subdue all the Greek states that do not capitulate, but he does so on the *prophasis* of vengeance on Athens—again a reason that was sincerely felt as far as it went (6.94.1; cf. 5.105). It makes *prophasis* a useful word to introduce a sequence where explanations or justifications are in the air, but it is not yet clear whether they are the whole story, and we shall see something of this in book 4 (below, p. 126).

Elsewhere too the narrative suggests disingenuousness, but in an oblique way:

> When it was necessary for Apries to fall, it happened from a *prophasis* that I will recount briefly here and at fuller length in my Libyan account. Apries sent a great army against Cyrene and met with a disastrous defeat, and this led the indignant Egyptians to revolt, as they thought Apries had deliberately sent them into something that he could see would turn out badly: they thought he was contriving their deaths so that he could rule the rest of the Egyptians in greater safety. In anger at this the survivors turned to open revolt, along with the friends and relatives of the men who had died.
> (2.161.3–4)

So disingenuousness is indeed there, with those suspicions that Apries' motive for the expedition was to get rid of the army; but it is not at all clear that this really *was* his motive, and there is no mention of it when Herodotus does return to the topic in his Libyan narrative (4.159.3–4). In any case, the anger is real enough, and that is the explanation for the decisive revolt. Or at least part of the explanation: "when it was necessary for Apries to fall . . ." (ἐπεὶ δέ οἱ ἔδεε κακῶς γενέσθαι) may suggest that here there is a more cosmic perspective as well, and in that case this would be another case of triggering something with a deeper background.³³ In this case too there is a genuinely causal element: the developments would not have happened at that time without the trigger.³⁴ So *prophasis* is indeed a very useful introductory word, with a range that allows a variety of later developments.

If Herodotus wants a clearer word for "pretext" he uses *proschēma*, literally, "what is held forward," or its related verb form, *proischomai*.³⁵ Here he

10   HERODOTUS AND THE QUESTION WHY

more regularly gives an additional, usually more powerful explanation as well: the Persian Aryandes sent to ask who had killed Arcesilaus, and

> this charge (*aitiē*) was the reason that he put forward (*proschēma tou logou*), but it seems to me that the army was sent to conquer Libya. (4.167.3; BELOW, P. 125)

The Greek ambassadors to Gelon remind him of the current threat:

> You doubtless know about the man who is campaigning against Greece—that Persian who's going to yoke the Hellespont and bring all the eastern army from Asia to fight against Greece, putting forward the reason (*proschēma*) that he's making for Athens, but in fact having in mind to bring the whole of Greece under his power. (7.157.1)

Miltiades takes an Athenian army and sails to Paros,

> with the *prophasis* that the Parians had started it by joining the Persians and sailing a trireme to Marathon. That was what he put forward in what he said (*proschēma logou*), but he also bore a certain anger against the Parians on account of Lysagoras son of Teisies.... (6.133.1)

So in each case the alleged reason contrasts with something deeper.

Still, even these *prophasies* and *proschēmata* do carry some explanatory power: note the "also" in the last of those instances.[36] Quite often, in Herodotus and elsewhere, it can be the case that an attack is waiting to happen but will not start until a pretext is available: the case of Cambyses, long waiting for his *prophasis* to attack Croesus (3.36.3; above, p. 9), is often replicated on the international scale, as it is in the case of Athens seizing the *prophasis* to denounce Aegina when they offer Darius earth and water (6.49.2) or indeed of Darius attacking Greece on the *prophasis* of vengeance on Athens (6.94.1; p. 9). In such cases pretexts do matter: they may explain less than the underlying reasons for attack, but that attack would not have happened now without them. We shall find something similar in the Hippocratics, where again there are often cases of underlying dispositions and triggering stimuli (pp. 98–99); *prophasis* is often the word for those stimuli, and there too it carries some secondary explanatory force (chapter 5[a], esp. pp. 82–84).

Still, the lexical analysis of these nouns takes us only so far. There are also those little words for "because" or "for," words like ὅτι and διότι and εἵνεκα and γάρ, or just the use of participles to convey a crucial fact: the Persian usurpers wanted to make Prexaspes their ally "because" he had been so badly treated by Cambyses and "because" he was the only person who knew the truth about Smerdis' death, and he was also especially respected by the Persians (3.74.1); the citizens of Dodona may have called their female visitors doves "because" they spoke in an incomprehensible, birdlike tongue (2.57.1); the Libyans do not eat female animals "for the same reason," literally, "because of the same thing," as the Egyptians (4.186.1).[37] Motives and other thought processes are also conveyed by purpose-clauses: the Milesians are given the task of watching the passes "so that the Persians might have guides to take them to the heights of Mycale" if needed, though a further consideration was to prevent them causing trouble in the camp (9.104, where notice again the casual assumption of double causation). Simple statements such as "the X learned this custom from the Y" again offer explanations—and quite often there the learners are the Greeks, appropriating customs and habits from foreign powers in ways that may often have taken Herodotus' readers and listeners aback, "wondrous" things indeed.

There are many more complex ways too in which so skilled a narrator can engage the reader in making sense of events. That is particularly true if we look for explanations not just why wars begin the way they do but why they end the way they do, for words like *aitiē* and *prophasis* do not then come into play; the time for talking may not be over, as there may still be diplomacy to be done, but it will not be talking in those terms. Themes such as Greek freedom and Persian "softness" will surely have a part to play in explaining why the great events of 490 and 480–479 ended the way they did, but their narrative presentation is anything but straightforward for a reader to interpret. And Herodotus surely does expect a very active reader, one who is given plenty to work on and plenty to puzzle at. Even in cases where he seems to advance a clear and explicit motive, Emily Baragwanath has made a strong case for thinking that this does not close off other possible ways of looking at the action. In fact, she argues, the rest of the narrative may often seem to be pulling against the explicit textual diagnosis, and the reader is left to puzzle.[38] If so, that has its own mimetic quality, as we are put in the same position as characters within the text itself: they too have to puzzle in order to explain and to understand and to predict, and if our provisional judgments frequently need revision, so it is in life, and so it was in the life that the narrative represents. But so dynamic and complex a reading process demands an approach that goes some way beyond collecting those passages where causal explanations are made explicit.

(C) NARRATIVE: SHOW, NOT TELL

This discussion has already brought us to narrative. Ancient historiography was to be a predominantly narrative genre, and it was Herodotus who did so much to make it so. That is one reason why Homer's poems, those archetypal narrative masterpieces, loom so large in the background of his work and will therefore be a recurrent theme in this book as well.[39] Sometimes Herodotus interrupts the flow to incorporate passages of explicit, "dissertative"[40] causal analysis: we have already referred to some of these. But there is a good deal more to his technique than that. Like most Greek and Roman historians—indeed, like most good narrators, then as now—he prefers to show, not tell: to let his audiences draw their own inferences from the way that people talk and think, events develop, and outcomes work themselves out.

One important feature is the narrative's habit of reliving its own earlier phases. Solon's wisdom (1.30–33) comes back in the story of Polycrates of Samos and again when Artabanus speaks to Xerxes at Abydus, with many verbal echoes in both cases:[41] it is hardly rash to suggest that Solon, with his insights into the mutability and vulnerability of human life, offers some keys for understanding those later sequences. There is also a series of "Warners" in the text as expeditions loom. They do not all say the same thing, but they often form variations on two cases found in book 1, "You are taking on an enemy in an area where they are strong and you are weak" (Bias or Pittacus—Herodotus is not certain which—at 1.27), or "You are attacking a country where there is little to gain and much to lose" (Sandanis at 1.71). Yet the kings attack anyway, or most of them do; and time after time they take a step too far and meet catastrophe.[42] The bigger the event, the more resonant the echoes of the past: as Xerxes' expedition begins, there are particularly sharp relivings of the early stages of Darius' expedition against the Scythians (below, pp. 119–120).

What are we to make of these recurrent patterns? We have already seen that this narrative is thoroughly engaged with causal explanations, of different sorts and in varied combinations. It would be a sluggish reader who failed to wonder if those patterns did not contribute to our understanding of "what they were fighting each other for"—why, recurrently, these great kings behaved in tellingly similar ways; and also, if we turn to the outcomes of these campaigns rather than their launches, why they lost when they did. The question is the more pressing because the individuals concerned are very different,[43] and so it is not a crude matter of a "tyrannical stereotype": Croesus' intellectual curiosity, Cyrus' decisiveness and drive, Cambyses' madness, Darius' sustained control, Xerxes' apprehensive but thoughtful vacillations—there is no single pattern there. The recurrent shaping is of their actions, not of their characters, and even then the patterns operate in ways that diverge as well as cohere: in that aphorism rightly or wrongly attributed to Mark Twain, history does not repeat but it does rhyme. Is this rhyming then because of something in the Persian system? Or the Persian character? Or human character in general?[44] Will Greek states fall into the same pattern? Will Athens?

Good questions: good enough, indeed, to keep Herodotus' readers fascinated for a full nine books—and perhaps further still, even after they put aside the final book-roll. And good enough, I hope, to justify a book-length treatment here.

(D) EXPLANATION: A GAME FOR TWO

One further point does emerge from that earlier analysis of the words. It is striking how many of them have a rhetorical tinge. We saw how often *aitiē* and *aitios* conveyed blame: even in the Hippocratics they are much more often used for something regrettable than for something neutral or good. Whatever the etymology of *prophasis*,[45] its usage generally focuses on things put forward in excuse, sometimes true, more often false, sometimes a bit of both. *Proschēma* even more clearly refers to pretexts or excuses. All these have a lot to do with saying or speaking. To explain something, in the historians as in the physicians, is characteristically to do something verbally, and it is a game for two: it is an appeal to another person's conceptual range (either more emotional, "blaming," or more cognitive, "explaining") and an attempt to make a phenomenon intelligible by accommodating it within what the other person is already set up to find reasonable.[46] If we do this in a conversation, we take into account the assumptions or knowledge of the individual we are talking to; if we do it in a book or a talk, we gear what we say to the readers or listeners we have in mind. It is a rhetorical thing, a contribution to discursive exchange. That is why this book will so often talk of "explanation," for that too is a game for two, something done for the benefit of someone who hears or reads.

Modern writers, historical or medical, generally prefer "cause," or more rarely "reason," preferring the latter word especially when talking about causes that are a matter of human motivation. To talk of "causes" redirects attention not to the rhetoric but to the facts of the case: a causal sequence is something inherent in the events themselves, irrespective of what anyone may choose to say or not to say about it.[47] Greek writers can do this too: sometimes—and particularly in the Presocratic philosophers[48]—there is also talk of an *archē*, a "beginning," and that is something that resides in the things themselves, not the mouths that talk about them. That becomes particularly important for Polybius (pp. 104–105), but Herodotus can speak in that way too. Still, when he does it is also striking how similar the thinking is to that of his *aitiē*-talk. The Persians say that the *archē* of their animosity towards Greeks was the Trojan War (1.5.1): that rounds off the discussion of who were the ones who were *aitioi* for the rift (1.1.1). Herodotus prefers to rush on to the person who "began (ὑπάρξαντα, a word from the same root as *archē*) unjust deeds against the Greeks" (1.5.3), and that is Croesus: so *archē* here links easily with "unjust deeds," just as we saw *aitiē*- language often combining with talk of injustice and conveying a strong sense of blame. Blame is again called for when "for a second time evils began from Naxos and Miletus to strike the Ionians" (5.28.1), and there the culprits are very clearly Histiaeus and Aristagoras. But, just as later for Polybius, for Herodotus too the word *archē* usually belongs at the last stage of a causal chain, once the war (and it usually is a war) breaks out, and it is time for the talking and the arguing and the making of excuses to stop.

That rhetorical texturing means that we too need to give a lot of attention to Herodotus' audience—the second player in this game—as well as to Herodotus himself. That is why so much of this book will be given to other authors who shaped or reflected the audience's mindset: to Homer, to Hecataeus, to tragedy, to orators, and—particularly important for any analogy between scientific and historical explanation—to the earliest medical works in the Hippocratic corpus, building as they do on conceptual foundations laid by Presocratic philosophers. Such affinities give some guidance as to what counted as an adequate explanation, what sort of assumption could be taken for granted as enough to render something more intelligible.

Even if modern thinkers prefer to talk of "causes" rather than "explanations," audience expectations can still be central. In their classic discussion of "Causation in the Law," Hart and Honoré argue that the concern of causal analysis is "often to *apply* generalizations that are already known or accepted as true and even platitudinous to particular concrete cases."[49] That is similar to Herodotus' preoccupation with seeing how certain axioms—balance, symmetry, growth and decay, even the interest of the gods—apply to specific phenomena, whether those were features of the world around one (prolific or unprolific animals, a flooding river, the thickness of skulls) or sequences of past events. In the law courts, the application usually involves delivering a "dissertative" argument of the sort that ancient historians generally eschewed, but judges and advocates are also very aware—just as Cicero and Quintilian had been[50]—of the value of a powerful narrative.[51] How those various platitudinous causal principles interact in Herodotus' narrative history will indeed be a complicated story—and "story" is the right word, with a consummate storyteller to weave them together.

In this story, too, the ways in which large and familiar principles—blameworthiness, reciprocity, balance, ethnic differences—play out in practice are often messy, and they take people by surprise, both the people who are characters in the text, and (we can often infer) the people who would have read or heard the text as well. That does not mean that events lack explicability: in retrospect we can form an idea of how those principles were operating. But it does mean that they lacked total predictability,[52] however wise the figures in the text were who tried to forecast outcomes and however pertinent their warnings. This contrast between predictability and explicability will again be a recurrent theme in what follows. In modern thinking it may indeed be a basic difference between scientific and historical explanation, for in science we do tend to assume that a repeated experiment should predictably produce the same results. We will return to these questions in chapter 3.

(E) HISTORICAL CONSCIOUSNESS

One point is clear. The audience were used to thinking about history and accepting that it had something to say about the present: that was why the Stoa Poikile at Athens could depict the heroes of Marathon alongside those of the Trojan War (p. 202), and why Simonides' *Plataea* could echo Achilles when he sang about the Greeks marching out to fight the battle for freedom (p. 59). As the Greek world expanded during the colonization period, two principal idioms for conceptually "placing" these new areas were those embodied in Hecataeus' two works in the early fifth century. There was his *Guide to the World*, describing them geographically in space, and there was his *Genealogies*, relating them to the culture-heroes from which they came, normally Greek ones, and thus bringing them into the Greek intellectual compass in time.[53] Those past heroes could validate or elevate what was happening in the here and now, and this was not just a matter of simple curiosity: such ancestries could play an important role in kinship diplomacy, in establishing claims to territory or property, or providing legal precedents to settle disputes.[54] States that appointed civic "remembrancers" or "sacred remembrancers" did not do so simply for the joy of distant tales:[55] the past mattered. Tragedy too deals with the past but gestures towards the present, though it does so in a careful way, avoiding jarring anachronisms by hinting at present realities in language that is deliberately vague;[56] yet there is no doubt that past and present relate to one another. Indeed, the tragic plots themselves show the past hanging firmly and ominously over their dramatic present, and not just a vague timeless past but particular events and developments within it: Atreus' banquet in Aeschylus' *Agamemnon*, Phaedra's Cretan ancestry in Euripides' *Hippolytus*, Laius' murder in Sophocles' *Oe-

dipus Tyrannus. Exactly *how* the past is working may be unclear, and a polyphony of views may be available, all played with at different moments. If we ask why Agamemnon has to die, some explanations will start from what happened at Troy, some from Aulis, some from Atreus' dinner table, and some from decisions taken by the gods; some might involve too much success, or too much pride, or too much moral blindness. All can play a part, and explanation is not simple but multiple and complicated—and Herodotus may not be too different.

There was already a taste too for making sense of current realities by explaining how they had come about, one that Herodotus' speakers reflect when they use tales of the past in advising on contemporary issues.[57] In a way this goes back to the Presocratic philosophers' preoccupation with coming to be and passing away, explaining the physical cosmos in terms of its genesis; we can see parallels in the Hippocratics when they explain how the human body formed in the way it did.[58] On a less grand scale, it is first cousin to the taste for "aetiology," finding or fabricating stories to explain the origin of particular monuments or institutions. This extended to reflection on the whole current state of humanity. Hesiod's myth of the ages[59] explained how life had become miserable, and Empedocles too looked back to a Golden Age when Love prevailed over Strife. By the fifth century more upbeat notions were also in the air, ideas of human progress such as that in *Prometheus* or in Euripides' *Suppliant Women* or in *Antigone*'s πολλὰ τὰ δεινά ode ("there are many extraordinary things, and nothing more extraordinary than a human").[60] A positive outlook had already been possible for Xenophanes: "The gods did not reveal everything to mortals at the beginning, but in time, by searching, mortals make discoveries for the better" (DK 21 B 18). The Hippocratic *On Ancient Medicine* is insistent (3, 12, 14) that medical science has improved through successive discoveries and hopes that it will continue to do so. In the *Sisyphus*, probably a satyr play, a character even explained religion as the invention of a "shrewd and intelligent man" in order to dissuade people from wrongdoing even in secret (*TGrF* 43 F 19):[61] there is no way of telling what happened to so bold a speaker in the play, but such ideas could be put into the air.

It was not necessary to take such an account literally. It could instead be a sort of historical modeling, capturing the essentials of a complicated process in a simplified version. We later see that carried through in Plato's *Protagoras*, using a mythical narrative to explore how justice and mutual respect came to be on this earth as a way of cementing the order necessary for a community's survival. A similar historical modeling of "social contract" ideas will also figure at the beginning of *Republic* 2.[62] It is not far from the manner of Hobbes or Rousseau. "Modeling" is indeed a reasonable way of putting it, for these pictures resemble an economic or a sociological model that cannot be true in absolutely literal terms—reality is always so much messier—but nonetheless aspires to capturing something insightful and genuine.[63]

Herodotus' story of Deioces the Mede does something similar at 1.96–101, with its picture of how monarchy could come about.[64] Deioces makes himself available to administer justice, first in his village and then more widely among the scattered Median communities, and does it so well that he is soon indispensable; he then retires, but is persuaded to return by the offer of the throne. Installed as king, he insists on a fine palace for himself in the center of a single great Median city, introduces a strict court ceremonial and creates an aura of majesty about his own person, taking care rarely to be seen in person and now delivering his judgments only in writing.

How exactly this works as a "model" within the *Histories* themselves is another question, coming as it does so early in the narrative: is this a pattern for all society and all times? Or just for an early, primitive stage, before a more sophisticated population can develop laws and institutions for themselves? Or just for the East, as the narrative turns to the growth of the Persian empire, allowing the possibility that the Greek world could be less geared to monarchy? It will take the rest of the work to answer such questions—or to begin to do so. But all such thinking at least shows a sort of historical consciousness, with its readiness to look to the past to understand the present. Herodotus did not burst upon a world that was wholly unprepared.[65]

(F) RECONSTRUCTING MENTALITIES

Of course there are pitfalls in reconstructing audience assumptions, and nobody should fall into loose talk of what "the Greeks thought. . . ." Our comparisons will be with authors of different ages and milieux; not all their audiences will be the same as one another or as the various audiences who would hear or read Herodotus; there may be generic variations, just as audiences of comedy might cheerily accept chains of fantastic events that in a different mindset they knew were wholly illogical. Still, one should not overstate these problems. Homer's poems may have been around for two and a half centuries already, and the stories for even longer: they still clearly played an important role in forming people's mindsets, giving benchmarks for gauging contemporary behavior even in a very changed world. Even if tragedy, comedy, and lyric could be felt as different genres, for they had different performance contexts, it need not follow that prose literature yet dealt in "genres" in so clear-cut a form.⁶⁶ If we do think of performance, then some at least of the Hippocratic texts seem to have been intended for public display before a general audience;⁶⁷ they are not just for medical students. These include the works most illuminating for Herodotus, *Airs Waters Places* and *On the Sacred Disease*. That audience was not necessarily so different from that of Herodotus.

What should we make of such affinities, especially those with the Hippocratics? Sometimes they simply point to an ingrained assumption that historian and physicians share with the rest of their society: one that will be important in this book is an expectation that an organism might carry in it from birth the qualities that would lead first to strength and success and then to decay and eventually demise—a "unifocal" mode of looking at things, dwelling on the strengths and fragilities of that single body and finding explanations within itself for its ups and downs. When an Achilles or an Oedipus or an Antigone is finally undone by the same characteristics as constituted his or her greatness, we are not far away from such ideas; and the same may apply with Herodotus' Persia or for that matter with Thucydides' Athens.

There are times, though, when the contact with the Hippocratics is more specific, for instance when Herodotus gestures towards the climatic determinism that we see in *Airs Waters Places* (pp. 96–97).⁶⁸ "Soft places tend to produce soft people," says Cyrus in the enigmatic retrospect that closes the *Histories*, urging the Persians not to move from their harsh homeland (9.122; pp. 92–93); Egypt has customs that are the reverse of everyone else's, "along with their climate being different and their river having a different nature from other rivers" (2.35.2); the people there seem to be the healthiest in the world except for the Libyans "on account of the lack of changeability in the seasons, for diseases occur especially when there is change of any sort and in particular seasonal change" (2.77.3); the extremities of the world have received as their lot (ἔλαχον) the finest features, "just as Greece received as its lot the mix of seasons that is by far the best" (3.106.1). It is true that most of these are indeed gestures, and (except perhaps for 2.77.3) they do not indicate firm commitment to a deterministic view. We may not know quite what to make of Cyrus' rhetoric, especially as he has earlier shown himself shrewd in the use or acceptance of very different arguments from luxury (1.126, 1.155–156; below, p. 93);⁶⁹ the Egyptian contrariness can be a matter of analogy or harmony between climate and customs, not cause;⁷⁰ and that "just as" at 3.106.1 leaves it vague exactly what sort of link there may be between the "seasons," where Greece has the finest, and the other features which appear at their best in the extremities. Maybe it was a *divine* balancing in the original distribution that the phrase "received as their lot" suggests, for divine foresight plays a part a little later in the discussion of the relative fertility of timid and vicious creatures (3.108.2).⁷¹ But an *acquaintance* with that thought-world still seems clear, and the snappy allusiveness of the phraseology suggests that Herodotus expected many of his audience to be acquainted with it too.

Let us take a more elaborate test case, one to which we will often have reason to refer (pp. 96, 169, 175, 199): the passage where *Airs Waters Places* deals with what is seen as an eastern lack of bellicosity.

> I now turn to the lack of spirit and courage—the fact that Asians are less warlike than Europeans and gentler in character. The seasons are most responsible for this, in that there are no great variations in heat or cold, but all the parts of the year are similar. There are therefore no mental shocks nor strong changes in the body, which are more likely than continual sameness to make the temper fierce and impart to it an uncalculating passion. For it is changes of all things that stir up the human intellect and do not allow it to rest. For these reasons, it seems to me, the Asians are unwarlike; and also because of their institutions, for most of Asia is governed by kings. Where people are not their own masters and independent and ruled by others, they direct their efforts not to military training but to avoiding an appearance of being warlike: for the dangers are different for those who are warlike and those who are not. The warlike are likely to be made to go on campaign with all its hardships, and to be forced to die for their masters, far from children, wife, and other friends. And all their good and brave deeds serve to make their masters great and raise them up; but they themselves reap danger and death. Besides, men like this inevitably find their own land turning into a desert, because of the enemies and the neglect: so that even a man who is naturally brave and spirited finds his mentality changed because of the institutions. Let me give you a clear indication of this: consider the Greeks and barbarians in Asia who are *not* ruled by masters but are independent and toil for themselves. These are the most warlike people of all. For they run dangers for their own sake, they bear the prizes for their own bravery, and similarly the punishments for their cowardice. You will also find differences among the Asians themselves, some being better and some being worse: and the reason is the changes in the seasons, as I said earlier.
> (*AIRS WATERS PLACES* 16 I. PP. 114–116 J = II. PP. 62–66 L)

It is not hard to find analogies here with Herodotus' thinking, especially with his explanation that "while the Athenians were held down they willingly played the coward because they were working for a master, but once they were free each wanted to achieve something for himself" (5.78).

Those are analogies we shall explore in more detail later (pp. 91–93, 169–170), along with some differences; it may well be, for instance, that *Airs Waters Places* is concerned to work backwards from that eastern lack of bellicosity and explain where it came from[72] (the simple racist generalization that they are *naturally* inferior would not be enough, and Greeks and barbarians alike are "the most warlike of all" when free of tyranny).[73] Herodotus is more concerned to work forwards and see how it worked out in events[74]—if indeed it did, and we shall see the qualifications there too. For the moment, it is enough to see the light this can cast both on the shared intellectual interests—national differences, constitutions, climate, and the effect of each on behavior—and on the assumptions Herodotus might be dealing with. That need not mean that Herodotus meekly accepts those prejudices of easterners' lack of courage or of the glories of self-interested freedom: premises can always be challenged, and in both cases we will see qualifications as well as acknowledgement of their force. The author of *Airs Waters Places* too might well have thought of himself as challenging stereotypes in that insistence that some barbarians, those living under the right conditions, could be the bravest of all. But had Herodotus chosen to adopt the prejudices and the stereotypes, many of his audience might have accepted them as explanation enough.

For there comes a point when explanation can stop, perhaps has to stop; where one has to accept that no further explaining is necessary, because life is simply like that. (And life can be very various: the ethnographies help to make that point, setting out so many customs that one may find strange but that are just there.) One can trace things back to their origin, but there may still be questions to ask—up to a point. Herodotus can accept that Cleomenes' gruesome self-mutilation and death, "turning himself into sausage meat" (6.75.3), came because he was mad, but he can still ask why he went mad and whether that madness fits into some larger pattern. There are several possible explanations, each rehearsed in turn (6.74.3, 84). Most of those explanations imply some notion of payback, *tisis*, or a rebalancing justice, *dikē*, to use those two terms that we have already seen to be deeply ingrained (p. 4). Perhaps it was divine payback for his treatment of the Argives; perhaps for a similar sacrilege at Eleusis; perhaps—and this is Herodotus' own preferred view—for his perfidious treatment of Demaratus, which (we might add) also involved bribing of the Pythia.[75] One does not need to ask any further why such a rebalancing of the scales needed to occur, or why Heaven might be involved, any more than one needs to ask why divine forethought has maintained a balance in nature by making the most vulnerable creatures the most prolific (3.108; p. 86) or why the Nile might be expected to be analogous to the Danube (pp. 2–3) or why an organism might carry the seeds both of its greatness and of its decline. That is simply the way the world is, and the challenge is to see the ways that principles of balance or symmetry or growth-and-decay apply in particular cases.

So these are "life-is-like-that explanations," ones that place a phenomenon by seeing it as an example of a shared and acknowledged aspect of experience. As in the Cleomenes case, they often complement "origin explanations," tracing that phenomenon back to where it comes from, in one sense Cleomenes' own actions and in another the gods. One can already see the combination in one of the most moving passages of the *Iliad*.[76] Achilles and Priam muse on the suffering they share; one has lost his friend, the other his son. If one looks for the origin of such suffering, there will of course be human causes: the *Iliad* explored those in plenty, not least in the human interactions of Achilles himself. But Achilles puts more weight on the gods, and as so often thinking about the gods is a way to understand the human condition too.

> That is the lot the gods have spun for poor mortals—to live with pain and grief. They themselves have no cares. There are two urns on Zeus' threshold, one of good things and one of bad. To one person Zeus the thunderer gives a mix, to experience good at some times and bad at others; but the person who is given bad is hapless, driven by foul hunger around the god-nourished world and wandering without honor from gods or from humans . . .
> (*IL.* 24.525–533)

Priam and Achilles should be grateful that they have been among the luckier ones, as they had some good things too. There is no point in lament, and no need to ask more about why the gods give misery, or even why they grant at least a measure of goodness to one person but not to another. Life is like that, and knowing that helps one to "place" one's current miseries. That is understanding enough.

CHAPTER 2

TO BLAME AND TO EXPLAIN:
NARRATIVE COMPLICATIONS

(A) THE PROEM

The expectations of Herodotus' audience would not have been restrictive. They would have been used to authors—Acusilaus, Pherecydes, and others—combining everything they had to say into a single book; they would have been used, too, to ethnographers joining together anything that was interesting about a culture, monuments, customs, achievements, and events into a single collecting of "things about the Egyptians," for instance, or "the Libyans" or "the Indians"—*Aigyptiaka, Libyka, Indika*.[1] But a more precise horizon of expectation would have to form as they read or heard onwards; it would be generated by the text itself and by the narrator that it reveals. It is important to put it that way, because Herodotus' self-characterization itself plays such a big part in molding that expectation. Herodotus presents himself, in more or less subtle ways, as interested in everything and putting questions to everything, and that helps to infect the audience with a similar cast of mind.

The process begins with the proem:

Ἡροδότου Ἁλικαρνησσέος ἱστορίης ἀπόδεξις ἥδε, ὡς μήτε τὰ γενόμενα ἐξ ἀνθρώπων τῷ χρόνῳ ἐξίτηλα γένηται, μήτε ἔργα μεγάλα τε καὶ θωμαστά, τὰ μὲν Ἕλλησι, τὰ δὲ βαρβάροισι ἀποδεχθέντα, ἀκλεᾶ γένηται, τά τε ἄλλα καὶ δι' ἣν αἰτίην ἐπολέμησαν ἀλλήλοισι.

This work sets on display the researches of Herodotus the Halicarnassian.[2] The purpose is to save things that originate from humans from fading with time and to preserve the glory of great and marvelous achievements, some displayed by Greeks, some by barbarians, including in particular why they came to war with one another.
(PROEM)

Several aspects of this manifesto would have struck the audience. The first is the nature of the self-projection: we get a strong sense of Herodotus' authorial personality, and not just because of the prominence given to his name and city. His role is the "setting on display" (ἀπόδεξις) of his researches; they will preserve the great and marvelous achievements "displayed" (ἀποδεχθέντα, a participial form of the verbal equivalent of the noun ἀπόδεξις) by both Greeks and barbarians.³ A mirroring of narrator and doer is insinuated—perhaps an equivalence, for the narrator's role is seen as a vital one, preventing human accomplishments from "fading" or "losing their glory," becoming ἀκλεᾶ. That last word conveys a strong sense of the epic too. These mortal achievements win glory, *kleos*, with all that word's Homeric overtones, and the narrator's role is that of Homer, or indeed of Achilles himself, singing of "the glorious deeds of men," the *klea andrōn*, at *Iliad* 9.189. This is not a demure introduction, then. Herodotus' audience might have half-expected him to compete with Hecataeus; his modern critics stress his affinity with the tragic poets.⁴ But the first comparison that Herodotus invites is with Homer himself.

What Herodotus will set on display is his "researches" or "inquiries," his *historiē*: not "History" in its modern sense, but a word that focuses on the gathering of material as well as on its exposition. Not just any gathering, either: *historein* is to ask questions, and Herodotus presents himself as an inquirer. The audience will also be struck by the range of material into which he will inquire. This is not going to be limited to "things about the Egyptians" or "Libyans" or any one people; it is to include great and marvelous achievements of Greeks and barbarians, therefore of several peoples. Dionysius caught this aspect well, contrasting Herodotus with his predecessors and contemporaries (p. 58):

> But Herodotus of Halicarnassus chose not to write up an inquiry into any one city or race, but to bring together a variety of many different actions from both Europe and Asia, collecting them within the scope of a single enterprise.
> (DIONYSIUS OF HALICARNASSUS, *ON THUCYDIDES* 5)

Persian expansionism here provided a helpful organizing principle when so many peoples were to be covered: then the Persians attacked the Egyptians (so let me tell you about the Egyptians), and so on.⁵

The material to be included will be of a wide range in other ways, and the proem heralds that variety. The work will accommodate anything that is an *ergon*, literally, a "doing," something that is wrought or achieved by mortals, provided only that it is "great and marvelous." An *ergon* can as naturally be a building or a monument, perhaps even a custom, as an historical event.⁶ The work may include anything that is γενόμενον ἐξ ἀνθρώπων, "originating from humans": another interesting formulation, for that γενόμενα ἐξ, "originating from," again finds room for buildings and monuments as well as for chains of consequences springing from particular actions.⁷ Yet even this description will turn out to be too restrictive, as there will be room, as we have already seen, for investigating natural phenomena as well: the silting up of the Nile, for instance, is not something that originated from mortals, nor is its annual flood.⁸ So this is already a case of "revision in stride," something that we will later see much more often (chapter 5[c]). The emphasis on "humans" will itself need qualification and extension (pp. 107–108): we shall have to bring in a godly dimension as well, and do so very soon (1.8.2).

So there will be broadening—but for the moment the rhythm is different, with the successive clauses narrowing things down.⁹ Thus "the great and marvelous achievements" defines more sharply "the things that originate with humans"; the "some displayed by Greeks and some by barbarians" clarifies "the humans" from which they originated. The last clause continues this sharpening process as we focus on the reason "why they came to war with one another": the question Why. That of course suits the theme of this book, and this is why so much was made of it in the first pages of chapter 1, building on Myres' vignette. Still, we should remember the "other things" as well as the "reason" that the proem promises (p. 1). There is nothing to suggest that the work will limit itself completely to "the reason" for their conflict, and of course it will not:¹⁰ there are many other things that are of interest in their own right, simply because they are "great and marvelous" (hence the title of Rosaria Munson's Herodotus book, *Telling Wonders*);¹¹ and a large part of the narrative will be devoted to the wars themselves, not merely the "reason" for their inception. Nor does "how they came to war with one another" tie even that aspect to τὰ Μηδικά, the successive Persian invasions of Greece: wars of easterners against Greeks start much earlier than that, as early indeed as Book 1.¹²

The emphasis on "the reason" is still important. The Homeric echoes have led us to expect a great war; this now tells us that the focus will be on the war's "reason" *as well as* on its course. As we have seen (pp. 5–8), *aiti-* language can readily suggest "blame," and here the *aitiēn* is picked up in the first sentence of the narrative: "The experts in tales (*logioi*)¹³ among the Persians say that it was the Phoenicians who were to blame (*aitioi*) for the breach" (1.1.1). That recalls the opening of the *Iliad*, where the end of the proem—"from the point when they first stood divided in strife, the son of Atreus, lord of men, and divine-blooded Achilles"—was picked up by that initial question, "And which of the gods was it that sent them together to fight in strife?" (*Il.* 1.8). Here it is the *aitiē–aitioi* play that formulates the first question that Herodotus puts to his material and draws his audience into putting as well.

It is a useful first question, too, for Herodotus' expositional strategy: to ask, "Who is to blame? Who started it?" invites a narrative answer—a return to the beginnings and a telling of the tale.¹⁴ Here again, however, there is redefinition to come,¹⁵ and it starts very soon, as the next chapters illuminate how such "blame" really works.

(B) THE EXCHANGE OF ABDUCTIONS (1.1–5)

These Persian "experts in tales" blamed the Phoenicians for starting it all. That is the first paradox, for the Phoenicians were a people who did not fit exactly into either the "eastern" Asian category or the western "European"—those two peoples who "came to war with one another." The Phoenicians had originally come from the Persian Gulf (1.1), from the southeast rather than the East or the West; by the time of the abduction they had come to Asia, but they still occupy something of an intermediate position. A little later Croesus, the Lydian king who is intrigued by Greek wisdom, will fill a similar intermediate place as we move into more historical time (p. 114): like the Phoenicians, more eastern than western, but still a Mr. In-between.

The Phoenician traders, they said, arrived in Argos, and the captain was taken by the sight of the local princess Io; she and some of her companions were seized and carried off to Egypt. "That is how the Persians say Io reached Egypt—this is different from the Greek version—and this was the first of the outrages" (*adikēmata*, "injustices"). Then they say that some unnamed Greeks arrived in Phoenician Tyre and carried off the king's daughter Europa: "These people would be Cretans." "So far the account was equal, they say; but then the Greeks were to blame (*aitioi*) for the second outrage (*adikiē*)." They sailed to Colchis in a "long ship" and "once they had conducted their business"—an extraordinarily low-key way to describe the Argo and the mission of the Golden Fleece—they abducted the princess Medea; her father, the king, sent to Greece and demanded satisfaction (*dikai*), asking for the return of Medea; but the Greeks replied that they had received no satisfaction for Io and would therefore give none for Medea.

Next came the affair of Paris. He had heard, they say, of all this, and therefore decided he wanted a wife from Greece; he knew that he would not have to give any satisfaction (*dikai*) for that. So he seized Helen, and when the Greek messengers came to protest they were told that they had given no satisfaction for Medea and should not expect any for Helen. "So far it was merely a question, they say, of mutual abductions; then the Greeks became greatly to blame (*megalōs aitioi*). For they mounted a campaign against Asia before the other side did the same against Europe." That was the origin, they say, of the Trojan War; and since then they have always regarded Greece as their enemy. "For the Persians claim Asia and the barbarian peoples within it as their own, whereas Europe and everything Greek they regard as separated."

There is a lot of "blame" around here. The Persians blame the Phoenicians; the Phoenicians, we go on to learn (1.5.1–2), claim Io is just as much to blame. A tally is kept; when there is one abduction on each side, they say that the score was level (ταῦτα μὲν δὴ ἴσα πρὸς ἴσα σφι γενέσθαι, literally, "that this was equal against equal for them," 1.2.1). The concepts with which this *aiti-* language keeps company are, as so often (p. 6), those of "injustice," *adikiē*, the sort of outrage one blames people for, and of claiming satisfaction, *dikai*—perhaps compensation, perhaps revenge.

The question "Who is to blame?" has thus invited this narrative answer, "Who started it?"[16] That is not unfamiliar in quarrels: we shall see something similar in Antiphon's *Third Tetralogy* (p. 71), and in fourth-century lawsuits too a crucial question was who started it, who struck the first blow. The principle was even enshrined in Attic law.[17] In a way it also has parallels with scientific explanations, given the preoccupation of the early cosmologists with tracing things back to their "beginnings," *archai*, and tracing the steps that led to the current state of things (p. 13). However, complications soon set in, and "starting it" does not end the inquiry. After one abduction apiece, the next "starters" (this time the Greeks) are as blameworthy as the original Phoenicians, and the Greeks become "greatly to blame" for launching an army: that sort of escalation is important in explaining the future, for the Persians themselves therefore date the beginning (*archē*) of their anti-Greek hostility to the Trojan War (1.4.4, 1.5.1), not to the point where the Phoenicians "started it." There are thus several places when "blame" adheres, and that singular *aitiē* in the proem, looking for the one "reason" or "blaming" that may explain everything, already looks insecure, yet another candidate for rethinking in stride.

It is problematic, too, how far the "blaming" really influences people's actions. A pendulum is swinging here, and it is tempting to express this as a sequence of "retaliations"[18]—tempting, but inexact. The Cretans are not retaliating for Io; it is just that the balance is level after their performance. It is the Persian experts who are keeping the score, not the Cretans themselves. Memories of Io do affect the abduction of Medea, but they do not inspire the seizure itself: instead the point comes into the argument afterwards—"you did not give satisfaction for Io, so we won't for Medea." Paris, too, is influenced by memories of Medea, but once again there is no suggestion of revenge; he was simply led by this to conclude that he might get away with it, just as the earlier abductors had done. "Blame" is already slippery; it drifts so readily from a genuine motivational force into the sphere of rhetoric, self-defense, and semblance.[19] It is not *just* talk, for it also affects what people do: Paris would not have acted in this way but for the earlier exchanges. But it affects it in indirect ways, and give-and-take may mask motives as often as constituting them.

These chapters are also important in introducing the contrast between East and West, Persia and Greece. That final explanation—"the Persians claim Asia and the barbarian peoples within it as their own, whereas Europe and everything Greek they regard as separated"—is carefully phrased. For one thing, it avoids collapsing two distinctions into one: the geographical Europe/Asia distinction is not the same as the ethnic Greek/barbarian distinction, for there were Greeks in Asia too,[20] but the Persian claim is limited to the "barbarian peoples" within the Asian continent. Then "claim as their own," οἰκηιοῦνται, refers in the first instance to a *political* claim (and one that already insinuates the looming Persian expansionism),[21] but the word can also project an intellectual view of geographical or ethnic unity; it is this second nuance that is picked up in the other part of the sentence, "regard as separated." Even the tense of "separated," the perfect κεχωρίσθαι, is telling: that captures a present state that is the result of a "separation" in the past, and so it has not necessarily always been so "regarded"—a matter of *nomos* then, "convention," rather than *physis*, "nature."[22]

Both the Europe/Asia and the Greek/barbarian distinction will later be significant. The geographical point certainly matters: the crossing of the Hellespont will be particularly marked, as the aggressor moves from one continent into another.[23] But it will also be important that the barbarians of Asia can in some sense be regarded as all the same thing, just as all Greeks hang together, including Asiatic Greeks; otherwise, for instance, the Lydian Croesus' attacks on Asiatic Greeks would not be a plausible antecedent for the Persian invasion of the Greek mainland. That would not have struck a contemporary audience as the only possible way of looking at it—it might have been more natural to think of a distinction between (all) Greeks and (all) barbarians, not just easterners[24]—but has been carefully prepared here. In these opening chapters, then, the Colchians, Trojans, and even the Phoenicians all stand in one tradition, the easterners, shortly to be joined by the Lydians Candaules and Croesus; Cretans, Argonauts, and (presumably) Spartans fit into another, the Greeks.[25]

The most striking feature of this beginning is that it is virtually all in indirect speech, two-and-a-half pages of it, perhaps five minutes in performance: this is an astonishing way of beginning a dramatic narrative work, but one that signals this as *what others say*, the version of these Persian "experts in tales." Herodotus does not present it all passively; he interjects that "these must have been Cretans"; he observes that "this is different from the Greek version"—very different indeed, his audience would have added, as they noted this extremely rationalized, humanized, sanitized version of some of the most familiar Greek myths.[26] Still, so long a passage of indirect speech has something programmatic about it. Whatever else Herodotus will do, he will λέγειν τὰ λεγόμενα, "tell us what people say" and deploy different versions against one another—here, a new, foreign version (or so he claims)[27] against those that the audience know already. What people say matters, not just as a way of getting at the truth but also because their opinions, right or wrong, drive their conduct: what the Persians "claim as their own" offers part of an explanation for what they do, "what they are fighting one another for."

Then there is a further version, that of the Phoenicians themselves. They do not agree with the Persians about Io: they claim that there was no violent abduction but that she willingly had sex with the captain, then ran away with him when she learnt she was pregnant (1.5.2). What is striking there is not what the Phoenicians disagree with but what they accept.[28] Io's departure still starts it all; it is just that she was a willing partner, that she too was "to blame." It is still a story of lust between captain and local girl, not of a passionate Zeus and a metamorphosis into a cow (cf. p. 107). The Phoenicians give just as blatantly self-serving an account of the rights and wrongs as the Persians. So far, it looks as if Herodotus is using judicious criticism of a small detail to showcase his critical capacity and raise his audience's confidence in the accuracy of the rest—the sort of technique that we associate with a Cicero or a Tacitus.

Yet this is another false start.[29] The next sentence makes a new series of moves:

> I am not proceeding with any intention to say that these things happened in this way or any other way; I shall indicate the man who I myself know began unjust deeds (*erga*) against the Greeks, and then go forward to the rest of my narrative, moving through cities of humans, small and big alike. For those cities that were big long ago have for the most part become small; and those that were big in my own day were small in the past. I therefore know that human prosperity is always unstable, and I will mention both sorts equally.
> (1.5.3–4)

So much for all those elaborate abduction stories: he now dismisses them, saying that he will pass instead to the man who he knows started unjust deeds against the Greeks—Croesus, we soon discover—and, brutally, the minute difference between the two versions is used as a springboard to dismiss everything he has so far said. He has shown that he can play these rationalistic games, and play them well (there may well be a gesture at Hecataeus' expense here, at least in affecting something of his manner of downplaying the divine,[30] even if Hecataeus did not tell any of those particular stories[31])—but it is not the work that he has chosen to write. That will instead begin with Croesus; and the emphasis on personal knowledge and the reliability of material is another programmatic step, another adjustment of the horizon of expectation.

All the same, such material has been dismissed because its detail is unreliable, not because it is the wrong sort of explanation in principle.[32] It remains for the moment a possibility that the Persian "experts" had the right sort of explanation but applied it to the wrong sequence of events; as yet, the audience will not be sure; things will become clearer, though only gradually, as they hear more.

Homer is also brought back to mind in this closing paragraph. This is one of several ways in which ring composition marks the end of the section,[33] but the phrasing marks a progression of thought rather than a mere repetition, and a continuation of that narrowing that was already visible in the proem. *Erga*, "what people have done," were signaled in the proem; now it is more precisely the *adika erga*, the unjust deeds that Croesus began against the Greeks, for the Persian experts have acclimatized us to thinking of these as important in this world of blame. Human activity, τὰ γενόμενα ἐξ ἀνθρώπων, was the project in the proem; now it is more precisely the "cities of humans," ἄστεα ἀνθρώπων, that Herodotus will cover.

He will do so, too, in a way that echoes Odysseus, that heroic figure who "saw many cities of humans and came to know their minds" (*Od.* 1.3). We have moved from the initial *Iliad*, with its glory and its fighting, into the peacetime *Odyssey*, with its traveling and its broad experience.[34] Initially the proem had linked the ἱστορίη, the inquiring, and the ἀπόδεξις, the exposition; here the gathering of information and the presentation are even more smoothly connected, because the description of his presentation is couched in metaphors of physical movement. "I am not proceeding . . . I shall then go forward . . . moving through cities of humans . . ." He will now move through the cities in his exposition, just as before he moved through them in his travels:[35] the two activities are intimately connected. Once again this narrowing does not exclude the broader themes with which we began, any more than it did in the proem—but it is an indication of the sort of material we can expect first.[36]

The nature, however, of this connection between travel and exposition is another surprise. The audience would not be surprised that Herodotus' travel could be claimed to provide his material, but their first instinct would be to take this in a different sense: they were used to ethnographic works and would interpret the proem's "great and marvelous *erga*" as the wondrous curiosities that the world had to offer. But Herodotus explains that travel has also given him something more, an insight into human stability and "prosperity," *eudaimoniē* (p. 76). His spatial wanderings have taught him a lesson about temporal change.[37] Before long we will find a further character who reminds us of the Herodotus we are seeing here: Solon, who had "traveled great distances in the pursuit of wisdom and for contemplation" (1.30.2) and who similarly had learnt, and tried to impart, a lesson about human prosperity and vulnerability.[38] Solon tries to teach Croesus, who learns his lesson too late, just as Herodotus' text might point to a similar lesson about human mutability.

We have come some way, then, since the first sentence. We see the possibility not just of recounting great and *marvelous erga*, but of placing them in a coherent pattern and of extracting a conclusion about human experience. That sort of insight will not wholly displace the sorts of "explanation" that we have so far seen; the desire to find someone to blame will continue to be one way of rendering activity intelligible. Yet there is also an indication of a different sort of insight, one that the proem had not led us to expect. The emphasis on human mutability is a generalization borne of experience, but it also helps to make sense of that experience, to locate it, just as we saw Homer relating individual catastrophes to a pattern of what human life is like (p. 21). That is a different register of explanation, a different way of rendering events intelligible. At the moment the two registers do not interact; they are both there. The nature of their coexistence will become clearer in Croesus' story.

(C) PAYBACK AND ITS COMPLICATIONS

We are already seeing that the blame game is more complicated than we might have thought. The ways that the blamers speak and think explain a lot, but that does not mean that the audience point the finger of blame in the same way, or agree that the best way to understand events is to identify who started it or even who is most culpable. The same is true if we move on to the actions that so often follow when one side thinks the other is to blame—the principle of *tisis*, that pattern of payback. This again often figures in the characters' minds, usually in terms of revenge, the concern to make the other person or nation pay for the suffering you have just experienced at their hands and are blaming them for. The idea is basic to that reciprocal give-and-take, the "model of repayment in kind," that John Gould has highlighted as a basic principle of Herodotean explanation.[39] There was something of that in the picture of mutual abductions as payback succeeded payback—the sort of "and then A did to B, and then B did to A . . ." sequence Aristophanes would parody in *Acharnians* (496–556). It is understandable, though I think it mistaken, that the *Acharnians* speech is often taken as a riff on Herodotus himself: the two passages certainly have something in common (pp. 215–216). Yet we have already seen the complications, as payback has become exaggerated and distorted (the Greeks becoming "greatly to blame" when they launch a whole war)—and anyway it has become a matter of semblance and excuse, as much as a genuine motive, as Paris' desire is not for retaliation but for Helen.

In any case we soon begin a new sequence as we turn to Croesus: he is seen to be the one who "starts it" in a different series, the first person to initiate "unjust deeds" against the Greeks (1.5.3). Is this going to be a series of ebbs and flows, with Croesus starting aggression in one direction, then the Greeks pushing back, then Persians taking over the eastern mantle in their own aggression against the West? No, not really, or at least only partly. Give and take is overlaid by a further model, and Croesus turns out to be more significant for different reasons, showing a pattern of imperialistic overreach that—again in an unstraightforward way—will be paradigmatic for the Persian empire (chapter 8) and will be reflected in that narrative patterning in which events seem to repeat themselves (chapter 1[c]). Whereas give and take was a matter of two sides, each having a turn to give and then to take, imperialism is closer to that unifocal organic model (p. 18) that finds explanations in the growth and decay of a single body. Of course those expansionist moves involve another side as well—the Massagetae or the Ethiopians or the Scythians or the Libyans or, finally, the Greeks. That certainly does not *exclude* matters of reciprocity, particularly the reciprocity of vengeance: this is particularly important when the spotlight returns to Greece, and Darius seeks vengeance for the Athenian and Eretrian burning of Sardis (5.105, 6.94.1; pp. 10, 104); earlier too we can see it in play, though not in straightforward ways (pp. 123–128). But still the imperialist power is quite capable of causing its own disasters through ill-judged overreach. A tale of reciprocity has not disappeared (that is why "overlaid" is the right word, not "displaced"),[40] but it has moved off-center—in some ways, but only in some, as reciprocal vengeance has to move off-center in the *Oresteia*, with the institution in *Eumenides* of a civic law court to provide a more peaceable way of settling disputes. In Aeschylus' trilogy the move is to explore better ways to cope with such vindictiveness in the future; in Herodotus it is to understand why things happened in the past.

"Payback," τίσις, is indeed often most illuminating and cataclysmic when it does not quite work, or works in paradoxical ways. There is payback in Croesus' fall, certainly: but not payback of any sort that his story might lead anyone to expect, payback for instance for unjust aggression (1.26.3) or for ill-judged imperialistic aspiration: no, it is payback for something that happened five generations earlier and that everyone, probably including the reader (chapter 7[b]), had forgotten. That something was the outrageous behavior of Candaules, showing off his naked wife to his chamberlain Gyges (1.8–12), and Candaules certainly got his just deserts—but the eventual payback followed from the actions of Gyges, and Gyges was trapped by "necessity" into doing what he did (1.12.1). But then Greek payback does not need to be fair in modern terms, any more than it needs to be predictable.

If we jump to the end of the *Histories*, the story of Masistes' wife (9.108–113) forms a structural ring with that opening story of Candaules.[41] Once again we have intrigue at court centering on a king's lust; there too the queen plays a driving role. The king this time is Xerxes, and his desires are more typical of tyranny in that they are directed towards someone else's wife rather than his own, the wife of his brother Masistes. Like the wife of Candaules, the woman is never named; like her too, she has a strong sense of honor and propriety, and she resists Xerxes' advances. In the hope of easier access, Xerxes arranges for the woman's daughter, his niece Artaÿnte, to marry his son Darius. Then matters become more complicated because Xerxes falls for the niece instead, and this time "he gets" the woman (9.108.2).

Trouble hits. One day Xerxes visits Artaÿnte when he is wearing a fine robe woven by his wife Amestris. Delighted both with the robe and with his lover, he promises to give her whatever she wants. She—predictably for the reader, though evidently not for Xerxes—demands the robe. Bound by his oath, he cannot avoid giving it to her, and she wears it with pride. Unsurprisingly, Amestris recognizes it and is not pleased. A few days later it is Xerxes' birthday, when Persian custom requires him to grant any gift requested over dinner. Amestris seizes her opportunity and demands—this turn is less predictable—not Artaÿnte herself, but her mother, who she thinks is the one to blame (*aitios*, 9.110.1; p. 7). Xerxes again cannot get out of it. He tries to soften the blow by offering Masistes his own daughter if he divorces his wife. Masistes refuses—he has no complaint against his wife—and Xerxes withdraws the offer but still demands an end to Masistes' marriage. Meanwhile Amestris has ordered her bodyguard to bring her the woman and mutilates her horribly, cutting off her breasts, nose, ears, lips, and tongue and throwing the breasts to the dogs. Masistes rides off to Bactria with his sons and some others to stir up a revolt: Xerxes traps him on the way. Masistes, his children (παῖδες), and his soldiers are all slaughtered.

Payback? Yes, in a way. Outrageous actions bring consequences. But the people most responsible would seem to be Xerxes and Artaÿnte for starting it, and then Amestris for escalating it. There is no explicit mention of payback visiting any of them (for the "children" are most likely just Masistes' sons, the ones who accompanied him on his path to revolt, not Artaÿnte). The ones who suffer are Masistes' wife, who had the courage to resist Xerxes' advances; Masistes himself, who honorably defends his marriage; and the sons and soldiers, who simply do what they are told. Yet the very way that payback has become travestied and distorted is most telling, for it shows so much about the court—the power, the sexuality, the brutality, the shattering consequences that personal loves and hates and caprices can bring, yet also the kingly respect for Persian custom—which only makes things worse.[42] There is a pointer too to something more supernatural at play: Artaÿnte demanded the robe "for it was necessary (ἔδεε) for things to turn out badly for her whole house" (9.109.2), another echo of Candaules (1.8.2; pp. 107–108). By that stage of the narrative we shall have seen many similar features in the "Persian stories" (chapter 9) told of previous kings: these are the ways of the court, and they explain a lot.

What they explain includes a further aspect of payback. There is indeed no *explicit* mention of Xerxes suffering for this, but many will have known what eventually happened to him. In 465 he was assassinated. The details are controversial—different sources give different versions, all of them replete with familiar literary motifs[43]—but it was clearly a matter of court intrigue: the ringleader was Artabanus, commander of the royal bodyguard. Somehow Darius, the crown prince, was involved. Perhaps Artabanus just killed Darius first and then Xerxes (Arist. *Pol.* 5.1311b37–39); but perhaps Darius was accused of being the assassin himself and murdered for it by his brother Artaxerxes (Ctes. *FGrH* 388 F 13.32; Justin 3.1; Diod. 11.69). Darius, of course, was the hapless husband of Artaÿnte: a minor player in the drama of the robe, to be sure, yet still a player, and one who had no reason to be impressed by his father's behavior.[44] The Bactrian revolt that Masistes had hoped to stir did not happen, but Herodotus leaves no doubt that it might easily have done. Many of his audience would have picked up the hint that there were further troubles to come, and this glimpse of the ways of king and of court help to explain why.

So yes, payback, but again coming in a way that is more complicated than a chain of strike and then counterstrike or outrage and then vengeance, even though human vengeance plays its part as well—the vengeance misdirected by Amestris, the thwarted vengeance of Masistes, the ultimate vengeance involving Darius. To understand how it could happen in so oblique a way, one again moves to that more unifocal model of an organism—Xerxes' court—that carries its own dangers and vulnerabilities. The models are different, but they interact, and in a way that depends on the reader or hearer—that second party in the explanatory game for two—doing his or her part to fill in the gaps.

(D) WHOSE FAULT IS IT ANYWAY?

Let us return to blaming. We saw in the first chapter how central that was to thoughts of *aitiē* (pp. 5–8); we also saw that it was often thrown around for specious or inadequate reasons while still having big consequences. The queen decided that Masistes' wife was to blame (*aitios*, 9.110.1): that was unjust (p. 7), but it mattered a good deal.

Sometimes the extension of *aitiē* is such that any suggestion of blameworthy offense is a mere waft in the air. When Oroetes decides to move against Polycrates of Samos, it is explicit that he "had not suffered anything at his hands, nor heard any slighting remark, nor even ever seen him before": yet this too is described as "because of an *aitiē* along the following lines" (3.120.1). The first explanation then offered centers on the abuse that Oroetes had at court for letting Polycrates become so powerful, and his pain at such an "insult" (3.120.4). There is a second version too, which has Polycrates treating Oroetes' messenger with insulting dismissiveness (3.121). This alternative more directly shows Polycrates himself giving offense, but both explanations are described as alternative *aitiai* (3.122.1), and the implication is that the word would have fitted the first as well. So is the "blame" that Oroetes himself suffered at court playing a part in the appropriateness of the word, even though he is eventually the inflicter of violence rather than the sufferer? Perhaps; the case of Cyrus and Astyages (p. 8) may suggest something of that sort of transferability.

We see something similar at the beginning of book 3, giving the Persian version of the *aitiē* for the Egyptian conquest: the "Egyptian man" who stirs up Cambyses against Amasis has his personal grievance (3.1.1), but it is eventually Cambyses' own resentment of Amasis' trickery that has the more substantial effect (3.1.5). The difficulties of pinning blame may also add an extra nuance to 6.3.1, when Histiaeus avoids telling the Ionians the true *aitiē* behind his mischief-making and tells a false tale instead about what Darius intends to do to them. There the word primarily conveys just "the real explanation," but there is certainly blame that *should* attach—and to himself rather than to Darius. But if so it is indeed just a waft in the air, and the explanation has moved some way beyond a simple picture of blameworthy transgression followed by vengeful or punitive payback.

Here too we are not too far from the world of Homer, where there is blame in plenty. The Trojans as a whole blame Paris (*Il.* 3.453–454); so, in particular, does Hector (3.38–57, 6.280–285 and 525); even the herald Idaeus blames him too (7.385–397). The Trojans blame Helen as well, so Helen herself tells us (24.768–775). Helen even blames herself, though not without a touch of manipulation—she is especially good with elderly or more powerful men (3.171–180, 6.344–359), and Priam shows a susceptible old man's indulgence in assuring her that it was "not her fault but that of the gods" (3.164–165).[45] Hector blames himself too, for camping one night too many in the plain (22.104).

On the Greek side, blameworthiness for the quarrel continues to be something for characters to brood over. Thersites' blame is uncompromising and directed at Agamemnon (*Il.* 2.225–242). The god Poseidon blames Agamemnon too (13.108, 111–113); so, unsurprisingly, does Patroclus (16.273–274); so, by implication, does Odysseus, picking the right moment to say it to Agamemnon's face (19.181–182). Phoenix thinks the right thing to say to Achilles himself is that his anger would be reasonable but for the offer of recompense that Agamemnon is now making (9.515–523): on that view it is in book 9, not book 1, that Achilles is going too far. (Compare the movement within Herodotus 1.1–4: the Greeks become "greatly to blame" when they escalate the exchanges, p. 25.) No such fine distinctions, though, for Achilles himself, especially once Patroclus is dead: he just blames himself, deeply (18.97–126).

Nor is blameworthiness without its explanatory force. It doubtless matters that Paris was in the wrong, and that goes towards explaining the outcome of the war,[46] just as Pandarus' oath-breaking transgression of the truce allows Agamemnon to express his conviction that Troy will fall (*Il.* 4.158–168, 234–239). Others agree, Trojan (7.351–353) as well as Greek (4.269–271, 13.624–625). Still, for the plot developments that absorb the reader or listener most, the deeper significance of blame is in the light it casts on the blamers and their interaction.[47] In understanding how the quarrel escalates, it does not matter how much *we* blame Achilles or Agamemnon; it matters how much they are blaming each other. In the terrible tirade that Achilles launches against himself in book 18, blaming himself for letting Patroclus and his Myrmidons down, it similarly does not matter whether he is right: it matters that he feels that way, throwing blame at himself as he is so ready to throw it at others (11.654, 21.275–278), and that his feelings are now driving him back furiously to the fight.

The Trojan War continued to be a test case for blameworthiness. In Herodotus' own day, Gorgias, with whatever degree of seriousness, allowed Helen to give a virtuoso demonstration of the reasons why she was not to blame at all (pp. 72–73). It was probably a little after his day that Euripides would stage an equivalent in his *Trojan Women* of 415 BCE, with Menelaus as judge, Helen pleading her innocence, and an implacable Hecuba insisting on Helen's guilt. How much it all explained is a different matter. The *Iliad* does not lead us to think that the Trojan War is really explained by whether Helen was herself to blame. Gorgias may be playfully demonstrating that if you can argue that, you can argue anything. Euripides' Hecuba is only too clear that, even if she wins the argument before Menelaus, that may not seal Helen's fate (pp. 73–75).

Herodotus' treatment of Helen is intriguing too, and again shows how complicated blame and reciprocity can be in practice. She figures in that initial exchange of abductions and plays a minor part there in complicating the picture of masculine exchanges. The learned Persians thought that the Greeks' escalation into a full-scale war was silly, comments Herodotus, "because they thought it clear that women would not be abducted if they did not want to be" (1.4.2). That may not be the most tactful way to put it, and is certainly not likely to appeal to a modern ear: but in its way that remark is an overture, perhaps in a different key, to the role that Herodotus' strong and decisive women will play later in their men's world. We see the first of these soon enough, and it is Candaules' wife (chapter 7[a]).[48]

In book 2 the story of Helen comes into its own, with the extended treatment at 2.112–120.[49] Here again, as in the abduction sequence, it is when the men take over, fired by their own desires and indignations, that events escalate catastrophically and reciprocity becomes unstraightforward. Certainly Menelaus is fired by a desire for vengeance, and certainly the story comes to embody a paradigmatic imposition of a great punishment for a great outrage, one administered by the gods themselves (2.120.5). Yet the mortal level of the narrative dwells not on reciprocity achieved and balance restored but on reciprocity misfiring or frustrated; the agent of the frustration is, even more paradoxically, the one man in the story who is most concerned with reciprocal justice, the Egyptian king Proteus. For it is he who retains Helen in Egypt, determined that Paris should not benefit from his crime: he would even have wished "to take vengeance on Paris for the Greek man's sake" (ἐγὼ ἄν σε ὑπὲρ τοῦ Ἕλληνος ἐτεισάμην—notice the use of a root of *tisis*). He is deterred only by the higher duty he feels not to kill visiting strangers (*xeinoi*, 2.115.4), and again one contrasts Paris and the outrage to his *xeinos* Menelaus. Despite all Proteus' efforts, human reciprocity fails everywhere. The first transgression was that of Paris himself, repaying Menelaus' welcome with injustice, ἀδικίη (2.113.3; cf. 2.115.3): "You received the gifts of hospitality (*xeinia*)," Proteus tells Paris, "then did the most impious of deeds" (ξεινίων τυχὼν ἔργον ἀνοσιώτατον ἐργάσαο, 2.115.4). Menelaus then seeks his own vengeance, and on arriving in Troy "claims justice" (or "recompense," *dikai*) "for the injustices" (2.118.3). But that vengeance comes in the most quizzical of ways. The Trojans assure him that they do not have Helen, for she is in Egypt—"and it would not be just for them to be brought to justice" or "pay recompense" (καὶ οὐκ ἂν δικαίως αὐτοὶ δίκας ὑπέχειν) for the person they do not have. The Greeks are unimpressed, Troy eventually falls, and Helen is indeed not there; Menelaus has to collect her from Egypt on his return, along with the treasure that Proteus has impeccably kept safe for him. Yet Menelaus then himself repays Proteus appallingly, sacrificing two Egyptian children to secure a wind for sailing (2.119.2–3). The language echoes the phrases we heard of Paris a few chapters earlier. Menelaus too received "great gifts of friendship" (ξεινίων ἤντησε μεγάλων, 2.119.1), as well as the return of Helen and the treasure, yet "after receiving these things, Menelaus behaved unjustly towards the Egyptians" (τυχὼν μέντοι τούτων ἐγένετο Μενέλεως ἀνὴρ ἄδικος ἐς Αἰγυπτίους) and "contrived an impious deed" (ἐπιτεχνᾶται πρῆγμα οὐκ ὅσιον, 2.119.2). Even the unexpected winds point to the parallel, bringing Paris to Egypt (2.113.1) and then preventing Menelaus' departure (2.119.2).

Menelaus is clearly no better and no worse than Paris, and the true protector of reciprocity and Greek values is the Egyptian Proteus. But that very championing ensures that the human level of reciprocity misfires at every stage. If Paris does eventually receive his comeuppance, it is only because the gods intervene: ". . . to express my own view," says Herodotus, "it was because the supernatural (*to daimonion*) was ensuring that they should be utterly destroyed and make it plain to humans that great injustices produce great acts of vengeance from the gods" (2.120.5).[50] This is a rhythm that we will see is typical of Herodotus' narrative, with a story beginning on a human plane but finally only making sense if a divine level is also brought into play (chapter 10).[51]

That shift to the divine level is important. Human reciprocity naturally leaves unfinished business, with one party resenting the previous step in the sequence and alert for an opportunity to strike a new blow. That was why the Trojan War could so naturally fit into the wider series of East-against-West abductions at 1.1–4; and even though the war is the final step in that series, it is still marked as having an important consequence: the eastern perception of the Greeks as their natural enemies (1.4.4). Once the gods have been brought in as the agents of vengeance, however, the story stops there. Vengeance is complete and annihilating (thus the victims are "utterly destroyed," 2.120.5); and, even if they had not been, the quest for any further strike against the gods would be catastrophically fruitless. This sequence can act as a warning example for later generations (2.120.5 again), but that is the only interest in the future.⁵² Once the divine becomes central, the causal picture becomes much closer to the self-contained organic model, where an explanation is sought in terms of an individual entity and when that entity dies, the story stands a chance of being complete. Finishing a human chain of vengeance can be much more difficult. That, after all, is what the *Oresteia* is largely about—and there too the gods have to be brought in to bring some sort of answer.

(E) THEM AND US

A Greek audience would certainly find much in this treatment of the Trojan War that was arresting, even bemusing. It is a new insight into the most familiar of Greek myths, and it is owed to its Egyptian point of view. The story is drawn from the mythical period that Herodotus normally eschews, that indeed he made a great show of eschewing at 1.5.3. To offer it here, in this Egyptian context, continues his insistence that reliable Egyptian memories stretch further into the past than anything Greece may "know."⁵³ Some features of his style, notably his use of direct narrative rather than indirect speech, indicate even more confidence in this story than in the rest of his early Egyptian history.⁵⁴

That is not the only way in which parochial Greek assumptions are put firmly in their place. Egypt had been introduced as the home of inversion and the topsy-turvy, where everything is put into reverse, where in particular Greek customs are firmly avoided (2.35.2, 2.91.1). Yet by now it is seeming more Greek than Greece, a country where Greek moral values are more revered than they are at home. This is a place where suppliants are respected (2.113.2);⁵⁵ where not merely Proteus but also his official Thonis is outraged by Paris' affront to hospitality (2.114.2–115.4); where Proteus then respectfully keeps Helen and the treasure for "the Greek *xeinos*" (Menelaus, 2.115.6), as if he is already bonded even before his arrival; where he eventually gives him lavish gifts of guest-friendship, *xeinia*, and restores everything he has lost (2.119.1).⁵⁶ Even the shape of the story feels Greek, although Herodotus claims Egyptian sources (2.113.1, 116.1, 118.1, 120.1), and many of the audience would be sensing affinities to Stesichorus' famous version that Helen never went to Troy—it was only a phantom.⁵⁷ The effect is not far removed from that of Sophocles' *Philoctetes*, where the audience are transported to a wild place, on the margins of the civilized world—and yet find Greek civilized values more securely respected there, by the man who has been deserted for ten years, than they were in the Greek community that sent Odysseus and Neoptolemus on their mission.

The final paradox is that Menelaus repays all this with human sacrifice—the sort of human sacrifice that, Herodotus has already brought out, ignorant Greeks falsely ascribe to the Egyptians (2.45.2, where the Busiris story is in point).[58] No one at that point could fail to think of Aulis and that other human sacrifice perpetrated by Menelaus' brother Agamemnon. Menelaus' brutality is clearly not a momentary aberration, but a Greek pattern; and it is the antithesis of those values embodied in Proteus himself. Greek values are found in the Other more than in the Self, and Egypt continues to play the subtle role it is developing for herself in the *Histories*, a place where, despite the initial intimation of simple inversion, the parallels and contrasts for both Greek and Persian experience are rich and complex.

We shall see that this is not the only challenge to Greek moral smugness, and these cross-cultural comparisons are important for explanation too. Anyone inclined to explain the Greek victory over Persia as all down to some moral superiority is given pause; parallels with other cultures can suggest that behavioral features, including the most brutal and unpleasant, require an explanation that goes deeper than complacent talk of national characteristics. "Platitudinous generalizations" (p. 14) will still be playing a part in audience reactions; that Hippocratic interest in similarities and differences between Greek and foreign cultures may suggest that not just the platitudinous stereotypes would be familiar but also their questioning and qualifying (chapter 1[f])—some barbarians, we remember, are there the best fighters of all. The same is suggested when Euripides' Andromache denounces "you Greeks, you inventors of barbarian atrocities" (*Trojan Women* 764) in 415 BCE, just a few years after Herodotus' *Histories* probably reached their final form. So such thinking can still fit within the expectations that audiences would bring to this explanatory game for two. But it is hard to think that they would fit *comfortably*, at least for many or most of those readers and hearers.

Nor is this the last time that they will find themselves rethinking ideas, whether those are their own preexisting assumptions or just those suggested by Herodotus' own earlier narrative. We shall see a lot more of that later. But in the next few chapters we should think about some broader questions, both where such ideas might come from and, first, how one can possibly know what explains anything anyway.

CHAPTER 3

HOW CAN YOU POSSIBLY KNOW?

(A) PUTTING IN THE WORKING

Generations of schoolchildren have been taught to "put in their working" or "show their work" when solving mathematical problems. You need not just to get the right answer but to show how you got there. That is what historians are so often reluctant to do. This is partly because such explicit working would not fit comfortably into a narrative genre, one whose business was showing not telling (chapter 1[c]); but even the passages of "dissertative"[1] analysis are often reticent, "telling" the audience the answer but hardly "arguing." Thucydides states bluntly "the truest explanation" for the war: the Athenians became great and by frightening the Spartans forced them towards war (1.23.6). He does not say why he prefers this to alternative explanations—this was Pericles' war, or the Spartans' or Corinthians' fault for overreacting, or all because of Megara—though his narrative allows readers to do something to work that out.[2] Nor does he make it clear why the Sicilian expedition was "not so much an error of judgement about the choice of enemy as a failure by those at home to make the right follow-up decisions . . ." (2.65.11), and in that case critics have found it more difficult to find support in the narrative.[3]

Even that mightiest of figures in causal analysis, Hume himself, tended not to make his working clear. In his philosophical works he explored at length how, in his view, the mind notices a "constant conjunction" and infers a causal connection of events that still "belongs entirely to the soul." Yet when he wrote the *History of England* for which the philosophy was a propaedeutic, he was content to talk about many causal connections that were out there, features of the world rather than of his own soul:[4]

> But whether we are to account for that measure [William's return to Normandy so soon after the conquest] from the king's vanity or from his policy, it was the immediate cause of all the calamities which the

English endured during this and the subsequent reigns, and gave rise to those mutual jealousies and animosities between them and the Normans, which were never appeased till a long tract of time had gradually united the two nations, and made them one people . . .
(HUME 1762, CHAPTER IV)

That national spirit which prevails among the English, and which forms their great happiness, is the cause why they bestow on all their eminent writers, and on Bacon among the rest, such praises and acclamations as may often appear partial and excessive.
(HUME 1762, CHAPTER XLIX, APPENDIX)

One reason for that lack of explicit working is that historical methodology is so elusive, not least because "constant conjunctions" are difficult to identify amidst history's mass of singularities. In that first passage in particular, Hume's causal claim does not radiate verifiability: how could he, or his readers, possibly be sure that this was the crucial factor? Even if one puts weight on that "immediate," how can we know how it would have been if William had remained solidly in Westminster? Might there not have been troubles anyway? The younger Hume might well have tartly told the older that such a "conjunction" indeed belonged entirely to his own soul.

Herodotus contrasts with Hume here, for he sometimes does let us see his working, both on scientific matters and on the history of events.[5] Scientifically, there is the discussion of why the Nile floods (2.20–25), impressive in its logic even if it reaches the wrong conclusion. One explanation falls down on Hume's ground of "constant conjunction"—the trade winds have sometimes failed to blow, but the Nile has still flooded—and also because it explains too much: if it were a matter of winds, then other rivers too should behave the same way, and they do not. That is an example of what logicians call "denying the consequent" or *modus tollendo tollens*:[6] if p then q, but not q, so not p either. Another is rejected on grounds of verifiability; when someone, presumably Hecataeus (pp. 2, 64), adduces "Ocean-stream," he is just pushing the analysis into the unclear (ἐς ἀφανές, 2.23), and "I at least do not know of any such stream." A third simply fails to accommodate the theory within the audience's preexisting assumptions: to explain it in terms of melting snow ignores the way that it is flowing from the hottest regions to the cooler, and certain other pointers to melting snow are also absent.

The explanation he does favor (2.24–25) affords a better accommodation, relating it to the perceived trajectory of the sun (cf. 4.50.3–4). We saw in chapter 1 that this adopts the Presocratic principle of using the perceptible to infer the unknown (p. 2). There are analogies too with argumentative patterns in the Hippocratics: if the "sacred" disease were genuinely more "sacred" than any other, it ought to strike all classes of people equally, but in fact it particularly afflicts the phlegmatic (*On the Sacred Disease* 5 pp. 150–152 J = 2 VI pp. 364–366 L)—so *modus tollens* again; if Scythian impotence were really the result of a divine visitation, it would afflict all classes equally, or perhaps the poor even more than the rich (*Airs Waters Places* 22 I p. 128 J = II pp. 78–80 L).[7] Thomas has analyzed these Hippocratic analogies powerfully,[8] and I will say no more here.

Herodotus can show his work when talking about historical events too.

> Here necessity compels me to make clear an opinion that most people will find invidious (ἐπίφθονον), but I will not hold back from putting it in the way that appears to me to be the truth. If the Athenians had taken fright at the approaching danger and abandoned their land, or even if they had not fled but stayed there and surrendered to Xerxes, nobody would have made the attempt to take on the Persians at sea. Then, if there had been no opposition at sea, what would have happened on land would have been something like this. No matter how many covering walls the Peloponnesians had put up across the Isthmus, the Lacedaemonians would have been given up by the allies: that would not have been from choice but through necessity, as the naval force of the barbarians would have picked them off city by city. So the Lacedaemonians would have been left to fight alone, and once isolated they would have performed great deeds—and died an honorable death. Either that would have happened, or they would first have seen all the other Greeks Medizing and they too would have come to terms with Xerxes. Either way, the Persians would have conquered Greece: for nobody can tell me what use the walls across the Isthmus would be if the king dominated the sea. As things are, anyone who called the Athenians the saviors of Greece would not be wrong, for the choice they now made was going to be what tilted the scales. That choice was for Greece to be free and to survive, and it was they that roused all the rest of Greece, excepting the Medizers, and thus—second only to the gods—repulsed the king. Frightening and alarming oracles from Delphi were not enough to persuade them to abandon Greece: no, they stayed, and they were willing to face the invader in their own country.
>
> (7.139)

That tells us something both of Herodotus, who feels so strongly, and of his audience, who will not like what they are hearing: a "game for two," indeed.

There is a good deal going on in that passage beyond the surface analysis: hints of the Athenian imperial future, for that is why most people will find such ideas "invidious" (though ἐπίφθονον suggests that that is a matter of envy as much as moral disapproval);[9] the author's refusal to buy into the tropes of Athenian "finest hour" or "beacon of freedom" rhetoric, for if the Athenians saved Greece it was simply because they did not run away when they might have done; the pointers to the danger of Greek fragmentation, to the understandability of Medism, and to the vulnerability of the Peloponnese to sea power.[10] As so often, the richest explanatory passages explain more than the single context in which they figure.[11]

Still, let us stay for the moment with the surface argument and particularly that interest in "virtual history"—the things that did not happen but might have done. Herodotus knows that such counterfactual thinking matters, that indeed one cannot analyze historical causes without it.[12] To say that $p \to q$ implies that if p had not happened, q would not (in the case of necessary causes) or might not (in that of sufficient causes) have happened either, and that involves counterfactual speculation.[13] True, even when we are convinced that q would/might not have happened without p, we may not yet have found a cause, for both p and q may be effects of an antecedent cause C; but it is a pretty good start. If one formalizes the present case, it would be in terms of a *necessary* cause. The Athenian steadfastness was doubtless not sufficient to explain the outcome; apart from anything else, the gods had a role to play ("second only to the gods," 7.139.5); and the Athenians' choice would "tilt the scales" one way or the other, no more. Still, if they had left, the Greeks would have lost no matter what else happened (at least as far as the human level is concerned: the implications of that "second only to the gods" are not traced through, and we will return to that later [p. 156]).

We can see similar counterfactual thought-experiments in cases of the physical world.[14] Once again (cf. pp. 2, 41), the Nile flood is a good example. Why does the Nile show a phenomenon that its counterpart the Danube does not? It is because of the sun's path: if that ran to the north rather than the south the Danube would behave in the way that the Nile does now (2.26). A little earlier he has played with another counterfactual thought-experiment in discussing the silting of the Delta: if the Nile flowed the other way into the Arabian gulf, "what would prevent that from silting up, given the passing of twenty thousand years? I think myself that it would happen within ten thousand" (2.11.4).[15] There is an element of counterfactuality too in discussing that explanation in terms of the prevailing tradewinds (p. 41), just as there always is in *modus tollendo tollens*. If that were right, what else would be the case? Other rivers would react to the winds in the same way—but they do not.

There are other historical examples of such "virtual thinking." It may be a simple matter of rejecting a report: it cannot be true that Xerxes ordered his noble followers to jump overboard in a storm, because if the ship really needed to be lightened he would have sacrificed the rowers instead, and he did not: this is another form of *modus tollendo tollens* (8.118).[16] The same goes for Herodotus' conviction that Helen could not really have been in Troy: if she had been, the Trojans would have given her back (2.120).

When facts are not in doubt, counterfactual thinking can extend to more elaborate cases of explanation. The Phocians did not Medize: why not? Simply because the Thessalians did, and the Phocians hated them; if the Thessalians had stayed on the Greek side, it would have been the Phocians who would have gone over to Xerxes (8.30.2). In formal terms, that should imply that this explanation is both necessary and sufficient, the only cause that came into play: whatever else might have happened to complicate matters, the Phocians would have been on the opposite side to the Thessalians. Why did the Corinthians take part in the expedition against Samos? It followed an incident where the Samians had foiled some Corinthians who had been taking a cargo of Corcyrean youths to be castrated, but that is not enough to explain it:

> If the Corinthians had been on good terms with the Corcyreans, they would not have taken part in the expedition against Samos for that reason (ταύτης εἵνεκεν τῆς αἰτίης); but in fact they are at odds with one another and have been continually ever since they first colonized the island. (3.49.1)

That continuing bad feeling would not have been enough in itself to explain the Corinthian participation, as it would not bring Samos into it at all; but the incident of the Corcyrean youths is not enough either, so neither cause is sufficient.[17]

There are more straightforward cases too, where he is simply trying to recreate the thinking of agents when they were planning for various contingencies: their planning naturally ranged over the alternative futures, including the ones that did not go on to happen as well as the one that did.[18] At 5.65.1 he speculates on what would have happened if the Peisistratid children had not fallen into enemy hands in 508: the Spartans would not have forced the Peisistratids out but would have gone home quickly, for they were not thinking of a long siege—otherwise they would have come with more food and drink. At 6.30.1 he describes how the Persian satrap Artaphrenes and his general Harpagus decided to execute Histiaeus without further ado; this was because they feared what would happen if they sent him up alive to Susa, for—so Herodotus thinks (δοκέειν ἐμοί)—Darius would have forgiven him because of his earlier services. Herodotus is presumably extending his own speculation in order to reconstruct the thinking of the Persians.

Then at 7.168 he is explaining the temporizing of the Corcyreans in 480, when they put to sea with sixty ships but did not get as far as to link up with the main fleet. The Corcyreans explained this in terms of prevailing winds, but Herodotus prefers to interpret this lingering as a deliberate ploy, carried through in the expectation that Xerxes would win. (Just before he has explained the behavior of the Syracusan Gelon along similar lines, though in that case Gelon was assuming that either result was possible: 7.163–164.)[19] Herodotus speculates on what the Corcyreans would have said to Xerxes (itself an indication of the importance of rhetoric in his and his audience's thinking)—"we didn't want to do anything that you would have disliked"—and thinks that Xerxes would have found this plausible enough to treat them better than the other Greeks ("that would indeed have happened, so it seems to me," 7.168.3). That such an alternative future can be imagined, and could have been imagined by the Corcyreans at the time, therefore gives credibility to the interpretation of their thinking that Herodotus accepts and leads him to reject the excuse (σκῆψις) that the Corcyreans proffered.[20]

On the face of it, the logic of these different counterfactual steps is different. In the Phocian case (8.30), he is assuming the cause—the hatred—and inferring the consequence—they would have been on the other side. It is not an argument *for* positing hatred as the cause (that would require other possible explanations to be considered): it is *assuming* that hatred is the only plausible explanation and using the speculation to underline its intensity. The same could be said about those thought-experiments concerning the Nile, even though he does there consider other explanations: the counterfactual aspect is an arresting way of stating a conclusion reached on other grounds.[21] With the instances of Corinth and Corcyra (3.49) and of Athenian leadership (7.139), he is altering one variable in a complex confluence of conditions to work out how much difference it would have made, then arguing back from that speculation to gauge the importance of that variable. The Phocian and Nile examples are presentational ploys, and good ones: they help the audience to grasp and remember the claim that is being made.[22] The Corinthian and Athenian ones are more clearly heuristic, conveying the logic that supports the causal claim in the first place.

Yet the different cases have more in common than that distinction might suggest, and not just because the Athenian case in particular carries a powerful presentational rhetoric of its own. The Phocian and Nile instances have a heuristic element as well, for there too the argument is based on asking "what else would we expect to be the case if the postulated explanation is true?" and then "are we prepared to accept those implications?" The answer in each case is Yes: we can believe that the Phocians would have been on the other side, that the Danube would behave similarly, and that the silting would have happened on the east coast of Egypt just as it does on the north. Similarly with the cases of Histiaeus' execution (6.30.1) and the Corcyreans' temporizing (7.168): can we believe that such an alternative future (Darius' or Xerxes' forgiveness) was possible enough to be contemplated? The answer in each case is Yes, and so the reconstructed motive can be accepted. The heuristic—the readers' heuristic as well as the writer's—and the rhetorical cannot ultimately be distinguished, for it is the invitation to ponder those causal implications that adds presentational persuasiveness, underlining that there is cool and rigorous reasoning behind the claims that are made.

(B) SCIENTIFIC AND HISTORICAL EXPLANATION

All this raises questions of verification. In this fantasy world of alternative futures, how could Herodotus or his audience possibly know? How could they be sure what would or would not have happened if the Athenians had left or if the Thessalians had stayed loyal or if the Corinthians and Corcyreans had been on good terms, any more than Hume could know what would have happened if William had stayed in London?

A commonsense answer would be in terms of—common sense, the application of understanding of how the world is; and, suspicious though one should be of talk of "common sense," so often a mask for something that is neither common nor sensible, that move is not wholly wrong. It is a version of that application of general, often platitudinous principles that we discussed in chapter 1 (p. 14): in these cases, it would be our understanding of the way that humans behave, while the explanation of the Nile flood depends on the way that silting works or the melting effect of the rays of the sun. Local or kinship animosities can be deep enough to decide a community's decisions about war and peace, and that is a general "life-is-like-that" observation (pp. 20–21): one can see that the hatred of the Phocians for the Thessalians or of the Corinthians for the Corcyreans really is that deep, and that is more specific. Sea power allows strategic mobility and leaves coasts vulnerable, and that is general (and an insight of Thucydides' Archaeology too: Thuc. 1.1–19); Sparta's allies would be particularly vulnerable if the Athenians took their fleet away. There are reasons why the audience might be primed to find all those generalizations cogent, and we will return to those in the next section.

That is not the end of our difficulties, for how could Herodotus or his audience be clear how much difference any single factor made anyway? It is evidently not enough just to use the "but for" approach that lawyers sometimes use as a rule of thumb:[23] *X* would not have happened "but for" *Y* happening first. There are any number of things "but for" which a later thing would not have happened. The murder would not have happened if the murderer's father and mother had never met, or if the victim had not decided to dash out for a burger at the wrong moment. Many different chains of events need to come together, and the chances of any single individual thing ever happening are always microscopically small. So how can we go about working out which bits of those chains are the ones that explain most, which are the "hot" but-fors and which are the "cold"?

Here we seem to run into an empirical difference between scientific and historical explanation. One can run a scientific experiment over again to check the same result or alter a crucial variable to see what difference it makes. (At least one can do this some of the time: one cannot start the universe over again in a new way, and unless one is evil or insane one cannot unleash an interesting new virus on an unprotected population.)[24] But one cannot run ancient society over again without slavery to allow a better idea of its economic impact, nor erase the French Revolution from the eighteenth century or impose a British revolution on the nineteenth to explore the effect of revolution on industrialization.

One can see why that makes historical causation so epistemologically puzzling. How can one know how much the Treaty of Versailles contributed to the genesis of the Second World War twenty years later? Or, to return to counterfactuals, how different Britain's history would have been if Catherine of Aragon had borne a son? Or how much difference a Great Man or Woman made, a Churchill or a Cleopatra? No wonder some theorists have preferred to think of "narrative codes," fitting events into story patterns that writers or their audiences are preconditioned into finding attractive, possibly simple ones like "pride goes before a fall," possibly more complicated ones concerning, say, the merits or the dangers of regulating your economy or of how electors in a society respond to the rich or the posh or the female.[25] Yet this in turn risks reducing a historian's causal analysis to a matter of arbitrary preference, not too far from deciding which of the alternative endings of *Casablanca* we find more pleasing, or whether the seventeenth century was right to prefer a happy ending to *King Lear*. It is surely not just a historian's self-regarding fantasy to think that some causal analyses are better than others and to find a nonaesthetic justification for such a preference. We could hardly function in everyday life if we did not accept that a routine choice—choosing which pizza to order or which digits to press on one's phone—would have a regular consequence, and in such cases we have no doubt which "but-for" is making the difference.

These are deep issues. So is the further question of how we find a way to defend a concept of historical causation without a further commitment to historical determinism: how can we "explain" the outbreak of the First World War or the collapse of the old Soviet Union without also implying that the arrangement of the pieces could never have had any other outcome in 1914 or 1989, and that if only observers had been intelligent enough they would have known it in advance? Yet highly intelligent observers, far more in tune with their contemporary realities than later generations could ever hope to be, quite evidently could not predict those outcomes with any certainty. John Buchan once claimed that

> events do not follow each other only in succession of time. Even from the point of view of art, history must have its own inevitableness; and from the point of view of science, it must aim at representing the whole complex of the past as a chain, each link riveted to the other by a causal necessity.[26]

But few will agree. There are just so many other ways that history could have happened: yes, events are linked—but the links have more of the daisychain about them than the rivet.

Yet in science there is far more of the rivet, and often explicability, inevitability, and predictability come close to being the same thing.[27] "Often," but by no means always, and "close to," but by no means identical: scientific predictability can become a matter of statistical probabilities rather than certainty, especially in quantum physics.[28] There often has to be room for chance as well: ornithological science can explore the reasons why migrating birds can predictably find their way to their best breeding grounds, but escaping predators en route and finding a suitable spot on arrival can still be a chancy matter. Still, if adding one compound to another in specific quantities has a particular result on Monday, we should normally predict it to do the same if we repeat the process on Tuesday and on Wednesday. There can therefore be talk of "causal laws" for science, and that is the case even when we think in the nondeterminist terms appropriate to quantum physics:[29] such talk would be anathema for most historians.[30]

How, then, can we have retrospective explicability in history without implying either the inevitability of scientific causation or, a slightly different point,[31] prospective predictability? And yet it is hard to think that one cannot. There may be a myriad of possible ways that events could have developed, just as there are of different patterns a football match could take after kick-off;[32] one cannot believe that even omniscience would allow firm knowledge that the first touchdown or goal would come in the sixteenth minute. That, however, does not mean that a maneuver's success or the result of the game is inexplicable once it has happened. Still, if that retrospective explicability is not dealing in 100% certainty that something was always bound to happen, what *is* it doing? One can again see why some prefer to make that move into thinking of fitting events into "narrative codes" with which the audience would be familiar; and in that case we may be getting back to that ancient idiom of rhetorical terminology, what can be made persuasive, after all (chapter 1[d]).

This is a book about Herodotus, not a work of philosophy: there will be no attempt to solve these issues here. Still, both these questions—verification and predictability—are worth taking further even if we narrow the inquiry to the assumptions that Herodotus and his audience might share. First, any idea of predictability would not have seemed so clear-cut in the context of Herodotus' contemporary science, where thinkers readily allowed an element of chance to coexist with an underlying necessity. Plato pointed out this feature of earlier cosmology (*Laws* 10.889b–c), and Aristotle criticized his predecessors for not thinking through what they meant by "chance" (*Phys.* 2.196a11–b9); Empedocles had said that "it is by the will of Chance that all things have acquired thought" (DK 31 B 103) and had given the workings of accident an important role in his account of animal physiology; for Democritus, particles would always be in motion, predictably borne on by their own momentum, but that need not mean that any specific collision was predictable within the limits of human intelligence.[33] Coincidences and accidents mattered, and this insight did not pull against an interest in establishing firm patterns of causation—indeed, it played a basic part within those explanatory schemes. When we reach the Hippocratics, we will see not merely an insistence that the outcome was unpredictable in particular cases—that would be common ground between ancient and modern physicians—but also an acknowledgement that causes could operate in combination, with different explanatory chains intersecting in a way and in a sequence that would not be predictable (chapter 6[a]).[34]

Second, *aitiē*, that tension between explicability and predictability mirrors something in the historians' own texts. Wise figures know how difficult it is to predict the future: Herodotus' Solon knew that particularly well and tried but failed to pass on that wisdom to Croesus (1.30–33). Wars are unpredictable, says Thucydides' Archidamus, here agreeing with what the Athenian ambassadors have just said (Thuc. 1.78.1, 1.84.4, 2.11.4); his Hermocrates thinks "the uncertainty of the future" is the most valuable prompt to caution in one's aggressiveness (4.62.4); and his Pericles produces the memorable formulation that "events can proceed ignorantly," they haven't read the script (1.140.1). Aristotle knew that too: it is probable that the improbable will happen (*Poetics* 25.1461b15).

That unpredictability, indeed, creates many of those Herodotean "wonders," *thōmata*. Croesus' fall may be explicable in retrospect: it was evidently something that, despite all the clues, Croesus himself found impossible to foresee, and we will later see that readers too would not find the explanation in the text to be quite what they expected (chapter 7[b]). Resisting Persia might be a matter of *agnōmosunē*, "a failure to think straight" (6.10, 9.4.2; p. 178); one of the greatest "wonders" is that the Greeks still won—and there will be some explanations in the air for that too. Historiographic theorists now worry about events that are overdetermined, but just as substantial an issue with Herodotus and Thucydides is the way that the biggest things are *under*determined. Those freedom-driven Greek states could so easily have fragmented into self-destruction rather than gloriously winning; the Athenians could so easily have won in Sicily, for that too was just a matter of a few meters in the wall construction at Thucydides' Syracuse (7.2.4).

And verification? One indeed cannot run the experiment of replaying history but altering one crucial variable. There are still vaguely equivalent thought-experiments that one can do by comparing different but similar sequences from the past or from imaginative virtual history. Why did the Spartans make so much fuss about keeping the Athenians on board in 480 but seem to care much less in 479? Herodotus identifies the critical variable there as the construction in the interval of the Isthmus wall (9.8.2). It may also be a matter of finding constants rather than variables, such as that animosity between Corcyra and Corinth (3.49.1; pp. 3, 226). Narrative may also allow more elaborate comparative exercises, especially within the Persian empire, with those different kings and their recurrent patterns of campaigning (p. 12). We shall see more of that later in this book, and we shall also see that an implicit procedure may underlie those imaginary counterfactual speculations. Why should we believe that hatred or self-interest would be so powerful with the Phocians or the Thessalians? The answer will involve a more or less conscious awareness of the way such factors have operated in other sequences in real history (section [c] below and chapter 15[b]).

Here there is a strange overlap between this type of approach and that of "narrative codes." Either way, the relation of one set of events to comparable sequences is crucial to understanding them, and this takes us back to scientific explanation. For in science too we accumulate material and test theses in ways that are not dissimilar, and the Hippocratics theorized this as well as anyone—theorized it, indeed, in a way that is helpful for historiography too. Several works explore the methodology of comparing parallel case histories:

> Some diseases arise from regimen, some from the air that we breathe to live. The way of telling the difference is as follows: when many people are attacked by one disease at the same time, one must assign the explanation (*aitiēn*) to the element that is most common and that we all use

most, and that is what we breathe. For it is clear that our individual regimen cannot be responsible (*aitia*), because the disease strikes everyone in turn, young and old, men and women alike, wine drinkers and water drinkers, those who eat barley cake and those who feed off bread, those who take most exercise and those who take little. So regimen cannot be responsible (*aitia*), when people with all types of regimen are attacked by the same disease. But when many different types of illness happen at the same time, it is clear that individual regimen is responsible in each case, and one must treat them by opposing the visible cause (*prophasis*) of the disease . . .
(ON THE NATURE OF MAN 9 IV PP. 24–26 J = VI PP. 52–54 L)

The principle is one of analyzing similarities and dissimilarities (*homoia kai onomoia*, *Epid.* 1.20 I p. 176 J = 1.9 II p. 660 L): shared features point to an explanation in what is common to all, distinctive ones mean that you try to identify something more specific. "Similarities or differences" are indeed the first words of *In the Surgery*, outlining what a physician should look for (III p. 58 W = III p. 272 L): the phrase may well have been a mantra of the trade.[35]

How you deal with those individual features becomes clearer in a passage in *Epidemics 6*:

> The essential point comes from the diseases' origins and departures. One summarizes as many cases as possible and one's painstaking analyses of these cases, and discovers whether they are like one another; and one also analyzes the dissimilarities, to see if there are patterns of similarity even among the dissimilarities so that they can be reduced to a single similarity. That is the way of verifying what is correct and exposing what is wrong.
> (EPID. 6.3.12 VII PP. 238–240 S = V P. 298 L)

Thus, even among the dissimilarities you look for patterns, features that are shared with other case histories. At least this far, modern "evidence-based" medicine still does much the same, exploring the similarities and dissimilarities in outcomes and side effects of particular treatments.

Elsewhere in the *Epidemics* we can see the procedure at work: thus an author notes that victims never suffered Group *B* of symptoms without also suffering Group *A*, but often suffered Group *A* without suffering Group *B* (*Epid.* 1.10 I p. 162 J = 1.4 II p. 630 L, cf. 6.7.1 VII p. 272 S = V p. 336 L).[36] This recalls that argument in *On the Nature of Man* that it cannot be regimen that is responsible when a particular disease strikes everyone alike, but regimen may be responsible when many different types of illness happen at the same time (9 IV pp. 24–26 J = VI pp. 52–54 L).

There is similar methodological thoughtfulness in other works. One of the earliest texts, *On Ancient Medicine*, has an interesting and elaborate discussion of the problems of distinguishing causal and contingent factors (17–19 I pp. 42–52 J = I pp. 612–620 L).[37] Too many people jump to causal conclusions if the patient has done anything unusual around the day of his illness, taking a bath or a walk or eating strange food.[38] What they need is a more firmly based understanding of the effects of a badly timed bath. That understanding is built up by an accumulation of cases, as the observer notices which factors (such as badly timed baths) recur in similar cases and which do not. If a person accustomed to taking lunch is deprived of it, he or she will suffer certain symptoms: the causal link is established by the observation that *all* lunch-takers suffer similarly in similar circumstances (10–11 I pp. 30–32 J = I pp. 592–594 L). This is not very different from Hume's insistence on the need to seek "constant conjunction" and pin down repeated sequences,[39] except that the Hippocratic writers dwell on *simultaneity* of cause and symptom, their "origins and departures" (*Epid.* 6.3.12 VII pp. 238–240 S = V p. 298 L; p. 51),[40] while Hume talks about antecedents. That question too has been of considerable interest to philosophers, with Kant arguing that some but not all causation was simultaneous: Kant would seem to be right, at least within the limits of human perception.[41]

It is worth noticing too that it is a sign of the good physician to suffer "wanderings and uncertainties" in the analysis of such similarities (*Epid.* 6.8.26 VII p. 286 S = V pp. 352–354 L). The procedure is not meant to be easy, and general explanations are not asserted with confidence.[42] There are some lovely cases in the *Epidemics* where we can see what have been called "scientific soliloquies,"[43] as the physicians leave themselves and their successors the equivalent of post-it notes:[44]

> The symptoms of Menander's vine-trimmer were similar [to the case of the patient already described], except that his bowel movements were initially loose, then stopped completely, and so did his urine: he reached his crisis; he did not suffer a shivering fit on the seventh day—was this because his stomach had already been disturbed?
> (EPID. 4.1.25 VII P. 118 S = V P. 168 L)

> Concretion [of stones in the kidneys] tends to happen after urination more in the case of children: is that because they are hotter?
> (EPID. 6.3.7 VII P. 238 S = V P. 296 L)

> On the same side of the body are localized pain in the ribs, straining in the hypochondrium, swelling in the spleen, nosebleeds, and most problems of the ears; the same is true of eye problems. Is this true in all circumstances, or is it affections that move *upwards* that stay on the same

side, such as those affecting the region of the jaws, eye, or ear, but affections that move downwards do not stay on the same side? Yet cases of angina, erythema, and pains in the ribs stay on the same side. Is it that affections moving upwards from below the liver stay on the same side, such as those striking the testicles and the varicose veins? These questions require thought—where it takes place, where it comes from, and why.
(*EPID*. 6.2.5 VII P. 226 S = V PP. 278–280 L)

Notice how these radiate provisionality: "If I see anyone die, I shall mention it; the ones I know about for the moment have survived" (*Epid.* 2.2.24 VII p. 42 S = V pp. 96–98 L). All this is very close to Karl Popper's view of scientific causal analysis, building up a predictive hypothesis, seeing if it can be falsified, and if necessary making "compensatory adjustments."[45]

We shall look more closely at Hippocratic theorizing in chapters 5 and 6, but the general outline is clear. One builds up a picture over as wide a range of cases as possible but is aware that this is provisional and the next case may turn out to revise the picture. In a particular instance analyzed by Helen King, the picture is first that nosebleeds are good for women; but then we come to a case where they are not, and the picture is revised by observing that the woman is a virgin: hence, the adult channel from vagina to nose is not yet established; hence, she is not really a counter-example after all but an instance of a more refined pattern.[46] We are building up a narrative code, if one wants to put it like that, as we accumulate parallel sequences—women do well from nosebleeds; no, not quite true, nonvirginal women do well from nosebleeds.[47] A "compensatory adjustment" has been necessary. In a similar way a compensatory adjustment is necessary for Herodotus to explain why Scythian oxen are irregular in having no horns—it is because the climate is too cold to promote growth (4.29)—or why the Nile does not follow the norm of flowing smaller in summer. But in all these cases too we would hope that, at least if the science had been any good, we were deciding that one code is better than another because of something that is true rather than simply "belonging entirely to one's soul," something inherent in the nonvirginal female body or the physiology of oxen or the effects of the sun's rays: the compensatory adjustment has brought one closer to the truth.

This is not at all unlike the process whereby the *audience* of Herodotus notice that (say) tyrants, especially Eastern tyrants, tend to behave in similar ways. (Let us limit the point to the audience; it may well have been true of the writer too, but we are on firmer ground with the intellectual exercise encouraged by the text or by its oral form.) One after another, these tyrants tend to get carried away by a run of success, get overconfident, try one campaign too far and take on an enemy where whatever there is to gain is far less than what there is to lose, and they come unstuck (chapter 1[c]). Is this because they are just similar people, perhaps have something like that in the blood? No, because they are in fact very dissimilar people: so it must be something else, perhaps something in the system, something about tyranny or perhaps just about power. Or is it more something about the East, so that it is distinctively eastern tyrants that behave like that, and ultimately falter? In particular, will the Athenian empire turn out to be one that is similar or dissimilar, *homoion* or *anomoion*? Or will it perhaps be similar in its character but dissimilar in its ultimate fate? If so, what will be the further dissimilarity that might explain it, something perhaps to do with freedom or democracy or even with Greekness?

That last question in particular may not be answered in the text: but one can see the analogy with Helen King's nosebleeds, and here too we might hope that the explanatory "code" will correlate with something in the facts of the case, not just be some novelistic literary trope that we happen to find we like. The same goes for other patterns that recur too often to be coincidental—nations prepared to fight enthusiastically for freedom, or states brimming with bellicosity against their neighbors. There may be differences as well: eastern states may give up aspects of their freedom more readily, Greek neighborly animosity may be even more furious. Those too have their explanatory power.

Oratory too collects and explores "similarities and differences," for instance, in the elaborate way that Apollodorus constructs his scandalizing stories of mother Neaera and daughter Phano to mirror one another in [Dem.] 59:[48] this makes both stories more credible, and it insinuates an idea of explanation too—in that case, it will indeed be something in the blood, just as it is in those Athenian dramas that play on similarities between self-willed Clytemnestra and self-willed Electra. A symbouleutic example would be Andocides' *On the Peace with Sparta*, tracking the differences between the present situation and 404–403 when a Spartan peace led to the disastrous rule of the Thirty, and the similarities with the years before the Peloponnesian War when peace was accompanied by prosperity:[49] the audience are encouraged to draw conclusions about what peace is likely to lead to now, and so it is a matter once again of cause and effect.

For a more elaborate example, take Demosthenes' speech (21) against Meidias. One important concern is to establish that what Meidias has done—publicly slapping Demosthenes at a festival—counted as *hybris*. That is a very charged word: if the case can be made, it will make a big difference to the jurors' view of why Meidias acted in the way he did and therefore also to the consequences for Meidias. Demosthenes' argument depends on looking at possible parallels and arguing how they are similar and how they, or some of them, are different.[50] Some of these are taken from real life: compare the case of Euaion who killed a Boeotian (21.73–76). That was *hybris* too and was similar—but Meidias is even worse because. . . . Sometimes the real-life example is taken from further back in history: just look at Alcibiades, famous *hybristēs* as he was (21.143–150)! Then some are imaginary and hypothetical: "Suppose it were someone quite unlike Meidias . . ." (21.128); "would not a normal person have kept his head down after the vote against him of impiety?" (21.199); "what would it be like if people like him were in charge of the state, and an ordinary person were on trial for attacking one of them?" (21.209).[51] Such comparative thought-experiments were not just the stuff of philosophical mind games: they could be important in real court cases, where one person's honor and the other's whole future were at stake.

As a contribution to causal analysis, the point still has value if we concentrate on this heuristic matter of how we identify causes, or at least how we would if our intuitions in a particular instance were challenged. (It is a further ontological question whether such principles of regularity are basic to what causation *is*—it may well be something conceptually more "primitive." But let us leave that aside.) If we relate, say, the rise of Nazism to the Wall Street crash, we then have to ask why it did not have a similar effect in France or England, and we are into a study of "similarities and dissimilarities" in rather the Hippocratic fashion, wherever that path may eventually lead us.

This approach may also be the best way forward in distinguishing those hot but-fors from the cold but-fors.[52] We in fact apply, pretty unconsciously,[53] a sort of mix of historical thinking and virtual history:[54] "Has p, when it occurred in other cases that were relevantly similar, been followed by q sufficiently often? Might p, if replicated in other virtual cases that were relevantly similar, be expected to be followed by q sufficiently often, or if p had not been replicated, might q be expected to follow anyway?" Of course, we then need to define what counts as "relevantly similar"[55] and "sufficiently often" to justify those "expectations," and so it just pushes the issues one level further back; but it is an important pushing-back, as it suggests that even in this modified "scientific" approach we are taking the narrative we are trying to explain and relating it to other narratives, including imaginary narratives.[56] For an explanation to have power and carry conviction, it is implicitly not stand-alone: it is piggybacking on other narratives, just as it would be if we went down the "narrative code" avenue and appealed to story patterns with which the audience would be familiar.

(C) STORIES IN CAHOOTS

Where, then, do these other narratives come from? We already have some answers. Some come from Herodotus' own earlier narrative: one campaign recalls earlier campaigns; one Warner reminds us of other Warners. Some are added from Herodotus' imagination, the alternative futures that might have happened but did not. But the audience bring something to the party too. Real life can always make one more sensitive to the currents of the past. (A modern parallel is the way that Sir Ronald Syme gestured towards 1930s power politics to add cogency to his interpretation in *The Roman Revolution*, published in 1939.)[57]

This interplay between past and present is a topic that we will revisit much later in the book (chapter 15), but it should already be clear that recent experience could underpin several of the examples of this chapter. Those who remembered the bitter animosities between Corinth and Corcyra in the late 430s (Thuc 1.24–55) would be all too willing to accept that "they are at odds with one another and have been continually, kinsmen as they are, ever since the Corinthians first colonized the island" (3.49.1; p. 226) and accept that this could play a part in that brush over Samos. They knew too what a massive fleet could achieve through their experience of the Athenian empire; by the early 420s they would have seen the effect of the seaborne attacks on the Peloponnese (Thuc. 2.17.4, 2.23.2, 2.25, 2.30, 2.56);[58] if Herodotus were still writing and reciting in the later 420s, they would know the more dramatic impact of Demosthenes' and Cleon's successes at Pylos (Thuc. 4.1–41). Both are relevant to Herodotus' dismissiveness about the Isthmus wall at 7.139.

What about the Phocians? Could they really hate the Thessalians so much that they would always be on the opposite side (8.30)? Some at least would remember that they had been among the Athenians' allies when they tried to intervene in Thessalian stasis in the mid 450s (Thuc. 1.111.1); but by 431 alignments had changed, and the Phocians were on the Spartan side (2.9.1), the Thessalians (generally) on the Athenian (2.22.2, 3.93.2, etc.). Then at Thucydides 3.101.2 (426 BCE) "hatred of the Phocians" plays a part in directing conduct not of the Thessalians but of their nearer neighbors the Locrians of Amphissa. The Phocians, it seems, were good haters now and good at being hated, and it makes it all the more believable that they were good haters back in 480 too. Accommodation within an audience's conceptual scheme is always easier when it relates to further events within their own experience, for as Aristotle so sagely observed, "It is clear that what has happened is possible, for if it were impossible it would not have happened" (*Poetics* 9.1451b17–19), and this extends to the believability of explanations as well as that of the stories themselves. We are not far here from Hume's "constant conjunction" of events. That is what would have happened, because it always, or at least so often, does.[59]

This is another case, too, where we can compare the practice of fifth-century science. As *On Ancient Medicine* puts it, you are much likelier to accept a medical explanation when it maps on to your own experience: "Then it is simply a matter of remembering what happens to yourself" (2 I p. 16 J = I pp. 572–574 L).[60] *On Ancient Medicine* itself appeals to the audience's memories of what it is like to have a cold (18 I p. 46 J = I. p. 614 L) in order to make a point about nasal inflammation and its causes, while the recollection of how one drinks fluids can help us to infer what bodily structures are best equipped to absorb liquid (22 I pp. 56–58 J = I p. 626 L). *On the Nature of Man* argues for seasonal shifts in one's constitution on the grounds that phlegm is most visible in winter (colds, white swellings) and blood in spring (nosebleeds) (7 IV p. 18 J = VI pp. 46–48 L). *On the Sacred Disease* supports its view of air circulation by appealing to the experience of numbness in the extremities when the circulation is cut off (7 II p. 154 J = 4 VI p. 368 L). *Airs Waters Places*, arguing that the sun draws off the lightest part of water, points out that exposed skin is drier in sunny weather than skin covered by clothes (8 I p. 90 J = II p. 34 L).

So for historians as for physicians, what you have seen for yourself always carries particular impact; but we all know more than that. Knowledge of human experience can come from stories too, and this is where intertextuality becomes important.[61] We shall often find cases where Herodotus' narrative remolds patterns familiar from, in particular, Homer, though sometimes more generally from myth (as in the case of Agariste's wedding, 6.126–131, reminiscent of stories of the wooing of Helen and of the competition Pelops won for the hand of Hippodameia),[62] reinforced as myth so often was by performances on the tragic stage. This even finds an echo in modern analysis of the behavior of juries: juries are more likely to find a case plausible if it recreates a story pattern that is familiar, though these days it is more likely to be familiar from film or television rather than from the *Iliad* or the theater.[63] Nor need that process always be conscious, any more than jurors are conscious of why they find an advocate's story persuasive. Some readers or hearers would be aware of an echo of the *Iliad* in a battle scene (pp. 202–203); some might think explicitly of tragedy when Astyages serves up Harpagus' son to him at a banquet (1.119; p. 114); but it would not matter much if they did not. Subconscious familiarity with story patterns would be just as effective in reinforcing their cogency.

Homer occupies a special position here, not just because of the prime role the poems played in Greek cultural education and awareness but also because they were the great model for an extended and complicated narrative. But there would be other works and genres too that would be part of the intellectual landscape. Let us next look at some of those.

CHAPTER 4

ADVENTURES IN PROSE

(A) SOMETHING DIFFERENT?

"There was no Herodotus before Herodotus," proclaimed Momigliano.[1] He was probably right: Dionysius of Halicarnassus, who had access to a range of pre-Herodotean authors that we lack, insisted that there was something new and special about Herodotus (*On Thucydides* 5). For Dionysius that newness consisted in Herodotus' drawing material together from local traditions and records. Whether or not he puts it in the right way,[2] that idea of "bringing together" is important (and may mirror a parallel development in poetry, if the *Ionika* of Herodotus' uncle or cousin Panyassis is rightly thought to have been more inclusive than its more locally focused predecessors).[3] Earlier writers might concentrate on a particular region or country, or produce "genealogies" or *Periēgēseis Gēs*; Herodotus' greater scale allowed him to combine material of all types, genealogical, narrative, geographical, scientific, and whatever else he might choose, and draw it from all over the world that he knew.[4]

One of the basic questions for this book—how far his investigation of history operated in the same way as that of scientific phenomena—is made possible by that expansive mindset. We might put it in terms of his combining "genres," perhaps of allowing one genre to "enrich" another, and we might compare the way that tragedy was drawing on and gesturing towards other genres to deepen its suggestions.[5] Herodotus himself would not have had the vocabulary to put things in that way, and anyway prose literature had not yet settled down into such conventionally delimited kinds (pp. 17–18). It is still reasonable to think that Herodotus' scope did allow him to see new combinations and connections, and to explore them with a curiosity and intellectual ingenuity that can still seem breathtaking. This all-embracingness is indeed another feature that he shares with epic, the "genre" *par excellence* that explored human experience on the largest scale.

Yet Herodotus' work did not burst upon a world that was wholly unprepared. We have already seen something of that in chapter 1, in particular the readiness in several areas to look back in time, or look across to other cultures in the present, in order to cast light on present realities. To explore all the possible models against which his audience might gauge his work would require a book much longer than this. Skill in narrative was becoming the stock-in-trade of orators, and so was the subtlety and ingenuity of their techniques in slanting it in the direction they wished. Evocation of the legendary past was not infrequent; that was probably already the case with, in particular, the Athenian funeral speech.[6] The same was true of orators' glorifying treatment of the Persian Wars themselves. Herodotus presents a more qualified view,[7] though not without acknowledging that some of those glories were real (p. 223).

It is increasingly clear too how many other poetic genres, not just epic, had used narrative; in the seventh century an elegy of Mimnermus had treated a battle of Gyges against Smyrna (frr. 13–13a W²); Simonides' *Salamis* and *Plataea* had now extended such treatments to the themes that Herodotus himself would treat.[8] Simonides' evocation of Achilles in the *Plataea* suggests a "heroizing" of these achievements in line with that of the Stoa Poikile (pp. 15, 202) and of fourth-century orators[9]—and Herodotus is again more nuanced. Such analogies between legendary past and present were familiar in epinician victory odes as well. That suggests a patterning of past and present where each can illuminate the other, and that again is something we will find in Herodotus.

There are other kinds of writing, too, that scholars have claimed Herodotus is "writing against" and implicitly exploiting to define what is special in his own work: "Aesopic" low literature;[10] the poets in general;[11] "other purveyors of mythical material";[12] the sort of proto-biographic big-man writing that Stesimbrotus of Thasos and Ion of Chios, two rather different animals from one another, were producing.[13] That may be the case with all of these, and with each there would be more to say about Herodotus' debts as well as his originality. In cases where these relationships are especially relevant for "explanation," there will be an opportunity to do so later in the book.[14]

In this chapter we will limit discussion to two areas where the precursors covered particularly similar grounds.[15] One of these will concern the orators and "sophists" and, particularly, their interest in questions of responsibility and blame. First, though, let us look at his prose predecessors in treating genealogy and ethnography, who have often (rather imprecisely) been called *logographoi*: here Hecataeus will be especially important.

The -*graph*- in that *logographoi* immediately suggests a qualification. These authors indeed "wrote." Hecataeus foregrounded his writing in his proem: "I write (γράφω) these things as they seem to me to be true" (*FGrH* 1 F 1, p. 62, below). Yet it is now widely and wisely accepted that most of the material that Herodotus drew on was oral, not written, or at most "semi-oral"—written reports of oral tradition, or oral traditions that had interacted with written.[16] Some think that the introduction of writing was crucial for the development of historiography itself, allowing as it did the "cross-checking and confrontation" of different traditions[17] and encouraging the development of a tradition of prose writing that would prove more amenable to sophisticated critical discussion. How much does that complicate our discussion of "explanation"? Does Herodotus' own medium mean that he can explain things in ways that were qualitatively different from those he found, and that his audience knew, in previous versions of the same events?

The straight answer is that we cannot know: by definition we have no access to those oral traditions to tell us the answer. My suspicion, though, is that the answer is "no," or at least "not to any great degree." In the African traditions that Jan Vansina studied, he found little "attempt . . . to establish relations of causality between historical events," but rather a tendency to view history as static, with little sense of continuous development;[18] but we have already found much more sense of historical change in Greek culture, both oral and written (p. 16). It is in any case easy to overstate the impact of writing, at least in its early stages.[19] True, it could allow the development of more elaborate and more detailed genealogies (which does not mean that these were more accurate);[20] true, too, writing could facilitate the wider and quicker spread of ethnographic detail as experience of distant lands accumulated. The first could help Herodotus' chronological endeavors, and those might suggest links between individuals and cities that might carry explanatory force;[21] we should certainly not underestimate the value of such a "chronological scaffolding" for the development of historiography.[22] The second may have generated further material for thought-provoking comparisons with other peoples, and we shall often see that such comparisons have their explanatory function.

Yet chronology itself, as opposed to the stories that attached to the figures that needed chronological fixing, will play little part in this inquiry (little, but not none: this is relevant for instance to the question how much the Greeks learned about the gods from Egypt or the Pelasgians, 2.43–45 and 2.52.3–53); and the richest material for ethnographic comparison came from Egypt, an area long familiar to Greek travelers and traders, and from Persia, familiar enough to a writer from Halicarnassus. Oral traditions may tend to present changes as sudden rather than gradual and associate them with culture-heroes;[23] but in Herodotus that affects his passing references to the distant past more than his treatment of more recent history.

Nor should we overstate the indispensability of writing and reading, or even of prose, to incisive critical debate. "It is hard to imagine Hecataeus writing down his criticism of Hesiod in hexameters!" writes one scholar[24]—but perhaps it is not so hard, if we remember that, even in a world much more used to prose, Lucretius found hexameters perfectly attuned to hard-edged debate. Xenophanes and Empedocles were already finding it possible to couch critical discussion in verse, one suspects largely for an audience of hearers rather than readers. Much, too, of the Hippocratic corpus, argumentative as it is, may also represent works originally written for agonistic public display,[25] and in a well-known passage of the *Phaedo* Socrates refers to a public reading of a book of Anaxagoras (Plato *Phd.* 97b8–c2). It is very likely that the *Histories* themselves are elaborated from versions that were meant for oral delivery: they surely envisage an audience that could pick up points on hearing rather than reading.

Comparative study can certainly illuminate certain aspects of oral tradition, in particular the way that "social memory" favored (without being confined to) stories with relevance to current realities and the taste of localities for giving stories their own tendentious slant.[26] Herodotus himself knew as much, and there are indications that he expected his audience to know it too.[27] Oral transmission will also have shaped stories in ways that made it easier for Herodotus to develop the ideas that he did: features of one tale may infect one another, for instance—"collective memory simplifies by fusing analogous personalities or situations into one"[28]—and attract clichés and stereotypes,[29] and this will have given the impression of clearer and more recurrent patterns in, say, Persian court politics or Greek freedom-fighting than really featured in the messiness of life. There may be certain elements that characterize oral storytelling as well—some repetitiveness,[30] perhaps, or a readiness to use analogies with what the audience will find familiar. But these are traits of written literature as well, the more so in an author such as Herodotus working on the cusp of written and oral culture.

We have already seen, too, how many features of Herodotus' technique are already there in Homer's epics, and those were "oral" both in tradition and in performance. It is true that, as with Homer, writing played a part in allowing Herodotus' work to become a fixed text, or relatively fixed; even if Herodotus may have adapted or selected material from that work for a specific audience, a text of this sort will be less geared than a one-off oral display to any *particular* performance context.[31] Writing will also be part of the explanation for Herodotus' length (as again with Homer—perhaps!), and we saw earlier in this section that this expansive scale did matter. But I would be reluctant to go further in the search for any fundamental differences that writing may have made.

So let us turn to those writers of prose. The prominence that Herodotus affords to Hecataeus[32] means that he demands a treatment all his own.

(B) HECATAEUS

Hecataeus of Miletus was clearly an important precursor with his *Genealogies* and his *Guide to the World* (*Periēgēsis Gēs*),³³ one who very likely deserves prominence as one of historiography's intellectual parents or grandparents; but, as with real genetics, it is not straightforward to identify exactly where characteristics originated or how they have blended or mutated. At times Herodotus seems to be defining his own work against that of Hecataeus and in its terms, but there too his tone is hard to catch. Sometimes it seems captious: both authors use the striking phrase "gift of the river" to explain the geomorphology of the Nile Delta, but Herodotus seems to be suggesting that it required little insight on Hecataeus' part to realize that much:³⁴

> It is evident even to anyone who has not heard about it before and just uses his eyes—anyone with any sense, that is—that the "Egypt" to which the Greeks sail is ground that has been acquired, and the gift of the river.
> (HDT. 2.5.1; CF. HECATAEUS FGRH 1 F 301)³⁵

Later in the book Herodotus tells a story of Hecataeus visiting Thebes and telling the priests about his ancestry, reaching back to a god in the sixteenth generation: the priests retorted by showing 345 wooden statues of chief priests who had succeeded one another as son to father, with not a god in sight (2.143 = T 4 Fo.).³⁶ Most readers find Hecataeus there the butt of the story, with his divine pretentions and his trademark genealogy.³⁷ Equally, it is possible to take a more generous view, with Herodotus acknowledging Hecataeus as a pathbreaking pioneer, investigating the world and the past with open-minded curiosity, finding foreign truth to correct or qualify Greek perspectives (including any claims to recent divine ancestry), and showing a capacity to apply learning to current affairs when he appears as a narrative figure during the Ionian Revolt of 499–494 BCE, advising the Ionians of the importance of their sea power (5.36, 5.125–126 = TT 5–6 Fo.).³⁸ Very likely both approaches are right: this would not be the only time when an author blazoned his appreciation of a predecessor by trying to outdo him, with the implication that this was the intellectual benchmark that mattered and these were the points that were worth scoring.³⁹ If Herodotus himself is in Thucydides' sights at 1.20.3 (and he surely is), that is very much the same technique.

Some aspects of the inheritance are clear enough. There is the self-conscious pride in critical intelligence.⁴⁰

> Hecataeus of Miletus speaks as follows: I write these things as they seem to me to be true: for the tales the Greeks tell are many and laughable, so it appears to me.
> (HECATAEUS FGRH 1 F 1 J = 1 FO.)

That evidently figured early in the *Genealogies* and may have been the first sentence. We can duly trace Hecataeus' correctives to various Greek myths, "rationalizing" them in a way that makes them sit more comfortably with the expectations of normal life:[41] Danaus did not have fifty sons, as Hesiod said; I say it was fewer than twenty (F 19)—notice again that confident first person; it was a nasty snake at Taenarum that became known as "Hades' dog" and was taken by Heracles to Eurystheus (F 27).

That proemial sentence of the *Genealogies* seems itself to be echoed by Herodotus at the beginning of book 2.[42] He is telling the story of the Egyptian king Psammetichus, who was keen to find out the earliest language and set up an experiment with two new-born children. They were given to a shepherd to bring up, with strict instructions that no one should say a word to them: eventually, at the age of two, they ran to the shepherd and said *bekos*, which turned out to be the Phrygian word for "bread." That is what the priests at Memphis say, but there is another version too:

> The Greeks say many silly things, including the version that Psammetichus cut out the tongues of some women, and it was these that he instructed to take care of the children.
> (HDT. 2.2.5)

Not for the only time,[43] the two versions are more notable for what they agree on—the experiment and, presumably, its outcome—than on the point of difference; but the echo of Hecataeus is intriguing, and it invites the same duality of approach. Is it simply marking out Herodotus as a follower of Hecataeus, correcting Greek ideas with more credible, if less sensational, versions? Or was the purveyor of the tongueless alternative Hecataeus himself[44]—that is, "Yes, the Greeks do tell many daft stories, just as Hecataeus said; and here's one, told by that Greek Hecataeus himself"?[45] Either way, or both ways (for again the combination is perfectly possible), that once more looks like a programmatic gesture so early in Herodotus' Egyptian *logos*. If he is the new Hecataeus, it is because he can do Hecataeus so much better.

How Hecataeus managed explanations, though, is not so clear. Evidently the works included pieces of narrative. We might expect these to figure more in the *Genealogies*, attaching stories to great figures from the past, than the *Guide to the World*, but in fact it looks likely that the two books were more similar in texture than we might expect, and the *Guide to the World* too would tell tales while the *Genealogies* included snatches of ethnography.[46] The narratives in the original text were clearly anything but dry:[47] Dionysius of Halicarnassus notes "theatrical reverses" as a feature of his and others' work (*On Thucydides* 5 = T 17a), and "Longinus" talks of his readiness at intense moments to move into direct speech without any introductory "he said" (*On the Sublime* 27.2 = T 20; F 30 is the example he cites). But in the surviving fragments the narrative elements are very sparse. Such as they are, they suggest the odd motivation statement, but these do not go beyond the obvious. Orestheus son of Deucalion came to Aetolia to become king (F 15); Ceyx "took badly" some outrage and ordered the Heracleids to leave (F 30); the Athenians saw the high quality of the land that the Pelasgians had worked locally, and in their jealousy and greed for the land forced them out of Attica "without offering any other *prophasis*" (F 127 = Hdt. 6.137.2). In that last case it would be interesting if that remark about *prophasis* were Hecataeus' own, for it might suggest that he drew a distinction between true and false explanations;[48] but that might equally be Herodotus' own gloss on a matter where Hecataeus was simply silent,[49] in contrast with the self-justifying Athenian version that he goes on to give. "Explanations" of events and actions were clearly there, then, but we can say little about them.

What is clear is that Hecataeus gave "explanations" in a broader sense: explanations of names, with etymology figuring heavily in both *Genealogies* and *Guide to the World*; and the "rationalizing" approach to myth can itself be seen as a type of explanation, making it intelligible why such a story should have arisen. There is explanation of natural phenomena too, such as that passage explaining the Nile Delta as the result of silting— "the gift of the river" (F 301, p. 62). He also seems to have offered an explanation of the Nile flood in terms of its waters flowing from "Ocean": at least, the nameless representative of "some Greeks who wanted to make a name for themselves for their wisdom" (Hdt. 2.20.1) and argued along those lines (2.21) looks like Hecataeus, who did make the Nile flow from Ocean (F 302), and it fits the interest in Ocean that we can trace elsewhere in the fragments (F 18).[50] The explanation moved Herodotus to ridicule, as he dismissed the idea of Ocean as the invention of Homer or some other poet (2.23, p. 2); that though also reflects the way in which Hecataeus would be trying to explain the physical phenomenon in terms familiar to his audience, for the idea of an encircling Ocean from which "all rivers and all the sea and all springs and all deep wells flow" is indeed as old as the *Iliad* (21.194–198; cf. 18.607–608), or at least the *Iliad* that Hecataeus and his audience will have known.[51]

We can see a similar accommodation to his audience's knowledge if it was Hecataeus who described the Black Sea being "like a Scythian bow" (F 197 J = T 12a Fo.), which may be meant with no more literal precision than when Herodotus described Scythia as "square-shaped" (4.101) or when we speak of Italy's "toe" or "heel."[52] Explanation, as we saw in chapter 1, is a game for two, relating the unfamiliar to the receiver's conceptual schemes, and the same is true of descriptions: similes and analogies are a good way of doing so in a world where texts did not include maps or diagrams.[53]

Nor, indeed, was Hecataeus' explanation of the Nile flood so crazy. Herodotus' criticism is that it "refers the story to the realm of the nonevident," the *aphanes*[54]—that is, it offends against the principle that "the evident phenomena are a sight of what is unclear" (p. 2)—and therefore is unverifiable (2.23). There is something in that, as we saw in chapter 1; but it is not always so bad a strategy to explain *obscurum per obscurius*, if the explainer acknowledges that the *obscurius* feature is one for which no explanation has yet been found. Hecataeus' thinking was presumably that the Ocean was tidal in a way that the Mediterranean was not, for reasons that were in his time unclear; if the Nile flooding was regarded as a mega-tide, it was not stupid to think that this might be a secondary phenomenon depending on the broader *explanandum* of Ocean tides. Nearly two centuries later Dicaearchus was still taking the Nile to flow from Ocean (fr. 113 W, specifying the Atlantic); Ps.-Scylax, writing probably around the same date, may well have done the same.[55]

The *Guide to the World* is divided into two volumes, *Europe* and *Asia*. There may be more to that than simple convenience based on the size of book-rolls, as some of the division looks counterintuitive. In particular, he counted most (not all)[56] of the islands of the eastern Aegean as belonging in "Europe" (FF 140–143), whereas the coast itself was "Asia";[57] later authors put the dividing line between Europe and Asia further west, and given the close interaction between islands and their adjacent coasts (*peraiai*) Hecataeus' division would have seemed very odd. Something seems to be at stake here, just as something may well be at stake if it is Hecataeus who is in Herodotus' sights (it probably is)[58] when he criticizes the "Ionians" for their treatment of Egypt, including their definition of the Nile as the dividing line between "Asia" and "Libya" (2.15–17). Maybe it is geopolitical, reflecting that division between the Persian and European/Greek sphere of interests that we find at the beginning of Herodotus' *Histories* ("the Persians regard Asia and the people who live there as theirs, but Europe and the Greek world as separated," 1.4.4); if so, such thinking may also surface when "Hecataeus" is made to advise the Ionians to take to the ships and fortify the island of Leros, with its insight that the landlubbing Persians will find a seaborne attack difficult to mount (5.125).[59] Or maybe it is ethnographic, a foretaste of the view we find in *Airs Waters Places* that, with some qualifications, Europe and Asia produce different types of people (pp. 19–20, 96–97).[60] Either way, it looks as if this embeds an implicit attempt to explain *something*, whether it is the limits of the Persian world or the human characteristics of the continent's inhabitants.

There is a broader point too, one already hinted by that strong overlap of interests between the two works. We tend to regard geographical and historical works as different intellectual endeavors.[61] In the Greek world it was different.⁶² One can see genealogies and geographies/ethnographies as inspired by similar concerns, the desire to place peoples and customs as Greek knowledge of the world expanded (p. 15). Geographies and histories were often written by the same people; histories included geographical and ethnographic material (we limply label them "digressions"), and geographies included historical sketches of the places they described. Within Herodotus himself we often see that disputes about the past intermesh with disputes about space and place. A site of memory—a *lieu de mémoire*—was all very well, but your *mémoire* may not be my *mémoire*, and it can matter a lot to both of us as we lay claim to the same *lieu*. Very early in the *Histories* Herodotus makes it clear how the inquiries intertwine: his travels through place have given him insight into mutability in time, for he has seen how small cities have become great and great become small (1.5.3–4; pp. 28–30).

That returns us to a basic question of this book. How far do historians' attempts to explain events and actions follow the same lines as their attempts to explain other features of the world? How far is explaining what we call "history" felt as different from explaining anything else?

(C) OTHER PEOPLES AND THEIR PAST

Hecataeus was not alone. "The invention of prose"⁶³ was a complex business, and Dionysius of Halicarnassus could marshal an impressive roster of names when he listed Thucydides' predecessors and contemporaries (*On Thucydides* 5; cf. p. 58). How much he really knew about those authors is another matter—but he knew more than us, and for us tracking the work of the likes of Pherecydes of Athens, Xanthus of Lydia, Cadmus of Miletus, Charon of Lampsacus, and Dionysius of Miletus is a frustrating task, though one made easier by Robert Fowler's monumental work on the early mythographers.⁶⁴

Clearly some interests were shared. Other writers as well as Hecataeus wrote on the sources of the Nile and the reasons for its flood.⁶⁵ Works like *Aigyptiaka* and *Persika* probably included some history of events as well as what we would call ethnography or geography; at least, that is what we might infer from a work described as *Things After Darius* (τὰ μετὰ Δαρεῖον of Dionysius of Miletus, *FGrH* 687 T 1). Some writers were concerned to develop a chronological system, aided no doubt by the increased accessibility that writing allowed to the collective memories of different nations.⁶⁶ Nor should we assume that their storytelling was always dry, however primitive their manner seemed to the sophisticated tastes of those few later writers who may have read them (especially Cicero, *de Or.* 2.53): it was not just Hecataeus in which Dionysius found those "theatrical reverses" (*On Thucydides*

5; p. 63). The fragments duly include several "merry tales,"[67] and in some cases we can see some similarities to the storytelling technique of Herodotus.[68] As is the way with good stories and as was the way with Hecataeus, various actions were made intelligible: a motivation here,[69] a setting in context there. All that is "explanation," of a sort.

At a deeper level, we can see that the past, mythical or historical or both, was being used to make sense of familiar features of the present day, cosmological (the role of Chaos or Gaia or Erōs in creation), astronomical (catasterisms), geographical (the Nile again), onomastic (place names), or institutional (Hellanicus, best seen as a longer-lived contemporary of Herodotus, had a lot to say about the Athenian Areopagus).[70] Genealogies too could dwell on the origins of families of particular prominence: Hellanicus traced the ancestry of Andocides back to Odysseus (*FGrH* 4 F 170), and Pherecydes of Athens has been seen as taking a particular interest in and friendly attitude towards the ancestors of the politician Cimon.[71]

Still, there are uncertainties everywhere: uncertainties of dating,[72] of title, even (with Cadmus of Miletus)[73] of the writer's very existence. It would be interesting to know if writers who dealt with the geomorphology of the Nile did so in the same works as they collected Egyptian events; Xanthus seems to have included discussion of geological phenomena in his *Lydiaka* (*FGrH* 765 FF 12–13a) as well as showing some concern with the chronology of events, though it is unclear how elaborate his narratives were (FF 30, 32). That sort of "bringing together" might allow at least the opportunity to investigate the causes of events with parallel techniques to those applied to geology—but we cannot tell if the opportunity was taken. It would be interesting too if Charon of Lampsacus and Dionysius of Miletus, who treated some of the same Persian events as Herodotus (Astyages' dream, Charon *FGrH* 262 F 14 ~ Hdt. 1.108; Pactyes, *FGrH* 262 F 9 ~ Hdt. 1.156–160; Athens' involvement in the Ionian Revolt, *FGrH* 262 F 10 ~ Hdt. 5.97–102; the conspiracy of the Magi, Dionysius *FGrH* 687 F 2 ~ Hdt. 3.61–79),[74] developed a distinctive Persian coloring in those stories. It would also be good to know if the linear narrative in such authors progressed beyond that "and then . . . and then . . . and then" for which the epic cycle was derided (p. 216). It would be particularly fascinating to discover exactly what Ephorus meant by saying that Xanthus gave Herodotus his *aphormai*, his—as we would put it—"launching pad" (*FGrH* 70 F 180). But we cannot tell.

It was in considering this group of authors that Momigliano pronounced his dictum that "there was no Herodotus before Herodotus" (p. 58). There is no indication that he was wrong, and if any of these nebulous figures had had anything of Herodotus' imaginative breadth we might have expected to hear more about them. But we cannot be quite sure.

(D) RHETORICAL FINGER-POINTING

Fowler still extracted enough from those scanty fragments to identify features of Herodotus' "voiceprint." He put special stress on Herodotus' investigative energy in weighing different accounts, something hard to find in those other early prose writers: "He discovered the *problem* of sources."[75] This, he plausibly suggested, should be linked to the emerging "science of rhetoric" that was "furnishing a theoretical framework and a practical set of tools for use in such arenas. The orators argued from analogy, from contrast, from probability, from experience—just like Herodotos."[76] We have already suggested adding "explanation" to those features of his voiceprint (p. 5), and these intellectual tools were equally useful here. That was especially so when it was a matter of blame or exculpation, so often central to forensic oratory. Understandably, orators focus on blaming *people*: it is after all a person who stands accused, and the question is whether he or she (more rarely "they," as in Thucydides' Plataean debate, 3.52–68) should be condemned or not. It is reasonable to see Herodotus as broadening those forensic techniques to investigate phenomena on a less personalized level—features of whole societies and their institutions, for instance, or even physical phenomena.[77] This will be a sort of mirror equivalent of the way in which he draws techniques from the investigation of physical phenomena and applies them to human events, and in each case the familiarity of his audience with such models will be as important to his persuasiveness as that of the author himself.

Indeed, the weighing of blame has something in common with that characteristic weighing of sources and evidence. In each case, ideas of what is *eikos*, "reasonable," become important, even if "reasonable" expectations deal with factual plausibility in the one case and moral responsibilities in the other. Quite often the two investigations become indistinguishable. To claim I am not αἴτιος τοῦ φόνου, "responsible for the killing," can boil down to "I did not do it," and that is a matter of simple fact. This is the case, for instance, with Antiphon's *On the Murder of Herodes*: whoever killed Herodes, it was not me. Even in that speech, though, one can see some parallels to Herodotus' methods. Historical parallels have their place, tracking similarities and differences from the present circumstances (68–70), just as later orators would collect past *homoia* and *anomoia* in comparison with their present cases (pp. 54–55). There is counterfactual thinking too, and several passages in the speech elaborately paint alternative scenarios (21–28, 41–45, 52–56, 63): if I had really been guilty, the slave's testimony would not have taken that form only under torture; there would have been blood on the boat; a shout would have been heard; I would not have come back to

Athens; my voyage would have ended in shipwreck because of the pollution. The last two arguments also have analogies in Andocides' *On the Mysteries* (399 BCE): if I were guilty I would not be here (1–5); the gods would have shipwrecked me if I were guilty (137–139). The form is that of the *modus tollendo tollens* argumentation we have already seen in Herodotus (p. 41)—if p then q, but not q, therefore not p.

More interesting are those cases where the facts are not in doubt, but the causality and the assignment of blame are not straightforward. Antiphon's *Tetralogies* here are fascinating. Their exact date is uncertain, and they may date shortly after Herodotus, but if so it will only be by a few years: Antiphon of Rhamnous—if this is the same man—was executed in 411, and the *Tetralogies* may be among his earliest works.[78] In any case, the sophistication of the argument suggests a honing of skills by rhetoricians that has taken place over several generations.

The three *Tetralogies* each consist of four speeches, two on each side of a case, and range over the different sorts of arguments that might be used. The first *Tetralogy* covers a case of murder and the only question is whether the defendant did it, and so here the issue is one of fact, as in the *Murder of Herodes*. All depends on *eikos* arguments, including counterparts of ones we know to have been aired earlier in the fifth century by the Sicilians Corax and Teisias.[79] Here as in the *Murder of Herodes* some counterfactual speculations are used to support the various *eikos* arguments: if it had been cutthroats, the victims would not have been found still wearing their cloaks; if it had been a fellow drinker, the others would have known; if it had been a quarrel, it would not have taken place there and then (*Tetr.* 1 α.4; further argument along these lines at β.5–6, γ.2, δ.4–5). On the other side, had I been guilty, I would not be here but would have gone into exile (β.9; response at γ.6)—a version of an argument we have already seen in *On the Murder of Herodes* and in Andocides.

The second and third *Tetralogies* move on to different cases and ones more illuminating for this book, cases where most of the facts are regarded as established but questions of responsibility and blame remain. The second deals with what we would regard as an accidental death, a case where a boy was killed when hit by a javelin throw in the gymnasium. This may well have its basis in a real-life incident, if the story is true that Pericles and Protagoras argued about it at length (Plut. *Pericles* 36.5)—a further indication that such discussions would have been familiar within Herodotus' own lifetime whatever the date of the *Tetralogies* themselves, as Herodotus almost certainly outlived Pericles. Someone needs to be designated as *aitios* and removed if the city is not to remain polluted: but who? The thrower, who is accused of involuntary homicide? The boy himself? Further refinements, not dealt with in the speeches but (so we are told) considered by Pericles and Protagoras, are that "on the most correct reasoning" (κατὰ τὸν ὀρθότατον λόγον) the organizers of the games were *aitioi*, or alternatively that the javelin should be designated as the inanimate *aition*.

In the *Tetralogy* counterfactuals are again brought into play to specify the crucial *differentiae* of the present case: if the javelin had landed outside the proper area or if the thrower had been doing something forbidden or throwing out of turn, he would clearly be guilty (*Tetr.* 2 β.4, 7); if the boy had been standing still rather than running, or if he had run across at the proper time, it would not have been his own "mistake" (*hamartia*, β.5, 8, countered at γ.10). As for blame, it is clearly relevant: the dead boy's father claims limply that the thrower was guilty of "indiscipline," *akolasia*, though it is not clear why (γ.6). But it is not *very* relevant.[80] Everyone agrees that the thrower had no intent; the one person who seems most blameworthy, the trainer who called the boy across the landing area, is explicitly not being accused of anything (γ.7), though this is slightly qualified in the final speech of the four (δ.4). Identifying the person who is *aitios* goes beyond blame, and it means identifying the perpetrator of the action that made the real difference. That is what will decide who was the "doer" (ὁ δράσας) and who was the "sufferer" (ὁ παθών, β.7, γ.3)—language that will recur in Gorgias' *Helen* (§7)[81] and at a poignant moment in a later tragedy, when the aged Oedipus argues passionately that he was victim rather than "doer" (Soph. *OC* 538–540).

One solution does not seem open, the one that would seem most obvious to us: that nobody is to blame, that this is the sort of thing that sadly but familiarly can just happen—a "life is like that" explanation, in fact. Nor is a version acceptable of Priam's line to Helen or Croesus' to the unfortunate Adrastus, "It's not your fault, it's the gods" (*Il.* 3.164–165, p. 35; Hdt. 1.45.2). The possibility of divine ill-will is aired—but that only makes it worse, for it would be wrong for the jury to impede the "assaults of the gods" (γ.8). The perils of pollution hang over the whole collection,[82] and that is an important reason for identifying a single figure who is *aitios*: the community will be threatened unless the right culprit is identified to satisfy the anger of the dead, and that puts particular weight on the jurors to decide "piously." (This is put particularly colorfully in the *Third Tetralogy*, α.3–4.) Herodotus, we shall see, is less concerned always to pin an explanation upon a single person and is much more content with causes operating in a complex amalgam. But with Herodotus too we shall see some intertwining of human and divine levels with neither excluding the other, even if for him they interact in rather different and more enigmatic ways (chapter 10).

The third *Tetralogy* deals with the aftermath of a drinking quarrel. A young man struck an older one, and some time later he died. Part of the argument dwells on the rights and wrongs of the quarrel: was it justified homicide or not? The accused claims that it was the older man who started it, *Tetrology 3* β.1–2, 6. The prosecution seems to accept the importance of this who-started-it issue, as this is the one area where the facts themselves are put in question: the rejoinder is that it is much more likely to have been the younger man (γ.2), using similar sorts of *eikos* argument to those of *Tetralogy 1* (and decidedly weak ones, as the defendant's friends point out, δ.2). The language recurs here of who is the "doer" and who is the "sufferer," δ.6, 8. We have seen some of the who-started-it thinking in the first chapters of Herodotus as well, but the difference is that it is quickly complicated and overlaid in his narrative (pp. 26–29). There is just a little complication in the *Tetralogy* too, with the argument that the striking of the fatal blow is more important than that of the start of it (γ.4), but the argument then moves swiftly on.

Then there is the complication that although the victim received medical attention over the "many days" that he survived, the physician is claimed to have been incompetent (β.3–4).[83] Who then is *aitios*, the striker of the blow or the physician who failed to save him? A bit of both, we might naturally say—and Herodotus, open to a confluence of different causes (chapter 6[b]), would have no problem with that. In the world of the *Tetralogies*, this is again not an option, and a single person to suffer must be identified. In this case the expected answer becomes clear: the accused goes into exile before delivering his second speech, which is delivered by his friends.

If we compare the *Tetralogies* as a whole with Herodotus, some of the features are ones that are natural enough in a forensic setting, even if it is only fictionally forensic. The concentration on persons—*who* is *aitios* rather than *what*—is to be expected: it is after all a person who is in the dock. Nor should we be patronizing about the concentration on a single culprit rather than dwelling on the possibility of joint responsibility.[84] Some of that is doubtless to be connected with that preoccupation with pollution and the need to fix on the right object of the avenger's wrath—"just as one cannot be only partly polluted, so one cannot be only partly a killer"[85]—but even a modern court would have to answer the simple "guilty or not guilty?" question for the one person who is in the dock.

What the *Tetralogies* certainly show is a facility in handling charges of blame and responsibility, and particularly in deflecting them, for it has been observed that the defense arguments tend to be more sophisticated than those of the prosecution;[86] and an awareness of how important counterfactual speculation can be in such thinking. They also suggest an awareness of how slippery and difficult such arguments can be, and how eventually "blame" may not be the only thing that matters. The alertness to arguments on both sides of a case was a trademark of the sophists (Protagoras' *Opposing Speeches*—*Antilogiai*—were well known,[87] and the surviving *Dissoi Logoi* are an exercise along these lines), and one that went with a claim to "make the weaker cause into the better one" that was easy for Aristophanes to satirize in the *Clouds*. It still shows a knowledge that these issues were *complicated*, and that these blame games were often much less straightforward than they might seem.

Gorgias' *Helen* is a more flamboyant display piece that suggests the same. This too probably dates from about the time that the *Histories* were taking their final form, or only a few years later.[88] It is a virtuoso demonstration that Helen is innocent, that someone or something else (so here there is already a move to less personalized explanations) is to blame for the Trojan War. There are four possible reasons why she is not to blame: it was Aphrodite's and the gods' fault, or that of the man who abducted her, or that of the powerful *logos* that persuaded her, or that of irresistible love and lust, *erōs*. It is all skillfully constructed so as to suggest that if one claim is accepted, then the next one, usually more paradoxical, ought to be accepted too. The underlying assumption centers on duress: if Helen was acting under coercion—by Paris, by Aphrodite, by *logos*, by *erōs*—then she should be excused; but was she? The listener is left to judge. We shall see similar concerns in Euripides' *Trojan Women*; they recur in the puzzles about free will in Thucydides' Plataean Debate (3.52–68), where the Plataeans elaborately argue, then the Thebans equally elaborately deny, that the Athenians left their smaller ally no choice but to act as they did.[89] We shall find equivalent preoccupations in Herodotus too (p. 177).

The purpose of Gorgias' work is uncertain, as indeed is that of the *Tetralogies*.[90] Perhaps they are just displays of the author's brilliance. If either Gorgias or Antiphon is writing a "teaching text" for aspiring orators, it will not be in the sense of providing a straightforward model for imitation, for these would not be the most persuasive ways of arguing in a real-life court;[91] it would be more a matter of pushing pupils to think harder about the principles involved. In Gorgias' case, the implication may be that the conclusion is evidently absurd, and of course Helen must be guilty—but now the problem is to show where the argument has gone wrong. That approach works well for another of Gorgias' writings, *On Not-Being*, where the conclusion is that nothing exists, that if it did we could not know of it, and if we could know of it we could not communicate that knowledge. The conclusion is evidently not to be believed, but that makes the argument more of a challenge: this way, the author's brilliance shines even more brightly, and pupils and listeners are left to set about the disentangling.[92] Or it may all just be a joke: that is the way he rounds off this "encomium of Helen—and my bit of playfulness" (*paignion*, *Helen* 21).[93] Most likely, it is a mix of several of these.

What matters for us is again the spirit of intellectual experimentation, and the facility with which these exculpatory ploys are handled. Something of the same is seen in Gorgias' *Defense of Palamedes*, which also shows the way that counterfactuals can so easily be brought into play: if Odysseus really thought me a traitor or really had the interests of the Greeks at heart, the moral position would be quite different (*Palam.* 3); then there is a long list of possible motives that Palamedes might have had for such treachery, none of which can plausibly apply (12–21).

Nor should we think that such interests were limited to refined intellectuals. Tragedy was aimed at a general audience, and in his *Trojan Women* of 415 BCE Euripides stages a version of that same debate about Helen's guilt.[94] The escalation of the captive women's misery is reaching its height. The virgin Cassandra is assigned to the lustful Agamemnon, and now Hector's model wife Andromache is given to the son of her husband's killer: she is hauled away, leaving her young son Astyanax to his awful fate. After the debate the boy's broken body will be brought back for his grandmother Hecuba to bathe and mourn. Euripides is too good, and too tragic, a playwright to interpose a discussion that his audience might find trivial or distracting. Yet this is when Hecuba and Helen engage in their own version of Gorgias' debate (and this is probably the right way to put it: there are indications that Gorgias is not just in Euripides' own mind but in those of at least some of the audience).[95] The audience are clearly expected to care.

The judge is to be Menelaus, who has been given the choice whether to execute Helen or to take her back to Greece. Helen, dragged in by Menelaus' men, speaks first (*Trojan Women* 915–965). Her reflex, as in Gorgias, is to deflect the blame on to someone else. The first culprit is Hecuba herself, for giving birth to Paris; the second is an old man, apparently a herdsman, who had the chance to kill him as a baby. This might have seemed less unreasonable to the audience than it does to us, as this goes back to the first play of the trilogy, the *Alexander*: a dream had there revealed to Hecuba how much damage the new-born Paris would cause if allowed to live, and Priam had handed him over to the herdsman to expose, rather as in Herodotus' tale of the young Cyrus.[96]

Then Helen turns to the story of the divine beauty contest, with Aphrodite offering Helen herself as the prize. Counterfactuals come in here, though less to establish causation than to turn blame into gratitude: Greece might otherwise have been subject to eastern tyranny, for that was the alternative offer that Paris had from Hera. Real-life court cases offer similar dwellings on alternative futures: if Andocides had not denounced those that he did, not merely his own family but many other innocent men would have died and the four men he named would probably have been denounced anyway, *On the Mysteries* 52–53, 57–59, 68; if he had not patriotically made timber available, the ships that fought at Arginusae would have not been built and the city would now be fighting for survival, *On His Return* 11–12.

Menelaus too—Euripides' Helen continues—should take some of the blame, for leaving Helen and Paris alone while he was away in Crete: that is a bold stroke, but we can compare Thucydides' Plataeans, blaming the Spartans themselves for forcing them into alliance with Athens (Thuc. 3.55.1, echoing the Corinthians at 1.69.1). Counterfactuals play a further part as Helen's speech nears its end, though this time it is the lack of alternative futures that comes into play. What else was she to do when the gods were using her in this way? Go on—just try yourself to punish the goddess and do better than Zeus (*Trojan Women* 948). And anyway (so she claims) she has done her best to create an alternative for herself but has failed: she has tried to escape to the Greek army but has been caught each time.

Hecuba's riposte (970–1032) is largely concerned with denying the factual premises, and many of her *eikos* arguments have an element of *modus tollendo tollens*: if Helen's story was true, what else would have to be true?[97] Testing those corollaries can then involve looking for believable explanations for each in turn. If the divine contest had really taken place as Helen described, what explanation would be on offer for Hera or Athena? Trying to get a better husband than Zeus? In Athena's case, trying to get any husband at all? Hardly. (This is rather like the catalog that Gorgias' Palamedes gives of impossible motives, counterfactual alternatives that could never plausibly have come into play.) If Helen's story of being forced were right, what would she have done? Let out a scream in Sparta—but nobody heard her. Or tried to escape—but nobody caught her in any attempt. Or to hang herself, the way any well-bred woman would—but she had not. And if she were so honorable, how would she be dressed now to face Menelaus? Not like this. In each case, her story would imply a corollary that cannot be believed. No: it is her own lust that became her "Aphrodite," along with her greed for eastern luxuries. Finally, Menelaus should think causally forwards as well as backwards: this is his chance to set a grand precedent for posterity, establishing death as the proper punishment for deserting a husband. (Both Thucydides' Plataeans and his Thebans similarly urge the Spartan judges to decide in their favor and therefore "set an example to the Greeks," 3.57.1, 3.67.6.) Menelaus immediately announces his verdict in Hecuba's favor.

A lot is going on in this scene, and the audience's interest will not be limited to weighing the arguments for their own sake. The way the speakers argue characterizes them too, and Helen's insensitive refusal to take any responsibility (she is very different from the Helen of the *Iliad*) emerges as clearly as the sheer anger of Hecuba. The rift of understanding between all involved is also telling. Nothing could be more crass on Menelaus' part than his decision to crack a joke:[98] Why should she not come on board my ship? Has she put on weight since I last saw her? (1050).

Once again, too, as in Herodotus (chapters 2, 8[c]), blame is more important for what it tells us about the situation and the blamers than for whether it is justified or not. For how much does it all matter now anyway? Menelaus has decided that Helen must die, though he will take her back to Greece first. But will he keep to that? *Don't travel in the same ship*, Hecuba urges (*Trojan Women* 1049). She knows all too well what will happen if they do; from the beginning of the debate she has been nervous of what the sight of Helen's beauty may do to him (891–893). Menelaus agrees (1054–1055). But the audience know the *Odyssey* and will remember that scene of postwar domestic tranquility when Menelaus and Helen together will host young Telemachus (*Od.* 4). They will understand that, for all the anger and whatever the claims of justice, other emotions are the ones that will win.[99] The plight of Thucydides' Plataeans is again all too similar: whatever they say and whatever the justice of their case, the Spartans there decide their fate—seemingly have already decided—on the basis of expediency. "Virtually all the Spartans' decisions about Plataea were taken for the sake of Thebes, for they thought that the Thebans were valuable for the war that was then in its early stages" (Thuc. 3.68.4).

Still, it is reasonable to assume that viewers will find the arguments thought-provoking *as well* and recognize the skill and the slipperiness of the rhetorical gyrations on both sides.[100] Explanation, we remember, is a game for two: Herodotus' explanatory strategies work because they already fit, to a degree, into the causal schemes and assumptions already in his readers' and listeners' heads. In Athens at least, forensic speakers were addressing large juries, and dramatists were putting on tragic plays for large audiences. These audiences clearly understood both the importance of blame and how problematic its assignment could be; nor would they be unused to counterfactual speculations even when these became elaborate—what alternative futures were on offer, what else would have to be true if a claim were well founded. It would be no surprise either if a blame game turned out to be not merely difficult but also tangential, if other emotions and issues needed to loom larger in one's mental schemes. Much of this will come back in Herodotus too, though in ways that are not so focused on individual personalities. But he was leaning on doors that were, if not open, at least partly ajar.

(E) SAMENESS AND DIFFERENCE

μέν . . . δέ . . . : "on the one hand . . . on the other hand . . ." Greek conceptualization dealt easily in twos—"most human things come in pairs," Alcmaeon DK 24 A 3—and juxtaposition and contrast came easily to mind.[101] Those prose investigators were now finding many "theres" and "thens" to suggest polarities and analogies with the here and now. As investigative techniques later became more theorized, an important category became what Aristotle calls the *epamphoterizonta*, "those belonging both ways," things that straddled a divide and did not fall neatly on one side or the other.[102] That systematized a feature that had long been familiar: after all, a typical μέν . . . δέ . . . sentence says two things that one might not expect to go together (hence the contrast) but in that particular case do. It would certainly be no surprise either for Herodotus or for his audience to find elements of both sameness and difference between "there" and "here" and between "then" and "now."[103] This became even more interesting when the sameness and the difference were causally related: where, for instance, the continuities of human nature could explain the forms that human development had taken as societal circumstances had changed, or the different ways in which peoples had reacted to their varying climates or political systems.

Travel broadened the mind: that was so for Herodotus, with that insight into human mutability that his journeys had brought (1.5.3–4; p. 30), just as it is for his Solon (1.30.2) and his Anacharsis (4.76.2); it had already been true too with Thales, said to have brought geometry into Greece from Egypt (DK 11 A 11), with Pythagoras who allegedly imported "philosophy" from the same country (Isoc. *Busir.* 11 28 = DK 14 A 4) and travelled both there and to Babylonia "for the sake of *philomatheia*" (Strabo 14.1.16),[104] with Democritus "who journeyed through the most distant lands in his quest for learning" (Cic. *Fin.* 5.50 = DK 68 A 13),[105] and doubtless with others too.[106]

The prototype was Odysseus, with those many wanderings in which "he came to know the mind of men" (*Od.* 1.3). The gathering knowledge of other people's customs naturally played a part in the debates about *nomos*, "custom" that could be adapted if humans so chose, and *physis*, embedded "nature," that were central to many questions of how features of life were to be explained.[107] That was already the case with Xenophanes when he observed that Ethiopians imagined their gods as snub-nosed and black, Thracians as red-haired and blue-eyed; if they could, lions would imagine their gods as lions and horses as horses (DK 21 B 15–16).

We depend on fourth-century sources for much of our evidence on Herodotus' contemporaries, but it is credible enough when Xenophon makes Hippias and Socrates debate what to make of laws that had worldwide acceptance, such as honoring the gods and one's parents, with abhorrence of incest a more doubtful case (*Mem.* 4.4.19–20).[108] In the *Symposium* (dramatic date 416 BCE) Plato's Pausanias adduces the various approaches to pederasty in different Greek cities and among the barbarians and relates them to the different national characters: in Elis and Boeotia people are bad at persuasion, so that is why it is defined as good there to give in to seduction; barbarian nations and other tyrannies are opposed to pederasty, just as they are to philosophy and physical exercise, because it is dangerous for too many friendships and too much spiritedness to develop (*Symp.* 182a–d). We have already seen that the Hippocratic *Airs Waters Places* could take a similar overview of Greeks and barbarians and make a similar point about tyrannies and spirit (pp. 19–20). There may well have been further medical debates about similarities and differences with other cultures, especially Libya and Scythia, again in the interest of exploring a universal human nature that might issue in different customs or physiques in different environments.[109] That is not very different from the way in which Herodotus, seeking to explain the extraordinary behavior of the Nile, looks for a cause that reflects a universal physical law, one that would lead other rivers such as the Danube to behave similarly if the same conditions applied (2.24–27; pp. 2–3, 43).[110] In this way, certain underlying human traits—an awareness of divinity and its personalizing in familiar terms, the universality of sexual desire and its institutionalizing in a way that suits the local character, the tendency to spirited self-assertion unless repressed, the self-protection of the powerful when they can—do indeed help to explain those individual variations, and sameness and difference hunt closely together.

Conclusions could be more far-reaching: how different were Greeks and barbarians anyway? Not very, it would seem, according to the sophist Antiphon—possibly the same man as the author of the *Tetralogies*, more probably not:[111]

> We are equally adapted by nature to be both Greek and barbarian . . . in all this, there is no firm dividing line between barbarian and Greek: we all breathe out into the same air through our mouths and noses, we all laugh when we are happy and cry when we are sad, we take in sounds through our hearing, we see with the same rays of light, we work with our hands, we walk with our feet.
> (ANTIPHON DK 87 B 44B)[112]

Admittedly we do not know the context, and there may have been counter-arguments to follow; we should also note exactly what is said—not "we are all the same," but "we are equally adapted by nature to be the same," which is rather different. Antiphon could still acknowledge that Greeks and barbarians had ended up behaving very differently—otherwise the paradox of the statement would disappear—but he does seem to be insisting that the distinction between Greek and barbarian is a matter of *nomos* rather than *physis*. It would appear that Gorgias' pupil Alcidamas said something similar about slavery in a fourth-century speech about the Messenians: "God has made all people free; nature has made nobody a slave" (fr. 3). Doubtless not everyone would agree; Aristotle later took a very different view (*Politics* 1252b6–9, 1254a17–55b15). If Alcidamas was speaking to the Spartans they probably did not agree either, seething as they would be at the rebellion of their Messenian serfs. But such things could be said.[113]

So customs could be the same, and customs could be different. If they were different, one could ask why, and the answers could be disturbing. That does not mean that Herodotus' first audiences were wholly ready for what they would read or hear. If they had been, there would have been less room for the "wonder," *thōma*, that can itself be so important to explanation: the world is full of wondrous things, and that is itself a life-is-like-that insight that the audience are led to accept. When Darius makes a point about how Greeks and Indians think wholly differently about how to treat their dead fathers and concludes that *nomos* is lord of all, listeners and readers would be shocked (3.38; pp. 142–143). It would be discomfiting too to find suggestions that Athenian democracy and Persian tyranny might not be so diametrically opposed as one might think, and there might again be underlying human characteristics, not very pleasant ones, that surfaced in both (chapter 13). But these would not be the only shocks and discomforts of this sort that the intellectually curious had experienced, and once again Herodotus was operating within thought categories that his audience were primed to find plausible.

Such analyses also imply an element of historicizing even if it is not spelled out. If Heaven did not differentiate Greeks and barbarians or free and slave, something or someone else must have;[114] if *erōs* is universal but practices diverge, then that must be because people in Elis or Boeotia have instituted things differently from those living under tyrannies.

The spelling out becomes clearer if we return to those historicizing models discussed in chapter 1 (pp. 16–17), cases where features of the here and now are explained in terms of how things have come about. For the character in the *Sisyphus*, human religion was imposed by a "shrewd statesman," alert to the cohesion that a shared fear of the gods could give. Plato's Protagoras and Glaucon explain the development of human society in similarly historical terms: after a period of injustice and unfettered self-seeking, the need and value of cooperation was felt. Herodotus' Deioces has something in common both with *Sisyphus* and with Plato's discussions, shrewd as he is in manipulating for his own advantage that societal desire for order and justice (p. 17). But there are continuities too to explain the changes: for believers in progress, a society's quest for survival and prosperity, the ingenuity of human researchers and leaders, the goodwill of the particularly friendly deity like Prometheus;[115] or in Hesiod's picture of decline, the grimmer aspects of humanity that doom one generation after another to self-destruction.

That too can be seen as a reflex of some Presocratic philosophers' thinking, in this case the assumption that the single element from which everything is composed—air, water, fire, or whatever it might be—might carry in itself an implied explanation of how it could come to take such different forms.[116] In Herodotus as well we will find continuities as well as differences, and continuities that explain the differences between the Homeric world, the times he was describing, and his own day (chapter 14[e]). That steering between sameness and difference is again done in a way that would not be wholly unfamiliar.

Jean-Pierre Vernant argued that there were particular reasons why the "tragic moment"—the time when tragedy developed into so dominant a genre—came in the fifth century.[117] For him, it was a matter of a sense of a past heroic code of values coinciding with a new sensibility for the needs of the community.[118] Something similar can be said about Herodotus:[119] we shall later sense some Herodotean ruminations on how new and how different this world really is (pp. 201–205).

We can go further. So many strands in the intellectual excitement of the fifth-century come together in ways that create a "historiographic moment," an intellectual world that was waiting for a Herodotus to come along: scientific and medical investigation of causes; an alertness to the importance of the past yet an awareness of change; the speculation on the origins of society; the exploration of the limits of human achievement in tragedy; the humor and wryness of comedy; an eye on the great experiment, for good or for ill, of Athenian democracy; and not least the bewilderment of what had happened in 480, looked back on with an awareness of how much had changed since. None of this "explains" Herodotus himself; if there was no Herodotus before Herodotus, there was no guarantee that there would be one now. But it was not coincidence that Herodotus happened now; nor was he writing for an audience that would find his thinking too alien to accommodate.

CHAPTER 5

HIPPOCRATIC AFFINITIES

(A) MEDICAL SCIENCE

We have several times talked broadly about "science" or "scientific explanations." By this we often meant the Presocratic philosophers, with their ideas about the origins and functioning of the natural world: any separation of natural philosophy, or what would later be called "science," from other sorts of philosophy lay some distance in the future. But we have also referred to the considerable "Hippocratic" medical literature that survives, some of it clearly from Herodotus' own day or very soon after.[1] Then as now, physicians were unsurprisingly very interested in causes:

> On examination the notion of spontaneity (τὸ αὐτόματον)[2] disappears; for everything that happens would be found to be happening because of something (διά τι),[3] and in this "because of something" spontaneity is shown to have no reality but to be just a name. Medicine operates with these "because of somethings" and with forecasts, and therefore is shown and will always be shown to have reality.
> ([HIPP.] *THE ART* 6 II P. 198 J = VI P. 10 L)

Herodotus is interested in physicians and medicine and describes clinical phenomena and diseases carefully.[4] He finds it fascinating that in Egypt "everything is full of physicians," with specialists for eyes, headaches, teeth, stomachs, and "the nonvisible diseases" (2.84). Particularly egregious roles are played by the unnamed Egyptian eye physician whose advice indirectly led to Cambyses' Egyptian campaign (3.1.1) and then by Democedes, the man who cured Darius and then egged on Atossa to urge an invasion of Greece (3.129–138). He notes too that Croton, Democedes' city, was held to be first among Greek cities for medical expertise, with Cyrene second (3.131.3).[5] (Alcmaeon too, soon to figure in this chapter, was a native of Croton.) The madness of Cambyses and then of Cleomenes engages him greatly: whole chapters are given to the various explanations on offer in each case (3.33 and 6.84; cf. pp. 159–160).[6]

Doubtless he talked to physicians at length, and he may have heard the public display lectures that were a feature of agonistic medical culture (p. 18); it would be odd if he never learned from them. Still, such questions of influence are not our main concern. When we see affinities of thought and method, it may simply be that such thinking was in the air, common to various areas of intellectual inquiry just as similar explanations were assumed to apply in different fields (chapter 1[a]). What matters more is that they point to assumptions and expectations that Herodotus' audience might share, aspects of their mindset that they too would bring to the explanatory game.

Affinities there certainly are, in plenty.[7] We have already seen some. As we saw in chapter 1(f), *Airs Waters Places* discusses the differences in martial culture between barbarians and Greeks, placing weight on the constitutional impact of tyranny as well as on climate and national character (16 I. pp. 114-116 J = II. pp. 62-66 L; pp. 19–20): that is a passage to which we will return several times in this chapter and the next. There is a broader parallel too in the simple interest in foreign peoples, exploring similarities and differences to illuminate the human *physis* that they share (chapter 4[e]). Chapter 3 explored some parallels in investigative technique, especially the use of *modus tollendo tollens* argumentation (pp. 41–42) and the development of a methodology for discriminating causal from contingent factors (pp. 50–54), and we also saw similarities in the ways historians and Hippocratics exploit appeals to an audience's own experience (pp. 56–57).[8]

On other points too it is easy to find analogies. Like Herodotus, physicians also deal in explicability rather than predictability, for (despite that dismissiveness about "spontaneity" in this chapter's epigraph) it is acknowledged that chance can play a role (p. 49): a physician is not left without a riposte if a skeptic points out that treated patients sometimes die and untreated patients sometimes get better,[9] nor when someone claims that an outcome often depends on luck rather than on the practitioner's expertise.[10] Herodotus and the physicians share a loose "empiricism," in the sense that both stress the importance of evidence and both could be impatient with claims that are unverifiable,[11] but both too are ready to go beyond the perceptible to infer the invisible: "things that escape the sight of the eyes have been captured by the sight of the mind" (*The Art* 11 II p. 208 J = VI p. 20 L; cf. Hdt. 2.33.2).[12] The Hippocratics lay emphasis on identifying the *krisis*, the critical moment when the future outcome of a disease is determined:[13] it is also vital to know the right time, the *kairos*, to apply the treatment that will make the crucial difference.[14] That is not far from Herodotus' identification of the tipping point in 480 BCE as Athens' decision not to desert the Greek cause (7.139; pp. 42–43), or his interest in pinpointing the decisive moment in a battle (7.225.2, 8.89.2, 9.63.2).[15]

It is basic too to Hippocratic technique to identify the differences in particular cases that come from environment or physical make-up, but to penetrate below these to find universal truths about the human body. That is much the same mindset as we saw in Herodotus' steering between sameness and difference (chapter 4[e]), including the insistence that the shared universal characteristics can explain the differences: the human body is set up in such a way as to respond to airs or waters in certain ways, or to suffer particular ailments if any factor disturbs its balance. Many of these are conceptual features that we have already seen in the Presocratics, and this is part of that Hippocratic debt to the likes of Empedocles that is particularly clear in such early works as *On Ancient Medicine*.

The explanatory vocabulary is also similar, though not identical. The most general word is the adjective *aitios*, often in its neuter form *to aition*. The connection with "blaming" (pp. 5–8) is not forgotten, but it is even more felt with the noun equivalent *aitiē*. The act of ascribing is also more felt with *aitiē* than with the adjectives: it is possible to say that bad physicians ascribe the *aitiē* to the wrong factor, being ignorant of *to aition* (*On Ancient Medicine* 21 I p. 56 J = I p. 624 L).[16] As that passage shows and as in Herodotus (p. 7), such blame language can transfer from people, the most obvious targets for "blame," to things or concepts. Thus skeptics find the physician "to blame" when things go wrong, while the physician blames, in less personal terms, the nature of the patient or the indomitable nature of the disease (*The Art* 11 II p. 210 J = VI p. 20 L). Often, though, the element of blame recedes, or at least is irrelevant to explanation or treatment. An *aition* can be either a proposition (e.g., "that morning mists destroy the clearness of the water," *Airs Waters Places* 6 I p. 82 J = II p. 24 L, or "that the wound and the surrounding area become free of swelling," *On Fractures* 26 III p. 156 W = III p. 504 L) or a thing (e.g., "the stiffness of the body and the hardness of the digestive organs," *Airs Waters Places* 4 I p. 76 J = II p. 20 L, or just "what we breathe," *On the Nature of Man* 9 IV p. 26 J = VI p. 54 L).[17] As we shall see in the next chapter, such *aiti-* language is the favored way of describing a "predisposing cause" when several explanations combine.

Such predispositions often work together with a more immediate cause, and these triggering causes are often categorized as *prophasies*, though in some of the corpus that word is used more generally of any sort of explanation:[18] as Galen puts it, "Hippocrates sometimes uses *prophasis* in the ordinary-language sense of falsely attributed causes, but he often applies it to the clearly visible causes (*tas phaneras aitias*), and sometimes straightforwardly to all causes" (*Commentary on Epidemics* 1, XVII p. 52 K).

As Galen there says, a Hippocratic *prophasis* is often something visible, or at least perceptible or easily deducible from perception.[19] That stress on perceptibility helps to explain why some diseases can be said to strike without a *prophasis*, with no visible warning,[20] just as Thucydides' plague sometimes struck healthy people "from no *prophasis*," 2.49.2. But this should not lead us to play down the causal implications in cases where a *prophasis* can be perceived.[21] Most telling here are the prepositions most often used with it: διά, "because of" or "through," and ἐκ or ἀπό, "from," which in some cases might simply mean "after" but more often suggests a causal connection. An explanatory aspect duly seems hard to avoid in cases such as *Prorrhetikon* 2.16 VIII p. 256 P = IX p. 42 L, "if the marrow of the back becomes diseased after a fall, or after any other *prophasis*, or from chance," or 2.24 VIII p. 272 P = IX p. 56 L, "when a lesion occurs in the womb, either after giving birth or from an abscess or from some other *prophasis* . . . ," or *On Female Diseases* 2.29 XI pp. 348–349 = 2.138 VIII pp. 310–312 L, "any *prophasis* is sufficient to displace the womb, if it has a defect—coldness in the feet or groin, or dancing or winnowing or cleaving wood or running uphill or downhill"—though that last case shows that such causes coexist with the underlying "defect" that leaves the womb susceptible.

It is understandable, too, that the Hippocratics should often show more interest in a *prophasis* than in an underlying disposition, as in many cases (not in all) it is the *prophasis* that is more treatable or avoidable (just as a judge or legal philosopher will be more concerned with the burglars than in the social conditions that drove them to crime, for one cannot put a whole society in jail; p. 95): a girl can avoid running uphill more easily than she can change her basic physical constitution. "Obvious explanation" might be a good English translation, and just as in Herodotus (pp. 8–9) a *prophasis* can convey something that is true. Sometimes the obvious explanation is also the right one.

Still, it need not be the only one that is right, and we have already seen some cases where diseases are explained in terms of both an underlying predisposition (often an *aitiē*) and a triggering stimulus (usually the *prophasis*).[22] That sort of analysis is particularly useful in cases where physicians apply a schema that we have already noted as a favorite, that "unifocal" idea of an organism carrying the seeds not just of its growth and flourishing but also of its decline (p. 18). Growth and decay are all very well; they can even be developed to posit rather more elaborate types of bodily change. In this way *On the Nature of Man* explains that the elements commingle in different ways, and occasion different imbalances, according to a person's age and physique as well as to the seasons of the year (9 IV p. 26 J = VI p. 54 L). But this takes us only so far. Unifocal analysis can explain why a body will be vulnerable to arthritis or epilepsy or the common cold; it may even explain why a cold is more likely to come in winter, or arthritis strike those of a certain age. To jump ahead, it may also explain why Persia is likely to be expansionist, or why Athens is likely to land itself in a war. That still does not explain why I am healthy on Saturday and sick on Sunday, or why Persia attacked in 490 and 480 rather than 500, or why Athens was at peace in 432 and at war in 431. This will require a different sort of analysis, looking more closely at those triggering stimuli—the sort of visible precursors, in fact, that the physicians saw as *prophasies*—and an acknowledgement of causes acting in combination.

But we are indeed jumping ahead, and we will return to this in the next chapter. First let us look at one particularly important Hippocratic assumption, the idea that an organism is regularly made up of a number of different elements or constituents that need to be in balance with each other, not least because their natural state can easily be one of conflict or at least tension. Here too we are close to the world of the Presocratics, especially Empedocles' picture of a world dominated by Love and Strife (p. 16). Such ideas were familiar enough to Plato's audience to be parodied in the speech of the medical man Eryximachus in Plato's *Symposium* (esp. 186d–187c, 188a). They would have been familiar to Herodotus' audience too.

(B) HARMONIOUS BALANCING

What keeps health together is an equality of rights (*isonomia*) between the various powers—wet and dry, cold and hot, bitter and sweet, and so on; what creates disease is a monarchy among them, for the monarchy of any one of two qualities is destructive. Disease (he says) comes about as follows: if we ask *by what*, by an excess of heat and cold; if we ask *from what*, from too much or too little nourishment; if we ask *in what*, in the blood of the marrow or the brain. Sometimes, he says, disease arises in them because of external causes (*exōthen aitiai*), from a certain sort of water or locale or fatigue or force or something similar. Health he regards as a proportional blending of the qualities.
(ALCMAEON OF CROTON DK 24 B 4)

An "equality of rights," *isonomia*: the similarity to the language of politics is plain (p. 4). So is the readiness to acknowledge multiple causes, or at least multiple ways of looking at causation, even if the slickly precise way of putting it—by what, from what, in what—may be owed to the authors who transmit the paraphrase (Aëtius, Stobaeus, and Ps.-Plutarch) or their predecessors, not to Alcmaeon himself.[23] But let us concentrate on that notion of a "proportionate blending" of qualities—hot and cold, wet and dry, bitter and sweet—that might be expected to be in tension or even in conflict with each other. When the balance is equal or correct, the body is healthy; when it becomes disproportionate, disease sets in. So to a degree health and disease are both explained "unifocally," in terms of the make-up of the individual organism, though it is also important that sometimes—not, clearly, always—it may be an external stimulus that knocks that balancing out of kilter.

This picture continues to dominate within the Hippocratics. Once again, as with Alcmaeon, we are often dealing in twos—"most things come in pairs" (Alcmaeon DK 24 A 3; pp. 75–76)—even if there are several pairs in tension within the same body, hot and cold as well as wet and dry. The picture is generally of several simultaneous tugs of war, with each pulling against each other on different ropes; it is not so often a triangular or quadrilateral tugging match, with each element pulling at a corner of a more complicated shape. Sometimes the figuring is one of "tension," with two forces struggling against one another; sometimes it is more a question of "balancing" or "blending" in appropriate proportions, as in the Alcmaeon fragment.[24] There are important differences between the two figures,[25] but they are closely related, especially when things are going wrong: the one force or the one constituent in the blend becomes too strong for the other, and the organism ceases to function as it should.

Perhaps the clearest case of binary polarities is offered by one of the earliest texts, *On Ancient Medicine*. Its author inveighs against pathological explanations in terms of the hot and cold and the wet and dry, but what he objects to is not the polarizing but the unverifiability of that set of antitheses. He replaces them with a new and more extended set of internal polarities, giving a tension of, for instance, the sweet and the bitter, the astringent and the insipid, "and a vast number of other things with all sorts of qualities, both in number and in strength" (*On Ancient Medicine* 14 I p. 38 J = I p. 602 L). Binary polarities are equally widespread where the emphasis falls on blending rather than tension. *On Regimen* I, for instance, develops an elaborate schematism of different human types in terms of the blending, in varying proportions, of the two elements fire and water.

Of course the blending or the tension can go wrong, and this is where the physician has to put things right. "Pain is caused both by the cold and the hot, and both by what is excessive and what is deficient," and the best form of therapy is often simply to repair the imbalance, cooling the hot parts or moistening the dry: "Pains are made healthy by their opposites" (*On the Places in Man* 42 VIII p. 84 P = VI p. 334 L). "To put it in a nutshell, opposites cure opposites: medicine in fact is subtraction and addition, subtraction of what is in excess and addition of what is deficient" (*On Breaths* 1 II p. 228 J = VI p. 92 L).[26] Equally, however, there is an implication that the "natural" state is to be in balance, and that this can sometimes be restored by simply giving the body time to cure itself ("natures are the physicians of diseases" sounds proverbial, *Epid.* 6.5.1 VII p. 254 S = V p. 314 L); the turning of the seasons, for instance, might be enough to do the trick (*Epid.* 3.15 I pp. 254–256 J = III pp. 98–100 L; *On the Nature of Man* 12 IV p. 36 J = VI 12 p. 64 L).

Sometimes, it is true, the picture goes beyond the binary. *On the Nature of Man* posits a quartet of physiological constituents, blood, phlegm, yellow bile, and black bile. A picture of proportional balance still holds, but this time in more of a quadrilateral manner: all four elements need to be in equilibrium, and an excess or deficiency in any of them produces an uneven "commingling." Pain is caused when any portion of an element is left uncommingled or has to shift elsewhere in the body to fill a space left empty during the commingling process (*On the Nature of Man* 4 IV pp. 10–12 J = VI pp. 38–40 L): one notices the very visual, literal way in which the process is envisaged, and the idea is still one of the need for the balance that is intrinsic to a body's natural and healthy state.

Such assumptions would be familiar to audiences of historiography too. When, for instance, Herodotus explains that the most lethal animals have their deadliness compensated by also being the less fertile (3.108–109), the assumption of natural balance would be easily recognizable (there it is a matter of "divine forethought," τοῦ θείου ἡ προνοίη);[27] some sort of natural balance seems also to be in play just before, where the ends of the earth are said to have the most beautiful natural phenomena, whereas central Greece has the most beautiful climate (3.106; p. 18). That can even be seen as a cosmic form of "payback," *tisis*, compensating a deficiency in one area by righting the balance in another.[28] When Thucydides describes the constitution of the Five Thousand as "a reasonable commingling (*xynkrasis*), respecting both the few and the many"[29] (8.97.2), a medical tinge might well be felt;[30] but even if it just reflects a broader understanding that proportional mixing is good in any sphere, be it wine, cooking, politics, or health, that too is telling for the audience mindset. One can understand why that is felt as healthy, and why Thucydides should go on to claim, rightly or wrongly, that "this was the first thing that promoted the city's recovery from its degraded situation." One can understand too why his Alcibiades should think it persuasive to argue that a blending (ξυγκραθέν) of the three different sorts of citizen in the state should be a source of strength (6.18.6).[31]

We can go beyond such lexical points. Thucydides' Athens is a blend of tyranny, the tyrant city (pp. 144, 189), and democracy—or is it more a matter of "tension" between the two? While he is alive, Pericles by his own position is able to keep the two aspects in some form of balance, given that "it was becoming in name a democracy, in fact rule by the first man" (2.65.9). Other Thucydidean balances and tensions are visible too, and usually an underlying binary structure can be sensed: that between the risk-taking enterprise that made Athens great and the cautious strategic restraint that is now wise; that between private ambition and public service; even that between thoughtful reflection (*logismos*) and the necessity, in warfare, sometimes not to think too much.[32] In all these cases a balancing act is possible, but it is not easy, and the pressure of war makes it particularly hard.

Thucydides may provide the clearer cases of such antithetical thinking, but some of Herodotus' thinking can be put in similar terms: the tension in a city or in Greece as a whole between freedom's inspirational power, with all people fighting for themselves, and its dangers, as all follow their own interests; the tension in a democracy between self-belief and silly impulsiveness; the tension in one-man rule between its directed sense of purpose and the obstacles in the way of hearing good advice. In those cases the strengths and the weaknesses are closely related; both indeed result from the same defining features of the institution.

When we notice such conflicts, we are easily tempted to think that the historians are exposing fault lines in Athenian democracy or Greek libertarianism or Persian autocracy. That need not be so. There is obviously a danger that such inherent instability may eventually prove decisive and fatal, just as Thucydides' Pericles fears "our own mistakes more than anything the enemy may devise" (1.144.1) and just as it does, eventually, in a human body that dies of a chronic condition. But the philosophical and medical parallels should remind us that in itself there is nothing wrong with such conflicting forces, that indeed such tension and balancing can be productive and can even be an indispensable ingredient for health and success providing—what is not easy—that the balance can be maintained. Brooke Holmes has written of the physical body as conceptualized as "a terrain of unruly forces" that "can be seen as hard to control and potentially dangerous even when they are accomplishing something good."[33] That goes for historiography too.

We can go further. Medical writers could assume that investigating the origins and constitution of the human body will be *the same inquiry* as that into the causes of disease:

> Some physicians and sophists say that nobody could know medicine without knowing what a human is.
> (*ON ANCIENT MEDICINE* 20 I P. 52 J = I P. 620 L)

The author of *On Ancient Medicine* has no time for that view, but only because it puts things the wrong way round: one should start not with philosophical speculation but with medicine itself, because exploring illness, seeing where things may go wrong, is the best way of discovering "what a person is, by what causes a person is made, and similar points, in precise manner" (pp. 52–54 J = I pp. 620–622 L), and therefore of analyzing their health as well. In a way this reflects that basic Greek insight that a person's strengths may eventually prove destructive and fatal (p. 18). For Herodotus and Thucydides too the same tensions may explain both glorious success and deep vulnerability, and notions such as freedom, tyranny, democracy, and empire may all be best explored when subjected to peril and stress— once again, just like the human body. Perhaps we should not be surprised that there is such lack of agreement about, for instance, whether Herodotus is pro- or antidemocracy. He is more concerned to analyze, to investigate, and to explain than to praise or to blame, and strengths and faults exist and emerge side by side.

(C) CORROBORATION AND REVISION

We are already seeing that Hippocratics can see and explain things in several different ways; in the next chapter we will see that some works, especially *Airs Waters Places*, can even develop two explanatory strategies that come close to being contradictory (pp. 96–97). Both features are made easier by a favorite presentational strategy, dubbed by G. E. R. Lloyd "corroborative argument."[34] Typically an author sets out a hypothesis very early, often baldly or dogmatically: the basis of everything is wind (*On Breaths*) or the four humors (*On the Nature of Man*) or fire and water (*On Regimen* 1); seasons, winds, and waters define what diseases one can expect to find in a place (*Airs Waters Places*). Then evidence is fed in where it suits or supports, such as those appeals to an audience's own experiences (pp. 56–57). A variation is to begin with the opponent's hypothesis, the view perhaps that bodily constitutions and diseases can be reduced to one or two elements (*On Ancient Medicine*) or that epilepsy is a sacred sickness (*On the Sacred Disease*). In that case, evidence comes in where it counters or undermines. Either way, an explanatory train of thought can be carried through and elaborated as far as it can go, and if there are different explanatory strands, then evidence can be deployed as it becomes appropriate. This is not an exact opposite of modern "evidence-based medicine," because in a way the theses are still tested by evidence; but it is certainly starting from the conclusion rather than the evidence, and it makes it easy to shut one's eyes to contradictory indications or alternative explanations that would explain the evidence just as well.

Take *On Breaths*. That work begins by claiming that all diseases have a single character and the same essence and cause:

Human and animal bodies have three forms of nourishment: these are called food, drink, and wind (*pneuma*). Wind in bodies is called breath, and outside bodies it is called air. In everything, this is the greatest lord of all.
(ON BREATHS 3 II P. 230 J = VI P. 94 L)

Evidence is then adduced, again appealing to familiar experiences. Air is more important than food or drink, for a person deprived of air dies more quickly than one deprived of nourishment (*On Breaths* 4); belching shows that air is taken in with food (7); fevered patients gape because air whisks around the system and then unbolts the mouth (8). It ends by echoing the opening formulation: breaths are the greatest busybodies, and everything else is only jointly or secondarily responsible (*sunaitia kai metaitia*, *On Breaths* 15 II p. 252 J = VI p. 114 L; cf. p. 100). The initial thesis has not been falsified and has appeared to be corroborated: it will therefore do.

Just as interesting, though, are the cases where the evidence does *not* wholly fit, or at least renuances as well as corroborates: there can then be progressive redefinition of that initial firm statement. Even in *On Breaths* there is some mild revision in stride of this sort: by the end there is the extra nuance of those other causes that are "jointly or secondarily responsible," presumably features such as food, water, and blood, the last of which has just been acknowledged as central to consciousness (14 II pp. 248–252 J = VI pp. 110–114 L).

Elsewhere the revision of the initial thesis can be more far-reaching. The second part of *Airs Waters Places* begins with the program "to demonstrate how much Asia and Europe differ from one another in every respect, and to show that there is no similarity at all in the physical appearance of the two peoples" (12 I p. 104 J = II p. 52 L). Yet the evidence later adduced greatly qualifies this: we go on to see many internal differences within each continent, and there are times when a people of one comes to be very similar to a people of another.[35] This is not simply an "extra nuance," as it was in *On Breaths*: this is progressive correction, where an initial thesis is thoroughly refined as we measure it against real experience. It is in fact a presentational equivalent of that Hippocratic heuristic method that we earlier identified: the formation of a provisional hypothesis and its testing and if necessary revision against the accumulation of experience (pp. 52–53).

We can already see some revision in stride in Homer: even the assumptions embedded in that initial question—"Which of the gods was it that sent them together to fight in strife?" (*Il.* 1.8; p. 24)—quickly need rethinking once the narrator has skillfully insinuated that the quarrel of Achilles and Agamemnon was one that was waiting to happen, given the simmering resentment of both men. On a bigger scale, the initial suggestions of strong differences between Greek and Trojan give way by book 24 to an emphasis on how much they humanly share (pp. 21, 145). In Aeschylean tragedy we could similarly say that our understanding of Agamemnon's death deepens as wave after wave of explanation washes through the action, though there too the earlier explanatory strands are complicated and enhanced rather than simply rejected (p. 16). One can find parallels in Thucydides as well.[36] There is even some analogy with the Platonic *elenchos*, where an initial proposition is subject to examination in the light of further considerations, often in that case other assumptions and insights that the interlocutor shares (or can be brought to share). There too an initial assumption may not be wholly false: by the end of the *Republic* the naïvely formulated ideas aired in book 1—justice is "giving each person their due" (but what is their "due"?), or "the interest of the greater person" (but what makes that person greater?), or "the other person's good" (but that may turn out to be your own good too)—may all turn out to be true, but in ways that by then seem very different.

And Herodotus? We can certainly see something similar on the small scale. He begins his treatment of Egyptian customs by insisting that they do things in a topsy-turvy way, "in general doing everything in the opposite way to other peoples" (2.35.2). Yet within a few chapters he has passed on to overlaps between Greek and Egyptian culture, with a particular interest in those features that the Greeks draw from Egypt.[37] When the topsy-turvy idea returns, ringlike, towards the end of the section, it is in an adjusted form: the Egyptians "avoid using Greek customs and, so to speak, those of any other peoples" (2.91.1), a formulation that leaves it open for similarities to remain—but because the Greeks are using Egyptian customs rather than the other way round. Here again that attention-grabbing initial strong proposition has needed to be redefined by the harder and more complicated realities. We shall see something similar in the way he introduces Croesus, "the first man to begin unjust deeds against the Greeks"—except that he had some precedents (1.5–6; p. 106).

That can be taken further. It may not be extravagant to see that strong initial statement in the proem, searching for "the reason (*aitiē*) why they came to war with one another," as itself one of those over-straightforward first bids: will there really be only one? Nor is that the only aspect of the proem that will later need some renuancing or broadening (chapter 7[a]). We have also already seen that there is quickly some revision of that initial suggestion that the explanation is to be sought in terms of aggression and revenge; we talked of "overlaying" that way of looking at it with a more unifocal emphasis on the imperialistic mindset, the tendency of a great power to expand until it encounters decisive reverse (p. 31). We shall later often see that one of the most basic questions of all—how different are Greeks and barbarians, anyway?—can itself be the subject of deep rethinking as the work progresses, rather again as it does in the *Iliad* (pp. 145, 211).

Something of the same applies to the theme of eastern "softness" that, to a degree, Herodotus shares with *Airs Waters Places*.[38] Had he wished to see a lack of bellicosity in terms of Persian easy living and develop it straightforwardly as a major explanation of Persian defeat, *Airs Waters Places* suggests that he would have found receptive ears (pp. 19–20). There are plenty of other indications too that Persian luxury and ease, (*habrotēs*) were an object of fascination: the number of *habro-* words in Aeschylus' *Persians* (472 BCE) is "quite remarkable,"[39] and nearly half a century later Aristophanes had fun with the idea in *Acharnians* (65–90).[40] Sometimes, but by no means always,[41] that could be linked with lack of military toughness: a few generations later Xenophon reported the Arcadian Antiochus' remark that Persia had many cooks but no fighters (*Hell*. 7.1.38), and for all his admiration of Cyrus he would end the *Cyropaedia* with reflections on the intensity of Persian decline. And develop it Herodotus duly does—but straightforwardly?

As with so many leading ideas, it first comes with Croesus. The wise adviser Sandanis points out what folly it would be for him to attack Persia, a land at the time lacking in all luxuries—no wine, no fine food, nothing but leather clothing.

> "If you win, what will you take from them? For they don't have anything. But what if you are beaten? Let me tell you how much you will lose: for once they have tasted our good things, they will embrace them and there will be no way of holding them back. For myself, I thank the gods for not putting the idea into Persian minds of attacking the Lydians." But Croesus was not persuaded. For the Persians, before they conquered Lydia, had no luxurious goods at all.
> (1.71.3–4)

The passage has its oddities, not least because Croesus already thinks that the Persians *do* have it in mind to attack Lydia (1.46.1);[42] nor does it yet intimate that other side of *habrotēs*, the notion that the hard life of one's poverty-stricken opponents may make them more formidable a foe. That idea comes soon enough, when Cyrus, by now victorious, is persuaded by Croesus not to be too harsh on the rebellious Lydians but instead . . .

> forbid them to possess arms to fight with; order them to wear tunics under their clothes and dainty footwear[43] on their feet, and tell them to play the lyre and pluck the harp and teach their children to be shopkeepers. And swiftly, sire, you will see them becoming women rather than men, and there will be no danger at all of rebellion.
> (1.155.4)

The Lydians used to be the luxurious ones (Sandanis); now they need to be made even more so. Cyrus is persuaded, just as he is when Croesus suggests a more tactical use of luxury to trick the Massagetae in his last campaign (1.207, 212).

So much for Lydia: what of Persia itself? Their wealth is clear: all that Persian gold and silver (7.27–28, 7.83.2, 7.190, 9.22.2, 9.80–82, 9.109.3, among other passages), affording Mardonius a ready fund that he could have used, had he so chosen, to bribe the powerful men in the Greek cities (9.2, 9.41.2–3). So is their luxury: it was there early in the *Histories* for Cyrus to exploit against the Massagetae; it is there at the end, with the comparison of Persian sumptuous fare with a frugal Spartan meal that so impresses Pausanias after Plataea (9.82; pp. 170, 210). That can be regarded as a pointer to softness:[44]

> They go into battle wearing trousers and with turbans on their heads: that's how much of a pushover they are.
> (ARISTAGORAS AT 5.49.4)

But Aristagoras is not an especially reliable judge, and his Ionian rebels soon discover to their cost that the Persians are anything but a "pushover."[45] At Marathon the Persians thought the Athenians must be crazy, for they actually *ran* eight stades to close with the enemy.

> They were the first to withstand the sight of Median dress and the men who were wearing it: until that time even the name of the Medes was enough to instill terror.
> (6.112.3)

That dress promoted fear in the opposition, not confidence or contempt. We shall see more later to suggest that Persians were anything but soft when it came to battle, including that final decisive battle of Plataea (p. 170). Any easy assumptions about Greek toughness and Persian feebleness should by that time have been thoroughly questioned and revised.

What, too, of the final chapter of all? Ringlike, it goes back to a much earlier period, the moment of Cyrus' victory over Astyages. The Persians have a chance to exploit that victory and move from their rough and meagre terrain to occupy much better land: thus, said a certain Artembares, "we will be *thōmastoteroi*," more of an object of wonder. Cyrus however "felt no wonder (*thōma*) at the idea."

> "Do this," he said, "if you wish to prepare for a future of no longer ruling but of being ruled: soft lands tend to produce soft men. The same land cannot produce wonderful (*thōmaston*) fruit and good fighters." The Persians saw the wisdom in this, and gave up the idea and went away, acknowledging that Cyrus had won the argument. Their choice was to live

in a poor land and be rulers rather than be plain-dwellers and be other peoples' slaves.
(9.122.3–4)

Plenty of "wonder" there, *thōma*, that key Herodotean idea; and the work ends on that contrast of rulers and slaves that, we shall see, has by then become so critical (chapter 12).

It is an extraordinary ending.[46] Moreover, it is richly suggestive—but of what? How, for instance, are we to reconcile this Cyrus with the man who in book 1 gave his men a day of hard labor and then a day of sumptuous feasting and used the attractions of the easy life to persuade his Persians into revolt against the ruling Medes (1.126; cf. p. 175)? Is it just that he is a sort of resident expert on luxury, able to see both its exploitability and its dangers, and to apply whichever insight is needed to persuade a particular audience? Or is this final chapter not about luxury at all, but about some other reason why they might become "soft"?[47] And did the Persians continue in their reluctance to move, and does that explain their continued vast rule? Or did they move, did they become soft, and does that help to explain their failure in Greece? If so, why did they make that initial move? Was it to take over Lydia, and if so do we assume that Cyrus had come to change his mind, and Persia their customs, for the worse? Or was Croesus simply wrong at 1.46.1 (p. 116) to assume that Cyrus had such expansionist ideas at his expense?

What, too, of the present day, where the new "ruler" of a large part of the Greek world was Athens: Athens, not perhaps as sumptuous as Persia but still with the chryselephantine statue of Athena gazing down from the glorious acropolis; Athens, the new "tyrant city" (pp. 144, 189); Athens, where "because of the greatness of the city everything comes in from the whole world, and we can take our own enjoyment in the fruits of everyone else's products as much as of our own," while pride might be taken in "our relaxed mode of life" ("Pericles" at Thuc. 2.38.2, 2.39.1); yet Athens, so proud of its own record of being an indigenous people who had never moved their dwelling place—even if that could be seen as a result of the poor quality of their land (Thuc. 1.2.5–6)?[48]

Lots of questions, then; and as to answers, readers and listeners are on their own. If they have become accustomed—perhaps by that point even *trained*—to think and rethink as they go on, there is no reason for them to stop as they close the work or leave the lecture. Nor, indeed, were those readers and listeners given a gentle start. Some of the most demanding cases for rethinking in stride came in the first half of book 1. In chapter 7 we shall go back to the beginning; but, first, some more on how both Hippocratics and Herodotus explored cases that resisted reduction to only a single cause.

CHAPTER 6

EXPLANATIONS IN COMBINATION

(A) HIPPOCRATICS

Chapter 3 explored how one might identify a cause, and David Hume was there the great name in the background. But both Herodotus and the Hippocratics knew that causes often operate together, most obviously in that distinctive combination of "predisposition" and "trigger." It is time to move from Hume to John Stuart Mill:

> It is seldom, if ever, between a consequent and a single antecedent, that this invariable sequence [i.e., a pattern of regularity of the sort he has defined as an indicator of causation] subsists. It is usually between a consequent and the sum of several antecedents; the concurrence of all of them being requisite to produce, that is, to be certain of being followed by, the consequent. In such cases it is very common to single out only one of the antecedents under the denomination of Cause, calling the others merely Conditions.

Yet that sort of discrimination is not straightforward:

> All the conditions were equally indispensable to the production of the consequent; and the statement of the cause is incomplete, unless in some shape or other we introduce them all.

And most people are distressingly sloppy about it:

> Nothing can better show the absence of any scientific ground for the distinction between the cause of a phenomenon and its conditions, than the capricious manner in which we select from among the conditions that which we choose to denominate the cause. However numerous the conditions may be, there is hardly any of them which may not, according to the purpose of our immediate discourse, obtain that nominal pre-eminence.[1]

Whether or not we too call it "caprice," the choice of which condition to emphasize will also depend on why we are bothering in the first place. For instance, that Hippocratic model of predisposition and trigger has something in common with a distinguished modern reapplication of Mill's language of "condition" and "cause," that of Hart and Honoré in *Causation in the Law*.[2] It may be that an arsonist would not have been successful but for a breeze in the right direction, or more basically the presence of oxygen; a burglar would not have been successful if the back door had not been left open; a poisoner is only able to operate because he was able to buy arsenic. The breeze, the open door, and the availability of arsenic are for Hart and Honoré conditions, and the arsonist's or burglar's or poisoner's own action is the cause. It may be that the social deprivation that drove the criminal to crime would count as a condition too, or at least part of what Hart and Honoré call the "stage already set" before the criminal's "intervention."[3] A judge will there be more interested in what they call the "cause" and we might call the trigger, and that is the predominant interest of Hart and Honoré too (it is notable how often they write of "mere" conditions): the social analyst or historian's interests are likely to go the other way, with interest in the social deprivation (in court, that might at best be adduced in mitigation) or the level of neighborhood trust that might leave back doors open; the psychologist may be concerned with the links between the two, the nature of the interaction itself. We similarly saw in the last chapter that the Hippocratics can be more interested in the *prophasis* than in an underlying bodily defect where the *prophasis* describes what is treatable (p. 83). The dominant interest of each is more than "caprice."[4]

How "capricious," then, are the Hippocratics, and how do they set about making their explanations less "incomplete" by bringing different explanations together?

They have several ways. First, the most combative: it is not *A* or *B*, it is *C*—what we might call the politician's line, it's not our fault, it's the last government's. Second, the most accommodating: it is all of *A*, *B*, and *C*. Third, the most mechanically elaborate: *A* and *B*, and perhaps *C* and *D* as well, are interacting, and we can see how (so that "predisposition and trigger" analysis falls within this category). This can sometimes lead to a sort of hierarchy or league-table ranking: *A* is more important than *B* or *C* or *D* and so exercises that sort of "preeminence" that elicited Mill's disdain. All these approaches are found in both early and later Hippocratic works and can sometimes be found in different parts of the same work.

(i) *It's not A, it's not B, it's C.*

This is the "politician's line"—and the forensic orator's, as we saw in the case of Antiphon's *Tetralogies* or Gorgias' *Helen* (chapter 4[d]). If one is trying to get oneself off the hook or to get one's enemy on to it, nuanced multiplicity of explanation is not likely to be appropriate: that hook is either appropriate or it is not. It was important for a Hippocratic physician too to have the rhetorical skill to fight one's corner, sometimes to defend one's whole craft against those who were skeptical of medicine's claims, sometimes just to promote one's own interpretation and reputation and to defeat one's rivals.[5] There were even display competitions where rival theorists would put their case for regarding the basic bodily constituent as air or fire or water or earth (*On the Nature of Man* 1–2 IV pp. 2–8 J = VI pp. 32–36 L). The bigger your prestige, the more clients you would attract—and your livelihood would depend on it.

That insistence on *your* explanation, excluding alternatives, duly appears in particular arguments. For instance, *On the Sacred Disease* notes that experienced sufferers hide their heads when they feel an attack of the disease coming on, and do this "from shame and not, as most people think, through fear of the divine" (15 II p. 171 J = 12 VI p. 382 L),[6] while dissection reveals a moistening of the brain in diseased goats that shows that "it is not the god harming the body but the illness" (14 II p. 168 J = 11 VI p. 382 L).[7] As we saw (p. 51), *On the Nature of Man* argues that it is not regimen that is responsible for a particular disease because it strikes everyone alike (9 IV pp. 24–26 J = VI pp. 52–54 L), and *On Ancient Medicine* provides an elaborate guide for setting aside factors that look like causes but are really coincidences (17–19 I pp. 42–52 J = I pp. 612–620 L). Those display pieces arguing that the basic constituent of the human body is fire or air or water or earth are insistent that it is one rather than the others.

*(ii) A and B and C as well: multiple coexistent causes,
but with no attempt to bring them into a coherent scheme.*

Take here *Airs Waters Places* 16 (I pp. 114–116 J = II pp. 62–66 L), which we discussed at length in chapter 1 (pp. 19–20). That explains the lack of bellicosity among Asian people in terms of the pleasant climate—but it is also (*proseti*) a matter of their institutions, for people who live under an autocrat are less willing than free people to risk everything just for their master's sake. The argument is purely additive: it is just an additional point, *proseti* (Jones' Loeb translation "are a contributory cause" suggests a clearer schematism than there is in the Greek). There is no attempt to explain the connection by, for instance, suggesting that the climate and the easy life it encourages might make people more willing to accept such institutions.[8]

There is a broader point too about *Airs Waters Places*, one that extends to whole explanatory strategies.[9] Sometimes we find a "causal" model, whereby (say) bad or changeable climates cause disease but may also generate a toughness in those who can resist them (e.g., 13 I p. 108 J = II p. 56 L; 15 I p. 112 J = II p. 62 L; 19 I p. 122 J = II p. 72 L; 23 I p. 132 J = II p. 82 L; 24 I pp. 132–134 J = II p. 86 L). This continues the causal register of the first half, where climates generate bodily types: cold water develops a stiff body, for instance (4 I p. 76 J = II p. 20 L). Sometimes, though, we find rather an "analogy" or "harmony" model, where we find a pleasant climate generating a pleasant life in all respects, including a pleasant freedom from disease (esp. 5 I pp. 78–80 J = II pp. 22–24 L).[10] At the end of the work we duly find that diversity in seasonal weather has come to generate, not tough types, but diverse ones (24 I p. 134 J = II p. 90 L). The author feels no need to bring his two schemes together: where he is concerned to explain physical variations in changeable climates he exploits his analogy model, and when he is explaining tough physiques he uses his causal model.[11] All this is made much easier by that "corroborative" presentational strategy (chapter 5[c]), matching evidence to the theory it supports and using it in the context where it fits.

A smaller example is *Airs Waters Places* 7 II pp. 82–88 J = II pp. 26–32 L, discussing the qualities of water. Most attention is given to the terrain where the waters originate, the best coming from high places and the worst from marshy ground; but then "I particularly praise" those flowing to the east while the worst are those flowing to the south, especially if prevailing winds are southerlies too. There may be an implication that terrain is the primary explanation and aspect secondary, as Jouanna puts it,[12] but that is indeed Jouanna's formalization, not that of *Airs Waters Places* itself, and the end of that discussion leaves us with aspect again defining which are the best waters, which the second-best, and so on (8 I p. 88 J = II p. 30 L). The two different causal schemes simply coexist without needing to be reconciled.

Other works are not dissimilar. *On Ancient Medicine* spends most of its effort in explaining health and disease in terms of conflicting "powers"— the sweet and the bitter, the astringent and the insipid, and so on; but its closing chapters pass to a different type of analysis, explaining how the different structures of different parts of the body produce pains and other bodily phenomena. There is no attempt to relate the two modes of analysis to one another; he does not say, for instance, that the bodily structures create conditions for flatulence and its location, and the conflict of "powers" triggers it on a particular occasion. It is just that some ailments come from powers and some from structures (22 I p. 56 J = I p. 626 L).

On the Sacred Disease is especially interesting here. Its argument could easily be taken to be that this "sacred" disease is not sacred at all, but in fact it is not quite that: it is that this disease is no more and no less "divine" or "sacred" (*theion*) than any other, for divinity is behind everything. As in *Airs Waters Places* when it discusses the "female disease" of the Scythians (*Airs*

Waters Places 22 I pp. 126–130 J = II pp. 76–82 L), the author needs to tread carefully here.[13] He cannot say, "It is not the gods at all," as that would get too many pious lips to purse among his listeners. It is a different matter with that assertion that sufferers "hide their heads from shame, not from fear of the divine" (15 II p. 171 J = 12 VI. p. 382 L; above, p. 96), as this is a claim about human behavior rather than the gods themselves—rather as Herodotus is prepared to give "the names" of the Egyptian gods (2.3.2), as these are what mortals use, while retaining his usual cautious reticence about the gods themselves.[14]

Yet *On the Sacred Disease* also provides powerful reasons why divine explanation is not a helpful way of looking at it, in keeping with his sustained attack on "supporters of magico-religious medicine":[15] natural causes explain why particular people are attacked by it, just as in *Airs Waters Places* they explain why that female disease happens in Scythia and nowhere else. If it were the gods, then why would the sacred illness particularly affect phlegmatic types? If the female disease were divine, then why do not the poor suffer more than the rich, for it is the rich who can make the sumptuous sacrifices that win the gods' favor? It is open to debate how far this argument points to genuine "religiosity" in either work and how far it is just *ad hominem* along the lines "if you believe in the gods, you cannot also believe that they would punish people so randomly."[16] Either way, one can see how the argument exploits both our first category, not-*A*-not-*B*-but-*C*, and our second, *A*-and-*B*-and-*C*: it is the second that allows the formulation that the disease can be divine as well as having identifiable secular causes, but it is the first that furnishes the argumentative armory to dismiss his opponents' causal analysis and demonstrate that divinity cannot carry any helpful explanatory force.

(iii) A interacting with B and C in an identifiable way: hence, not just accumulating explanations, as in (ii), but seeking to reduce them to a finite schema.

The favored scheme here is that familiar one of predisposition and trigger, with a susceptibility caused by an internal predisposition and then an outbreak stimulated by an external cause. Hard digestive organs make you susceptible to pleurisy, but your abscesses on this occasion may have been triggered by any type of immediate cause (*prophasis*, *Airs Waters Places* 4 I p. 76 J = II p. 20 L). A child's predisposition to epilepsy comes from the body's internal imbalance, but this particular epileptic attack may be owed to a sudden change in the wind to the south, an unexpected noise, or a failure to catch the breath when he or she is crying (*On the Sacred Disease*, esp. 13

II pp. 164–168 J = 10 VI pp. 378–380 L). There are times where this taste for the binary—a sort of μέν-δέ thinking—leads to simplification. *Airs Waters Places* has traced the causal chain further back to climate, which both encouraged this physical type and then also produced the cold water that combined badly with the dry body; *On the Sacred Disease* has spent time on where that predisposing bodily structure may come from, stressing the part played by heredity, and on giving pathological explanations for particular symptoms such as fluxes of phlegm and bile; there is also that further divine level of explanation. But when each work comes to specify a particular causal interrelation, it deals with a simple binary polarity, a predisposition and a *prophasis*. As so often in Greek conceptualization, "most things go in pairs" (pp. 75, 85).

There may be other variations of interaction too, often quite subtle ones. Take the discussion of the "Long-heads" (Macrocephali) in *Airs Waters Places*:

> No other race has heads like these. Originally it was custom (*nomos*) that was most responsible (*aitiōtatos*) for the length of their heads, but now nature contributes as well as custom. The custom aspect is as follows. As soon as a child is born, they mold the head with their hands while the body is still tender and the head is still soft, and they force it to become longer: they do this by applying bandages and suitable appliances, which spoil the roundness of the head and increase its length. That is how custom originally achieved this result, so that nature was forced to develop in this way; but as time went on it became part of nature, so that custom no longer imposed any compulsion. For seed comes from every part of the body, healthy seed from the healthy parts, diseased seed from the diseased parts. As a general truth bald parents have bald children, grey-eyed parents have grey-eyed children, squinting parents have squinting children, and the same goes for other bodily features: so why should not long-headed parents have long-headed children? But these days long-headedness is less common than it was, for custom no longer exercises so powerful an effect because of the contact with other peoples.
> (*AIRS WATERS PLACES* 14 I P. 110 J = II PP. 58–60 L)

So custom, *nomos*, and nature, *physis*, work together. Originally the physical feature was imposed by the people's custom, but as time went on what was originally driven by *nomos* became part of nature—as we might say, it entered the genetic code. But *nomos* clearly continues to contribute too, for long-headedness has become less common because the custom is no longer so "powerful" (*ischuei*) because of contact with other people, presumably implying that this has led the Macrocephali to change their traditional ways.[17]

That *aitiōtatos*, "most responsible," already has something of the "league table" ranking mentality about it, not just sketching how causes collaborate but putting their respective contributions in order of merit. That can be taken much further, as at the end of *Airs Waters Places*:

> These [i.e., acute climatic changes from one season to the next] are the greatest factors in creating differences in people's natures; next comes the land in which a person is brought up and its waters, for in general you will find types and characters of people varying according to the nature of the land. . . .
> (AIRS WATERS PLACES 24 I P. 136 J = II P. 90 L)

Or the end of *On Breaths*, quoted in the last chapter (p. 89):

> So breaths are seen to be the greatest busybodies (*malista polypragmoneousai*) in all diseases, everything else is only jointly or secondarily responsible (*sunaitia kai metaitia*), and I have demonstrated the underlying cause of the disease to be such as I say.
> (ON BREATHS 15 II P. 252 J = VI P. 114. L)

It is not usually made explicit why these are the hierarchies, and there is no such sophisticated methodology articulated for ordering causes as there was for identifying them in the first place (pp. 50–53); still, we can usually infer from the surrounding argument why the author is putting the explanations in that order. In *On Breaths* wind has been a recurrent feature in various contexts, for breaths are those "greatest busybodies": blood-movements are crucial too, but it is air that stimulates an irregularity (e.g. regarding fevers, 7–8, or epilepsy, 14), or is at least what makes a laceration painful (14). The logic is not irreproachable,[18] but it is not just a case of accumulation; it is rather a pyramid hierarchy with breath at the top.[19]

All these different modes of combination hunt together. We have already seen something of that in *On the Sacred Disease* (above, pp. 97–98), and if we return to a famous passage in *Airs Waters Places* on the female disease (22 I pp. 126–130 J = II pp. 76–82 L), we see something of the same. There is the same facility as in *On the Sacred Disease* in explaining why a divine explanation is not illuminating: the widespread distribution of the disease shows that it is no more divinely caused than any other. There is accumulation of causes too. The illness is prevalent there because Scythians go in for bloodletting behind the ear, with unfortunate consequences; it is also because the men wear trousers, and hence find it inconvenient to masturbate; and it is also cold and tiring because of the climate. There is the third category too, with *A* interacting with *B* and *C* in an identifiable way, here quite a sophisticated one. Thus, the central core of the argument is that their horse riding causes the swelling of the joints. Humans respond in one way by the bloodletting, which has the side effect of reducing the flow of semen. Then psychology cuts in as well, because the men accept that they are impotent and start dressing as women.[20]

That ready coexistence of all these different approaches should warn us against regarding any of them as more developed or more sophisticated or simply better than the others. We may tend to regard the third category, at least the analysis of the interaction if not the league-tabling, as the most acute and serviceable. It is not clear that Herodotus or his contemporaries would have agreed: the capacity for seeing things separately, for keeping different explanatory types in nonoverlapping compartments mirrors habits of thought in other genres. In a classic article Ben Perry argued for the "early Greek ability for viewing things separately,"[21] and Christopher Rowe has perceptively analyzed Hesiod's thought in terms of "multiple approaches": that is, "a thing's being described or explained in more than one way in the same context, where the descriptions or explanations are not brought into connection with each other, and where they may appear to be—sometimes, I may add, actually *are*—mutually inconsistent."[22] We have already found something similar in tragedy (pp. 15–16).

Nor, indeed, should we feel that our own conceptual world is so very distant. Our everyday existence is full of phenomena that invite explanation in different, coexisting registers. If we explain why a particular selection of people should all be in the same room at 4 o'clock to discuss (shall we say) Herodotus, one explanation might deal with neural antecedents, another with the participants' educational backgrounds, a third with the reasons for the timetabling; some might even, less plausibly in this case than in others, adduce the will of God. It is no mark of sophistication to want to bring all those ways of looking at it into a single scheme. They are "incommensurable."[23]

So if we find that Herodotus too develops different explanatory strands that he can, but feels no need to, bring together into a coherent single scheme, we need not be surprised. One effect is indeed to facilitate the polyphony that is associated with sophisticated historical consciousness, the awareness that there is not one single way of looking at complicated issues, that multiple voices and insights can be a strength in a writer or observer rather than a weakness. Pick-and-mix is so much better than one-size-fits-all.

(B) HERODOTUS

Herodotus too was happy to pick and mix.[24] There are times when he firmly rejects one explanation, sometimes but not always to prefer another. When he discusses the Spartan and Athenian maltreatment of Xerxes' heralds, he goes on to trace the aftereffects of this half a century later (7.133–137). The Spartans went to considerable lengths to atone for the impiety, but

> I cannot identify any bad thing that happened to the Athenians after they had treated the heralds in this way, other than the fact that their land and city was devastated—but I do not think this happened for that reason (ἀλλὰ τοῦτο οὐ διὰ ταύτην τὴν αἰτίην δοκέω γενέσθαι). (7.133.2)[25]

And when a certain Athenades kills Ephialtes, the traitor who showed Xerxes the path at Thermopylae, he did so "for a different reason" (*aitiē*) "but was no less honored for it by the Lacedaemonians" (7.213.3). (One again, incidentally, notices that waft of "charge" and "blameworthiness" that comes with *aiti-* language; if these *had* been the reasons, Athenades and the Spartans would have been acting to avenge a perceived offense.) He can also enumerate alternative explanations without implying that all are valid: several possible reasons are aired for the Argives' failure to join the common enterprise in 480 (7.148–152), and even if more than one may carry some truth it seems unlikely that they all do. This is parallel to his caution about accepting causation within the ethnographic or physical domains when it might be just a matter of correlation: the Egyptians still celebrate a particular festival, "but I cannot say whether this is why they do it" (2.122.2); the Libyans cauterize the veins in children's heads and "that, so they say, is why they are the healthiest people of all; and it is true that the Libyans are the healthiest people we know, but I cannot say whether it is for that reason" (4.187.3). It is such thinking that makes possible the delightful ambiguity when Mardonius explains that he has sidestepped the implications of an oracle, one that had foretold Persian devastation of Delphi followed by their total defeat: now he has spared Delphi, so "we shall not be destroyed for this reason" (or "this grievance," ταύτης τε εἵνεκα τῆς αἰτίης οὐκ ἀπολεόμεθα, 9.42.3). Mardonius is now confident that they will win, as he goes on to say, but there is more truth in his words than he realizes: not for *this* reason, perhaps—but they might still be destroyed for another.

There are equally times when Herodotus is quite content to accumulate different explanations, without ordering them into a hierarchy or explaining how they interrelate:[26]

> Many and great were the factors that roused Cyrus up and urged him on: first, his birth, the impression[27] that he was something more than human; second, the good fortune he had enjoyed in war; for wherever Cyrus launched a campaign, that nation found it impossible to escape. (1.204.2)

Mardonius eventually won over Xerxes and persuaded him to do what he said (i.e., to invade Greece): for other considerations too played a part and worked as his allies in ensuring that Xerxes was persuaded. For one thing there were messengers from Thessaly from the Aleuadae, urging the king to move against Greece and promising him their enthusiastic support (these Aleudae were kings within Thessaly); for another there were the Peisistratids who had come up to Sousa, arguing the same things as the Aleuadae. . . .
(7.6.1–2)

For Herodotus knows that choices can be overdetermined. Demaratus played his part in securing the succession for Atossa's son Xerxes rather than his elder half-brothers, but . . .

> it seems to me that even without this advice Xerxes would have become king: for Atossa controlled everything.
> (7.3.4)

Often, too, we get different causal threads at different points, all reasonable and persuasive, without any immediate interest in discriminating which matters more or most. Mardonius is eager to fight at Plataea while his superiority in numbers is overwhelming and before more Greeks can gather (9.41.4); only later do we learn from Alexander of Macedon that it is not just a matter of numbers—the Persians are also running out of food (9.45.2). Croesus is fearful of Cyrus' growth and launches a preemptive strike (1.46.1); later it is also "in desire for land, wanting to add to his own territory, and in particular trusting in the oracle and wanting to take vengeance on Cyrus for Astyages" (1.73.1). That should not be seen as contradiction, for there can indeed be multiple causes for events; and the bigger the events, the more complicated that accumulation of causes can be.[28] The defensive explanation is appropriate at 1.46.1, for defensive necessity is most likely to shock Croesus out of his grieving for his son; the aggressive land-hunger suits at 1.73.1 because it sits so suggestively with Sandanis' warning at 1.71, pointing out the poverty of the people who would be the target. The later explanation does not exclude or replace the earlier, but each is developed where it is most appropriate in narrative terms.

Sometimes though he does firmly state that one explanation is more important or powerful than another, though in those cases too the secondary factor has some explanatory power as well.[29] We have seen that already in a few cases: even if *prophasies* or *proschēmata* retain some explanatory power, they clearly explain less than, say, the Persian drive to conquer Libya (4.167.3; p. 10). Nor is it just the ambassadors before Gelon who claim that

Athens and Eretria may be the named targets but the Persian ambitions are broader (7.157.1; p. 10): we might suspect that they would say that, wouldn't they, to convince Gelon, but Herodotus also expresses the same judgment in his authorial voice.

> These cities (Athens and Eretria) were the reason that was put forward (*proschēma*) for the expedition, but they had it in mind to conquer as many of the Greek cities as they could.
> (6.44.1; CF. 6.94.1)

> In name (*ounoma*) the king's expedition was represented as a drive against Athens, but the target was all of Greece.
> (7.138.1)

It would be a mistake to regard the singling out of Athens and Eretria as *only* a matter of "name."[30] When Darius instructs his slave to remind him daily before dinner "sire, remember the Athenians," it is not a mere pretext that is his concern (5.105.2). Vengeance on Athens continues to figure especially large when Xerxes raises his invasion plans for debate (7.8β: below, pp. 121–123), and such vengeance talk is not just a matter of pure anger: Mardonius can reasonably point out the empire-wide dangers of allowing those "Ionians who live in Europe" to make the Persians a laughingstock (7.9.1–2). But the language throughout also makes it clear which explanation matters more, and that is the aim to conquer all Greece, just as it was earlier the aim to conquer Libya (p. 10). A Thucydidean reader would have found it easy to formalize Darius' motives in terms of "more *A* than *B*" or "not so much *B* as *A*" (cf. Thuc. 1.9.1, 1.88.1, 2.65.11, 7.57.1). It is interesting, too, that such an insistence on the greater power of the imperialistic drive recurs with special frequency in those two contexts, first the Libyan campaign and then the Greek war itself. This is not the only way in which that Libyan campaign serves as something of an overture to the bigger war that is to come (below, pp. 125–128).

In such passages, too, that schema of predisposition and trigger is not far away. True, he does not formulate this as precisely as Thucydides, or for that matter Polybius, would do. Thucydides' famous proclamation about the origins of the Peloponnesian War is particularly straightforward to recast in predisposition-and-trigger form: Spartan fear of Athens explains why the war was going to happen some time; Potidaea and Corcyra explain why it happened in 431 rather than 440 or 425.

We can, however, say that the explicit later theorizing of Thucydides and Polybius is building on, and operates with much the same mindset as, what we are already seeing in Herodotus. It would have been easy enough for a reader of a Thucydidean mindset to put the outbreak of hostilities in book 5 in terms of an underlying "disposition," that Persian expansionism to which we have become accustomed over four books, and an immediate "trigger," the machinations of Aristagoras and the stirring up of Ionia. A Polybian reader could also have added the "beginning," the *archē*: those ships that Athens sent to Ionia in 499/8 BCE, which Herodotus calls "the start of sufferings for Greeks and barbarians" (5.97.3), echoing the Homeric ships that were "the beginning of evils for the Trojans and for Paris himself" when they abducted Helen (*Il.* 5.62–63).[31] The origins of the war clearly go much further back, but these can still count as the "beginning": they mark the start of the (fairly) continuous movement and sequence of "sufferings for Greeks and barbarians" that culminate in the events of 490;[32] rather as for Polybius Saguntum will be the beginning of the continuous story of the Hannibalic War (3.6.1)—and, for that matter, Thucydides will mark the beginning of his war as the attack on Plataea ("This is the point at which the war starts," 2.1.1). Herodotus may not formalize his scheme with the same methodological persnicketiness as his successors, but they are still standing on his shoulders.

So Herodotus is prepared to let explanations coexist, he is prepared to arrange them in a hierarchy, and he is prepared from time to time to rule certain explanations out completely. There are times too when he simply leaves it open which of these may be the case, particularly when a divine explanation may be in play and caution is therefore especially pertinent. Was Cambyses' madness payback for his sacrilegious treatment of the Apis bull? Perhaps, but it may be just one of those bad things that often happen to mortals (a life-is-like-that explanation), and anyway they say that he may *also* (*kai*) have suffered from a congenital disease . . . (3.33). That initially looks like a case of either-*A*-or-*B*-but-not-both, but then that significant "also" allows the possibility of an accumulation of real explanations.[33] We shall see further cases in chapter 10 where divine and secular registers intertwine, yet it is anything but clear exactly how they do so.

The Hippocratic parallels confirm that his audience too would be at home with all those varieties of disjunction and conjunction as they opened his book or heard him begin his lecture. Which of these patterns will he develop most, or at least develop first? They are soon given some clues.

CHAPTER 7

EARLY MOVES

(A) CROESUS AND CANDAULES

In chapter 2 we left Croesus as "the first man to begin unjust deeds against the Greeks" (1.5.3–4; pp. 28–29).[1] Except that he wasn't. The text immediately goes on to list some precursors. It was Croesus who reduced the Ionians, Aeolians, and Dorians of Asia Minor and made them pay tribute (1.6.2), but there had earlier been the Cimmerians' attack on Ionia, "not a destruction of the cities, but a plundering attack" (ἐξ ἐπιδρομῆς ἁρπαγή, 1.6.3); there had been Gyges, who attacked Miletus and Smyrna and took the town of Colophon (1.14.4); Ardys had taken Priene and invaded Miletus (1.15); Sadyattes and Alyattes had again attacked Miletus (1.16–18). So this is an unusually clear case of revision in stride (p. 90), and the way it is deepened includes a revision of the categories as well as the introduction of other individuals.[2] We now see that there are various degrees of "unjust deeds," with mere ravaging expeditions belonging in a different category from the escalation involved in conquest and the imposition of tribute[3]—a new discrimination, in fact, of categories of escalating aggression to complement that already seen in the first chapters. There too the abductions had been described in the language of "injustice," and these—at least until the escalation of the Trojan War—had been presented as casual "plunder"; the same word, *harpagē*, had been used. Those chapters had made it clear that plunder was one thing, full-scale war another, and now Herodotus insinuates the more nuanced idea that subjection, not plunder or transient fighting, is the important historical stage. This is another case, too, where the contemporary experience of Herodotus' readers would make them readier to accept the validity of the analysis (pp. 55–56). No one familiar with the Athenian empire would doubt that subjection and tribute bearing constituted a new category that made, if not all the difference, at least a difference that mattered a lot.[4]

These backward steps take us to Candaules, and the famous story of

Candaules' wife (1.8–13) also does something to set the scene for the rest of the *Histories*. A narrative that will so often include tales of tyrants and their sexual transgressions begins with a paradoxical version of that—the man who falls for his own wife (ἠράσθη τῆς ἑωυτοῦ γυναικός, 1.8.1). The story has many other aspects of interest that look ahead, not least the way that Gyges tries so hard to evade the inevitability that the king lays upon him but finds that he cannot; such are the ways of the court. We shall see a good deal more of these ways of the court later, ways that so often eventually, somehow or other, turn against the king himself (below, chapter 9).

Especially interesting is the way that so much of this reminds us of the early four chapters, and through them of the *Iliad*. Once again, things begin with a woman, or rather with a man who is consumed with a woman's beauty and led by this to an arrogant assertion of his will. Once again, great and lasting consequences spring from this domestic, erotic start. Once again, too, there is more than a touch of rationalism about the way this story is told. An alternative version—very likely the earlier,[5] even more likely the more dominant in Herodotus' day—was different in texture, more fairytale, less human and tragic. That version portrayed Gyges as a simple shepherd who discovered a ring of invisibility, which he used to seduce the queen and kill the king. Plato tells an elaborate version at *Republic* 2.359c–360b.[6] Another rendering, also very likely old, had this magic ring foiled by a dragon-stone owned by the queen, or possibly by her own gift of the evil eye:[7] she would in that case have been able to see Gyges even after his ring had made him invisible to others. Herodotus has no magic ring, no dragon-stone;[8] the only "invisibility" is that which Gyges has to try and secure for himself, by slipping out of the room before the queen can see him.

Yet there are also substantial differences from the way in which Herodotus developed in 1.1–5 the model of catastrophic sexual affairs and abductions. In one sense there may once again be rationalism, rather as there was in 1.1–5 (p. 28); the world of the fairytale has disappeared. But this is not the sort of rationalism that reduces all to a human level.[9] Here there is a further revision of the terms of the proem, which had given us to understand that Herodotus' focus will rest on humans rather than gods, "the things that originate from humans." That had anticipated a feature of that early abduction model, the way in which several of the most god-ridden Greek myths were reduced to a human level: this Io was not transformed into a cow (1.1.3–2.1), this Europa was not transported by a bull (1.2.1), this Medea had no magical powers and no golden fleece (1.2.2–3), this Paris judged no goddesses (1.3.1–2).[10]

Now this restriction has turned out to be delusive, and in this Gyges story we have a strong hint of a supernatural dimension: "It was necessary that things should turn out badly for Candaules" (1.8.2).[11] The audience may be unclear about the texture or origin of this necessity, but they will find it hard to interpret it in wholly human, nonsupernatural terms (p. 146). The divine intrudes again at the end of the sequence, with Delphi foretelling that punishment will fall on the fifth generation (1.13.2): the Lydians (Herodotus adds) later forgot this as the events unfolded, and Herodotus' audience may go on to forget it too (pp. 112–113)—but, for the moment, the effect is powerful and clear. We saw (p. 89) that the initial question and answer of the *Iliad*, "which god brought them together to fight in strife? It was the son of Leto and Zeus . . . ," is in some ways a false start; the poem looks for a god who started the quarrel, but finds that it largely originated from humans. Here the false start works the other way around. Rationalism has its bounds; however much one may insist on the human elements of the story, the supernatural level will also come into play, with figures and events as momentous as these.

There is new light on the women too. In the abductions they were mere possessions, things to be "seized" (the basic sense of the *harpagē* root); there was no interest in the women as thinking, feeling personalities. That is remarkable, especially with Medea or Helen, whose emotional depth had already excited such literary interest. Candaules' wife is similarly passive in the other versions of the story: Gyges turns invisible in Plato's version and so *of course* can seduce the queen; that leaves no interest in what she thought about it all, or whether she could have done, or wanted to do, anything about it.[12] In Nicolaus of Damascus' account, perhaps from Xanthus of Lydia,[13] the queen initially shows enough outrage to denounce her "seducer" Gyges; yet after the murders they still become husband and wife, and there is no further interest in her reactions.[14]

At first, Herodotus' presentation of the queen seems similar too. She is not named.[15] She is simply "his wife" or "the queen"; she is her husband's pride, something for him to show off—Beauty personified,[16] no more. But in Herodotus things then change, and we are led to see it from her viewpoint. Arrestingly, she becomes a personality;[17] and instead of things simply starting "with" a woman, she begins to initiate as well as to suffer. In the initial chapters, the avengers were the males who felt outraged; now the woman takes her own revenge. Later too influential women, many of them named, will play a part in starting important movements.[18] Atossa, the Persian queen, will point her husband Darius in the direction of Greece (3.134); Xerxes' wife Amestris will exact a terrible revenge on Masistes' wife, heavy in its suggested but unmentioned consequences for the king (9.108–113; pp. 32–34). A momentous chain of events also has its origin in the bedroom of a Spartan king, with the dispute between Demaratus and Leutychidas over the succession to Ariston (6.63–70), including an enigmatic speech in which the Spartan queen mother sets out her side of the story.

So to understand events fully we need a good deal more than the sketchy beginnings of 1.1–4, and that is what we are gradually given: we need more on the gods; we need more on the personalities of the humans, including the females. Herodotus will continue to give us both.

Finally, blame. That was complicated enough in the sequence of initial abductions: we saw that in chapter 2. In this story there is much less explicit interest in attaching blame than there was in those abductions. Who, after all, can straightforwardly be blamed here? Hardly Candaules' wife: we are led to see things so much from her point of view. Candaules himself is blameworthy, certainly, and he pays for it. But the story does not end with his death, for it will have repercussions five generations later, and who is to blame for those? Not the fifth descendant, or not in any way that we can so far gauge: the "vengeance" or "recompense" will come for what Gyges has done to the Heraclidae (1.13.2) and is fixed long before anything that Croesus does. As for Gyges, it is certainly his action that triggers this, but it is hard to think that he is blameworthy. Too much stress has fallen on the necessity for him to act in the way he does, articulated not merely through his own perceptions or those of the queen but also through Herodotus' own authorial comment ("there was no way out," 1.12.1).[19]

We therefore have a chain of consequences where the implications of the proem's *aitiē* and the first sentence's *aitious*, with their hinted link between origin and blame, would be inapposite. Not that we have heard the last of blame; it will become highly relevant when the five generations are complete, and the search for an explanation for Croesus' fall becomes insistent once more (p. 111). But, for the moment, the narrative's interest has shifted towards different explanatory modes.

These early chapters, then, are full of feints and redirections. Is it a simple question of blame, of who started it? Initially yes, in the alternative versions of Persians and Greeks; then complications set in, with the blameworthiness of escalation in the first four chapters; then hardly at all. Do we have to go a long way back to find the starting point? Initially yes, to the Trojan War and beyond; then no, only to Croesus, much later; then yes again, or at least a little further back than Croesus. Do we leave the gods out? Initially yes; but then we cannot. Is it a matter of give-and-take, payback, revenge? Initially yes; then no, as payback becomes more a question of rhetoric than motive; then yes again, but with the woman as a personable individual taking the initiative rather than the outraged males. And is it a matter of distinctively tyrannical, monarchic behavior? Not at all at the beginning, where the abductors are a mix of traders and nobles and princes; but there is an increasing hint of it at the end, with Candaules' pride in his own felicity that will recur with other, very different tyrants, starting with Croesus himself.

So already any initial suggestions are being overlaid by different ways of looking at it. "Overlaid," though, is again the right word, just as it was for that complicating of the initial picture of revenge (chapter 2). Those initial suggestions and gestures are not wholly rejected or dismissed,[20] for many will come back, combining with and complementing other explanatory registers. In other words, this is a narrative equivalent of the second, not the first, of our ways of combining explanations (chapter 6[a]), a case of "both A and B" rather than "not A but B."

(B) CROESUS: PRIDE, AGGRESSION, DOWNFALL

What further redirections, then, do we get once we return to Croesus himself and those "unjust deeds"—deeds that, as we earlier saw, involved bringing charges against one Greek state after another, justified when he could, slight and factitious when he could not (1.26.3; pp. 7–8)? In a work so rich in explanation, it is striking that no explanation is given for his aggression. Such behavior, escalation though it may be when compared with its preceding counterparts, is not felt as something that needs explanation at all: no mention of ancestral enmities, for instance (contrast 1.4.4) or of defensiveness (contrast 1.46.1) or of vengeance or of desire for land (contrast 1.73.1). So is it restraint, not aggression, that presents the special case, the one where motives need probing?[21] If that is so, there is a danger that the proem's focus on the great war's *aitiē* may be homing in on a non-question. If it is seen as a simple act of imperialistic aggression, then why not just regard it in the same light, a continuation of those earlier aggressions that are just the sort of thing that life is like, just the way that humans, or at least easterners, instinctively behave? This would then be a new register that would trump and replace—no subtle "overlaying"—other ways of explaining why wars happen, an "explanation" that would work by denying the need for any *specific* explanation at all.

Of course it is going to be more complex than this, not least in giving us more reasons for that "eastern aggression," ones in which Greeks too have played a part (p. 124). But first we are introduced to some other aspects of human experience that may not require specific explanations every time they occur, for it is now that we are introduced to Solon and his programmatic wisdom. His dialogue with Croesus (1.29–33) is deep, with a conversational dynamic that is itself expressive: however relevant Croesus' "unjust deeds against the Greeks" may be to the narrative or to what we might infer about Solon's thinking, a wise man speaking to a tyrant is hardly likely to dwell on that tyrant's bad behavior, and we can sense a certain skillful indirectness in the way he speaks.[22]

His words ooze wisdom, and they have many poetic touches.[23] They will also be echoed later in particular narrative sequences, particularly that of Polycrates of Samos in book 3 and in the words of Artabanus at Abydus in book 7,[24] then in the desperate Greek graspings for hope as Xerxes relentlessly approaches (7.203.2). If we try to pin down exactly what Solon's moral might be, it proves strangely elusive—perhaps, indeed, because it is *not* exact. Life is mutable; anyone's fortune may change, for no day in a life is the same as any other (1.32.4). Heaven is "envious and turbulent" (1.32.1): envious, one presumes, of those who come closest to divine prosperity and turbulent in destroying them. The most prosperous human beings act or think in particular ways, and those ways contribute to their destruction. Those three theses are not identical with one another, but they are all there, and they overlap;[25] any or all of them may turn out to be true in the various events that are to come.

By the end of the Croesus narrative, Croesus himself feels that Solon has touched on the truth of his coming catastrophe, as he solemnly intones "Solon" three times as he sits, set there alive, on the pyre (1.86.3). He may even be suggesting, rightly or wrongly,[26] that Solon even predicted it: "It had all turned out as Solon had said" (1.86.5). But which of the various inflections that Solon's wisdom could be given has been most apposite here?

That question of explaining Croesus' fall is hardly subdued or inexplicit, for the victorious Cyrus allows Croesus to send to Delphi to ask Apollo, "the god of the Greeks" (1.90.2), "whether it is the custom of the Greek gods to be ungrateful" (1.90.4). Apollo, not just the reader, takes that as a request for an explanation, for Apollo's answer does not confine itself to the charge of ingratitude: in explaining why it is not his fault, he goes further, and says what *does* explain Croesus' fall.

As Apollo begins to speak, the reader or hearer will surely have no idea what any answer might be. There have been so many different strands in speech and narrative. Will it emerge that Croesus is responsible for his own fate, and if so how? Is it punishment for over-ambition, crossing the natural bounds of his kingdom? Or for presumption in "testing" the oracle, for to ask such a question and expect an answer is un-Greek,[27] even if a little less un-Greek than his earlier testing of the oracles?[28] Or for the even greater presumption now in reproaching the god? Or for thinking that the Greek god would care so much for material goods or apply so crude a model of gift exchange, in using language such as "Croesus has given you gifts worthy of your discoveries . . ." (1.53.2)?[29] It would be no surprise, either, if Apollo's answer had echoed Solon's wisdom, interpreted in any or all of our various ways. Croesus' fall could have been presented as the turning of Fortune's wheel; there might even have been a hint of divine envy of such prosperity, though Apollo might have found it difficult to admit to that directly; there might certainly have been further suggestions of punishment for Croesus' presumption in counting on that prosperity. The more recent hints of transgressive and self-destructive tyrannical *action*, the "yearning for land" (1.73.1; above, p. 103) or the failure to spare the guiltless (1.26.3; above, pp. 7–8, and 1.76.2; below, p. 117) might also have come into play. Or it might have emerged as vengeance for the Greeks who had initially been Croesus' victims; this is, after all, the god of the Greeks, described as such by Croesus himself (1.87.3, 1.90.2, 1.90.4). There are so many ways in which Apollo might have made it clear that an explanation need not include any "ingratitude" on his own part.

What Apollo does say comes as, at least partly, a surprise. There is no suggestion of any divine punishment of the individual king. Far from showing disdain for Croesus' lavish gifts and resentment at Croesus' remonstration, Apollo answers the remonstration civilly, and suggests that he was indeed grateful for the gifts[30] and had done what he could. As for any suggestion of divine envy, or of divine punishment of presumption,[31] or of divine distaste for aggression, all are wholly absent. The answer is quite different: "Croesus has paid for the mistake (or fault or failing: *hamartas*) of his ancestor in the fifth generation back, who was a guard of the Heraclidae, followed a woman's deceit, killed his master, and took over a position to which he had no right" (1.91.1).[32] It all goes back to Gyges: *that* is the explanation, at least the first explanation, of it all.

We had certainly been told of this at the beginning; there had been the prophecy of the five generations, and even the notice that the Lydians forgot all about it until it was fulfilled (1.13.2; above, p. 108). Still, it is an odd reader who has been thinking about this in the more recent narrative. Several of the earlier parts of the narrative have been recalled, but not this one;[33] we have not, for instance, been prepared in any way to understand what "holding destruction back for three years" might mean. In retrospect we might understand this as referring to the death of Croesus' son Atys, which (it is perhaps implied at 1.46.1) delayed Croesus' fatal campaigning for two years,[34] and the preparations for the campaign might (though Herodotus does not tell us so) have required a further year. So maybe Apollo, unable to delay destruction to the next generation (1.91.2), delayed it by destroying the next generation instead. But no reader could have sensed that dimension in the Atys narrative itself: that is introduced as an act of divine indignation (1.34.1), not of oblique favor.[35]

So the effect of this narrative is rather similar to that which Stanley Fish thought-provokingly suggested for *Paradise Lost*, arguing that the audience of the poem, finding Satan so seductive and God's rhetoric so lackluster, effectively *reenact* for themselves man's original sin.[36] Here too the audience forget, just as the Lydians forgot, until it all becomes clear. That is high-level *mimesis*, indeed, inducing the audience to mimic the forgetting that plays a role in the text and therefore to understand this explanatory strand with extraordinary clarity.[37]

It is easy to think of Herodotus as toying with his audience here, starting all sorts of ideas that prove to be red herrings and false (or at least less true) leads; nor is that formulation wholly unfair. However, this game is a productive one, drawing the audience into essaying their own interpretations and measuring them against what turns out to be the case. The human audience, like human observers at the time, can only grasp so much; there may be a broader scheme as well, transcending several generations in a way that is visible only to the gods and then later, retrospectively, to the historian.[38] But we should also be clear that even those first ideas were not useless, including all those strands in Solon's wisdom. Even if they proved not to be the ones that mattered most on this occasion, it does not mean that they have no purchase at all; Herodotus does not operate with a system where a single thoroughgoing causal explanation excludes all others, and any or all of the strands may be relevant later. They may even have been relevant here, for the cross-generational explanation need not wipe out all others just because it is finally seen to be the most powerful one, validated by no less an authority than Apollo himself.[39]

Even after apparently finishing with explanations, Herodotus adds another story in the next chapter, one that dates back to the dynastic unrest when Croesus took over the throne, and a particularly barbarous punishment—death by "carding," that is tearing the flesh as one would card or comb wool—that he inflicted on a man who had intrigued on behalf of a rival claimant (1.92.2–4). This is a new slant again on Croesus, and one that brings his behavior (the torture) and predicament (dynastic intrigue)[40] closer to those that will typify the later tyrants who "transgress customs and kill without trial" (3.80.5).[41]

The questions that the audience have come to ask, and the explanations they have themselves essayed, therefore remain questions and explanations for their future reading and hearing, and during that process they may come to look back to past sequences and explore again the lessons that might be drawn for later narrative developments.[42] Apollo's answers do not end the procedure here, but they do remind the audience that historical explanation is a very provisional, very elusive, and very challenging business.

CHAPTER 8

EMPIRE

(A) CROESUS AGAIN

Croesus is not a Persian. He is a Lydian, even if it is he who starts the chain of "unjust deeds against the Greeks" (1.5.3; above, p. 28).[1] He may still set a pattern for later events as his narrative place is taken by Persian kings, and that pattern may take several forms. One of these may be in that pattern of cross-generational payback that emerged towards the end of his *logos* (pp. 112–113), especially as the narrative of Cyrus soon goes on to deal with a story redolent of the world of Greek tragedy, introduced by that same word *hamartas* that Apollo used ("mistake" or "fault," 1.119.1; cf. 1.91.1). This is the tale of Astyages' punishment of Harpagus by murdering his son and serving up his flesh for the unwitting father to eat: any Greek reader or hearer would think of Thyestes' banquet, rich as that gruesome episode was in its cross-generational consequences for the house of Atreus. But the clearer way in which Croesus sets a pattern is in that aggression against Cyrus, and the disaster that this brings upon himself, his country, and his house; and this is not a matter of unjust deeds against *the Greeks* at all. The focus has shifted eastwards.

The emphasis shifted in fact quite soon after those first "unjust deeds" of 1.26 (above, pp. 7–8); for once he has taken Bias/Pittacus' restraining advice (1.27; p. 12), we hear more of Croesus' interest in Greece not as a target for aggression but as a source of wisdom and insight,[2] first that of the mortal Solon, then that of Delphic Apollo. His *himeros* (a strong word for "desire," almost "yearning") to question Solon (1.30.2) is as striking as his *himeros* for more land (1.73.1; p. 103). Croesus does not grasp the true import of what he hears, at least for the moment, but he does *care* about interrogating the Greek sage and the Greek god. That initial note of Croesus as Greece's archetypal eastern enemy has turned out to be less than a half-truth. It is then this final war with Cyrus, a war with an enemy further east for which Croesus has even gained Greek promises of support, that contributes more than those "unjust deeds against the Greeks" to our understanding of the great wars that are to come. That encounter helps to explain the growth of Persia; at the same time, it introduces both the expansionism and the self-destruction that set a pattern for the future.

This shift of emphasis is reflected in the way Herodotus divides Croesus' wars into two, first the western ones (1.26–28), then, as the gaze shifts eastward, the rest (1.71–85). Something of the same applied to his father, Alyattes—western wars at 1.16–25, war against Cyaxares at 1.74. But the shift also contributes to the structure of the whole work. We have already seen how the early chapters introduce the theme of East against West (chapter 2[b]), and those early chapters of the Croesus episode did indeed deal with aggression against the Greek states. The East/West emphasis persists in a different way during the treatment of contemporary Athens and Sparta (1.59–68), introduced by the simplest of transitions: encouraged by Delphi, Croesus investigated the relative strength of contemporary Greek states, and this is what he found. Herodotus is informing us on the way in which both sides in the ultimate conflict, eastern and western, are shaping up.

Yet this East/West emphasis soon drifts out of focus; by the time the spotlight shifts to Cyrus the narrative is controlled by Persia's expansion, with only the odd glimpse westwards. Greece comes back into focus a little in book 3, with the panels on Polycrates of Samos and Periander of Corinth (3.39–60), but Herodotus fails to take opportunities there to bring the audience up to date on what is happening in the rest of the Greek world.[3] Occasionally, but only occasionally, Greece looms as the endpoint of Persian expansion, "always at the end—as ultimate goal, and as ultimate risk," as Huber beautifully put it.[4] Atossa's bedroom conversation with Darius—she *so* wants those Greek maids, 3.134.5—points to the importance of Greece as that target, and *this* might be expected to prompt Darius to something immediate. In fact, it takes several books for that preparation to lead to anything, a feature that has sometimes worried even the most sensitive of critics[5] but in fact has good Homeric precedent.[6] Herodotus prefers to leave most of his Greek material to books 5 and 6, as the Greek theme returns to center stage with the Ionian Revolt, and he there gives elaborate retrospects first of Athens and then of Sparta. This is really a form of ring composition, introducing themes at the beginning that will be mirrored at the end, but allowing them to drift out of focus in the middle.[7]

This shifting focus is important for historical explanation. As long as the East/West conflicts are central, a "payback" model of aggression and counter-aggression retains its plausibility. As Greece drifts out of focus, such a sequencing of give and take will disappear as well. As we concentrate on Persian expansion, it is likely that any explanations will come to be points about Persia or about expansion, not—or not yet—about Greece. Our gaze becomes more unifocal, or bifocal only in the sense that it turns to a series of other two-sided encounters that do not involve Greece. So it turns out to be less of a paradox after all that the later stages of the Croesus story are more suggestive for the future than his aggressiveness against Greece, for our next few questions must be put to eastern, not western, behavior.

Croesus' attack on Cyrus thus initiates an imperialist pattern that has already been mentioned (pp. 12–13). Despite warnings, a ruler launches a new war against a foe in which the dangers outweigh the potential gains; he crosses a natural boundary, often with a disdain for the brute facts of nature; and he runs immense risks, which may (but do not always) destroy him. The pattern will recur with Cyrus, with Cambyses, with Darius, and with Xerxes.

Yet the pattern is here introduced in an off-key way, one that has little to do with any presumption or overconfidence or pride—that *Selbstsicherheit*, "self-certainty," that has so often been thought the hallmark of those later tyrants.[8] The first we hear of Croesus' enterprise is very different:

> Croesus lay sunk in deep grief for two years after his son's death: then the destruction of the empire of Astyages son of Cyaxares at the hands of Cyrus son of Cambyses, together with the growth of the Persians, delivered Croesus from his grief, and made him think of stopping the increase in Persian power, if he could, before they became great. (1.46.1)[9]

As here presented, this is to be a preventive war, one inspired by prudence rather than self-deluded pride—a case of self-protective "diffidence" rather than "competition" or "glory," in Hobbes' tripartite division of the reasons for conflict.[10] The later imperialists will, at least in some cases, be carried away by their runs of success: that is explicitly one of the motives influencing Cyrus (1.204; pp. 102, 119). Croesus too has had his successes (1.26–28), but there is no mention of that here. When he gets carried away, it is by one of the oddest things of all: by that craze for Greek oracular wisdom. "For once he had grasped the truth of the oracle, he was besotted with it" (ἐνεφορέετο αὐτοῦ, 1.55.1). That is as bizarre a version of tyrannical transport and excess as Candaules' lust for his own wife (p. 107): a first instance, here as there, that is almost a parody of the theme that will later be familiar.

Still, as the narrative goes on Croesus comes to fit, and introduce, the later pattern more closely, especially once his "yearning for land" is added as a further motive (1.73.1; p. 103): Cyrus, Cambyses, Darius, and Xerxes will certainly be driven by a similar desire for territorial expansion.[11] In those later episodes the hints of a preventive war may carry a flavor of disingenuousness or self-deception, such as Xerxes' fear that the Athenians might attack Asia (7.11.2–3)—as unreal at that time, after the débâcle of the Ionian Revolt, as the fantasy of Bias/Pittacus that the islanders might attack Lydia (1.27). (What, ironically, made it more realistic a decade or so later was the aftermath of Xerxes' invasion itself, with Athens launching its maritime enterprises of the 470s, 460s, and 450s; more on these in chapter 15.)

The emphasis on the crossing of the Halys river (1.75)—Croesus' natural boundary, as a chapter on the geography of Asia makes clear (1.72)[12]—again prefigures the way in which later aggressors initiate their wars by crossing a natural boundary, a river, a strait, or a desert.[13] Herodotus tells the story that it was the brilliant ploy of Thales that got him across, diverting the river into two streams, and this prefigures the tampering with nature that we will see with Cyrus at the Gyndes (1.189) and particularly with Xerxes at Mt. Athos and at the Hellespont (7.22–24, 7.34–35; p. 158). Yet even this takes an unexpected turn, for Herodotus deflates this version,[14] thus, it might seem, abandoning all the narrative advantages that he has carefully prepared by this attack on nature:

> When Croesus arrived at the river Halys, he then—in my version—put his army across by the bridges that were already there; but the general version among the Greeks says that Thales of Miletus put them across . . . (1.75.3)

In particular, Herodotus points out that one variant—that the old stream was dried up, and the whole river was diverted behind the waiting army—cannot be correct: how would they have been able to get back? (1.75.6). So once again a major thematic pattern is introduced in a strange way.

Some things, though, fit more straightforwardly. Croesus "took the city of the Pterians and enslaved it, captured the neighboring cities, and displaced the Syrians *though they were not to blame*" (Συρίους τε οὐδὲν ἐόντας αἰτίους ἀναστάτους ἐποίησε, 1.76.2). Warfare is like that, and we should not be too unworldly in blaming Croesus for such insouciance. Still, this is the same indifference to genuine blameworthiness as when Croesus was trumping up grievances against the Greeks (1.26.3; pp. 7–8), and he is reverting to a type that will again come back with the later imperialists, especially Xerxes at 7.8γ.3: "They will be conquered, alike those who are blameworthy and those who are not." This "displacing" of whole peoples is another prefiguring of a habit that will typify the conquering Persians, whether by forced migration (3.93.2, 4.204, 5.14.1, 6.119.1–2, etc.) or by creating refugees (1.177.1, 7.118). That gruesome carding (1.92.4; p. 113) also strikes a note of brutality that will become familiar: within a few chapters we see a childhood equivalent of it when the ten-year-old Cyrus, playing king in a boys' game and angry with a playmate who did not do his bidding, "set about him extremely harshly with a whip" (1.114.3).

But Croesus knows when to stop, or thinks he does. Before, it was the advice of Bias/Pittacus that brought him to desist; now, it is the drawn battle of Pteria, and his perception that it would be safer to wait for more allies, those from Egypt and Babylonia, before renewing the fighting (1.77). This is the cautious Croesus we already know. Yet he never suspects that Cyrus might come to him (1.77.4), though that early emphasis on a preventive war against the threatening neighbor might have led us, and him, to expect it.[15] Indeed, that motive is displaced to the other side, for it is a similar quest for a preemptive strike that now motivates the shrewd Cyrus (1.79.1). An omen indicates danger (1.78.1). Croesus, again characteristically, sends envoys to a shrine for clarification, this time, the shrine at Telmessus. By the time the envoys return it is too late, Sardis has fallen, and the initiative, together with the narrative focus,[16] has switched decisively to Cyrus.

So Croesus' story does serve as a useful overture, but not all the themes are quite as we will later see them, nor will we ever see all the elements recurring in quite the same combination. If even Croesus himself does not wholly fit the patterns that he prefigures, each later instantiation of a pattern is likely to have its own atypical elements as well. Every king and every campaign will be different;[17] it is not a question of "the" pattern, but a number of patterns that will often—not always—recur. These are *potential* patterns, not inevitable ones,[18] just as Solon's insight that disaster can strike anyone (1.32) does not mean that disaster will strike everyone. With states as well as individuals, even if overreach can lead to disaster, there are also many times when it does not: all those campaigns of Croesus against the Greeks, or of Cyrus against the Assyrians, or of Darius against India and Babylon and then the rebellious Ionians. Even if ultimately "absolutism was bound to fail,"[19] it did not follow that it was going to fail on any particular occasion or campaign, for history was not so deterministic. Such failures are explicable, but that need not mean complete predictability.

Nor do the reverses all happen in the same way. The reasons for the Scythians' victory are particularly singular, with a strategy to baffle the invader that is all their own. Just like a Hippocratic physician comparing a fresh case to those recorded in the *Epidemics* (pp. 50–53), Herodotus' reader or hearer has a lot of work yet to do to isolate what features are really recurrent and what is specific to an individual king or campaign—and, very importantly, to work out the precise way in which an initial pattern may be working in any of those later cases, the "how" as well as the "which."[20] The complexities of history allow different sequences to show traces of the same mold; but like the jelly that comes out of the mold and would not be shaped without it, they can all still wobble.

(B) FROM CYRUS TO XERXES

The narrative of Cyrus' reign is many-faceted, and includes several aspects to which we will return (pp. 141–142, 149–153).[21] When we reach his own final campaign, launched against the Massagetae and their queen Tomyris, there is a clear indication of multiple motives in a passage that we have already quoted (p. 102):

> Many and great were the factors that roused Cyrus up[22] and urged him on: first, his birth, the impression[23] that he was something more than human; second, the good fortune he had enjoyed in war; for wherever Cyrus launched a campaign, that nation found it impossible to escape. (1.204.2)

There will be mixed motives and explanations for the subsequent big campaigns as well. Cambyses has reasons for complaint against the Egyptian king Amasis, who tricked him by sending him not his own daughter, but the daughter of his predecessor Apries (3.1); Darius is seeking revenge from the Scythians "because they had started the injustice by invading the land of the Medes and defeating them in battle" (4.1.1); he also wants to punish the Athenians and Eretrians (5.105.2; p. 104), and so does Xerxes. We have, though, seen several times that such motives can readily coexist with an imperialist drive, and that revenge talk can be a matter of rhetoric as well as of genuine motivation. In the Scythian case, the wording of 4.1 itself suggests there is more to it ("Asia was blooming with manpower, large sums of money were coming in, and Darius conceived the desire to take revenge"), and later the Scythian messengers to the neighboring kings have good reason to suspect that Darius has them in his sights as well (4.118). Still, blame talk continues to be relevant when those kings reject the request, perhaps for self-serving reasons but publicly on the grounds that the Scythians were to blame (*aitioi*) for starting the wrongdoing (*adikiē*), 4.119.4—another case, then, where blame and revenge play a part in explanation while being anything but the whole story.

We have seen, too, that those Persian kings are very different individuals (p. 12): Cyrus' bundle of motives, like his traits of character, would not recur in quite the same way with each of them. Yet their actions *are* repetitive in that patterned way, and sometimes the echoes are especially marked. In particular, the early stages of Xerxes' campaign echo features of Darius' Scythian expedition, with a similar bridging (Bosporus for Darius, Hellespont for Xerxes), a similar warning from Artabanus (4.83.1, 7.11), and a similar response when a loyal grandee tries to beg his son or sons off the expedition: Darius slaughters all Oeobazus' sons to "leave them behind" as their father had requested (4.84.2), Xerxes cuts Pythius' son in two and marches the army between the halves (7.39).²⁴ In both cases we also have a bizarre echo of Solon's story of 1.30.4–5, where the mother of Cleobis and Biton prayed to the gods to give her sons whatever was best for mortals, and they fell down dead. In these cases too a parent asks for a boon: when a Persian monarch plays god, the outcome is even grimmer. It is all very different from Aeschylus' *Persians*, where Darius appears as a character to rebuke Xerxes' rashness and to contrast his own record of caution. For Aeschylus' Darius, Xerxes is an aberration; for Herodotus, he is playing the Persian national game.²⁵

So the attentive reader of Herodotus, noticing *homoia* and *anomoia* in the same way as that physician who compares new cases with those recorded in the *Epidemics*, will by book 7 be finding much that is familiar. That impression is reinforced by the way that imperialism has emerged more and more explicitly as the Persians' preoccupation: that readiness to acknowledge multiple motivation has shifted, with an increasing emphasis on conquest as the primary aim—a move, in the categories of chapter 6, from $A + B + C$ to a league-table ranking of A more than B and C.²⁶ But it has taken time for such clarity to build, and initially the narratives of Persian campaigns dwelt more on the singularities—those different motives, for instance.²⁷

For Fornara, it is book 7 that makes the difference, with Herodotus only now turning to the "psychology behind the expansion of nations."²⁸ In his view, Persian expansion began as an organizational principle, allowing Herodotus to treat each people as they were brought into the empire but now changes to the theme of his history.²⁹ Fornara makes this a point about Herodotus' intellectual development: his thinking became progressively more ambitious, and he grew "into the historian of the causes of man's actions rather than of actions achieved."³⁰ Thus, for instance, Xerxes' bluster about the need to enslave just and unjust alike (7.8γ.3) is "amoral," and it reveals a capacity to think "beyond the specific" and an understanding of "the cancerous nature of imperialism" that has developed as Herodotus wrote.³¹ Yet we have already seen how the arc of the narrative has been pointing towards the Greek wars long before we reach them; once we do get there, many of the features recall the actions and words of others, and for instance that remark of Xerxes shows the same mentality as Croesus (1.26.3; pp. 7–8).³²

It is better to see this gathering clarity as a presentational point, and symptomatic of the way that Herodotus has handled, even trained, his audience: it is they who have gradually built this picture and seen how many features of Xerxes' campaign need to be related to broader patterns of empire and of power. We have seen this before, with Homer, with the Hippocratics, with tragedy, and with Thucydides: themes are not set out all at once, initial statements are just first bids and are constantly revised in stride (chapter 5[c], esp. p. 90). We can later find something of the same in Thucydides, whose initial, broadly stated view of the origins of the Peloponnesian War (1.23.6) is then refined in the detail of the narrative itself.[33]

All this lends particular importance to the great debate when Xerxes airs his plan to invade Greece (7.8–11), with so many links to previous events and suggestions. Xerxes, we note, was not himself initially so keen on invading Greece, though—just as in Darius' conversation with Atossa (3.134; p. 136)—it was not a doubt about aggression as such, simply a question of prioritizing targets: he wanted to attack Egypt first (7.5.1). But he is prey to self-interested people. One is Mardonius, with his desire to become governor of Greece (7.6.1); there are also the exiled Peisistratids, with their oracle-monger Onomacritus reporting only the favorable prophecies, and messengers from the Aleuadae of Thessaly (7.6). These are not the first dissident Greeks to egg on invaders in their own factional interests. There was Democedes of Croton, exploiting Queen Atossa to persuade the king because he wants to get home (3.132–134); there were Aristagoras and Histiaeus in the Ionian Revolt. (Nor indeed is it just Greeks: it is "an Egyptian man" who for personal reasons stirs up Cambyses against Amasis at 3.1.1–2, and the Egyptian Phanes also has a lot to answer for at 3.4; so do the Paeonians Pigres and Mastyes at 5.12–13.)

The atmosphere of the court is such that these eggers-on are likely to find a ready ear: we shall see more of that in the next chapter. The doubters, with their compulsory circumlocution and obliquity, find it all so much more difficult. Mardonius thus finds the right tunes as he urges Xerxes on to invade[34]—the need for vengeance on the Athenians for their part in the Ionian Revolt, the shame if they get away with it, the need to deter others who might take on the might of Persia, the glory that awaits, the ease of the expected victory, and (particularly attuned for Persian ears)[35] the beauty and fertility of the country (7.5, 7.9). Contrast what the Spartan Demaratus later says about the poverty that has always attended Greece (7.102.1)—but then Mardonius only got as far as Macedonia in his previous campaign a few years earlier (7.9α.2), so how could he know?

This speech of Mardonius can well be described as "smoothing over" (we might use a different decorating metaphor, "putting a fine gloss on") "Xerxes' own opinion" (7.10.1), for Xerxes himself has by now made that "opinion" clear, and those earlier doubts about the project seem to have passed away. He has summoned the council "so that I might pass on to you what I have in mind to do" (7.8α.2), and he sets out all the arguments for action.[36]

> This is what must be done: but, in order that I might not seem to you to be self-willed (ἵνα δὲ μὴ ἰδιοβουλέειν ὑμῖν δοκέω), I put forward the matter for general discussion (ἐς μέσον, literally, "into the middle"), and

I encourage any of you who wish (τὸν βουλόμενον) to make clear what he thinks.
(7.8δ.2)

The phrasing there reeks of democratic debate, where matters were regularly put "into the middle." At Athens debate was introduced by the question, "Who wishes to speak?" and another canonical phrase invited anyone who wished (*ho boulomenos*) to initiate a legal process.[37] But the atmosphere of this debate could not be less democratic. It will become clear what most of the counselors think: when, for reasons we shall have to consider later (pp. 153–156), Xerxes changes his mind overnight and announces that the expedition will not after all take place, they fall on their knees and pay obeisance in joy (7.13.3). But for the moment all except one "kept silent and did not dare to express a view contrary to the one before them" (7.10.1).

The exception is Xerxes' uncle Artabanus, and his words ooze caution. It is always better to hear the opposite view, he says, just to check the superiority of the right one. There are risks in bridging the Hellespont and moving into Europe, just as there were when Darius bridged the Bosporus (and so that parallelism of the two campaigns, shortly to be intimated by narrative shape, is made explicit), and then too, continues Artabanus, I urged caution on Darius. Better to dissolve the council and think it over, for good decision-making is priceless. Heaven tends to strike the biggest animals and houses and trees with its lightning bolts; haste brings mistakes. All as tactful as can be, with lots of generalizations,[38] even though the message is clear: the forceful language is reserved for his concluding diatribe against Mardonius, and the contrast of the two tones is strong, ending with a fantasized picture of Mardonius himself lying dead in defeat, torn apart by dogs and birds—an appalling threat that recalls the proem of the *Iliad* (*Il.* 1.4–5), and the echo underlines the momentousness of the "great harm you will have brought on the Persians" (7.10θ.3).

That is as bold as a counselor can go: it is too bold for Xerxes himself, who immediately loses his temper. Lucky for you that you're my uncle; otherwise you would really suffer for those "stupid" (or more literally, "pointless," "vain," *mataia*) words (7.11.1). There is no going back:

I will drive against these men whom even Pelops of Phrygia, slave of my ancestors, conquered so completely that to this day the people themselves and their land carry the name of their victor.
(7.11.4)

That is magnificent—but, once again, it is not the way to elicit free, frank, good advice, especially from those who do not enjoy avuncular immunity.

Artabanus is certainly wise: when he says that "land and sea" are their greatest enemies, his phrasing captures a great deal of truth, both cosmic and secular (pp. 157–159). Still, the issues are not wholly clear-cut, and it may be that Artabanus is not unequivocally right.[39] True, a warning is not a prophecy and an unrealized danger may have been a danger nonetheless.[40] Doubtless, too, there is more to it than awarding marks for being "right."[41] But a narrative history still encourages one to measure the history that happened against the futures that were feared, and noticing how the worst does not always happen can point to broader themes: how hard it is to gauge the right course, for instance, when such wisdom is so elusive; how even the best informed of predictions may miss the mark without rendering the eventual outcome inexplicable.[42] Xerxes may at times read history crudely,[43] and he is not yet adopting the calmness of his later encounter with Artabanus at Abydus (7.44–52; p. 141). Still, there is already something of that insight and that argument here:

> Men of Persia, I am not the first to introduce this tradition (*nomos*) among you; I have taken it over and will follow it. We have never yet kept still—that is what I hear from my elders—since the time when we took over this empire from the Medes after Cyrus' defeat of Astyages: no, a god drives us on, and combines with us as we take on many things to guide them to a happy outcome.
> (7.8α.1)

Blithe, perhaps—but not nonsense, and the issues are not straightforward. That "tradition" is there; Xerxes is himself alert to the pattern that Herodotus' own text has come to suggest. There are also risks, especially for a new monarch, in abandoning that pattern, just as there are in following it: more on this in the next chapter (pp. 140–142). The phantom that then appears may suggest too that "a god" may indeed be "driving them on"—another topic to which we will return (pp. 153–156). Both on the human and on the divine level, it is very complicated.

It is all the more complicated because we have by now gathered that this is not just a matter of Xerxes himself. It is the culmination of something much bigger. Is that bigger something a point about Persia? Or about tyranny? Or about power? Or about the gods? Or, most likely, about more than one of these, perhaps about all? That may become clearer when in the next chapter we look more closely at Herodotus' presentation of the Persian court. First, let us return to that question of blame.

(c) BLAME?

Talk of imperialistic aggression can readily suggest a fingering of blame, just as the Persians themselves blamed the Scythians when they invaded and "everything was laid desolate through their *hybris* and arrogance" (1.106.1; cf. 4.1.1 and p. 119). If aggression is so much a cross-generational tradition, should it not follow that *of course* the Persians are to blame?[44] Were they not the ones who "started it"? Even in cases where they did not, as perhaps in the case of Athens' involvement in the Ionian Revolt, were Persians not so clearly spoiling for an imperialistic fight that it was evidently their fault, just as the decisive escalation in those initial abduction stories was the Greeks' fault (p. 26)?[45]

Well, perhaps. But we should also see how Herodotus complicates that simple picture. First, there is the sense that the Greeks do a lot to bring it on themselves: there are those meddlers at the court (p. 121), and there will be many more cases when Greeks care more about their petty factionalism than about any Panhellenic cause (chapter 12). Greek tyrants in particular tend to look eastwards to bolster their own power.[46] Then there is the ease with which the Athenians allow themselves to be talked over by Aristagoras (5.97), or the earlier readiness of Sparta and Corinth to be sucked into aggressive behavior in the eastern Aegean (1.69, 3.47–48). That is just one of several examples where it is the Greek states themselves that first attract the attention of the Persian invader.[47] This should not be overstated, and it does not add up to the level of "the Greeks had it coming"; it is not as strong as Thucydides' more explicit claim that "the allies had themselves to blame" for Athenian aggrandizement in the years between the Persian and Peloponnesian Wars (1.99.3).[48] But there is something of the same.

Blame also plays a more complicated role in the particular episodes, in line with the more complicated plays we have already seen with blame and blamers in those early stories of book 1, and indeed with the Homeric Helen (chapter 2[d]); this affects too the way in which revenge and payback are figured.

One case has already been discussed, that of Oroetes and Polycrates (3.120–121; p. 34): blame is in the air there, as we saw, though it may be as much the blame that Oroetes had incurred from Mitrobates as any reason he had for blaming Polycrates. In any case, this triggers a stream of consequences, including not just Polycrates' own grisly end but also the deaths of both Mitrobates and Oroetes himself (3.126–128). The power vacuum left in Samos then plays its part in creating the conditions for Persia's advance, for Polycrates' brother Syloson persuades Darius to give him the island as reward for an earlier favor (3.139–140; p. 8). That ends bloodily, and the Persians play a large part in that bloodshed (3.146–147, 3.149); this is understandable enough, for their elite troops have been massacred in a surprise attack after a peaceful deal had been agreed (3.146.3). As a result, their commander Otanes "deliberately forgot" the instructions he had received from Darius to avoid killing and enslavement and to hand over the city unharmed (3.147.1). Herodotus' view is not just that this was predictable but that it was what the treacherous Samian leader Maeandrius was counting on (3.146.2).

If we are looking for culprits here, more blame attaches to the Samians than to the Persians, "for they did not—it seems—want to be free" (3.143.2).[49] We shall look at their behavior later, symptomatic as it may be of the difficulties of handling a new-found freedom (pp. 179–180); it is sufficient here to notice that there is a lot of blaming in the Samians' own wranglings as well, with invectives against Maeandrius first for his presumption in granting Samian *isonomiē* (3.142.5) and then for missing an earlier chance to take the Persians by surprise (3.145). The Persians have in contrast done their best, both with those initial eirenic instructions of Darius and in Otanes' immediate readiness to accept that peaceful deal. So the whole story has blame and payback in abundance: Mitrobates' blaming of Oroetes, Syloson's positive payback for his good turn to Darius, the blame of his own countrymen for Maeandrius, and finally the indignation of Otanes and the Persians at Samian faithlessness. It is anything but a straightforward matter of blaming the Persians for any initial imperialistic urge.

The Persian advance into Libya is an even less straightforward case. This, we noticed earlier, is a sequence where distinctions between the explanations proffered, *prophasies* or *proschēmata*, and the more important imperialistic drive are unusually explicit (p. 104).[50] The Persian commander of Egypt, Aryandes, has been approached by Pheretime of Cyrene. Pheretime's son Arcesilaus, the king of Cyrene, has been killed by his political enemies at the neighboring city of Barca: she now wants Persian aid to exact vengeance from the Barcaeans. Aryandes agrees. At first his reasons seem emotional, "he pitied Pheretime" (4.167.1), and there is no reason to exclude that "pity" completely from the web of explanations. Arcesilaus' death is duly the point raised in the initial negotiations. Aryandes sends to Barca to ask who had killed Arcesilaus, and they reply that "they all had: for they were suffering greatly and grievously at his hands" (4.167.2). But this is where we are told that this was merely the reason put forward (*proschēma*), and the army was really sent to conquer Libya (4.167.3; p. 10), a land that Herodotus goes on to describe in such a way as to end with those fertile parts that an invader might find particularly attractive (4.198–199). So once again talk of vengeance is seen as the stuff of semblance, and the identification of who is to blame ("who had killed Arcesilaus?") would seem no more than secondary for the Persians. Straightforward expansionism seems the key.[51]

Yet vengeance is not irrelevant. Only a small amount of the elaborate Libyan *logos* (4.145–205) is concerned with the Persian attack, but that is the point heralded in the first sentence of the *logos*, 4.145.1: "... at the same time there was another great military expedition, directed against Libya, and I shall put forward its explanation (*prophasis*) after first setting out the following" ("the following" turns out to be various foundation stories). The range of *prophasis* (above, pp. 8–10) is most useful here: it is so far unclear not merely what the "explanation" will be but also whether it will be true, false, or (as often) part of the truth.[52]

When he comes to set out the narrative background, the element of vengeance becomes clear: for even if there is something bogus about the *Persians'* talk of vengeance, one cannot doubt the genuineness of *Pheretime's* desire to get her own back once her son had had the worse of a complicated period of *stasis* and had met his end in exile (4.164.4). That was the point at which Pheretime turned to Aryandes, "for there were certain good services that Arcesilaus had done for Cambyses son of Cyrus" (4.165.2).[53] "When she arrived, Pheretime supplicated Aryandes, urging him to avenge her, putting forward the explanation (προϊσχομένη πρόφασιν) that her son had been killed for his Medism" (4.165.3). The language—προϊσχομένη more than πρόφασιν (pp. 9–10)—suggests that the claim is false, and indeed there has so far been no suggestion that "Medism" played any part in Arcesilaus' downfall.

Herodotus then flashes forward to tell us what happened later to this Aryandes. He presumed to mint silver in Egypt in a way that seemed to rival the Great King's own coinage, "and when Darius realized what he was doing, he brought a different charge (*aitiē*) against him, claiming that he was plotting against the throne, and killed him" (4.166.2). When the narrative later resumes, we see Aryandes' general Amasis demanding the ringleaders and being refused. A trick secures the city's defeat, Pheretime exacts a further brutal vengeance, and the Persian army withdraws. The book ends with a note of Pheretime's own subsequent horrible death, eaten alive by worms that seethed all over her body: this shows "that, in mortal life, excessive acts of vengeance arouse the envy of the gods" (ὡς ἄρα ἀνθρώποισι αἱ λίην ἰσχυραὶ τιμωρίαι πρὸς θεῶν ἐπίφθονοι γίνονται, 4.205)—an unusually explicit acknowledgement, stamped with narratorial authority, of direct divine involvement in human affairs.[54]

So vengeance and reciprocity are everywhere. Arcesilaus' killers are avenging their comrades; the Persians are avenging Pheretime (*timōroi*, 4.200.1) and paying back Arcesilaus' services; Pheretime is avenging her son, and that is how her retaliation is finally described (τεισαμένη ... τιμωρίαι ... τιμωρίη, 4.205). Even the final role of the gods can be seen as an extension of reciprocity, escalating to a different level, rather as at 2.120.5 (p. 147): there is some appropriateness when her humiliating mutilation of her enemies results in her own mutilation, with her body invaded by worms, the humblest of creatures.⁵⁵ No human actions could have secured that appropriateness.

As usual, too, vengeance and reciprocity introduce an element of blame, and here that comes with some sophisticated distinctions. Blame does not attach simply to those who are physically responsible for a killing: all the Barcaeans accept that they share responsibility, for all were suffering at Arcesilaus' hands (4.167.2, p. 125); then the Barcaeans refuse to give up "those responsible" (*aitioi*) "for the killing" as "the whole mass of the people shared the responsibility" (*metaition*, 4.200.1; p. 7). There are also degrees of blameworthiness recognized by the participants themselves: when Pheretime eventually exacts her revenge, there seem to be three groups (4.202–203.1): "the most blameworthy" (*aitiōtatoi*) who are impaled and whose wives are mutilated, "the rest of the Barcaeans" who are enslaved, and a group who "were Battiadae and had no share in the blame for the killing"⁵⁶ who take over the city.

Still, Herodotus' own narrative weight falls not just on those true motives of vindictiveness but also on falsity, pretext, and semblance—Pheretime's claim, not supported by the narrative, that Arcesilaus was killed for Medism; Darius' false charge against Aryandes; Aryandes' own propaganda, not acknowledging his true imperialist ambitions. Claims are displaced from their natural place and placed in mouths where they ring false: we would have believed in a vengeance motive had it been articulated by Pheretime but not when it is put forward by Aryandes; we might have accepted that Arcesilaus' killers were "seeking *dikai*," but it sounds unpersuasive when the claim is made by Arcesilaus himself (4.164.1). So again blameworthiness and vengeance quickly become part of the rhetoric of justification and excuse. This is not too far, in fact, from those early cases where we saw that blame was only a waft in the air, when it was not the attacker's blaming but that of others that contributed to a complex *aitiē* (p. 34).

There is also the question of outcome rather than origin. Even before the fighting begins, we are given to understand that the Persian attack will be unsuccessful. "Most of the Libyans give no thought now to the king of the Medes and gave no thought then" (4.197.1): any Persian infiltration is clearly not going to last. Once Barca has fallen, we duly see the Persians pull back (4.203). Why, then, does it all peter out so quickly? The narrative gives only gentle suggestions. The invading commanders are divided amongst themselves, with the admiral Badres urging an attack on Cyrene and the land-general Amasis pointing out that Barca was the only "Greek city"⁵⁷ against which they had been sent. Badres' position fits the expansionist model; Amasis' has some respect for the proferred justification in terms of vengeance on Barca. Those in command are themselves unclear about the relative importance of these different aims and the stage at which they should define their mission as accomplished. So they dither, they move on, then they change their minds and attack Cyrene again, and the Cyreneans resist; a panic attacks the Persian army, and they dash away for eight miles; then a message comes from Aryandes recalling them to Egypt. The Libyans harry and kill them as they retreat.

In miniature there are several suggestions here of the nature of Persia and Persian command. One is that very proliferation of motives: the disagreement of the commanders suggests that there can be times when weighing their relative importance really matters, however difficult that may be. We also see the indirection in the absence of a single overall commander on the spot.[58] Xerxes' later view—that the presence of the commander makes all the difference to an army (8.69.2, developing the themes of 7.103.4; p. 181)—is anything but stupid, and builds on Persian reality: that will again be clear at Plataea (9.63.2).

But—finally—it is important that the reasons for such a failure are to be sought within the Persian army itself. Persia attacks, and Persia withdraws. This is unifocal, the ebb and flow of a particular people;[59] if the Libyans harry the retreat, they are only intensifying a Persian development that is already happening, for thoughts of conquest are already past. Reciprocity, the give-and-take between different peoples, has little to do with this, however much it may illuminate the internal Libyan conditions that made the Persian enterprise possible. It fits that "unifocal" model that we noticed with the Hippocratics, where an organism has embedded within it the seeds of its growth and then of its destruction, and the external factors are just a stimulating trigger.

Will this, then, be a unifocal pattern that recurs with the greatest expansionist campaign of all, with the Greek wars? Or to explain both origins and outcome will we there have to make more of the other side, reasons for Greek provocation and success as well as for Persian aggression and failure? We shall have to see. That resonant final sentence of the Libyan *logos*, proclaiming the way that Pheretime's punishment showed "that, in mortal life, excessive acts of vengeance arouse the envy of the gods" (4.205; p. 126), also suggests that we must bring in the divine perspective more fully (chapter 10). But first there is more to say about Herodotus' Persian stories.

CHAPTER 9

HERODOTUS' PERSIAN STORIES

(A) THE WORLD OF THE COURT

These "Persian stories"[1] are familiar ones: the exposure and saving of Cyrus as a baby (1.108–113), then his recognition by Astyages at the age of ten and the king's cruel reaction (1.114–119); Cyrus' organizing of a successful rebellion (1.125–130); the various crazy actions of Cambyses and then his death (3.1–38, 3.66); the conspiracy that put Darius on the throne (3.67–88); the story of Intaphernes' wife as she chooses to save brother rather than children, a tale that has reminded many people of Sophocles' *Antigone* (3.118–119); Darius' pillow talk with Queen Atossa as she urges him to invade Greece (3.134); Darius' irritation at the news of the burning of Sardis and "the thing with the bow," as he shoots an arrow into the air to mark his desire for vengeance (5.105); the role played by Atossa in securing the accession for her child Xerxes rather than Darius' older sons (7.2–3); then, crucially, that debate on whether to invade Greece (7.8–11, discussed in the previous chapter), followed by the night-time phantom that persuades the king that he has no choice (7.12–19, pp. 153–156). Finally, there is the tale of Xerxes falling in love first with his brother Masistes' wife and then with their daughter Artaÿnte, one of those "ill-judged promise" stories where his offer to Artaÿnte turns badly wrong, with a hint of Xerxes' own looming assassination (9.108–113, pp. 32–34). That story near the end of the *Histories* mirrors the tale of Candaules' wife at the beginning, a similar case of ill-judged braggadocio in a besotted royal lover. Candaules was not a Persian but king of that in-between country Lydia, but we saw in the last chapter that those stories of Lydian kings, especially Croesus, can to an extent prefigure those of the greater eastern monarchy to come.

These stories have a distinctive atmosphere, and it is very un-Greek. This is the world of a court and courtiers, usually flattering, sometimes bold; of harems and bedrooms; of viziers and conspiracies. Women play a big role.[2] It is a world of the indoors, very different from Xerxes' outdoor scenes once he is on his great campaign, overlooking his massed troops at Abydus (7.44–52) or the naval battle at Salamis (8.88–90), perilously storm-tossed at sea as he crosses back to Asia (8.118–119).

The stories also have a distinctive narrative shape, which used to be called a "novella":[3] the self-contained story, told with all the seductive charm, and sometimes some of the folk motifs, of a fairytale. They typically concentrate on a charismatic individual, often the king, and a few one-on-one encounters; they are often rich in direct speech; they frequently but not always center on abrupt changes of fortune.[4] There are plenty of one-on-one encounters once Herodotus turns to the Greek narrative, but the shape there is usually different, more seamless and less episodic: when we do get something similar, it is usually in flashbacks or diversions.[5] The vivid theatricality of these scenes makes it unsurprising that some of these Persian characters have proved the stuff of drama and of opera,[6] much more so than the Greeks.[7] Handel's *Serse* (1738) is only the most famous example.

What explains this difference of texture? Reinhardt's answer centered on Herodotus' source material. For him, Herodotus' "Greek genius"—shades of 1940s racialism (cf. p. 274 n. 1)—lay in distilling his "Asiatic" sources in one eastern novella after another. There may well be something in this. There is no reason why Herodotus should not have been familiar with genuine Persian material (whether or not he needed an interpreter), perhaps in textual form, perhaps through oral tradition.[8] Halicarnassus after all was on the cusp of the Persian empire. A good case has been made for his acquaintance with a version of Darius' accession close to the king's own version preserved on the Behistun inscription high on a mountain in Iran; if so, one can see how skillfully he has molded it to fit his own narrative.[9]

Here too, if this is on the right lines, his "distilling" for a Greek audience has interesting features. Noticeably, for instance, he has not played up the "exotic" as much as he might. When Candaules plays his ill-judged trick involving his queen, there is nothing of the glamor of the palace: no maids to help her undress, no chamberlain hovering at the door, no gold-plated bedsteads or thrones. She just comes in, takes her clothes off, and puts them on a chair. We might be in a suburban apartment.

Elsewhere too a modern reader, eager for the titillation of the harem, is going to be disappointed. "Harem" culture is taken for granted but mentioned only when it is relevant, and not much is made of it. After the dispatch of Ps.-Smerdis, it is agreed that the seven conspirators can have access to the king "unless he is in bed with a woman" (3.84.2, 3.118.1). The rebellious Intaphernes tries to take advantage of this but is barred by the "gatekeeper and the messenger" from entry on the grounds that this is how the king is occupied (3.118.2): hardly the most exoticizing description of an antechamber's retinue, and we never discover if what they said was true, only that it worked (though with unhappy consequences for the two servants, subject to casual mutilation at the hands of the frustrated Intaphernes).

Earlier the Egyptian king Amasis was unhappy to send his daughter up to Cambyses, "knowing very well that the king intended to keep her as a concubine rather than a wife" (3.1.2), and so he sent Nitetis instead, the daughter of his predecessor Apries. Cambyses was not pleased when he found out. An alternative story is then told of "a Persian woman" who "goes in" to visit Cyrus' wives and compliments one of these wives, Cassandane, on her children; the indignant Cassandane replies that, despite being mother of such fine specimens, her husband treats her with less regard than the Egyptian Nitetis. Her eldest son Cambyses hears and promises that Egypt will suffer for it—so Herodotus has heard, but he does not believe it (3.3). If either version is right,[10] the harem had big consequences and needed mention—but the treatment is hardly lubricious. This is a very different manner from that of the Book of Esther, lavish on the scouring of the land for pretty virgins, then their year-long beauty treatment to ready them for Xerxes' pleasure (*Esther* 2).

The same is true after Cambyses has died and his mysterious successor is on the throne. Otanes suspects that this is not the king but a usurper, a criminal who had earlier been punished by having his ears cut off (3.69.5). The time comes for Otanes' daughter Phaedymiē to take her turn in the king's bed. Pluckily, she does as her father has asked, feels in the dark, and confirms that he has no ears. The father's outrage is unbounded: "Here we are, ruled by this Median fellow, a Magus—and one with no ears!" (3.73.2). That is magnificent, as are his earlier words to his daughter: if this is the man who I suspect it is, "there is no way that he should get away with sleeping with you and being master of Persia! He must pay for it!" (3.69.2)—one notices the order, with paternal fury taking rightful priority. Once again, the harem is mentioned because it matters.

As for Darius, his important moment in bed is with his wife, Atossa, when she is chatting away about her wish for new staff and urging her husband to be more successful in order to get them. We are not far off the modern suburban world once again, this time with some 1960s-style sexist stereotyping of the pushy wife of a rising executive (others may think of Emma Bovary). So, if this is an exotic and distant world, Herodotus does what he can to bring it closer to home. The wonder in this eastern world, the *thōma*, is not in its gold-plated accoutrements or even in the troupes of women awaiting their sexual turn; it is more that Cambyses and Darius, whatever they may have available in the back room, nevertheless have a home life not so different from those an audience can recognize.

Whatever its origin, how genuinely Persian is this material? We have come to understand more about the Persian world since Reinhardt, and it is clearer that Herodotus' picture is often a caricature or a travesty, though with glimpses of genuine history.[11] Here too one cannot help feeling that a lot of the distinctive aspects are features less of the real Persian court or even of real Persian stories, more of a Greek construct of that eastern world. Heleen Sancisi-Weerdenburg demonstrated that brilliantly as far as the portrait of women is concerned, showing how little we know about women from Persian sources and how much of the image of feminization is owed to the Greeks.[12] She argued much the same for Xenophon's *Cyropaedia* and for other fourth-century sources such as Dinon and Ctesias.[13] That construct is very likely one that is not wholly Herodotus' own—Sancisi-Weerdenburg brings out that he is one of the least stereotyping of Greek writers[14]—but still one that he takes over from image more than from reality. It is not for nothing that Herodotus, along with Aeschylus, figures in Edward Saïd's *Orientalism* as a progenitor of that broad, stereotyped, undifferentiated portrayal of "the East" that has been so prevalent in western thinking[15]—though doubtless Saïd overdid the picture of undifferentiated stereotyping, and we may later see that he did not get Herodotus wholly right either.

That does not make Herodotus' narrative "distilling" any less interesting. If he paints a different world and then brings it closer to home, that is a process of defamiliarization followed by refamiliarization that has parallels in later paradoxography,[16] extending right up to the early modern intellectual processing of the New World charted in Stephen Greenblatt's *Marvelous Possessions*.[17] First you look at, or present, something new as curious and different; later you see that it is not so different after all, and the really amazing thing is how it helps you to understand at a deeper level something you know already—perhaps even yourself.

It may already be clear where this argument is heading. The Persian stories are like that not, or not only, because the source material was like that but because the world they depict was like that—or Herodotus wished his audience to think it was. Where one man wields such untrammeled power, his personality commands speculation and almost inevitably suspicion: what influences him, and more especially who influences him? What happens in the dark of his bedroom? Feeling in bed for a royal ear will not happen often; whispering into one may be happening every night. Stories will be told, shaped, and improved. Human nature being what it is, misdemeanors will be particularly fascinating. Conspiracies will be suspected; some will be detected; some will have been real. Momentary episodes will have vast consequences. The episodic "novella" will be the perfect narrative form.

It may be enough to leave it at that and not extract any bigger interpretative implications. Not everything in Herodotus needs to be related to the conflict of East and West; when he says in the proem that he will recount "other things and the reason why they came to war with one another," we should take and translate that literally (pp. 1–2). If something is a *thōma*, that is reason enough for its inclusion, and these are riveting, wonderful stories. Yet, in a work so saturated with explanation, it is natural to expect that the character of this world will have consequences once East and West come to war.

Often the feminizing was assumed in Greek stereotyping to be the origin of Persian feebleness and ultimately defeat, and Sancisi-Weerdenburg was right to protest against so simplistic a causal chain.[18] It is another question how, and how far, this works in Herodotus, less given than most (we remember) to such casual stereotyping; and another question again how such explanations may bite not merely on the outcome of the campaign but also on its genesis. Why such imperialist expansion? Why should it be Greece that brought failure and defeat?

(B) BIOGRAPHY?

The questions raised by narrative shape can be taken further. Twenty years after Reinhardt, Helene Homeyer argued something similar about a Persian origin for Herodotus' material, but with a focus on "biography" rather than the "novella."[19] Ten years after that, Arnaldo Momigliano gave her ideas greater currency in his influential *Development of Greek Biography*.[20] They concentrated on the "biographical" texture of Herodotus' early books, with the narrative so often organized around the actions of the king. This is particularly true of book 1, with the focus given first by Croesus and then by Cyrus;[21] Cambyses then dominates the first half of book 3, though the strong linearity is broken by the glances across to the Greek world and the doings of Polycrates and Periander. If Darius is then less of an organizing presence, that is partly because his reign extends over three and a half books, weaving in a vast amount of material and shifting attention increasingly to Greece. No Greek figure, not even Miltiades or Themistocles or Pausanias, is used to control the narrative to a similar degree.[22] For Homeyer and Momigliano, this feature of the early books was again a consequence of the source material; neither quite said that Herodotus knew a Persian biography of Cyrus (though Momigliano almost did), but they were clear that there was a strong one-man focus in some Persian material that he would have known. Homeyer went on to explain the different texture of the later material in terms of a lack of similar material; the implication was that Herodotus would have constructed his Greek narratives in a similar biographical way if only such a source had been available to him.[23]

Once again there may be something in this contrast of source material. We know of Persian narratives centered around the king's person, often couched in autobiographical terms: the Cyrus cylinder, switching from third person to first person in midnarrative, and Darius' Behistun inscription are the best-known cases. Other Near Eastern cultures show similar examples,[24] and Cyrus in particular seems to have served as a magnet for folktales, perhaps even epics, in oral circulation.[25] What is more difficult to believe is that this is *why* Herodotus organized his narrative in the way he did, and—more difficult still—that he would have controlled his Greek material in the same way if only he had had the sources. For one thing, he probably did have some material of that type: we know very little of Stesimbrotus of Thasos' *On Themistocles, Thucydides* [son of Melesias], *and Pericles*, but there is every likelihood that Herodotus had heard or read it in some form.[26] But it is more telling to think of how different his later narrative would look if there had been any attempt to mold it in that way. There is just too much material that could not be shoehorned into any sort of biographical pattern: the troubles of Athens and Aegina, the false start of the war with the march into Thessaly and back, the preliminaries of the 479 campaign, the fighting in Mycale. Greek history was simply too messy, with too many different strands interacting, as each city went its separate way and each had its own concerns, often involving fierce enmity with a neighbor.

One can see this in the shape of book 6.[27] Once the Ionian Revolt is over, the narrative is piecemeal, even meandering:[28] the focus is one moment on Sicily, the next on the Chersonese, then briefly on Persia again and Mardonius' campaign, then extensively on Sparta, then on Athens and Aegina. A firm forward movement comes only with the Marathon campaign, and that is given not by the Persian generals on the spot—Datis has a few mentions, Artaphernes almost none—but by the momentum of the expedition itself. (Here we might contrast the narrative of the Libya campaign in book 4, with—as we saw in the last chapter—much less firm a sense of direction: the decision there to get involved does not go back to the king, 4.166–167, and the Persian commanders are less clear about the campaign's objectives, 4.203.2.) So that linear directedness in book 6 too goes back ultimately to Darius, firmly resolved as he was on vengeance on Eretria and Athens: we remember "the thing with the bow," and the slave whose job every evening was to say, "Sire, remember the Athenians" (5.105). Darius, one suspects, did not need much reminding.

We can even see Herodotus going out of his way to avoid too much "biostructuring."²⁹ It would have been easy to introduce some of the major players of books 7–9 as early as book 6, but they are held back: Leonidas is not even mentioned at the time of his accession on the demise of Cleomenes (6.85.1); and Themistocles' arrival on the public scene, presumably in his archonship of 493/2, is not given until 7.143.1 with the airy *neōsti*, "recently." Earlier, Miltiades' doings in the Chersonese were similarly not told at their chronological place but delayed until after the Ionian Revolt (6.39–41, with another problematic *neōsti*):³⁰ by then the Marathon campaign can already be sensed as looming. True to a general principle of Greek storytelling,³¹ Herodotus prefers to hold each person back to the time when they become most relevant.

In other ways too Herodotus could have done more to control his narrative around those individuals. Cleomenes' story is spread over several phases in two books and has little linearity; his last mention in the narrative in fact deals with the earliest of his actions (his advice to the Plataeans to turn to Athens, 6.108). In book 6 he shares the Spartan limelight with Demaratus and indeed with the court intrigue of the last generation (6.61–65). Miltiades' role at Marathon is limited to his pressure on Callimachus to bring on the battle (6.109–110); more could probably have been done with a part he played in the preliminaries at Athens (p. 196), and if he had anything to do with the tactics followed in the battle, notably the thinning of the center (6.111.3), Herodotus does not tell us so. There was a good deal more to say about Themistocles' career in the 480s as well, not least his long-running rivalry with Aristeides: Plutarch found quite a lot on this over half a millennium later,³² and Herodotus shows that he knew about it too (8.79.2)—but he keeps it to himself, preferring to hold Aristeides back for that dramatic moment on the eve of Salamis. It is not rash to think of him as deliberately writing "not-biography," distancing himself from the forms of narrative structure being developed by his contemporaries Ion of Chios and Stesimbrotus of Thasos.³³

Still, that is the point. For Greece, that is possible, even desirable. We have a sequence of people, all with their moments in the sun, Miltiades, Leonidas, Themistocles, Pausanias: earlier we had Cleisthenes and Cleomenes. In the East there is only one big player, dominating not just one episode but a whole reign. (In Herodotus' narrative, book 9 is a partial exception, though one could argue that Mardonius comes to show some kinglike characteristics; p. 183.) Biostructuring fits the one, just as the novella suited individual episodes within it; it does not suit the other. So again form and content go together: the differing narrative shape reflects the features of freedom, generating a complex of separate stories as each city pursues its own path, then a single more glorious one as the unified command of the enemy monarch seizes hold of Greek history and makes it, just for a season or so, one single story rather than a jumbled mesh.[34]

(c) BE CAREFUL WHAT YOU SAY...

Narrative shape, then, can carry explanatory power: different types of narrative point to different worlds and help the reader or listener to understand what those worlds are like. It will not be difficult to regard these as points about outcome, suggesting strengths and weaknesses of both sides that will come out when they confront one another: we shall return to that later (pp. 200–201). But what about the origins rather than the conclusion of the Greek campaign, or of all the other campaigns that Persia undertakes? Is there anything distinctive about these Persian stories that makes it more intelligible why these expeditions should have been launched?

First, not much needs to be explained. Many campaigns and invasions just happen, with no explanation at all. That was true of Croesus' first moves against the Greek states (1.26.3; pp. 7–8, 110): we are not told his motive, only that he deployed genuine grievances when he had them and made them up when he did not. No special explanation is thought necessary for Cyrus to attack the Assyrians (1.178.1) or for the "three expeditions" that Cambyses planned against Carthage, Ammon, and the Ethiopians (3.17); nor for Phraortes when "he did not think it sufficient to rule over just the Medes but launched an expedition against the Persians, attacking these first and reducing them first to be the Medes' subjects" (1.102.1); nor in many other cases, so that Mardonius can later acknowledge, almost in passing, that Persia's usual way had been to conquer "because we wanted to acquire extra power" (7.9α.2). The Persians attack the Perinthians because "they did not want to be Darius' subjects" (5.1.1): no further explanation is needed. When Atossa seeks to persuade Darius to invade Greece, any hesitation is not based on doubt about the case for aggression (3.134.4–6); it is just a matter of which nations to target first. The same question of prioritization comes up at the beginning of book 7: which should come first, Egypt or Greece (7.5.1; p. 121)?

Nor is this just a Persian feature. Greeks share the same bellicose tastes. Once the Spartans are strong enough, they naturally think of attacking Arcadia (1.66.1), and the only explanation needed is their confidence that they will win. Greek wars happen at the drop of a hat, and it does not take much for Athens to take on Aegina or for Sparta to attack Argos. Sometimes reasons or motives are given, as for the Corinthians or Spartans when they move against Samos (3.47–49) or for the Spartans when they propose moving on the dangerously democratic new Athenian regime (5.91; cf. 5.74.1); sometimes these motives too are similar to ones seen in the East, as in the "envy and yearning for the land" that Hecataeus used to explain the Athenian attack on the Pelasgians (φθόνος τε καὶ ἵμερος τῆς γῆς, 6.137.2). Frequently, though, Herodotus gives no motives at all. Once Miltiades is established in the Chersonese, he first built a wall for protection against the Apsinthians (so a motive *is* given there, a defensive one), then "fought a war against the Lampsacenes first among the others" (6.37.1)—much the same language as is used for Croesus "taking on the Ephesians first among the Greeks" (1.26.1) or Darius "taking Samos first among Greek and barbarian cities" (3.139.1). In West as in East, when an explanation is given, it is often a sign of the momentousness of what is about to happen (Cyrus against the Massagetae, Xerxes against Greece, the renewal of the Aegina-Athens conflict) rather than of the difficulty of understanding it any other way.[35]

What needs explaining is not any attacking but any desisting from attack. Ernst Badian put the point with characteristic trenchancy:

> Imperialism in some sense is as old as the human race, or at least as its social organisation. The extension of power by one's own group over others is only a special case of the victory of one's own side over others: in human terms it does not call for an explanation. . . . What does call for an explanation, when it appears in history, is that relatively high level of sophistication that *rejects* opportunities for the extension of power.[36]

It is therefore in these contexts of looming aggression that Herodotus deploys his "Warners."[37] The first, the Greek Bias or Pittacus, is successful, and Croesus' plan to attack the islanders is abandoned (1.27); the second, the Lydian Sandanis, is not (1.71), and Croesus falls. Later one of the great set-piece Greek debates concerns whether Sparta should *not* attack Athens and strangle the newborn democracy at birth; Soclees finds the right reasons, or so it seemed to most of the Peloponnesian allies at the time (5.91–93). On the Persian side, the great Warner is Artabanus, but he fails to dissuade Darius from his Scythian campaign (4.83) and then fails again with Xerxes (7.10), despite all Xerxes' uneasy second thoughts (7.12–18).

So perhaps that is what we should be looking for: not so much Persian reasons for attack but Persian reasons why there is so rarely restraint? Soclees and the Peloponnesian allies can restrain Sparta, just about; the Greek allies can even put all their usual wars aside in 480 and 479, though the squabbling in camp gives a clear idea of what might be expected once the danger has passed.[38] It is not hard to find reasons why this might be more difficult at the Persian court. A tyrant is simply so difficult to talk to, so difficult to persuade—at least unless it is in bed and one happens to be the queen. It is no coincidence that the word used to characterize the new-found Athenian freedom is not *dēmokratiē* but *isēgoriē*, equality of speech (5.78: p. 164); nor that one of the proudest slogans of Athenian democracy was *parrhēsia*, the ability to speak out, the right of any citizen to respond when the call comes in the assembly, "Who wants to speak?" (Eur. *Supp.* 433–441). That is what is lacking when one is dealing with one man, and his subjects know it. The Spartan Demaratus cautiously asks Xerxes whether he "should speak the truth or tell you what will give you pleasure," and even that formulation is bold (7.101.3; cf. 7.104.1, 5); the Mytilenean Coes asks Darius "whether it is welcome to him to hear the opinion of one who wishes to give it" before offering advice that may be unwelcome (4.97.2) and then puts what he has to say very carefully indeed (of course there is no danger that you might be defeated *in battle* . . . For myself, there is no way that I would be left behind . . .). A courtier needs to be quick on his feet. Cambyses asks his embarrassed retinue how he is regarded in comparison to his father Cyrus (3.34.4). Most reply with the safe answer that Cambyses is the greater, but Croesus produces an even more diplomatic reply: Cyrus is the greater "as you do not yet have a son so great as he left behind in you" (3.34.5). Croesus, of all people, understands the ways of courts.

Often enough the awkward dynamics of conversation at court may be sensed, whether it is the roundabout and gingerly way in which Solon couches his advice to Croesus (1.30–33; pp. 110–111) or Croesus his to Cyrus (1.207), or the orderly silence of the Persian council before Salamis and the malicious glee of others when Artemisia gives advice that they expect Xerxes to reject (8.67–69).[39] The great debate in book 7 is itself a prime example: we saw in the last chapter how carefully Artabanus needs to tread. Mardonius, so sycophantic in that debate, can later be seen to be picking his words just as carefully after Salamis, when he fears for his own safety as instigator of the whole expedition: there is no reason to be disheartened, he says, and the Greeks have no chance of escaping punishment; this was not the Persians' fault, and "if Phoenicians and Cyprians and Cilicians were cowardly"—one can hear the sneering delivery of the words in recitation—"that defeat has nothing to do with the Persians" (8.100.3–4).[40] *Logos* is travestied in such discussions; it is no way to ask for or get or act on good advice. Xerxes' outburst says it all, when the cautious Artabanus urges restraint (7.11; p. 122): if you weren't my uncle, you'd really get what you deserve for advice like that. Not that Greek discourse is without its travesties too, as the Greeks' own council before Salamis shows (pp. 183–184), but this is not for want of speaking out. That does not reduce the force of the point about Persia.

(D) OVERCONFIDENCE?

So tyrants are not easy to restrain once they have set their mind on something. If we ask why they have set their mind on conquest in particular, we already have a good answer: there is nothing special about wanting empire, and what is unusual about tyrants is that they have the power to achieve it—or at least to think that they can do it, and scholarship has often fastened on that last aspect. To go back to classic German scholarship, a key word was *Selbstsicherheit*,[41] that "self-certainty" in which Greek moralizing so often sensed danger: we touched on this in the previous chapter (p. 116). One of Cyrus' several motives for attacking the Massagetae, we are told, was his run of success in wars: "wherever he aimed a campaign, it was impossible for that nation to escape" (1.204.2; pp. 102, 119). Or, once again, so he thought, and the Massagetae proved his downfall. It would be understandable if, surrounded by flatterers who are fearful of saying anything the great man does not want to hear, such self-preening overreach recurrently becomes part of a king's mindset.

But does it? These kings are not stupid nor (except for Cambyses) insane; however obliquely the warning advisers have to speak, they are not always ignored and the kings are not always reckless. Croesus, we saw, is driven by caution more than overconfidence when he takes on Cyrus (p. 116). Cyrus himself then takes Croesus' advice on the Massagetae campaign, which favors what is presented as the more cautious option even if it does not go so far as urging complete withdrawal (1.207.3; pp. 141–142). Darius sets out to exact vengeance from the Scythians only when his resources are strong enough (4.1.1). Xerxes is "chafed" by Artabanus' warning as he broods about it the following night (7.12.1) and tries to draw back—but cannot, for reasons that are evidently complicated and to which we shall return (pp. 153–156). Even Cambyses is sensible enough not to attack Carthage without the willing support of the Phoenician fleet (3.19.3). The kings recognize dangers too, even when those Warners have had to skirt around them. Cyrus knows the risks before attacking the Massagetae and entrusts his son Cambyses to Croesus for safekeeping "in case the crossing against the Massagetae does not succeed" (1.208); Darius listens to Coes, and that is why he ties sixty knots and instructs the Ionians to undo one a day, leaving only when the last knot is untied (4.97–98). So, however nervous court rhetoric may be, this is not yet enough to explain why restraint so rarely works.

We should not neglect the gods here. "A god drives us on," says Xerxes, "and combines with us ourselves when we take on many enterprises" (7.8a.1; p. 123). ". . . And brings them to a happy conclusion," he adds: he will be wrong about that, but he may still be right about the first part.[42] In the enigmatic scene that follows, a supernatural phantom appears to him in the night to tell him that he cannot draw back (7.12.1). That cannot be rationalized away: Artabanus tries to do so, pointing out that people dream about what has been preoccupying them during the day (7.16β). That is sensible, and it is wrong. The phantom appears to Artabanus too, menacing his eyes with hot irons: that proves very persuasive (7.17), and the god indeed drives the Persians on to what awaits them in Greece. One could trace too the rising curve of Greek confidence that the gods will favor their side (pp. 166–167). So yes, the gods may be driving the Persians not just onwards but ultimately downwards too.

Still, we shall see in the next chapter that Herodotus' narrative encourages us to look for human explanations as well, and look for them first: sometimes we just have to bring in the gods—too many things, like the rain shower that saves Croesus (1.87.1–2), would be less, not more, explicable if one did not—but there is almost always a human dimension too. Even Xerxes' phantom, as enigmatic as ever, tells him, "You are not doing well to change your mind, nor is there one here who will forgive you" (. . . οὔτε ὁ συγγνωσόμενός τοι πάρα, 7.12.2). Who is, or are, these unforgiving figures? It sounds eerily more than a reference to the phantom itself (p. 155).

For what, after all, is the alternative? The human dangers are clear if a king wavers or seems to be weak, and the narrative leaves the impression that Xerxes is still fresh on the throne (the beginning of book 7 jumps quickly over several years). Queen Atossa knows how to needle her husband in that bedroom conversation:

> My king, your power is so great—yet you are sitting here, not acquiring for the Persians any new nation or any new power. You are a young man, the master of vast wealth: you ought to be seen to be doing something to set on display, so that the Persians too may learn that they are ruled by a real man. There are in fact two reasons for doing this, both so that the Persians may know that their ruler is a real man and so that they should be worn down by warfare and not have the time on their hands to plot against you. . . .
> (3.134.2)

That echoes a theme from early in the *Histories*—the anguish of Croesus' son Atys when he is forbidden to go to the hunt. "What sort of face can I put on when I go out in public to and from the marketplace? What sort of person will I appear to my fellow-citizens, and what sort to my newlywed wife?" (1.37.2–3).[43] Atys may be overdoing it, for it is no grand campaign that is relevant there: but it already makes the point that appearances *mat-*

ter, that sitting idly at home is not an option for a king, nor even for a crown prince like Atys.

That can coexist with a recognition of the risks. Take Xerxes again, this time in a quieter mood when he speaks with Artabanus at Abydus. As before in the Council (p. 123), he is no fool even if he begins disconcertingly (as disconcertingly as Thucydides' Alcibiades, who may be echoing him: 6.18.3).

> It is better to be confident about everything and to suffer half of the terrible things that might happen than to be fearful about every possibility and never suffer anything at all. . . . We are human: how can we identify anything stable? In no way at all, I think. Gains tend on the whole to come to those who are willing to take action, and not to those who consider everything and are apprehensive. Look at Persia! Do you see how powerful it has become? If my predecessors as king had thought the way you do, or even without thinking like that had had other advisers like you, you would never have seen it advance so much. It is by taking risks that they have brought it so far. Great success tends to be won through great dangers. . . .
> (7.50.1–3)

There is grandeur there[44] and also insight. It is not only a run of his own successes that drives a king on to do more, it is also the triumphant history of his predecessors. As he said in the first debate, "We have never yet kept still" (7.8α.1). Reinhardt put it well: Xerxes has "the curse of being a descendant."[45]

Much earlier in the narrative, something of the same underlies Croesus' advice to Cyrus. By now Cyrus is set on that final, fatal campaign against the Massagetae, and the issue is whether he should choose to fight on the further or the nearer side of the river Araxes, for Queen Tomyris has given him the choice. (One notices again the importance of the natural river boundary.) Most urge the nearer side, within Cyrus' own domain; Croesus takes the opposite view. He may or may not be right;[46] what is interesting here is the way he argues it. Most of his speech is clearly well judged for Cyrus' ears,[47] but it begins in a curiously oblique way.

> O king, this is not the first time, since Zeus gave me over to you, that I have promised to do what I can to turn away any mistake that I see within your house. My experiences, unwelcome as they were, have become lessons for me. If you think you are immortal yourself and lead an army of immortals, there would be no need for me to give you my advice; but if you recognize that you are human and you lead others who are human too, your first lesson should be that there is a cycle in human

affairs, and its rotation does not allow the same people always to enjoy good fortune. . . .
(1.207.1–2)

All very Solonian and very wise, but how does this affect the question of which side of the river to fight on? No wonder scholars have suspected confusion or a combination of incompatible variants,[48] and the latest discussion regards it as hopeless to look for coherence.[49] In part, this defends Croesus' right to speak at all: his is the voice of experience. Still, it is expressive that these opening remarks look as if they are leading to a quite different conclusion, one in the vein of those earlier Warners Bias/Pittacus and Sandanis (p. 12), advising Cyrus to abandon the expedition altogether. After all, Cyrus himself knows the risks involved (p. 139). This is a quintessential example of one of those campaigns where there is far more to lose than to gain, and Croesus himself goes on to comment how poor the Massagetae are in the good things that the Persians have at home (1.207.6). But it is too late for that. Abandoning the campaign is unsayable, just as it is unthinkable for Cyrus himself. All Croesus can do is move on to the second-best option.

In a sense these kings are prisoners of history, not without choices or chances of escape—evidently there *are* choices, and this is where the different targets come into play—but these choices are heavily predetermined to go in an aggressive direction, whatever the precise blend of motives in each case. Prisoners of history: that may not amount to a "curse on the Achaemenid house," though there may be a hint of a supernatural perspective as well; nor is it quite a counterpart of that Lydian five-generational payback that begins with Gyges and ends with Croesus, but a more human and secular equivalent that operates across the generations on a similar timescale.[50] It is not just Heaven that points a king in a direction that, as even he may know, may turn out to be catastrophic as well as glamorous.

(E) BUT ARE WE SO DIFFERENT?

This may so far seem very triumphalist: will unrestrained megalomania, even cautious unrestrained megalomania, not be riding for a fall?[51] No wonder the Greeks won. But Herodotus is rarely that simple. Take Darius' seminar on comparative anthropology. Indians and Greeks are at his court, and he asks how they would treat the bodies of their dead fathers. The Greeks would burn them; the Indians are horrified. The Indians would eat them; the Greeks are horrified. Custom is king, Herodotus concludes, and one would have to be mad to laugh at the ways that other peoples do things

(3.38). What is even more telling, and very Herodotean, is where this comes in his narrative.[52] We have just seen Cambyses behaving with brutal insensitivity to Egyptian customs;[53] a Greek reader or listener might be feeling culturally superior. But here it is a Persian, Darius, who is the sensitive one, and the Greeks at his court who emerge as too prejudiced to realize that their own views are just as culturally determined.[54]

That is not the only time that any Greek readerly smugness is put firmly in its place. There is a similar rhythm at 7.135–137, where the Spartans' proud words championing Greek freedom of spirit are followed by a sequence where Xerxes comes out very well and another Greek city, Athens, very badly (p. 224). We might also recall his treatment of Helen, where the moral hero is the Egyptian Proteus (chapter 2[d]). As Edward Saïd might have said but did not, Herodotus was a father not just of western Orientalism but also of its critique.

Later too a Greek audience might find plenty to wonder about the planks in their eyes. The Greeks' own debating habits do not come out too well: if the Persian council before Salamis is over-docile, the Greek one is over-rambunctious (pp. 183–184). In fact it is a shambles, and what eventually decides the issue is not rational argument but Themistocles' threat to sail away (8.60–64). Not that it matters anyway, as the Greeks soon go back on their decision, and Themistocles needs a second ploy (8.74–6; p. 171). There is every chance that the alliance will break up: if everyone and every city is free to do what they want, they will act in their particular interest rather than that of the collective—a theme we will return to in chapter 12. The Greeks are prisoners of history too, in their case the history of intercity hostilities and jealousies and the ever-present threat of fragmentation that these bring. One of the greatest "wonders" of all was that Greece managed to stay together in 480–479 and, to a very qualified degree, united.

What is more—again to anticipate a later theme, that of chapter 15—the audience's knowledge of Greek history after 479 would make them aware that Greeks too could be bullying, brutal, and overconfident. If these Persian tyrants set up a "despotic template" against which Greek rulers can be gauged, the implication is often that those Greeks measure up to those eastern counterparts all too closely.[55] Certainly it is taken as read that Greeks want to be tyrants too: that is assumed at 5.11.2 and will extend to Aristagoras (not just Miletus, 6.5.1, but aspirations for Naxos too, 5.30.3), and, if the rumors were right, Pausanias ("all of Greece," 5.32).

So these points are more about power than about Persians[56]—or indeed than about Medes, for it is the parable of the Mede Deioces that first explores, in a simplified and historicized pattern, the factors that can construct a tyranny (1.96–101; p. 17), just as Astyages then goes on to model a way in which a king's own arrogance and brutality can bring about his own destruction (1.107–130). It is no coincidence that the closest we come to an eastern-style "novella" in Greece concerns the shenanigans in the sixth-century Spartan royal house and the consequential disputes over the succession (6.61–70); the next closest might be the stories of Polycrates' ring (3.40–43) and of Periander and Lycophron (3.50–53). In each case we are dealing with kings or tyrants and, in the cases of Sparta and of Periander, with their tensions close to home.

The drive to power, to conquest, even to brutality is therefore not limited to Persia nor to tyranny;[57] nor are the dangers that come with it. If we think forward to the world of Thucydides, Aristophanes, and Euripides—the world that was familiar to Herodotus' audience and shaped their expectations—even those dangers are shared: the Athenian *dēmos* too is susceptible to flattery, and its courtiers (the demagogues) have to play along; the *dēmos* too tends to overreach, has an appetite for war, is carried away by a run of success, and can be brutal to its functionaries if they fail to match its expectations.[58] Nor is it easy to make the *dēmos* listen when it is set on a path, and one has to be oblique and indirect; that is what Nicias tries to do, and it does not work (Thuc. 6.20–23). The Thucydidean and Aristophanic conceit of the "tyrant city" goes deeper than one might realize, and the points recur often enough to suggest that they are part of a familiar stereotype, one that Herodotus' audience would have known.[59] Even the pressure of expectation created by one's predecessors, that "curse of being a descendant," has parallels: think of the nostalgic attraction of Aristophanes' *Marathōnomachai*,[60] or all those appeals to "the ancestors" in Attic oratory.[61] Not everything may be universal: for instance, Deioces' adoption of a remoteness and inaccessibility to enhance his mystique may be impractical in the greater openness of a Greek city.[62] Nor does that story, modeling a process whereby society needs a single ruler for justice to flourish, map on to Greek ideas of the development of civilized society.[63] But a great deal is shared.

What Persia offered was the clarity of extremes:[64] a prism for examining what happens when power is concentrated to the highest degree. For similar reasons, Plato takes a tyrant figure in the *Gorgias* to illustrate the appeal and the peril of absolute self-gratification,[65] and Xenophon takes Cyrus the Great to explore possibilities of government and the administration of justice.[66] Persia could be "good to think with" for Greek intellectuals.[67] And—another point, a big one, but again one that must be left until a later chapter (13)—now Athens might be offering a similar clarity at the opposite pole from tyranny, not the rule of the one but the rule of the many. How that would end, nobody could yet tell.

Reinhardt commented that the Persian stories helped one to find "Self in Other,"[68] and he was right. The Persian court might seem very different from the Greek city, and in many ways it was; what it led to was not so different at all. It is indeed that pattern of defamiliarization and refamiliarization (p. 132), but at a much more elaborate level. Nor is it new. It is not so different from the *Iliad* itself, with Trojans beginning by seeming to be very different from Greeks—their excited chatter as they go into battle against the grimly silent Greek war machine (*Il.* 3.1–9), Paris wearing his fine leopard-skin jerkin but then recoiling when faced by the lionlike Menelaus (*Il.* 3.10–37)—but ending by not seeming so different at all, when it comes to the important aspects of humanity that Achilles and Priam realize they share (*Il.* 24.468–676, esp. 518–551; p. 21). National nature may be one thing, and it matters; human nature is something bigger. Thucydides would have agreed.

CHAPTER 10

THE HUMAN AND THE DIVINE

(A) DIVINE PERSPECTIVES

It was his belief in the gods that really first made Herodotus into a historian.
(FOCKE 1927: 57)

Hartmut Erbse thought that "this insight should be printed in gold letters before every modern discussion of Herodotus."[1] We have seen places where a religious dimension is inescapable. There was Pheretime's horrible death, demonstrating that "in mortal life, excessive acts of vengeance arouse the envy of the gods" (4.205; p. 126); there was that five-generation payback for the wrongdoing of Gyges (pp. 108, 111–113); there was the conviction in the first story of the *Histories* that "it was necessary that things should turn out badly for Candaules" (1.8.2; pp. 107–108), something we surely take supernaturally,[2] just as we do with similar remarks later about Apries, Scyles, Demaratus, and Artaÿnte (2.161.3, 4.79.1, 6.64.1, 9.109.2).[3] Sometimes fish might have human jewelry in their stomachs, but it is not going to be coincidence that it is this fish, with this ring, that is brought to Polycrates (3.42.4: "He realized that there was something divine about it"); nor is it going to be coincidence that a mysterious cloud of dust is seen rising from Eleusis and moving towards Salamis, accompanied by the sound of a mystic song (8.65); nor that a rainstorm comes to quench Croesus' pyre in answer to his prayer to Apollo (1.87.1), even if sometimes rainstorms do burst from a cloudless sky.[4] True, that is given as just "what the Lydians say," but the quenching is also referred to in the report of what the priestess of Apollo said, 1.91.3, and Herodotus takes narratorial authority for that: "This is what the Pythia responded to the Lydians," 1.91.6.[5]

Herodotus also makes plain his own conviction about the Trojan War. He has just explained why he prefers the version that Helen was never at Troy at all and therefore the Trojans could not give her back:

To make my own view clear, it was because the supernatural [(*to daimonion*): we might say "Heaven"] was seeing to it that the Trojans should be totally wiped out and make it evident to mankind that great wrongdoings excite great acts of revenge from the gods. That is the way it seems to me.[6]
(2.120.5; pp. 37–38)

Like the verdict on Pheretime and the word of the Pythian priestess, this comes at the end of a complicated narrative sequence, one in which (as in those other two cases) a pattern of human-level explanation had been traced. The human level is where we start, and for most of the time it is where we remain; but, at the end, there are those times when the gods really have to be brought into it, just as in explaining the noncoincidental neatness that payback for Spartan impiety in 480 should fall on the sons of the heralds involved (7.137.2; pp. 220, 224).[7]

Generally, it is true, Herodotus is careful to introduce his more supernatural stories with "it is said that," and sometimes to make it clear who does the saying.[8] The Persian survivors of their attack on Delphi reported that they were chased on their retreat by two hoplites "of greater than human stature, pursuing them and killing them"; the Delphians themselves say that these were two of their local heroes, Phylacus and Autonous (8.38–39). There is some disagreement on how exactly the fighting at Salamis began:

> And this too is said, that a phantom of a woman appeared to them and urged them on, loudly enough for all the Greek forces to hear, after first rebuking them with the words, "You fools! How much further are you going to carry on backing water?"
> (8.84.2)

When Pheidippides was running to Sparta to call on them to come to the Marathon campaign, he "said himself and reported to the Athenians" that he had met Pan on a mountain: Pan called out his name and asked why the Athenians were neglecting him when he bore them such goodwill. "The Athenians believed this to be true," and when all was over they founded a temple and an annual torch race in Pan's honor (6.105).[9] And "I have heard a story" that Epizelus, who went blind at Marathon, "said himself" that he saw a vast hoplite towering over him, with his beard casting a shadow over his shield: the phantom passed him by and killed the man at his side (6.117).

So these are reports of what other people said and believed. Still, it is a mistake to think of Herodotus as "distancing" himself in such passages, as if such claims were all likely to be suspect. We have seen enough passages where he is prepared to commit himself, and anyway "it is said" need not always indicate reserve:[10] the words of the Pythia in book 1 made that clear (p. 146). In the Delphic story of book 8, for instance, there is already a plentiful amount of the supernatural that is told directly, with no hedging around. The sacred weapons of the god somehow moved themselves outside the temple. As the Persians attacked, they were struck by lightning from on high, and two peaks of Parnassus fell on them with great carnage; a shout and cry were heard from the temple of Pronoia (8.37). The stones that fell from Parnassus were still visible in Herodotus' own day (8.39.2). "It is said" can also indicate respect and awe: people are still telling the tale; it still matters.[11]

Any reserve is rather a matter of the caution that is always required with divine phenomena: caution in reporting them, caution in making sense of them.[12] Some reports may be unreliable; not all will be, and even those that are may still convey the numinous air of those momentous times. One can understand why the Persians should have believed in those giant hoplites or Epizelus in his supernatural adversary, why Pheidippides should have thought he met Pan on a mountain top and why the Athenians should have believed him. Even when there is a "wonder" about which Herodotus has no doubt, he often makes it clear that his interpretation is only a matter of opinion, just as he does in interpreting the Trojan War as an act of crime and supernatural punishment (2.120.5). Similarly, the fighting of Plataea drifted towards the grove of Demeter:

> It is a wonder (*thōma*) to me how it could be that when they were fighting by Demeter's grove not a single one of the Persians was seen entering the sacred domain nor dying there, but most fell in the unhallowed ground around the temple. I think that, if one has to express any opinion about divine matters, it was the goddess who would not let them in, because they had burnt the shrine in Eleusis.
> (9.65.2)

So divine matters require particular caution, especially for one of such an empirical cast of mind as Herodotus. His normal suite of techniques, *gnōmē*, *opsis*, and *historiē* ("intelligence," "sight," and "inquiry," 2.99.1), can only take him so far: "sight" can show him the temples, "inquiry" tell him what people say, but "intelligence" can draw only very cautious inferences. No surprise, then, that when he comes to Egypt he can express reluctance to set out "the divine aspects of what I heard, except for just the names of gods, as I think that all humans know the same amount about them" (2.3.2)—as much as one another, and as little. No surprise, either, that he often gives more space to what we might call religious anthropology, how humans think about the gods, than to the gods themselves;[13] or that he prefers to speak of *to theion*, "the divine," than to categorize actions as the workings of particular named gods.[14]

It is important, though, to stress that his empiricism leads him to *belief* in gods and in their effect on the world, not to doubt or to skepticism:[15] "There are many indications (*tekmēria*) of divinity in human affairs . . ." (9.100.2)—*tekmēria*, a quintessentially empirical word.[16] Would it make what happened to Croesus on the pyre more credible rather than less credible if one took the god out of the explanation? Or—the instance that Herodotus is discussing in that passage at 9.100—the rumor of the Greek victory at Plataea spreading far away at Mycale on the very day it happened? Or what happened to Arion, saved so miraculously on the back of a dolphin (1.24–1.25)? Or even what happened for the Greeks in 490 and 480–479? Similarly in the *Odyssey* the possibility of divine help makes it more believable, not less, that Odysseus could have survived that journey on his raft.[17] For Herodotus, as arguably for Aeschylus, "a divine explanation . . . is a *diagnosis of something actually observed in human behaviour*, and not a piece of mumbo-jumbo independent of observed phenomena."[18] There may be limits to what can be said, but there are some insights that he thinks important and right, and many center on the biggest things: the Trojan War, the defense of Greece.[19]

It is that same empiricism, too, that leads him to insist that gods communicate with mortals through oracles:

> When I look at cases like that, with Bacis speaking so clearly, I do not myself dare to argue against the validity of oracles, nor do I accept argument from others.
> (8.77.2)[20]

To foretell is not in itself to predetermine or cause, and so oracles are less relevant for our inquiry than the other supernatural passages we have been considering—or rather, what becomes causally relevant is the human attempt to interpret them and the human choices that result. Still, this at least reinforces that impression of a divine realm that cares a great deal about what happens on earth and what humans do to one another.

(B) ENIGMATIC DIVINITY

So Herodotus treads cautiously but sometimes feels the divine is inescapable. His narrative has less explicit ways of encouraging readers and hearers along similar lines.[21]

Take his treatment of Cyrus' childhood. He begins by saying he is avoiding more inflated versions (he says he knows of three others), preferring what is said by "those who do not wish to exalt (*semnoun*) Cyrus' history but to tell the truth" (1.95.1). The word *semnoun* normally has a divine tinge and suggests that the relevant writers had decked Cyrus out with the sensational details appropriate to a god. Rather like the proem of Tacitus' *Annals*, dwelling on the "fear," "hatred," "anger," and "partisanship" (*metus, odia, ira, studium*) that characterize earlier works on the principate, the formulation here makes points about both subject and writer. Cyrus is the sort of figure who invites "exalting," just as the principate invites hatred and distortion; such is the nature of court historiography, and such is the manner that the narrator proclaims his intention to avoid. Here the idea of "exalting" recurs a little later, concerning the grand ceremonial with which the shrewd Deioces surrounded his throne (1.99.2, *semnoun* again): that is the majestic style of oriental monarchs (cf. 2.173.2), and it is also the style of the overstated tales that they inspire, told to them (7.6.4) or of them (3.16.6–7). Court and story normally share the same manner. Yet this work is to be different, precisely because the author (again like Tacitus) has an eye for the dangers.

The point recurs when we reach the description of Cyrus' birth and salvation. Herodotus' version has as saviors a cowherd, Mitradates, and his wife, whose name was "Cyno" in Greek or "Spako" in Median (Herodotus explains that the Median for "dog" is *spaka*: 1.110.1). When Cyrus is finally restored to his Persian family:

> He said that he had been brought up by the cowherd's wife, and he continued always to speak of her in the highest terms; Cyno was always on his lips. His parents seized on this name, and they spread the story that a dog (*kuōn*) took Cyrus when he was exposed and brought him up: their purpose was to give the Persians the impression that their son had been saved more supernaturally (*theioterōs*). That was the origin of this tale. (1.122.3)

Note the comparative "*more* supernaturally": that need not exclude the possibility that there was *something* supernatural about the unvarnished truth.[22] But Herodotus' emphasis still falls on the deflation of the divine element, not on any irreducible supernatural residue. This, evidently, was the sort of "inflated" version which was in circulation (and which surfaces, unqualified, elsewhere in the tradition)[23]—and which Herodotus will play down, rather as the early chapters of book 1 showed him toying with rationalized versions of familiar myths (pp. 28–29). Once again there are suggestions here of the way that dynastic politics works. Such divine stories are the stuff of propaganda, semblances, political rhetoric: in this case, the rhetoric used by Cyrus' natural parents. Herodotus uses it to point not to an underlying divine reality but to the self-interested manipulations behind the throne.

We might again be reminded of the humanizing texture of those early abduction chapters as we reach the "Thyestean banquet" (1.119–120), with Astyages serving up Harpagus' murdered son to his unsuspecting father. As Reinhardt observed,[24] the equivalent stories in Greece would present this as an outrage before gods as well as humans. Here it triggers Harpagus' desire for vengeance, and the consequences are pursued on, for the moment, a wholly human level. It is understandable that Reinhardt should have isolated this as a Persian element in the story, avoiding the divine register that the Greeks would instinctively have expected.

But one wonders. There are those times when the divine simply has to be accepted; a listener or reader, even one who has been acclimatized to treading carefully, would be unwise to dismiss the divine out of hand. Often in tragedy too one is aware of a supernatural level operating when events turn out in a way too neatly and suggestively to allow coincidence; and that may be true even if no particular god is named and even if the characters themselves seem insensible to the suggestions.[25] The same seems true here. Is it really just coincidence that Cyno/Spako produces a stillborn child precisely on the crucial day? This turned out, "somehow as heaven would have it," says Herodotus (κως κατὰ δαίμονα, 1.111.1): the words are unemphatic, even casual, but they may hint at something supernatural at work.

Then we have a coronation game that the ten-year-old Cyrus played with other children: that choice of game again seems more than coincidence. So does the failure of the Persian seers to warn that danger remains from this young Cyrus (1.120.5): this is the more remarkable because their advice (1.120.6) to pack him off to the Persians hints at some continuing unease,[26] but this action seems exactly the one most likely to make Cyrus a more formidable danger, another indication that a higher force is guiding events.

By then Astyages has already taken his "Thyestean" revenge on Harpagus, and here too one senses something supernatural at play, for it is noticeable how strangely these events reenact those of ten years earlier. Here too a child is brought in a vessel (1.119.4 ~ 1.113.1); here too it is "revealed" to the bereaved parent (ἀποκαλύπτειν, 1.119.5-6 ~ ἐκκαλύψας, 1.112.1); here too Harpagus responds to the king with a meek, but delusive, acquiescence in his will (1.119.7 ~ 1.108.5); and he goes home to bury his own child, just as he had originally been told to bury the infant Cyrus (1.119.7 ~ 1.108.4).[27] Some of this is Astyages' stagemanaging: the punishment is made to fit what Astyages sees as the crime. But once again it looks as if there is more to it. The mirroring is too neat; something larger is at work.

After Harpagus has set his trail of vengeance in motion, he sends a furtive message to Cyrus and puts to him that "the gods are watching over you: otherwise you would never have enjoyed so much fortune" (1.124.1). Cyrus himself takes the hint and uses similar language when urging the Persians to rebellion: "I think that I now take this enterprise in hand as one born by some divine chance" (θείῃ τύχῃ γεγονώς, 1.126.6). Much later in the narrative the theme will recur, and it will become clear that Cyrus really believes in his divine origin, at least by then (1.204.2; p. 119). Admittedly, the audience do not know that yet, and they may be wondering if this is another case of divine language being the stuff of rhetoric and semblance; but the nexus of "coincidences" has already encouraged suspicions that Harpagus' and Cyrus' words might be literally correct.[28]

A chapter later, and the hint grows louder. Astyages marshals his forces to meet the Persian threat, and "as one who is stricken by the gods" (ὥστε θεοβλαβὴς ἐών, 1.127.2)[29] selects Harpagus himself to be his general, forgetting the harm he has done him. Harpagus himself had envisaged his selection as a possibility but had not been confident (1.124.3). Divinity is active after all, and the audience can find retrospective confirmation that all the "coincidences" were not just coincidental. From the first steps that Astyages took to meet the dangers presaged by his dreams, all his actions turned out to be precisely those necessary to make the dreams come true.[30]

There is also a strange mirroring of the Atys and Adrastus story: Croesus is concerned to preserve his heir, Astyages to destroy his, but in each case it is not merely hopeless to try to avoid the consequences a dream presages, it is also those attempts that seal the victim's fate.[31] The parallelism extends to the marriages that each arranges: Astyages avoids choosing a Median husband for his daughter to reduce the threat from any offspring (1.107.2), but the result is the "mule" Cyrus (1.91.5–6); Croesus marries off his son to keep him busy (1.34.3–35.1), but the fear of losing face before his bride is one of Atys' reasons for going on the hunt (1.37.3, p. 140).[32] In the Atys-Adrastus story Herodotus made it explicit that something divine was at work ("a great indignation from god," ἐκ θεοῦ νέμεσις μεγάλη, 1.34.1; cf. p. 112). The notion of Astyages 'stricken by the gods' tells a similar story, and memories of that earlier sequence, and of the irreducible involvement of the divine elsewhere in the Croesus-*logos*, might themselves reinforce the conviction that divinity is at work.

Herodotus' initial dismissiveness of any "inflation" has thus been overtaken by the narrative's subsequent suggestions. The rhythm is indeed similar to that seen in the early chapters of the work: a provisional, programmatic pointer to the exclusion of the divine lends extra weight and persuasiveness to the emergence of a divine strand when it can no longer be avoided.

It is again important, though, that the divine strand in no way negates or usurps the role played by human factors, and indeed the divine element becomes explicit at the moment when human factors are also at their most active. The extreme situations are the ones that most clearly reveal the elements at play, and those elements can be both human and supernatural. That was true of Croesus on the pyre, where his insight into Solon's human wisdom and the kings' human interaction were crucial in the scene where Apollo's intervention was also at its most irreducible. This is again the case now. Astyages is "stricken by the gods," and otherwise he would have chosen differently; but it would have made little difference, and for human-level reasons. Harpagus was not confident that he would himself be chosen—but he assured Cyrus that, whoever was selected, that general would be happy to play the same treacherous game (1.124.3). Harpagus is not truthful in all that he says,[33] but if this particular claim overstates, the exaggeration is only slight.[34] Astyages has only himself to blame. The narrative stresses his "harshness," *pikrotēs* (1.123.2), seen particularly in his taste for ruthless vengeance, first and most chillingly on Harpagus, then on the luckless seers who had given him poor advice (1.128.2).

> Such was the end of Astyages' reign after thirty-five years, and the Medes bowed before the Persians thanks to this man's harshness . . .
> (1.130.1)

The human register dominates at the end.

Let us take a second example that is equally laden with enigma, and this takes us back to Xerxes' Council at the beginning of book 7. We left that as Xerxes changed his mind (p. 122): he felt nighttime doubts, with Artabanus' advice "chafing" him (7.12.1). He decides, in fact, "that he has no business launching a campaign against Greece," and he falls asleep. But then, so the Persians say—again a "so they say" to introduce a divine element—he has a dream. A tall, handsome figure stands over him and rebukes him:

> You are not doing well to change your mind, nor is there one here who will forgive you. No, stick to the path that you decided to take during the day.
> (7.12.2)

Initially unimpressed, Xerxes reconvenes the Council the next morning, and announces his decision not to invade after all. He explains his outburst of anger in terms of his "youth," which "boiled over" when he heard what Artabanus had said, and this is the point when the counselors fall to their knees in delight (7.13.3; p. 122). But the next night the dream visits him again:

> Son of Darius, so you make it clear among the Persians that you have abandoned the expedition, and are dismissing my words as if they come from a nobody? Be sure of this, if you do not launch the campaign imme-

diately, this is what will befall you: just as you became great and mighty within a short time, so swiftly will you be humbled once again. (7.14)

Now, seriously rattled, he leaps out of bed and summons Artabanus to tell him what has happened: he asks Artabanus to change clothes and sleep in the king's bed, to see if the same dream comes to him. Artabanus' response is coolly rational. One tends to dream about the things that have been preoccupying one during the day,[35] and anyway there is no point in changing clothes, as any divine being is not so simple as to be taken in and can just as well appear to me in my own clothes and my own bed (7.16). (There may well be deeper reasons, based on Mesopotamian ritual, for his reluctance to wear the king's clothes,[36] but if Herodotus knows of these he does not go into them here.) But Xerxes insists; and the dream duly appears to Artabanus too.

> "Are you the one who is urging Xerxes not to campaign against Greece, as one who cares about him? But you will never—not now, not hereafter—get away with deflecting what has to come about. What Xerxes must suffer if he is disobedient, he has already been told." And, so Artabanus thought, after delivering these threats the figure made as if to burn out his eyes with hot irons.
> (7.17.2)

This persuades Artabanus too. He goes to Xerxes and says that he is now persuaded that a "god-driven destruction is overtaking us" (7.18.3). The next morning Xerxes announces that they will campaign after all, and Artabanus gives him his full support.

Once again, the divine element here seems irreducible,[37] at least if "what the Persians say" is correct. It is true that not all dreams are heaven-sent; but ones that make it into Herodotus' narrative, or for that matter any other ancient historical narrative, do tend to come from the gods and are there because they come true.[38] Artabanus after all tries to rationalize it away, and he is clearly wrong (p. 140).[39] There is also something supernatural in the air in what immediately follows, for Xerxes has a third dream, one in which he is crowned with an olive wreath that sprouts branches that reach over the entire earth, and then the wreath disappears (7.19.1). The dream interpreters take this as a good sign, but a Greek audience would see that as a woeful underinterpretation: the wreath disappears, so any domination is not to last; moreover, the olive is the symbol of Athens, with the olive tree that will so portentously sprout again two days after it is burnt on the Acropolis (8.55).[40] Perhaps the dream interpreters are afraid to spell out the clear implications:

that suits the uneasy atmosphere of the court.[41] But it may also be some divine clouding of the wits, some *atē*, that makes it so difficult for them to draw the implication they should.

So once again we have a narrative that draws the audience irresistibly into accepting a divine dimension. We seem in fact to have two counterpart stories one after another, one explaining the expedition on the human level and one on the divine. That still leaves questions to be answered. One is posed by that phrase "nor is there one here who will forgive you" (7.12.2). What does the phantom mean? Is this still on the divine level, with the phantom referring to itself? Or does that pick up on a *Realpolitik* point about the human level, of the dangers that loom for any king who sits at home (pp. 140–141)? Notice the way it is put: "Son of Darius, so you make it clear among the Persians . . ." (7.14; p. 153). "Son of Darius," that father he needs to live up to, with a hint at that inherited need for expansion; "you make it clear," emphasizing that he has now gone public. The courtiers do indeed show their delight at the abandonment of the plan, but it may still be the case that so swift a change of mind is damaging to prestige. U-turns are not good for the image: modern presidents and prime ministers know that as well as ancient rulers. That touches on the deeper question of the relation between the two sequences, if indeed there is any clear relation at all. If Heaven is now determined to bring Xerxes down, is that supernatural resolve independent of the first Council? In that case, might it be that Heaven was already stagemanaging that Council to drive Xerxes in the desired direction? Maybe—but there has so far been no indication of that in the text. Or is that divine determination itself prompted by what happened at that Council, with the gods feeling that Xerxes' imperialistic thinking must be punished whether or not it turns into action? That would not be out of keeping with other strands in the *Histories*: Croesus, after all, was struck by *nemesis* from the divine for "thinking himself the most prosperous man alive" (1.34.1), a matter of thought rather than action; book 1 tells how the oracle of Branchidae was so offended by an impious inquiry from Aristodicus of Cumae that it replied endorsing the impiety, "so that through your unholy action you might die all the quicker and not come again to the oracle to enquire whether you should surrender a suppliant" (1.159.4).[42] In both those cases the mere thought was enough.

The straight answer is that we just cannot tell how independent the two scenes are.[43] The divine sequence re-sorts and reassembles some elements of the human, and they are juxtaposed in such a way that both levels, the human and the divine, clearly matter. Neither can be collapsed into the other. But the nature or even the existence of any causal link between them is left as enigmatic as so many other features when historian, or reader, ponders the role of the divine in human affairs.[44] It is as difficult for the reader or listener to grope for the truth as it would have been for participants at the time, rather as we saw in the Croesus narrative that readers might forget or misread clues just as the figures in the story did. This is high-class *mimēsis* indeed.

(C) HISTORICAL EXPLANATION?

Where does this leave the gods in historical explanation? The answer has to be "somewhere," at least some of the time. When Heaven plays a part, it matters a lot, often decisively. We cannot even say that the gods are used only to explain things that are also fully explicable on the human level, however helpful that approach often is for tragedy; there are too many cases like Apollo's rain shower or Xerxes' dream or Delphi's self-moving weaponry and tumbling peaks that resist explanation in human terms.[45] What we can say is that divine explanations and human explanations intertwine, and when one is at its most intense, we tend also to find the other.

It is also often true that the human level is treated more elaborately than the divine,[46] however much more decisive the divine level may in fact have been. That was arguably already the case with Homer, where—however active the gods are in setting up that final encounter of Priam and Achilles—it is the human drama of their meeting that is really absorbing. Even Herodotus' careful discussion of the Athenians' contribution to the Greek victory left the pious phrase "second only to the gods" unexplored (μετά γε θεούς, 7.139.5; p. 43):[47] there is no discussion of *how* the gods could have saved the Greeks if the Athenians had defected, understandably as that is so unknowable and the divine world is so difficult to access. The gods' own reasons for actions are usually stated only when they are straightforward to infer.[48] Demeter is protecting her own temple (p. 148) or Apollo his shrine at Delphi (p. 147); no surprises there, then.

Apollo's elaborate explanation at 1.91 (pp. 111–113) is in fact a rare exploration of divine motivation in a case where the answer would not be obvious, and there it is the account of the Pythia that allows Herodotus such atypical knowledge. If we go back to our dissection of Solon's wisdom (p. 111), the aspect that is least recurrent is that of simple divine jealousy, *phthonos*, of prosperity for its own sake, without any concern for what the humans actually *do*:[49] even in that vignette of Pheretime (4.205; p. 126) it is explicitly the transgressions that evoke the *phthonos*, not the prosperity alone. Artabanus talks of *phthonos* too at 7.10ε, but we have already seen how circumlocutory he is being, and it is anyway human action—or, as he would prefer, inaction—that he is concerned with. A focus on envious gods would make it too much a matter of divine mindset, and that is not Herodotus' primary focus. Divine thinking was just so difficult to find knowable at all, at least if it went beyond the obvious or the oracular when that was explicit. Transgressive mortal mindsets are more within his purview; transgressive mortal actions, more still.

Nor is the way that human and divine levels interact always clear. Sometimes the "intertwining" is so close that they resist disentangling. Take Artabanus again, this time his warning at Abydus. There are two things, he tells Xerxes, the greatest of all, that are our biggest enemies. The army and fleet are vast, and he would not want any more:

> If you were to gather more, those two things become even worse enemies. These two are land and sea. There is no sea harbor great enough anywhere, as far as I can gather, to have room for this fleet if a storm attacks and to be able to guarantee saving the ships. And yet it's not just one you need, but harbors along all the continental shore that you are sailing past. So, without harbors to receive you, you must learn that it is circumstances that govern humans, not humans that govern circumstances. So much for the one; now for the other. This is the way in which land is your enemy, and if you meet no opposition, it becomes more and more your enemy every step onwards that you take, always stealing that extra distance; for mortals are never content with the good fortune they already have. Yes, I am saying that, with no opposition, as the distance increases the land will generate more and more hunger.
> (7.49)

The tone and language are more forthright than before, though no less gnomic. Xerxes has indeed calmed, and Artabanus knows it. And, once again, he oozes wisdom. His point is a thoroughly secular one: the forces are too big for comfort, and neither land nor sea can support them. That secular level returns often enough in the narrative, with notes of the immense cost of feeding the army (7.118–120) and of rivers drunk dry (7.43.1, 7.58.3, 7.108–109, 7.127.2, 7.196).

Artabanus' language presages, though, another register in which land and sea are Xerxes' enemies, one that picks up on earlier cases when tyrants take on nature.[50] The pattern goes back to Cyrus at the Gyndes (1.189; p. 117) and before that to the time when the Cnidians try to dig through their isthmus to protect themselves from Harpagus but the workmen are afflicted by an excess of injuries hard to explain in natural terms. Delphi tells them to desist, for "Zeus would have made you an island, had that been his wish" (1.174.5).

By now Xerxes has launched his own assaults on sea and land, changing Mt. Athos into sea (7.22–24) and the Hellespont into land (7.34–35, prefigured in the bridging of the Strymon at 7.24). In the case of Athos, the enterprise was unnecessary (7.24.1),[51] and land and sea take their revenge. This first comes when the fleet has to double-park off the Magnesian coast, and "a wind they call the Hellespontian" (surely a significant name, stressing that dividing point of the continents) suddenly breaks the calm, dashing the ships against the shore, "an irresistible business of a storm" that lasts three days and nights. No fewer than four hundred ships are destroyed (7.188–192). Then another storm breaks in the night after the battle of Artemisium, driving debris and corpses into the Persian fleet in the harbor and causing havoc among the detachment sent to sail around Euboea (8.12–13). Later, especially on the return journey to Persia, the extreme shortage of food is similarly stressed (8.115). There is a further occasion too, this time at Potidaea, when the sea first changes into land and then, catastrophically for the Persians, back to sea again (8.129; cf. p. 239 n. 25). This, then, is one occasion in which Artabanus is proved right, even if the Persians might well have gone on to win despite taking all these logistical risks.

But is he right simply for the secular way that he put it? Or is there something divine, almost magical, at play too, as we see how a king toys only at his peril with such natural givens as land and sea? The Delphians were told by the oracle to "pray to the winds," "for these would be great allies of the Greeks" (7.178.1); then it is said (another typical "it is said") that the Athenians had prayed to Boreas, the North Wind, married in legend to an Athenian bride Oreithyia, even though Herodotus is typically cautious about the link with the storm off the Magnesian coast:

> If it was for this reason that the North Wind fell upon the barbarian force at anchor, I cannot say; but the Athenians certainly say that the North Wind had helped them before and did so then with this effect, and on their return they founded a shrine to Boreas by the river Ilissus. (7.189.3)

So again, typically, he is more confident about human behavior, the Athenians' gratitude, than about the divine.[52] He is less cautious, however, about the inrush of the waters at Potidaea, where the locals explained it as punishment for the Persian desecration of a temple and "they seem to me to be right in saying that this was the cause" (*aition*, 8.129.3; cf. p. 239 n. 25). He is less cautious still with the Euboean storm:

> Everything was done by the god (ἐποιέετό τε πᾶν ὑπὸ τοῦ θεοῦ) to make the Persian force equal to the Greek rather than much bigger. (8.13)

"To make them equal," one notes, not to give superiority, far less victory:[53] the humans still have to do their bit too, and it is a very big bit indeed. The winds are the "allies" (7.178.1, above), but they will not do everything. Still, we can clearly not leave the gods out of it. As on the medals that Queen Elizabeth I struck after the defeat of the Spanish Armada "God blew, and they were blown asunder."[54]

So this is a case where divine and human are intertwining closely. Again, it is when the supernatural is most in the air—the Strymon, Athos, the Hellespont—that Herodotus also stresses the human-level points, with hunger or voracious demands or rivers drunk dry.[55] That coincidence of weather disruption with a major battle also seems too neat to be coincidental.[56] This is not a case of the divine overriding the secular but of the two pulling in the same direction, and how, or how much, the gods need to intervene is left as hinted but unexplored.

Elsewhere too it is unclear exactly how the two levels are interacting. Take two stories that surely mirror one another,[57] those of the Persian Cambyses and the Spartan Cleomenes. Both went mad; that is clear. Cambyses was "not sane even before" (3.30.1), and Cleomenes earlier "a little on the crazy side" (6.75.1). Then a trigger came upon these dispositions, driving them over the edge. In Cambyses' case the Egyptians say that it was because of his injustice (*adikēma*) to the Apis bull (3.30.1), and the narrative rhythm makes the reader inclined to believe it, though other, possibly complementary explanations are acknowledged (congenital disease, or just "one of the many bad things that happen to people," 3.33; p. 105). Deranged behavior certainly intensifies after the Apis episode, and forces soon gather against him on the human level. But not just the human: it will not be coincidence that he is finally wounded in precisely the same part of the body that he wounded the bull, or that it happens in "Agbatana," fulfilling in an unexpected way a prophecy he was given long before (3.64.3).[58] Reinhardt thus thought this "the most religious of Herodotus' Persian stories" (1940: 156). Human derangement seems certainly to play a part in that final episode, as in a frenzy he leaps on to his horse to ride straight off "on campaign" (στρατεύεσθαι, 3.64.2) to Susa (all the way from Egypt!): as he leaped, his sword inflicted the wound. But are we to think that the gods have encouraged his deranged behavior, then and before, to precipitate his fall? We are not told.

Cleomenes' craziness was even more spectacular. Whenever he met another Spartan, he would strike him in the face with his rod of office. The ephors "shackled him in wood" (6.75.2),[59] but a helot was intimidated into giving him a knife: Cleomenes promptly killed himself by cutting his legs and working upwards, "slicing himself into sausage meat" (6.75.3). Not pleasant. But why? What was the "trigger" for the madness? Most Greeks say it was because of the shady part he had played in bribing the Pythian priestess (6.75.3), a story Herodotus has just told at length (6.61–70); the Athenians say it was because of sacrilegious damage to a shrine at Eleusis; the Argives, that he disrespected the sanctuary of those men of Argos whom he had defeated in battle and who had taken refuge in a sacred grove, killing them deceitfully and mercilessly (6.76–80). The Spartans themselves say that there was nothing supernatural about it (ἐκ δαιμονίου μὲν οὐδενὸς μανῆναι Κλεομένεα, 6.84.1), but that he had picked up the habit of heavy drinking from some Scythian ambassadors, and that this was the explanation.

> That is what the Spartans say about Cleomenes; but my own view is that he was paying some payback [*tisis*] for [or "to"] Demaratus.
> (6.84.3)

So this, clearly, is another case where different explanations are run against one another, and each body of people takes the self-centered and self-justifying line that one would expect. Of course the Spartans would be the ones who deny any divine punishment; they are the least likely to admit there was any wrongdoing, local or international, to be punished for.

Nor is this a case where all the explanations can be equally true. Herodotus' "own view" at the end is clearly contrasted with the Spartan version as a superior alternative ("but my own view is"). This Spartan view is presented as incompatible with the others ("nothing supernatural about it"), while those Athenian and Argive views were originally introduced as contrasting alternatives to the view stressing the bribery of Delphi (6.75.3): a first reading would therefore suggest that all these options are rival ones.[60] Yet they need not have been. If there is payback for the bribery and for Demaratus (or for that matter for Eleusis or for Argos), then the gods would have found their way to orchestrate the punishment, and madness might easily be their way to do that. Cleomenes' Scythian-style drunkenness could equally be their means of inflicting that madness, rather as an Aphrodite or a Dionysus of tragedy finds a chink in a mortal character and exploits it to wreak the destruction that they seek.

Herodotus, however, says nothing along those lines. Mortal and divine perspectives are set side by side; he makes it clear that the divine explanation is in his eyes the one that works best. Anything more by way of explaining the divine mechanisms is left for the reader or listener to supply. So, if we recall those different ways of handling multiple or competing causes (chapter 6), we have something of a mix: one explanation, the divine, is better than another, the purely secular; the different levels may however be interacting, but if so Herodotus does not tell us how; yet, even as the divine perspective is allowed and emphasized, the focus of the narrative has remained on the human level, tracing the steps by which Cleomenes (like Cambyses) has become more and more distant from normal human behavior.

It is less paradoxical than it may seem that divine explanations are sometimes inescapable and when they exist can be the ones that matter most, yet the focus and the interest so regularly remain on the human level. The gods are very difficult to know about, beyond the basic fact that they exist and that they can do extraordinary things, some of the time. Mortals have to struggle as best they can to acquire what knowledge they can. We see them often wrestling to make sense of oracles, and the gods do not make it easy: there too the narrative emphasis falls on the mindsets of the mortals as they struggle for insight, not of the gods who set the puzzle.[61] A focus on the matters most susceptible to human investigation makes sense, just as on a temporal and spatial level Herodotus concentrates on the nearer periods and regions, however fascinating he acknowledges distant legends and (particularly) distant lands to be.[62] In a way, too, this may recall *Airs Waters Places* and *On the Sacred Disease* (pp. 97–98), in which the acknowledgement of a divine level did not preclude the emphasis from falling on the clinically human, for that is where human inquiry stands the best chance of success.

The gods anyway regularly leave so much to humans to sort out for themselves: even in the great war they are concerned only to equalize the forces to give the Greeks a fair chance (8.13; p. 158) or to intervene momentarily to protect or avenge their own shrines (p. 156). Themistocles may think it prudent to say that "it was not we who won our victory, but the gods and heroes, who felt jealousy (*phthonos*) at the notion that one man might rule over both Asia and Europe, and an impious and outrageous man at that" (8.109.3). Themistocles may even be right about the divine envy, sparse though that idea has been (pp. 156–157)—but the narrative has not led us to believe that "it was not we who won" it *too*.[63] He spoke more accurately, and perhaps less disingenuously, before Salamis: "When people take bad counsel, not even the god tends to help what they are thinking" (8.60γ). The gods, like the heroes, are "allies," no more (7.178.1 of the winds; 8.64.2 of the Aeacidae; 8.143.2 of "the gods and heroes"). When mortals do trust in the gods alone they tend not to prosper, just as the Athenians do not prosper who, trusting in the wooden walls, sit tight in the Acropolis (8.53.2). Moral behavior is certainly no guarantee of survival, nor even of divine goodwill: the Chians at the beginning of book 6 do nothing, it would seem, to deserve their appalling run of bad luck (6.15–16, 27).[64]

Was Focke right, then, and was it Herodotus' belief in the gods that turned him into a historian (above, p. 146)? Maybe—but if so, only in a rather filtered and nuanced way. Belief in the gods may have fostered a belief that all human events may make a sort of sense, even if that "sense" sometimes offended one's moral sensibility (as the gods of tragedy so often behave badly by mortal standards). That "making sense" is a matter of explanation, not justification. But if you believe in the Greek gods, you also believe that there is not much there to be relied on: gods are whimsical in their earthly interventions, except when their own interests are concerned. One may understand in retrospect why they acted, yet it is rare that one can predict that in advance. That balance of explicability without predictability fits comfortably enough in the world of the Greek gods.

A suitable humility finds a home there too:[65] those gods demand and expect deep human thought as we puzzle over their oracular utterances, and we need to accept both that there is insight to be gained and that it is never going to be easy. Herodotus too will puzzle, and expect his readers and hearers to puzzle too, over the complex events he describes, and he allows us to share the different ways of looking at them and making sense of them. There will be times when we too may agree that putting all the mortal clues together is not enough to make us feel that we have got to the answer or indeed to any answer; we can acknowledge the attractions of that intelligently humble honesty. All that said, his primary focus remains those "things that originate from humans," τὰ γενόμενα ἐξ ἀνθρώπων (pp. 23–24). Whether or not that emphasis "really made him a historian," it makes him the historian who lays the path to Thucydides and Polybius.

CHAPTER II

EXPLAINING VICTORY

On the whole, we have so far been exploring reasons why the Persians invaded, and the reasons why they might, sooner or later, be heading for a fall. Some of these centered on court dynamics, some on the nature of imperialism itself, some on the dangers and transience of success, some on the gods. But the Persians did not usually fail:[1] they had not failed in Babylon or in Egypt or against the rebellious Ionians. Many of the audience would recall that they had not failed in another Egyptian campaign in the 450s, one that had ended in humiliation for Athens (p. 218). In Herodotus' narrative there have certainly been setbacks—among the Massagetae, in Scythia, then in Libya—but none has been as spectacular as the one that now looms in Greece. In the early books we might indeed have the impression that the most dangerous enemies are the most "primitive" when judged by Greek standards, especially the Massagetae and the Scythians; ancient and sophisticated civilizations like Babylon and Egypt have fallen much more easily. Are there reasons why it should be this civilized adversary and this campaign that should have delivered that fall for which they were riding? Could it have been any of Persia's victims that turned out to be the victim too far? It is time to make the inquiry less unifocal and extend the gaze to the Greeks' side. Why did they win?

Several possible explanations beckon, and one can find traces of each in the text. Perhaps it is a question of freedom:

"Hydarnes," they said, "your advice [to capitulate] is not given on an equal footing, for you know one of the alternatives but not the other. You know how to be a slave, but you have never yet experienced freedom and seen whether or not it is sweet. If you knew it, you would be telling us to fight for it not just with spears but with axes too."
(THE SPARTAN HERALDS, TALKING TO THE
PERSIAN GOVERNOR HYDARNES, 7.135.3)

Those heralds are in fact making their way to what they (as it turns out, wrongly) assume will be their deaths: they were volunteers to atone for the murder of Persian heralds fifty years earlier.

Or perhaps the explanation is to be sought in the equality that typifies, in particular, democracy, itself coming to be associated with freedom (p. 191). Thucydides' Pericles was later to proclaim a sort of "democratic courage" (2.36.5–46, esp. 39–40, 43).[2] Is that already there in Herodotus?

> It is clearly a universal truth, not just a matter of one single case, that equality of speech (*isēgoriē*) is something to be taken seriously, if the Athenians too were no better in war than any of their neighbors as long as they were under tyrannical rule, but once they were rid of the tyrants became vastly preeminent. That shows that while they were held down (*katechomenoi*)[3] they willingly played the coward because they were working for a master, but once they were free each wanted to achieve something for himself.
> (5.78)

It is true that the emphasis there falls on freedom rather than democracy;[4] it is also true that Athens was exceptional, and most of the cities would indignantly have denied that they were democracies. Still, the whole alliance could in some ways[5] be seen as a sort of democracy of states under Spartan leadership, each city very ready to speak up for itself.

In both the passages cited above we see a mode of argument familiar from earlier chapters, weighing a situation against others that are close enough to be comparable while different in the crucial element. In the Spartans' response the pictured alternative is fictional: "if you were free" but otherwise the same. In Herodotus' own assessment, the comparison is one over time, of the Athenians before and after the expulsion of the Peisistratids. The Spartans create a fictional alternative world; Herodotus compares two scenarios that happened successively in historical fact. When only one variable is altered, one can see in the facts, or speculate in the fiction, how much difference is made. The first technique recalls the great deployment of counterfactuals at 7.139, discussing how much difference it would have made had the Athenians gone over to Xerxes (pp. 42–43): there, as with the Spartans talking about staves and spears, we are in a world of might-have-been. The second is similar to 9.8.2 (p. 6), comparing the Spartans' strategy in 479 with that of a year earlier, where we are again dealing with historical actuality before and after a critical change.

Those two parallel cases of 7.139 and 9.8.2 suggest a further way of explaining victory. Both concern strategy: so is an explanation to be sought not in ideology but on the military level, despite Xerxes' apparently crushing numerical superiority? Did the Greeks simply read the demands of the campaign better? Or was it perhaps their superior tactics, given their weighing of options before choosing to fight at Thermopylae (7.175) or at Salamis (8.56–64, 74) or their deliberations on how to exploit the topography of Plataea (9.51)?

Perhaps, though, it was rather a matter of Greek toughness, bred in a hard land and more than a match for the softness (*habrotēs*) of easterners.

> The barbarians have no courage while you Spartans reach the greatest heights of excellence (*aretē*) in warfare. This is how they fight, with arrows and short spears: and they go into battle wearing trousers on their legs and turbans on their heads. That's how much of a pushover[6] they are.
> (ARISTAGORAS AT SPARTA, 5.49.3–4)

> Greece has always been brought up together with poverty, with excellence (*aretē*) brought in, the product of wisdom and of powerful law: that is how Greece defends itself from poverty and from serving a master.[7]
> (DEMARATUS TO XERXES, 7.102.1)

Demaratus reverts to *nomos*, "law" or "custom," at the end of that encounter, explaining more about how it wards off such despotism:

> They are free, but not free in every way: for over them there is a master, law (ἔπεστι γάρ σφι δεσπότης νόμος), and they fear this even more, far more, than your people fear you. They therefore do what that tells them to do, and it always tells them the same thing, not allowing them to flee in battle no matter how numerous the foe but ordering them to stay in line and to win or to die. And if this seems nonsense to you, I am willing to stay silent in future: I have spoken now because you compelled me.
> (DEMARATUS TO XERXES, 7.104.4–5)

Xerxes laughs:[8] he just does not get it.

There are other aspects of Greek, or at least Spartan, custom—for custom also is embraced within *nomos*—that the king finds equally hard to fathom. Before Thermopylae a scout reports that he has glimpsed the Spartans outside their camp:

> He saw some of the men exercising, some combing their hair. He looked carefully at this and found out their numbers. Having learnt everything in detail, he rode back unmolested, for nobody pursued him or took much attention, and when he got back he reported everything to Xerxes. The king could not make out what was going on, because they were pre-

paring to kill or be killed to the best of their ability. But he thought what was going on was laughable—and so he sent for Demaratus. (7.208.3–209.1)

Demaratus recalls their earlier conversation, just as the reader will: "You made me a laughingstock then, when you heard my prediction of how matters would turn out" (7.209.2). But Xerxes will not be laughing after Thermopylae.

Demaratus was speaking "not about everyone but about the Lacedaemonians alone" (7.102.2; cf. 104.2), and his remarks do show a distinctive Spartan tinge—all that emphasis on kill-or-be-killed and fighting no matter what the odds, perhaps that grim stress on fear.[9] The preparation for Thermopylae is clear. It is a further question how far his words can be extended to the whole of the Greek alliance, and even how far they are true of Sparta itself: more on this later (pp. 172–174).

Other aspects of "custom" are Hellenic, not just Spartan, and these too can be dumbfounding. News arrives in the Persian camp that the Greeks are celebrating the Olympic Games despite the looming threat. What is the prize? An olive crown:

> At that point Tritantaichmes son of Artabanus expressed an opinion of the noblest sort, though in the king's eyes it stamped him as a coward. On discovering that the prize was a crown rather than money, he could not keep silent but said for all to hear, "Oh, Mardonius! What sort of men have you brought us to fight, when they compete not about money but about excellence (*aretē*)!"
> (8.26.2–3)

"Excellence": *aretē* again—and again the king does not understand. One recalls the gulf of misprision that separated Croesus' idea of happiness from that of Solon, though here the focus has shifted to dwell more on honor and "excellence."

Recalling Croesus might suggest a different strand again, for it was after all "the god of the Greeks" that he took to task (1.90.2; p. 111). As the crisis comes, Greek trust in the gods is on a rising curve. At the beginning of the Ionian Revolt Dionysius of Phocaea dares only to hope that the gods might allow an equal playing field, θεῶν τὰ ἴσα νεμόντων (6.11.3); before Marathon Miltiades uses the same words (6.109.5). In the storm before Artemisium that hope was realized, and with a strange literalness: Persian ships are destroyed, and

> everything was done by the god to make the Persian force equal to the Greek rather than much bigger.
> (8.13; ABOVE, P. 158)

But do the gods do more? After Salamis the trust is growing stronger:

> Go and tell Mardonius that this is what the Athenians say: as long as the sun follows its same path in the heavens, we will never come to terms to Xerxes. We will go out to fight, trusting in gods as our allies and the heroes, whom he scorned when he burnt their dwellings and statues. (8.143.2)

Is this, then, one of those cases where, try though one may to find an adequate explanation, one eventually has to assume that Heaven was at work (chapter 10)?[10] Are the Greek gods on the Greek side, and are they enough to win?

So there is no shortage of ideas, and any Greek listener or reader in search of triumphalism and self-celebration could find plenty to make the heart sing: how great to be the champions of freedom, of democracy, of self-expression, of honor; how good to be the tough ones, how good to scorn greed; how fine, and how appropriate, to be the favorites of Heaven. Aren't we simply *better* than them, and isn't that explanation enough?

We have seen enough earlier in the book to doubt whether matters can be quite so simple, and we shall see more. The events regularly play out in a way that complicates all of those views. Still, one further lesson from earlier chapters is that simple views can be overlaid or renuanced, but that does not mean that they are wholly contentless. There is something, no doubt, in all of those approaches that will survive, no matter what the buffeting offered them by the often paradoxical, often grimy, often inglorious reality of what actually happened. We have learnt too not to expect monocausality: this is a world, and this is an author, very comfortable with causes in combination (chapter 6). Sometimes they can be ranked in order, sometimes the machinery of their combination can be tracked—but sometimes they just are all there, sitting comfortably alongside one another.

A final lesson has been not to expect explanations to be determinist: even when events turn out to fit a familiar pattern, that pattern was always a *potential* for recurrence, not one that was certain to come again. Time and again, it could easily have been so different. The decision to fight at Salamis was taken by a hair's breadth. Plataea might have gone the other way. Many of the conditions operating in 490 and 480–479 were already in place for the battle of Lade in 494: then too freedom was at stake; then too the Greeks had a savvy commander; then too the Persian fleet had a numerical superiority, though a less impressive one than later at Salamis; then too there was division and dissent among the Greeks. Yet Lade was an overwhelming Persian triumph. So might Marathon have been; so might Plataea.[11] Unpredictability, though, to remind ourselves again of that mantra, does not mean inexplicability; any or all of these strands of explanation for victory can still have purchase, and most of them do.

The qualifications remain important, and so let us revisit those categories in reverse order. First, the gods. Many of the complexities here are already familiar from the preceding chapter: it may be that one finally cannot escape bringing in divinity, but looking at the human level comes first. Even those confident claims at the end of book 8 have a strong human dimension, for the emphasis falls on the obligation that the gods lay upon the humans. There can be no thought of collaboration with the enslaver of Greece:

> There are many great obstacles forbidding us to do that even if we wished. First and greatest there are the statues and dwellings of the gods that have been burnt and destroyed: we have an obligation to do our best to avenge them rather than make terms with the man who did these things. Then there is Greekness, a matter of common blood and common language and the shrines of the gods and the sacrifices and the similar customs that we share. For Athenians to betray all this would not be good. (8.144.2)

The gods and heroes will fight beside them as their allies (*summachoi*), comrades to inspire trust (8.143.2; p. 161). But it is still the humans who have a free decision whether to "betray" or not, even if that choice is for the moment presented as one that they are bound to make one way. A little later, though, the Athenians speak as if they are going to decide the opposite, telling the Spartans that they will take thought for their own safety unless an army is sent to relieve them (9.6–8). That may well be bluff—the Athenian women's response to Lycidas when he proposed coming to terms had been to stone his family to death (9.5), and that does not suggest half-heartedness[12]—but the Spartans find it credible (9.9–10). The emphasis falls firmly on the human side, and on the Athenians' shifting rhetoric as well as on what they may believe.

That "trust" in the gods still turns out to be justified, but it is important to see why. The Athenians themselves know the answer: it is because Xerxes has destroyed the gods' own shrines. As events unfold we get more unmistakable hints of the gods in action, cautious though Herodotus is in the way he records them (above, pp. 147–149): again, these are mainly cases of gods taking care of their own interests and particularly their dwellings, with Apollo protecting Delphi (8.37–39; p. 147) and Demeter protecting her grove (9.65; p. 148). Once or twice there are hints that gods might help their favored cities, Pan at Marathon, for instance (6.102), or—so the Athenians say—Boreas sending his wind to save Athens (7.189; p. 158).

There is little suggestion, though, of the gods favoring Greece because they are Greeks. After all, Apollo, that "god of the Greeks," was on the Trojan side in the *Iliad*, not the Greek. Plutarch records that Delphi took more of an active role to support the Greeks at Plataea, suggesting the right terrain for the battle (*Arist.* 11): that version of gods as active helpers may well be early,[13] but Herodotus passes over such material in silence. His emphasis falls rather on the gods' concern to punish the sacrilegious Xerxes, and that takes us back to Persian unifocality.

None of this means that the gods were unimportant: they may even have been decisive. But that rests in the unverifiable, appropriate for Herodotus' distinctive diffidence. Gods must never be forgotten, any more than they were in that cautious "second only to the gods" at 7.139 (p. 156). But, as in that passage of Herodotean analysis, the emphasis in his narrative falls on the human sphere, where mortal inquiry and reflection can hope to obtain purchase.

What, then, of Greek values, that concern for honor rather than wealth that so impressed Tritantaichmes (8.26; p. 166) or the toughness and valor that Demaratus thought was necessary to ward off poverty (7.102.1; p. 165)? In fact, the Greeks are hardly impervious to the attractions of wealth, Themistocles least of all when he keeps most of a bribe for himself (8.4.1–5.1) or when he "would not cease from grasping" what is effectively protection money from the allies (8.112). Nor, certainly, are Spartans impervious to a well-directed bribe—Cleomenes, who needs to be stopped by his daughter when tempted by Aristagoras; Leutychidas, caught with a glove full of silver; even the supreme commander in 480 Eurybiades, who happily accepts five talents from Themistocles.[14] The Thebans' advice to Mardonius to "send money around to the powerful men in the cities" in winter 480–479 (9.2.3) was not stupid; it might well have worked,[15] and Mardonius is guilty of "thoughtlessness" or "folly" (*agnōmosunē*, 9.3.1; cf. 9.41.3) when he makes a different choice. "Poverty," then, had less positive results as well as contributing to the valor of which Demaratus was so proud.

Were the Greeks so much tougher than the Persians anyway? The author of *Airs Waters Places* did not think it straightforward: for him the "most warlike people of all" were easterners, both Greeks and barbarians, provided that they were free of tyrannical rule (16 I pp. 114–116 J = II pp. 62–66 L; pp. 19–20). We saw earlier that the last chapter of Herodotus' work was ambivalent too (9.122; pp. 92–93): after all, the last sentence is "the Persians chose to be masters while living in poor country rather than to sow the plain and be other people's slaves"—poor country rather than rich. Aristagoras was dismissive of Persian fancy clothing (5.49.4; pp. 92, 165), but the truth emerged at Marathon. Full marks are awarded to the Athenians for their extraordinary run into battle, for

they were the first to withstand the sight of Median dress and the men who were wearing it: until that time, even the name of the Medes was enough to instill terror.
(6.112.3)

The dress was terrifying, not enfeebling. Eventually, it is true, it turns out to play a part at Plataea, but for a purely practical reason. It was not that it emblematized weakness or lack of courage—the Persians fought very well at Plataea (p. 173), as they had at Salamis (8.86)[16] and went on to do at Mycale (9.102.3)—it was just that it was less fitting for combat than hoplite armor. They were like "naked men fighting hoplites" (9.63.2).[17]

Let us consider another scene that looks as if it will tell an emblematic tale of eastern softness. After Plataea Pausanias is struck by the luxury he discovers in the Persian camp, and he instructs the Persian chefs to prepare the dinner they would cook for Mardonius and the Spartan servants to produce the Spartan equivalent. Then he calls in the Greek generals to look at them (9.82.1–2). The difference is eloquent, but eloquent of what? We might expect Pausanias to draw a conclusion along the lines of "no wonder we won," fighting softies like that.[18] In fact it is more "why on earth did they bother? Was the prospect of meals like this really worth it?" (cf. 9.82.3). That tells a tale about Pausanias, whose own taste for Persian luxury was later to be notorious (pp. 209–210). It also picks up on the wise words of earlier Warners, especially Sandanis at 1.71, advising against campaigns where there is much to lose but little to gain from a poorer culture.[19] That throws the focus firmly back on to the Persian side: unifocality, once again.

Perhaps, then, it was less a matter of toughness, more of superior Greek strategy and tactics, with a better understanding of the demands of the campaign? Yet the point of the passages quoted earlier—7.139 on sea power, 9.8.2 on the Isthmus wall—was that the Greeks, or at least an important part of the high command, did *not* understand the strategic facts: otherwise they would not have pinned so much hope on the Isthmus wall but realized that without control of the sea, the wall was useless. Herodotus knew that (7.139) and so did Chileos of Tegea (9.9)—but the Spartans, and others too, took a lot of convincing. In the event, the Isthmus wall played no part in the outcome.

More important might be the choice to fight at Salamis, protecting the cities that would fall if the Greeks retreated further and exploiting the advantages of joining battle in the narrows, giving the chance to pick off the Persian ships in sequence rather than facing all together. Themistocles makes this explicit at the Greek council:

> Listen to what I say and compare the two options. If you fight by the Isthmus, you will join battle in the open sea, and that is not at all to our

advantage with ships that are less maneuverable and fewer in number. You will also lose Salamis and Megara and Aegina, even if everything else goes well, for the land army will follow the fleet, and thus you will lead them against the Peloponnese: you will be putting all Greece at risk. But if you do what I say, you will find these benefits as a result: first, you will fight in the narrows with few ships against many, and if the combat goes as we might expect we shall win a great victory: fighting in the narrows benefits us, in open water benefits them. Then Salamis is saved, where our children and wives have been evacuated. The point you are most concerned about follows too: if you stay here, you will fight just as much for the Peloponnese as you would at the Isthmus, and if you are sensible you will not draw the enemy towards the Peloponnese. (8.60α–β)

Fine, sensible words, and well geared to their audience, formally the commander Eurybiades (the "you" is singular, except for a plural in the "the point you are most concerned about"), but for all the council to hear:[20] notice the focus on the Peloponnese, with Salamis, Megara, and Aegina treated as if they were adjuncts, people "you" might lose, rather than part of a broader "we." The cramping in the narrows duly goes on to play a part in the victory, though in a way that was not spelled out by Themistocles. When the first ranks of the Persian fleet turned to flight, those behind became entangled with them (8.89.2), compounding the initial disorder as they sailed into battle (8.86).[21]

Still, those tactical considerations did not drive the decision.[22] They are not even Themistocles' prime arguments: what persuades first him and then Eurybiades is that unless they fight here, the Greek force will break up, each city acting for itself (8.57.2, Mnesiphilus to Themistocles; 8.58.2, Themistocles to Eurybiades). It is only because "it would not have been in order (οὐκ ἔφερέ οἱ κόσμον οὐδένα) for him to denounce the allies in their presence" (8.60.1) that he resorts to the tactical argument, which is only his second-best. (*Kosmos*, as we shall see, becomes a keyword in this section of the narrative, both in debate—not that there is much "order" on the Greek side; pp. 183–184—and in battle.)

Nor does the tactical point decide the debate itself: that is settled by Themistocles' threat to sail away to Siris in Italy unless he gets his way (8.62.2). Even after that there is a further failure of nerve (8.70.1), and Themistocles has to short-circuit a further debate by sending Sicinnus to tell Xerxes that the Greeks are planning to "run away in terror" and that this is his chance to forestall them (8.74–5). Both the threat (Siris) and the message (Sicinnus) are all too believable; indeed, Sicinnus' message is largely, not wholly, the truth.[23] There had already been such "scattering" of Greek forces before

Thermopylae, when there had been a similar "splitting" (ἐσχίζοντο) of opinion, and those who did not wish to stay took matters into their own hands (7.219.2). Eventually what brings on the battle is not the tactical advice, wise though it was: it was the threat of Greek fragmentation, with each city free to concentrate so much on its own self-interest. This is not the only time when the worst Greek characteristics, not the best, contribute most to their ultimate success.

What, then, of discipline during combat itself? Was Demaratus more on the mark when he spoke of the Spartan obedience to *nomos*, their readiness to stand their ground and fight or die (7.104.4–5; p. 165)? Nobody could doubt the courage and constancy of the victors of Marathon, nor of the Three Hundred at Thermopylae,[24] nor of those singled out for praise in the summaries at the end of battles (a sort of "mention in dispatches": 7.226–227, 8.17, 9.71–73). At Salamis every commander was proud of what he had done, each indeed thinking that he had been the bravest of all (8.123). It is crucial that the Greek ships keep order—*kosmos*, that word again—when the Persians do not (8.86). But there is also the failure of discipline of the Ionians before and during the first encounter of these Greek wars, the battle of Lade, as they cannot face the prospect of more training under the hot sun (6.12), then suffer desertions in the fighting itself (6.14). Nor, before Marathon, is Miltiades confident that Athenian resolve will last if battle is delayed (6.109.5): more on this later (p. 188).

The most spectacular failure of discipline of all comes before Plataea and is perpetrated by the Spartans themselves, those whom Demaratus was singling out for that obedience to *nomos* (7.102.2 and 7.104.1; p. 166). Pausanias had his reasons for ordering his troops to withdraw and regroup, but one captain, Amompharetus, simply refused: he would not be the one "to flee before the foreigners and disgrace Sparta" (9.53.2). In one way Amompharetus is indeed following *nomos*, that tradition of standing one's ground,[25] but now it is pulling against military discipline rather than reinforcing it: it was not for Amompharetus to second-guess his general's reasoning.

The result is chaos. The Athenians on the other wing see that the Spartans are not doing what they had agreed. This fits all too well their "convictions about the character of the Spartans, men who said one thing and did another" (9.54.1)—that typical distrust of one Greek city for another. Their messenger to the Spartans finds "that their leaders had reached the stage of quarreling with one another" (9.55.1), with Pausanias calling Amompharetus "a madman, quite out of his mind" (9.55.2). Madness has figured before on the Greek side, notably at Sparta itself with Cleomenes and his gruesome end (pp. 159–160)—but that was a local embarrassment, not a cause of danger in the face of the enemy. Then at Marathon the Persians had thought the Greeks—in that case, the Athenians—quite mad for running into battle (6.112.2). They thought the same about the Greek naval attack at Artemisium (8.10.1). But in those cases the Persian perception turned awry, at Marathon terribly so. Here Pausanias' abuse seems all too justified, and Spartans and Athenians alike find themselves in a situation of terrible confusion, desperately moving to and fro as the Persian cavalry engage (9.57). No wonder Mardonius looks on and wonders how all this fits the Lacedaemonian reputation for military preeminence (9.58; p. 182).

Yet, paradoxically, it is this Greek disorder, not any firm and measured stance at the battle's outset, that helps them to victory: it prompts Mardonius to instruct the Persians to "cross the river Asopus at a run" (δρόμῳ, 9.59.1) in a strange reversal of Marathon, prompting the rest of his army as well to lose their own order as they follow (9.59.2). So this is a further case where it is a Greek failing, not a strength, that contributes more to a crucial victory. It is still a near-run thing, with the Persians "not inferior in spirit and strength" to the Greeks (no lack of toughness there, 9.62.3). It is only when Mardonius himself falls that the tide turns (9.63). But whatever decides that battle, it is not Greek strategy and it is not Greek discipline.

Once again, though, to qualify is not to reject. There is plenty to suggest that Greece has rather less to be proud about and that it could all have been so very different. But yes, the gods may still have played a part; yes, Persians would have done better if they had been armed less prettily; yes, Themistocles knew what he was about; yes, there was maritime orderliness at Salamis; yes, there were Greek heroics on the battlefield; and yes, they were pretty tough, even if the Persians were tough too. And we still have our first two categories to explore more thoroughly: freedom and democracy. These are important enough to deserve chapters of their own.

CHAPTER 12

FREEDOM

(A) INSPIRATION

Day, borne on white horses, came over the land, clear to see. First came a sound of joyful song from the Greeks, and the echo sang out loud in reply from the island rocks. Fear came over all the barbarians, for their judgment had proved false: for there was no hint of flight as the Greeks then sounded their solemn battle hymn, but they surged forward to battle in confident good cheer. The trumpet blared, inflaming it all. A moment later came the sound of babbling oars as they struck the surface and sent the foam flying from the deep as the boatswain called the rhythm. Quickly they were all clear to see: first the right flank led the way, disciplined (εὐτάκτως) and in good order (κόσμῳ), then the whole fleet came out against us, and a great cry could be heard together: "Come, children of the Greeks! Free your country, free your children and the seats of your ancestral gods and the graves of your forefathers! Now everything is at stake." A babbling in the Persian tongue met them from our side, and it was no longer a moment for delay.
(AESCH. PERS. 391–407)

Thus spoke the messenger in Aeschylus' *Persians*, telling the Queen and court of the beginning of the débâcle of Salamis. It is highly visual—the daybreak creeping over the land, the "inflaming," the flying foam, the Greek ships coming into view—but the sense of sound is just as important: the joyful song, the echoing rocks, the battle hymn, the trumpet, the confused "babbling" of the Persian language that echoed the "babbling" of the Greek oars, the proud words uttered perhaps by the Greeks themselves or perhaps, as in the report recorded by Herodotus (8.84.2), by a supernatural voice. Aeschylus gives a modern-day turn to the start of the fighting in the *Iliad*, where the excited birdlike clamor of the Trojans as they go into battle contrasts with, there, the grim, purposeful silence of the Greeks (*Il.* 3.1–9; p. 145). Here as there, one side is already looking and sounding like the winners. The emphasis on Greek order recurs in Herodotus, as we saw (p. 172), but in Aeschylus the culmination is not silence but that cry. Cry freedom!

So what about this freedom, so clearly in Aeschylus contrasting with the "slavery" and "subjection" and "yokes" that have typified the world and ambitions of Xerxes?[1] Is this, as a distinguished scholar has claimed, for Herodotus too the most powerful explanation of all?[2] And if Salamis prefigures the outcome of the whole war, rather as Hector's death prefigures the fall of Troy (*Il.* 22.410–411),[3] does it also suggest that freedom is the reason why the Greeks won?

Those words of the Spartan heralds live in the memory: if you knew freedom as we know freedom, Hydarnes, you would tell us to fight for it not just with spears but with axes (7.135.3; p. 163). But in fact freedom was not only a western taste any more than tyranny was confined to the East,[4] and Herodotus knew it. So, once again, did the author of *Airs Waters Places*, drawing attention to those easterners, both Greeks and barbarians, who were independent of tyranny and were "the most warlike of all" [16 I pp. 114–116 J = II pp. 62–66 L; pp. 19–20]. In Herodotus the Medes had themselves set the pattern as they rid themselves of the yoke of Assyria, "in one way or another (κως)" showing themselves "good men as they fought for liberty: they thrust off slavery and were freed" (1.95.2). That κως, "in one way or another," marks an inferential reconstruction;[5] the detail was evidently irrecoverable, but Herodotus infers that this is the way it must have been, and similar language will recur when the focus switches to the west (5.2.1, of the Perinthians; 5.109.2–3, of the Cypriotes). Then Cyrus knew the right way to round off his deft ploy with the day of toil and the day of banqueting: "Now follow me and become free" (1.126.5; cf. p. 93). The Persians duly "took him as their champion and won their freedom, long since resenting being ruled by the Medes" (1.127.1), and the Medes are now the ones to be the "slaves" rather than the masters (1.129.3–4; cf. 1.120.5). This was Cyrus' great achievement: "You have made the Persians free instead of slaves," Darius' father Hystaspes tells Cyrus, "and rulers of everyone rather than ruled by others" (1.210.2). Darius himself uses it as his clinching argument in the constitutions debate, as he sums up the merits of monarchy as opposed to the alternative possibilities of democracy and oligarchy:

> Let me summarize everything in just a single word. What was the source of our freedom? Who gave it to us? Was it a *dēmos*, or was it an oligarchy, or was it a monarch? My proposal then is that, as a single man gave us our freedom, we should continue that same principle; and, besides, that we should not abandon our traditions when they are good ones. For that way lies harm.
> (3.82.5)

Those cases suggest a further point: that once one has freed oneself one does not stop there but goes on to try to assert oneself over others in a "sequence of empires." That too, as we shall see (pp. 185–186), is not confined to the East.

Removal of freedom is also a theme from early on, with a clear indication of what it means:

> Croesus was the first barbarian we know of who reduced some of the Greeks to paying tribute, and made some others his friends. . . . Before the rule of Croesus, all the Greeks were free.
> (1.6.2–3)

That imposition of tribute is clearly an important step, an important escalation from mere ravaging expeditions;[6] such an imposition recurs with the Scythians when they expand at the Medes' expense, though with their ranging nomadic existence they did a fair amount of ravaging too (1.106.1).

Losing one's freedom, though, amounts to much more than a financial obligation. Both Herodotus and especially his characters regularly cite "slavery," *doulosunē*, as the real or anticipated consequence of conquest,[7] and—once again—not just in the East.[8] True, this is affected by the Greek preconception that everyone in the Persian empire, perhaps the whole world,[9] was regarded as the king's "slaves," including grandees as great as Pythius (7.39.1), Mardonius (8.102.3), and indeed Hydarnes himself, the man who according to the Spartan heralds "knew only the one alternative, slavery" (7.135; p. 163).[10] The degree of slavery doubtless varied greatly even at a much lower level.[11] In most cases it would be enough to acknowledge suzerainty, pay tribute, and contribute military service when required; in others it could be a matter of wholesale deportation, as was threatened for Athens and happened at Eretria (6.94.2 and 119), or at least of the selection of the best-looking girls for removal to, presumably, a harem, while the most handsome boys were castrated (the Ionians at 6.32).

The urge to empire is taken as natural and expected (pp. 136–137), but when it leads to success, it can easily go further, with a danger of "injustice." Thus Croesus' moves against the Greeks can be regarded as "unjust deeds," *adika erga* (1.5.3; pp. 28, 106), with the king fabricating justifications in cases where he had no substantial grievance (1.26.3; pp. 7–8). The king of the Ethiopians accuses Cambyses similarly: there is no way that he can be a just man, enslaving as he does people from whom he has suffered no wrong (3.21.2).

Similar thinking underlies the response of neighboring kings to the Scythians when these neighbors were asked for assistance against Darius: they would have given help had the Scythians not been the first to *adikeein*, for they had launched an unprovoked invasion of Persia; as it is, the Persians had due cause to do the same to the Scythians now that they could (4.119).[12] Astyages' resentful rebuke of Harpagus again dwells on the notion of due cause: he had his own reason to avenge Astyages, but he should not have enslaved his own people (the Medes) to the Persians, as they had no share in what Astyages had done (1.129). Artabanus then advises Xerxes against leading the Ionians against Athens, for "either they would have to be the most unjust of humans if they enslaved their mother-city or the most just if they joined in freeing it" (7.51.2): predictably, Xerxes is unmoved. Themistocles rebukes the Ionians in similar terms for "campaigning against their fathers and seeking to enslave Greece" (8.22.2).[13]

Those criticisms do not go so far as to imply that *any* conquest or even any enslavement is immoral:[14] it is doing so without a grievance that is unacceptable, imposing that yoke on one's own kin or on people who have done nothing to provoke it.[15] And Herodotus is very ready to give credit to conquerors and even tyrants—when they deserve it, and so often they do not.[16]

Nobody could be expected to welcome such aggression when it was heading in one's own direction, and what is morally bad is to offer no resistance. Contempt for those who give in too easily can come from all quarters: from the Egyptian Sesostris, who on his victory inscriptions added female genitalia under the names of those peoples who gave in too quickly (2.102.5); from the Scythians, who called the Ionians "if they were free, the most disgraceful and cowardly men alive, or if they were to be counted as slaves, the most master-loving slaves of all and most reluctant to run away" (4.142);[17] from the Greeks, with accusations of cowardice at Salamis furiously thrown and strongly rebutted (8.94), with cities' retrospective attempts to cover up the shame of missing Plataea (9.85.3), and with a swift move to exact retribution from the Medizing Thebans (9.86–88).

There are limits: the children of the Theban arch-Medizer Attaginus can be excused, for Pausanias proclaims that "children had no share at all in responsibility for the Medism" (τοῦ μηδισμοῦ παῖδας οὐδὲν εἶναι μεταιτίους, 9.88; cf. p. 7). The power of necessity is also acknowledged (just as it was in Homer, *Od.* 22.351–353, 356, and in sophistic oratory, p. 72), and when the Greeks swore an oath to sacrifice one in ten of the Medizers, they explicitly excused those that had no choice (ἀναγκασθέντες, 7.132).[18] Thus, people such as the Thessalians, left unprotected in the path of Xerxes' advance, are acknowledged to be acting out of "necessity" (7.172.1, 3); so are the Phocians, "Medizing not because they wanted to but because they had to" (9.17.1). It can still be noted that the Thessalians went on to Medize "no longer hesitantly but enthusiastically[19] . . . so that it became clear that they were most useful to the king as events developed" (7.174; cf. 7.138.2). It does not sound as if the historian approved.

For Herodotus does not conceal his own feelings. The states that chose to resist are, uncompromisingly, "those that took the better view about Greece" (7.145.1). When Cleomenes moves against the Medizing Aeginetans, he is "laying the preliminaries for the good of Greece" (6.61.1; p. 188); the Athenians' refusal to go over to Persia made them the "saviors of Greece," and he knows that other states will resent such praise (7.139; pp. 42–43). His sentiments are also clear when he lists the Peloponnesian cities that sent help for the Salamis campaign: Sparta, all Arcadia, Elis, Corinth, Sicyon, Epidaurus, Phlious, Troezen, and Hermion: "The rest of the Peloponnesians did not care. The Olympia and Carneia had already happened" (8.72)—that last phrase eliminating the possible excuse that they were delayed by a festival as the Spartans had been at Marathon (6.106, 120). He then lists the seven "races" of the Peloponnese: "Of these seven races the rest of the cities, apart from the ones I have listed, remained neutral. If I may speak freely, by remaining neutral they were in fact Medizing" (8.73.3). That "freely," *eleutherōs*, carries an edge.

In other cases too his sharpest criticisms are directed at those whose behavior lets others down who are keen to fight for the common cause. "There was nothing healthy in the Eretrians' thinking" when they called for Athenian help despite being still divided among themselves, some wishing to take to the hills and some to betray the city for private gain (6.100.1–2): either way, the four thousand Athenians who were sent would have been left to fight the Persians alone. Credit goes to the Eretrian Aeschines who warned the Athenians and told them to depart (6.100.3). It is the duplicity, not the Medizing itself, that is there so bad:[20] there are no harsh words just before at the expense of the Carystians, who swiftly gave up their words of defiance, only some wry irony as "they came around to the Persian way of thinking" (6.99.2).

Even when there was more choice involved, Herodotus understands the immense risks involved in taking on Persia's might. To do so was "folly" for the Ionian rebels, *agnōmosunē*, a failure to use one's *gnōmē* or thought processes (6.10); Mardonius thought in the same terms of the Athenians if they were to fight on in 479 once their territory was in his hands (9.4.2), though by then he is guilty of some "folly" of his own (9.3.1; p. 169). Herodotus had used the same word of the Aeginetans when they rebelled from Epidaurus in a further intercity quarrel (5.83.1), and of the Getae when they resisted Darius' advance and were immediately "enslaved" (4.93). But even there he had applauded the Getae, these "bravest and most righteous" of the Thracians (ἀνδρηιότατοι καὶ δικαιότατοι), for choosing to fight. The Ionians too who took up the fight at Lade win his respect, especially the Chians who "performed brilliantly in the battle and did not play the coward" (6.15.1; cf. 14.1). If this was folly, it was folly of the most glorious sort.[21]

The Athenians, we saw, fought so much better once they were free, because now each man was achieving something for himself rather than working for a master (5.78, quoted at p. 164). But, just as a taste for freedom is found in the East as well as the West, so the Greek commitment to freedom is itself variable: Peisistratus found support among those "who welcomed tyranny more than freedom" (1.62.1); when in 480 the Argives were not offered a partnership with the Spartans on the terms they wanted, "they say ... that they chose to be ruled by barbarians rather than making any concession to the Spartans" (7.149.3); and the Ionians, initially inspired by Dionysius of Phocaea's freedom rhetoric, soon wilt when forced to train under the scorching sun, saying to one another that "it is better to put up with the coming slavery, whatever it may be, than to continue with this one that we have now" (6.12.3). That is not too different from the behavior of the Median nobility, ready to abandon to the Persians their freedom in order to escape from Astyages' ruthlessness: "Later, however, they regretted what they had done and revolted from Darius, only to be defeated once again in battle" (1.130.1–2).

The most elaborate and thought-provoking case is that of Samos, in turmoil after the fall of Polycrates. In Herodotus' version,[22] rule passes to a certain Maeandrius. Wanting to be "the most just of men," he sets up an altar to "the Zeus of Freedom," Zeus Eleutherios, and proclaims a free state: "I did not approve of Polycrates when he was master of men who were similar to himself, nor do I approve of anyone else who does that" (3.142). Instead he will place power "into the middle," *es meson*, and establish *isonomiē*, "equality with regard to the law" (3.143.2)—both democratic slogans, and we shall return to those democratic aspects later (p. 191). But Maeandrius' gesture turns into a shambles. A prominent Samian called Telesarchus springs to his feet: "You are not worthy to be our ruler, you low-born, ruinous creature: you ought rather to be looking to render account for the money you got your hands on" (3.144.5). No word of freedom there. Maeandrius realizes that if he gives up control someone else would seize the tyranny, so he resorts to more conventional tyrannical means, tricking his local enemies into his power and imprisoning them (3.143.1). A nasty family tangle develops between Maeandrius and his brothers; the prisoners are killed; the Persians arrive with their own nominee for power; the result is a particularly bloody Persian takeover (pp. 124–125). A final irony is that it is imposed by Otanes, that champion of democracy in the constitutions debate (3.147).

"The Samians, so it seems, did not want to be free," acidly comments

Herodotus (3.143.1). Perhaps that is a wry way of saying that they were incapable of the resolve and self-restraint necessary for managing freedom; perhaps he means it literally—they would prefer a tyrant, though hardly one imposed in this uncompromising way; or perhaps it is shorthand for "they were not ready," "they did not want freedom *enough*."[23] In any case, it is no way to take on the might of Persia.

Still, many Greek states certainly did "want to be free." Herodotus' readers too may thrill to such stirring words as the Athenians utter at the end of book 8 to Mardonius' messenger Alexander of Macedon, cataloging all those bonds that tie the Greeks together (8.144.2; p. 168):

> We ourselves know that the Mede has many times larger a force than we do: there is no need to be rude to us about that. But still we shall strive for freedom and fend him off as best we can. Do not try to persuade us to make terms with the barbarian: we will not be persuaded. Now go and tell Mardonius that this is what the Athenians say: as long as the sun follows its same path in the heavens, we will never come to terms to Xerxes. . . . Be very clear about it, if you did not realize it before: as long as a single Athenian remains alive, we shall never make terms with Xerxes. (8.143.1–2, 144.3)

And Alexander says nothing more—not yet. He is allowed a further vignette before Plataea, where he rides up to the Greek camp at dead of night (a sort of Sicinnus in reverse: cf. 8.75), giving them the important information that Mardonius is about to run out of food (9.44–45). That suggests that, at least in Herodotus' eyes, he was motivated by genuine concern for the Greeks: "I am myself Greek by ancient descent and I would not want to see Greece enslaved instead of free," he says (9.45.2). We should probably take that at face value while also understanding why Alexander's Greek hearers might have their suspicions.[24]

We have heard before of Alexander's parading of Greek descent, when he made a scene, and won it, about his eligibility to compete at the Olympic games (5.22). And Alexander, of all people, should understand how deep a taste for freedom can go. He had shown it himself when—so Herodotus tells us—some Persian envoys were behaving with appalling crassness at his father's court, demanding the presence of women at a banquet and assuming that these respectable ladies were to be available for their postprandial pleasure. Alexander had taken action, replacing the women by some young friends who turned out to be less available, and indeed less female, than the Persians had expected: the envoys were killed, along with their retinue (5.17–20). Their disappearance left the Macedonians in terrible danger, though Alexander then had the deftness to deal with it by sending a well-judged bribe (5.21).[25]

If even a man like that has come by the end of book 8 to think that the Athenians would do well to make terms, this too underlines the risk they are taking. Readers and listeners will admire them the more for taking it, and if they thrill to the freedom rhetoric, they will understand why the Athenians did so: this is a simpler version of that "mimetic" readerly experience that we noted with Croesus (pp. 112–113) and with Xerxes' and Artabanus' dreams (pp. 155–156), with an audience's emotions coming to mirror those of the people in the story. Then Herodotus constructs his following narrative in such a way that even the appearance of backtracking, when the Athenians tell the Spartans that they will make terms after all (9.6, 9.11.1), does not destroy that admiration. If there is duplicity here, the assumption is more likely to be that they are disingenuous in what they say now to the Spartans than in what they had replied to Alexander (p. 168).[26]

So inspiration? Yes. But, again, there is another side to it.

(B) THE UNRULY FREE

We have seen some of that other side already when looking at Greek order and discipline (pp. 172–173). When everyone is "achieving something for himself," it is understandable that all will indeed pursue their own interests or at least their own view of what is right. Even Amompharetus was right by his own lights at Plataea (p. 172), but it is no way to run an army. In that exchange with Demaratus, Xerxes too is talking sense:

> Come, let us be reasonable. How could a thousand, ten thousand, even fifty thousand oppose an army as big as this, given that they are all alike free and are not ruled by a single man? We outnumber them by more than a thousand to one, as they number five thousand. If they were under a single ruler as we are, there is a chance that they might be so afraid of him that they would outstrip their own nature and go against a larger enemy force when driven forward by the whip. But as it is, they are let loose to be free, and would not do either.
>
> (7.103.3–4)

Xerxes is thinking in Persian, as that mention of the whip shows. That is a Persian specialty,[27] fitting that assumed ideology that regarded all the king's subjects as slaves and therefore whipping boys.[28] To use it is such second nature that Xerxes even orders the Hellespont itself to be whipped, with "barbarian and outrageous" words as accompaniment (7.35; cf. 7.54.3). Whips are duly used at Thermopylae, with disastrous effect: they contribute to the confusion as the rear ranks are whipped forward and get tangled up with those in front (7.223). Xerxes is also wrong about his enemy's vulnerability, for the reasons that Demaratus gives. But he is not *that* wrong.[29] Herodotus had said something similar himself about the Thracians, the most numerous nation except for the Indians: "If it were ruled by one man or could achieve unanimity, in my opinion it would be invincible and the most powerful of all" (5.3.1).[30] Xerxes is right about the cohesion that only an unquestioned chief command can give, just as he will be right in claiming that his own presence makes a difference to his men's discipline and courage (8.69.2; cf. 8.86); he is simply wrong about the reasons why the absence of a single command would be a weakness on the Greek side, not so much in any reluctance to fight as in a difficulty in getting a unified direction either of strategy or of tactics. It is an understandable mistake: Mardonius gets it wrong similarly, noticing the chaos among the Spartans at Plataea and inferring that it is because of cowardice rather than of the commanders' disagreement (9.58).

There Mardonius thought they were "running away," *diadrantas* (9.58.2), and he was wrong. The phrase, however, picks up on a broader "running away," *drēsmos*, that has been in the air for some time, a matter of strategy rather than tactics or indiscipline. In that case, it is an unfriendly way of referring to the option of retreating southwards, ultimately into the Peloponnese; but it is not only the policy's opponents who describe it like that but also Herodotus himself (8.4.1, 8.18, 8.23.1, 8.60.1, 8.75.2, 8.80.2). The word seems pejorative when used of Aristagoras (5.124.1);[31] it would now be a paradoxical sequel to the glorious "running" (*dromos*) into battle at Marathon (6.112.1), especially as now, figuratively, "they are running the race on which the whole issue will depend" (*dromos* again, 8.74.1). That paradox, though, is itself symptomatic of that perpetual tension in this coalition of the free: free to run into action, free too to run away. But it does not happen. The one who runs away is Xerxes, and this again is described in the same terms (8.97.1, 8.100.1). Yet at Lade, at the start of it all, it had been the Greeks who deliberately played the coward, or many of them (6.13–14). That could so easily have happened again.

The way people speak is, as so often in Herodotus, most telling (as are the constraints on speaking:[32] one remembers Demaratus' reluctance to speak openly, 7.101.3 and 7.104.1, 5; pp. 138, 165).[33] When Alexander comes with his message at the end of book 8, he is delivering from Mardonius an offer sent down by the king:[34] it is a message within a message within a message, with the boundaries of each carefully marked (8.140). The hierarchical pyramid is clear. The Greek response is in strong contrast: the Athenians wait for the Spartans, let them have their say, and then speak out frankly and freely—and for themselves (8.143–144). This is freedom at its best, and the substance of what the Athenians say lives up to its delivery (p. 180).

Still, speaking out frankly and freely can have a downside too, and earlier in the book the debate before Salamis has shown it.[35] There too we have a contrast between the Greek and the Persian manner. The Persian council of war is a model of order and discipline,[36] not without a strong element of inhibition. It starts with the counselors sitting quietly in order (κόσμῳ ἐπεξῆς ἵζοντο, 8.67.2), each in the place assigned by the king, and continues with Mardonius asking their opinions in turn (8.68.1). Most give the answer that they know Xerxes wants; Artemisia alone speaks out in opposition, speaking good sense but tailoring it diplomatically to the king's sensibilities.[37] Even so, everyone expects her to suffer for it, with some delighted by the prospect and some distressed (8.69.1). This is again the air of a court, so familiar from earlier in the narrative (chapters 8–9).

There is something of the same even when it is not the king but the general Mardonius who is reluctant to take advice:[38] "When he expressed that view, nobody spoke again, so that he carried the day: for he was in command, not Artabazus" (9.42.1). In a melancholy dinner conversation at Thebes, a man from Orchomenus asks a Persian fellow-guest why, if disaster is clearly looming, nobody tells Mardonius and the Persian grandees about it. The reply is that they will not listen, no matter how persuasive the argument: "Many of us Persians know the truth and follow because we must" (9.16.4). Authoritarianism seeps down the hierarchy. It does not foster open and honest disclosure of one's views.

The Greek debate before Salamis could not be more different. Themistocles knows he cannot tell the truth about the danger of fragmentation, for that would not have been "in order" (οὐκ ἔφερέ οἱ κόσμον οὐδένα, 8.60.1)—"order," *kosmos*, that keyword again (pp. 171, 172). There is not much that is "orderly" in the debate itself. Eurybiades had summoned it, but before he even states the topic, "Themistocles flooded the place with words" (πολλὸς ἦν ὁ Θεμιστοκλέης ἐν τοῖσι λόγοισι, 8.59).[39] Adeimantus of Corinth scornfully rebukes him—"athletes who break too soon are whipped"—but Themistocles is uncowed: "Those who are left behind don't win any crown." He puts forward his strategic argument, second-best though it is (p. 171). Adeimantus jumps in again even as he speaks,[40] telling him to keep silent now that he is a man without a city (for Athens had been occupied) and urging Eurybiades not to put it to the vote. Themistocles' retort is less gentle this time: he showers abuse on the Corinthians (all the Corinthians, not just Adeimantus) and tells them he has a city and a land greater than theirs as long as he has two hundred ships, for no Greeks could resist them if they attacked (8.61.2). Then his threat to decamp to Siris (8.62.2; p. 171) abruptly terminates the debate. It seems that the decision is not even put to the vote, even though this was clearly what Adeimantus had expected: "Eurybiades . . . chooses that proposal, to stay there and fight it out at sea . . . Now that Eurybiades had decided . . ." (8.63–64.1).[41] Perhaps this was just as well, for the multiplicity of voices and of self-interested views has made it unlikely that the right strategy would be followed.

The whole debate has been a mess: Herodotus' own word for it is *akrobolisamenoi*, "skirmishing" (8.64.1). Nor, in any case, is it the last word, for the Greek nerve will break, and the debate will be reopened (8.70.2, 8.74; p. 171): this time it is described as a "great pushing and shoving of words," ὠθισμὸς λόγων πολλός, 8.78), a phrase that will recur in the arguing before Plataea over the place of honor in the battle line (9.26.1). These are military terms: the Greeks are wasting their bellicosity on words. *Logos*—frank, open, constructive exchange of arguments—is travestied just as much on the Greek side as on the Persian, though the travesties are tellingly different.[42] *Isēgoriē* can well be contrasted with tyranny, but this exchange shows what happens when "equal speaking" gets out of hand.

Nor is this the end of the bad-mouthing, for there are recriminations after the battle too. "The Athenians" there accuse Adeimantus and "the Corinthians" of cowardice, fleeing from the battle in its early stages (8.94–95): plural nouns for both the abusers and the abused, just as Themistocles accused "the Corinthians" and not merely Adeimantus in the debate. "The rest of Greece" supports the Corinthians in denying the charge (8.94.4), but its truth is again less significant than the bad feeling that the episode betrays. So again "blame" carries more explanatory force because it is the characters who do the blaming, not the narrator (cf. chapter 2[d] and pp. 123–128).

Admittedly, not all the verbal exchanges of civic pride were so acrimonious. There are fierce disagreements about who had fought the best at Salamis (8.123), but at least every voter puts Themistocles second after putting himself first, and Sparta crowns him with unparalleled acclaim (8.124). That second "pushing and shoving of words" before Plataea clearly matters greatly, and it means a lot to Athens to be given a place of honor ahead of Tegea (9.26–28.1); but neither side contends the right of the Spartans to the most honorable place of all, and the Athenians finish their speech by a dignified statement of readiness to submit to the Spartans' judgment and accept whatever station they are granted (9.27.6). They had already done the same the year before in ceding command of the fleet to Sparta, despite their overwhelmingly greater contribution in ships (8.3).[43] Herodotus' first audiences might reflect that such mutual goodwill and restraint had not survived to their own day.

(C) FREEDOM FROM AND FREEDOM TO

There is more to say about those angry words of Themistocles in the Salamis debate: his city was greater than the Corinthians', for with two hundred ships no Greeks could resist their attack. Fighting words, indeed; and "no Greeks," not "no Persians" or even "no enemy." The ships' value for the here and now is not neglected: "the whole war depends on the ships," Themistocles tells Eurybiades (8.62.1). But that idea of fighting against Greeks glances ahead, and in a different direction. Perhaps it looks forward no further than to that threat to leave and go to Siris, but then Themistocles also stresses that "Siris is ours from ancient times" (8.62.2), and we might expect a city of kin to be welcoming and violence to be unnecessary.[44] Maybe it is simply the language of the kindergarten playground: my city can beat your city any time it likes. Yet it looks forward further too, to times when the "skirmishing" and the "pushing and shoving" go beyond words and become real. This is not the only time in the *Histories* when it is highly relevant that the animosity of Corinth and Athens was central to the precipitation of the Peloponnesian War.[45]

Such a future was hinted at 5.78 itself, ". . . the Athenians too were no better in war than any of their neighbors as long as they were under tyrannical rule, but once they were rid of the tyrants, became vastly preeminent" (p. 164). "Vastly preeminent," literally, "by far the first":[46] excessive language for the moment, but that is the path on which the Athenians are headed. The Spartans are soon fearing something similar, though they put it, naturally enough, in terms only of equipollence. That is frightening enough:

> The Spartans knew the oracles and could see that the Athenians were not at all willing to defer to them, now that they were growing more powerful; they reflected that if it was free the Attic race could become as powerful as their own, but if held down (*katechomenon*)[47] by a tyranny would be weak and obedient . . .
> (5.91.1)

Thanks to Soclees, their proposal to reinstate the Peisistratids is rebuffed: but the Corinthians are warned, rather magnificently, that they will learn the lesson all too well, when they will be the ones to miss the Peisistratids more than anyone else. Once again, the brushes between Corinth and democratic Athens in the 430s will be in the audience's mind.[48]

Even the inspirational words of Miltiades before Marathon tell the same tale. All depends on the polemarch Callimachus:

> This is the greatest crisis the Athenians have ever faced. If they bow down before the Medes, their fate has already been decided. They will be handed over to Hippias. But if this city survives, it can become the first city of all Greece. . . . If you come over to my view, you have a city that is free and the first among the cities of Greece; but if you choose the pro-

posal of those who want to avoid fighting, you will have the opposite of every good thing that I have said.
(6.109.3, 6)

For freedom is a continuum. As 5.78 makes clear, once you have cast off the yoke of subjection to others, you do not stop there but go on to dominate others:[49] that quest for empire, we remember, is natural. One force destroying freedom is the drive for freedom itself, as one nation's freedom becomes another's slavery.

The idea is by no means new in the *Histories*. We saw it in the sequence of Medes and Persians in book 1 (p. 175); we saw it when Bias of Priene proposed that the Ionians should sail away to Sardinia and found a single city there, and thus "prosper, freed from slavery, living in the largest island of all and ruling others" (1.170.2).[50] We will see it again in the closing chapter of the *Histories*, where the choice facing the Persians is one between ruling and being ruled (9.122; pp. 92–93). It is the world of Gorgias in Plato, defining the greatest good as persuasion, "responsible (*aition*) both for people's own freedom and for their rule over others in their own city" (*Gorg.* 452d). It is the world too, extending beyond one's own city, of Thucydides' Diodotus, speaking of "the greatest things of all, freedom or rule over others" (Thuc. 3.45.6); and of the bilious so-called "Old Oligarch," impatient with the *dēmos* who "want to be free and to rule" rather than be "slaves in a well-ordered city" (Ps.-Xen. *Ath. Pol.* 1.8). In a favorite modern formulation, "freedom from" has developed into "freedom to":[51] freedom from others' domination becomes the freedom to do what one likes, and there is no thought that one free people ought to respect the freedom of another.[52] Three centuries later Polybius would know what this would lead to: musing on the Peloponnesian past, he finds it explicable that there has been so little peace.

> It is no surprise that this has been their experience: for all[53] who are natural rulers and lovers of freedom fight one another incessantly, not yielding an inch as they struggle for primacy.
> (5.106.5)

Is there any suggestion that Athenian imperialism will be any less brutal than the Persian, or any more welcome to the other Greek states? That is a question to which we shall return (p. 231).

What will give Athens so many opportunities, just as it now gives Persia, is that Greek fragmentation. When Persian forces are there in arms, the antagonisms are just a matter of words, though they still compromise the alliance. We remember those Phocians and Thessalians, one of whom was certain to Medize because the other would not (8.30.2; p. 44). It will not take much for the hostility to burst into arms once that external constraint disappears and each state is really "free" to act in its own way.

There are many hints of that bloody future in books 7–9 (chapter 15), but we already know what is coming even before the glories of Marathon:

> For under the reigns of Darius son of Hystaspes and Xerxes son of Darius and Artaxerxes son of Xerxes, those three generations, more evils befell Greece than in the twenty generations that preceded Darius, some coming from the Persians and some from the head Greeks themselves fighting for the empire (ἀπ' αὐτῶν τῶν κορυφαίων περὶ τῆς ἀρχῆς πολεμεόντων).
> (6.98.2)

"The" empire, one notices: it is as if there is always one and only one, and the question is whose it will be. In 480 the contention over "rule" concerns the command in the war against Persia, and it is amicably settled when Athens defers to Sparta (8.3; p. 221). But the similar wrangling with Gelon of Syracuse (7.157–162) has no such resolution, and the Greek envoys are sent away with a stinging rebuke: they seem to have rulers (*archontes*) but nobody for them to rule (7.162.1).[54] Too many leaders, and at each other's throats: those next fifty years will see plenty more of that, and not only in words.

Those contentions will be among "the head" Greeks, *tōn koruphaiōn*, through those three generations: that is a word that can naturally be used of "the head" citizens in a single state, as in the constitutions debate when Darius warns about the dangers of an oligarchy where "every individual wants to be the head" (3.82.3).[55] Now the cities as a whole, in particular Sparta and Athens, are programmed to act similarly.[56] That reflects an analogy between city and individual that is embedded in Greek consciousness (p. 4), one that was to surface in its most sophisticated form in Plato's *Republic*, where state and citizen share a tripartite pathology of "reason," "spirit," and "desire." In many authors, both city and individual can be "sick": here in Herodotus the shared aspiration for primacy is producing a broader distemper, a Greek malaise. The coalition of the free is very fragile indeed.

At that point in book 6 the shape of the story has itself been making the point (p. 134). The fighting between Aegina and Athens has been meandering on, with failures and successes on both sides (6.87–93):

> The Athenians, then, had engaged in war with the Aeginetans; the Persian was attending to his own business . . .
> (6.94.1)

—a business that was, in fact, preparing the invasion. It is as if the Greek states are lost in a world of their own, one that is about to be in mortal peril. Once that invasion starts, the narrative is seized by a new direction, driven firmly on until Marathon is decided; there will be a similar firm forward thrust in the narrative of books 7–9. But it takes the initiative of a king, knowing what he wants and with the power to command it, to impose that strong direction. That is very much what Xerxes says to Demaratus (7.103.3–4). He is talking a lot of sense.

There is a further irony and a further reason why Herodotus allows such space to that fighting between Aegina and Athens. Predictably, it resumes once Marathon has been won, even though it did not take much shrewdness to know that Persia would come again. Yet:

> This was then the salvation of Greece, for it forced the Athenians to become a sea people.
> (7.144.1)

It was—says Herodotus—all thanks to Themistocles. "Much money" came in a windfall from the silver mines in 483/2. Instead of a general distribution to each citizen, Themistocles persuaded the people to build two hundred ships for "the war, meaning by that the war against the Aeginetans." Themistocles, we are given a strong hint,[57] himself had a different war in mind, and so it proved: "These ships were not used for the purpose for which they were made but were there for Greece at the time when they were needed" (7.144.2). If it had not been for that hatred of Aegina, so embedded that Athenian citizens were prepared to take the hit in their own pockets, Themistocles would not have won the crucial argument; rather as earlier Cleomenes' "envy and malice" had driven a campaign against Aegina in which he was "laying the preliminaries for the good of Greece" (6.61.1; p. 178).[58] In both cases, it is not the best qualities of Greece, nor even of freedom, that save the day. It is the worst.[59]

It was "the Athenians" whom Themistocles persuaded to do this:[60] all of them, or at least all the citizens who voted. But within that single city we can also see that fragmenting. If we return to Marathon and Miltiades' speech to Callimachus, his crucial argument for fighting the battle is not what we might expect: no appeal to heroism, no rhetoric of "we shall never surrender" or "beacon of freedom to all," but something more down to earth:

> If we fail to engage now, I expect that some great division among themselves (*stasis*) will fall upon the thinking of the Athenians and shake them into Medizing; but if we engage before something rotten is born within one side or other at Athens, then—provided that the gods allow an even fight—we can win the day.
> (6.109.5)

So something "rotten" (*sathron*) may "fall upon" and "shake" the ship of state: this is nautical language of failing timber and storm at sea.[61] Then Herodotus has no doubt that someone—not the Alcmaeonids but someone—played the traitor and held up the shield to alert the Persians (6.124.2). That suggests that Miltiades' words were more than scaremongering. Miltiades himself had reason to know how bitter the divisions of big men even in a democracy could be, as he had been put on trial once (6.104) and would soon face a second capital charge (6.136). More on democracy in the next chapter; for the moment, let us just note again that it is the worst qualities, not the best, that drive a decision that turns out to be critical.

So: does freedom save the Greeks? Yes, perhaps, but in strange and paradoxical ways. We have several times seen that strengths and weaknesses can be intimately connected, whether in an organism, a human personality, or a larger body, perhaps even in the Persian empire itself. The same qualities make an Achilles or an Antigone great but then drive his or her fall (p. 18): this may be a converse case, one where qualities that could be a debilitating weakness turn out to be the cause of Greece's greatest achievement. Freedom could have bad consequences as well as good; its inspirational power was not universal and not unsullied; but it mattered, and mattered greatly. Still, we are left in no doubt that the outcome was a close thing and could easily have gone the other way—provided the gods had allowed it, and this verges on the inscrutable. If it had, freedom would have had something to do with that too, just as it did when everything went wrong in Samos or at Lade. Greek success was explicable in these terms, but that does not mean that it was predictable.

So good and bad need to be kept in balance: that also chimes with what we saw earlier as a prerequisite for a healthy organism (chapter 5[b]). This leaves open the possibility that some of the same qualities could later turn very nasty indeed, just as they do when a body becomes sick; and for Herodotus' contemporaries that thought would come close to home, as democratic Athens, after all those heroics in 490 and 480–479, turned from the role of freedom's champion to being the new aggressor, even the new tyrant city. Not even its own citizens shied away from that sinister labeling (p. 144). Sparta now could pose as the "liberator of Greece" (Thuc. 2.8.4): the liberator from Athens. That story is familiar to us from Thucydides. Herodotus' first audience would not need to wait for Thucydides to know its substance.

CHAPTER 13

DEMOCRACY

(A) DEMOCRACY AND FREEDOM?

For modern politicians "democracy" and "freedom" are bosom companions, so much so that in political speeches "democracy'n'freedom" often sounds like a single word.[1] It is not just moderns that connect the two:

Freedom is the foundational principle of democracy: that is what they usually say, implying that this is the only constitution where people have a share in freedom.
(ARIST. *POL.* 6.1317A40–43)

One notes Aristotle's reserve: this is just what "they" say—and who are "they"? In one way, study of Herodotus can be a valuable inoculation against that lazy habit of conflating "democracy" and "freedom." Most of the states struggling to remain free were anything but democracies, and Greek oligarchs and even tyrants can use freedom rhetoric just as readily as democratic Athens. The Soclees who speaks "freely" and invokes "the gods of Greece" against the prospect of Spartan-imposed tyrannies (5.92; p. 196) is the representative of Corinth, probably at the time an "unusually narrow oligarchy,"[2] while "the tyrants of Cyprus" speak resonantly to their Ionian allies of the prospect that "Ionia and Cyprus might be free" (5.109.2);[3] then the coalition has no hesitation in approaching Gelon, tyrant of Syracuse, to "come to the aid of those liberating Greece and become a joint liberator" (7.157.2).[4] The threat of externally imposed domination is usually in point when such stirring appeals are made;[5] Soclees has not a word to say about democracy as such, even though it is newly democratic Athens that he is defending. One can see why Thucydides' Phrynichus was able to separate democracy and freedom so readily: "They [the allied cities] would not want to be slaves under either an oligarchy or a democracy rather than to be free under whichever of the constitutions they happened to have" (Thuc. 8.48.5).

In another way, though, Herodotus can help us to see how the conflation of democracy and freedom came about. Kurt Raaflaub has powerfully argued that the association of the two began around the third quarter of the fifth century[6] and that is the time that the *Histories* were taking shape. We can even see it happening in Herodotus' text, not least because both "democracy" and "freedom" could equally serve as the antonym of "tyranny." When Maeandrius, "wanting to be the most just of humans," tries to give up the tyranny in Samos, he does so not merely by "placing rule into the middle" (*es meson*) and "announcing an *isonomiē*," "equality with regard to the laws,"[7] both democratic slogans:[8] he also establishes a cult of "Zeus of Freedom," Zeus Eleutherios (3.142), but "the Samian people, so it seems, did not want to be free" (3.143.2; pp. 179–180). When Herodotus' Spartans come to regret their part in the liberation of Athens and propose restoring a tyranny, they too link freedom and the power of the *dēmos*: "It is to an ungrateful *dēmos* that we have handed over the city: now that—thanks to us—they have been freed, they have raised their head" and started asserting themselves even against our own king and ourselves (5.91.2; cf. 5.74.1). Herodotus' own judgment at 5.78, the passage that often figured in the last two chapters and will again be important in this, similarly couples *isēgoriē* with "now that they were free": that chimes with the concentration of Euripides' Theseus on the capacity to speak out in the assembly as definitional of freedom (τοὐλεύθερον)—"what is more equal (ἰσαίτερον) for a city than that?" (Eur. *Supp.* 438–441).

So democracy inspires: the people's "heads" are indeed "raised," as those Spartans gloomily can see. But that is not all that Herodotus thinks about democracy,[9] for heads can be turned, not just raised. In book 3 Megabyxus had put it memorably: at least a tyrant knows what he is doing, but that is impossible for an uneducated *dēmos*—it just jumps in and "tosses matters around like a river in flood" (3.81.2). Suitably enough, the first we heard of the Athenian *dēmos* had been at a time long before the establishment of democracy, when they were "deceived" (1.59.5) by Peisistratus into granting them a bodyguard. Nor did it end there: after being exiled again, Peisistratus and his new ally Megacles

> contrived for his return the most simple-minded thing I have ever heard of (given that the Greek race has been marked out from the barbarian since ancient times as smarter and freer of childish simple-mindedness) . . . (1.60.3)

They dressed up a beautiful and statuesque woman, Phye, as Athena, and proclaimed that the goddess herself was bringing Peisistratus back into the city. And it worked.

Nor has the *dēmos* learned to be any less gullible since, for in 500/499 the slippery Aristagoras arrives in Athens to try to enlist the city's support for the Ionian Revolt. He has been rebuffed in Sparta, despite a hint that Cleomenes was tempted, but now

> it seems to be an easier pushover to put one across a crowd than a single individual, if Aristagoras was unable to put one across the one man Cleomenes of Sparta, but could do so to 30,000 Athenians. (5.97.2)[10]

So the Athenians took their fateful decision to send aid to the Ionian Revolt; and "these ships were the beginning of evils (*archē kakōn*) for Greeks and barbarians" (5.97.3)—a modern-day equivalent of those Homeric "evil-beginning ships" that brought Helen to Troy (*nēes archekakoi*, Il. 5.63), with the allusion marking the solemnity of the moment. Not that they stay long: within a page the Athenians are "forsaking the Ionians completely" and refusing Aristagoras' pleas for further help (5.103.1). But the damage is done. We are on the path to Marathon, an exploit that turned out to be glorious for Athens but could so easily have been catastrophic.

(B) CHARACTERIZING THE *DĒMOS*

A clear picture of the Athenian *dēmos* was soon to become familiar: they are *tachybouloi* and *metabouloi*, swift to decide and swift to change their mind (Ar. *Ach.* 630, 632; cf. their deposition and then election of Pericles "as a crowd likes to do," Thuc. 2.65.4); they are easily flattered and won over by a smooth-tongued orator (cf. Ar. *Ach.* 634–640, and Cleon's dazzling denunciation of his audience for being misled by dazzling oratory, Thuc. 3.38); they are warm in pity towards victims (cf. Plat. *Menex.* 244e; Dem. 24.170–171)[11] though not always effective in helping them (Thuc. 3.68.5: "Such was the end of Plataea's story in the ninety-third year after becoming Athens' allies," with all that that elegiac phrase suggests; p. 227). We can already see something of the same in Herodotus, with the Athenians' swift recrimination of their envoys for offering Persia earth and water (5.73.3; cf. 5.96.2), or their election of Miltiades as general so soon after he was on trial for his life (6.104.2), or even their outpouring of grief for the fate of Miletus after failing to give them the help they needed (6.23.2). Nor does the Athenian *dēmos* do much better on the other occasions when we see it debating: thanks to Themistocles, they build the ships that prove crucial in 480 but not because they had that war in mind (7.144; p. 188); they do get the "wooden-wall" oracle right, but again it would have gone the other way but for Themistocles' smartness (7.143).[12]

The word *dēmokratiē* itself figures much less than we might expect.[13] With Maeandrius it is *isonomiē*, equality with regard to the laws (p. 191); when Aristagoras gives up his tyranny at Miletus he similarly creates *isonomiē* first in Miletus itself, then in the other cities of Ionia (5.37.2). At 5.78 the new Athenian institution is *isēgoriē*, equality in speech (pp. 164, 191). When the Spartans are anxious to undo the reforms, Soclees speaks of the new constitution as *isokratiē*, equality in power (5.92α.1). Nor did we find the word *dēmokratiē* in the constitutions debate in book 3: Otanes spoke more generally of "the many ruling" (πλῆθος δὲ ἄρχον) and of "increasing the power of the many" (τὸ πλῆθος ἀέξειν), and again used the positive slogan *isonomiē* (3.80.6, 3.83.1); democracy's critics just talked of the "useless crowd" (ὁμίλου . . . ἀχρηίου, Megabyxus at 3.81.1) or "the badness that inevitably arises when the *dēmos* has power" (Darius at 3.82.4). Then Cleisthenes' reforms at Athens are described in terms not of democracy but of the "tribes" that they established (5.69–70). Still, when Herodotus later returns both to Otanes and to Cleisthenes he makes no bones about it: Otanes' proposal was that "the Persians should have democratic rule," *dēmokrateesthai* (6.43.3), and Herodotus there defends that version by pointing out that Mardonius "imposed democracies," *dēmokratias*, on the cities of Ionia; Cleisthenes is the one "who established the tribes and the democracy at Athens" (6.131, coupled with a pointed reference forwards to his kinsman Pericles). Herodotus clearly thinks too that others thought of Athens in similar terms, stressing the *dēmos*: as we saw, the Spartans objected to the bad treatment they had received at the hands of an "ungrateful *dēmos*" (5.91.2).

There may be several reasons for that initial avoidance of the word. One is that it may not have been the best way to capture any of these early projects. Maeandrius' proposal may have been "an aristocratic rather than a democratic move";[14] it is anything but clear what Aristagoras did in Ionia, or said he was doing.[15] Still controversial is exactly how "democratic" Cleisthenes' reforms should be seen as being,[16] and whatever exactly Otanes suggested (and if indeed there was any such debate at all), it would not have had much in common with democracy as Herodotus' audience would know it.[17] Nor indeed is Otanes very precise about what he is proposing anyway.[18] All this still leaves unexplained why Herodotus is so ready to use the term in those later, retrospective passages to refer to Otanes' proposal and Cleisthenes' reforms.

A better explanation is emotive. "Democracy" was not yet a good word. In retrospect, Herodotus can acknowledge that this was what was at stake, but at the time proposers of such measures might tiptoe around it. Certainly, many of the word's early uses are hostile or at best neutral, especially in Herodotus when they are focalized through the eyes or mouths of his characters.[19] At the end of Darius' Scythian campaign, the tyrants of Ionia, collected at the bridge over the Bosporus, have the chance to destroy the bridge and leave Darius stranded:

> Miltiades the Athenian was there as commander and tyrant of the Hellespontine Chersonese, and he urged them to do what the Scythians asked and free Ionia; Histiaeus of Miletus took the opposite view, arguing that as things stood each of them was tyrant of a city, but if Darius' power was destroyed, he would not be able to continue in power at Miletus, nor would any of the others be able to rule anyone: each of the cities would want to be a democracy (*dēmokrateesthai*) rather than a tyranny. (4.137.2)

It is there taken as read that democracies are what the people in the cities want: that does not make them a good thing, at least as far as Histiaeus is concerned, and it is no surprise that he uses the unembroidered word *dēmokrateesthai*.

Isonomiē is by contrast a good word, never used pejoratively[20]—"first of all, the rule of the many has the fairest of names, *isonomiē*," as Otanes puts it (3.80.6), or "a fair-seeming name, political *isonomiē*," as Thucydides describes the principle paraded by a *dēmos* (Thuc. 3.82.8). *Isēgoriē* is not quite so unambiguously favorable—critics could denounce the excesses when such principles get out of their hand[21]—but still carries much of the same positive charge; the same was probably true of *isokratiē*, though the word is rare. Otanes and Maeandrius therefore speak of *isonomiē* because they want to be persuasive, while Aristagoras' motive is explicitly "so that the Milesians might willingly join him in his revolt" (5.37.2). Herodotus himself uses *isēgoriē* as he dwells on its inspirational power, and Soclees talks of *isokratiē* because he is indignant at the prospect of the Spartans destroying it.

These slogans, too, are particularly suited to the contrast with tyranny,[22] just as in the drinking song that celebrated Harmodius and Aristogeiton "when they killed the tyrant and made Athens *isonomoi*" (*PMG* 896); just, too, as Euripides' Jocasta was to respond to her ambitious son Eteocles' paean on "Tyranny, biggest of the gods" with an even more eloquent speech in praise of *Isotēs*, "Equality" (*Phoen.* 528–585). Tyranny is important in all these Herodotean contexts: the tyranny from which the Persians had just escaped, the tyranny that Maeandrius was trying to give up, the tyranny of the Peisistratids from which Athens had been freed and which Soclees now sees the Spartans trying to reinstate. In each place the *iso-* words carry a heavy suggestion of what the system *is not*—tyranny—without giving any precision on what it *is*; in particular, it leaves untouched the vital question *who* is entitled to such "equal" provision.[23] That contrast with tyranny is also the central idea of a passage that 5.78 is echoing, 5.66.1—"Athens was great before, but now that it was rid of the tyrants became much greater"— and then of the Spartans' fear of the growing power of a free *dēmos* in contrast with the deferential weakness "if constrained by a tyranny" (5.91.1; p. 185). One sees again why democracy and freedom should be concepts that couple easily, especially when democracy is denoted by those glowing *iso-* words.

So "democratic," "pro-freedom," and simply "antityrant" rhetoric and ideologies are beginning to blur together. Doubtless they were infecting one another too, and it may well be that Herodotus heard a particular amount of antityrant and pro-freedom rhetoric during any visits to democratic Athens.[24] But this very blurriness creates a danger too. For most modern readers, democracy glistens, at least as an ideal: it is easy to assume a similar mindset in the Greeks themselves, and where Herodotus uses these *iso-* words to suggest a negative—non-tyranny—we put more weight on the positive, democracy, that they were coming to connote. Yet even an Athenian audience, politically alert and proud of their system as many were, might find it more comfortable to have ideals sketched as general "civic" values, those of the *polis*, than anything more distinctively "democratic";[25] and many of Herodotus' audiences would not be Athenian, nor particularly in sympathy with Athens.

(C) DEMOCRACY IN AND OUT OF FOCUS

It is unsurprising, then, that comparatively little emphasis falls on "democracy."[26] Perhaps Herodotus too is more interested in what it is not than in what it is, along with the values that an Athenian democrat would share with the citizens of any free *polis*, and those are further reasons for his preference for those *iso-* words. When Athens does come out well, there is no mention of the *dēmos*: perhaps those resonant words at the end of book 8 (p. 168) were uttered in the Council of Five Hundred that prepared the assembly business, perhaps in the assembly itself,[27] but Herodotus does not bother to say. What matters is that this is what "the Athenians" said or did, just as it is when he praises them for their decision not to sail away at 7.139. There is no interest in how they took that decision, and certainly not in suggesting that democratic procedures were what explained such admirable choices.[28] When he speaks of the Athenians' readiness to take and endure "many troubles" for the sake of Plataea, he implies a continuity of such excellent choices across the periods before and after the Cleisthenic reforms (6.108).[29]

We can detect other cases too in which Herodotus makes a good deal less of anything "democratic," or of the *dēmos*, than he might have done. There are some indications that Miltiades' arguments for fighting at Marathon were delivered in a speech at Athens to the *dēmos*,[30] for fourth-century orators refer to a "decree of Miltiades" that required the Athenians to "take food and march" (Cephisodotus, quoted at Arist. *Rhet*. 3.1411a9–11; cf. Dem. 19.303). There is no suggestion of that in Herodotus' narrative, and Miltiades' rhetoric is delayed to the battlefield itself, delivered to Callimachus as polemarch and very likely in private[31] (6.109–110). The animosities of the big men, including those of Xanthippus and Miltiades (6.104.2, 6.136) and then of Themistocles and Aristeides (8.79.2), could happen under any constitution: similar things had happened under the tyranny, with friction between Miltiades' family and the Peisistratids themselves that culminated in the murder of Miltiades' father (6.35.3, 6.103.3).

Nor, as we saw, is any emphasis put on the democratic aspects of Cleisthenes' reforms during Herodotus' initial sketch of these, important though that aspect now seems.[32] It is as a tool in those big-man antagonisms that the *dēmos* comes into play with Cleisthenes: he was engaged with Isagoras in *stasis*, civil strife, and "recruited the *dēmos* to his faction" (5.66.2): "With the addition of the *dēmos* he was much more powerful than his factional rivals" (5.69.2). That meager narrative leaves no impression of the significance of the power accruing to the *dēmos* itself, and the first hint of that comes at 5.97 and then, more emphatically, in the retrospect at 6.131.1. The Spartans are vehemently indignant about "the ungrateful *dēmos*" (5.91.2; p. 185), but that is not the focus of the debate that follows: it is tyranny and freedom that are the focus of Soclees of Corinth in his great speech (5.92), and it is no coincidence that Herodotus describes him as "speaking freely" (5.93).

Soclees ends by calling on "the gods of Greece" and appealing to "justice," *to dikaion* (5.92η.5), rather as Aristagoras had pleaded with Cleomenes in the name of "the gods of Greece" to save them from enslavement and make them free (5.49.2). Freedom can be described in these terms, at least when it is removed without due cause (p. 176); that is something to which Greece as a whole might feel attachment and regard its championing as a matter of "justice." But is democracy "just"? That is less clear. Maeandrius' offer of *isonomiē* was inspired by "his desire to be the most just of men" (3.142.1), and the similar move of Cadmus of Cos is described in the same way (7.164.1), but that can be more a matter of their giving up tyranny, conceived as "unjust" (cf. Soclees at 5.92α1), and in Maeandrius' case proclaiming "freedom" (Zeus Eleutherios), than an unequivocal commitment to the "justice" of tyranny's opposite pole. Herodotus' various audiences would have had their own views on that, and they would not all be the same.

Nor is there much interest in the tos and fros of Athenian domestic politics after the removal of the tyrants, and rather less interest than in the frictions within Sparta; this is not the only time that Herodotus shows more interest in Sparta than in Athens. There is nothing for instance on the Athenian ostracisms of the 480s except for that of Aristeides (8.79.1); no background on the animosity of Themistocles and Aristeides, just the note that Themistocles was "no friend of his but an extreme enemy" (8.79.1). The *dēmos* is occasionally mentioned, but not much is made of it: that casual remark on Miltiades escaping from the danger of his first trial and "thus becoming *stratēgos*, chosen by the *dēmos*" (6.104.2), does not turn Miltiades into a popular hero.

Herodotus is sparse, too, in any detail on the new constitution's mechanisms in action. Thus, we do not know what body fined the tragedian Phrynichus and forbade any reproduction of his *Fall of Miletus* (6.21.2), nor what the procedure was for trying Miltiades (6.104.2, 6.136.1–2).[33] (Admittedly, Herodotus himself might not have known either.) Then, as we saw, a crucial part of Miltiades' argument to Callimachus focused on the danger of Athenian *stasis* (6.109; pp. 188–189). Yet Herodotus does not go into the texture of that *stasis*, and there is no suggestion that it might be "democrats" against others. If anything, one would conclude that it was the usual sort of clash among the big families, with one group—not the Alcmaeonids (6.121–124) but someone else—keener than the others on the Peisistratid return. In dismissing the charge of treachery against the Alcmaeonids, he mentions one possible argument that mentions the *dēmos*: "Or perhaps the family had some cause for recrimination against the people and therefore betrayed their country?" (6.124.1). He thinks the idea ridiculous.

The link of democracy and freedom is still there but not as a *necessary* link. It is more that democracy allows a prism for seeing freedom pushed to the limit, just as tyranny allowed a prism for looking at the opposite extreme of a people at the mercy of unrestrained power (p. 144).[34] Tyranny is the rule of one; democracy, of the many. Tyranny suppresses (*katechei*); democracy equalizes (those *iso-* words), even allows the many to "raise their heads." Freedom can inspire whole cities; in a democracy it can inspire every individual, as there is a deeper sense in which everyone is "trying to achieve something for himself," for everyone has a stake in it. Free peoples can make mistakes: thirty thousand people are more likely to make them than one. Free debate can be rowdy and lead to decisions of which people swiftly repent; a democracy may be especially prone to that, as the experience of the infant (and later the adult) Athenian democracy may suggest. Democracy can be hard to cope with, especially at first: the experience of Maeandrius at Samos on the rebound from tyranny showed as much, for "the Samian people, so it seems, did not want to be free" (3.143.2; pp. 179–180).

Yet none of these features, good or bad, is confined to democracy: debate was rowdy enough, and changes of mind quick enough, in that debate of the coalition commanders before Salamis. Nor is internal squabbling, or allowing internal squabbles to compromise national interests, any more characteristic of democracies than anywhere else. Spectacular internal rifts are also seen in the tyranny at Corinth in book 3 and in the Spartan royal houses in book 6. But democracy shows all these features in a particularly glaring light.

So in their different ways both tyranny and democracy allow the clarity of extremes. Persia's story has shown one way in which strengths and weaknesses can combine, even interact: the same qualities that generate Persian success can persuade a ruler to overreach. Will the experiment of Athenian democracy turn out to have a different end, once—after the end of Herodotus' *Histories*, but clearly anticipated within it (chapter 15)—the Athenian empire has grown? Or will it be the same, because the underlying imperialistic urge is so similar? Could anyone in Herodotus' day, Herodotus himself included, possibly know? The answer to those questions was still unclear when the first audiences heard or read his work.[35] Whatever the answers turned out to be, the strengths and weaknesses of freedom would do something to make either success or failure more comprehensible. Nothing was yet predictable; that did not mean that the outcome, when it came, would be inexplicable, and reading Herodotus would be helpful in providing some clues and precedents to help readers to understand whatever that outcome turned out to be.

These are themes to which we will return.

CHAPTER 14

INDIVIDUALS AND COLLECTIVES

(A) SELF-EXPRESSION?

The great thing about freedom, so Herodotus said, was that everybody was now trying to achieve something for themselves—so much better, evidently, than "working for a master (*despotēs*)" (5.78; p. 164). Subjects of a master would "play the coward," he there explains (*ethelokakeon*), and that was why the Athenians became "vastly preeminent" now that they were free. The "masters" in that passage were the Peisistratids at Athens, but the quintessential "masters" in the *Histories* are the kings of Persia, and the same word *despotēs* is used when Xerxes and Demaratus debate the advantages of the King's unified command at 7.102–104 (pp. 165–166, 181). Yet we have seen that it is too simple to think of Persians being "soft" or "cowardly" as a result of that constitution; the author of *Airs Waters Places* may have accepted this as at least a partial explanation, and that was probably a popular view as well (pp. 19–20), but Herodotus' Persians are pretty tough and pretty effective (pp. 169–170).

Is it possible, though, that 5.78 could be preempting a broader theme that will become clearer later, rather as its notion that Athens was "vastly preeminent" seems premature rather than false (p. 185)? Will we find it true, and will we find it important, that the western world of Greece allows more self-expression than the monarchic East? That, with fewer institutional constraints, there is more scope for creative and independent thinking? If Mill is right that "genius can only breathe freely in an atmosphere of freedom" and that individual liberty is essential to allow "scope for spontaneity, originality, genius, for mental energy, for moral courage,"[1] will those qualities be seeded particularly in a free state—perhaps even in a democracy, though Mill himself, fearful as he was of "the tyranny of the majority," would not have taken this step?[2] Perhaps we are even dealing with a precursor of "Great Man" theories, with a Miltiades or a Themistocles or a Pausanias able to influence events for good, or an Aristagoras or a Histiaeus for bad, in a way that an Artaphernes or a Mardonius cannot—but, if we move the gaze forwards to Herodotus' own early readers, that a Pericles or an Alcibiades can too? This too requires a chapter all to itself.

(B) NARRATIVE SHAPE

The king of Persia would not have taken kindly to any suggestion that his rule left no scope for individual success—provided that the success was his own. The monarch could proclaim his brilliance in first-person accounts, as in the Cyrus cylinder and on Darius' Behistun inscription, and we saw earlier that Herodotus' own narrative shape shows a certain "biostructure," reflecting the strong forward thrust that an energetic monarch can give (pp. 133–136). That would seem to push the argument in the opposite direction from the one for which we were looking, for the individual drivers of events are more often Persians than Greeks. Those insights on the monarchic side are uncomfortably near the truth: unified command is what makes the difference (Xerxes to Demaratus, 7.103.4; pp. 181–182); at least a tyrant knows what he is doing (Megabyxus in the constitutions debate, 3.81.2; p. 191). Nor is it just the kings themselves: Mardonius makes more of the decisive calls in the Plataea campaign than Pausanias, restricted as the Spartan regent is by the indiscipline of his troops (pp. 172–173).

Yet we have also seen that, even on the Persian side, it is a good deal more complicated. As Xerxes realizes, or half-realizes, when he talks to Artabanus at Abydus (7.50), they are in the grip of Persian history: there is that "curse of being a descendant" (pp. 141–142). So eastern monarchs indeed make the choices that drive events, but those choices are often ones that will be made only one way. Narrative shape, then, teaches more than one lesson, and the recurrent rhythm of those kingly narratives shows how limited that control of events can really be. Many of the hardest choices taken in Greek tragedy by the men of power suggest the same.

Outcomes too are not within that control. The king can launch expeditions, and many of them succeed; that, as Xerxes says at Abydus, is what made Persia great. But some fail, and the Greek adventure is the most prominent failure of all. No one individual controls the whole other side of the tale, and the Greek story is not biography or even a series of biographies. Yet this may be the point: Greece can produce a series of individuals, each able to dominate the stage for the moment that matters (pp. 135–136). Much later, Livy could develop a related theme in explaining his conviction that the fourth-century Romans could have fielded a series of generals who would have been more than a match for Alexander the Great, despite all those advantages of single command that the king enjoyed (9.17–19).³ (Related but not identical, for Livy's emphasis falls not on "individuality" but on Romanness, with Alexander facing leaders who all showed the same traditional military virtues.) So there may after all be room for an emphasis on free individuality, all the more effective because it can come back in different forms as one leader follows another. We need a closer look.

(C) INDIVIDUALS AND COMMUNITIES

"Individual" is a slippery term: it is no wonder that so many centuries have been hailed as seeing "the discovery of the individual."⁴ Fifth-century Greeks did not really have a word for the concept anyway.⁵ Even if we use it for our own heuristic purposes, it is hard to be sure exactly what we are looking for. Sometimes it points to *individuality*, the characteristics that mark one out as distinctive; that is a matter of personality. Sometimes it is more a question of *individualism*, a pursuing of one's own values rather than being bound by those of society: that can be put positively as being true to oneself, or negatively as egotistic selfishness. In discussions of literature, it may be *individuation*, the deft sketching of a person's traits to make sure that he or she stands out from the crowd of other characters. In the present inquiry we are likely to be looking to those features of "spontaneity, originality, genius, mental energy, moral courage"⁶ that Mill thought freedom could generate. In most of these senses there is an implied juxtaposition with a collective, the society or community as a whole: the collective from which the individual is marked as different; the collective whose values the individual chooses not to find binding; the collective from which the individual is made to stand out; the collective that can only rarely provide a man or a woman of such creative imagination or such mental energy.

Greek culture here provided one clear benchmark: Homer. There was a whole society depicted there with a value of "always being the best and always outdoing the others" (*Il.* 6.208, 11.784). If you wanted someone with a flow of ingenious ideas, you had Odysseus. If you wanted someone who would follow his own values even if it distanced him from the community, you had Achilles, and he would provide you with a fair amount of introspection and self-consciousness as well. If you wanted an author who could make characters, even minor characters, live in the memory, you had Homer himself. Not that the community was neglected or failed to matter: Achilles might take himself off to sulk in his tent, but he eventually knows he must come back because he has let down not just his friend Patroclus but also his men, the Myrmidons, sitting instead as "a useless burden on the earth" (*Il.* 18.97–126, esp. 102–104). Earlier, the plea that came nearest to making him relent was that of Ajax, who could not understand why he was letting down his friends and comrades (*Il.* 9.624–642, esp. 630–631): that at least leads him to say that he will come back when fire reaches the ships (650–653).

The *Odyssey* too, so the proem tells us, will be the tale of Odysseus' attempts to protect his own life and get his comrades home (*Od.* 1.5): he is brilliant at the first and much less so at the second, but it certainly mattered that in the old days he was "kind, like a father" to his islander subjects (*Od.* 2.47, 2.234, 5.12). The Trojans, Hector most of all, are fighting to save their city and their people. Prowess in battle was a prime value, but a great motivator was the thought of what others—the community—would say about you; good counsel, *euboulia*, was prized too, the counsel that was good for everyone.[7] So even in Homer the individual is never as individual as all that, never quite distinct or separable from the collective.

The Persian Wars were the new Trojan War, the stuff of legendary heroism, of epic valor, even of divine epiphany. Well before Herodotus they had been treated in terms that evoked Homer. An epigram on a monument probably from the 470s already commemorated the dead in Homeric language;[8] Simonides began his elegy on Plataea with a hymn to Achilles;[9] in the 460s the Athenian Stoa Poikile included a panel on Marathon alongside a scene from the Trojan War and another of Theseus fighting the Amazons.[10] Athenian ideology may have told against too much emphasis on individual achievement: these were the glories of the whole city. No Athenian individual is named in Aeschylus' *Persians*.[11] But that did not stop the artist of the Stoa Poikile from focusing on particular heroes: a scene from the Marathon panel seems to lie behind a representation on a sarcophagus now at Brescia,[12] and it shows Miltiades and Cynegeirus, both known from Herodotus to have played prominent roles. Elsewhere we are told that the polemarch Callimachus was also depicted on the Stoa; so was the Greek fighter Epizelos who was mysteriously blinded, so were the Persian generals, and so were Heracles, Theseus, and a local hero Echetlus.[13] The Homeric setting itself demanded as much, to give these modern-day heroes the same prominence as those godlike figures of legend. When one thought in Homeric terms, individuals did indeed explain a lot.

Herodotus too evokes Homer, particularly in these great battles. As Marathon reaches its climax and the Greeks are about to set fire to the Persian ships, deft choice of language evokes the moment in the *Iliad* when Hector is about to set fire to the Greek sterns:[14] that is a turning point in the poem, for this is when Achilles had said he would return, just as it will now be a critical moment at Marathon. The most Homeric battle of all is Thermopylae, that climax of Spartan heroism for which Demaratus' words to Xerxes had so clearly prepared (p. 166).[15] In particular, the fighting replays aspects of the struggle over Patroclus' body in *Iliad* 17–18, with great "pushing and shoving" (*ōthismos . . . pollos*, 7.225.1), this time in the right martial setting (contrast 8.78 and 9.26.1; p. 184), corpses falling over one another, the recurrent turning of the enemy, and threatened or real decapitation of the dead general.[16] There is even recurrent lion imagery in the Homeric version, suitable enough for this *Leonidas*: and his undying fame is marked by a *stēlē* with a lion, emblematically where the Greeks took their final stance (7.225.2: cf. the *stēlē* simile at *Il.* 17.434–435). Herodotus' text was to be an even greater commemoration.

Undying fame, *kleos*, that hallmark of epic, is very much in Leonidas' own mind, or so Herodotus thinks:

> My own opinion tends in this direction: when Leonidas saw that the allies had no enthusiasm to stay and share the danger, he ordered them to go but told them that it would not be right for him to leave himself: for if they stayed, great glory (*kleos*) awaited him, and the prosperity of Sparta would not be wiped out (*ouk exeleipheto*).
> (7.220.2)

For an oracle had predicted that either Sparta would be destroyed or its king would die

> . . . and Leonidas wanted to lay down glory that would belong to the Spartiates alone (*kleos katathesthai mounōn Spartiēteōn*), and so he sent away the allies rather than have a difference of opinion followed by a disorderly departure of those who would go.
> (7.220.4)

The words are carefully chosen. "Lay down," *katathesthai*, is another poetic allusion, it seems;[17] "would not be wiped out," *ouk exeleipheto*, recalls Herodotus' own mission that great human achievements "would not become faded (*exitēla*) with time" and that wondrous deeds should not lose their *kleos* (proem).[18] The king and the historian work in concert, both committed to preserving that *kleos*: it is a miniature version of the way both author and characters put wondrousness on "display" (p. 23). And it has worked. Two divisions of the Greek army still wear badges on their regimental caps recalling great moments of Thermopylae.[19]

Leonidas, then, is as concerned with his future fame as the Homeric Helen and Hector (*Il.* 6.357–358, 22.305). But there is a crucial difference, and it focuses on this role of the individual. Helen knows that she will be a subject of song; Hector wants to achieve something that future generations will remember about him. But Leonidas wants the *kleos* to be for "the Spartiates alone,"[20] a matter not of "him" or "her" but of "them." One of those cap-badge phrases, "in the shade," is similarly mentioned as a "memorial" (*mnēmosynon*) of Thermopylae (7.226.2), but it is left by another Spartan, one Dieneces, and what it commemorates was the resolve of three hundred men, not just one—though Dieneces won his own glory too.

Another key Iliadic word, *mēnis* ("wrath"), has a role to play too. It is the response of the Spartans as a whole to Aristodemus, one of the two men among the three hundred who missed the battle because of severe ophthalmia: Leonidas had ordered them to remain in the camp (7.229). The other man, Eurytus, had nonetheless demanded his armor and was led by a helot into the battle line, where he died. When Aristodemus returned to Sparta, he was "shunned";[21] nobody would light him a fire or spare him a word; he was known as "Aristodemus the runaway" (7.231). Herodotus muses counterfactually that the Spartans would not have been so furious with Aristodemus if it had not been for Eurytus;[22] here the point is the way that this fury is described. In the *Iliad mēnis* was largely a word for the gods and for Achilles.[23] Now it has passed not merely to more ordinary mortals but to the collective, and it is their response that eventually drives Aristodemus back to the fight, desperate at Plataea to redeem himself with a glorious death (9.71.3). With Achilles it was his own wrath, once its target had shifted from Agamemnon to Hector, that drove him to return; now it is the wrath of the community as a whole. At least to a degree, the world has changed, and not to the advancement of "the individual."

Still, this is Sparta; and it was Sparta that Demaratus explicitly had in mind with those words to Xerxes that so clearly presaged Thermopylae (7.101–104, esp. 7.102.2; p. 166). Sparta of course had had its individuals too, notably Cleomenes, but that had not ended well. What about Athens, especially Themistocles? Might it be that in this newly freed state a different form of individuality might flourish, one less damaging and more constructive than the strangely perverse sort of Sparta's Cleomenes? Might, even, that have something to do with democracy—in which case "the collective" would come into play again, but in a different way?

(D) AN ATHENIAN VIRTUE?

Themistocles has his Homeric analogue too. His inventiveness, his capacity to find the right words for a particular hearer, the shrewd eye to his own advantage, the ruthlessness when it suited him—all this has the whiff of a new Odysseus. At one point a more specific echo of an *Odyssey* scene may be sensed, when the slaughter of the cattle on the Euboean shore (8.19) evokes the killing of the cattle of the Sun (*Od.* 1.7–9, 12.260–425). That, indeed, is a case in which Themistocles outdoes Odysseus,[24] as he remains in control whereas Odysseus was prevented by a divinely imposed sleep from restraining his men. The consequences for Themistocles were good; for Odysseus, disastrous. This is part of a wider truth, for Themistocles' ingenuity is the salvation not only of himself but also of his country and his men; Odysseus got home alone. Again, as with Leonidas, we see that the collective is adding a dimension to Homeric individualism that is not wholly different—Ithaca had missed Odysseus' fatherly care—but is still greatly enhanced.

There are other ways too in which individual and collective intermesh. An individual can embody his city's characteristics: that was true with Leonidas, so clearly displaying at Thermopylae those Spartan characteristics highlighted by Demaratus (p. 166), and even with Amompharetus, applying his less well judged version of Spartan constancy (p. 181). To an extent the same is true of Themistocles and Athens,[25] though in this case the qualities mirrored are those that will be more conspicuous in the postwar years that Herodotus prefigures rather than narrates (chapter 15). Themistocles' capacity to mingle energy and self-enrichment will certainly typify the imperial city; he is uncompromising in his treatment of Andros, threatening its people with those inexorable deities Persuasion and Compulsion and unmoved by their pleas of Poverty and Impossibility (8.111), and this is a harbinger of things to come once the Athenians' "protection racket" was firmly in place.[26] Nor does Themistocles stop there, moving on swiftly to Carystus and Paros, "for he was unceasingly on the make" (*pleonekteōn*). The Athenians' taste for self-seeking was already clear when Miltiades appealed to them to give him ships for a mission he would not tell them about, but it would "easily"—*eupeteōs*, that "pushover" word that is a danger signal[27]— bring them untold wealth (6.132). That too turned out to be Paros, though on that occasion it did not end well (6.135.1).[28]

This "mirroring" effect[29] of city and individual should not be overstated: a taste for self-enrichment is hardly limited to Athenians. Aristagoras rightly thinks that similar promises would prove attractive to the Spartan Cleomenes (5.49), even if there he is ultimately rebuffed, and systematic Persian bribery is effective in states of all complexions (p. 169). Other qualities of Themistocles, in particular his quick-witted inventiveness, are not specially mirrored in the collective. It is Thucydides' Athenians who are distinctively enterprising risk takers, always on the look-out for something new (1.70.2): when Herodotus introduces the notion of the Athenian people as particularly smart, it is only to deride it and find them guilty of simplemindedness in falling for Peisistratus' trick (1.60.3: p. 191), and if the Athenians take risks in embroiling themselves in Ionia, they are also swift to draw back (p. 192). It will indeed be Thucydides and then Plutarch who will take this systematic mirroring of city and individual further, especially in their portraits of Alcibiades.[30] When Plutarch tells a story of the *dēmos* being delighted when Alcibiades brings a quail into the assembly and cheerfully helping him recapture it when it escapes, one has a much stronger sense of a *dēmos* and a demagogue that are thoroughly in tune (*Alc.* 10.1–2).

Tunes can, however, change; individuals and their cities are not always so harmonious, and that is already the case in Herodotus. Another recurrent theme is the way that cities do not always find it easy to get on with their great men, partly because the same characteristics so often go on to initiatives with less salutary results:[31] the greatest moments can carry dangers of a swift fall from glory and grace, and past achievement may not suffice to protect. When Miltiades is put on trial a second time, his friends "spoke a lot about the battle of Marathon and his capture of Lemnos—how he captured Lemnos, took vengeance on the Pelasgians, and handed the island over to the Athenians" (6.136.2). He does escape with his life but is given a monstrous fine and dies shortly afterwards. These were familiar dangers to Herodotus' audience. Pindaric odes remind the victors of the perils of success and the envy that it brings, and they often hint at the difficulties of reintegrating the victor with his community;[32] the charismatic Brasidas duly ran into such jealousy, *phthonos*, from the Spartan elite (Thuc. 4.108.7). Athenian ostracism too is based on the principle that an individual can become too great for comfort. Others besides tyrants may feel the need to strike off the tallest ears of corn in the way that Thrasybulus advised his fellow-tyrant Periander (5.92ζ).

We are left in no doubt that Themistocles' career too has a downward arc to follow. When he persuades the Athenians out of pursuing Xerxes, it was because "he wanted to have something in the credit bank with the Persian, so that if anything happened to him at the hands of the Athenians he would have somewhere to turn to; and that is what happened" (8.109.5). Herodotus' first readers and listeners would know what that referred to. It is the story that we know from Thucydides, the way that Themistocles was first ostracized and then accused of Medism, so that he fled to Corcyra and then to the court of Xerxes himself. There he persuaded the king that he had been his great benefactor, claiming that it was thanks to him that the Hellespont bridge had remained intact, and so he ended up as "a great man at his court, greater than any Greek before . . . ," the recipient of three cities as his reward (Thuc. 1.135.2–1.138). With these great figures Herodotus is generous in his narrative economy. Book 6 ends not with Miltiades' death but a flashback to that conquest of Lemnos (6.140), and the last we hear of Themistocles[33] does not concern that sinister future but his acclaim at Sparta (8.124). Or rather that is almost the last, for Herodotus there adds a note of Timodemus, a man of the Attic deme of Aphidnae, who snidely tells Themistocles that at Sparta he had bathed in Athens' glory, not his own (8.125). Themistocles has a telling retort, but that too prefigures the ill-will that awaits in his own city.

What, then, of democracy? Is there any sense that Athenian democratic culture allows individual initiative to flourish in a way that less liberal and permissive cultures do not? Or, contrariwise, that the dangers of such friction are particularly great when it is a *dēmos* that has to cope with so towering a figure?

No, not really. At Sparta too there is plenty of individuality, in its various senses, even if it does not usually end well. If Odyssean tricksiness is in point, the Spartan Ariston is prepared to manipulate his best friend into giving up his wife (6.62–63); if individual initiatives, Cleomenes launches a series of state interventions (including bribing the Pythia, 6.66) for personal reasons and apparently without consultation; if egotistic individualism, Pausanias' self-seeking disgrace is clearly anticipated (p. 210), and there is no shortage of ruthless ambition in the struggles for the throne involving Cleomenes, Demaratus, and Leutychidas.

Nor are such features even confined to Greece. In navigating his path to the throne, Darius combines enterprise and insight with risky self-seeking, and one of the most Odyssean tricks in the *Histories* is that of his groom Oebares, finding a way to make his stallion neigh at the place and moment that would ensure his master the throne (3.85–87).[34] Another, again in the interest of the master rather than the trickster himself, is that of Zopyrus, prepared to mutilate himself to deceive the Babylonians and contrive the city's capture (3.150–160). One of the last episodes in the *Histories* is one where a smart Persian outwits his Thessalian hosts (9.89). Nor, in Herodotus' version, is it any mean feat for the false Smerdis to keep himself on the Persian throne by sustained deception (3.61–79); nor, in a different register, for the Egyptian thief to extract the treasure from Rhampsinitus' store (2.121); nor for the Persian general Amasis to trick the Barcaeans with a concealed trapdoor (4.201). Herodotus welcomes such "Schelmengeschichten"[35] ("rogue stories") wherever they can be found: a collection of sixty-nine "instances of trickery" in Herodotus shows almost exactly the same number of Greek cases and non-Greek.[36] And Persians too have their personal ambitions. Darius certainly did; so did Cyrus; so did Mardonius, for a "terrible yearning had dripped into him" to capture Athens a second time, and this led him to neglect that good advice to turn to bribery (9.3.1; p. 169). There too that master far away is in the front of his thoughts, for the desire is to "use beacons across the islands to send the news to Xerxes at Sardis that he had taken Athens": that prominence of the master may add an eastern tinge, but it is something special about Mardonius too, an individual and individuating trait.

Even at Athens, such qualities are not specially connected with democracy. Another "Odyssean" moment comes at Athens early in the *Histories*—but that is the trick of Peisistratus and his own Athena, in his case a make-believe one (1.60; p. 191), and so it is a matter of tyranny rather than democracy. Miltiades has one or two ingenious ideas, especially his singular interpretation of an oracle that wins possession of Lemnos (6.139–140),[37] but his Athenian career is not particularly related to "democracy" (p. 196), and the first we hear of him is as tyrant in the Chersonese (4.137–138), one who even by tyrannical standards is particularly ruthless in eliminating other men of power (6.39.2).

Nor is Themistocles especially associated with democracy and the *dēmos* in the events themselves, even if his characterization proleptically anticipates features of the later democracy. His various forms of persuasiveness—spoken words, bribes, written messages—work on a series of very different audiences: Eurybiades (three times), Adeimantus of Corinth, the Ionians (unsuccessfully), the council of generals (three or more likely four times), the Greek forces on the morning of Salamis, Xerxes (twice), and—ruthlessly—the islanders of Andros, Carystus, and Paros, among others.[38] Few of these involve the Athenian *dēmos*, and there is no clear suggestion that the *dēmos* is either easier or more difficult to persuade than any other body. There are two cases involving the *dēmos* when he is first mentioned (7.142–144): he convinces the Athenians that the seers' interpretation of the "wooden walls" is mistaken, for if a disaster really looms at Salamis, the island would not have been addressed as "divine," and this persuades the *dēmos* to accept the interpretation (not his own) that the "wooden walls" must be those of the ships (7.142–143). No deceit or even disingenuousness there, though perhaps we can sense a talent of this master of duplicity in sensing a double meaning that others had missed. Then, immediately, there is a flashback to Themistocles' earlier success in talking "the Athenians" into using their windfall from the silver mines to build ships rather than take it for their own pockets (7.144): that has his characteristic mingling of truthfulness and disingenuousness, for he is right in identifying the military need but points to a different war, the one with Aegina (p. 188).

A further case in which the mass of the Athenians comes into play is after Salamis, when the Greeks as a whole have taken the decision not to follow Xerxes to the Hellespont. "The Athenians"—presumably the *dēmos* rather than the *boulē*, though characteristically (p. 195) Herodotus does not say so—are on the point of launching a pursuit of their own; Themistocles talks them out of it, saying in effect that they should not push their luck too far: "It was not we that achieved this, but the gods and heroes . . ." (8.109). Why not wait instead to the spring, and set sail then? That again may well be correct about the gods and insightful about the strategy (pp. 43, 156),[39] even though he does not believe it himself—he had argued the opposite in the general Greek council—and even though he has a selfish motive (p. 206):[40] he was "putting one over on them," *dieballe* (8.110.1).[41] This is the same word that was used of Aristagoras when he found it so easy to persuade the thirty thousand Athenians (5.97; p. 192), but this time there is no such derision of the *dēmos*' gullibility. They are prepared to believe him because "when he had been thought wise in the past, he had genuinely been shown to be wise and his advice to be good" (8.110.1)—good enough reasons, one would think.

So Themistocles' capacity to persuade the people *in particular* is not especially foregrounded, and none of these are cases where Herodotus suggests that a democracy took a decision that another form of government would not. This is not a forerunner of Thucydides' Cleon and Athenagoras, both "most persuasive to the *dēmos*" or "the many" (τῷ τε δήμῳ παρὰ πολὺ ἐν τῷ τότε πιθανώτατος, 3.36.6; ἐν τῷ παρόντι πιθανώτατος τοῖς πόλλοις, 6.35.2). Themistocles too may be "most persuasive," or at least most adept at getting his own way—but with everyone, not just with the *dēmos* and not just with Athenians.

Nor is it just Athens or just democracies that find it less than straightforward to get on with their greatest individuals. Cleomenes does good things for Sparta as well as bad, with successes in Boeotia (6.108) and Argos (6.76–80), however dubious the moral circumstances of the latter. His role in liberating Athens (5.64–65) also proves important for Greece as a whole, however swiftly the Spartans might come to regret it (5.74.1, 5.91; p. 191). Later too he can be described as "preparing the way for good things for all Greece" (6.61.1) when he intervenes against the Aeginetans as "traitors to Greece" (6.49.2). (His reasons are mixed and partly personal, but Herodotus there concentrates on results rather than motives.)[42] Yet he too is finally at odds with his city: he has to be restrained, and dies a gruesome death (6.75, 84). Other prominent Spartans end in exile, sometimes through their own choice (Dorieus, 5.42–48), sometimes because life in Sparta has become intolerable (Demaratus, 6.70), sometimes in disgrace after condemnation in a court of law (Leutychidas, 6.72).

A similar fate awaits the victor of Plataea. Pausanias will be charged with Medism, with "desire for rule over Greece," and with conspiracy within Laconia itself: he will be recalled to Sparta and will be on the point of death when he is dragged starving from his sanctuary (Thuc. 1.128–135.1). In this case too, as with Themistocles, Herodotus finds ways to remind his audience of the story, though the allusiveness with which he does so shows that he knows it will be familiar: the Persian general Megabates had a daughter "to whom Pausanias the Lacedaemonian, if the story is true, was later betrothed, lusting to become tyrant of Greece" (5.32); once the war was over and the allies "were already moving the conflict to be one about Persian territory, they took the leadership away from the Spartans on the grounds of Pausanias' *hybris*" (8.3). With Pausanias too Herodotus chooses to leave him not in his disgrace but at his moment of triumph, showing magnanimity in victory even to the Thebans, rebuking Lampon for the suggestion of mutilating Mardonius' body (no, we are Greeks, we do not do such things), treating a captured concubine with an almost chivalrous courtesy (9.76–78, 9.88): "The epitome of the knight *sans peur et sans reproche*."[43] But the story Herodotus tells shortly before, that of the Persian and the Greek dinners, conveys a hint of the future to come (9.82). Pausanias cannot understand why the Persians would come so far when they could eat far better meals at home. His own tastes are clear, and they are not Spartan ones (p. 170).[44]

Thucydides would later treat the postwar stories of Pausanias and Themistocles in close juxtaposition (1.128–138), implicitly pointing the parallels. There is a gesture towards the same idea in Herodotus.[45] Timodemus' gibe at Themistocles (8.125; p. 207)—that he owed those Spartan honors to the city of Athens—recalls one of the charges laid against Pausanias, that in his victory epigram at Delphi he had claimed glory that belonged to the cities as a whole: "When the commander of the Greeks had destroyed the Persian host, he, Pausanias, dedicated this memorial to Phoebus." The irate Spartans[46] later erased the inscription and substituted the names of the cities (1.132.2–3). The remains of the monument can still be seen in Istanbul.[47]

So Herodotus leaves plenty of room for his great men to matter. Heroism is still possible; the Greeks owe a great deal to Miltiades, Themistocles, Leonidas, and Pausanias. The Spartans themselves know it: hence those honors they heap on Themistocles. But the individual is nothing without the collective, and the tension between the two can become so great that the bond may snap.

(E) NATIONAL CHARACTERISTICS?

What, then, about these collectives? Should at least some of the focus rest on the characteristics of different peoples, not of individuals? Or perhaps on features of particular cities, especially Athens and Sparta? If the first, this might align Herodotus with *Airs Waters Places* (pp. 19–20); if the second, with Thucydides. Or should we be putting weight not on the differences but on the analogies noted in the previous section, with individuality and individualism (in several senses) among Persians as well as Greeks and among Spartans as well as Athenians, and the men of achievement becoming uncomfortable presences in their communities, wherever they are?

As usual with Herodotus, it is a bit of all of these. Yes, national variations matter: Herodotus' Persian stories point to a world that has important differences from the Greek, not least in the ways that people speak and debate (chapter 9); brutality, especially mutilation and whipping, are especially Persian features; Greeks are beset by factionalism. Cities too vary. Demaratus' generalizations about virtue are, as he says, focused particularly on what is special about Sparta (7.102.2; p. 166); *isēgoriē* is a good thing "everywhere" (5.78), but Athens is the place that shows it best. As we have also seen, however, easy generalizations tend to flounder when measured against the complexity of events. The Persians are not so soft in the battle line; Spartan discipline can break; Athenians can be brutal too.

Even when those assumptions totter, though, they invite a reader to renuance rather than reject, and it may be the renuancing that generates the sharper points.[48] The Medes too could show themselves good men in fighting for freedom (1.95.2; p. 175); but they were soon ready to accept the rule of Deioces (1.98–100; p. 17).[49] The Persians in the constitutions debate and the Greeks of Samos may both show that "they did not want to be free," but in different senses, in one case by thoughtful reflection on what was and what was not the Persian way, in the other by not being mature or compromising enough to cope (Darius at 3.82.5; p. 175; Samians at 3.143.2; pp. 179–180). Tricksiness and personal motives can be found in both East and West, but Oebares and Zopyrus will play tricks for their master and Mardonius' desire is to send good news to the king, while Themistocles works for his city and for himself. Spartans may be distinctively tough, but the Spartan king Cleomenes can be surprisingly similar to the Persian Cambyses, and the regent Pausanias can hint at his taste for gourmet fare rather than lumpy broth.

So this is a further way that Herodotus may align with the Hippocratic presentational technique (chapter 5[c]): here again bluff generalizations and general impressions are qualified as the complexities crowd in. What peoples share becomes more visible, and more arresting, because of that initial emphasis on the ways in which they are different.[50] Nor, as we saw (p. 145), is the *Iliad* very different: what Greeks and Trojans share is deeper than what divides them, but that emerges only gradually as the human experience becomes more and more intense.

There are parallels with Thucydides too, and they similarly extend to presentation as well as substance. His Corinthians develop their punchy contrast of innovative, risk-taking, go-getting Athenians with cautious, traditionally minded, stay-at-home Spartans (1.70). That goes further than Herodotus, who may have the hint of such a picture but only a hint;[51] Themistocles may be an enterprising risk-taker, but there is not much of that in the Athenians as a whole (p. 205). Nor are Herodotus' Spartans generally reluctant to start a fight, especially with Argos,[52] and it is they rather than the Athenians who respond warmly to the overtures of Croesus (1.69–70).

Yet in Thucydides too this strong differentiation is only the first word, not the last, and by the end of book 1 the elaborate excursus on Pausanias and Themistocles makes the point that Athenians and Spartans need not always be too different. Under the pressure of events, too, both Athenians and Spartans will have to change their ways, with Spartan generals who are more enterprising (Brasidas, Gylippus) and Athenians ready by 411 even to give up their democracy. Their strategies too will develop, with the navally minded Athenians embroiling themselves in land campaigns, while the Spartans develop the naval power that will eventually bring them victory in 404. The main lines of that strong initial statement remain true and important: at the end of the narrative the Spartans still "proved the ideal enemy for the Athenians to have, for the two peoples were so different, one swift-moving and one slow, one energetically active and one risk averse, and this was especially beneficial in the case of a maritime empire" (Thuc. 8.96.5). But by then Thucydides too has refined his initial statement as the narrative unfolds,[53] partly as a matter of presentation—the two cities' characters were never as different as the Corinthians say—and partly as one of historical development, as people change in response to the changing texture of events.

There are, then, both continuities and differences across cultures. That is an insight that would hardly have come as unfamiliar to Herodotus' contemporaries, even if they found some of his developments of the idea uncomfortable (chapter 4[e]). Thucydides will be more explicit than Herodotus in his focus on the ways in which human nature works in everyone, however different they remain. This "human nature" may not always be quite so ruthless and uncompromising and raw as Thucydides' speakers make it out to be (1.76.1–2, 4.61.5, 5.105.2), but their generalizations encourage us to muse on the issues, and Thucydides himself emphasizes how important it is to his readers that human nature will remain the same and, to a degree, patterns of behavior will recur (1.22.3–4, 3.82.2; p. 231). Yet despite the difference between the two authors in explicitness, here too Thucydides' mindset is not so different from that of Herodotus. With Herodotus as well similarities matter, for peoples do not differ so much: it is not really surprising that Spartans can fear what the young Athenian democracy may menace if allowed to grow (5.91.1; p. 185) in much the same terms as the Lydian Croesus can fear the growth of Persia (1.46.1; pp. 103, 116) and Xerxes, however anachronistically, can fear a threat from Greece unless he stamps it down now (7.11.2–3; pp. 116–117); nor that a Persian and a Theban can share the same dining couch and reflect on the transience of human life in terms that both can understand and that will affect them both (9.16), modern-day counterparts of Achilles and Priam long ago (p. 21).

Nor is that Iliadic reminiscence a casual one. Such intertextual hints matter, and not only as an allusive game, bonding writer and audience as they exploit the cultural capital that they share. They contribute to interpretation too. The differences from the *Iliad* as values change help us to understand how Leonidas thinks and responds, and how the Spartans at home do too; in the next chapter we will find other subtle ways in which pondering differences can prompt a deeper understanding of events. The continuities matter too: continuities with the distant past, if heroism is still possible and if battles take a familiar Homeric turn: continuities across cultures too, if clever ideas can be found either in East or West, or a taste for freedom, or for conquest and empire. These continuities can be a pointer to when it is wise to stop looking for more, to decide instead that this is one of those life-is-like-that things that need no further explanation. It is enough to say that humans, however different, are naturally just like that—or most or enough of them are, most or enough of the time. There is a place for that sort of "explanation," too.

CHAPTER 15

THEN AND NOW: HERODOTUS' OWN DAY

(A) SHADOWS OF THE FUTURE

"Look to the end," advised Solon (1.32.9). Explanation and closure go closely together. You do not know what you have to explain until you know what sort of story you are telling; you do not know what sort of story it is until you have decided how to end it, and—if you are a historical narrator—where to end it.[1] Herodotus ends his linear narrative at Sestos and the Hellespont in 478. The Persians have come into Europe; now they have gone back to Asia.[2] But that is not the end of his text, and we saw in an earlier chapter what is added by the enigmatic final flashback to Cyrus (9.122; pp. 92–93). Nor is it the end of the story, or at least of the way that his story will be read, for he has laid an elaborate trail towards a future that his audience will know all too well. That future is one in which Athens will play a dominant role: as so often, a narrator makes it clear that one story's ending is another story's beginning.[3] That beginning is prominent in the text itself, as the final episode in the linear narrative highlights both Athenian power and Athenian brutality. The general Xanthippus nails the Persian Artaÿctes to an upright plank overlooking the Hellespont,[4] then has the dying man's son stoned to death before his eyes (9.120.4). The Athenians are the masters now, but their methods are disconcertingly similar to those of the Persians before them.

These gestures to the future are relevant to our inquiry in several ways. One is simply that they expand the range of what Herodotus may wish to explain—not only the rise and fall of the Persian empire but also at least the rise of the Athenian empire and perhaps, though this will require more discussion, also its coming fall. A second relevancy, though, is more a matter of contemporary events being used to "explain" the past: perhaps they suggest new perspectives, perhaps they corroborate interpretative strands already there, perhaps it is a blend of both as comparisons and contrasts highlight what was universal and what was special about those extraordinary, wonderful events of Herodotus' tale. This is a two-way street: past illuminates present, present illuminates past.

Intertextuality and contemporary allusiveness have a lot in common. Especially in the previous chapter, we have seen some of the ways in which intertextuality can deepen understanding, suggesting both underlying similarities to paradigmatic events and differences that point to historical change. Contemporary allusiveness does the same. The Artaÿctes sequence itself looks both backwards and forwards, for it is a shrine of Protesilaus that Artaÿctes has defiled. Protesilaus was the first Greek hero to die in the Trojan War, killed as he leapt ashore from the ship (*Iliad* 2.701–702).[5] It is a familiar closural move to nod back at beginnings, and the final chapter of the work will do the same as it recalls the beginnings of Persian expansion under Cyrus: a memory of Protesilaus, the man who opened that first great clash of East and West, is appropriate as this modern-day equivalent of the Trojan War comes, apparently, to its end. An eerie omen, with fish leaping in the pan as they are fried, also recalls earlier moments of the narrative as well as boding no good for Artaÿctes himself.[6] We might also wonder what it portends for all those new "fish" that will be caught over the years and made to dance to the new Athenian tune.[7]

When we talk of "contemporary allusiveness," what "contemporary" do we mean? That is less than straightforward. "Publication" in the ancient world was a more continuous process than in the modern. It is reasonable to assume that the work took shape over many years and that Herodotus would have given readings at different stages, adjusting them to changing circumstances and audiences. Some unevenness may be owed to such gradual alterations or to notes for particular performances that have been only roughly assimilated into a draft.[8] The physical difficulties of making such additions or adjustments in ancient conditions should not be underestimated: rather than thorough rewriting, we might rather think of annotations in the margin or, in extreme cases, a snipping through of a papyrus roll to sew in a new passage.[9] So what was contemporary in the 450s might survive in delivery a generation later, or at least in a written draft from which a lecturer could draw some items and choose to omit others.

Nor do we know when Herodotus' text reached its final form, still less when any particular sentence was first written; attempts to plot his intellectual development are generally now regarded as unconvincing.[10] The date usually given is "ca. 425," but this largely depends on what has been regarded as parody of Herodotus' opening in Aristophanes' *Acharnians*, performed in that year. That is probably a misreading. There is certainly parody of something when Aristophanes' Dicaeopolis gives his own tongue-in-cheek analysis of the origins of the Peloponnesian War, but it need not be Herodotus' text: a lot is a riff on Euripides' *Telephus*, a favorite store of material for Aristophanes in paratragic mood; a lot more is best taken in terms of Herodotus and Aristophanes *doing the same sort of thing*,[11] both extracting capital from audience familiarity with the ways that wars were popularly explained: they did x, and then we did y, and then they did z . . . and so on—the sort of thing that was ridiculed when it occurred in the cyclic epics.[12] We have already seen that Herodotus, like Homer before him, cuts a good deal deeper, and the "capital" that he extracts is more serious than that piece of Aristophanic humor.[13]

A better case can be made for parody of Herodotus in Aristophanes' *Birds* eleven years later, with a description of Babylon (1124–1131) that carries a strong sense of the description at 1.179 and couples it with a Herodotus-style interest in Egypt;[14] but that too is not decisive for recent "publication" then. If Herodotus' work was well-enough known to mean anything to more than a small fraction of the audience, it could be remembered for several years afterwards: it need not be a new book rather than the theme of *Birds*, with its escapist interest in the exotic and unknown, that prompted thoughts of Babylon and Egypt.

Still, that 425 date is unlikely to be far wrong: perhaps a few years too early, but only a few. As we shall see, the explicit references to later events peter out in the 420s. The latest event to which Herodotus indubitably refers is the killing of the Spartan envoys in 430 (7.137; see below), but his retrospect of three disastrous generations seems to take us down to the 420s:

> For under the reigns of Darius son of Hystaspes and Xerxes son of Darius and Artaxerxes son of Xerxes, those three generations, more evils happened to Greece than in the twenty generations that preceded Darius, some coming from the Persians and some from the head Greeks themselves fighting for the empire.
> (6.98.2; CF. P. 187)

That phrasing is normally taken as implying that Artaxerxes is now dead (424 BCE), and this is probably right: it is true that Greece's evils persisted for some time after that, but had Herodotus written it before he would have been more likely to say "have happened," *gegone*, rather than use the aorist tense appropriate for a finished past event, *egeneto*.[15]

A reference in book 9 also clearly reaches the 420s if not beyond. Mention there of a man from Decelea—the steadfast fighter Sophanes, so firmly resolved to stand his ground that he planted an anchor in the soil—prompts an apparently rather gratuitous[16] mention of the legendary past, when the people of Decelea were so outraged by Theseus' abduction of Helen that they told the invading Spartans where to find her:

As a consequence the Deceleans were granted freedom of dues and privileged seating in Sparta, and this has lasted continuously to the present day, to such a degree as to make the Spartans keep away (*apechesthai*) from Decelea when, in the war that happened (*genomenon*) many years later between Athenians and the Peloponnesians, they were ravaging the rest of Attica.
(9.73.3)

It is probably safe to assume that this was written before 413, when the Spartans occupied Decelea as their base—hardly "keeping away" or "holding themselves back from"—though one scholar concludes the opposite.[17] It is unsafe to go further, inferring either from Herodotus' language that the Archidamian War is now over,[18] which would point to a date after 421, or from Thucydides that Decelea was ravaged in 427,[19] and that therefore the sentence was written before Herodotus knew of that.

There are other passages that would certainly have more immediacy after particular events in the Peloponnesian War—more on these in the next section—but here too it is hazardous to infer that they *must* have been written in the light of those developments. Demaratus' advice to Xerxes to occupy Cythera and use it to "intimidate the Spartans" (7.235) is a good example. The Athenian Nicias occupied the island in 424 (Thuc. 4.53–57), and some have concluded that Herodotus must have written after that date;[20] but Nicias was not the first to sense that possibility, and it seems that the Athenians had already used the ploy in 455 (Paus. 1.27.5; cf. Thuc. 1.108.5). In any case, Athenian attacks on the Peloponnesian coast had been substantial in the early stages of the Peloponnesian War (Thuc. 2.56: four thousand hoplites and three hundred cavalry) and would show the damage such raids could do.[21]

Nor is it safe to argue that Herodotus would have found opportunities for mentioning events had he known of them, for instance, the killing of Aeginetans in 424 (Thuc. 4.57).[22] As Fornara fairly observed, the references that we do have are so sparse that we must assume that he is being highly selective.[23] There is nothing, for instance, on the brutal Athenian treatment of Samos in 440–439, despite Herodotus' great interest in Samos. That, of course, makes the choices that he does make all the worthier of examination.

The precise date of "publication" may not matter too much, whether we are looking for Herodotus' formative influences or, more importantly for this inquiry, for the experiences that might affect his audience's interpretation of the past. Such memories may be especially sharp when the most recent years are in point but will not be confined to them; the events that led to the Peloponnesian War may indeed be more thought-provoking than those of the war itself. One might compare the way that memories of the 1930s were especially vigorous in British minds during the crisis of 1956, with prime minister Eden convinced that he was dealing with a new Hitler in Colonel Nasser and that firm methods were necessary to reverse Egypt's nationalization of the Suez Canal.[24] Historical parallels can teach bad lessons as well as good.

"Thought-provoking"—but what thoughts might be provoked? It will be useful first to go through the explicit references to events beyond the linear narrative (in narratological language, cases of "external prolepsis"). There may well be implicit ones as well (hints of the Athenian empire in Croesus' imposition of tribute at 1.6.2, for instance);[25] some of the generalizations may also anachronistically anticipate points more relevant to the later period, such as the Athenians becoming "by far the first of all" (5.78; p. 164) and perhaps even being famed for their smartness (1.60.3; p. 191). But the explicit references will be a start.[26] In particular, we should note where they come in the narrative and what they contribute in their contexts. The juxtapositions with events in the linear narrative is often suggestive, sometimes amounting to what has been called "situational irony."[27] It will be valuable to take them in the order in which they come, not the order of the later events to which they allude: that may suggest a rhythm and development in the suggestions. There is a danger of overinterpretation here, for many of the forward allusions simply come at the point where a parallel becomes relevant, but even there Herodotus can adjust emphases in the surrounding context to suggest contrasts or patterns.

- 3.12.4, Herodotus has seen the skulls of Persians killed in the campaign of Achaemenes son of Darius against the Libyan Inaros (459 BCE). This comes in the context of Cambyses' successful Egyptian campaign: further Persian adventures in Africa are clearly to come. Though Herodotus does not mention it, that fighting also involved the Athenians, with catastrophic results (Thuc. 1.104, 109–110).[28]

- 3.15.3, Inaros' and Amyrtaeus' sons acceded to the throne in Egypt, despite all the damage their fathers had caused (after 449 BCE, for Amyrtaeus was still ruler of Lower Egypt at that date, Thuc. 1.112.3).

- 3.160.2, Megabyxus son of Zopyrus fought the Athenians in Egypt in the 459 campaign. His own son Zopyrus (Herodotus goes on to say) deserted from the Persians to the Athenians—a true "desertion" contrasting with the false one when the first Zopyrus pretended to desert to Babylon.

- (?) 4.43, Sataspes the Persian (so the Carthaginians say) tried but failed to circumnavigate Africa, and was executed by Xerxes. The date of this is uncertain, but may well be post-478.²⁹ Herodotus tells the story while discussing the place of Libya on the world map. This failed expedition contrasts with the success of Darius, who was responsible for the "discovery of most of Asia" (4.44.1).

- 4.148.4, most of the cities founded by the Minyans were "destroyed by the Eleians in my time" (probably around 460 BCE). This rounds off a complicated sequence where a series of Spartan attempts to accommodate their Minyan kinsmen have ended in violence and failure.

- 5.32, Pausanias was betrothed—"if the report is true"—to the daughter of the Persian magnate Megabates when he "lusted to become tyrant of Greece" (cf. p. 210). Megabates has been sent westwards because of Aristagoras' dealings with Artaphrenes and through him with Darius: these were a consequence of Aristagoras of Miletus' own desire to become tyrant of Naxos (5.30–31). Naxos and Miletus were thus the "start of many evils for the Ionians," 5.28.1.

- 6.72.1, Leutychidas died in exile in Tegea (ca. 469), after leading a Spartan campaign into Thessaly (perhaps in 478?) and being caught red-handed in a case of bribe-taking. This, Herodotus notes, was some sort of payback (*tisis*) for what he had done to Demaratus. *Tisis* is a recurrent theme in book 6, especially in Spartan contexts;³⁰ Leutychidas himself will tell a fable centering on the theme at 6.86, bringing out how payback may be slow but is relentless—a case of the wrong person saying the right thing.³¹

- 6.91.1, after a sacrilege, the god had still not been appeased when "the Aeginetans were expelled from the island." The Athenians are not named, but this refers to their expulsion of the islanders in 431 (Thuc. 2.27; p. 226). In the narrative the Marathon campaign, so glorious for Athens, is about to begin.

- 6.98.2, "many evils" came upon the Greeks during the three reigns of Darius, Xerxes, and Artaxerxes (p. 187). This relates to the Delos earthquake that might have been taken as portending the Persian defeat at Marathon but is instead interpreted by Herodotus as ominous of bad things for Greece rather than good.³²

- 6.118.3, the Thebans restore a statue to Delium "twenty years later" than the Marathon campaign.

- 6.131, the descendants of Megacles of Athens and his wife Agariste include first Cleisthenes "who established the tribes and the democracy for Athens" (p. 193) and later Pericles, whose mother dreamed during her pregnancy that she was bearing a lion. That image is one with various suggestions, both positive (strength) and negative (threat). (This is not strictly an "external prolepsis," as Pericles was born before 478, but it is Pericles the adult rather than the infant who will be brought to the audience's minds.)

- 7.7, Inaros kills Xerxes' brother Achaemenes, governor of Egypt, "many years later" (459 BCE?: cf. above, 3.12.4). Xerxes has just invaded Egypt and made it "much more enslaved than it had been under Darius," but this, like 3.12.4, looks forwards to troubles ahead there for Persia.

- 7.106, Mascames of Doriscus is rewarded by Xerxes; "his son Artaxerxes continued those rewards to Mascames' descendants." All the other Persian-imposed tyrants in Thrace and the Hellespontine region were expelled "by the Greeks" (early 470s). Xerxes is at this point advancing through these regions in 480; this again points to future Persian reversals.

- 7.107, Boges of Eion is highly esteemed by Xerxes for holding out to the last when besieged by "Cimon and the Athenians." When hope ran out, he built a pyre and immolated himself, family, and household (probably 476).

- 7.114.2, Xerxes' wife Amestris "in her old age" buries alive fourteen Persian noble youths. Xerxes has just buried alive eighteen local children at Ennea Hodoi.

- 7.137.2–3, two Spartan heralds, sons of the Sperthies and Boulis who were sent to Xerxes (pp. 163–164), are captured and killed by the Athenians along with Aristeas of Corinth (430). This is juxtaposed not merely with Xerxes' magnanimous treatment of their fathers but also with the praise of Athenians as the saviors of Greece in 480 (7.139). Herodotus there acknowledges that this will not be welcome hearing for many of his audience (7.139.1; pp. 42–43).

- 7.151, "many years later" Callias and other envoys from Athens are in Susa at the same time as ambassadors from Argos. The Argives ask Artaxerxes if the terms of their friendship with Xerxes are still valid, and Artaxerxes confirms that they are (perhaps 461, perhaps 449–448). The focus in the immediate context is on the Argives, not the Athenians, and Callias and his colleagues could have been passed over in silence. They were there "concerning another matter," Herodotus teasingly says. Whether or not a formal "peace of Callias" was then agreed, many of the audience would know or assume that this was a stage when the Athenians ceased to pursue the retaliatory war against Persia. This is not too far after that passage of praise for the Athenians for their role in 480 (7.139).

- 7.170.3, the battle between Taras and Rhegium in S. Italy saw "the biggest slaughter among Greeks that we have ever known" (473?). Shortly before in the narrative, the attempt to involve Gelon of Syracuse in the Greek resistance has foundered: this may have been partly because he was preoccupied with a threat from Carthage (7.165–167). The previous tyrant of Rhegium had played a role in stirring up that Carthaginian threat (7.165).[33] External dangers in 480 contrast with the internally generated bloodshed to come.

- 7.233.2, Leontiades' son Eurymachus was killed by the Plataeans after he had captured their city when in command of 400 Thebans. The Theban attack on Plataea was the event that triggered the outbreak of the Peloponnesian War in 431. The narrative of Thermopylae has just ended.

- 8.3, the Athenians gave up their claim to naval leadership when the allies objected so strongly, making Greece's survival their priority and realizing that disagreement over the leadership would be disastrous.

> And they were wise about this, for internal dissension is worse than a united war effort to the same degree that war is worse than peace. So it was appreciation of this fact that made the Athenians give way without making a fuss—but, as they later demonstrated, only for as long as (or "until") they badly needed them. Once Xerxes' invasion had been repulsed and they were fighting for his territory rather than their own, they deprived the Lacedaemonians of the leadership, citing Pausanias' arrogant behavior as their reason. But all this happened later.[34]

The "theys" and "thems" are ambiguous in the Greek as in the English: was it that "they," the allies, eventually needed "them," the Athenians, and "they," the allies, who then removed the Spartans from the leadership? Or that "they," the Athenians, for a time needed "them," the Spartans, and "they," the Athenians, then contrived a way to get that leadership? In any case, this was the reason why Eurybiades the Spartan had overall command. Immediately afterwards the Greeks plan to "make a run for it" to the Isthmus (8.4.1; p. 182): and so the Euboeans turn to the Athenian commander Themistocles after all, and his initiative leads to the decisive change of strategy (8.4–5; p. 169).

- 8.109.5, Themistocles ensures a future refuge in Persia "if anything happens to him at the hands of the Athenians": and "this is what happened" (p. 206). The narrative goes on to his moves against Andros, Paros, and

Carystus (8.111–112, p. 205), but this is also soon after his triumph at Salamis and before his acclaim at the Isthmus and at Sparta (8.123–124; pp. 206–207).

- 9.35.2, after becoming a Spartan Teisamenus fought five crucial combats: Plataea (479), against the Tegeans and Argives, against the Arcadians (both late 470s), against the Messenians (late 460s), and against the Athenians and Argives at Tanagra (457).

- 9.37.4–38.1, Hegesistratus of Elis is caught and executed by Spartans some time "after the events at Plataea." That is the only indication of date: it could therefore fall in 479–478, making this an "internal" rather than "external" prolepsis, but the chances are that it was later.

- 9.64.2, Aeimnestus or Arimnestus, the killer of Mardonius, later died fighting the Messenians; he was leading three hundred picked men (so shades of Thermopylae in particular).[35] This and the next three allusions are given in the context of the battle of Plataea.

- 9.73.3, the Spartans "keep away" from Decelea in the war "that came about many years later between the Athenians and the Peloponnesians" (p. 217).

- 9.75, Sophanes the steadfast Athenian dies "much later" fighting the Edonians "for the gold mines" (probably ca. 465).

- 9.85.3, a so-called tomb of the Aeginetans is erected at Plataea ten years later.

- 9.105, Hermolycus, the best Athenian fighter at Mycale, dies in fighting between Athenians and Carystus (probably ca. 472).

- 9.108–113, the elaborate story of Xerxes and Masistes' wife. The affair took place "as time went by" (9.109.1) after Xerxes' return to Susa; it also gives a forward-looking hint of Xerxes' own death in 465 (pp. 32–33).

The allusiveness to the future therefore becomes more insistent as the narrative progresses, and the emphasis also shifts even within these later books. In the first two-thirds of book 7, the glances forward often concern the end of the Persian conflict that is there beginning: they focus on the fall of the Thracian cities that Xerxes is now taking, then on the time when Athenians relaxed their naval activities against a Persian enemy. By the end of book 7 and in the last two books, the emphasis had moved to later fighting of Greek against Greek, involving both Athens (Edonians—where notice the hint of greed, "for the gold mines"—and Carystus) and Sparta (Tegea, Messenia), sometimes both (Tanagra, Decelea) and sometimes neither (Taras and Rhegium).[36] Both the Persian and the internal Greek dimension are introduced by the generalization in 6.98.2, with some of those Greek evils "coming from the Persians and some from the Greeks' own contention for empire."

These are, indeed, unremittingly "evils," just as those "evils" that came upon the Ionians from Aristagoras and Miletus at 5.28.1, and there is no triumphalist hint of a glorious war of liberation and revenge once the Athenians had moved in the 470s to the offensive. The Athenians, indeed, are not treated particularly generously. Even the "expulsion" of the Persians in the Thraceward region is done "by the Greeks" (7.106.2) and is not specially celebrated; the emphasis immediately moves to Boges' spectacular death, and here the darker aspects—the siege and the starvation—are more specifically the work of "Cimon and the Athenians." Credit is given to the Athenians for their role in 480, both their ceding of the naval leadership (8.3; cf. 9.27.6; p. 221) and their constancy in staying (7.139). Herodotus also stresses, however, that the praise will be unwelcome to those who hear it, and that points the contrast between goodness then and their later actions. Passages hinting at that later brutality tend to cluster close to moments in 480 showing them at their best. This has something of the same technique as in that mention of Themistocles' future troubles while he is still glowing with the triumph of Salamis (8.109.5; p. 206).

To be sure, anti-Athenian stridency is avoided as well. Sparta's future fighting against Greeks is highlighted too,[37] and the hint of Pausanias' future just after the victory of Plataea shows the same technique as with Themistocles (9.82; p. 210). There is no direct criticism of the Athenians when those envoys are at the Persian court "concerning another matter," and even those who read between the lines were as free to conclude "now their work was done" as "they were now abandoning the cause."[38] The ambiguities of 8.3 allow those friendly to Athens to explain their assumption of leadership wholly as a matter of the allies' choice, not of the Athenians' own manipulation. But those who took an unfriendlier view were not short of material to support it.[39]

(B) THINKING BACKWARDS AND FORWARDS

Intertextuality and contemporary allusiveness, we have already seen (pp. 57, 215), have a lot in common. The first looks backwards, especially to Homer; the second looks forward, to events known to the first audience from experience. In earlier chapters we have also found many cases of looking sideways, comparing Athenian patterns with Spartan or Greek with Persian. All of these point both to differences and to similarities. These are fascinating enough in themselves: in a work so full of and so dedicated to "marvels," there is no need to strain to find interpretative value in every contrast and every continuity. "Just fancy that!" is often a proper and adequate response.

Still, one often does not have to strain, and interpretation—explanation—is clearly deepened if we find such similarities and differences thought-provoking. The enhanced importance of the collective helps us to understand why Leonidas behaved as he did, with values just as heroic as those of the *Iliad* but now centering more on the *polis*; the changing functioning of *mēnis* (p. 204) similarly illuminates the Spartans' response to the hapless sole survivor Aristodemus. It may also help us to understand a gingerliness in the ways that people and states are still coming to terms with these changed values: witness the lack of sure-footedness in the Spartans' consultation of the interstate collective that they lead (5.91–93), another episode rich in Homeric echoes,[40] or the uncertainties in the decision-making process before Salamis (8.59–64; pp. 183–184).

What, then, of the forward-looking allusions? Do these too add illuminating perspectives? And what of those later events that must have been familiar to the audience, even if they are not specifically name-checked in the narrative?

One simple point may be made first: it can be a matter of narrative immediacy. The past still matters. Debts to it are still being paid as the audience read or hear. The curse on Aegina for sacrilege was laid to rest only when its inhabitants were expelled a few years ago; perhaps its aftereffects linger on, if the audience already know about that slaughter in 424 (p. 217). Those sons of the Spartan heralds had met their end only in 430, and there too those who wished could find a supernatural cause still operating. Others might be content to contrast Athenian behavior to Sparta now with the two cities' togetherness against Xerxes: in the 480s they had been linked in that shared sacrilege against the Persian envoys, but now the Athenians have been the ones to impose on Sparta the transgenerational payback when Xerxes himself had been magnanimous (7.136–137).[41] There even might—might—be a debt to the gods still to pay for the Athenian refusal to give up the Aeginetan hostages in the face of Leutychidas' warning (6.86).[42]

Not just the gods remember, of course: humans remember too, or should remember. The Spartans remembered their debt to the Deceleans, one going much further back than 479, and this was still visible in the way they were conducting the campaign (9.73; p. 217). If, too, 424 had already come and gone, the audience might recall the respect Datis had shown to the temple of

Apollo at Delium.[43] The sanctity of that temple was a flashpoint in the Delium campaign of 424, with Athenian and Theban claim and counterclaim of impiety (Thuc. 4.97–98). Such matters were still important—or, indignant observers of that 424 campaign might think, they should have been.

Other insights could come even closer to home. When Gelon of Syracuse rejects the Greek approach for an alliance, he tells the envoys to go home and report that "the spring has gone out of the year" (7.162–163). The surface meaning is clear: the hopes pinned on that alliance have disappeared. Yet many would remember that Pericles had used the same image to commemorate the young men of Athens, their hope for the future, who had been killed on a campaign (Arist. *Rhet.* 1365a31–33, 1411a2–4).[44] The envoys' words to Gelon had made him aware of Greek civic pride and the intercity jealousies that it fostered. The memories of Pericles brought home what consequences these would bring in the generations that followed.

These parallels, though, are not just a matter of immediacy. We have already seen (chapter 3[c]) that they give narrative cogency too. If an intertextual reminiscence suggests that something similar to Marathon or to Thermopylae happened in the *Iliad*, or if experience suggested that the Athenian empire was replaying some of the same moves as the Persian, an audience will be the readier to believe that the narration is getting things right. Whatever it may be, if it is happening now or if it happened in the distant past or even in myth,[45] it could happen in 490 or 480 as well. If any observer of the Athenian empire could sense the desire for freedom in resentful subjects, they would be more likely to believe Histiaeus when he says that all the tyrants' cities wish to be rid of them (4.137.2; p. 194) or that Aristagoras might play a populist game by suppressing tyrannies and imposing *isonomiē* (5.37.2; p. 193), overstatement though that second claim seems to be.[46] If civic pride and jealousies continued to be so strident, it would be very credible that they loomed so large in the 480s as well. Those sideways glances at other cultures can work in a similar way, for if a cunning ploy can have momentous consequences for Darius it makes it more plausible that it could for Themistocles too—and *vice versa*. In a way it is an application of that empirical principle that "the evident phenomena are a sight of what is unclear" (p. 2): the more familiar and universal the pattern, the more likely it is that it may have obtained on any one occasion.

Recurrence can help one not just to believe but also to understand or to favor one interpretative thread over another. Take Athens and Aegina. Their mutual sparrings take up a lot of Herodotus' narrative and played their paradoxical role in explaining why the Greek fleet was so well equipped to take on Xerxes (7.144; p. 188). But could any hearer or reader believe that Athenians really hated their neighbors so much? Anyone who remembered recent events would find it easier to believe. That expulsion in 431 was driven, according to Thucydides, by the Athenians' "charge that they were not least responsible for the war" (Thuc. 2.27.1). That would be enough to make it stick in the audience's minds, and they would also know of what Thucydides later calls "the hatred that had already existed" (4.57.4, explaining the executions of 424). Pericles, so we are told, had once said that Aegina, that "eyesore of the Piraeus," needed to be removed (Arist. *Rhet.* 1411a15). Herodotus lets us see that hatred in action two generations before, with each new exchange cementing it more. The past explains the present, why the Athenians are still so bitter; the present makes Herodotus' interpretation of the past all the more persuasive. The interpretative interplay is indeed a two-way street.

Those are not the only features of the late 430s that would be in the audience's mind. We saw (pp. 44, 56) that the animosities of Corinth and Corcyra, so important in the run-up to the Peloponnesian War, would add credibility to Herodotus' narrative of the sixth-century triangle of Corinth, Corcyra, and Samos: Corinth and Corcyra "are at odds with one another and have been continually, kinsmen as they are, ever since the Corinthians first colonized the island" (3.49.1).

Elsewhere too that recent sequence would be in the audience's minds. When Soclees speaks out against action to restore the Peisistratids, that recent experience gives extra point to Hippias' threat that the Corinthians will particularly rue missing this chance "when the time comes for them to receive grief at Athenian hands" (5.93.1; p. 185). When in a later sequence the Corinthians lent the Athenians twenty ships, Herodotus adds that "at that time Corinth and Athens were on the best possible terms of friendship" (6.89): that was worth saying, strange as it would sound to contemporary ears. If Thucydides' account of the Corcyrean debate at Athens (1.31–44) is anywhere near capturing what the envoys had actually said, the Corcyreans' canny hanging back from the conflict in 480 (7.168) would also strike a familiar note with anyone who was there (admittedly, that would be only a small minority of Herodotus' audience).[47] The islanders' record of refusal to get involved in alliances had then taken some explaining away: the Corinthian charge was one of isolationist selfishness (Thuc. 1.32.3–4, 1.37.2–4).[48]

Just as interesting are cases where there might have been parallels between past and present but were not. Demaratus' advice to Xerxes about Cythera was as valid now as it had been in 480; if Nicias had already conducted that campaign of 424 (p. 217), that made the point even clearer—and underlined how big an opportunity Xerxes had missed.

Correspondingly, there were moments when the past might still have been alive in present memories but was not. Take the extensive flashback explaining how Plataea first came in 519 BCE, on the encouragement of the

Spartan king, to be so closely linked with Athens (6.108). Plataea too had played its part in the outbreak of the war (Thuc. 2.1–6), as Herodotus finds a way of reminding us at 7.233.2 (p. 227); the animosities of Thebes and Plataea were as active in 431 as they had been in 519, and that aligns with those cases of continuity that we have just been exploring. The more moving and recent memory would be the Spartans' treatment of the city in 428, executing the males and enslaving the women. "That was the end of Plataea's story, in the ninety-third year of the Athenian alliance" (Thuc. 3.68.5). If Thucydides' account of the speeches can be trusted, appeals to the past figured heavily in the pleas made to the Spartan judges by both Plataeans and Thebans, not just the past of 519 but even more the debt the Greeks owed to Plataea because of 479. Herodotus' audience might have assumed as much, even if they did not know as much about those arguments as Thucydides' readers would later be told. Neither Sparta, inflicting the punishment, nor Athens, leaving Plataea to its fate after encouraging it to resist, comes out of that sequence with any moral credit.

There may be an even wider implication. Thucydides' Thebans argue that if the Plataeans were "good" in the Persian Wars, they deserve twice the penalty for being "bad" now (3.67.2). Such ideas were in the air: Thucydides' bluff Spartan Sthenelaidas applies them to Athens too (1.86.2), and Herodotus' own Athenians suggest something of the same in their speech before, perhaps not coincidentally, the battle of Plataea (9.27.4). Readers will have heard such things in the streets, gymnasia, and symposia. Sthenelaidas will not have been the only one to ponder in these terms the contrasts that the flash-forwards suggested between Athens, savior of Greece in 480–479, and Athens, brutal imperialist in the half-century that followed.[49] Others might think that the same was true of Sparta.

So the past still mattered, and that is telling: past and present explain one another. Even more telling is when the past did not matter but might have or should have mattered, as with Plataea or with Decelea or with Delium (pp. 224–225). It certainly made you think.

We earlier suggested that Herodotus' narrative works in a similar way to the Hippocratic *Epidemics* (pp. 50–54), clarifying the *homoia kai anomoia*, what is similar and what is not, and using this to identify the variables that are making a difference. We can notice what is constant in Persian kings— their power and position—and what is varied—their personalities; and if patterns of behavior are recurrent, this gives pointers to what is likely to be the most powerful explanation.

This can now be taken further, with backwards, forwards, and sideways glances all playing a part. A causal explanation gains cogency through its applicability not only to one sequence but to others as well,[50] not unlike the way that those ships that were "the start of evil" parallel those other, Trojan ships that brought so much suffering in their wake (p. 105). Equally, it loses cogency if it does not, and that is why the tradewind explanation of the Nile flood fails (p. 41). If one city's hatred for another recurs in different time frames and has similar consequences, one does not have to look much further for an explanation. If a talent for cunning trickery can be found across cultures, there is no need to resort to ideas of, say, Greek exceptionalism; the same goes for a taste for freedom or for conquest. Those may be matters of *physis* rather than *nomos*, aspects of experience that invite nothing beyond the simplest of "life-is-like-that explanations": humans are indeed like that.

Yet the dissimilarities, the *anomoia*, matter too. What may be explicable in terms of distinct cultures is the direction such cunning takes and the interests it promotes, one's master's or one's own; or the barriers that may stand in the way of freedom, ideas of tradition and national identity in the East, quarrelsome selfishness in the West; or the factors that may promote or impede successful conquest, on the one side firm one-man control, on the other knowledge that one is fighting for oneself. Heroism too may take a subtly different form in a changed world, with Miltiades or Themistocles not heroes in the same way as Achilles and Hector; even Leonidas will not think in exactly the Homeric way. One needs to invoke historical change to understand that; one may need to do the same to explain why Spartans and Athenians can both regard Plataea's past as less urgent a motive than the fierce necessities of the present. But it matters that, at least where less is at stake, memories can still live on, and Decelea can at least for the moment be spared. It matters too that heroism is still possible, that in battle after battle there will be those individuals inviting the lapidary praise of "he showed himself a good man." That capacity is again a feature of the human condition: humans are like that always and everywhere, or at least can be.

The comparison between Persian and Athenian empires can also be part of the education Herodotus offered in historical change. If the Athenians behave so badly as leaders after being so good as colleagues, why should that be? Human nature, perhaps, in its rawest form: they behave so domineeringly because they can and because it pays. Or are things different, or might they be different, because this is an empire of Greeks over Greeks, with masters and followers alike understanding freedom? Or because this is the rule of a democracy? Or are any such differences illusory, or at least infinitesimal? Perhaps the Athenians are not so different anyway: perhaps, given the power, they would have treated Aegina in the 480s in the same way as they did in 431. Or perhaps they have learned from the enemy, all too well.[51] All are good questions: were there yet any answers?

(C) BACK TO THE FUTURE

What we were doing in the last section was in the manner of a Hippocratic writer who appealed to his audience's knowledge of what a numbed hand felt like or how one drinks fluids or what it is like to have a cold (pp. 56–57). Familiar bodily experiences help one to understand what is more distant or difficult; present and recent events help Herodotus' audience to understand those of sixty years before. But evidently the other direction down this two-way street also mattered to the Hippocratics. One records past cases in order to aid one's diagnosis of new ones: that is what the collection of the *Epidemics* is for. The more cases one can gather and the more differentiated their description, the greater the understanding can be expected to be. A good physician knows too that such explanations are provisional, and a new case may require one's previous pattern to be revised (p. 53). Diagnosis also links closely with prognosis, predicting when a crisis is going to come and, where possible and with an acknowledgement of the uncertainties, what the outcome is likely to be. Medicine is about curing too, doing what one can to make that outcome a better one, and prognosis can only help: "The physician treats the patient best when he has foreknowledge of what is likely to result from the present condition" (*Prognostikon* 1 II p. 6 J = II p. 110 L). That passage also explains that good prognosis builds trust: when things develop as predicted that makes you "trust the physician more, so that people are prepared to entrust themselves to the physician."

What about Herodotus? The present, it will now be clear, can illuminate the past. How does the past illuminate the present? And what about the future? After all, in scientific matters, a correct understanding of the past—how the Nile delta silted up, for instance—allowed predictions, cautiously expressed, of the future: if the silting up continues at the same rate, one day a serious drought will hit the area downstream of Lake Moeris (2.13.2–14.1).[52] Might the same be true of human history?[53] If so, it would not simply aid us to see what is going to come; that element of "trust" in the physician would also have a parallel, as our recognition of Herodotean patterns in contemporary events as they develop would also promote confidence in his account of the past. The two-way street will be carrying traffic still.

In terms of diagnosis of Herodotus' present, many features would already be clear to his first audience. The outbreak of the Peloponnesian War may or may not have been predictable, but it was certainly explicable: those universal Herodotean patterns of a drive to conquest and an urge to defend one's freedom make it no surprise. Back in the 470s it might have been less predictable that the Athenian empire would turn out as brutal and uncompromising as it had; their own sense for freedom might have made a difference, but it had not, and a pattern had turned out to be more universal than its victims might have hoped. Less universal, more specifically Greek, might be the ubiquity of intercity tensions and quarrels and attacks; no surprise there either if they had escalated as they had. Some strategic and military clarities were also continuous between then and now. The Peloponnese remained as vulnerable to naval power as it had been; Cythera could still be critical.

On other matters the jury was still out, and the future was very uncertain. Sparta's military ethic was very traditional, as Demaratus had stressed; but history changes and values change with them, as even the case of Leonidas and Thermopylae made clear. Would those Spartan ways be equal to the task, or would they be outdated when it was a new and different sort of enemy, one imbued with that democratic ethos of fighting for oneself?[54] Even by the late 420s, nobody could yet know. As it turned out, Spartan military traditions eventually prevailed on the battlefield of Mantinea in 418, outdone in skill but decisively superior in courage (Thuc. 5.72.2): nor would Sparta be so hopeless at developing a naval power of its own when it had to. It was becoming clear that Spartan commanders too could be imaginative: Brasidas was showing that by 424.

Looming large in many minds would also be a very big question indeed: what about the gods? The Spartans were uneasy, so Thucydides tells us in a later context (7.18), about a war where they might be religiously in the wrong, for the Thebans had attacked Plataea during a truce, and the Spartans themselves had neglected the terms of a sworn peace: was this, they wondered, why they suffered the catastrophe of Pylos in 425? It was a Spartan speaker in Herodotus who opined that the ways of Heaven can be slow but relentless when oaths are broken (Leutychidas at 6.86). Those affronted gods might—might—be already on the move.

There were even uncertainties about Persia: was that organic decay complete? Was the chain of East-West vengeance finished? Both sides were putting out feelers to Persia (Thuc. 2.7.1, 2.67.1, 4.50), and Aristophanes would have fun with Athenian embassies in *Acharnians* (62–125). We can see that Persian satraps were keeping a close eye on Greek developments (Thuc. 5.1). Thucydides gives little attention to any Persian dimension at this stage of the war,[55] but some might already have wondered if Persia might still play a role in the Greek fighting. If so, they were right.

The jury was also still out on how it all would end. Prognosis was particularly difficult, and—except perhaps during the darkest days of the Athenian plague—the probable outcome would be far from clear. Empires had risen and fallen: Herodotus had laid that process bare. It is easy, and it may be right, to take him to be suggesting the same about Athens—"Herodotus warns the Athenians," as John Moles entitled a classic paper.[56] But empires do not lose all wars: Herodotus had also shown enough cases where empires had won. If there was any moral to be drawn, it might be rather that the time would come for Athens too and one day, in one war or another, their empire would fall.[57] It did not follow that this was that war. Thucydides' Pericles could grant that the empire would fall sooner or later (Thuc. 2.64.3); he was also sure that, if Athens did the right things in this particular war, they could "win through" (*periesesthai*, 2.65.7; cf. 2.65.13). An Athenian audience might anyway feel that it was a little late for any such warning about their empire, which "might seem unjust to acquire but is dangerous to abandon"—Thucydides' Pericles again (2.63.2; cf. 1.75.4). All that a warning could offer was that the Athenians *might* lose. They probably knew that already.

Yet it remains true that this empire was different in one important respect: it was an empire based on democracy and the Athenians' own freedom, both exercised in a particularly full-blooded form: and democracy, we remember, was the extreme test-case for the opposite of tyranny (p. 197). Just like that diligent Hippocratic empiricist, the wise reader or listener would know that patterns are provisional, that a new observation might require one to refine a pattern and identify a cause that would make a critical difference. Democracy might be that critical cause; so might freedom—*might*. It was unpredictable.

That, though, did not mean that the outcome would be inexplicable when it came.[58] Explicability without predictability: we have seen that in plenty. Whatever the outcome, future readers—even future listeners, with reperformance when Herodotus himself was no more—would find strands in the text to help them to understand.

It was Thucydides who made it explicit that he was writing for all time, a "possession for ever" (1.22.4), but the emphasis in Herodotus' proem suggests the same:[59] that "glory," that need to preserve wondrous doings from "erasure by time." The use of the past tense in 1.5.4 is telling: "Those that *were* big in my own day were small in the past" (p. 28). That is written from the perspective of the future, rather as letters often use a past tense for events that were in the present for the writer but will be in the past for the recipient.[60] In that case, the two-way street continues for Herodotus' future readers, us included, as they—we—ponder our own times; like Thucydides, he may help us to "see clearly into what happened and what will happen again, the human condition being what it is, in the same and similar ways" (Thuc. 1.22.4)—what happened and what will happen again, each illuminating the other, each helping to explain.

CHAPTER 16

WHY INDEED?

Arnaldo Momigliano did not think much of the way Greek and Roman historians handled the causes of war. He found them thoroughly disappointing on the subject, much thinner and vaguer than they were on constitutional developments.[1] The highest marks in this lackluster class he awarded to Herodotus, though some of the way he put it may seem surprising. "Herodotus' approach to the causes of the war is both concrete and subtle," alert as he is to "the interplay of disjointed factors." "He is quite unsystematic." His mental horizon is very wide, "but even more admirable is the dexterity with which he avoids being enmeshed in his own net, wide as it is."[2] Thucydides might be "acclaimed by the moderns" for trying to bring more rigor to his causal analysis, but for Momigliano they are wrong: "If there is something that Thucydides does not succeed in doing, it is to explain the remote origins of the conflict between Sparta and Athens."[3] Thucydides' "truest cause" of 1.23.6—the Athenians becoming great and forcing Sparta towards war—is just "vague"; no wonder Polybius tried to improve on Thucydides' causal distinctions, but his attempts are little better.[4] As for the Roman historians, they get only a couple of pages. Even Tacitus falls short of the mark: "If you look for a dull patch in Tacitus, you have only to open the pages of Book XII of the Annals on the origins of one of the wars between Parthia and Rome."[5]

There is some truth in this, but one cannot help agreeing with John Gould that Momigliano has missed something, and that this something is to do with narrative (or "storytelling," as Gould puts it).[6] These writers have their own ways of making the events intelligible, and formal articulation of causal distinctions is only part of it. The readers have some work to do too, and Herodotus engages them in the explanatory process as narrative patterns gradually reveal those "similarities and dissimilarities," *homoia kai anomoia*, that are so methodologically important. Sometimes that engagement can become almost mimetic, as the audience find themselves puzzling along similar lines to the ways that characters in the text would have puzzled (pp. 111–113, 153–156, 181), and that too has its own explanatory value as the forces driving events become increasingly clear. Sometimes, too, narrative shape can carry its own interpretative suggestions (chapters 9[b], 14[b]).

Is Herodotus really so "unsystematic"? He is flexible, certainly, but that flexibility extends to where to be systematic and where not. He certainly develops a plurality of explanatory strands, some unifocal and some involving mutual reciprocity, some to do with Persia, some with Greece, and some with universal human experience; one explanation can overlay another without reducing the second to valuelessness (chapter 2[b–c]). But he can also be explicitly systematic when he chooses: systematic in his use of counterfactual speculation or comparison of parallel sequences or *modus tollendo tollens* (chapter 3); systematic too in running different explanations against one another, perhaps to exclude, perhaps to prioritize, and perhaps to trace their interaction (chapter 6[b])—but, again, only when he chooses. There are equally times when he just leaves explanations to coexist, presenting them as different ways of looking at a complicated picture that may all be true (chapter 6[b] again). That is not out of line with contemporary practice in the Hippocratics, and it can be seen as a virtue, an alertness to the polyphony that will always be there when different observers look at complex events from different perspectives (p. 95). Of course we should not imagine Herodotus scratching his head, wondering whether this was a time to exclude or to accumulate explanations, to coordinate or to subordinate, nor would his audience keep count of how often he made each choice. It was just that his, and theirs, mindset was capacious enough to adopt whichever approach seemed most appropriate in each case. That is not a bad way to avoid becoming "enmeshed in his own net."

The Hippocratics have often proved useful in this inquiry. Our focus has been as much on the audience as on Herodotus himself, as we have tried to illuminate the conceptual assumptions and expectations that they might bring. This has not been a study of Herodotus' own intellectual formation, relevant though the material is to that investigation as well. Still, it is fair to say that any cross-grained listener intent on tripping Herodotus up, alert for times when he might be out-of-date or simpleminded in comparison with those sophisticated medical contemporaries, would find this a difficult task. It might rather be the similarities that would be striking (chapter 5): the interest in accumulating comparable cases and looking for significant differences, the facility with various argumentative techniques, the assumption that organisms might carry the seeds of destruction as well as growth, the eye for a harmonious balancing of contrary forces, the awareness that several causal chains may intersect, and above all the humble awareness of the provisionality of anything one might conclude. Any inference will be on a so-far-so-good basis. The next observation may mean that one has to revise or maybe even reject.

Such "revision in stride" or "progressive correction" extends to presentational strategy as well as to heuristics, and that again is shared with the Hippocratics (chapter 5[c]). Time and again, ideas and contrasts are gradually qualified without being wholly negated: Greek and barbarian, toughness and softness, democracy and tyranny, freedom's inspirational power and its damaging self-seeking. One of the revisions even covered that search in the proem for "the" *aitiē*: no, there will be several, all jostling together.

The technique is easy to misunderstand, and some of the readers of this book may feel that this pushes the principle of charity too far, allowing both the historian and the critic to get away with too much as we call it "revision in stride." Are we claiming sophistication for what is in fact muddle and inconsistency, verging on a pantomimelike "oh yes it is! oh no it isn't!"? Readers will make up their own mind on that. But I hope they will notice that the "revisions" that come in stride are for the better, adding nuance to what was originally over-simple, so that the qualifications strengthen rather than dilute the analysis; and that we are rarely dealing with contradictions, at least unless we pose very simple questions such as, "Does Herodotus think democracy a good thing?" to which the answer will surely be "yes and no." There is no muddle or inconsistency in thinking that freedom can have disturbing consequences as well as inspiring ones; this is more a matter of balancing opposites—and we have also seen that the insight that strengths and weaknesses can go closely together, building and then imperiling greatness, will be no surprise (pp. 18, 189). And if it was the worst as much as the best qualities of freedom that brought Greece salvation (pp. 170–172, 188), that too is not an incoherence of thought. It is just a paradox.

Intertextuality has also been important, and as more than an intellectual or aesthetic game. It has added to the store that the audience can exploit in registering "similarities and dissimilarities," pointing both to continuities that might suggest universals of experience—"life is like that"—and to differences that point to historical changes. Leonidas is a Homeric hero with a difference, just as Thermopylae is a Homeric battle with a difference (chapter 14[c]); both the sameness and the difference matter, just as they do when Herodotus turns his eye to different cultures, there too finding pointers to universal human truths that may underlie, and may even explain, the local variations (chapters 4[e], 14[e]).

Soon Herodotus' text would itself become an intertextual model for others, and one can then see Thucydides exploiting his audience's knowledge of Herodotus just as Herodotus exploited knowledge of Homer. Of course Thucydides has his own explanatory ways, the ones that Momigliano did not like. Thucydides does like to formalize the relative importance of explanations, where Herodotus preferred to let the narrative do its own work (p. 104), though Thucydides too knows how to use narrative and he too is no stranger to revision in stride.[7] He may sometimes, not always, close interpretation down more than Herodotus does, leaving the readers less opportunity to form their own view:[8] he has his own strong view on what is the right way of looking at things, and cares that his readers may share it. Readers might well notice the difference from Herodotus' texture; it is fair to say that in his presentation Thucydides is "defining himself" against Herodotus' more discursive, less disciplined manner.

Still, Thucydides is drawing on Herodotus too. He cannot do what Herodotus did and set out a number of comparable sequences and invite his audience to spot the parallels and the differences. Thucydides has only his one great test case to explore: the Peloponnesian War. But he can evoke Herodotus' narrative in, for instance, his treatment of the Sicilian expedition, so that Xerxes can become the *comparandum* for his audience to ponder;[9] and his figuring of Athens as "the tyrant city" (pp. 144, 189) again builds on his audience's awareness of the great tyrant and tyrannical power that Athens has succeeded. That audience familiarity will partly be owed to oral tradition, but much will be owed to Herodotus too.[10] Thucydides may allow himself an odd snipe at his predecessor's expense (p. 62), but make no mistake about it: he is piggybacking on what he knew to be giant shoulders.[11]

With that "tyrant city" motif he is taking further a suggestion already in Herodotus' text, with those inescapable suggestions of Athens as the new Persia (chapter 15). We have seen how the suggestions of Herodotus' own day can work in parallel ways to intertextuality. They add to that store of comparable historical sequences that illuminate the past just as the past can illuminate the present: a two-way street, indeed (p. 215). And the greater the urgency a reader might feel to compare present and past, the clearer another insight would be—that the past mattered greatly and mattered still (p. 224).

Could that help one to see the future? If Athens is the new Persia, will its story also end the same way? (Though one should emphasize again that Persia's story had not yet ended.) If so, could one do anything about it? Yes, perhaps one could, though we have usually been dealing in explicability rather than firm predictability, of potential rather than inevitable patterning (chapter 3[b]). Still, that same avoidance of determinism might leave room for humans to avert such an ending—unless, of course, it was already too late (p. 231). We can remember too that Herodotus' fiercest criticism was leveled at those who did not even try to affect events, however formidable the forces they faced (p. 178); and that at least his speakers, if not the narrator in his own voice, strive to extract practical morals for the present from the experiences of the past (pp. 16, 141–142).

Like Thucydides (p. 231), however, Herodotus was writing not only for his own times but for later generations, who would by then know how this great democratic experiment had turned out, offering the clarity of one extreme, freedom, just as Persia had offered the clarity of extreme tyrannical power. Those later readers would also have their own experiences to look back on and strain to understand, offering further "similarities and dissimilarities"—and one of the most unpredictable things of all was what those points of comparison would be with events that were future for Herodotus but past for his readers.[12] So, like Thucydides, Herodotus would in the end have agreed with Burckhardt: "It is not so much a matter of being smart merely for the next time, more of being wise for all time."[13]

NOTES

1. WHY DID IT ALL HAPPEN?

1. Gould 1989: 64.
2. Section (b) of this chapter.
3. Thomas 2000: esp. ch. 6.
4. Thus, rightly, A. B. Lloyd (1975–1986): ii. 103. Cf. Corcella 1984: 77–81 = 2013: 63–67; Thomas 2000: 182–185. See also below, pp. 41–42. The same could be said of his reluctance to accept that sailors rounding what we now know as the Cape of Good Hope would have had the sun on their right, i.e., to the north (4.42.4): Corcella 1984: 82 = 2013: 68.
5. On which see Barnes 1982: 538–540, characterizing this as "a *bon mot*, an aphorism neatly summing up the general spirit and optimistic hope of Ionian science; it is not a piece of serious philosophizing"; for Wolbergs 2012 it is less optimistic, offering a caution about the uncertainty of inferences based on fallible sense-perception (cf. Anaximander DK 59 B 21), and Wolbergs also doubts both the precise wording and the attribution to Anaximander. Still, the empirical principle—the phenomena are where you start—is an important one: cf. D. Müller 1981; Corcella 1984: 80–81 = 2013: 66–67; Gianotti 1996: 181–182. On the Hippocratics' application of this principle, see Lo Presti 2010 and esp. Jouanna 1999: 293–322; on Herodotus' use and its affinity with that of the Hippocratics, see esp. G. E. R. Lloyd 1966: 341–345; Corcella 1984: 57–66 = 2013: 44–53; and Thomas 2000: 200–211, discussing this Nile passage at 201, 206–207, and 224. Cf. also below, pp. 81 and 225.
6. But see K. Clarke 2018: 159–162, pointing out that Herodotus is careful not to apply that argument from Nile–Danube symmetry in an overmechanical way.
7. For instance, at 2.104 when he draws an inference about the distant past from his observation of the Colchians' present-day appearance (Diller 1932: 21–23 = 1971: 121–123); cf. also Hollmann 2011: 253–254. Thucydides does something similar at 1.6.2.
8. 4.8.2 then shows similar skepticism about the knowledge about Ocean that others claimed: "They say that Ocean starts in the east and runs around the whole world, but give no demonstration to prove what they say"; cf. 4.36.2. Still, Herodotus elsewhere seems to accept the likelihood of sea at the edges of the earth, esp. at 4.13.1: K. Clarke 2018: 99–100.
9. "Fundamentally, Herodotus' conception of history shows it to be an analogue (as well as a part) of nature, or *physis*, as a whole" (Immerwahr 1966: 15). Similarly Lateiner 1986: 12 and already Pagel 1927: 29–40.
10. As was strongly and influentially denied by R. G. Collingwood, "the historian

need not and cannot (without ceasing to be a historian) emulate the scientist in searching for the causes or laws of events" (1946: 214), and, with particular attention to predictability, Popper 1960 (though the "historicism" whose "poverty" he was exposing also insisted on differences between explanations in social and in physical sciences, and Popper himself was prepared to admit some methodological analogies as well as important differences, 130–143); similarly Berlin in Berlin and Hardy 2002: 94–165. For a critique of Collingwood, see Dray 1964: 10–15 and 43–47, but Dray too (chs. 2, 4) is skeptical of assimilating the two explanatory methodologies.

11. Cf. Guthrie 1962–1981: iii. 151, 167–169.

12. It is possible that *isonomia* is the wording of his excerptors rather than Alcmaeon himself (p. 262 n. 23): so Mansfeld 2013, suggesting the influence on later tradition of Herodotus' constitutions debate (3.80–82). But such language fits well enough into the fifth century, and the general view is that it is likely to go back to Alcmaeon: thus Guthrie 1962–1981: i. 346; Ostwald 1969: 100–101; Jouanna 1999: 327; Lévy 2005: 119; and now Kouloumentas 2014: 871, citing further literature.

13. E.g., *On Fleshes* 4 VIII p. 138 P. = VIII p. 588 L; *On Breaths* 15 II p. 252 J = VI p. 114 L, 3 II p. 230 J = VI p. 94 L; *On Ancient Medicine* 16 I p. 42 J = I p. 606 L, 20 I p. 54 J = I p. 624 L. There are many other examples.

14. G. E. R. Lloyd 1966: 210–221, 252–253.

15. Cf., e.g., Bakker 2002: 14–15, writing on the relation of Herodotus' project to the natural and medical science of his day: "We have to allow for the possibility that Herodotus borrows contemporary terminology to establish the authority of an enterprise that is entirely his own . . ."; Vegetti 1983; Lévy 2005: 120.

16. Beer 2009 (originally 1983), e.g., xxiv (preface to the second edition of 2000): "Materials are passed around and back from one field to another."

17. Lakoff and Johnson 2003 (originally 1980), speaking of "understanding one sort of experience in terms of another sort of experience" (116) as the basis for the cross-domain similarities that they rightly stress are essential for metaphor (pp. 244–245 in 2003 Afterword).

18. As Beer herself stresses, arguing that Darwin differs from the practice of earlier centuries where a "concept of universal analogy" obtained (2009: 76). Lakoff and Johnson 2003: 107–110 similarly recognize the alternative view of "abstractions being applied evenly to different domains" and give their reasons, perfectly good ones in terms of the modern linguistic world, for rejecting it. But that alternative view is, I suggest, closer to the Greek conceptual mindset.

19. Cf. Kurke 2011: 95–102, especially 98–101, applying Mary Helms' anthropological findings to Greek *sophia* and stressing the range that can be brought into the domain of "craft" and described in the same ways—"'skilled crafting' embraces not only carpentry, metallurgy, and weaving, but also medicine, hunting, seercraft, shamanic power, navigation, song making and dance, political oratory, and the arts of judge, mediator, and ambassador . . ." (99). All those different areas can be assumed, again at least provisionally, to work in similar ways. On the body/state analogy, see also Brock 2013: 69–82.

20. As it is, for instance, for Menenius Agrippa when he tells the fable of the belly and the other parts of the body in the first scene of Shakespeare's *Coriolanus* (drawn from Plut. *Cor.* 6): it is not likely that Menenius' or Shakespeare's audience would assume that this analogy between belly and nobility went beyond this momentary insight.

21. Cf. Guthrie 1962–1981: i. 90–91 on Anaximander, 131–132 on Anaximenes, and 278–279 on Pythagoreans; Guthrie 1962–1981: ii. 136, 190–191, 199 on Empedocles,

299–300 on Anaxagoras, 408 on Democritus; and G. E. R. Lloyd 1966: 210–232 and 1979: 247–248. Kirk, Raven, and Schofield 1983: 131–133 seem to me to play down too much the significance of Anaximander's "biological–embryological language"; see now A. Gregory 2016, insisting on the importance of biology to Anaximander's thinking and arguing that he is a "uniformalist"—"that is, in questions such as the origins of the *cosmos* or the origins of life, he adopted theories which invoke the same sort of processes which we can still find going on in the world today rather than theories which invoke unique processes" (esp. 41–50 and 118–189: quotation from 47).

22. As does Thomas 2000: cf. esp. her p. 21. Jouanna 2005 explores the possibility of "transfers" of medical models of cause and crisis into historiography but is very cautious on individual cases.

23. Contrast T. Harrison 2000: 235: "The landscape of causation in the *Histories* is very clearly a foreign country"—a strong overstatement, to say the least. For Herodotus' "voiceprint," see Fowler 1996, a seminal discussion, and below, p. 68.

24. See p. 82.

25. The Potidaeans' explanation, cautiously accepted by Herodotus himself (8.129.3), is there in terms of Poseidon's wrath for a past impiety; but the tsunami itself is a physical phenomenon, and that makes the repeated use of the neuter *aition* more natural. The neuter is also used of ethnological explanations for what are taken to be physical facts: the *aition* for the thicker Egyptian skulls is the exposure of their shaved heads to the sun whereas the Persians wear headgear, 3.12.2–5.

26. Croesus' defense of the Lydians at 1.155.3 follows a similar line: do not destroy Sardis, Cyrus, as the city is *anamartētos* ("did no wrong") in the case of both rebellions; I launched the first, and now the culprit is Pactyes whom you appointed as governor. Croesus is bold enough to hint that Cyrus should take some of the blame himself for making that appointment, but wise enough to leave it as no more than a hint. A similar argument is made in the opposite direction by the Theban Timegenides at 9.87, where he says that if the indignant allies demand money as retribution for the city's Medism the city as a whole should pay, as it was not just the leaders who were responsible.

27. Cf. Gagné 2013: 306–325 on this sequence, esp. 311 on the way that Herodotus aligns with Thuc. 1.126–127 rather than later writers in emphasizing the secular dimension of human fault-finding rather than the religious aspect of curse or pollution.

28. Just, once again, as the act of ascription of αἰτία is often felt within the Hippocratics: p. 82. Cf. also Baragwanath forthcoming.

29. It is thus a matter of comment when Gelon gave Syracusan citizenship to the wealthy who had initiated the war, but sold the people of Megara Hyblaea as slaves even though they had no share in the blame (not *metaitioi*, 7.156.2) and were not expecting to be punished. That is not the way things ought to happen, even if it fits what tyrants do.

30. For such disingenuous *aitiai*, cf. e.g., the case of Darius and Aryandes, 4.166.2 (below, p. 126), and for Croesus' nonchalance about blameworthiness note his later treatment of the Syrians, 1.76.2 (below, p. 117).

31. Cf. Immerwahr 1956: 245–247 = 2013: 161–162 and esp. Rawlings 1975: 19, arguing for "a semantic field approximating to English 'self-justification,' 'exculpation' "; 25, "a *prophasis per se* can be either true or false." Antiphon, *On the Murder of Herodes* (1) 21–22 offers an especially clear case where a *prophasis*—Antiphon's own motive for undertaking the voyage during which Herodes disappeared—is clearly presented as true; but a little later the word equally clearly designates a false pretext (26). On the Hippocratics' use of the word, see below, pp. 82–84.

32. "He claimed to be travelling to see the world," Waterfield. Moles 1996: 263–264 overinterprets in finding the desire not to annul the laws the "true" reason, and the second mention of *theōriē* only a sly restatement of the "frivolous" claim.

33. 4.79.1 may here be similar, where *prophasis* introduces the death of Scyles when, once again, "it was necessary for him to fall"—the same phrase. He was discovered celebrating Bacchic rites at a time when his house was struck by lightning. The case also illustrates the moral of 4.76.1, 80.5, the Scythians' hostility to "foreign ways": so it could be regarded as triggering a downfall waiting to happen, even without that extra suggestion of a cosmic dimension. This charge that the irate Scythians have against him is also described as *aitiē*, 4.80.1.

34. Another complicated case is 2.139.2, discussed at Rawlings 1975: 30. Sabacos has there dreamed that he was cutting all the priests in Egypt in two, and suspects that the gods are sending him a *prophasis* to tempt him into impiety so as to engineer his own destruction. There is disingenuousness there, in the assumed devious behavior of the gods; but had Sabacos acted on the temptation, it would have been the real cause of his behavior, and that would have been the real cause of his destruction. Rawlings 1975: 30–31 discusses such divine *prophaseis* more generally, quoting with approval Pearson 1952: 209: "It is as though the jealous gods, who have decided (for sufficient reasons) to destroy a man, have to find some formal justification like mere mortals."

35. There are several cases where *prophasis* and *proischomai/proschēma* are found closely together, as in 6.133.1, quoted above in the text, and the very charged instance of 8.3.2 (p. 210). It is reasonable in such cases to think that it is the *proischomai/proschēma* that gives the clearer suggestion of disingenuousness: cf. below, p. 10, on 4.167.3. Still, *proischomai* is not always disingenuous either: at 6.9.3 the Persian generals provide some Ionian tyrants with the arguments for defection that they should "put forward" to their own cities, promising them that they will not suffer for their original revolt and their sacred places will be spared, but if they persist, threatening slavery for themselves, castration for their sons, and deportation to Bactria for their daughters. These need not be false: the threats are duly fulfilled at least in part, 6.19.3–20, 25, 32.

36. So Pearson 1952: 208 is wrong to say that the *prophasis* here "is only a formal excuse." Such doubleness may already be there at *Iliad* 19.302, where the captive women weep "in *prophasis* for Patroclus, but each for their own sufferings": grief for Patroclus triggers their tears, but need not be wholly inauthentic, any more than it was for Briseis just before. Cf. Lohmann 1952: 26–27; Edwards 1991: 271 ad loc.

37. Gould 1989: 64–65 observes that Herodotus' backward-looking connectives—e.g., "because," "for"—are more than three times more frequent than forward-looking ones such as "and so."

38. Baragwanath 2008.

39. And there is a good deal more to say about that: see Pelling forthcoming (d), written as a companion piece to this book.

40. "Dissertative" is the term favored by White 1987: e.g., 27–28 in drawing a similar distinction.

41. Below, p. 111 and n. 22; cf. esp. T. Harrison 2000: ch. 2 and S. O. Shapiro 1996: 353–354.

42. "Persian kings in Herodotus' opinion were inclined to try one conquest too many," Sancisi-Weerdenburg 1985: 464–465 = 2010, 445. The classic discussion of such patterning is Immerwahr 1966; the data are usefully collected and tabulated by Lateiner 1989: ch. 8.

43. Cf. esp. Reinhardt 1940: 148, 165–166 = 1965: 338, 358; Dewald 2003: 40–47, esp. 43; Baragwanath 2008: 120–121; Zali 2014: 93–94.

44. Cf. Dewald 2012: 84.

45. Rawlings 1975, esp. 36–60, argued that there are two separate homonyms with different etymologies, one πρόφασις meaning "a 'preferred explanation' and deriving from πρό-φημι, and the other a 'preceding appearance' from προ-φαίνω." But that requires taking πρόφασις in two different senses within the same sentence at *On the Sacred Disease* 2 II p. 142 J = 1 VI p. 356 L; and could any linguistic community continue to distinguish two phonologically identical words, operating in a closely similar semantic range? See also p. 261 n. 19 on the Hippocratic usage.

46. My argument here owes something to "cognitive narratology," "tracing . . . the active deployment of cognitive strategies drawn from real-world experience and prior textual and generic models" (Fludernik 1996: 52, though Fludernik herself is reluctant to draw historical narratives into her model, 26, 38–41). Ryan 1991: 48–60 brings out the way that the plausibility of a narrative (there a fictional one) depends on its alignment with patterns of cause-and-effect familiar from everyday life and previous literature.

47. Thus some philosophers find it important to distinguish causation from causal explanation. "It seems right to say that causal explanation is mind- and description-dependent. It seems wrong to say that *causation* [her italics] is mind- and description-dependent" rather than something more "pragmatic" and "objective" (Paul 2009: 163).

48. As Fowler 2006: 32 points out, contrasting Herodotus' use of αἰτίη.

49. Hart and Honoré 1985: 10, cf. 91–93; cf. Gallie 1968: 108, 112–113. We might compare Gould 1989: 81–82 on Herodotean *gnōmai* or "proverbs," offering "a generalization, a summing-up of human experience," "pigeonholing some fact" in terms of a broader understanding of "the general fund of human wisdom"; but I am closer to Hart and Honoré than to Gould in finding such generalizations as causally central.

50. Cic. *de Inv.* 27–30, *de Or.* 2.81–83, 326–330, *Orat.* 124, 210; Quint. 4.2.

51. The papers in Brooks and Gewirtz 1996 are here highly illuminating. So is Posner 1988: 269–316 on "judicial opinions as literature," an art-form in which the choice of language for factual statements plays a large part: this can cover narratives not merely of the facts of the particular case but also of such extraneous matters as the framing of the United States Constitution or the fighting of the Civil War: for examples of each, see Posner 308–309 (facts of the case), 292–293 (constitution), and 295 (civil war).

52. Cf. Gallie 1968: 23–24, 26–27 and 89–90 on the way that a narrative story, and therefore on his view (below, p. 249 n. 25) history too, deals with conclusions: "What happens is intelligible, we see how and in a sense see why it happened: but it is not necessarily (and indeed not usually) predictable" (27).

53. "Their [the genealogists'] main purpose was always to explain relationships between people, cities, or concepts," Möller 2001: 251. Cf. Fowler 1998: 1: "Genealogy gives him [Peleus at *Il.* 7.127–128, who has just inquired about a visitor's ancestry] his bearings. For those in the system a genealogy is a map." This genealogical accommodation of Greek overseas expansion can also already be seen in the Hesiodic *Catalog of Women*: Bertelli 2001: 73–76. Peirano 2010: 40 notes how something similar is visible in Dionysius of Halicarnassus' treatment of early Rome. For the contribution such "cultural work" made in developing "a sense of what it meant to be Greek in the first place," see J. Skinner forthcoming.

54. Jones 1999: esp. chs. 2–3; Osmers 2013; cf. Hartog 1989: 124 and L. G. Mitchell 1997: 26–27.

55. We know of these in Tiryns and Mycenae in the sixth century and in several Cretan cities during the fifth century, and also in Herodotus' own town of Halicarnassus: Hartog 1989: 130–132, Gagarin 2008: 36 and 117–121, Papakonstantinou 2015: 78. Still, this is a thin crop, and they may have been mainly responsible for recording and making judicial decisions. Thomas 1989: 198 can reasonably claim that "ancient Greece is notable for its lack of official 'remembrancers.'"

56. Easterling 1985, 1997.

57. Esp. Soclees at 5.92 and Leutychidas at 6.86. Gould 1989: 40–41 notes how different this is from the manner of Thucydides' speakers.

58. Particularly in *On Fleshes*, but cf. also *On Regimen* 1.10 IV pp. 246–248 J = VI pp. 484–486 L: Craik 2015: 47.

59. I retain this description despite the objections of Currie 2012: 39, who prefers "the myth of the races." It is true that Hesiod's γένη are more accurately "kinds" of humans, but the connotations of "race" carry too much other baggage and obscure the important historical perspective as one "kind" succeeds another.

60. Hesiod, *Works and Days* 106–201; Empedocles DK 31 B 128, 130; [Aesch.] *Prom.* 436–506; Eur. *Supp.* 195–215 (Theseus); Soph., *Ant.* 332–375. Further examples at Kurke 2011: 161. For discussion, see Ubsdell 1983: 350–352; Blundell 1986: 165–202; Dunn 2005; Rosen 2016; and, classically, Dodds 1973.

61. The play is sometimes attributed to Critias and sometimes to Euripides: Dihle 1977 made the case for Euripides, Sutton 1981 and Whitmarsh 2016: 94–96 for Critias, and after a judicious discussion Davies 1989 found the issue "hard to decide" (28).

62. Plato, *Protagoras* 320c–8d, *Republic* 2.358b–61d. On Plato's use of such models, see Morgan 2012, esp. 234, with my commentary at Pelling 2012b: 361–363. It is a version of the "genetic definition" explored by Guthrie 1962–1981: i. 239–240, 456–457, ii. 181, and esp. iii. 143–145, analyzing the *logical* presuppositions of a functioning system and transposing them, for expositional clarity, into a historicist register. Such points could be made more fleetingly: cf. Antiphon DK 87 B 61 on "the people of the past" who saw the dangers of anarchy and therefore accustomed their children to the discipline that would be necessary when they reached adulthood.

63. Cf. esp. Farrar 1988: esp. 88–90.

64. On Deioces, see Meier, Patzek, Walter, and Wiesehöfer 2004 (with my review, Pelling 2007c); T. Harrison 2003: 149–150 and 2011a: 33–35; Thomas 2012: 244–252; and Provencal 2015: 223–225.

65. I say more about this historical consciousness in Pelling forthcoming (c).

66. The issues are complicated. I had my say in Pelling 2007b.

67. This has been a recurrent theme in the work of G. E. R. Lloyd. See also Jouanna 1984; Demont 1993; Thomas 2000: ch. 8; and below, p. 96.

68. On this, see esp. Thomas 2000: 86–114, who is careful not to overstate the similarities with Herodotus. Her emphasis rightly falls on the importance of *nomos* and changeability in Herodotus, though as she says (113) *nomoi* are also important in *Airs Waters Places* and qualify any extreme form of "determinism." Herodotus' hints of climatic determinism are also discussed by Munson 2001: 87–88, by Kingsley forthcoming: ch. 4 and by Irwin 2014: 36–37, who finds at 3.23.3 a Hippocratic approach to the importance of waters to health.

69. Pelling 1997c: 62 = 2013: 374–375; cf. Thomas 2000: 106–109.

70. *Pace* A. B. Lloyd (1975–1986): i. 166, ii. 146–147 (Egyptian topsy-turviness "determined by the peculiarities of their environment"): on this, cf. Immerwahr 1956: 279 and Thomas 2000: 70, 112 and 2001b: 217–218 = 2013: 344–345 ("Herodotus does not

actually make much use of . . . 'environmental determinism'"). Chiasson 2001: 55–68 similarly finds more analogy than aetiology in Herodotus' treatment of climate in relation to behavior. Not that this sort of analogy is un-Hippocratic either: cf. p. 97.

71. On such "balancing," see also below, ch. 5(b).

72. Thus Heinimann 1945: 24–25, 29–32, 172–180, emphasizing the greater interest in *Airs Waters Places* in the causal background; but he does not do justice to Herodotus' greater interest in the causal consequences.

73. Backhaus 1975: 178 is puzzled by this, thinking that the only really tyrant-free Asiatics were the Ionian Greeks and that the qualifying ἢ βάρβαροι is therefore not much more than a formal gesture; but there was considerable ethnic mix in and around those Ionian cities.

74. Cf. Thomas 2000: 67–68 and Chiasson 2001: 34 for a similar point about the Scythians: unlike *Airs Waters Places*, Herodotus is not interested in relating Scythian behavior to their climate, but he is very interested in tracing how their customs work out in practice, especially their nomadism and readiness to withdraw when attacked.

75. Cf. Hornblower and Pelling 2017 on 6.84, and on the general importance of *tisis* in this stretch of narrative, their introduction section 3; for its relation to principles of symmetry, Redfield 1985: 103 = 2013: 273–274.

76. As in several similar passages in other pre-Herodotean authors: Versnel 2011: 158–159, rightly observing that such resignation can readily coexist with more "hopeful expectation" (162) of divine benignity.

2. TO BLAME AND TO EXPLAIN: NARRATIVE COMPLICATIONS

1. Below, pp. 66–67.

2. Not "Thurian": see esp. Erbse 1979: 146–153, with strong arguments for regarding the variant Θουρίου as a Hellenistic conjecture.

3. Cf. esp. Moles 1993: 94; Bakker 2002: esp. 31; Thomas 2000: 221–228 and 260–264. Lang 1987: 203 is unwilling to find significance in the echo ἀπόδεξις/ἀποδεχθέντα, but the parallels she quotes (1.136.1 and 8.68α.1) tell the other way: in those cases too there is pointed verbal play. At 1.136.1 the Persian society responds to one sort of "display" (or "acknowledgement," another sense of the verb), that of producing children, by another, acknowledging such prolific paternity as a form of manly virtue (ἀνδραγαθίη) second only to prowess in battle; at 8.68α.1 Artemisia has served Xerxes with one sort of display, that of martial deeds, and that supports her claim and her duty to serve him further with another sort, that of advice.

4. Cf. esp. Stahl 1968; Rieks 1975; S. Saïd 2002; Griffin 2006; Sewell-Rutter 2007: ch. 1.

5. 2.1.2–2.1: Cambyses "launched a campaign against Egypt. The Egyptians, before Psammetichus came to their throne, regarded themselves as the most ancient of all mankind . . ." Transitions are of course often more sophisticated: cf. Drews 1973: 175–177. But even so the Persian advance normally provides the springboard for such ethnological explanation (e.g., at 4.102.1, 4.167.3). Cf. Fehling 1989: 53–54, and for Fornara's view (1971a: 32) that this organizational principle only later developed into a theme, see below, p. 120. For another way of looking at it, see Rood 2006: 294: "It may seem significant . . . that Herodotus holds up his narrative of the Persians' imperialist march by lingering on the customs of those who succumb to or resist them. It is as if his own narrative is opposing that relentless march."

6. Cf. esp. Immerwahr 1960; Drexler 1972.

7. Cf. Fowler 2006: 31. Contrast Thuc. 6.88.7, τὰ γιγνόμενα ὑπὸ τῶν Ἀθηναίων, which Stein 1901–1908 ad loc. cites as a parallel. That ὑπό formulation points to things being done "*by*" the Athenians, actions rather than other sorts of achievements.

8. Vannicelli 2001: 239–240; Pelling 2018: 199.

9. On this gathering precision, cf. esp. Pagel 1927: 5; Erbse 1956: 212–213; Lateiner 1989: 14.

10. Thus far I agree with Węcowski 2004: esp. 157–158. Erbse 1956: 216, followed by Hommel 1981: 280–282, lists cases (e.g., 1.80.1, 2.116.2, 6.68.1) where ἄλλα τε καί . . . formulations introduce narrative with an exclusive *focus* on the καί . . . element, but in those other passages Herodotus makes no promise to talk of the other cases; here he does.

11. Neer 2010 similarly stresses "wonder" as a distinctive aspiration of archaic and classical art. Kurke 2013 extends this interestingly to the way the tragic chorus was viewed, in particular by Plato in the *Laws*.

12. Immerwahr 1956: 251 = 2013: 166.

13. Nagy 1987 takes *logioi* here as indicating people who are expert in producing *logoi* themselves, tellers as well as connoisseurs of tales. Perhaps; but Luraghi 2001b: 156–158, followed by Węcowski 2004: 149 n. 38, has good reason for taking it more broadly as just "learned, cultivated, clever." Provencal 2015: 72–78 compiles a list of previous translations, and eventually (78) comes round to taking it as "skilled in words, eloquent" (LSJ s.v. II): true to his thesis (below, p. 258 n. 103), he concludes that "the Persians are being characterized as sophists learned in the art of argument."

14. Just as it prepares for a clear ending, when the scales of vengeance are finally leveled: cf. Erbse 1979: 196, on the advantages of this approach for fixing clear beginning- and end-points in a historical narrative. On the link of explanation and closure, see also below, p. 214.

15. Thus Lang 1984: 3 productively interprets Herodotus' proem as a directional marker: this is the narrative's first trajectory, no more. Cf. Immerwahr 1966: 63; Lateiner 1989: 233 n. 12. For Thucydides, see below, p. 120.

16. Cf. Williams 1993: 57–58.

17. Cf. Dem. 23.50, [Dem.] 47.47, 59.1; Lys. 4.11; Isoc. 20.1; Whitlock Blundell 1989: 37.

18. E.g., Walcot 1978: 139, "This account in which one act of rape provokes the injured party to retaliate with counter-rape . . ." Lateiner 1989 interprets the early chapters in terms of "revenge" (209; cf. his 194). Others have talked of the "tit-for-tat exchanges": Rood 2010: 55 n. 33 gives a list of culprits, including myself, and add J. E. Powell, *Lexicon* s.v. "ἴσος" 4 and Blondell 2013: 143–144. For correction of this emphasis, see Pelling 2000: 269 n. 26 and esp. Rood 2010: 55–58.

19. Cf. Baragwanath 2008: 156, on the way that vengeance can so often be a cloak for other, more profit-targeting motives; Hohti 1976.

20. This difference between the two distinctions is important for the criticism of *Airs Waters Places*: Thomas 2000: 90–98. Thomas goes on to make good points about the passage of Herodotus, 98–100.

21. Cf. Bornitz 1968: 178–179. Rood 2010 develops the point that geographical divisions, here that of Europe and Asia, are envisaged as originally dependent on human intellectual constructions: so also Friedman 2006: 165.

22. I am grateful to Emily Baragwanath for this point.

23. Hornblower and Pelling on 6.33 and 6.43.4–45.

24. The narrowing of focus through the proem already prepares this: "the great and

marvelous achievements of both Greeks and barbarians" suggest and prepare many things and many peoples, but "how they came to war with one another" is already focusing more sharply on Persia against Greece.

25. Here the adoption of a Persian viewpoint has helped. The Persian *logioi* might more naturally regard the Greeks or Europeans as "separate" than their Greek equivalents would regard the "Persians" as typifying and dominating a separate ethnic or geographical unit. Cf. Immerwahr 1966: 81; Fehling 1989: 55; Thomas 2000: 99.

26. Cf. Dewald 1999: 226–227; Blondell 2012: 143–145; below, p. 108.

27. Fehling 1989: 50–57 argues against the genuineness of these Persian λόγιοι, and thinks that Herodotus is here grafting Greek tales, deftly manipulated by himself, on to fictitious Persian mouthpieces. This raises issues too large to address here; they do not affect our present concern, which is Herodotus' argument and self-projection and the expectations these arouse.

28. Fehling 1989: 51, 54–55; Baragwanath 2008: 125. A similar technique is visible in Herodotus' criticism of (presumably) Hecataeus at 2.2.5: below, p. 63.

29. Cf. Pelliccia 1992 for this as "a false-start recusatio" with parallels in Pindar, Sappho, and Gorgias" *Helen*.

30. Lateiner 1989: 38: "a parody of Hecataean mythological investigation"; Pelling 1999a: 331–332 and n. 25; Thomas 2000: 268 (but see *contra* Węcowski 2004: 151; Rood 2010: 63). For more on Hecataeus and his "rationalism," see below, ch. 4(b).

31. Von Fritz 1967: ii. 117–121. But more direct hits at Hecataeus have often been assumed: Diels 1887; Jacoby, *R–E* vii (1912) 2740 = 1956: 222; Hellmann 1934: 18; Krischer 1965: 166–167.

32. Rightly emphasized by Gould 1989: 64 and 1991: 18 = 2001: 301–302; cf. Erbse 1979: 181, 185–186; Fowler 1996: 83 = 2013: 76–77.

33. Węcowski 2004: 146–148.

34. Woodman 1988: 2–3; Moles 1993: 92–98 and 1996: 264–265; Marincola 2007: 13–15 = 2013: 114–115.

35. As many have noted: see now at length Wood 2016.

36. Once again, cf. the perceptive remark of Lang 1984: 3; above, p. 244 n. 15.

37. Pelling 1999a: 332; Greenwood 2018: esp. 166–167. Dorati's claim (2011: 274) that "Herodotus himself never saw the fundamental link between travel and thought as an object of investigation" is very odd.

38. For the parallels between Herodotus and Solon, and between historian and Warner, cf. Redfield 1985: 102 = 2013: 272–273; Pelling 2006b: 145–146, with references to earlier literature at 145 n. 15; Węcowski 2004: 162 (Solon "the only sage in the *Histories* who is incontestably wise and who is always right").

39. Gould 1989, esp. chs. 3–4 (p. 44 for "the model of repayment in kind"); cf. also Gould 1991. It had been equally strongly stressed by Pagel 1927: 15–23. For one clear series of negatively reciprocal actions, see 6.136–140 with Hornblower and Pelling 2017: 292.

40. It can still be disputed how deeply any such "overlaying" buries the original ideas, even for the moment. Root 2011 for instance sees the suggestions of the abduction chapters in terms of "ironic humor," and imagines an audience thinking, "It really is ridiculous to imagine the causes of war with Persia as the mirror of image of the story of Helen, isn't it? How funny it is to have it all strung out in a pious sounding exposition. Ha!" Such a reading seems to me to press an "ironic" approach too far: for a judicious discussion of the issues, see Rutherford 2018.

41. Cf. esp. Wolff 1964, noting at 56 (= 1965: 674–675) the verbal echoes of Can-

daules; Sancisi-Weerdenburg 1983: 27–30 = 2013: 143–145; Welser 2009; Boedeker 2011: 220–222.

42. Cf. Baragwanath 2008: 279–280.

43. Briant 2002: 563–567.

44. Cf. Wolff 1964: 53–55 = 1965: 671–673, speculating that the version known to Herodotus may have been the accusation, marked by Ctesias as false, that Darius was the assassin himself. This would make Darius "a second Orestes," appalled by his mother's brutality and taking his own vengeance years later on a lustful parent. But Welser 2009: 364–365 points out that the more usual version, fingering the captain of the guard Artabanus, would more exactly mirror the initial story of Candaules and may well be what Herodotus and his audience would have in mind.

45. Roisman 2005: 108–109 builds a broader psychological picture of the old men who are trying to make themselves agreeable to the beautiful young woman.

46. As is emphasized by Lloyd-Jones 1971: 7–8 and others, e.g., Allan 2006.

47. More on this in Pelling forthcoming (d). This relates to the remark of Kullmann 2001: 390 that "past and future are emphasized far more in the epic characters' direct speech than in narrative." The past becomes relevant through what people think and say about it.

48. Cf. Blondell 2013: 146–150.

49. On Helen in book 2, see esp. de Bakker 2012 and de Jong 2012, with references to previous scholarship, and Blondell 2013: 150–158.

50. The *Cypria* had claimed that the Trojan War was brought about by the gods to reduce surplus human population (fr. 1). Herodotus' alternative justification may be conceived as a reply to the *Cypria*, and/or both passages may reflect the way in which that war was regarded as a test case of divine justice, as (in a way) so often in Tragedy. The familiarity of that moral issue would give added weight to Herodotus' pronouncement here.

51. Another case involving human and divine reciprocity will be that of Euenius (9.93), the shepherd who is blinded by his countrymen for neglecting his watch and losing his sheep; they are punished for this excessive punishment by a famine and by a failure of their livestock to reproduce. Told to give Euenius whatever recompense he should choose, they trick him into accepting a local estate, and he is furious when he realizes what has happened. Again reciprocity has been heavily in point, but has been several times travestied or perverted on the human level: the story ends when the gods requite Euenius with a different sort of boon, granting him the gift of prophecy. On Euenius, see esp. Stadter 1992: 792–793 = 2013: 343–344 and A. Griffiths 1999.

52. There is not even any interest in what will later happen to Menelaus. Would the audience reflect on the traditions they knew of the resumption of contented home life with a fascinating Helen (the *Odyssey*) or of translation to the Isles of the Blessed (Eur. *Hel.* 1676–1679; cf. *Od.* 4.561–569)? It is hard to think so. Such thoughts would qualify, perhaps even undermine, the strong picture of the divine as upholders of reciprocal vengeance; and, even if Herodotus can accommodate such complexities elsewhere, such exploratory complexities seem alien to the texture of book 2. We should at least have expected some more explicit signaling of this particular paradox.

53. This confirms that for Herodotus there is no simple *spatium historicum*, with secure knowledge beginning at a single point, and no suggestion that different things happened in some earlier *spatium mythicum* (cf. von Leyden 1949/1950). The extent of any *spatium historicum* depends both on the type of story and on the record or mem-

ory that preserved it: the criterion is one of what is knowable. See T. Harrison 2000: 198–205 and Baragwanath and de Bakker 2012b: 19–29, esp. 27–28 on Egypt, with references to previous scholarship at 25–26 n. 95, and S. Saïd 2012: 88–90 on the Trojan War. Still, even in Egypt those traditions are of course tested by Herodotus' own *gnōmē* (Corcella 1984: 61–62 = 2013: 48–49), and the "enormous *spatium historicum*" that Egypt offers allows partition according to the varying degrees of certainty (Vannicelli 2001: quotation from p. 240). African culture also shows cases where mythical and historical "periods" are accepted as coexisting side by side: Vansina 1965: 101, 157.

54. de Bakker 2012: 122–126; cf. de Jong 2012: 131–132.

55. On the intrusion of Greek assumptions here, cf. Sourdille 1910: 36; Fehling 1989: 64; and West 2007: 14–16. A. B. Lloyd 1975–1986 on 2.113 is inclined to accept the existence of contemporary Egyptian asylum, largely on the basis of this Herodotean passage: that does not convince.

56. On the Greek coloring of the *xeinia*-emphasis, cf. A. B. Lloyd 1975–1986 on 2.114, and for its foregrounding in this episode, see Vandiver 2012: 146–155.

57. On Stesichorus' *Palinodes* and their background in legend and earlier literature, see Davies and Finglass 2014: 299–317. This Greekness was one factor that led Fehling 1989: 59–65 to argue for disingenuousness here, with Greek assumptions and traditions misleadingly being grafted on to those Egyptian sources. We should, however, consider the possibility that the Greekness, here as for instance in the constitutions debate (Pelling 2002b), is *expressive*, something that an attentive audience would recognize and reflect upon as they see how easily Herodotus' reading can be accommodated within their accustomed view of the facts. It need not follow that those Egyptian sources are a fabrication, as Fehling thinks, only that any genuine Egyptian material has been extensively remolded to fit with the presuppositions of Herodotus' Greek audience. Cf. Kannicht 1969: i. 45–49, especially 45: "Die Geschichte ist also ihrer proägyptisch-antigriechischen Tendenz nach offenbar eine ägyptische Geschichte. Aber sie ist mit griechischem Material, also für Griechen erzählt" ("The pro-Egyptian and anti-Greek texture presents this as an Egyptian story; but it is told with Greek material, and therefore for Greeks").

58. Cf. Munson 2001: 143–144. The connection of the two passages is already noted by Plutarch, *Herodotus' Malice* 12 857a–b, who regards it as symptomatic of Herodotus' bias towards barbarians (οὕτω δὲ φιλοβάρβαρός ἐστιν . . . , 857a): that is a crude way of phrasing this challenge to complacent Greek assumptions, but is not without insight.

3. HOW CAN YOU POSSIBLY KNOW?

1. For the word, see p. 14.
2. Further discussion at Pelling 2000: 82–111.
3. Cf., e.g., Hornblower 1991–2008 ad loc.; Andrewes in *HCT* v: 368.
4. Sometimes, it is true, Hume is prepared to speak in such terms even in the philosophical works: Garrett 2009: 74, 82, 84–85. That makes "constant conjunction" a heuristic technique for examining something "independent of, and antecedent to the operations of the understanding," and he writes as if it were absurd to think of causality as purely a matter of the observer: "As if causes did not operate entirely independent of the mind, and would not continue their operation, even tho' there was no mind existent to contemplate them, or reason concerning them"! (Hume 1739/1740: 1.3.14). But we need

more clarity on what sort of "constant conjunction" could underpin those sweeping historical causal statements.

5. Thomas 2000: 173–174 is right to single out this feature of Herodotus' presentation and set it in the context of Presocratic and Hippocratic thinking.

6. Thomas 2000: 183. Not very acutely, Diodorus later tries to out-Herodotus Herodotus by using the same *modus tollens* argument against his own thesis: if the idea of the dipping sun were really the explanation, would one not expect other rivers of Libya to show the same phenomenon (1.38.11–12)? The answer should be no, one would not: their sources are presumably not nearly so far south. See also Priestley 2014: 136–137, who assumes that Diodorus draws this argument from Agatharchides.

7. For the Hippocratics' use of *modus tollens* arguments cf. G. E. R. Lloyd 1979: 25, 27–28; Deichgräber 1971: 122; and below, p. 98.

8. Thomas 2000: 136 and ch. 6, esp. 182–185; 2006: 63–64. See also Corcella 1984: 77–81.

9. Gallie 1968: 114 notes the tendency for historians to include such explicit causal argumentation at times when they are countering received ideas: that fits Herodotus' self-portrayal here.

10. Pelling 2013b: 13–16; cf. Rutherford 2018: 26. On the counterfactual component in 7.139, see also Baragwanath 2008: 227–228 and 236.

11. The same could be said about the nearest equivalent in Thucydides, 8.96.3–4, where again the argument illuminates a good deal more of the war's strategic background than just its present context.

12. Hence an interest in counterfactuals has become a leading theme in philosophical discussion of causation during the last generation: it is surveyed by Paul 2009. The work of David K. Lewis has been particularly influential, esp. 1973a and 1973b. The extensive Postscript to 1973b in Lewis 1986, further refined in Lewis 2000, is important: for historical explanation his refinement in terms of "chancy causation" is particularly relevant if we are to avoid determinism (1986: 175–184), a tweak that has something in common with the "on the whole" (ὡς ἐπὶ τὸ πολύ) approach that has been found in Aristotle's scientific as well as his ethical thinking (Henry 2015). "Chancy causation" refines the syllogism in terms of the chances of q being "much less" if p had not occurred. This attempts to deal with atypical cases (a golf ball hitting a branch [p] will reduce the chances of its ending in the hole [q] but may exceptionally deflect it to do exactly that), and may serve as a rule of thumb. On counterfactual thinking in Greek thought and argument, see the essays in Wohl 2014, especially Tordoff 2014 on Thucydides and Gagarin 2014 on rhetoric.

13. Or, if we wish to take account of "chancy causation" (see previous n.), we should add a "probably" or a "normally" in both cases.

14. So Lateiner 1986: 14, bringing out the analogy with the Hippocratics and emphasizing that Herodotus' use of counterfactual thinking extends both to scientific and to historical investigation.

15. Here not merely the counterfactual element but also the use of numerical calculation is interesting as a method of reconstructing the past, here the geomorphological history of the Delta: see Sergueenkova 2016: esp. 128–129.

16. Not a good argument: the nobles would doubtless have been useless oarsmen.

17. On the complicated web of motivation statements here see Baragwanath 2008: 88–96, exploring the ways that a critical audience may be drawn in to a critique of Herodotus' analysis and an evaluation of the motives he assigns. On the importance of gifts and reciprocity in the sequence, see Gould 1991: 17 = 2001: 299–300.

18. An interesting variation comes at 7.47, when Xerxes invites Artabanus to consider a counterfactual *past*: what would you have said if that dream-vision had not come to you (7.17–18)? Cf. Grethlein 2011: 117–118 and 2013: 196. Artabanus shows his courtier's skill in sidestepping the question, but also shows Herodotus' own manner in extracting a further explicatory strand: land and sea are still their enemies (below, pp. 157–159).

19. On this sequence, see von Fritz 1965: 11–15. The plausibility of that reconstruction is unaffected by the question whether Gelon's refusal to help was conditioned by the Greeks' refusal of a leadership role (7.153–162) or by his preoccupations in Sicily itself (7.165: on Herodotus' technique here, cf. Baragwanath 2008: 217–220 and Zali 2014: 213–227). Either way, once Gelon had decided not to help it made sense for him to prepare for the alternative futures.

20. There may here be a recollection of the Corcyrean debate at Athens in 433, where the Corcyreans' avoidance of past entanglements became a flashpoint: see p. 226.

21. For a similar use of counterfactuals for arresting presentation, cf. 4.99.4–5: the Taurians inhabit the coastal region of Scythia "as if another people and not the Athenians were to inhabit Sounion in Attica" or "another people and not the Iapyges were to cut off and live in the extremity between Brentesion and Taras." On this see K. Clarke 2018: 75–76.

22. A similar case where counterfactual speculation emphasizes a conclusion reached on other grounds might be 7.229.2, explaining the Spartans' wrathfulness with Aristodemus after Thermopylae. The crucial factor, so Herodotus thinks, was that two invalids had been excused from the battle, but the other man had insisted on fighting anyway and had died: see p. 204.

23. Though there are many problems in elevating the "but for" principle to more than that rule of thumb: Hart and Honoré 1985: ch. 1, esp. 21 n. 16.

24. Cf. Mumford and Anjum 2013: 109–119, esp. 116 on the limits of experimentational possibility.

25. See esp. Gallie 1968 ("as in the sciences there is always a theory, so in history there is always a story," 2), esp. ch. 5, and Mink 1987; cf. the thoughtful discussion of "narrative as explanatory" at Atkinson 1978: 128–139, emphasizing (135–136; cf. 162–163) that new perspectives lose their cogency if they depart too far from the questions and insights already acknowledged to be valid. This approach chimes with the great attention paid to rhetoric in recent historiographical theory: the works of Hayden White, esp. White 1973 and 1987, have been particularly influential. Cf. esp. White 1987: 43–44 on the way in which the "aggregation of themes" generates "plot structures" against the background of "the various story types cultivated in a given culture" and these in turn give a "production of meaning": "the effect of such emplotment may be regarded as an explanation," but one in terms of "the *topoi* of literary plots, rather than the causal laws of science." White 1973 was an elaborate (and to my mind overschematic) attempt to classify such literary modes and tropes. White 1999: 87–91 then preferred to talk of later historical events as "fulfilling" earlier ones, as figures are fulfilled in a narrative, rather than "caused" by them.

26. Buchan 1929: 8. But Buchan's lecture then goes on to list various cases where, with more or less plausibility, he ties vast events down to trivial beginnings; all depends on counterfactual virtual-history speculations, which would seem to imply that it all could have happened quite differently. Cf. J. Assmann 2011: 209, discussing texts from Egypt, Israel, and the Near East as well as Greece and the difference from modern thinking: "The concept of causality suggests an automatic and a natural progres-

sion from one event to another, but this is the exact opposite of what we find in ancient texts. . . . In all cases, the focus is on requital, not on causality," with "requital" interpreted in terms of reward for the good and punishment for the bad. This seems to me badly overstated: a more nuanced view of "causality" is called for in the modern as well as the ancient context, and requital is anyway one acceptable form of causal explanation. But Assmann is right to question any expectation of "an automatic and a natural progression" in ancient texts.

27. Thus Popper 1960 insisted on predictability as the factor that most distinguished the claims of natural and of social sciences: cf. pp. 237–238 n. 10.

28. A standard example is the predictability that (say) a radon atom will decay within a particular time period: cf. Anscombe 1971; D. K. Lewis 1986: 233. The statistical likelihood is determinable even if that excludes certainty that x will happen in a particular case: radon has a half-life of 3.8 days, and if one starts with a million radon atoms half will be gone within 3.8 days, but there will still be about a thousand left after 38 days and a reasonable expectation of having one left after 76 days. Current scientific thinking is that the last remaining atom would be indistinguishable from all the others and would still have a 50% chance of decaying in the next 3.8 days. I am most grateful to Professor Robin Nicholas for advice here.

29. Because the *probability* of an atom's decay is fixed by such a "law": see previous note.

30. So White 1987: 60: "In general [historians] do not claim to have discovered the kinds of causal laws that would permit them to explain phenomena by viewing them as instantiations of the operations of such laws, in the way that physical scientists do in their explanations."

31. Different because predictability must also take into account the human inability to know all the relevant facts or to compute those that are known.

32. As most elegantly argued by Gallie 1968: 91–102, though his sporting parallel of choice is cricket.

33. Cf. Guthrie 1962–1981: ii. 161–164 and 414–419, esp. 417; Barnes 1982: 418–426, esp. 425–426; Warren 2007: 144; Hankinson 2008: 448–450.

34. That point is of course valid: cf. Popper 1960: 117 on the confluence of several different causal sequences to explain (say) why Newton's apple fell at that moment.

35. Deichgräber 1971: 80–81.

36. Thus Deichgräber 1971: 37–40 was right to say that the methodological principles articulated in the later *Epidemics* 6 are already traceable in the earliest books of *Epidemics*, 1 and 3: cf. also *Epid.* 1.17 I p. 170 J = 1.8 II pp. 648–650 L, 3.16 I p. 256 J = III p. 102 K.

37. "Arguably the most sophisticated statement about causation to be found anywhere in the Hippocratic Corpus," Schiefsky 2005: 288. Cf. G. E. R. Lloyd 1979: 53–54, arguing that similar assumptions underlie *On the Sacred Disease*.

38. Cf. *On Regimen* 3.70 IV p. 384 J = VI p. 606 L, *patients* often unjustly blame whatever they were doing at the time the illness struck. There too the implication is that adequate medical experience enables one to distinguish coincidence from cause.

39. And it is therefore vulnerable to the same objections, e.g., that constant conjunction, especially in cases of simultaneity rather than antecedence, does not demonstrate which is cause and which is effect, or discriminate cause and effect from collateral effects of an antecedent cause. But, heuristically, it is a good start.

40. Cf. *On Ancient Medicine* 19 I p. 48 J = I pp. 616–618 L: the fever will cease when

the discharging fluids thicken; and "we must consider the causes (*aitia*) to be those things whose presence necessarily means that there will be a complaint of a particular kind, and whose change into a different mixture means that the complaint will cease"; *On Breaths* 14 II p. 248 J = VI p. 110 L, when blood remains stable consciousness remains too, and when blood changes consciousness changes; *On Crises* 16 IX p. 282 P = 16 IX p. 282 L (a later and derivative work but one that often repeats material virtually verbatim from earlier works), the clues given by the times when urine changes its color and when it changes back again.

41. One of Kant's examples, much quoted in the later literature, was that of a lead ball falling on and depressing a cushion. Cf. e.g., Mackie 1974: 7–8, 109, 161; Brand 1980; Huemer and Kovitz 2003; Kistler 2006: 39–44.

42. Langholf 1990: 219.

43. Deichgräber 1971: 38: "ein wissenschatfliches Selbstgespräch."

44. These self-directed questions recall an introductory technique characteristic of works such as the Ps.-Aristotelian *Problems* or Plutarch's *Greek Questions* and *Roman Questions*: "self-directed" rather than "rhetorical," as they do not imply a particular answer but may prompt a number of alternatives.

45. See esp. Popper 2002 (first published 1959), a theory that has (of course) led to much discussion. For the Popperian analogy, see also Corcella 1984: 78, 84 n. 89 = 2013, 64, 70 n. 89 and on falsifiability 1984: 79 n. 74 = 65 n. 74; for a similar approach to narrative, see Gallie 1968: 43–44. It also fits the model of "predictive processing" developed against the background of contemporary neuroscience by Clark 2016: this suggests that in everyday real-world transactions the brain initially predicts experience on a probabilistic basis and then exploits ongoing sensory signals to "refine and nuance the guessing as we go along" (5). We identify what is most "newsworthy" in a new experience and use this to correct predictive error: "a kind of bootstrap heaven" (19). In our case these new experiences will largely be those afforded by the reading process but may also include those drawn for comparison from contemporary experience: on this, see ch. 15.

46. King 1989.

47. Another case, also concerning a nosebleed, is the daughter of Philo at *Epid*. 1. 19 I p. 174 J = 1.9 II p. 658 L: a number of symptoms, including nasal haemorrhage or copious menstruation, tended to be a good sign, "and I know of no case of a woman who died when any of those symptoms took place properly: for the daughter of Philo, who died even though she had suffered a violent nosebleed, had dined rather unseasonably on the seventh day." So Philo's daughter is no true counter-example: there was another causal factor at play.

48. Spatharas 2009.

49. Andoc. *On the Peace with Sparta* (3) 2–12. The account is historically wild, a good example of the confusions that can lodge in oral history (Thomas 1989: 119–123), but that does not affect the present point.

50. Here compare and contrast the general point made by Gallie 1968: 106 to distinguish historical from scientific explanation: "The hypothesis that a particular politician's actions over a certain period must be attributed to his temporary insanity is not one that we can imagine historians proceeding to test, systematically for truth or falsity, on other partially similar manifestations of political ineptitude on the part of other politicians." I am not sure that Gallie is right about that; in any case, this is pretty well what Demosthenes does with Meidias, there testing for *hybris* rather than ineptitude.

51. Cf. also *Against Meidias* 36–41, 58–65, 71–76, 165, 175–183.

52. That would therefore constitute some defense against the scorn of John Stuart Mill for "the capricious manner in which we select from among the conditions that which we choose to denominate the cause" (1843: ch. 5): see p. 94.

53. Or perhaps the process is so unconscious that it would be better to say we "imply" rather than "apply" it: cf. Mackie 1974: 77–80, arguing that such regularities may so far be unobserved, and are certainly not in our mind when we make a simple causal statement. Still, if challenged we might naturally defend such statements by invoking or looking for or constructing such parallel cases: cf. Hart and Honoré 1985: ch. II, arguing that "in the last resort" (61) causal claims invite "defence by generalizations" that they "exemplify" (56, 58). See also Atkinson 1978: 110–115 and 151–158, sympathetic to the view that causal intuitions are based on the accumulation of experience (156) but rightly insisting (113; cf. 154) that they retain their focus on individual cases and do not amount to the construction of any causal "laws."

54. Thus Popper 1960: 95 was prepared to allow an element of "experiments, carried out in our imagination in that case to trace "different attitudes in different historical periods." (These might of course have important causal implications.) In David K. Lewis' similar construction (p. 248 n. 12), "virtual" cases are replaced by cases that are nonfictional but true in some alternative spatio-temporal world. To a non-philosopher this seems too high a price to pay.

55. This will depend on the way that we describe both cause and effect. In general it is true that the fuller the description of the cause, the more demonstrable it will be that the cause is sufficient, whereas the fuller the description of the effect, the more demonstrable that it is necessary (Davidson 1967: 698 = 1993: 82); but it is a matter of selection as well as fullness.

56. This is relevant to an issue that has attracted philosophical attention, the question of how "fine-grained" a description of a cause needs to be: differences of emphasis can point to causal differences, for "Socrates *drinking hemlock* at dusk" caused his death whereas "Socrates drinking hemlock *at dusk*" did not (the example is drawn from Achinstein 1983: 193–217). Other narratives of drinking hemlock include death; narratives of drinking at dusk, thankfully, do not.

57. Or so I argued in Pelling 2015.

58. Cawkwell 1975: 54, 69–70; cf. Hornblower 1991–2008: i. 328–329 on 2.56.1.

59. Cf. here Lateiner's observations (1989: 191–196) about "analogy" as an important heuristic principle, 1989: 191–196, and more generally Corcella 1984.

60. *On Ancient Medicine* is particularly insistent on the indispensability of such appeals to familiar experience if an explanation is to carry conviction: Barton 2005.

61. Thus Ryan 1991: 54–57, discussing the way that a reader's preconceived "system of reality" underpins the believability of cause-and-effect sequences in fiction, rightly insists that those preconceptions may be drawn equally from other texts and from reality.

62. See Hornblower and Pelling on 6.126–131.1, and more generally the papers in Baragwanath and de Bakker 2012a.

63. Dershowitz 1996; cf. Pelling 1999a: 343–344. Gagarin 2003 and Spatharas 2009 show how important this principle is to the storytelling techniques of Attic orators.

4. ADVENTURES IN PROSE

1. Momigliano 1966b: 129 = 1960: 31, echoed by O. Murray 1987: 101 n. 12 = 2001: 27 n. 28, by K. Clarke 2018: ch. 1, and by others.

2. That question has attracted a large bibliography: see esp. Fowler 1996; Marincola 2012: 3–11; and several contributors to Luraghi 2001a.
3. Thus, E. Bowie 1986: 32 and 2001: 49–50.
4. It may be that Hippias of Elis—certainly a polymath—attempted some similar "drawing together" in his Συναγωγή of material hitherto treated separately to produce a "fresh and multiform *logos*" (*FGrH* 6 4 = Clem. Al. *Strom.* 6.15.1), but we know very little about it: cf. Guthrie 1962–1981: iii. 283; Fowler *EGM* i. xxxii–xxxiii; E. L. Bowie 2018b: 73–74.
5. For a recent stimulating discussion, see Swift 2010.
6. Loraux 1986; Thomas 1989: ch. 4.
7. Grethlein 2010; cf. Zali 2014: 311–316.
8. Fowler 1996: 65 = 2013: 51; E. L. Bowie 1986: 27–34, 2001, and 2018b; K. Clarke 2008: 187–191, and on Simonides the papers in Boedeker and Sider 2001. For a list of "poems on historical themes," see Marincola 2006: 25.
9. Isoc. 4 (*Paneg.*) 83; Dem. 60.10; Hyp. 6.35. Cf. Thomas 1989: 221.
10. Kurke 2011; cf. Griffin 1990.
11. Grethlein 2010; cf. Marincola 2006: esp. 14, 21–22.
12. Baragwanath and de Bakker 2012b: 31.
13. Pelling 2007b, 2016a, and forthcoming (a).
14. Especially with proto-biography: below, ch. 9(b).
15. For a helpful survey of Herodotus' relation to these two areas, see also Zali 2014: 19–29.
16. Cf. esp. O. Murray 1987 = 2001 and the other papers in Luraghi 2001a; "semi-oral" is the description favored by Giangiulio 2001: 127, 132. West 2011: 256 warns against assuming that Herodotus had access to texts of writers such as Charon, Xanthus, and Dionysius of Miletus.
17. Bertelli 2001: 67, cf. 84, 93. See Bertelli's paper and Fowler 2001 for references to earlier discussion. More generally, the work of J. and A. Assmann has frequently stressed the importance of writing in giving form and shape to collective memory: see conveniently J. Assmann 2011, esp. chs. 2 and 7, and A. Assmann 2011, esp. ch. 8. In classical scholarship this approach is particularly associated with E. A. Havelock, e.g., Havelock 1976, 1982, and 1986.
18. Vansina 1965: 104–105. Cf. J. Assmann 2011: 246 (cf. 261): "Writing, which in Israel led to the monolithic crystallization of tradition, led to fluidity, controversy, and hence to a variety of traditions in Greece."
19. As Thomas 1989: ch. 1 emphasized, esp. 15–34. Cf. Luraghi 2001b: 153–154, 159, and esp. J. Assmann 2011: 239–246 and 273–275, insisting that the impact of writing took a different form in Greece from in Egypt or Israel: in Greece texts "do not flaunt their 'writtenness'; on the contrary, they emerge from and return to physical, live voices and interactions" (241). Thus "foundational texts"—Homer's epics, the tragedies, Plato's dialogues—are represented as reproducing oral speech.
20. Thomas 1989: 181–195, followed by, e.g., Bertelli 2001: 93 and Fowler 2001: 103: cf. Thomas 2001a: 200 and Hartog 1989.
21. Möller 2001: 251: cf. above, p. 15.
22. The phrase of Fowler, *EGM* ii. 685, discussing Hellanicus.
23. Vansina 1965: 104–105 and 1985: 130–133.
24. Bertelli 2001: 79.
25. Cf. p. 242 n. 67.
26. Cf. e.g., Vansina 1965: 76–113, 164–173 and 1985: ch. 4.

27. Cf. esp. Luraghi 2001b. A particularly clear example is 6.84, where each locality gives the version most favorable to itself: see pp. 159–160. Equally, there is a better chance of accurate recall in the localities where the events are presumed to have taken place: Vansina 1965: 196. Ironically, these points would be even more forceful if Fehling 1989 were even partly right in suggesting that some of the oral traditions Herodotus reports are too good to be true—that is, so exactly what one might expect that they are likely to be fabricated. In that case, Herodotus would be playing to those audience expectations, and this is itself telling for what they found familiar. Cf. Luraghi 2001b: 144.

28. Vansina 1985: 21. The muddles in Andocides' versions of his own family history provide some examples: Thomas 1989: 118–123, 139–144, 204–205.

29. Vansina 1985: 139–146. Some of his examples are clichés about kingship and royal courts; cf. his p. 108 on the tendency of oral tradition to concentrate on "great men" and p. 176 on the way that events can become personalized as doings of the king himself.

30. Vansina 1965: 55 and 1985: 69–70, 76.

31. Fowler 2001: 105–113: "It will work for any audience, anywhere" (108).

32. Nicolai 1997 points out that our picture of Hecataeus as a great originator is owed to implications drawn from Herodotus himself rather than to any explicit ancient tradition. On the attention paid to Hecataeus in, particularly, book 2, see now Dillery 2018.

33. On the titles, see Fowler *EGM* ii. 660.

34. Similarly A. B. Lloyd 1975–1986: ii. 37–38; J. G. Griffiths 1966: 57; Dillery 2018: 34–35; and Jacoby *FGrH* ad loc. also accepts the Hecataeus reference. West 1991: 159 notes that "the expression could by Herodotus' time have become a commonplace": true, but that need not preclude a hint of Hecataeus, especially if 2.2.5 too is taken as barbed (p. 63). If so, both passages may be taken as a programmatic staking out of ground, presaging several further barbs in the Egyptian *logos*.

35. Hecataeus references in the form "F 301" refer to the *FGrH* numbering; where a fragment or testimonium is included by Fowler in *EGM* the reference is given in the form "F 197 J = T 12a Fo."

36. The truth of the story has been doubted, and Herodotean imaginative creativity has been suspected: cf. esp. West 1991: 145–154; Fowler, *EGM* ii. 661. But Moyer 2002 and 2011: 42–83 has shown that the story chimes with genuine Egyptian material, especially extensive genealogies and at least some ancestral statues; cf. also J. Assmann 2011: 170–171. The mistake may have been in an assumption that each of the 345 represented a different generation, when at least some may have operated in different regions at the same time.

37. Thus, A. B. Lloyd 1975–1986: i. 127: "Malicious joy there certainly is in II, 143 . . ." Similarly Fowler, *EGM* ii. 661 and 2006: 35–36; Bertelli 2001: 91 n. 77, and Moyer 2002: 83 = 2013: 315. For cataloguing as a general feature of Hecataeus' work, cf. Ceccarelli 2016.

38. West 1991: esp. 159.

39. Similarly here Dillery 2018: esp. 44–49, seeing Herodotus as acknowledging that Hecataeus had the right approach but suggesting that in that case he ought to have done better, and K. Clarke 2018: 15–17. Rutherford 2018: 41–42 finds an "uncertainty of tone" that "may indicate that Herodotus was not completely confident of his ability to eclipse Hecataeus with his own work."

40. On this "regime of critical intelligence," cf. Bertelli 2001: 83–84, adopting a phrase of Detienne. I am less convinced by Bertelli's suggestion that Hecataeus' γράφω (above, p. 59) marks "the difference between his own written redaction and the 'λόγοι of the Greeks'"—but those Greek λόγοι will have included both written and spoken versions.

41. Cf. Bertelli 2001: 84–89 and esp. Fowler, *EGM* ii. 665–668, who makes important qualifications; also Fowler 1996: 71 = 2013: 60 on the "quaver in the voice" with which Hecataeus puts forward such rationalistic interpretations. "Rationalization" is a term often used overcasually, but Hawes 2014 draws some important and illuminating distinctions. For some tentative suggestions of my own see Pelling 2002a: ch. 7, with particular reference to Plutarch's *Theseus*.

42. Cf. A. B. Lloyd 1975–1986: ii. 9 ad loc.; Dillery 2018: 27, 33. If this is right, it qualifies Nicolai's claim (1997: 154) that nobody in antiquity attached the least importance to this proemial statement.

43. Cf. 1.5.2 and p. 28.

44. Thus, tentatively, A. B. Lloyd 1975–1986 ii. 9; against, but with a very weak argument, Jacoby, *R–E* vii (1912) 2679 = 1956: 192.

45. It is similarly likely that Herodotus "throws this laughter" [i.e., that implied by Hecataeus' "laughable," γελοῖοι] "back at Hekataios with his own laughter at 4.36.2," there targeted on "the many people who have written *gēs periodoi*, none of them sensible": Fowler, *EGM* ii. 680. Cf. also 6.53.1, where ἐγὼ γράφω may well echo Hecataeus' preface and be a similar allusive gibe: cf. Hornblower and Pelling 2017 ad loc. "Some others of the Greeks," cited for a version at 2.134.1, may also refer to Hecataeus: Nagy 2018: 110.

46. Cf. Zali 2018: 126. Thus, the *Genealogies* apparently included details on places and their etymologies (FF 3–7, 10–12) and on local diet (F 9); *Guide to the World* apparently included material on city-founders and their families, or on mythical visitors (FF 102c, 107, 119, 128–129, 139–141, 302, 308). But in many cases, it is hard to see which work a fragment belonged to: K. Clarke 1999: 61–62; Purves 2010: 110–111; and on Herodotus' story of Hecataeus in Egypt, see Fowler, *EGM* ii. 664–665.

47. So, rightly, C. W. Müller 2006: 38–39.

48. Not that a *prophasis* need always be false: pp. 8–9. But in this case, the implication would be that, if the Athenians had offered any such *prophasis*, it would have been a mere mask for the jealousy and land-hunger.

49. Cf. Fowler 1996: 77–78 = 2013: 69, commenting on Pherecydes.

50. Cf. A. B. Lloyd 1975–1986: i. 128–129 and ii. 100 ad loc. ("That Hec. is the person here criticized is certain"). On this passage, see also Munson 2001: 237 and Dillery 2018: 35–37.

51. D'Alessio 2004 has good arguments for the view that the version without 195 is there primary, making not Ocean but the Acheloüs the source of the world's waters, but he allows the possibility "that the presence of Ocean in this section (line 195) goes back to a period not much later than its appearance within the monumental poem" (p. 33 with n. 59). The idea of the encircling Ocean is made likely by its depiction around the rim of the Shield (18.608).

52. Similarly von Fritz 1967: 64–65. F 197 J = T 12a Fo. (= Amm. Marc. 22.10) in fact ascribes the "Scythian bow" analogy to "Hecataeus and Ptolemy and other detailed investigators." It may also be, as confidently stated by, e.g., Jacoby, *R–E* vii (1912) 2680 = 1956: 192 and A. B. Lloyd 1975–1986: i. 130 and ii. 54–55, that Hecataeus compared the

shape of Egypt to an axe: thus, Ps.-Scylax 106.3. But this is anything but certain, and Shipley 2011: 15 (cf. 185) comments on how little Ps.-Scylax seems to owe to Hecataeus.

53. And the practice therefore continued in later authors: Strabo is particularly rich and imaginative in his geographical similes (Dueck 2005).

54. Waterfield has "obscure and dubious," de Sélincourt "depending on an unknown quantity."

55. Ps.-Scylax 105.1: so Shipley 2012: 128 and n. 80, restoring the lacuna to make the Nile flow either "from the Red Sea" (then taken as including Persian Gulf and Indian Ocean) or, less likely, "from the outer Ocean"; cf. also Shipley 2011: 183 ad loc.

56. For Lade was in "Asia," F 241.

57. On this, see Ceccarelli 2016, with references to earlier scholarship.

58. Cf. Jacoby on *FGrH* 1 F 301; A. B. Lloyd 1975–1986: ii. 83 on 2.16.

59. Cf. Ceccarelli 2016: 70. This point holds even if the story comes from Herodotus' imagination, as West 1991: 154–156 suggests: Herodotus would be reconstructing advice that fitted his idea of the historical individual.

60. Thus, von Fritz 1967: 58.

61. Though these assumptions have come under challenge in the last few decades: cf. Schlögel 2016.

62. K. Clarke 1999. Cf. also Fowler 2001: 97. A major theme of Thomas 2000 is also the lack of a firm line between different types of inquiry, scientific and medical, philosophical, and historical; similarly now Kingsley forthcoming.

63. The title of Goldhill 2002, presenting the emergence of prose as "a trendy, provocative, modern and highly intellectualized form of writing" and "integral to the cultural revolution we call the Greek enlightenment" (1). Goldhill emphasizes the search for causes as a fundamental feature of such developments (8, 13, 19, 28, etc.).

64. Fowler, *EGM* i–ii: cf. also his important paper on their relation to Herodotus: Fowler 1996.

65. Diodorus 1.37.3–4 says that not just Hecataeus but Hellanicus, Cadmus, and "everyone like that" (πάντες οἱ τοιοῦτοι) treated the Nile flood and the river's sources. The "everyone like that" need not be taken too seriously, but E. Almagor (on Cadmus, *BNJ* 489 F 1) may be overskeptical. Diodorus' implication was that all three gave explanations that remained "mired in myth" (the phrase of F. Pownall on Hellanicus, *BNJ* 4 F 173 = 608a F 4). The topics had also been discussed by Thales, Anaxagoras, Oenopides of Chios, Diogenes of Apollonia, and Democritus: cf. A. B. Lloyd 1975–1986: ii. 91–93, 98–101; Anon. *On the Nile*, *FGrH* 647 F 1 with the *BNJ* comm. of S. Gambetti.

66. Above, p. 60.

67. The phrase of P. Ceccarelli in *BNJ*, discussing Charon *FGrH* 262 F 1 (a story of dancing horses).

68. So C. W. Müller 2006: 42–43 and Fowler, *EGM* ii. 723–724, both discussing Pherecydes *FGrH* 3 F 105.

69. Including quite elaborate ones: Aphrodite's support for Troy was a feint, as she hoped to ensure the city's total destruction to give a future kingship for Aeneas, Acusilaus *FGrH* 2 F 39 (cf. Fowler, *EGM* ii. 361–362). Other fragments especially rich in motivation are Acusilaus *FGrH* 2 F 22, Pherecydes *FGrH* 3 FF 10–12 (Danaë and Acrisius), 13 (Alcmene and Amphitryon), 34 (Cephalus and Procris), and 114 (Melampous), and Hellanicus *FGrH* 4 FF 26, but there are plenty of other examples.

70. *FGrH* 4 FF 38, 169 (= 323a FF 1, 22) with Fowler, *EGM* ii. 447–455.

71. Thus Fowler, *EGM* ii. 469, 476–477, 708–709, following Huxley 1973: cf. Thomas 1989: 161–173, esp. 165. Pherecydes traces that lineage at *FGrH* 3 F 2. For this preoccupation with heroic forebears, modified by but surviving into the Athenian democracy, see Thomas 1989: 106–109 and index, s.v. "legendary ancestor, role of."

72. That of Charon of Lampsacus (*FGrH* 262) is especially disputed, but see Fowler 1996: 67 = 2013: 53–54 and Möller 2001: 249–250 for a defense of a pre-Herodotean date; Ceccarelli in *BNJ* prefers to classify him as a "younger contemporary" of Herodotus.

73. See Almagor, "biographical note" in *BNJ* on Cadmus *FGrH* 489 (again in my view overskeptical: cf. p. 256 n. 65).

74. The conspiracy of the Magi also seems to have been treated by Dionysius of Miletus, *FGrH* 687 F 2.

75. Fowler 1996, esp. 76–80 = 2013: 66–72; quotation from 1996: 86 = 2013: 81 (his italics). Cf. Apfel 2011: 165–172.

76. Fowler 1996: 79 = 2013: 71.

77. And not just Herodotus: much the same could be said about Polybius' tour-de-force denunciation of Fabius Pictor on the causes of the Second Punic War (3.8.8–11). That is very forensic in its use of *modus tollendo tollens* (cf. pp. 68–69) and counterfactual argumentation—if Fabius had really been right, the Carthaginians would have responded differently to Rome's demands for the surrender of Hannibal—but in the interest of *disproving* Fabius' pinning of responsibility on human personalities, in that case, Hasdrubal and Hannibal.

78. As is often thought: cf. Dover 1950: 56–59 = 1988: 29–34 (balancing different views but tending towards an early date if the work is genuine); Gagarin 1997: 8–9. On one Antiphon or two, see also p. 77.

79. Corax, Arist. *Rhet.* 1402a. Teisias: Plato *Phaedr.* 273b with Bryan 2014. Corax's example was a fight between a strong man and a weak one: the one side would claim that it was *eikos* for the strong man to be the attacker, the other that the strong man would have known that he would be the natural suspect and would therefore not have done it. Here cf. *Tetr. 1* β.3: because I was known to be the man's enemy, they might think it *eikos* for me to be the culprit, but it was even more *eikos* for me to know I would be the chief suspect. The examples are much discussed: cf. esp. Gagarin 2014.

80. See the interesting discussion of Williams 1993: ch. 3, esp. 60–64, arguing that the modern law of tort here offers a closer parallel to such thinking than our criminal law: one can be legally and financially responsible for the consequences of one's actions even when there is no question of criminal intentionality.

81. Cf. Blondell 2013: 167–168, 178.

82. So much so, in fact, that this religious principle overrides the precise details of Attic law, which would have been more generous to a perpetrator of such an involuntary killing than the speeches assume (there was a specific provision covering "death at the games," though it is disputed what this covered). This may be because the focus on more general principles would be more thought-provoking, but we cannot exclude the possibility that even in real-life cases the fear of the gods might occupy minds, and fill speeches, more than the letter of the law. Cf. Caizzi 1969: 25–44; Parker 1983: 104–110, 115; Gagarin 1997: 23 and 2002: 52–62.

83. The case is strikingly similar to two discussed in a modern study of legal causation, one where a victim of a stabbing assault was given the wrong drugs in hospital and died (*R. v. Jordan* 1956), and one where a woman was taken to hospital after an assault and died from scarlet fever caught from a nurse (*Bush v. Commonwealth of Ken-*

tucky 1880): Hart and Honoré 1985: 96, 98, 341–342 and 356. In both cases, the defendants were acquitted, but in the first case only on appeal.

84. "Dwelling on," because some possibility of joint responsibility is momentarily acknowledged in the *Second Tetralogy*: if it is right to blame the boy for running across the area, then it is also right to blame the thrower; the boy has already been punished by his death, and the thrower must now be punished too (γ.10). But not much is made of it.

85. Gagarin 2002: 111.

86. Caizzi 1969: 45.

87. Guthrie 1962–1981: iii. 180–182; Apfel 2011: 52–57, with reference to previous scholarship.

88. At least, it seems to pre-date Euripides' *Trojan Women* of 415 BCE: see n. 95.

89. Cf. Macleod 1977: esp. 244–245 = 1983: esp. 120–121.

90. See the excellent discussion of Blondell 2013: ch. 8.

91. As Dover 1950: 59 = 1988: 33 observed for the *Tetralogies*: neither the diction nor the fuzzy relationship to the real laws is appropriate for the Attic courts. Witnesses too would in a real-life case be important. Gorgias' pushing of the argument to extremes would also strain any jury's sense of reasonableness.

92. Aristotle duly disentangles an important step in the argument at *NE* 3.1110b9–17, 1111a21–b3: the important distinction is between coercion by external forces and by one's own internal drives, for if the second counts as "coercion" no room is left for voluntary choice. He may or may not have Gorgias in mind, but anyway demonstrates the continuing interest in the issues.

93. This idea of a joke is taken by Blondell 2013: 176 as a "safety net" in case any of the audience were tempted to take Gorgias seriously.

94. It is discussed by Blondell 2013: ch. 9.

95. Cf. Goldhill 1986: 236–238; Croally 1994: 155; *contra*, M. Lloyd 1992: 100–101. Notice 998 (Hecuba), "You say that my son took you by force." In fact, Euripides' Helen has not said this, but Gorgias' Helen did.

96. Eur. *Alex*. TT iii K. (*POxy* 3650), ivb. Cf. Scodel 1980: 20–28; Cropp in Collard, Cropp, and Gibert 2004: 36–37.

97. Cf. M. Lloyd 1992: 32–33 on this characteristically Euripidean use of a "hypothetical syllogism."

98. Or so I read it, as do Burian in A. Shapiro and Burian 2009: 21 n. 32 and Blondell 2013: 198; *contra*, Kovacs 1998; J. Gregory 1999–2000: 69–72.

99. So also Burian in A. Shapiro and Burian 2009: 20–21; *contra*, M. Lloyd 1992: 111–112, "The point . . . is to leave no secure impression of what is to happen to her."

100. So Goldhill 1986: 237–238. Cf. M. Lloyd 1992: 19–36 and 99–112; Croally 1994: 153, "While we saw some slick moves in Helen's speech, Hecuba is very slippery indeed."

101. G. E. R. Lloyd 1966.

102. G. E. R. Lloyd 1983: 44–53.

103. Questions of "alterity" have recently been much discussed: see the survey of scholarship in Provencal 2015: 2–6. I had my say in Pelling 1997c; for a similar line argued differently, see Gruen 2011b. Provencal himself argues that "the cultural grid constructed by Herodotus is more complex and systematic, and thus both more fluid and more rigid, than has been recognized" (6). I would say "more thoroughgoing" rather than "more systematic" and would question "rigid," but it will be clear that I agree about complexity and fluidity. But Provencal follows through this approach in a way that seems to me insufficiently multitextured, emphasizing the parallels that he finds between Persian culture and "the sophists."

104. For other texts associating Pythagoras with Babylonia and Persia, see Guthrie 1962–1981: i. 253–254.

105. Cf. DK 299 A 1 (D.L. 9.35), 9, 11–13, 16; Guthrie 1962–1981: ii. 386–387 and 387 n. 1.

106. Thus Ubsdell 1983: 359–374 saw Herodotus as "working parallel to the sophists" (374) in his use of foreign customs as a prompt to intellectual reflection on human nature. His entire ch. III ("Herodotus and the sophistic movement") is extremely valuable.

107. On these discussions, cf. esp. Heinimann 1945; Guthrie 1962–1981: iii. 55–134; and, with especial focus on Herodotus, Kingsley forthcoming chs. 3–4.

108. Incest seems to have been regarded as a particularly troubling test case in such discussions: Kingsley forthcoming ch. 3.

109. So Thomas 2000: 42–74, collecting the signs of this in the Hippocratic corpus: the indications are admittedly sparse, but she makes a good case. Libya and Scythia are regions of particular interest to Herodotus too, especially in book 4.

110. Corcella 1984: 80–81; Thomas 2000: 139.

111. So Pendrick 2002: 1–26; the unitarian position is set out by Gagarin 2002: 37–52. This is not the place to enter that old controversy.

112. As supplemented by *POxy* 3647: see Pendrick 2002 ad loc.

113. See also Thomas 2000: 122–134 for further ways in which barbarian customs figured in contemporary sophistic debate about νόμος and φύσις, especially in the so-called *Dissoi Logoi*.

114. Cf. the perfect tense κεχωρίσθαι at 1.4.4; p. 27.

115. On all this, see esp. Dodds 1973 and above, p. 242 n. 60.

116. Not that any such "explanation" was always made clear, as Aristotle complained in the case of Empedocles (*Metaph.* Γ 1000b12–13): Hankinson 2008: 442–445. Cf. Guthrie 1962–1981: i. 54–71 (discussing Thales but pointing to this as a more general feature of the Milesians' thinking) and index s.v. "hylozoism."

117. Vernant 1988 (1972).

118. Cf. J. Assmann 2011: 274, discussing the vitality given to Greek culture by the familiarity with Homer: "Holding onto Homer as a foundation even in the age of the Polis meant living in two times and two worlds at once."

119. Or so I argued in Pelling 2006a.

5. HIPPOCRATIC AFFINITIES

1. This is not the place to discuss the intricate problems of dating particular works. In her authoritative survey Craik 2015 gives the following as the most probable dates for the works mentioned in this book: *Airs Waters Places*, "mid to late fifth century" (Craik 2015, p. 11); *On Ancient Medicine*, "the final decades of the fifth century" (285); *On the Sacred Disease*, "mid to late fifth century" (195); *Epidemics* 1 and 3, "around 410" (90–91); *Epidemics* 2, 4, and 6, "around 400" (90–91); *The Art*, "the final decades of the fifth century" (40); *On Places in Man*, "a comparatively early date, perhaps around 450 BC" (162); *On the Nature of Man*, "last decades of the fifth century" (212); *On Fractures* and *On Joints*, "the second half of the fifth century" (111); *On Regimen*, "late fifth or early fourth century" (275); *On Regimen in Acute Diseases* "the end of the fifth century" (6); *Prorrhetikon* 2, "at the end of the fifth century" (244); *On Breaths*, "the final decades of the fifth century" (102); *On Fleshes*, "450–400 BC" (48); *On Affections* and *On Female Diseases*, "late fifth or early fourth century" (19, 206).

2. Translation is difficult: Jones translates "spontaneity" (Loeb); G. E. R. Lloyd, "the spontaneous" (1979: 33); and Jouanna, "le spontané" (Budé); J. E. Powell's *Lexicon* has "of its own accord." The notion is of something happening in and of itself, as wild plants might grow (Hdt. 2.94.1, 3.100). C: cf. 7.9γ: "Nothing is αὐτόματον, but everything that mortals achieve comes through trying." Cf. Holmes 2010: 142–147; Mann 2012: 150–153. But Herodotus would have agreed with *The Art* that the impression of spontaneity can be misleading: at 2.14.2 the Nile floods αὐτόματος, but that does not exclude an extended discussion of why this should be (2.20–27; pp. 2–3).

3. Cf. G. E. R. Lloyd 1979: 32–33, noting the contact with Leucippus DK 67 B 2 and *Airs Waters Places* 22 I p. 126 J = II p. 76 L. But not everyone agreed that everything had a cause. Diocles of Carystus thought that many things were more properly described as "beginnings" rather than *aitia*, that causal analysis was not always central to treatment, and that a cause should only be ascribed in cases that admitted it (fr. 176). That contrasts with the preoccupation with causal explanation in, for instance, *On Ancient Medicine* (p. 52), where it seems clear that every disease has a cause (Rawlings 1975: 48–49); cf. van der Eijk 2005a: 85, 89–92.

4. Lateiner 1986: 9–10; Dawson and Harvey 1986; Grmek 1989: 41, 76–77, 108, 126–127, 163–164; Thomas 2000: 28–42; Jouanna 2005: 3–6; Demont 2018.

5. If that passage is genuine: Hude marks it as corrupt, and Wilson regards it as one of those passages that may be a later or marginal addition of Herodotus himself (cf. p. 215).

6. On the Cambyses case, see Thomas 2000: 34–35 and, taking a different view on several aspects, Jouanna 2005: 6–10; McPhee 2018; Demont 2018: 187–190.

7. See esp. Thomas 2000. Lateiner 1986 was an important forerunner (see also Lateiner 1989: ch. 9); others too have observed that Herodotus' description of clinical phenomena and diseases is careful (Dawson and Harvey 1986; Grmek 1989: 41, 76–77, 108, 126–127, 163–164).

8. For further parallels in argumentative technique, see Thomas 2000: ch. 6.

9. *The Art* 4–8 II pp. 194–204 J = VI pp. 6–14 L. But there are signs of a lively debate about exactly how much should be attributed to chance: "If a person knows medicine in this way, he waits the least upon chance, but with or without chance everything would be done well," *On the Places in Man* 46 VIII pp. 92–94 P. = VI p. 342 L. Cf. Holmes 2010: 142–147; Villard 1996; and Wenskus 1996: esp. 416.

10. *The Art* 4 II p. 194 J = VI p. 6 L. The response—bad luck tends to come after bad treatment and good luck after good—will remind golfers of the retort attributed to Gary Player when an onlooker said that a bunker shot had been lucky: "It's funny, the more I practice the luckier I get." Themistocles too says something similar: Hdt. 8.60γ.

11. Lateiner 1986. Thus, Herodotus' dismissive approach to untestable claims about Ocean (p. 2) has much in common with *On Ancient Medicine*'s impatience with opponents' airy claims about the constitution of the human body (p. 85).

12. Cf. *On Breaths* 3 II p. 230 J = VI p. 94 L: the power of air is "invisible to sight but visible to reason," with Mann 2012: 27–28 and Thomas 2000: 204–206. The principle is in line with the Presocratics: above, p. 2. Spatharas 2007: 160–161 thinks that the passage in *The Art* is an echo of Gorg. *Helen* 13 (the *meteōrologoi* who "have made unbelievable and invisible things appear to the eyes of opinion," τὰ ἄπιστα καὶ ἄδηλα φαίνεσθαι τοῖς τῆς δόξης ὄμμασιν ἐποίησαν): perhaps, but it is more likely that both are echoing an intellectual cliché.

13. E.g., *Epid.* 1.22 I pp. 178–180 = II. 1.9 pp. 666–668 L; 1.26 I p. 184 J = 1.12 II

pp. 678–682 L; 2.1.6 VII pp. 20–22 S = V p. 76 L; 4.1.2 VII p. 92 S = V p. 144 L; 4.1.6 VI p. 94 S = V p. 146 L; 4.1.20 VI p. 108 S = V p. 156 L, etc.

14. *On the Places in Man* 44 VIII pp. 88–90 P = VI pp. 338–340 L; *On the Sacred Disease* 21 II p. 182 J = 18 VI p. 394 L; *On Affections* 47 V p. 74 P = VI p. 258 L, 50 V p. 76 P = VI p. 260 L. The first Hippocratic aphorism continues after "Life is short, the art is long" by saying that the *kairos* is short-lived, dealing with it is tricky, and judgment is difficult. For other Hippocratic views on *kairos* see Craik 1998: 209–210 on *Places in Man* 44.

15. Jouanna 2005: 22–24 discusses the possibility that Thucydides is influenced by Hippocratic ideas of *krisis* at 1.23.1 (the Persian Wars has a speedy *krisis*, decided by two battles on land and two at sea) but does not discuss any Herodotean analogies.

16. Similarly *On Regimen* 3.70 IV p. 384 J = VI p. 606 L, where a patient does the same (τοῦτο αἰτιῆται οὐκ αἴτιον ἐόν); *On the Art* 7 II p. 202 J = VI p. 12 L.

17. But when different causes are being systematically evaluated, the *aition* tends to be formulated more as a thing and less as a proposition. Cf. Frede 1987: 128–129.

18. Cf., e.g., *Airs Waters Places* 16 I p. 114 J = II p. 64 L; 21 I p. 124 J = II p. 76 L; *On Regimen in Acute Diseases* 17 II p. 74 J = 5 II p. 260 L; Deichgräber 1971: 16. *Aitiē* and *prophasis* are particularly hard to distinguish in *On Ancient Medicine*, so much so that in two textual cruces, 11 I p. 30 J = I p. 594 L and 16 I p. 42 J = I p. 606 L, either word may be possible (Rawlings 1975: 51 n. 94). Schiefsky 2005: 215–216 favors *prophasis* in both cases but not because of the word's meaning: "In VM [i.e., *On Ancient Medicine*] there is no discernible semantic distinction between πρόφασις and αἰτίη/αἴτιος" (215). The general sense of *prophasis* is even more frequent in later works (Rawlings 1975: 55).

19. Rawlings 1975: 38–48; cf. Lohmann 1952: 20–30. Deducible rather than immediately perceptible: e.g., *On Joints* 41 III p. 280 W = IV p. 180 L, 53 III p. 324 W = IV p. 236 L, etc. So, of the two possible etymologies for πρόφασις (p. 241 n. 45) the Hippocratic evidence would in itself favor προ-φαίνω (Rawlings 1975: 44–45), but it is still hard to believe that this remained uninfected by any sense of πρόφημι. It is revealing that Weidauer 1954: 11–15, arguing for a προ-φαίνω derivation of Hippocratic πρόφασις ("zum-Vorschein-kommen"), glosses his interpretation as the "Grund, den man dafür angeben kann" ("grounds that one can adduce for something"). That comes very close to a natural way of expressing a πρό-φημι interpretation, and hints how close the two notions can come to each other. Cf. Diller 1955: 10 = 1971: 483; Rawlings 1975: 57 n. 106.

20. E.g., *Epid*. 3.3 I p. 240 J = III p. 70 L; 7.120 VIII p. 410 S = V p. 464 L; *Prorrhet*. 2.12 VIII p. 248 P = IX pp. 32–34 L; 2.24 VIII p. 272 P. = IX p. 56 L. It is thus possible to describe a disease as striking "with a *prophasis*," a visible precursor: e.g., *Epid*. 3.1 case 3 I p. 202 J = III pp. 38–40 L; 3.4 I p. 240 J = III p. 70 L; 3.17 case 11 I p. 276 J = III p. 134 L. Cf. Rawlings 1975: 46–47.

21. Contrast Heubeck 1980: 226: "Die medizinische *prophasis* ist auf Grund ihres Wesens niemals die Ursache einer Krankheit und sie sagt ebensowenig über die wahre Ursache einer Krankheit (τὸ αἴτιον, ἡ ἀρχή) etwas aus" ("Medical *prophasis* is essentially never the cause of an illness and says equally little about the true cause of an illness"); Rawlings 1975: 47, "very little causal force" but also 49, "the causal significance of *prophasis* is clearly minimal, yet it does exist." I would put it higher than "minimal."

22. Those words are rich in Thucydidean resonance, but notice that at 1.23.6 Thucydides with typical contrariness reverses the more natural application of the words, using *prophasis* of the underlying reasons why a war would come some time and *aitiai* of the particular stimuli that provoked it in 431. The element of "blame," however, is

relevant enough to those stimuli too—Corcyra and Potidaea were "grievances" in the minds of Sparta and even more her allies, especially Corinth. Cf. Sealey 1957: 4 ("a suggestion of oxymoron"); Heubeck 1980.

23. Cf. Diels 1879: 233, claiming that the categories simply reflect the peripatetic distinction of four causes. It is true that the "from what" may approximate to an Aristotelian exciting cause and the "in what" to a material cause, but there are three categories rather than four, and the match is not precise. Stoic vocabulary has also been detected, e.g., συνεκτικήν for what "keeps health together." On this fragment, and Alcmaeon in general, see Guthrie 1962–1981: i. 341–359, esp. 345–346; Ostwald 1969: 97–106; G. E. R. Lloyd 1975; Cambiano 1983; Longrigg 1993: 47–62, esp. 52–53; Zhmud 2012: 357–361; Mansfeld 2013; Kouloumentas 2014; and above, p. 238 n. 12.

24. Cf., e.g., Jouanna 1999: 325–328; Vlastos 1947; Müri 1950: 190–201 = 1976: 125–138 (discussing *On the Nature of Man* and *On Ancient Medicine*); G. E. R. Lloyd 1966: 20–22; MacKinney 1964; Ostwald 1969: 102–105; and Schiefsky 2005: 248–249, n. on *Ancient Medicine* 14.4. Cambiano 1983: 442–443 and Kouloumentas 2014 emphasize the coexistence of different tensions within the same body.

25. Cf. Vlastos 1953: 345–346 and Cambiano 1983: 446–447, observing that the "tension" figure implies an equilibrium of forces on the same level, whereas "harmony" *can* (as for instance in Plato) be more hierarchical, with higher forces dominating the lower.

26. Cf. also, e.g., *On Ancient Medicine* 13 I p. 34 J = I p. 598 L, observing that it is not so simple as helping the hot against the cold or the dry against the moist; *On the Sacred Disease* 21 II p. 182 J = 18 VI pp. 394–396 L; *On the Nature of Man* 9 IV p. 24 J = VI p. 52 L; Kühn 1956: 59; G. E. R. Lloyd 1966: 21–22; Ferrini 1996: esp. 21–23.

27. As it is with Epimetheus' forethought in the similar argument at Plato *Prot.* 320d–321b (Protagoras' great myth).

28. Thus Pagel 1927: 30–33, stressing the analogy with the way Herodotus views matters of politics or society; cf. Immerwahr 1956: 243–244 and 250 = 2013: 159 and 1966: 172, 312–313, and index s.v. "balance, in world."

29. Not just "between" or "of" the few and the many, as commentators often take it: it is a commingling ἐς τοὺς ὀλίγους καὶ τοὺς πόλλους, with ἐς functioning as in Pericles' καὶ ὄνομα μὲν διὰ τὸ μὴ ἐς ὀλίγους ἀλλ' ἐς πλείονας οἰκεῖν δημοκρατία κέκληται (2.37.1), government for the people rather than of the people. The phrasing of Andrewes *HCT* v: 339 is careful and correct: "This clause assures us that the interests of the people were given proper consideration." In medicine too a "blending" need not necessarily be in equal proportions: above, n. 25.

30. Thus Hornblower 1991–2008: iii. 1035 ad loc., citing further literature.

31. Cf. Jouanna 1980: 301–304 = 2012: 23–25. Jouanna makes a strong case for a thread of therapeutic analogy running through the whole of the Nicias–Alcibiades debate. The way Alcibiades describes the three sorts—τό τε φαῦλον καὶ τὸ μέσον καὶ τὸ πάνυ ἀκριβές—is striking and problematic but cannot be discussed here.

32. Strategic restraint: Pericles at Thuc. 1.144.1, 2.65.7. *Logismos* generally an Athenian strength: Pericles at 2.40.3. But not always: Demosthenes at 4.10.1; cf. Alcibiades at 6.18.3.

33. Holmes 2010: 146, illustrating the point from *On the Places of Man* 33 VIII p. 74 P = VI p. 326 L.

34. Cf. esp. G. E. R. Lloyd 1979: ch. 3.

35. Cf. Thomas 2000: 87–98: see also p. 264 n. 10. Critics of *Airs Waters Places* have often been puzzled by similar phenomena: cf. the unease of Diller 1934: 39–40 (though at 81–82 he observes the value of the introductory statement as an attention-grabber)

and von Fritz 1967: 92. Some problems in the text and ordering of *Airs Waters Places* of course remain. For further parallels in presentation between *Airs Waters Places, On Breaths* and Herodotus, see de Jong 2013: 264–267.

36. Rood 1998: index s.v. "correction, progressive"; Pelling 2000: 82–94 and below, pp. 211–212.

37. Cf. A. B. Lloyd 1990: 229–230, though he misses the presentational technique. Parallels between Egypt and one particular Greek city, Sparta, will also be important in 6.56–60, esp. 60: see Hornblower and Pelling ad loc.

38. Cf. esp. Redfield 1985: 109–115 = 2013: 281–288.

39. Hall 1989: 81; cf. Hall 1996: 15 and Garvie 2009: 62–63 on Aesch. *Pers.* 41–42.

40. Hobden 2013: 91–93 brings the *Ach.* passage into contact with Herodotus.

41. As Gorman and Gorman 2014 strongly argue, making many good points (though see also nn. 44, 47, and pp. 283–284 n. 7). Persian military indiscipline is certainly seen in *Persians* (Hall 1989: 79–84, and below, pp. 174–175), but there is no clear link with the *habrotēs* theme: cf. Garvie, cited in n. 39.

42. Thus, von Fritz 1967: 227; Heuss 1973: 397–398.

43. Κόθορνοι is often translated "buskins," but the word's suggestions are more of effeminacy than of theatricality: cf. Hornblower and Pelling 2017: 273–274 on 6.125.3.

44. Or so I assumed in Pelling 1997c: 62 = 2013: 374, as have many others. Gorman and Gorman 2014: 108 n. 61 take a different view, thinking this just "a reference to the barbarian armory not the barbarian lifestyle." That seems to me one of several cases where they close down the suggestions of a Herodotus passage too definitively. The "armory" point will indeed eventually emerge as the important one rather than any emblematic implications, but only eventually: below, p. 170.

45. For defense of this translation of εὐπετέες, see Pelling 2007a: 177–183.

46. So extraordinary that some have doubted whether Herodotus really intended to end here, most influentially Jacoby 1913: 375 = 1956: 192 and Pohlenz 1937: 164; but it would be even more extraordinary if so rich and enigmatic a retrospect had been intruded anywhere other than in so prominent a position. Particularly illuminating discussions are Bischoff 1932: 78–83 = 1965: 681–687; Redfield 1985: 114–116 = 2013: 286–288; Raaflaub 1987: 244–246; Lateiner 1989: 48–50; Moles 1996: 273–277; Dewald 1997: 67–82 = 2013: 385–401; Thomas 2000: 106–109; Chiasson 2001: 62–68; Flower and Marincola 2002: 311–312; Gorman and Gorman 2014: 81–86; Kingsley forthcoming: ch. 4. I had my say in Pelling 1997c: 61–64 = 2013: 373–377.

47. So Gorman and Gorman 2014: 81–85, fairly observing that there is no explicit mention of luxury in the passage. They prefer to take it in terms of agricultural life, not easy by any means but not so likely to instill martial skills such as horsemanship. I agree with them that most interpreters have been too clear-cut in assuming that the point was Persian luxury, but excluding that possibility also seems to me to close down interpretation too firmly.

48. "The names of Cyrus and the Persians are interchangeable with those of Pericles and the Athenians": Momigliano 1979: 149 = 1984: 72. That puts it more strongly than many of the original audience would have accepted, but the analogy was still close enough to make Athenians uneasy.

6. EXPLANATIONS IN COMBINATION

This chapter covers some of the same ground as Pelling 2018: there is some overlap of material.

1. Mill 1843: ch. 5 (though the "caprice" is swiftly qualified by Mill's acknowledgement of the different purposes that lead one to concentrate on one "condition" rather than another: cf. Hart and Honoré 1985: 18–19). See also above, p. 252 n. 52.

2. Hart and Honoré 1985: esp. chs. I–V. One of their examples—a man with an ulcerated stomach who then eats parsley and consequently suffers indigestion (35–37)—is particularly close to those of the Hippocratics. Yet there is indeed "something" in common with the Hippocratic distinction, but not everything: some "predispositions," including that ulcerated stomach, could in some circumstances be called "causes" by Hart and Honoré, and a "condition" need not for them preexist a cause—a breeze springing up after a lighted cigarette had been discarded and therefore contributing to a forest fire would still count as a "condition" (72). For a critique see Mackie 1974: 117–142, together with Hart and Honoré's reply in the introduction to their 1985 second edition (xxxvii–xlii).

3. Hart and Honoré 1985: 80. This is similar to what Mackie 1974: 34–36 calls "the causal field."

4. Similar points are made by Collingwood 1998 (1940): 303–307 and Atkinson 1978: 159–160. Collingwood went so far as to claim that all causal analysis involves a distinctive "standpoint" of this sort (for him, typically that of someone able to intervene to interrupt the causal process): "For a mere spectator there are no causes" (307). That would seem to exclude the historian from any causal analysis at all. Cf. Dray 1964: 45–46.

5. On such debates, see esp. G. E. R. Lloyd 1979: 92–94; cf. p. 242 n. 67.

6. Hornblower 1991–2008: iii. 186 notes the striking similarity of this to Thuc. 5.70, where the Spartans march to *aulos* music "not for the sake of the divine" but to keep in step. See also below, p. 98.

7. In fact, it shows no such thing: a god might be acting by moistening the brain. Cf. G. E. R. Lloyd 1979: 24. A similar oversimplifying polarity is posited at the end of *Sacred Disease* 16 II p. 172 J = 13 VI p. 386 L.

8. von Fritz 1967: 93.

9. This assumes what I cannot here argue, that the first and second parts of *Airs Waters Places* cohere as a single work. Certainly these different types of strategy should not be used as an argument against such coherence. On the unity question cf. Grensemann 1979, a sensitive discussion.

10. Cf. Müri 1947: 71–74 = 1976: 100–103. One possible way of reconciling the two principles would be to explain the "harmonious" analogies collaterally, with climate working both on land and people in parallel ways (so Diller 1934: 31–33), but that suits some of these cases, e.g. ch. 13, better than others. A different set of mismatches is identified by Thomas 2000: 87–98, who sees a combination of two theories, one "continental" and one "environmental." Those could be seen as a subdivision within the "causal" register.

11. *On Regimen* 4 similarly combines two unrelated explanatory schemes: Langholf 1990: 120–121.

12. Jouanna 2012: 164.

13. Laskaris 2002: 114–116, 123–124 is good on this need for cautious phrasing. On the similarities between the religious thinking of the two works, see van der Eijk 1991, with the important qualification made by Laskaris 2002: 148: *Airs Waters Places* can allow the possibility of divine favoritism, at least towards the rich; *On the Sacred Disease* cannot, because its stress on heredity would allow an opponent to claim that the gods

may still be sending the disease as punishment for some ancestral transgression. That in itself need not preclude the possibility (no more), accepted by van der Eijk, that the two works are by the same author: the "favoritism" can just be an additional *ad hominem* point against the traditionally minded that the argument allows in the one work but not in the other. Jouanna 2012: 105 similarly suggests that the difference of tone between the two arguments is a matter of rhetorical appropriateness, and (107) that the conception of the divine is so similar that it points to a single author.

14. Thomas 2000: 275 and 280.

15. The phrase of Jouanna 2012: 103: see his discussion, 101–112, also emphasizing that this insistence is never in conflict with "the religion of the great sanctuaries" such as Delphi.

16. Cf. the conflicting views of van der Eijk 1990 and 1991 (genuine religiosity) and Laskaris 2002: 113–124, 156 (*ad hominem* rhetoric; cf. Deichgräber 1971: 127 and G. E. R. Lloyd 1979: 55). I tend to side with Laskaris, but it is in the nature of effective rhetoric that one cannot be quite sure about such questions of sincerity.

17. Unless this is a discreet way of referring to miscegenation. Elsewhere too *Airs Waters Places* shows a taste for *physis–nomos* contrasts and interplays: Thomas 2000: 87–88, 92–93.

18. G. E. R. Lloyd 1979: 149 n. 119.

19. The reasons for that final ordering in *Airs Waters Places* are admittedly more elusive. The work has indeed stressed seasonal change but not in such a way as to suggest that it is more important than the land and its waters: the second emphasis has dominated most of the work. Perhaps the point is simply presentational, and the ordering should not be taken too seriously. Seasonal change here comes first, waters and places second and terminally. In the introduction to this second section, waters and places were the first and introductory point, and seasonal change the second (12–13 I pp. 104–108 J = II pp. 52–58 L). The chiastic ring is complete, and symmetry is preserved. On the importance of ring composition in this work, see Grensemann 1979: 426–431, stressing rather the symmetry of ch. 24 with ch. 1, and Wenskus 1982: 174–180.

20. For further parallels between this passage and Herodotus' own favored argumentative techniques, see Thomas 2000: 33–34, 178–180. Jouanna 2005: 10–13 concentrates on the comparison with Herodotus' own much briefer treatment of the "Enareis" (as he calls them) at 1.105.

21. Perry 1937; cf. Detienne 1996, arguing that a "principle of non-contradiction" then developed to "overthrow" the receptiveness to ambiguity typical of earlier ethical thinking.

22. Rowe 1983: the quotation is from p. 127. Rowe however seems to me to go astray in distinguishing this firmly from the approach of philosophy, science, and history: "No one of them can leave different descriptions or explanations of the same thing standing side by side, but must relate them to each other . . ." (126, cf. 134–135; Rowe is followed by Bertelli 2001: 82–83). Fifth-century philosophy, science, and history would not have regarded matters as so clear-cut. (Here I find myself largely in agreement with Versnel 2011: 213–218 and the vigorously pluralistic approach of Apfel 2011.)

23. To use the term of Apfel 2011: 12–16, developing ideas of Berlin. On its application to causal schemes, see Apfel 2011: 123–125.

24. For Herodotus' treatment of multiple causes, see also Apfel 2011: 172–177: her emphasis falls on accumulation of multiple causes, some of them "incommensurable" (cf. n. 23), but she does allow some degree of ordering and evaluation as well (176–177).

25. This formulation leaves open the possibility that the causal nexus is not yet complete, for payback may be yet to come: Munson 2001: 193–194; Boedeker 2015: 109–111.

26. For further cases, see Apfel 2011: 174–176.

27. For the elegant ambiguities in the Greek here, see Pelling 2006b: 164 n. 85.

28. Nor should it be seen as progressive, along the lines of Fisher 1992: 358 n. 74 ("Originally his intention had been more defensive, to check the expansion of Persian power [1.46], but his ambitions have grown with his confidence"), nor even as an "increase in understanding": Immerwahr 1956: 257 = 2013: 172. The "progressive" interpretation would only work if Croesus' original defensive strategy were firmly in the audience's mind through 1.72–73, so that they would notice the change; in that case, they would also notice the inadequacy of Sandanis' remarks in 1.71, for (whether or not expansionism was now Croesus' motive) if the 1.46.1 perception of Cyrus' aggression were correct then it would be impossible to leave the Persians be (cf. n. 91). Lateiner 1989: 207 sensibly brings out that the aggressive and defensive elements can easily coexist. Cf. also Baragwanath 2008: 126 for the accumulation of motives that need not be mutually exclusive: contrast Raaflaub 1987: 243, who notes the different motives but thinks that "the desire for more" of 1.73.1 is "considered decisive by the historian."

29. Cf. also Apfel 2011: 176–177.

30. So, rightly, T. Harrison 2011: 120–121, noting the frequency of harming enemies as a theme in Persian royal inscriptions. S. Saïd's words are carefully chosen, 2002: 143, "It [revenge] is less a cause than a pretext, as is said not only by the Greek envoys to Gelon (7.157.2) but by Herodotus himself (7.138.1)": *less* a cause than a pretext, perhaps, but not just a pretext, and something of a cause as well.

31. Cf. Fowler 2003: 317; Pelling 2006a: 79–80.

32. Cf. Demaratus' threat at 6.67.3, telling Leutychidas that his taunt would "be the start of vast harm or vast prosperity for the Spartans." The whole point there is that the bad feeling goes back much earlier.

33. McPhee 2018 elaborates the way in which the explanations of Cambyses' death could be taken as accumulative rather than alternative: the gods may be behind it all.

7. EARLY MOVES

1. I have treated the Croesus-*logos* in depth elsewhere (Pelling 2006b) and extract only a few points of particular importance for the argument here. Some other aspects are attacked by Stahl 2012: esp. 147 n. 23 and 149 n. 24; cf. below, p. 273 n. 41 and p. 277 n. 46. See now also the full treatment of Gagné 2013: 325–343, with bibliography.

2. Thus, rightly, Lattimore 1958, comparing, e.g., 1.16.1 and 18.2, 5.99.1–2, and 8.113.3, and M. Lloyd 1984, followed by T. Harrison 2000: 202.

3. Wardman 1961: 136–137 emphasizes that Herodotus makes this lasting and persistent constitutional change his important criterion; cf., e.g., Hellmann 1934: 24–26; von Fritz 1967: 209–210; Bornitz 1968: 180; Erbse 1979: 197; Ubsdell 1983: 79. Hellmann and others insist that there is no "flagrant contradiction" in Herodotus' presentation, as Jacoby 1913: 335 had claimed; but Shimron 1975: 45–46 correctly insists that *adika erga* would normally be a fair description for the capture of cities and marauding raids, actions which typified Croesus' predecessors. Shimron seeks to avoid contradiction by stressing *oida*, "I know," and inferring that Herodotus purports to "know" more securely about Croesus' aggression than about that of his predecessors; yet nothing in the text suggests any doubts about the historicity of the earlier attacks. (Thus,

there is no need to follow H. I. Flower 1991: 61 = 2013: 130 in thinking that Herodotus "is distancing himself somewhat" from what he says about Gyges and his early successors.) But "contradiction" is too crude a word for this technique of progressive revision.

4. Thus, Moles 1996: 260–261; Stadter 1992: 795–796 = 2013: 345–347 and 2006: 248; Ruffing 2011: 93–94. Cf. also below, p. 218.

5. On this, and on much of what follows, cf. esp. Reinhardt 1939. Von Fritz 1967: 212 objects that the primitive *Märchenmotiv* of the invisible ring might have become attached to the historical Gyges at any time, and it need not follow that Plato represents an older stage of the tradition; Laird 2001 and, differently, Pontier 2013 suggest that Plato is drawing on and adapting Herodotus for his own purposes (and adaptation would certainly have been needed: Herodotus' version would not at all give Plato what his argument required, a Gyges who had the ability to do what he wished without being noticed). But Herodotus' version, with the stress on the need for Gyges to stay out of sight behind the door, looks like a rationalizing of the invisibility theme, and if so invisibility was already part of the dominant tradition. Cf. Smith 1902: 281–282, 361; Reinhardt 1939: 176–178 already seems to be assuming and countering such an objection.

6. Though Plato's text seems to tell this story of "an ancestor of Gyges" rather than Gyges himself (359d). Laird 2001 defends that reading, but in view of Plato's later reference back to "the ring of Gyges" at 612b it seems better to assume textual corruption. In his 2003 Oxford text Slings obelizes.

7. Ptolemaios Chennos ap. Phot. *bibl.* 190 p. 150b (*FHG* iv.278): cf. Smith 1902; Seel 1956.

8. Here he is following the example set by Homer: Griffin 1977 brings out how much less of the miraculous there is in the *Iliad* and *Odyssey* compared with the epic cycle.

9. Unlike that in a quite different version again, that of Nic. Dam. *FGrH* 90 F 47.1–11. The king (here Sadyattes) is about to marry and sends the young Gyges to bring his new bride to court. Gyges falls in love with his charge and seduces her on the journey; on her arrival she denounces him to the king, who plans to kill him the next day; Gyges, informed of the plot by a besotted maidservant, swiftly kills the king, mobilizes support, and takes over queen and kingdom. This rationalism produces a sensational enough story, though with little of Herodotus' psychological and conceptual depth. Much of it may well go back to Xanthus of Lydia (cf. Jacoby *FGrH* ad loc.; Diller 1956), though the rapidity and excitement will owe something to Nicolaus' own contribution: cf. Toher 1989.

10. Cf. T. Harrison 2000: 31–33 and esp. Węcowski 2004: 149–154, who sees this as an ironic gesture of Herodotus, one of several aspects of the first four chapters that are set out only to be rejected: "In his abduction stories, he light-heartedly dismisses the tendency of some of his predecessors and contemporaries to deprive the world of its ethico-religious aspect" (153). I agree with Węcowski about the humor but would not see the human-level approach as so firmly dismissive: cf. p. 268 n. 20.

11. Stoessl 1959 productively stresses "Herodots Humanität"—the phrasing of distant or mythical material in very humanist terms—as a programmatic strand of these early chapters; but he fails to do justice to the limitations of this "Humanität," which are equally programmatic. Cf. Harder 1953: 449 = 1965: 374 n. 13 on the Candaules episode: "Daß die Götter fehlen, ist nur scheinbar" ("The gods' absence is only apparent").

12. This is admittedly required by Plato's context; his argument requires a device that can enable its owner to fulfill, without further trouble, any desire.

13. Above, n. 8.

14. Nic. Dam. 47.11 notes merely that Gyges bore no grudge for his bride's earlier denouncing.

15. She is named elsewhere in the tradition, as Tydo, Mysia or Nysia, Habra, or Clytias: cf. Smith 1902: 367–368 and n. 5. Some compare the unnamed "Queen" in Aeschylus' *Persians*; it is unlikely that the non-naming would itself generate a "tragic" atmosphere (thus Cataudella 1957: 114), but in each case the non-naming initially concentrates the audience on the woman's position and status. Masistes' wife too is not named at 9.108–112 (cf. pp. 32–34), and Larson 2006 suggests that the non-naming shields both queens from culpability.

16. Stahl 1968: 391–392.

17. Boedeker 2011: 231 highlights Herodotus' interest in such women who turn out less passive than their complacent menfolk had assumed.

18. Cf. esp. Dewald 1981.

19. It is true that his action is marked by Apollo as *hamartas* (1.91.1: p. 112), and such talk of "fault" implies to a modern mind an element of choice; but for Herodotus, as in Greek tragedy, such matters are complicated. See Sewell-Rutter 2007: 9 (Gyges) and ch. 6 (tragedy).

20. Cf. p. 31. This is where I part company with the valuable analysis of Węcowski 2004, who regards the suggestions of the early chapters as developed only to be dismissed: above, n. 10. See also Baragwanath forthcoming, for a sensitive account of the way that various suggestions of the early chapters are both echoed and renuanced in the Libyan *logos* (4.145–205). Gagné 2013: 341 approaches the Croesus-*logos* similarly: ancestral fault is important, but "one pattern of causality and retribution among many others." One again is reminded of Greek tragedy, e.g., the successive patterns of explanation in *Agamemnon* (pp. 16, 90).

21. Cf. Badian 1968, quoted below, p. 137, and discussion there.

22. Pelling 2006b: 152 and 2006c: 105–106; doubted by Versnel 2011: 533–534, and for a less favorable view of Solon's tact, see Dewald 2012: 79, finding Solon's speech "long-winded, ungracious, and pedantic."

23. Pelling 2006b: 142–143. Ellis 2016: 113–117 notes that Herodotus' language is often at its most poetic when suggesting the sort of general insights into human experience that Aristotle (*Poet*. 1451a36–b11) regarded as more appropriate to poetry than history.

24. Notice in particular Amasis' apprehension about Polycrates' "good fortunes" (*eutychiai*) because "the divine is envious" (3.40.2), and his look for mutability, with good fortune alternating with bad: no one with such a consistent run has failed to "end badly," 3.40.3, destroyed "root and all" (πρόρριζος, echoing 1.32.9). Artabanus' emphasis on συμφοραί and the diseases that cause "turbulence" (συνταράσσουσαι) so that they make a "short life seem long" then picks up various Solonic themes at 7.46.3; so does his emphasis on divine envy (ὁ δὲ θεὸς γλυκὺν γεύσας τὸ αἰῶνα φθονερὸς ἐν αὐτῷ εὑρίσκεται ἐών, 7.46.4). That word *aiōn* ("age" or "lifespan") also occurs in those three contexts and elsewhere only twice in Herodotus. Cf. Asheri, Lloyd, and Corcella 2007 on 3.39.3 and 3.40.2–3, and, e.g., T. Harrison 2000: ch. 2; Pelling 1991: 137 and 2006b: 142–143 n. 5.

25. I discussed this more fully at Pelling 2006b: 148, where I also emphasized that Herodotus' audience might not have bothered to discriminate them; so also T. Harrison 2000: 39–40. Versnel generously quotes that qualification in his critique of my arti-

cle (2011: 532–537 at 534), but then goes on to ignore it when taking me to task for looking for a clear-cut choice among these possibilities. (My discrimination of different elements in fact serves much the same expository purpose as Versnel's own at his p. 187.) Versnel's view of Herodotus' explanatory strategies does however remain different from mine, despite an overlap that he finally acknowledges (536–537). We both accept that Herodotus can accept multiple explanations at times, and that there are some instances where "there *is not* [his italics] one preferable solution" (his p. 537 n. 18); it is, however, important too that at times causes are evaluated and one explanation appears as more powerful than others, as (on my reading) the case of Croesus' question and Apollo's answer makes clear. Another case is the weighing of different explanations for Cleomenes' madness at 6.84: below, pp. 159–160. Nor is plurality of explanations the same as equipollence (". . . all of them [i.e., the 'many divergent insights' in the Croesus narrative] are equally true," his p. 535). So, ironically, Versnel's spirited defense of causal multiplicity eventually fails because he does not make Herodotus' mindset multiple *enough*: Herodotus has more than one approach to multiple explanations. For further criticisms of Versnel's approach as over-simple, cf. Gagné 2013: 336–337 and 341 n. 230; for defense of Herodotus' pluralism, Apfel 2011: chs. IV–V.

26. "Rightly or wrongly": I discuss these two ways of reading his remarks at Pelling 2006b: 158–159, where I also suggest that his description of Solon as "deriding" his wealth is questionable. For interesting further comments on this scene see Dewald and Kitzinger 2015: 99–100.

27. The reproaching is admittedly not so irregular (Parker 1998: esp. 114–116 and Hutchinson 2001: 341–343, though T. Harrison 2000: 80 can still reasonably comment on Croesus' "markedly peremptory tone" at 1.87.1); the testing and the cross-examination, more so.

28. Cf. Klees 1965: esp. 16–49 and 63–68, who extensively demonstrates that such testing (a) was genuinely carried out by non-Greeks, and (b) would have been most irregular for any Greek. Xen. *Cyr.* 7.2.15–17 makes it explicit that any such testing would naturally offend a god. For new evidence on Croesus' "testing," see Thonemann 2016, discussing a column drum found in 2005 excavations at Thebes (Papazarkadas 2014: 233–248). This seems to have been the base for a shield seen by Herodotus in the temple of Amphiaraus (cf. 1.49, 52). It carries verses from a rededication from ca. 500 BCE after, apparently, the shield had been stolen and recovered: Herodotus' report that Croesus respected τήν τε ἀρετὴν καὶ τὴν πάθην of Amphiaraus may reflect an original verse, restored as Ἀμ]φιαρέοι μνᾶμ' ἀρετ[ᾶς τε πάθας τ'ἀνέθεκεν ("dedicated to Amphiaraus to commemorate the man's excellence and his suffering"). I am not convinced by Thonemann's further suggestion that this "Croesus" was not the king but an Athenian aristocrat of ca. 530 BCE.

29. Cf. Klees 1965: esp. 63–66; Visser 2000: 23. For T. Harrison 2000: 61: "[Herodotus'] lengthy description of Croesus' dedications, each act of dedication compounding Croesus' certainty in his success, is inevitably a prelude to his 'betrayal' by Delphi"; cf. Nagy 1990: 274–275. Gagné 2013: 329 comments that Croesus' big mistake is to speak as if he is engaged in a reciprocal exchange between peers. Kurke 1999: 130–171 has a highly sophisticated argument that Croesus' view of gift-exchange is set at odds with a new, civic sensibility. The first-time reader—or rather different readers of varying sophistication—might well have sensed danger in one or more of these ways.

30. Thus, the language of 91.3: "He had done as much as the Fates allowed and granted these favors" (ὅσον δὲ ἐνέδωκαν αὗται, ἤνυσέ τε καὶ ἐχαρίσατό οἱ) echoes and

counters the charge of being ungrateful (ἀχάριστος, 90.4): Stahl 1975; 17, cf. Crane 1996: 77. Apollo does not reject the expectation of *charis*: if there is a "dialectic of divergent economies" at play here (Kurke 1999: 160–163), it is a dialectic where both economies are felt to be valid.

31. Thus, he does not condemn the testing as impious: cf. Christ 1994: 189–193 = 2013: 237–242.

32. See W. Hansen 1996, followed by Luraghi 2013: 101–103, for a most interesting suggestion that elements of Gyges' "crime" and of Croesus' punishment—respectively the illegitimate seeing and the breaking of silence on the pyre—originally formed parts of a single folktale, then separated into two temporally divided stories.

33. Sewell-Rutter 2007: 5–7.

34. Thus, Kurke 1999: 163 n. 68.

35. Vandiver 2012: 156–157.

36. Fish 1967. See also Montemaggi 2016 for a recent reading of Dante with something in common with this: in that case, it is a matter of the reader's response contributing to the poet's own salvation.

37. This therefore is a mild qualification of Grethlein 2013: 202, playing down the mimetic element in Herodotus; but Grethlein does acknowledge that "suspense" (a rather different matter) can there embrace the "how" if not the "what" of events as they develop.

38. Cf. Dewald 1993: 69–70 and 2012: 77–78.

39. So, rightly, Sewell-Rutter 2007: 11 and Gagné 2013: 341. I should have made this point more explicit at Pelling 2006b: 163–164.

40. Notice how little there is on dynastic intrigue within the bulk of the Croesus-*logos* itself, even if the advice of 1.89.2 suggests that Croesus knows the dangers. At 1.51.5 Herodotus mentions in passing the statue of "the bakerwoman" that Croesus gave to Delphi. Plut. *On the Pythian Oracles* 401e–f explains the statue as representing a bakerwoman who saved Croesus from conspiracy. If Parke 1984: 219 is right in arguing that the story predates Herodotus, the absence of this explanation at 1.51.5 confirms this general lack of interest in Croesus' internal difficulties.

41. Similarly, Munson 2001: 104: "This entirely new story . . . rectifies the domesticated portrayal of the Lydian king in the preceding narrative and regularizes his membership in the analogical category of absolute rulers that dominates the rest of the *Histories*." I am not sure about "rectifies" or "domesticated," but the last point seems to me exactly right. For the way this analogical category works, see esp. Dewald 2003.

42. Cf. Baragwanath forthcoming, discussing the ways in which the Libyan logos of book 4 retraces some of the same moves and themes, with both Arcesilaus and Aryandes unmindful and forgetful in ways that recall Croesus.

8. EMPIRE

1. For Lydia as an "in-between" country, see Pelling 1997c: 56 = Munson 2013: 367 and Moles 1996: 262.

2. It is no coincidence that six of the (possibly later) canon of "seven sages" crop up in the first part of book 1, Bias, Pittacus, Solon, Chilon, Thales, and Periander: cf. Benardete 1969: 17–19 ("we would seem to be presented with wisdom itself at the very beginning of his *Inquiries*"); Rieks 1975: 28; Asheri, Lloyd, and Corcella on 1.27.2.

3. Especially Sparta, where the references to Cleomenes (3.39.1, 44–47, 54–57, 148) could have prompted a much fuller treatment.

4. Huber 1965: 128: cf. 1.153, 3.134.

5. E.g., Immerwahr 1956: 271 n. 60 = 2013: 185 n. 60, "The difficulty is real . . ."

6. Cf. Schadewaldt 1938: 1–28 on the elaborate preparation given in *Il.* 11. Zeus' promise at *Il.* 11.186–194 would seem to point to success immediately after Agamemnon's removal from the battlefield; 11.284–309 seems to be delivering on that expectation—but then Hector himself is removed, and his real *aristeia* only begins in book 15. "The poet deceives the listeners over the distance of the path in front of them" (Schadewaldt 1938: 15), but the long-distance preparation is itself a mark of the momentousness of what is to come. Cf. also de Jong 2013: 283.

7. Ring composition was profitably investigated by Myres 1953 and Immerwahr 1966, but Myres' "geometrical" analysis suffered from over-schematism, while Immerwahr concentrated sharply on the transitions into and out of particular episodes. For attempts to extend treatment to a larger canvas, see Herington 1991, and for more microscopic analysis, Beck 1971.

8. Marg 1953. Some reservations about *Selbstsicherheit* will be aired in the next chapter.

9. For the relation of this passage to the final chapter of the work, cf. p. 93.

10. *Leviathan* (1651), ch. 13.

11. K. Clarke 2018: ch. 6 brings out how such "desires" are often complemented by a stress on what is "beautiful" in the land that is the object of such yearning: she argues that the over-passionate pursuit of such desires is a distinctively Persian trait. Cf. below, n. 35.

12. Cf. K. Clarke 2018: 104, 203 n. 83. The language emphasizes this notion of a natural division: Cappadocia as the boundary (οὖρος) of the Lydian and Median empires, cutting off (ἀποτάμνει) the western part of Asia, as a neck (αὐχήν) of land. It seems that Herodotus overstates the narrowness of this "neck" (see comms.): the effect is to exaggerate the degree to which it forms a natural boundary.

13. Cf. esp. Immerwahr 1966, index, s.v. "river crossing"; Gianotti 1996; K. Clarke 2018, esp. ch. 5.

14. His commentators thus make more of this "act of moral transgression" (*hybris*) (Asheri, Lloyd, and Corcella 2007 ad loc.) than Herodotus does himself. Cf. K. Clarke 2018: 205–206.

15. Cf. Stahl 1975: 10, "The discrepancy between reality and Croesus' concept of it is reaching its peak."

16. This switches, very emphatically, at 1.79.1, Κῦρος δέ . . . , some time before the end of the Croesus narrative. From then on matters are seen largely through Cyrus' eyes and are controlled by his movements. Even the summary of Croesus' reign, with strong closural force, has Croesus as the sentence's grammatical object, with the Persians expressively in control (1.86.1): "The Persians thus took Sardis and captured Croesus, who had ruled for fourteen years and been besieged for fourteen days, and—in accordance with the oracle—had brought his own great empire to an end."

17. Cf. Cobet 1971: 177–178, rightly insisting that patterning should not exclude attention to singularity. This, then, is a mild correction of Fowler 1996: 82 = 2013: 82, "History has no irregularities. Instead it has patterns." Herodotus' patterns are such as to allow for irregularities as well, and he does not smooth away all the bumps.

18. This recalls the principle of "chancy causation" that has become important in philosophical discussion (cf. p. 248 n. 12), as well as the role that Presocratic philosophers were content to attribute to chance (p. 49).

19. Immerwahr 1966: 45, quoted with approval by Lateiner 1989: 185: cf. Moles 1996:

279, quoted at p. 277 n. 51. But even this overstates: in Herodotus' day the Persian monarchy, like many others, was showing no signs of collapsing any time soon, and both Herodotus and his audience would have known it. When it did collapse a century later, it was at the hands of another monarch, Alexander the Great of Macedon.

20. Cf. Baragwanath 2012: 48, there talking about the *mythic* "plupast" (she goes on to explore how similar this is to a "plupast" falling in more historical times): "Not only does the *Histories* frequently stage contests over *which* mythic paradigm is apposite . . . but also over *how* a particular paradigm should be brought to bear."

21. I also touched on some further aspects in Pelling 2006b.

22. ἐπαείροντα, a disturbing word: Chiasson 2012: 230–231.

23. For the elegant ambiguities in the Greek here, see Pelling 2006b: 164 n. 85: is δοκέειν impersonal, "it seemed that" he was more than human, or personal, "he thought" he was? Chiasson 2012: 231 n. 57 is unconvinced.

24. This may well reflect a genuine Near Eastern purification ritual, perhaps on this occasion apotropaic after the eclipse of the sun (7.37.2): cf. Masson 1950; Rollinger 2000; and esp. Thomas 2012: 235–244. Thomas plausibly suggests that the Pythius incident had been subject to "layerings of Hellenizing interpretation" even before Herodotus. For the echoing of Oeobazus, cf. esp. Bornitz 1968: 125–135; Hartog 1988: 35–40; S. Lewis 1998; Baragwanath 2008: 269–278; D. Murray 2016: 57–58.

25. Pelling 1997b: 15. For Rosenbloom 2006: 102–103 and 2011, followed by Balot 2014: 77–80, the Athenian audience may be alert enough to see through Darius' disingenuousness here. I rather doubt how much the average audience member would know about Darius' adventures in a distant land forty years before.

26. de Jong 2013: 274–276, tracking the progression from 5.102.1 through 6.32–44.1 to 6.94.1–2.

27. Fornara 1971a: 29–31.

28. Fornara 1971a: 87.

29. Fornara 1971a: 32.

30. Fornara 1971a: 39, building on the developmental hypothesis influentially argued by Jacoby 1913. Fornara suggests (86–87, 90) that this interest may have been inspired by the prospect or the outbreak of the Peloponnesian War. As several contributors to T. Harrison and Irwin 2018a remark, this developmental aspect is the aspect of Fornara 1971a that has worn least well.

31. Fornara 1971a: 88.

32. Cf. T. Harrison and Irwin 2018b: 4. Immerwahr 1956: 264 = 2013: 179 is similar to Fornara in finding books 7–9 better explained and better structured than what has gone before, but also insists that the explanations follow earlier patterns but on a grander scale (1956: 270 = 2013: 184).

33. Gribble 1998: 57; Pelling 2000: 82–94. Cf. below, p. 297 n. 53.

34. Zali 2014: 152. But this is not to say that he is simply an echo chamber for Xerxes' own thinking: see Roettig 2010: 32–33, 49–51.

35. Cf. K. Clarke 2018: ch. 6 on the way that a land's "beauty" is particularly stressed in contexts of Persian expansion: above, n. 11. Konijnendijk 2016 suggests also that Mardonius is playing to his audience's ears in arguing that "the Greeks find the most beautiful and smoothest land" and go there to fight their open battles (7.9β.1): not true, but well attuned to the Persian skill in cavalry warfare.

36. See Baragwanath 2008: 243–247 on the argumentative rhythm of the speech, starting with calm reflection and moving into a more emotional register as he turns to thoughts of revenge; for the combination of arguments, cf. also de Jong 2013: 276–281.

37. For "into the middle," cf. Detienne 1996: ch. 5 (though Rhodes 2018: 268, 275–276 is right to say that it is not *exclusively* democratic); for "who wishes to speak?" cf. passages collected by Olson 2002 in his n. on Ar. *Ach.* 45; for ὁ βουλόμενος, Rood 1999: 158. The phrasing is deftly parodied by Ar. *Wealth* 908 (where see Sommerstein 2001 ad loc.), and Eur. *Supp.* 438–440 echoes both phrases, though (typically for tragedy) not precisely, in Theseus' praise of democracy.

38. Bischoff 1932: 57–58; Pelling 1991: 132.

39. Or so I argued for Artabanus in Pelling 1991, as I did for Croesus in Pelling 2006b.

40. Grethlein 2009: 201 and 2011b: 107, followed by Stahl 2012: 138.

41. Thus Stahl 2012: 138 n. 14 is "not persuaded that Herodotus wants his reader to contemplate the question 'how far' Artabanus 'actually gets things right'" (he is quoting Pelling 1991: 134), though he is happy to talk of Croesus being "wrong" (see below, p. 277 n. 46).

42. "The elusiveness of wisdom" was thus one of my two emphases in Pelling 2006b. Grethlein 2009 is not far from that view, though he is harder on Xerxes than I would be; cf. also Grethlein 2011: 104–110, drawing the conclusion that it is easier to draw lessons from the past on what one should not do than on what one should.

43. Grethlein 2009.

44. Thus Stahl 2012: 132–133 speaks of Croesus' "unjust deeds against the Greeks" (1.5.3) as introducing "the *moral partisanship* [his italics] of the work. Justice is on the side of the Greeks throughout in so far as they are being attacked, and the attacking side is to be viewed as committing acts of injustice. One of the work's . . . guiding motifs, then, is the Greeks' *just* self-defence against *wrongful* aggression."

45. Cf. de Jong 2013: 271–272, seeing the *Histories* as "one long and detailed refutation of the thesis," aired by the Persians in the proem, that the Greeks started it all.

46. Dewald 2003: 38–40, 46–47. In Waters' list of 55 tyrants (1971: 42–44) 21 are marked as "Persian-supported or nominated."

47. Baragwanath 2008: 177–178: particularly striking is the allegation that Argos invited Xerxes into Greece, though Herodotus simply reports this as "something that is said" (7.152.3); cf. also Baragwanath 2008: 211–217.

48. For more elaborate comparison of Herodotus and Thucydides along these lines, see Pelling 2000: 94–103.

49. Cf. Immerwahr 1956: 269 = 2013: 183.

50. On much of what follows, see also Baragwanath forthcoming, giving a subtle analysis of the explanatory intricacies of the Libyan *logos*.

51. Though there remains some uncertainty about whether this particular piece of expansionism is owed more to King Darius' own thinking or to Aryandes' anticipation of his wishes: Baragwanath forthcoming. Cf. also Baragwanath 2008: 156 on the way that vengeance can more generally be a cloak for other motives.

52. On the blend of truth and semblance here, cf. Sealey 1957: 5–6.

53. In fact, Arcesilaus' gifts to Persia had been half-hearted and Cambyses himself had regarded them as unsatisfactory (3.13.4), but this is not brought out here.

54. Cf. p. 156. On the medical aspects of the description, see Demont 2018: 179–182.

55. Friedrich 1973: 99.

56. It is unclear whether this means that all the Battiadae had no share in the blame, or whether to escape enslavement one had both to be one of the Battiadae and uninvolved in the killing.

57. Notice the emphasis: that is one way in which the Greek/Persian focus is dis-

creetly kept before the audience. Such pointers tend to cluster at the beginning or end of sections (e.g., Darius and Atossa, 3.133–134; Megabazus, 4.143); at each point we may wonder if the Greek campaign, heralded as "always at the end" (p. 115), is to come next, but again the path before us is longer than we might expect (p. 271 n. 6).

58. How and Wells (on 4.203) feel that Amasis' nervousness about expanding the campaign is "inconsistent" both with the view that the object was overall conquest (4.167.2) and with the attack on Euesperides (4.204). That is wrong: we need assume only (1) that Aryandes did not share all his long-term thoughts with his subordinates, (2) that a Persian commander in the field would be apprehensive about going beyond his orders, and (3) that he might feel less concern about an attack on Euesperides than on a "Greek city." All these assumptions are plausible, and all pick up themes developed elsewhere. The historical truth of it all is quite another question, and there are reasons for believing that the Persian aims were always more limited and that the campaign was really a success: Tuplin 2018: 104–105.

59. Notice 4.204: this is the furthest that a Persian army has ever penetrated to the African West. The effect of the passage is not merely to underline the remoteness but, here as at 9.14, to set the campaign in a wider context of Persian history and to emphasize that the Persian expansion is here reaching its limits. Growth will now give way to contraction.

9. HERODOTUS' PERSIAN STORIES

1. The title of this chapter (much of it repeated from Pelling 2016b) echoes Karl Reinhardt's "Herodots Persergeschichten" (1940). That classic and perceptive work shows signs of its date of writing: in the first paragraph, "History means to be conscious of a nationally conditioned present time. . . . It involves polarities of one's own people ('Volkstum') and foreigners, of past and present . . ." and so on. It is to Reinhardt's credit, then, that this paragraph ends with praising Herodotus for his pathbreaking "recognition of Self within Other," surely not the most welcome theme in Nazi Germany. For his own retrospect of these years, see Reinhardt 1955, esp. on his agonizings in 1933–1934 about whether to resign his position in Frankfurt (1955: 46–54 = 1960: 388–397). Hölscher 1993: 298–303 then added a fragment of Reinhardt's melancholic reflections on the darkest years written in autumn 1945. For Reinhardt's obituary, see Hölscher 1958.

2. Cf. Boedeker 2011, emphasizing the importance of gender relations in the Persian court and generally as an "engine for historical, especially imperial, movement" (212).

3. That was the term used by Reinhardt 1940; the classic treatment was Aly 1921.

4. Cf. Trenkner's definition, 1958: xiii: "an imaginary story of limited length, intended to entertain, and describing an event in which the interest arises from the changes in the fortunes of the leading characters or from behaviour characteristic of them; an event concerned with real-life people in a real-life setting." For Trenkner, Herodotus is "the classic representative of the Greek novella of the preclassical period" (xiv; cf. 24–25). Her other examples largely come from much later novels.

5. As for instance in the stories of Arion (1.24), Alcmeon (6.125—at Croesus' court!), Hermotimus (8.105–106), Perdiccas (8.137), or Euenius (9.92–95); on Spartan royal tales (6.61–70), Polycrates' ring (3.40–43), and Periander and Lycophron (3.50–53); see below, p. 144. Cf. the comments of Cobet 1971 on Arion (145–152) and Polycrates' ring (160–164), observing that both contribute more to the worldview underlying the whole *History* than to their immediate narrative context.

6. On modern opera, see Bridges 2015: 191–192 and Pelling 2016b: 67–68. On the fragment of an ancient *Gyges* (*POxy* 2382; *TGrF* 2 *Adesp.* F 664), possibly pre-Herodotean but in my view more likely to be Hellenistic, see Griffith 2008: 69–70 and, with references to previous scholarship, Belloni 2000 and Travis 2000.

7. If we look later, Themistocles' arrival at the court of the Molossian king Admetus was rich in dramatic potential (Thuc. 1.136–137; Plut. *Them.* 24), redolent as it is of the plot of Euripides' *Telephus*; but I know of no such Themistocles play.

8. Cf. esp. O. Murray 1987 and West 2011. On such linguistic contacts, see D. M. Lewis 1977: 12–15, with the cautious comment of West 2011: 264. Ctesias too seems to have known such material: Lenfant 1996.

9. So Balcer 1987: esp. 32–34, 70–72; cf. Demandt 1972 and esp. Köhnken 1980. This is not to say that Herodotus knew a Greek version of the inscription itself: on this, see Asheri 1999. Köhnken 1990 also argued that the tale of Oebares (3.85–87) was similarly based on indirect knowledge of the Behistun version, one involving misinterpretation of a relief depicting horse and wagon of a king's attendant (3.88.3), which Herodotus then remolded and elaborated in distinctive style: cf. Rollinger 2018 for this and further near-eastern motifs in that story.

10. Herodotus leaves the impression that the first in particular may well be right: Immerwahr 1956: 260 = 2013: 174 is too quick to dismiss such a personal motive as "ludicrous."

11. For useful surveys, see M. Flower 2006 and Munson 2009; for an overview of recent scholarly discussion, see T. Harrison 2011a, with some criticism of Iranian specialists for "airbrushing" (49) away the complexities of Greek historiography.

12. Sancisi-Weerdenburg 1983. On the Persian evidence, especially that of the Persepolis tablets, see also Brosius 1996. Immerwahr 1954: 34 had already argued something similar concerning the dream-sequence at 7.12–19 (below, pp. 153–156), and Demandt 1972 had shown that the story of plucky Phaedymiē rested on an assumption embedded in Greek rather than Persian iconography, namely, that Persian monarchs' ears would usually be concealed by hair or headgear.

13. Sancisi-Weerdenburg 1985 and 1987. On Ctesias, see, however, Llewellyn-Jones and Robson 2010, esp. 22–32 and 68–87, with criticism of Sancisi-Weerdenburg along similar lines to T. Harrison 2011a (n. 11): they associate Ctesias with the novellas in Xen. *Cyr.*, seeing it as a work of "faction" (78) intended "to allow his Greek-speaking readers into another mindset" (82).

14. Sancisi-Weerdenburg 1983: 21 = 2013: 137.

15. E. W. Saïd 1978: ch. II.

16. I have here benefited greatly from discussion with Jessica Lightfoot. The increased knowledge of the East gained from Alexander's campaigns generated a similar process of marvel followed by progressive de-exoticizing: see Stevens 2016: esp. 147–148.

17. Greenblatt 1991; cf. Pelling 1997c: 640–645 = 2013: 377.

18. Sancisi-Weerdenburg 1983: 31, 32–33 = 2013, 146, 148.

19. Homeyer 1962.

20. Momigliano 1993 (first ed. 1971): he went so far as to say that Herodotus "includes several biographies" of eastern figures, especially Cyrus and Cambyses (12; cf. 21, 34–35). I discuss the Homeyer and Momigliano theses more extensively in Pelling forthcoming (a), section 5.

21. Cf. Munson 2009: 457 = 2013: 321, "his biography of Cyrus." 1.95.1 strongly marks the beginning of Cyrus' own story, and its wording itself suggests a biographical focus at least in part: "Our story now turns ask who this Cyrus was (τόν τε Κῦρον ὅστις

ἐών . . .) who destroyed Croesus' empire . . ." But the shift of narrative focus comes earlier at 1.79.1, Κῦρος δέ . . . : see p. 271 n. 16.

22. O. Murray 1987: 106 = 2001: 32–33 talked of "the biography of Histiaeus in the Ionian revolt (the only Greek example of a biography in Herodotus)," but Histiaeus cannot be said to dominate the narrative structure in the same way as Cyrus and Cambyses: cf. Dewald 2003: 46.

23. Homeyer 1962: 79–81. O. Murray 1987: 96–97 = 2001: 32–33 similarly explained the different textures in terms of the differences between Persian and Greek source material, though for him these were differing types of oral tradition: he suspected that the novellas and palace stories preserved a Persian storytelling form, "an account of Persian court life as the Persian aristocracy saw it" (1987: 113–114 = 2001: 42–43).

24. Pelling 1990b: 221–222 = 2002a: 305.

25. So Gera 1993: 13–22.

26. Pelling 2016a: 118–119.

27. For this and the next two paragraphs, see also Hornblower and Pelling 2017: introduction, section 2.

28. "Curiously fragmented and disjointed": Stadter 2006: 242.

29. I fear I am responsible for coining the ugly word: Pelling 1997e, discussing the degree to which Cassius Dio shapes his narrative around a series of life-stories of the leading figures, especially the emperors.

30. On the thorny chronological issues of that chapter, see Hornblower and Pelling 2017 ad loc.

31. Cf. Rood 1998 and Pelling 2000, indexes s.v. "delay, narrative" in each case. The classic treatment is that of Fraenkel 1950: 800.

32. Plut. *Them.* 3, 5.7, 11.1, 16.2, 20.2 and *Arist.* 2–3, 5.4, 7.1, 8.6, 9.5, 22.3–4, 24.6–7, 25.10.

33. Or so I have argued: Pelling 2007b, 2016a, and forthcoming (a). Contrast Millender 2002b: 3, "Herodotus' biographical approach to history."

34. Dewald 2003: 43 similarly comments on the way that the eastern tyrants give "a strong diachronic thrust to the narrative as a whole." Cf. M. A. Flower 2006: 274: "The Persians are the driving force of the history."

35. Cf. Immerwahr 1956, 280 = 2013: 193. Cyrus: 1.204; Xerxes: 7.7–19; Aegina-Athens: 6.87–88. The last is important because the war dribbled on into the 480s and provided Themistocles with his argument for shipbuilding, 7.144.

36. Badian 1968: 1; cf. Cawkwell 2005: 87.

37. Cf. esp. Bischoff 1932 and Lattimore 1939.

38. On the (qualified) Greek capacity to exercise restraint, see also K. Clarke 2018: 298–312.

39. Cf. respectively Pelling 2006b: 149–152 (Solon: cf. also p. 138) and 166–169 (Cyrus); 1997c: 56–57 = Munson 2013: 368–369 (the debate before Salamis) with pp. 183–184 below. I bring the points together in Pelling 2006c.

40. Xerxes' summary of Mardonius' argument is interesting too: closeted with Artemisia, he reports him as saying that "the Persians and the land army are not sharing the blame (*metaitioi*) for any reverse . . ." (8.101.2). "Sharing" with whom, himself or Mardonius or the allies? Had Mardonius heard the word *metaitioi*, his nervousness might not have been put to rest.

41. Marg 1953.

42. Cf. de Jong 2013: 278–279.

43. Cf. Boedeker 2011 on the way in which the Atys scene introduces that important theme of gender relations at the Persian court (p. 274 n. 2).

44. Carey 2016: 78–80 suggests there is a touch of the epic hero, contrasting with the lack of heroism that Xerxes goes on to show after Salamis.

45. Reinhardt 1960 (1940): 165 = Marg 1965: 358. Cf. also Marg 1953: 1109 = 1965: 298 and Baragwanath 2008: 244–245, 251–252 on these institutional pressures.

46. In Pelling 2006b: 169–172 I argue that he is not right and is learning the wrong lesson from his own experience. Stahl 2012: 147 and n. 23 rejects the argument (incidentally misrepresenting it: I suggested not "that Herodotus may agree with Croesus' advice" but the opposite, though I continue to find the issue less simple than Stahl), but he agrees that Croesus is wrong, as already in Stahl 1975: 23–30 and still in Stahl 2015: 83 n. 6. So also K. Clarke 2018: 291–292. S. O. Shapiro 1994, Schulte-Altedorneburg 2001: 158–161, and Grethlein 2009: 204 disagree; Grethlein 2010: 191–192 discusses further, with an emphasis on the episode as demonstrating "the limits of human wisdom" (192) that is close to mine (Pelling 2006b).

47. Pelling 2006b: 167, relating the rhetoric to the qualities of Cyrus that we have already seen at 1.204 (above, p. 102) and which Croesus evidently knows very well.

48. Literature cited at Pelling 2006b: 168 and n. 94.

49. Versnel 2011: 533–534, who finds "no understandable link with his ensuing advice" and criticizes the ingenuity of such attempts as my own (Pelling 2006b) to explain it.

50. Cf. Reinhardt 1940: 147 = 1965: 336–337 on the lack of an explicit religious dimension in Astyages' equivalent of "Thyestes' banquet."

51. Cf. Moles 1996: 279: imperialism "is immoral and it will always fail"; cf. Stadter 2012b: 11 and below, p. 286 n. 15.

52. For Herodotus' skill in exploiting such juxtapositions to create "situational irony," see A. Griffiths 2001. The reading I offer here of 3.38 has something in common with that of 3.17–21 given by Irwin 2014: 31–42: any readers who began by laughing at the naïveté of the Ethiopian king might end by feeling that the laugh is on them.

53. At least, that is how Herodotus portrays him. As is well known, this is an area where he may have got historical reality badly wrong: Briant 2002: 55–57; Kuhrt 2007: i. 104–106; Moyer 2011: 60; Konstantakos 2016 (but T. Harrison 2011a: 75–80 puts in a plea that rehabilitation may have gone too far). Thus Asheri finds it "unthinkable" (Asheri, Lloyd, and Corcella 2007: 427–428) that Cambyses killed the Apis bull as Herodotus describes at 3.27–29, though Depuydt 1995, after a careful reexamination of the Egyptian evidence, is inclined to believe Herodotus: "There are no incongruities between Herodotus and the archaeological record" (125). Ctesias' portrait of Cambyses seems to have been much more favorable: Lenfant 1996: 369–371.

54. For different views of Darius' characterization here, see Christ 1994: 187–189 = 2013: 235–237, "a crass and intimidating display of power," and Provencal 2015: 48–53, "Darius exhibits the same *indifference* [his italics] to *nomos* as had his predecessor Cambyses." Kingsley forthcoming: ch. 3 has a good discussion of the view that Darius' presentation implies: it is best seen as a plea for mutual toleration, but need not commit him to a strong "relativism" that takes every nation's customs to be as good as any others.

55. On this "despotic template," see esp. Dewald 2003. This is also the approach in Pelling 2002b, discussing the constitutions debate in book 3. The parallels between Sparta and Persia (Stadter 1992: 809 n. 68 = 2013: 366 n. 68) are particularly striking,

above all those between Cambyses and Cleomenes (A. Griffiths 1989; reservations at Demont 2013: 43 and 2018: 187–190); cf. Millender 2002b: 11–21 on broader parallels between Spartan and non-Greek kingship.

56. Boedeker 2011 reaches a similar conclusion about the depiction of Persian gender relations: except for polygamy, "it is not easy to pinpoint uniquely *Persian* characteristics in the elite gender relationships we have surveyed" (228).

57. Sourvinou-Inwood 1988: 182 n. 123 = 1991: 283 n. 123 argued similarly concerning the story of Periander and Lycophron: "In my view, the emphasis in Hdt. III.48 and 50–53 is very much more on the tyrant/king as a paradigm (a polarized figure suitable to the idiom of myth) for all men, than as an abnormal being standing apart from society." Cf. also Baragwanath 2008: 119 on Cambyses.

58. Flattery, playing to the popular gallery, and the *dēmos*' susceptibility: Thuc. 2.65.10; Ar. *Ach*. 637–640, *Knights* 1115–1120; Eur. *Supp*. 232–237, 414–415. Overreach and greed for more: Thuc. 4.21.2; Eur. *Supp*. 739–741. Enthusiasm for war: Thuc. 2.8.1, 6.1.1, 6.24.3; Eur. *Supp*. 479–485. Carried away by a run of success: Thuc. 4.17.4 (the Spartan ambassadors' view). Brutality when expectations disappointed: Thuc. 4.65.3, 7.48.3; and the Arginusae trial would show that the stereotype was not unfounded. Cf. Irwin 2014: 68.

59. Thucydides: thus Pericles ("your empire *is like* a tyranny," 2.63.2) and Cleon ("your empire *is* a tyranny," 3.37.2), and cf. Euphemus at 6.85.1. Aristophanes: the chorus' address to "Dēmos" at *Knights* 1111–1114. Cf. Raaflaub 1979; Tuplin 1985; and Kallet 1998: 52–54.

60. Ar. *Ach*. 181, 697–698, *Knights* 781, 1334, *Clouds* 986, *Wasps* 711, *Holkades* fr. 429 K-A: cf. Carey 2013.

61. See Loraux 1986: index, s.v. "ancestors": Isoc. *Paneg*. (4) 85–99 is perhaps the most elaborate example. Even Pericles' funeral speech begins with an emphasis on fathers and forefathers before shifting the emphasis strongly to the present generation (2.36; cf. 2.62.3).

62. Cf. von Fritz 1967: 282, 289. Compare the similar pomp and seclusion with which even the idealized Cyrus surrounds himself at the end of Xenophon's *Cyropaedia*.

63. As in Plato's *Protagoras* or *Republic* 2: cf. pp. 16–17. This has something in common with Darius' argument (3.82) that both democracy and oligarchy inevitably cycle into tyranny: there a reader with Greek assumptions might offer qualified assent, but raise a further question—what happens next?—where Greek and Persian experiences might diverge (Pelling 2002b: 150–152).

64. I elaborate this notion in Pelling forthcoming (d), comparing the way that the extreme clarity of Achilles' choice in the *Iliad*—he *knows* that if he fights he will die, and if he does not he will live a long life—sharpens rather than obscures the choices faced by ordinary mortals as they face battle with hope and fear rather than knowledge.

65. Plato *Gorg*. 470c–471d, cf. 525d; elsewhere cf. *Rpb*. 1.344a–c, *Apol*. 40d, *Euthyd*. 274a.

66. Thomas 2012: 252 here compares Herodotus' treatment of Deioces the Mede (1.96–100): Persia was "a potent and fertile source for thinking about political theory as well as thinking about the barbarian."

67. Thus Thomas 2011 argues that Herodotus' Persian ethnography, esp. 1.131–140, is deeply affected by the perspectives and presumptions of Greek sophistic speculation.

68. Above, p. 274 n. 1.

10. THE HUMAN AND THE DIVINE

1. Erbse 1979: 192 n. 30.
2. *Pace* Hohti 1975. The word "supernatural" is in some ways misleading (cf. Williams 1993: 130–131), especially as for Herodotus and his audience divine activity could be regarded as a perceptible phenomenon within "natural" human experience; but it is hard to find a better one to capture the range of phenomena that baffled explanation without gods or fate or *daimones*.
3. Other cases are listed at T. Harrison 2000: 231–232 and n. 22; cf. Hornblower 2013 on 5.33.2 and Hornblower and Pelling on 6.135.3.
4. T. Harrison 2000: 92–100 is good on the way that such natural phenomena may still, on grounds of their timing, profusion, or occasion, reasonably be taken as divine.
5. "Herodotus' reference to Lydian tradition on this episode is superficial; we may take it as a device to highlight a critical point in the narrative," West 2007: 14. On the use of indirect speech in this passage, see also Gould 1989: 37–38 and Ellis 2016: 119–121, though Ellis does find in it "traces of Herodotus' epistemological caution creeping in at the edges."
6. Echoed at Thuc. 7.87.6 but tellingly with the religious dimension removed; see Grethlein 2008 and 2010: 156–158 and 264–265.
7. Plutarch here provides an interesting comparison, both in *Herodotus' Malice* and in the *Lives* of Themistocles and Aristeides. He is critical of Herodotus for underplaying the contribution of the gods and records a good deal of independent divine material, though he is also happy to take over and adapt the items that Herodotus does relate: Marincola 2015.
8. "No story containing miraculous elements is delivered in the narrator's own voice": Fowler 2015: 201; see also Hornblower and Pelling 2017 on 6.61.4.
9. On Pan's epiphany, see also T. Harrison 2000: 82–83; Hornblower and Pelling 2017 on 6.105–106.
10. T. Harrison 2000: 25–27 and 248–250 has some good remarks on this; cf. also Mikalson 2003: 145.
11. Pelling 2006b: 157 n. 59; de Jong 2004: 109–110.
12. What Gould calls the "uncertainty principle" in matters of the gods (1985 and 1994: 94 = 2001: 362 = 2013: 186); cf. T. Harrison 2000: ch. 7.
13. Cf. Scullion 2006: 194: "the contrast between Herodotus' interest in ritual and his wariness of theology."
14. Scullion 2006, esp. 197–198: cf. Mikalson 2003: esp. 131–135 and 144–146; Hornblower and Pelling 2017 on 6.27.3; and, on the cases where he is prepared to pin down the individual god in question, Mikalson 2003: ch. 2 and T. Harrison 2000: 180–181.
15. So also Smolin 2018. T. Harrison 2000 brings this out well; his ch. 3 in particular explores what counts as adequate empirical evidence for assuming a divine dimension. Roettig 2010: 108–111, 114 similarly stresses that Herodotus is careful not to claim more than he thinks the evidence supports, and this is usually only that gods exist and their influence on the human world can be sensed: he rarely speculates on divine motives. On Herodotus' empiricism see also D. Müller 1981, esp. 315–317 on its religious aspects.
16. See Hollmann 2011: 13–15, 46–47 and esp. Thomas 1997 and 2000: 190–200, stressing that the range of *tekmērion* extends to inference from evidence as well as the evidence itself: borrowing from modern medicine, we might say "evidence-based."

17. Strasburger 1972: 23.

18. Thus Easterling 1973: 5–6, on Aeschylus.

19. Cf. Marincola 2015: 61–62 and 71–72 on the clustering of divine material around the narratives of Salamis and Plataea: but again in both cases "Plutarch outdoes Herodotus" (Marincola 2015: 72; on Plataea: cf. p. 279 n. 7).

20. If we assume that that passage is authentic, as I am inclined to do; but the issue is difficult. See the discussions of Asheri 1993, who defends the passage, and A. M. Bowie 2007: 166–167, who deletes it. In general, on Herodotus' treatment of oracles and divination, see Mikalson 2003: 52–58 and esp. T. Harrison 2000: ch. 4.

21. Cf. Hornblower 2013: 32–33 on the way that the absence of the divine from book 5 may be only apparent.

22. Chiasson 2012: 218–219; cf. the careful formulation at T. Harrison 2000: 176: "They staged—at least in part—a miraculous escape from death." T. Harrison 2000: 177 n. 71 goes on to make a rather different point.

23. Justin 1.4.10–11; cf. Ael. *VH* 12.42, Luc. *On Sacrifices* 5, etc.: Weissbach, *R-E* Supplementband iv (1924) 1139. In contrast Isocrates presents a much less flattering and wholly human-level version in *Philippus* (5.66, 132): Haussker 2017.

24. Reinhardt 1940: 147 = 1965: 336–337.

25. One might compare Reinhardt's own brilliant reading of the *Oedipus Tyrannus*, a play full of coincidences that are no coincidences and of "dramatic ironies" that suggest a divine force speaking through Oedipus' mouth, unaware as he is of the full implications of his words: Reinhardt 1979: 94–134. In Herodotus too there are sequences where events seem to fall out too neatly to be coincidence, but readers are left to draw that inference for themselves. Compare several cases in book 6 that look like, but are not explicitly described as, divine epiphanies: 6.61.3–4 (Helen), 6.69 (Astrabacus), and 6.135 (Timo); see Hornblower and Pelling 2017: 170, 179–180, and 291–292.

26. Cf. Frisch 1968: 11.

27. The verbal symmetries are much more extensive: Long 1987: 169–175.

28. Divine parenthood or origin is a frequent motif in parallel "exposure of the wonder child" folktales (cf. B. Lewis 1980: 212, 245–246): the audience may have known such tales, and if so this too will have predisposed them to suspect a divine aspect.

29. ὥστε in Herodotus should point to a genuine reason ("as" or "given that" = Attic ἅτε) rather than to one that is merely perceived or potential ("as if" = Attic ὥσπερ); cf. J. E. Powell, *Lexicon* s.v. and, e.g., 1.8.1, 1.73.3, 5.42.2, 8.118.2, 9.49.2, 9.76.1. Translations such as "blinded, as it were, by a god" (Evans 1991: 53) are too weak.

30. Beginning with the involvement of Harpagus himself. That is hard to explain realistically: why could not Astyages directly order a minion to carry out the execution, rather than involve the vizier (cf. Erbse 1992: 32–33)? That may already reflect a supernatural string-pulling, with Astyages blindly taking the worst possible path; or it may reflect a feature of Astyages' characterization, pointing to the same indecisive halfheartedness as is visible earlier after the first dream (1.107.2; Pelling 1996), and later after Cyrus' rediscovery (1.120.6–121.1). We need not follow Erbse in positing compositional awkwardness or confusion here.

31. Cf. Frisch 1968: 8; Pelling 1996: 75.

32. de Jong 2013: 288–289.

33. Cf. esp. 1.124.2: "Your survival is owed to the gods *and to me*."

34. Cf. 1.127.3: "Some of the Medes fought properly, those who had not been party to the plot." That will refer to commanders rather than troops: ordinary soldiers would

not have been brought in on the plotting, and the language seems to pick up 1.123.2, when Harpagus broaches the subject with "each of the foremost Medes."

35. A good Hippocratic principle: *On Regimen* 4.88 IV pp. 422–424 J = VI p. 642 L makes such dreams a sign of good health.

36. That is, the practice of "the Stranger on the Throne," where after bad omens a king might leave the palace and install a stranger in his place: whatever evil threatened would then strike this stranger instead (Kümmel 1967: 169–187 and 1968, Abramenko 2000): cf. Frisch 1968: 16; Pelling 1999b: 29 n. 13; Hollmann 2011: 92. This might chime with the suggestion of Baragwanath 2008: 251 that the dream represents a Persian or Persian-style explanation for Xerxes' decision whereas the debate moved in a register that was more Greek.

37. So also Carey 2016: 73–75.

38. Pelling 1997d, 1999b; cf. West 1987: 264 n. 11 and T. Harrison 2000: 135–136 n. 50. This tells against the suggestion of Pietsch 2001 that Xerxes should have suspected the truthfulness of the dream and a stronger personality would not have been cowed, or the similar argument of Schulte-Altedorneburg 2001: 187–193 that the content of both Xerxes' and Artabanus' dreams is a function of their own characters and that they should have resisted: see, *contra*, Roettig 2010: 46–79.

39. Mikalson 2002: 195–196. In Pelling 1999b: 18–19 I relate this to one of Todorov's categories of "the fantastic," the presence of a character to focus the doubtfulness that readers might themselves feel in any real-life equivalent (Todorov 1973: 31–34).

40. So also Carey 2016: 87–89, linking with other negative portents later in Xerxes' march. Köhnken 1988: 33–34 = 2006: 445–447 is also right to link the olive crown with 8.26, the admiration of Artabanus' son Tritantaechmes for the Greek crownings at the Olympics (p. 166), and with 8.124.2, Themistocles' crowning at Sparta (p. 184: the real glory of the campaign will pass to the Greeks and Themistocles at the end. It need not follow that Köhnken is right to deny the connection with the olive tree on the Acropolis.

41. Hollmann 2011: 84 (cf. 67 and 86) is good on this.

42. The elaborate tale of Glaucus (6.86) raises a similar issue, with the Delphic reply to an impious query that "to make trial of the god and to act in this way amount to the same thing" (6.86γ). But interpretation of that story in context is very difficult and cannot be gone into here: see Hornblower and Pelling 2017 ad loc. for fuller discussion.

43. "Bafflingly opaque": Scullion 2006: 197.

44. Cf. Immerwahr 1954: 30–36, speaking of Herodotus' "obfuscation of theological issues." That phrasing might mislead, but he clearly means "obfuscation" to be taken in its etymological sense as we are left "in the dark" concerning the dream's interpretation (36).

45. Though that is not to say that all the divine explanations are therefore "mumbo-jumbo independent of observed phenomena" (Easterling's phrase for what Aeschylus does *not* do; above, p. 149). Rain showers, threatening dreams and rockfalls are regular enough, and it is only the context that makes these less readily explicable in human terms (p. 279 n. 4). The same could be said of, for instance, Clytemnestra's dream at Aesch. *Cho.* 527–539 and the queen's at *Pers.* 176–199, and contrasts with certain irreducible divine interventions in the *Iliad*, such as Aphrodite's whisking Paris or Poseidon whisking Aeneas from the battlefield (3.380–382, 20.325–329).

46. Hence the concentration of Lateiner 1989: esp. ch. 9 on the human level is not

misleading, though (like T. Harrison 2000) I would put more weight on the religious dimension than he does.

47. Cf. Kleinknecht 1940: 249–250 = 1965: 552–553; Solmsen 1974: 166–167 = 1982: 105–106. Note, for instance, that he omits "the heroes," important though these are to the ways that Athenians normally thought of their divine helpers: Scullion 2006: 203. They will figure prominently at 8.143 (p. 167).

48. Mikalson 2002: 189; Scullion 2006: 199; Hornblower and Pelling 2017 on 6.27.3. On Demeter, see also Boedeker 1988: 46 = 2013: 576–577.

49. S. O. Shapiro 1996: 352–355 has good arguments for "the jealousy of the gods" as a recurrent theme, but she phrases this in terms of jealousy "of human excess" or "excesses" (355)—excessiveness of thought and deed, not just prosperity. The best candidate for jealousy of prosperity alone is the story of Polycrates, where divine *phthonos* is initially highlighted in Amasis' letters at 3.40.2 (above, p. 268 n. 24). We are then told plenty about Polycrates' actions, and they could be represented as transgressions, but Herodotus' own narrative could have laid much more emphasis on those in explaining his fall. Thus, fairly, T. Harrison 2000: 45–47 and Grethlein 2010: 195. For Fisher 1992: 362–363: "The overall picture is perhaps of a great king, whose crimes were sufficiently grave to render untenable the Amasis view that he met his fate simply because of his great success; but not serious enough to make just or apt his peculiarly unpleasant end." Dewald 2011 traces various ways that Solon's presentation of vulnerable human happiness recurs in later episodes; divine *phthonos* is not an emphasis.

50. This is a major theme of K. Clarke 2018; see already K. Clarke 1999: 31–32, and for doubts or qualifications, Scullion 2006: 193–194 and Romm 2006: 184–190, all emphasizing that Herodotus can nonetheless also admire some alterations of nature, especially when they are magnificent or carried through for benign purposes. Scullion may well be right in seeing such tyrannical behavior as a sign more of arrogance than of sacrilege (so also K. Clarke 2018: chs. 5 and 7); but the comeuppance that tyrants receive does often include a divine dimension, as we shall see. I discussed the land-and-sea theme more fully at Pelling 1991: 136–139.

51. Unnecessary but not pointless: see the good discussion of Baragwanath 2008: 254–265, observing that such a display of magnificence could be expected to have a daunting effect on Greeks who heard of it.

52. Cf. Immerwahr 1954: 27–30, observing that such theological interpretations are less clear-cut than in Aeschylus' *Persians* and arguing that this is because of the imponderables that human observers would feel in judging events as they develop: cf. above on *mimesis*, p. 156.

53. Cf. Mikalson 2002: 192: "What Greeks needed from their gods was a fair fight. The Greeks themselves could handle the rest." Immerwahr 1954: 53 similarly stressed that the storms were not themselves decisive.

54. *Flavit Jehovah et dissipati sunt.* Other medals were struck with slight variations of wording. Less portentous was a delightful parody of Caesar: *venit vidit fugit* ("he came, he saw, he ran away").

55. Pelling 1991: 138–139; cf. above, p. 152.

56. Though not humanly hard to believe: compare the summer storm that delayed D-day, or the autumn storm that broke just after Trafalgar. But in Herodotus the divine is sufficiently in the air anyway to make a difference: cf. p. 279 n. 4.

57. A. Griffiths 1989.

58. Cf. T. Harrison 2000: 85–86; McPhee 2018: 74–75.

59. Perhaps "the stocks," as translators take it, but it is unclear that Cleomenes' confinement was in public in the way that that suggests: see Hornblower and Pelling 2017 ad loc.

60. Though Herodotus' own view, stressing Demaratus, is not very different from the general Greek view that it was punishment for bribing the Pythia: the priestess was bribed to say what she did about Demaratus. See Hornblower and Pelling 2017: 189, introductory n. to 6.75.3–6.84, though we did not there explore the ways in which Herodotus might have chosen to bring the different views more closely together.

61. These human attempts at interpretation are successful more often than one might think: Hollmann 2011: 106 puts the success rate as three out of four.

62. Here cf. esp. Romm 1992, esp. 36–41, 54–60, and 69–70, and K. Clarke 2018: 50–58, 146–148.

63. This passage may therefore be less authoritative than Mikalson thinks (2002: 188 and 2003: 47, 80–83, and 138). Scullion 2006: 203 is more cautious: this is "the closest we get to a final judgement on Xerxes and the divine," but it "is doubly distanced from his narrative voice; it is embedded in a speech of Themistocles, and the speech is anyway a deception. . . . [A] tempting but uncertain judgement on the failure of the Persian invasion."

64. T. Harrison 2000: 55–56. It remains possible that they inherited the guilt of those earlier Chians who surrendered a suppliant (1.160): cf. Hornblower and Pelling 2017 on 6.2–5 and 16.2.

65. Here a similar conclusion is reached by T. Harrison 2018: 355.

11. EXPLAINING VICTORY

1. Raaflaub 2011: 25 similarly observes that Persia's failures attract more Herodotean attention than the successes: in his view that is because they convey more useful lessons to a Greek audience.

2. So Balot 2014.

3. The verb *katechein* is a *mot juste* for oppressive tyrannical rule: cf. 5.91.1 (p. 185), 1.59.1 with Gray 1997: 128–129, and esp. Forsdyke 2001: 332–341, who suggests that Herodotus' usage is influenced by Athenian antityrannical ideology. Cf. pp. 284 n. 9 and 293 n. 24.

4. Thus, Fornara 1971a: 48–49: "It is the freedom implicit in democracy which is 'worth taking seriously,' not the form of government giving power to the *dēmos* which here is praised" (though Hornblower 2013: 226 is right that this "tilts things a little too far:" democracy matters too). Cf. Rhodes 2018: 273–274. On the use of *isēgoriē* rather than *dēmokratiē*, see below, p. 193.

5. But only in some ways: cf. Munson 1988: 98, 101. The opinions of different states are certainly heard (cf. 7.219.2 before Thermopylae, 8.58–64 and 74.2, 78–82 before Salamis, and 9.50–51 before Plataea), and Baragwanath 2008: 310–314 can therefore speak of the "democratic texture" of the debate before Salamis at 8.58–63. But decisions often seem to rest with the Spartans alone: cf. 7.220–22, Herodotus' own opinion that Leonidas "sent away" allied contingents, and 8.63–64.1, Eurybiades making the decision at Salamis. But at 9.51.1 "the commanders" decide, and even at Salamis the decision-making process seems vague: see p. 183. Nor is open speech confined to democracies: p. 190.

6. On this translation, see p. 291 n. 10.

7. Gorman and Gorman 2014: 108–117 are right that poverty is not here seen as a

straightforward *source* of valor: valor has to be "imported," ἐπακτός. But it is still seen as contributing, for it is because of the poverty that valor is needed to ward it off. See also Thomas 2000: 109–111.

8. Usually a bad sign in Herodotus, especially for a despot: Lateiner 1977, esp. 178–179 on Xerxes and Demaratus; Hollmann 2011: 171–173. This laugh should be seen as scornful rather than "good-humoured" (Goldhill 2002: 17).

9. So, rightly, Millender 2002a and b; Forsdyke 2001: 347–350; and Balot 2014: 82–84. But I see no reason to follow these scholars in stressing distinctively *Athenian* ideology as a driving influence here (cf. p. 283 n. 3), still less in finding any disparagement of the Spartan values as the wrong sort of lawfulness (Millender 2002a) or alternatively as admirable but by Herodotus' day outmoded (Balot—but it was far from clear at that stage that the traditional Spartan military style was outmoded). It is better to follow von Fritz 1965 and 1967: 257; Cartledge 2002: 77 and 113; Raaflaub 2004: 233–234; and Provencal 2015: 8–9 in seeing Demaratus as presenting a Spartan variation on a more general Greek theme. Cf. also Lateiner 1989: 185, "Herodotus profoundly admired the unique and inimitable society of Sparta ruled by *nomos* and traditional institutions, not men"; Fornara 1971a: 49–50; Ubsdell 1983: ch. II. iii; Thomas 2000: 109–111; Stadter 2006: 246; Gruen 2011b: 69–70.

10. Thus, Momigliano 1979: 147 = 1984: 71: "The doom of Xerxes and his armies is willed by the gods. Xerxes' arrogance [as seen in the debate and dream of 7.8–18] is not so much a sin as an indication of divine disfavour."

11. Cf. Baragwanath 2008: 164–165.

12. Cf. Baragwanath 2008: 234–238.

13. This story is normally regarded as deriving from Delphic oral tradition, but Marincola 2016a has good arguments for tracing it back to the fourth-century historian Cleidemus (*FGrH* 323). Cleidemus is not likely to have been making it up from nothing. Marincola 2016b: 113–135 gives some other cases where Plutarch added further divine material to Herodotus' narrative of Plataea; the Dioscuri, for instance, march out with Achilles (fr. 11.30 W^2) in Simonides' elegy (p. 202).

14. Cleomenes: 5.51 (with Pelling 2007a: 188–189). Leutychidas: 6.72. Eurybiades: 8.5. Cf. Blösel 2018: 247–248, who finds Spartans more prone than other Greeks to giving and receiving bribes.

15. M. A. Flower 2006: 286.

16. At Salamis "both sides are internally disunited, but they are also brave to an equal degree": Munson 1988: 102.

17. Not that expensive weaponry was always so damaging: Masistius' gold and multilayered armor made him particularly hard to kill (9.22.2; cf. 9.20). Cf. also Pelling 1997c: 63–64 = 2013: 375–376, where I contrasted the treatment of Achilles' armor in the *Iliad*, first lent to Patroclus and then donned by Hector. That armor does not fit both figuratively and literally, for Hector eventually dies because it leaves a critical chink at the throat (*Il.* 22.322–325). In the *Iliad* the emblematic and the literal levels coexist; in Herodotus the literal is the level that matters.

18. And that is the inference made, e.g., by Raaflaub 1987: 245: "We are invited to extrapolate: the Persians, once a rough people in a rugged land, had . . . been softened by their wealth," and by Hobden 2013: 91: "The distinction between the indulgent Persians and the rugged Spartans is made manifest in their rival dining customs and brought to bear on their respective defeat and victory." Perhaps—but that is not the conclusion that Herodotus himself draws. See also Gorman and Gorman 2014: 90–94.

19. Cf. also Croesus at 1.207 and Artabanus at 4.83.1–2; Hellmann 1934: 96–98;

Bischoff 1932: 78–81 = 1965: 682–685. But Cobet 1971: 106–113 is also right to emphasize that there are subtle differences of emphasis among the different Warners.

20. On the mix of singular and plural verbs here and at 8.62, see Baragwanath 2008: 306–309.

21. That recalls what happened at Thermopylae in those other narrows (7.223), one of many ways in which the great battles mirror one another: see Hornblower and Pelling 2017: introduction to section 2 and introductory nn. to chs. 6–17 and 109–117.

22. On this and what follows, cf. Pelling 1997c: 57 = 2013: 368–369.

23. Much the same is the case with his second message, accurately telling Xerxes that the Greeks will not pursue him to the Hellespont but misrepresenting the decision as one that he had argued for rather than against (8.110.2–3).

24. The wisdom of that strategy at Thermopylae is another question: cf. 7.223.4, παραχρεώμενοί τε καὶ ἀτέοντες, with M. Clarke 2002, who plots the Spartan values against their Homeric forebears and speaks of "a warrior ethos that has been pushed beyond the limits of sanity."

25. Or rather an extreme version of this: as von Fritz 1965: 22 says, it is hard to think that such a νόμος could ever have been envisaged as excluding a move to take up a better position. Cf. Blösel 2018: 247.

12. FREEDOM

1. *Pers.* 24, 50, 71, 191, 196, 234, 594, 745. Contrast the Athenians, "who are called no man's slaves or subjects," 242. Cf. esp. Rosenbloom 2011: 361–364, who calls Athens here "a synecdoche for Hellas—Athens stands for, represents, and defends 'all Hellas'. . ." (362), and finds the combination of freedom, *isonomia*, *isēgoria*, and open speech distinctively "democratic" (364). For reservations about the search for such "democratic" ideology in Herodotus, see pp. 284 n. 9 and 293 n. 24; but that suggestion is more persuasive with a play performed before an Athenian audience.

2. Thus, Raaflaub 2004: 101: "In explaining their astonishing victories, the Greeks pointed most of all to the independence and strength they gained from the individual and collective freedom typical of their society. . . . All these aspects are present already in Aeschylus' *Persians*: elaborated, differentiated, and reinforced by scholarly explanations, they reappear in Herodotus and in Hippocrates' treatise *Airs, Waters, Places*." Similarly Moles 1996: 259; Cartledge 2002: 75–77; Cawkwell 2005: 91; and cf. T. Harrison 2018: 344 n. 53. Freedom is also the linking theme of the long ch. 2 in Ubsdell 1983.

3. Griffin 1980: 1; Schoeck 1961: 117; Pelling forthcoming (d).

4. Herodotus' alertness to an eastern taste for freedom was explored by Ubsdell 1983: 111–140, stressing *inter alia* that this alertness is unusual in fifth-century Greek texts (113–114). For Greek tyrants, see Waters' list of 55 (1971: 42–44: above, p. 273 n. 46).

5. So Stein ad loc.

6. Cf. pp. 106 and 266–267 n. 3.

7. Real: e.g., 1.27.4, 1.169.2, 1.174.1, 2.1.2, 3.21.2, 4.93, 5.49.2–3, 6.32, 6.44.1, 6.45.1, 7.1.3, 7.7.1, 9.90.2. Anticipated: e.g., 1.164.2, 1.169.1, 3.19.3, 6.11.2, 6.12.3, 6.22.1, 7.8γ.3, 7.168.1, 8.142.3, and in the last word of the history, 9.122.4. There are many other examples, especially in books 7–9. The mid fifth-century development of this "terminology of servitude" in interstate relations is tracked by Raaflaub 2004: 128–132: he relates it, plausibly enough, to the realities of the Athenian empire. For enslavement, and worse, as a normal consequence of a Greek city's fall, see van Wees 2011: 89–98.

8. Thus, 7.154.2, of Sicily; 9.27.2, of Greece in legendary times.

9. See now esp. D. Murray 2016, with reference to earlier literature, and for the claim to universal kingship in Old Persian inscriptions, Badian 1994: 110; Rollinger 2013: esp. 109; Bichler 2018a: 140.

10. Thus, Artemisia can refer dismissively to Xerxes' "slaves, who are counted as allies—Egyptians, Cypriotes, Cilicians, Pamphylians" (8.68γ): "allies" (cf. 7.96.2)—but clearly still "slaves," or as good as. It should be emphasized that this was a Greek conception of the way Persians thought, and real Persian ideology was more nuanced: "vassalage" is a better term. Cf. Balcer 1987: 44–45; Gould 1989: 27; Raaflaub 2004: 313 n. 189, with further bibliography.

11. Cf. Raaflaub 2004: 129; Hornblower and Pelling 2017 on 6.44.1.

12. The Spartans' thinking at Thuc. 7.18 is similar, though it is put in terms of "transgressions," *paranomēmata*, rather than "justice" and brings in the gods: the Spartans thought they had been in the wrong during the Archidamian War because the Thebans had started it by attacking Plataea and Sparta itself had refused the arbitration that Athens had offered. Now in 414 the position was reversed. On the continuities of thinking between Herodotus and Thucydides here, cf. next two notes and Drexler 1976: 30–35.

13. Cf. Euphemus at Thuc. 6.82.4, who even in a speech putting more weight on expediency than justice emphasizes that the Ionians deserved their treatment by Athens because "they came against us, their mother-city, with the Mede."

14. Except perhaps for 3.21.2: if Cambyses had been a just man, he would not have desired to possess any country beyond his own. But that is focalized through the voice of the king of the Ethiopians, and the weight anyway falls on what follows, ". . . or tried to enslave people *from whom he had suffered no wrong*." Ideas of the immorality of any empire are closer to the surface in Thucydides, but even there Pericles only claims that "acquiring" a tyrantlike empire "*seems to be* unjust, but abandoning it is dangerous" (2.63.2). Others, however, did hold all enslavement to be unjust: Xen. *Mem.* 4.2.14 (though I am less certain than Irwin 2018: 322 n. 100 that this points to a "general recognition at the time").

15. Cf. also 5.75.1. Contrast Moles 1996: 259, putting tyranny and imperialism together: "Herodotus emphasises that the conflict was between tyranny and imperialism and freedom and autonomy, and clearly regards the former as immoral (which does not necessarily make the unfree blameless)." Similarly Moles 2002: 36, for Herodotus "*arkhē* seems *intrinsically* unjust"; also Raaflaub 2002: 21 and 2004: 196, though at 1987: 241–242 he stresses the importance of *unprovoked* attack. The execution of prisoners of war raises a similar issue; it seems that there was no general feeling of unacceptability, and the question was whether they and their cities deserved it (van Wees 2011: 79–98).

16. "Then Peisistratus ruled the Athenians, not disturbing the honors that were in place nor changing the ordinances but administering and ordering the city on the basis of its existing customs in a fine and good way" (1.59.6); various measures of Artaphernes in 493 BCE were "extremely helpful to the Ionians" (6.42.1) and "making for peace" (6.43.1), including even the imposition of democracies (6.43.3); Datis treats Delos and Delian Apollo with great respect (6.97, 118.1). The balanced judgment of Strasburger 1955 is here exemplary, on tyranny (1955: 10–15 = 1965: 588–594 = 2013: 305–310) as in his wider discussion of Athenian democracy. It is no great overstatement to claim that Herodotus was "extraordinarily unprejudiced" (Fornara 1971a: 90). But Herodotus more often shows tyrants and conquerors behaving with brutality and without excuse: cf. esp. Lateiner 1984 and 1989: 163–186, and for Cartledge 2002: 76 despotic tyranny is in Herodotus' eyes "without qualification a bad thing."

17. The Scythians here may, understandably, be unfair to the Ionians as a whole: it is their tyrants, not the people themselves, who are taking these decisions. Cf. Dewald 1993: 66–67; Baragwanath 2008: 181. Still, the behavior of the Ionians at Lade suggests that the Scythians were not wholly wrong (Hornblower and Pelling 2017 on 6.12.2).

18. On the gathering emphasis on "necessity" in, particularly, book 7, see Baragwanath 2008: ch. 7.

19. Or possibly "not hesitantly but making haste": Baragwanath 2008: 209–210. In both the relevant passages, however, προθύμως is combined or contrasted with a phrase that indicates a mental process, here "no longer hesitantly" (lit., "doubtfully" or "with doubt," ἐνδοιαστῶς), and at 7.138.2: "not wishing to join in the war but Medizing προθύμως." Baragwanath interestingly suggests that at 7.138.2 the phrasing is focalized through, or at least affected by, the viewpoint of unsympathetic non-Medizers.

20. The criticism extends to all the Eretrians, not just those who Medized (101.2): cf. Hornblower and Pelling 2017 on 6.100.1.

21. Pelling 2013a: 31: cf. Hornblower 2013 on 5.83.1 and Hornblower and Pelling 2017 on 6.10.

22. The details, especially the projected cult of Zeus Eleutherios, are historically dubious: cf. Raaflaub 2004: 90–91, 110–111, and 316–317 nn. 228–229, with further bibliography. But I follow Shipley 1987: 103–105 in finding the outline plausible even if the hints of democracy are not (below, p. 193).

23. Wry way of saying that they were not disciplined enough: thus, Marincola ("apparent sarcasm") in his note in the de Sélincourt (1996) Penguin translation; cf. Shipley 1987: 103 and Pelling 2002b: 151–153, where I discuss the relation to the constitutions debate. Not ready for freedom: Ostwald 1969: 166 and Raaflaub 1987: 225–226, finding a contrast with Athens which *was* now ready (5.78). Baragwanath 2008: 102 combines both those aspects: "Were the Samians themselves to be held somehow responsible for this outcome, in not being *ready* for freedom?—in being unprepared to risk the absolute commitment that freedom requires?" Cf. also Barker 2009: 370–372 and my further discussion at Pelling 2011: 9 and n. 30.

24. Baragwanath 2008: 318–321 is good on the way that readers and listeners are drawn into "the difficulties in explaining his conduct": they will understand the doubts of Alexander's hearers at the time. Both the goodwill and the suspicions chime with Alexander's earlier characterization: "a person with interests and commitments in two directions" (Scaife 1989: 135), Athens and Persia. This fits well with the analysis of Alexander's advice at Tempe (7.173.3) given by Robertson 1976: Alexander may well have been colluding with the Medizing Aleuadae of Larisa, but still "the advice he gave, though not disinterested, was sound" (120). Badian 1994: 118–119 suggests that Alexander was playing a double game before Plataea: if the Greeks won, this would be remembered as a good deed; if the Persians, "no one would ever hear of the nocturnal incident: Alexander could make sure of that." Perhaps—though "making sure of that" might not be so easy. Alexander was Athens' *proxenos* (a foreign friend) and *euergetēs* ("benefactor"), 8.136.1, and at 8.140β.1 he refers enigmatically to some previous demonstration of his goodwill: for discussion of what that might be, see Meiggs 1982: 123–124; Badian 1994: 124–126; Zali 2014: 224–225; and Hornblower 2013 on 5.73.3. On Alexander's role, see also T. Harrison 2011b.

25. On the dubious historicity of all this, see esp. Badian 1994: 108–114.

26. For a different view, see Zali 2014: 231–232. The reading adopted here leaves open the likelihood that some irony would be felt, looking forward to the time when,

indeed, "Athens made peace with Persia to gain land and gold" (Fornara 1971a: 86): cf. p. 223 and p. 299 n. 38.

27. Thus, the Athos canal is dug by workers under whips (7.22.1), and the army are also whipped while crossing the Hellespont (7.56.1): Hartog 1988: 332; K. Clarke 2018: 242–243. Cf. also the young Cyrus at 1.114 (pp. 117–118); Xen. *Anab.* 3.4.25.

28. Above, p. 176. Cf. 4.3–4, where Scythians (so the story goes) rightly think that the very sight of a whip will be enough to cow some rebellious slaves.

29. Hence, in my view, we should not see Xerxes just as a negative example (Forsdyke 2001: 350); here I am in sympathy with von Fritz 1967: 257 and Romm 1998: 184–185. Still, Forsdyke is right to emphasize that Xerxes' point is not particularly pertinent to Sparta, where armies on campaign were usually under the command of a king.

30. Romm 1998: 184. Irwin 2007: 67–68, 79–82 similarly stresses the relevance of 5.3.1 to Greek affairs but sees it rather differently.

31. Cf. Hornblower 2013 ad loc.: "δρησμός (Attic δρασμός) is from διδράσκω, so perhaps 'he thought of doing a runner.'" That British colloquialism, or "make a run for it," captures the dismissive tone well: cf. the Phrygian at Eur. *Or.* 1374, βαρβάροισι δρασμοῖς, where Willink 1986: 307 comments that "the 'runaway' slave thematically depreciates himself and his 'cowardly' race"; Aeschin. *Against Ctesiphon* 21, explaining that a public official may not leave the country before his audit "to stop him grabbing the city's money or affairs and then making a run for it"; Plb. 5.26.14.

32. This is also a major theme of Zali 2014, emphasizing the differences between Greek and Persian patterns of speech-making and the contribution these make to historical interpretation. She observes (119–121) that, paradoxically, options are on occasion more openly discussed among Persians than among Greeks, and that this qualifies any easy stereotyping of each side.

33. Forsdyke 2001: 344 pertinently compares Aesch. *Pers.* 591–597 and 694–706.

34. Alexander's opening —"men of Athens, Mardonius says this: . . ."—even echoes a Persian royal formula, "thus saith the king": Fowler 2001: 110, T. Harrison 2011b: 70. We may catch some sarcasm in the Athenian retort, "go and tell Mardonius that the Athenians say this," 8.143.2.

35. Zali 2014: 68 contrasts the profusion of speeches before and after Salamis with their paucity in the narrative of Plataea in book 9 and suggests that this reflects the characters of the dominant city in each case: Athens fosters wordiness; Sparta, reticence.

36. Zali 2014: 97–98 emphasizes this formality of Persian debates, and notes Herodotus' tendency to present these in direct speech whereas their more numerous Greek counterparts have a mix of direct and indirect. Persians speak when invited to and are not interrupted: "The direct discourse and formality of the Persian debates reflect the inflexibility and strictness of Persian institutions."

37. Thus Artemisia deftly deflects any criticism for bending gender proprieties first by reminding the king of her services at Artemisium—sea battles, significantly, so she knows what she is talking about and would not be shirking from cowardice; and then by diminishing her own sex ("at sea their men are as superior to yours as men are to women," 8.68α.1). Flattery follows: "Good men tend to have bad slaves, bad men good, and you are the best of all men . . ." (8.68γ). The qualities of Artemisia's rhetoric are explored by Munson 1988, who finds in her skill and openness some Greek—she thinks particularly Athenian—qualities. Zali 2014: 158–163 brings out the sham qualities of the debate: the majority view is followed only because it coincides with Xerxes' own opinion.

38. Mardonius has already shown himself too headstrong to listen to sensible counsel (9.2–3, 41), and his "joy" at 9.49.1 also mimics the untimely delight shown by several kings (Flory 1978: 150: cf. Lateiner 1977; Grethlein 2013: 201–202). Cf. Zali 2014: 164–165; K. Clarke 2018: 234–235 and n. 40, 293 n. 59.

39. "Flooded the place" is a free translation to capture the nuance of πολλός applied to a single individual. It is appropriate to a strong flow of water or a raging wind or storm (2.25.4; *Il.* 10.6–7; Hes. *Theog.* 787; Plat. *Tim.* 43a), and when used of a person it "seems appreciably stronger than μέγας (as if the person were thought of as more than a mere individual)," enveloping one from several directions (Barrett 1964: 155 on Eur. *Hipp.* 1; cf. also *Hipp.* 443). It is also used of Gelon's forceful reply to the Greek envoys at 7.158.1 and Cleon's attack-dog rhetoric at Thuc. 4.22.2, and Demosthenes applies it to the vehemence of his opponents, *On the Crown* (18) 136 and 203.

40. Notice the tenses at 8.61.1, ταῦτα λέγοντος Θεμιστοκλέος αὖτις ὁ Κορίνθιος Ἀδείμαντος ἐπεφέρετο . . . , "while Themistocles was saying this (present) Adeimantus the Corinthian again kept attacking him" (or "began to attack," imperfect).

41. See Zali 2014: 110 and n. 19 on the lack of a clear "constitutional framework" here, and 138–143 on the disorder of the whole debate.

42. Pelling 1997c: 57–58 = Munson 2013: 368–369 and 2006c: 110–112; A. M. Bowie 2007: 144–145; Zali 2014: 116–117. Thermopylae saw a real ὠθισμός . . . πολλός, 7.225.1: see p. 203.

43. Ceding naval command to the outsider Gelon was another matter (7.161): p. 187.

44. Not that any kinship was very close: see A. M. Bowie 2007 ad loc. and Hornblower 2015: 363–365 on Lyc. *Alex.* 978.

45. Cf. 3.49.1 and 5.93.1 with pp. 44, 226.

46. Cf. the less strong formulation at 5.97.1, when Aristagoras arrives at Athens "which was the most powerful of *the other* cities" (τῶν λοιπέων ἐδυνάστευε μέγιστον), i.e., other than Sparta. Even that exaggerates ("obviously anachronistic and applicable only to a much later period," Raaflaub 1987: 238), but less so than 5.78.

47. For this choice of word, cf. 5.78 and p. 283 n. 4.

48. Cf. p. 226 and Buxton 2012, who rightly emphasizes the irony that *eleutheria*—the freedom that Soclees champions against tyranny and the freedom with which he speaks out—will also be the driving force behind the Athenian domineering that the Corinthians will come to resent.

49. Cf. Baragwanath 2008: 192–202, with references to earlier scholarship; though I am unsure that any "sense of paradox" (Baragwanath 194; so also Ubsdell 1983: 139) is here felt or implied.

50. There is no reason to follow Avery 1972: 532–523 and n. 10 in thinking that Persian ideas of freedom involve the domination of others whereas their Greek counterparts do not: Pelling 2002b: 146 and n. 71. Cf. Momigliano 1979: 149 = 1984: 73: "For Greeks or for Persians, the choice is between ruling or being ruled." I am also skeptical of Raaflaub's argument that the link between freedom and conquest was a distinctively Athenian rather than general Greek conception (2004: 187–193, 260–262), though— understandably, given Athens' unusual success—it is particularly easy to trace in Athenian sources and behavior. Polybius certainly found it plausible to apply the idea to the history of the Peloponnese (5.106.5, quoted in text below).

51. The classic treatment is that of Isaiah Berlin's 1958 inaugural Oxford lecture on "two concepts of liberty," distinguishing "positive" and "negative" liberty (Berlin and

Hardy 2002: 166–217). Harris 2013: 353–358, 366–367 surveys subsequent discussion of Berlin. M. H. Hansen 1989: 8–11 and Patterson 1991: xii, 220 see a closer analogy between Greek and modern ideas of liberty than Berlin himself found (e.g., Berlin and Hardy 2002: 32–34, 283–286, 318–319).

52. Cf. de Romilly 1963: 79–82.

53. Or alternatively "as they [i.e., the Peloponnesians] are all naturally both ambitious of supremacy and fond of liberty, they are in a state of constant warfare..." (Paton in the Loeb [1922–1927], left unrevised by Walbank and Habicht in the 2nd ed. [2010–2012]). It is unclear whether Polybius is making a point about the Peloponnesians (Paton) or about all humans who share a similar disposition.

54. On Gelon, see further below, p. 225.

55. Cf. 3.159.1 (Babylon); 6.23.6 (Zancle). See also Pelling 2002b: 144 n. 66 and Hornblower and Pelling 2017 on 6.98.2.

56. For such analogies, cf. Raaflaub 2004: 274–275. Otanes again offers half of a similar comparison with his observation that in a democracy bad people damage the state after "putting their heads together," συγκύψαντες, 3.82.4; in 480 the Greeks hope that the different states can "put their heads together" (συγκύψαντες) in the alliance that will save them, 7.145.2.

57. Herodotus is not quite explicit about this, but he introduces the story by describing Themistocles' "proposal" or "thinking" (γνώμη) as one that was "most excellent in its timeliness" (ἐς καιρὸν ἠρίστευσε), 7.144.1. That phrase does not suit a suggestion that just happened to turn out well in a way that its maker had not anticipated. Cf. Moles 2002: 45; Blösel 2004: 79; Baragwanath 2008: 291 n. 6.

58. That need not mean that "doing good for Greece" was Cleomenes' motive, only the result: cf. Hornblower and Pelling's (2017) nn. on 6.49.3 and 6.61.1

59. Cf. Lateiner 1989: 184: "The paradoxical advantage of non-autocratic governments is, Herodotus believes, that envy, strife, and disunity—among men and nations—promote human freedom..." Lateiner puts this, as does Immerwahr 1966: 199, in terms of the virtues of competitiveness and the energy it fosters: "Hellenic strength results from disunity and strife, even war." That interpretation will strike a chord with some modern readers, but I am not convinced that competitive strife is a motor of freedom for Herodotus rather than an unwelcome concomitant.

60. Cf. p. 195.

61. On the nautical language, see Hornblower and Pelling 2017 ad loc.

13. DEMOCRACY

1. Q. Skinner 1998 has interesting remarks on the process whereby what he calls a "neo-Roman" theory (for there was some basis in, e.g., Sallust and Livy for the idea that true freedom could only be found in a republic) came to "appropriate the supreme moral value of freedom and apply it exclusively to certain rather radical forms of representative government" (59) in, particularly, the seventeenth century.

2. Or in effect so if not in theory, as it was in the mid fourth-century BCE (Plut. *Dion* 53.4). The quotation is from Salmon in *OCD*⁴: cf. Salmon 1984: 231–239.

3. One of these tyrants goes on to defect, but the others do not: 5.113. Aristagoras is also explicitly "tyrant of Miletus" (5.49.1) when he delivers his freedom rhetoric at Sparta, despite his earlier gesture of abandoning that tyranny (5.37.2, p. 292 n. 14); admittedly, multiple ironies might there be felt (Baragwanath 2008: 167).

4. Cf. Pind. *P.* 1 (470 BCE), written for Gelon's brother the tyrant Hieron and celebrating his foundation of Aetna "with god-built liberty": Raaflaub 2004: 90.

5. See Q. Skinner 1998: esp. 49–57 for the later importance of the distinction between external and internal threats to freedom, particularly in the British Civil War, where "servitude" to an internal "tyranny" was in point, and in the American War of Independence, where it was a question of external imposition.

6. Raaflaub 2004: esp. 203–249. The association of the two is not found in our sources before about 430, but Raaflaub argues (esp. 205–221) that the 440s provided a historical context where the connection might easily take root in partisan exchanges between the elite, defending the "freedom" with which they had become familiar, and champions of the *dēmos*, arguing that only under democracy can their freedom be defended. Much of the argument is uncomfortably aprioristic: we should not (*pace* Raaflaub 206–207) draw any conclusions from the absence of the idea from Aeschylus' *Suppliant Women* (see p. 292 n. 16) and from Herodotus' constitutions debate (we should not associate that debate with any date earlier than the rest of the *Histories*, and anyway Otanes' house alone "remained free" as a result of his democratic stand, 3.83.3). But Raaflaub's general picture remains attractive.

7. Not quite "equality before the law" but often something more like "equal access to the law" (cf. Thuc. 2.37.1): "The term reflects the political norms and regulations by which ruler and ruled are equally bound, the statutes which are valid and binding equally on both": Ostwald 1969: 120. That need not mean equal political rights and privileges, though Thuc. 3.62.3–4 and 4.78.2–3 show that it can imply some involvement in government: cf. Vlastos 1953 and 1964; M. H. Hansen 1989: 16–17; Pelling 2002b: 137 n. 44; and Lévy 2005.

8. *Isonomiē* is "more of a banner than a label" (Vlastos 1964: 8 = 1973: 172–173) and comes to be particularly associated with democracy: cf. esp. Thuc. 3.82.8, 6.38.5 with Hornblower 1991– 2008 iii. 413, and Plato *Rpb.* 8.561e, 563b (Vlastos 1953: 352); Ostwald 1969: 97: "not a name for a form of government but for the principle of political equality, which, though it is of course more closely associated with a democratic constitution than any other, is not necessarily confined to it." But it is "*a* banner" for democracy rather than distinctively "*the* banner": as M. H. Hansen 1989: 23–24 stresses, it was not used often enough for that. For *es meson* cf. p. 273 n. 37, and for the echoes here of the constitutions debate Ostwald 1969: 107–108 and Pelling 2002b: 140 n. 54.

9. Badian 1994: 121 n. 15 distinguishes Herodotus' contempt for the *dēmos* from his admiration for democracy: the two are not so easy to separate, given that criticisms of democracy, both in Herodotus (Megabyxus at 3.81) and elsewhere (e.g., the Herald at Eur. *Supp.* 417–425 and 481–485 and Ps.-Xen. *Ath. Pol.* [the "Old Oligarch"] passim), typically center on the incompetence, lack of education, or self-interest of the *dēmos*. Cf. Vlastos 1953: 337–338 n. 1 for the way in which *dēmos* frequently figures in phrases where democracy, the system of government, is clearly in point. Vlastos there claimed that *dēmos* may actually *mean* the democratic form of government (cf. LSJ s.v. "δῆμος" III.2, J. E. Powell *Lexicon* s.v. 4), but Larsen 1948: 6 n. 16 and 1954: 14 n. 2 was right to say that this goes too far, and Vlastos later retracted this claim (1964: 4 n. 2 = 1973: 167 n. 17).

10. The translations "pushover" and "put one across" are over-colloquial but are better than more formal equivalents at capturing the range of εὐπετής, connected to πίπτω ("fall"), and of διαβάλλειν, not just "to slander" or "to deceive" but to use words in various ways to trick and mislead: Pelling 2007a.

11. On pity in oratory, cf. esp. Tzanetou 2005; on pity in Herodotus and Thucydides, Lateiner 2005 and Pelling 2012a.

12. I here differ from Balot 2014: 94–96: cf. p. 239 n. 28. For a balanced view, see Zali 2014: 107–108.

13. Vlastos 1953: 337–339 and 1964: 3 = 1973: 166–167 thought that the word did not exist when Herodotus or his source framed the constitutions debate but that it came into use before he wrote book 6. This is unconvincing: cf. Ostwald 1969: III n. 1 and 178–179; Pelling 2002b: 136 n. 35, with further references. See also below, n. 16. The root first figures in Herodotus' text at 4.137.2 (δημοκρατέεσθαι).

14. B. M. Mitchell 1975: 86; so also Shipley 1987: 104–105. Ostwald 1969: 107–109 however notes the importance of Maeandrius "proclaiming" it in an "assembly": the assembly has a democratic ring, but the need for this to be "proclaimed" suggests that "the *isonomiē* proclaimed by Maeandrius, however closely related to any pre-existing democracy, is not identical with it."

15. Cf. Hornblower 2013: 144–145 on 5.37.2, and Aristagoras is still "tyrant of Miletus" at 5.49.1 (p. 290 n. 3).

16. Cartledge 2016: 73–75 summarizes recent views. His own position is that the new constitution "was an early form of democracy—though not yet that in name" (75) and is indeed better described as *isonomiē* or *isokratiē*. The word *dēmokratia* itself may well date from the second quarter of the fifth century (Cartledge 74; Raaflaub 2004: 206, 213; Rhodes 2018: 267), though the evidence is indecisive. Little can be deduced from Aeschylus' *Suppliant Women* (?463 BCE), which makes many mentions of democratic procedures (Easterling 1985: 2–3) but avoids the word *dēmokratia*: that may well be because, as Easterling shows, tragedy typically avoids such "modern" words even in references with a contemporary ring, and we cannot tell whether the word was by then familiar in everyday speech. The first incontrovertible uses of *dēmokratia/-ē* are those in Herodotus, Aristophanes, Antiphon, and the "Old Oligarch" (Ps.-Xen. *Ath. Pol.*).

17. This much is fairly uncontroversial, though there is less scholarly consensus on what exactly was envisaged in any such historical debate: see Pelling 2002b: 128–129 and n. 20, with references to earlier literature.

18. Pelling 2002b: 138–139.

19. Cf. M. H. Hansen 1989: 7, 26–28; Cartledge 2016: 94–95.

20. The nearest to an exception might be Plato, *Rpb.* 8.561e, where Socrates has just described a fickle, undisciplined, "democratic" man and the interlocutor describes such a person as "indeed an *isonomikos* man"; Socrates himself has there defined democracy as "disbursing a sort of equality to equal and unequal alike" (558b), and there is no doubt about the disapproval. But the passage is so laden with irony, with many positive words given a sarcastic turn (Socrates goes on to define such a man as "fine and versatile," καλός τε καὶ ποικίλος), that there may be nothing negative in the word itself rather than the tone in which it is uttered.

21. Thus the "Old Oligarch" makes it a symptom of the lack of discipline at Athens that *isēgoria* has been granted even to slaves and metics (Ps.-Xen. *Ath. Pol.* 1.12), and the precocious young Cyrus says sarcastically that he now understands what the *isēgoria* at court really means—"for you would never shut up" (*Cyr.* 1.3.10). In the philosophical tradition Zeno denied the value of granting *isēgoria* to bad people at the expense of good (*SVF* fr. 288) and Chrysippus that of allowing *isēgoria* to the *amousoi* in a cultural discussion (*SVF* fr. 361).

22. Particularly *isonomiē*: cf. Larsen 1948: 7–12; Kinzl 1978: 120–121, 125, 317–318;

Pelling 2002b: 136–139; Lévy 2005. For instance, a polis elite might well resent the tyrannical preeminence of one of their number rather than, as they might put it, an *isonomië* of esteem among their equals (Raaflaub 1979: 247–248). But this is not to say that it *means* "lack of tyranny": this is a matter of connotation rather than denotation (Vlastos 1964: 7–10 = 1973: 171–174).

23. Cf. Moles 2002: 39; Tuplin 1985: 364–366; Pelling 2002b: 136–137; Raaflaub 2004: 94–95; Rhodes 2018: 268, 270—all with references to further literature.

24. Millender 2002b: 22–23, putting this very strongly ("virtually bombarded by Athenian democratic ideology and rhetoric"). Millender 2002a and b, like Forsdyke 1999 and 2001, therefore puts particular weight on Athenian democratic ideology as informing Herodotus' outlook (cf. p. 284 n. 9); similarly Balot 2014: 81–82 and, in the case of the antityranny rhetoric of 5.92, Luraghi 2013: 99–100 and 111, following Forsdyke; *contra*, Gorman and Gorman 2014: 106–107 n. 60. For the reasons given in the text, I doubt whether it is always possible to discriminate distinctively "democratic" aspects in so clear-cut a way. Still, it is of course reasonable to assume that Herodotus was influenced by what he heard at Athens, just as he was by what he heard in Ionia or in Thurii. See also Thomas 2000: 9–16; West 2011: 261; and J. Skinner 2018: 190–191 for similar warnings against overemphasizing the influence of Athens' cultural milieu.

25. Even in so communally charged an experience as attending the tragic theater. Here I am now in sympathy with the arguments of Rhodes 2003, differing from the emphasis of much recent scholarship (including my own) and seeing "Athenian drama as reflecting the *polis* in general rather than the democratic *polis* in particular" (119).

26. So Farrar 1988: 20: "The significant contrast is not between democracy and oligarchy or tyranny, but between freedom on the one hand, and irresponsible, despotic (and narrowly interested) rule on the other."

27. Kleinknecht 1940: 251 = 1965: 555 and others assume that this is an assembly, but Mardonius' next envoy Mourychides deals with the *boulē*, at that point removed to Salamis, at 9.5.1, and it was normal procedure for the *boulē* to receive ambassadors: Rhodes 1972: 20, 43, and esp. 54. Occasionally, it is true, the *boulē* could refer matters on to the full assembly, and according to Plutarch Aristeides brought the Spartan delegates before an assembly after proposing a decree; he then says that Aristeides himself delivered some (very Herodotean) fine words in reply (*Arist.* 10.4–6). Scholars have assumed that this material derives from Craterus' collection of Athenian decrees (Sansone 1989: 188) and if so it would carry some weight, but it may equally be that Plutarch is himself, by a typical technique (Pelling 2002a: 93–94), expanding the role of his central figure with no source authority. Rhodes 1972: 54 n. 1 is similarly skeptical of Plutarch's evidence here, but Zali 2014: 84 accepts it.

28. Kleinknecht 1940: 257 = 1965: 562 emphasizes that we hear nothing of the arguments that led to the proud proclamations of 8.140–144. I see no trace here of the stress on and admiration for democratic debate found by Balot 2004: 94–98.

29. The original decision to accept the Plataean appeal dates to 519 BCE, still under the tyranny (Thuc. 3.68.5): see Hornblower and Pelling's (2017) n. on 6.108.1. Balot 2004: 101 overlooks this when he includes that choice as a prime example of the democratic Athenians' "thoughtful, voluntary efforts on the city's behalf" along the lines of 5.78.

30. Hornblower and Pelling 2017 on 6.103.1.

31. "Miltiades went to him and said . . . ," 6.109.3: that could mean either "went up to him" in the council of ten generals (thus, apparently, de Sélincourt, "to Callimachus,

then, Miltiades turned") or "went to him" outside once the council was deadlocked. It is unclear whether Callimachus was present at the initial council at all: see Hornblower–Pelling's nn. on 6.109.2 and 4. Either way, it is hard to see this as testimony to the spirit of "open debate" generated by the shift towards democracy (thus Millender 2002a: 45–47): co-generals have to debate, and it can go well or badly, under any system (including the Persian: 4.203.2).

32. Larsen 1948 makes a good case for thinking that it was the Periclean age that first regarded Cleisthenes as the founder of democracy. It is symptomatic of modern assumptions that the 2500th anniversary of "democracy" was celebrated with verve in 1993–1994: cf. Grofman 1993, an introductory summary to a collection of essays in a special commemorative edition of *PS: Political Science and Politics*; M. H. Hansen 1994.

33. See Hornblower and Pelling 2017 on these passages. Herodotus' note on the constitutional position of the polemarch has also created a scholarly minefield (6.109.2). The initial description of Cleisthenes' reforms was very sketchy too (5.66.2 and 69.2, with Hornblower's notes): we are heavily dependent on *Ath. Pol.* for further details.

34. That polarity is one reason why "tyranny" continues to figure so heavily in the Athenian popular imagination even during the Peloponnesian War, at a time when (as the events of 411–410 showed) we might expect oligarchy rather than tyranny to figure as the real danger: cf. Ar. *Wasps* 417, 464, 487, and Bdelycleon's indignant riposte—"everything for you is 'tyranny!' and 'conspiracies' . . .": 488–499. Tyranny was "good to think with," a useful touchstone for evaluating its opposite. See Berve 1967: i. 194, 198; Raaflaub 1989: 46 and 2004: 203–205, 236; Pelling 2002b: 139 and n. 50; Tuplin 1985: 371–372, though Tuplin's overall point is that "tyrant" language is a less prominent part of the lexicon of political abuse than we might expect. He concedes that it was more frequent (373) in the fifth century than the fourth.

35. Cf. Dewald 1997: esp. 80–82 = 2013: 298–401 and below, p. 231.

14. INDIVIDUALS AND COLLECTIVES

1. The first quotation is from Mill, *On Liberty* (1859), ch. 3; the second is Berlin's summary of Mill (Berlin and Hardy 2002: 174).

2. The phrase was first used by John Adams (Adams 1787: 3.231); Mill 1859 quotes it from de Tocqueville towards the beginning of ch. 1. Cf. Berlin and Hardy 2002: 208–209. Berlin himself would not take this step either: "There is no necessary connection between individual liberty and democratic rule" (Berlin and Hardy 2002: 177). Q. Skinner 1998 explores the steps by which that problematic connection came to be assumed: cf. p. 290 n. 1.

3. Though there is more in that passage than meets the eye; Livy's cataloging of Alexander's advantages has a relevance to his own day as well, for now in Rome there was a great man who could harness the strengths of one-man power to those of Republican tradition: Augustus himself. See Pelling 2013b: 12, and for a different view of the contemporary relevance Morello 2002: 81–83.

4. In the preface to Pelling 1990a I collected examples of the claim from treatments of antiquity; the early Middle Ages; Renaissance Italy; and the sixteenth, seventeenth, and eighteenth centuries.

5. Ἴδιος and its cognates come closest, covering notions of *strange, unusual, peculiar, eccentric* (LSJ s.v. II.2–3); but individual people are not described in such terms until much later. Thus it is Plutarch, not Herodotus, who describes Themistocles as "wanting

to be ἴδιός τις in everything," *Them.* 18.8 (cf. *C.mai.* 25.2); when Herodotus describes a particular ἔθνος as ἴδιον, he means "having its own character" rather than that of the Scythians as a whole: 4.18.3, 22.1.

6. Berlin's summary of the argument of Mill 1859: p. 198 and p. 294 n. 1.
7. Schofield 1986.
8. *IG* I³ 503/4, well discussed by E. L. Bowie 2010 and Petrovic 2013; in the inscription "glory" or "talk" fills the earth (cf. *Od.* 9.19–20, 264) and there is mention of the "calf-bearing fertile land" (cf. *Il.* 9.141, 283; *h.Ap.* 21).
9. Fr. 11 W².
10. For the Stoa, see now Arafat 2013 and Arrington 2015: 201–203, with further references. The 460s date seems confirmed by the latest excavations: Camp 2015: 476–494.
11. Goldhill 1988.
12. So Vanderpool 1966, accepted by E. B. Harrison 1972 and many since: see Hornblower and Pelling 2017: fig. 1 on p. 4.
13. Paus. 1.15.3; Aelian *NA* 7.38; Plin. *NH* 3.57. See Hornblower and Pelling 2017: introduction to section 1 and nn. on 6.116 and 117.2–3.
14. 6.113.2–114, echoing *Iliad* 15.716–717: cf. Pelling 2013a: 25–26 and Hornblower and Pelling 2017: ad loc.
15. Boedeker 2003: 34–36; Munson 2001: 175–178; Carey 2016: 81–87; Marincola 2018; Pelling 2006a: 92–98, much of which is summarized in the next few pages.
16. For the details, see Pelling 2006a: 92–93 n. 48.
17. Cf. the hexameter at Plato, *Symposium* 208c, καὶ κλέος ἐς τὸν ἀεὶ χρόνον ἀθάνατον καταθέσθαι ("and lay down immortal glory for eternity").
18. Cf. Grethlein 2013: 186–200 on the way that Darius and Xerxes attempt to shape the memories of posterity by a degree of self-memorializing; Grethlein too brings this into contact with Herodotus' own project.
19. Namely, ΥΠΟ ΣΚΙΗ ("in the shade," the Greek Twentieth Armored Division), from Hdt. 7.226.2, and ΜΟΛΩΝ ΛΑΒΕ ("come and get them," i.e., if you want our arms you will have to take them from us, the Greek First Army Corps and the Cypriote Second Infantry Division), taken admittedly not from Herodotus but from Plutarch, *Apoph. Lac.* 225c, where it is attributed to Leonidas. The second of these has also become a favorite of tattooists.
20. For the reading (μούνων rather than μοῦνον) at 7.220.4, see Baragwanath 2008: 69 n. 39.
21. Flower and Marincola 2002: 233.
22. For the counterfactual element here, cf. p. 249 n. 22.
23. Cairns 2003: 31–33.
24. Blösel 2001: 185–186 and 2004: 158–160, 360.
25. As several scholars have suggested, especially Immerwahr 1966: 223–225 and Blösel 2001 ("a symbol for Athens as a whole," 196; "a mirror to the Athenians," 197) and 2004; see though Baragwanath's critique of Blösel, 2008: 315–322.
26. The phrase used by Cawkwell 1997: 24 and others, including Blösel 2001: 190.
27. Above, p. 192 and Pelling 2007a.
28. On the links between the two episodes, see Blösel 2004: 295–297.
29. The "mirroring" figure is used by Blösel in both his titles (2001 and 2004), echoing Hartog 1988.
30. For Thucydides, see Gribble 1999: ch. 3, esp. 174–175, 184–185; for Plutarch, Pelling 1992: 21–25 = 2002a: 125–128. Plutarch's portrayal of the *dēmos* in *Pericles* is sub-

tly different, there again mirroring the qualities of the man himself: Pelling 1992: 25–27 = 2002a: 128–130.

31. Thus, Ubsdell 1983: ch. 1 traces a pattern whereby many of the great figures—Miltiades, Cleomenes, Themistocles, Pausanias—are characterized by doublet sequences, the first salutary and the second more noxious.

32. This is a major theme of Kurke 1991.

33. Except for the brief retrospective mention in the Mycale narrative to "the same stratagem as Themistocles used at Artemisium" (9.98.4).

34. For Oebares, cf. p. 275 n. 9.

35. Köhnken 1990: 132 = 2006: 465. As Köhnken goes on to say, "Such stories are therefore, it seems, less characteristic of the particular persons or regions described than of Herodotus himself."

36. Hollmann 2011: 258–265.

37. Not that the story, as Herodotus tells it, quite matches the wording of that oracle: see Hornblower and Pelling 2017 on 6.140.1.

38. Eurybiades, 8.5.1, 58–64, and unsuccessfully 108; Adeimantus, 8.5.1–2, cf. 61; the council of generals, 8.19–20, 59–64, 108, and presumably 8.74 and 78; the Ionians, 8.22; Greek forces, 8.83. Xerxes, 8.75 and 110; Andros, Carystus, Paros, and other islanders, 8.111–112.

39. For the force and cogency of Themistocles' rhetoric here, cf. Baragwanath 2008: 298–304; for the strategy, see also Blösel 2004: 257.

40. But see the subtle argument of Baragwanath 2008: 289–322, suggesting that the previous narrative points to interpretations that complement, in her view even "undercut" (314), the authorial verdict of self-interest.

41. For the translation, see p. 291 n. 10.

42. See Hornblower and Pelling 2017 on 6.49.2 and 6.61.1.

43. Fornara 1971a: 62; cf. Irwin 2018: 284–287. The story of the captured concubine would have struck a particular contrast with the future for any reader or listener who knew the tale of his killing, albeit accidental, of a Byzantian maiden he had summoned to his bed: Plut. *Cim.* 6.4–5, *God's slowness to punish* 555c. Cf. Stadter 2006: 246.

44. So also Fornara 1971a: 65 and Gould 1989: 117. Contrast Momigliano 1979: 145 = 1984: 68: "Pausanias, who had previously despised Persian luxury (Herodotus 9.82) . . ."

45. So also Fornara 1971a: 62, Herodotus' Pausanias a "companion piece" to his Themistocles.

46. Or so Thucydides has it; in fact, it may have been the work of the amphictyony (Hornblower 1991–2008: i. 218–219) and therefore a more panhellenic rebuke.

47. ML 27 = Fornara 1983: 59; Stephenson 2016.

48. Cf. Pelling 2000: 208, followed by Baragwanath 2008: 241.

49. Buxton 2012: 585–586 n. 52.

50. Thus Cobet 1971: 99: "What binds people together is made visible because Herodotus takes their singularity seriously" ("das Verbindliche wird sichtbar dadurch, daß Herodot das Einzelne ernst nimmt"); he also (110–111) comments that the checklist of similar questions that Herodotus puts to different cultures itself implies an element of continuity, as each culture raises the same issues.

51. Or so I have argued, Pelling 2007a: 191–194: at 8.132 the Spartans thus draw back from pursuing any further eastwards than Delos.

52. *Pace* Munson 2001: 212–213. I treat Herodotus' and Thucydides' Sparta in more detail, along with Plutarch's, in Pelling forthcoming (b); see also Stadter 2006: 243–247 and Blösel 2018.

53. Just as, so it may be argued, his classic explanation of the war at 1.23.6 can be taken as a first bid that the narrative goes on to refine: Gribble 1998: 57.

15. THEN AND NOW: HERODOTUS' OWN DAY

1. Cf. esp. Mink 1987: esp. 47–48, 72, 136–137 and other literature cited at Pelling 1997f: 228 n. 1 = 2002a: 382 n. 1; for Herodotus, Dewald 1997: 76 = 2013: 395.

2. K. Clarke 2018: 64 comments on this Herodotean adaptation of a familiar type of narrative, that of a *nostos* or "return home." *Nostoi* are usually a matter of returning, Odysseus-like, to one's own specific home and family: here, for Persia, it is a matter of returning to the entire continent that they regard as "their own" (1.4.4).

3. The classic example is Dostoevsky's *Crime and Punishment*. It is striking how many modern novels begin at a funeral.

4. See Boedeker 1988: 41–42 = 2013: 371–372 on the precise location, given slightly differently at 7.33 and at 9.120.4.

5. See the subtle analysis of Boedeker 1988, esp. 34 = 2013: 363 on the Iliadic echoes.

6. Ceccarelli 1993: 49–54.

7. Moles 1996: 272–273.

8. Wilson 2015a: xi and 2015b: vii–viii; Hornblower and Pelling 2017: introduction to section 6.

9. Pelling 2002a: 43 n. 151.

10. Jacoby 1913 influentially argued for a development from an early interest in geography and ethnography to chronological historiography, and that was still broadly supported by von Fritz 1967 and Fornara 1971a. The argument especially focused on book 2, with a perceptibly different texture taken to point to an early date: see esp. Fornara 1971a: 17–23. More recently this has not worn well, as Harrison and Irwin comment (2018b: 2–4). A. B. Lloyd 1975–1986 i. 66–68 observed the weakness of arguments for an early date for book 2, and Ubsdell 1983: 447–452 pointed out that an equally good case could be made for putting it late; so also Cartledge 2002: 72. Those differences in texture can equally be taken as a consequence of adopting a manner felt to be in keeping with more "ethnographic" material: cf. Bowie 2018b; Bichler 2018b. For discussion of Jacoby's theory, see esp. Fowler 1996: 65–69 = 2013: 51–56 and Marincola 1999: esp. 291–292, and for a more general summary of views of the dating of Herodotus' work, see Harrison and Irwin 2018b: 10.

11. Pelling 2000: 154–155; similarly Węcowski 2004: 152 and Henderson 2012: 146–147. Nesselrath 2014 and Mash 2017: esp. 69–70 give me a hearing but are unconvinced.

12. *Anthologia Palatina* 11.130 (Pollianus),

I hate these cyclic poets who always say "and then" (αὐτὰρ ἔπειτα):
They're just muggers—of other people's verse.

On this feature in the epic cycle and the contrast with Homer, cf. Griffin 1977: 49–50.

13. At least in my view: cf. p. 31. For a firmer insistence on humor, see Root 2011 with above, p. 245 n. 40.

14. Fornara 1971b: 28–29; cf. Cobet 1977: 13–15; Pelling forthcoming (c). Nesselrath 2014 accepts that the parody is more thoroughgoing in *Birds* than in *Acharnians* but thinks that this is because *Ach.* draws on Herodotus' lectures and *Birds* on a published text.

15. See further Hornblower and Pelling 2017: ad loc.

16. Stein 1901–1908 ad loc. and Cobet 1971: 65 fairly commented on the looseness of the connection with Sophanes.

17. Pre-413: e.g., Evans 1979: 146; Hornblower 2010: 28. Post-413: Irwin 2013, who would push the date very much later, into the fourth century and later than Thucydides (cf. now Irwin 2018). I am not convinced.

18. As Fornara argued, 1971b and 1981: 149–150. I here side with Cobet 1977 and 1987 in assuming that γενόμενον can mean "that came about" rather than implying that it is concluded. The present ἀπέχεσθαι also allows the phrase to mean that "up to and including (ἐς) the war . . . the Spartans kept [and continue to keep] away from Decelea." Fowler, *EGM* ii. 683 n. 7 takes a similar view of the sentence's ambiguity.

19. Evans 1987 inferred this from Thuc. 3.26.3, where the Spartan ravaging covers "the parts of Attica that they had cut down before, including anything that had grown and anything that had been left out in the previous invasions." The inference is perilous: Thucydides may well simply mean smaller areas or farmsteads that they had inadvertently missed. *Hell. Oxy.* 12.5 comments that Attica as a whole suffered relatively mildly in the earlier attacks in comparison with those after 413.

20. Especially Fornara 1971b: 33–34. Cobet (1977: 6–7 and 1987: 510) thought that the argument should go the other way, as Herodotus would have mentioned Nicias' expedition explicitly had he known of it. Both inferences are insecure. On Cythera and the 424 campaign, see Fragoulaki 2013: 151–159.

21. Ruffing 2013: 206.

22. Thus, e.g., Evans 1979, following Jacoby 1913: 232 = 1956: 20 and How and Wells 1912: ii. 101. The relevant context is 6.91, the comment that Aeginetans were not able to appease the gods by sacrifices, try though they might, before they were expelled from the island (431). The butchering in 424 might seem even fiercer punishment, but the point is not one of punishment but of unsuccessful sacrifices: the expulsion of the entire community might seem a clearer sign of unappeased deities than the slaughter, as Thucydides puts it, of "all the Aeginetans whom the Athenians had caught." Many will have taken to the hills, as did the Lacedaemonian garrison (Thuc. 4.57.2).

23. Fornara 1971b: 34.

24. Selwyn Lloyd was Eden's Foreign Secretary at the time, and his "personal account" (Lloyd 1978) presents this viewpoint with particular clarity.

25. Moles 1996: 261–262; Stadter 1992: 795–796 = 2013: 345–347 and 2006: 248: cf. above, p. 106. It is also possible that the Persian tributary system served as a model for Athens to follow (Raaflaub 2009: esp. 98–101): neither hypothesis need exclude the other.

26. Cf. Rutherford 2018: 40. Most but not all are listed by Schmid and Stählin 1929–1948; i² 590–591 n. 9. Schmid and Stählin also list some fifty less precise references to institutions or phenomena that are still the case "in my time" (on this as a feature of the Herodotean "voiceprint," see Fowler 1996: 71 = 2013: 59), sometimes just indicated by a present tense. On what follows, cf. the exhaustive discussion of Cobet 1971: 59–78.

27. A. Griffiths 2001: cf. Rutherford 2018: 18–23.

28. There are other indications too that he knows a good deal more about Inaros than he says: Tuplin 2018: 108–109.

29. Cf. Asheri, Lloyd, and Corcella 2007: 612 ad loc.

30. Cf. Hornblower-Pelling 2017: introduction to section 3, and for the dates the nn. on 6.72.1.

31. Rutherford 2018: 20. This technique—wise words in an inappropriate mouth—was later to become a specialty of Tacitus: cf. Syme 1958: 209, 547 and Martin 1981: 94,

"It is one of the features of Tacitus' writing that the devil is given a fair share of the good tunes."

32. Cf. Hornblower and Pelling 2017: ad loc. Ubsdell 1983: 220–221 saw it as "surely a perverse" choice to take the omen as referring to Greeks rather than Persians.

33. See also Cobet 1971: 50–56 on the complicated narrative intermeshing here.

34. For the ambiguities here, see Munson 2001: 215–216, citing previous scholarship, and A. Bowie 2007: ad loc. For the reference to Pausanias' *hybris*, see p. 210.

35. Cf. Ruffing 2013 for this symbolic significance of "three hundred."

36. Cf. Cobet 1971: 64–66, 70. Stadter 2012a: 42–43 and 2012b: 2 observes that the references to the latest events, those of 431–430, concentrate in the last three books. That might have something to do with the time of their composition, as Stadter suggests, but might just be a consequence of the shift of focus in those books to the Greek world.

37. This point tends to be neglected in recent treatments, concentrating as they do on Herodotus' presumed view of Athens and its empire, but cf. Stadter 2012b and Blösel 2018.

38. Even the more generous "their work here is done" view leaves it open for the audience to reflect that Athenians were now turning against their Greek allies instead (Baragwanath 2008: 214–215 and Ubsdell 1983: 248–249 and 251–252 as, quoted there); but Herodotus leaves it to readers or listeners to draw that conclusion if they wish.

39. Cf. Dewald 1997: 79 = 2013: 398 on how differently Athenians and non-Athenians might respond to the end of the work.

40. Pelling 2006a: 101–103.

41. See Boedeker 2015 on this episode, esp. 108–109 on the "poetic/religious language" Herodotus uses to give it emphasis.

42. Thus Munson 2001: 190–191; cf. Hornblower and Pelling 2017: ad loc. Munson goes on to suggest (193–194) a hint that Athens might still be paying in the 420s for their own 480s sacrilege with the plague and the devastation of Attica: cf. Boedeker 2015: 110.

43. 6.97: cf. Fornara 1981.

44. Treves 1941 and Stadter 1989: 110 attribute this to the Samian campaign of 440–439; Fornara 1971a: 83 n. 12 to the historical counterpart of Thuc. 2.34–46, delivered by Pericles in 431–430. See also Munson 2001: 218–219; Pelling 2006a: 91–92; Grethlein 2006: 500–501.

45. On this, see Baragwanath and de Bakker 2012, esp. the editors' introduction.

46. See Hornblower 2013 on 5.37.2; Hornblower and Pelling 2017 on 6.9.2 and 6.43.3.

47. There may be further points of contact too with that debate. In Thucydides' version the Corinthians refer to their support of Athens when the rest of the Peloponnesian states wished to help Samos in 440–439 (1.40.5, 41.2). Luraghi 2013: 107 suggests that this might support the Corcyra-Corinth-Samos nexus in a reader's or listener's mind, and that it might also encourage a suspicion that the Corinthians were more influenced in 440–439 by anti-Samian feeling than these speakers admit. Hornblower 2010: 31 also speculates that 7.168.3, Corcyra's boasting that their fleet is second in size only to that of Athens, might recall the Corcyrean claim to have a fleet that ranks with those of Athens and Corinth (Thuc. 1.36.3)—or might even recall Thucydides' own version of that claim if Herodotus had heard an early recitation.

48. See also Baragwanath 2008: 220–222; Foster 2010: 59–60 n. 43; Bruzzone 2017: esp. 9–10. There may be other cases too: Raaflaub 2002 suggests that the debate of 7.8–11 and perhaps the Greek ambassadors' speech to Gelon at 7.157 might be influenced by an Athenian debate leading to the first Sicilian expedition of 427–424 (Thuc. 3.86, etc.); Hornblower 2010 wonders if the Potidaea narrative of 8.126–128 might be inspired not

just by the events of the late 430s and the siege of 430–429 (Thuc. 1.55–65, 2.70) but even by hearing a recitation by Thucydides himself.

49. Fornara 1971a: 57.

50. Cf. here Lateiner's observations about "analogy" as an important heuristic principle, 1989: 191–196.

51. Raaflaub 2009; cf. p. 298 n. 25.

52. Corcella 1984: 62–63 = 2013: 49–50. Corcella also observes (1984: 75–76 = 2013: 62) that 2.10.3 implies a similar ability to infer the future silting of the Acheloüs which "has *already* (ἤδη) turned half of the islands into mainland."

53. Here cf. also the insightful reflections of T. Harrison 2018.

54. Cf. Balot 2014: 82–84: see p. 284 n. 9.

55. Andrewes 1961; Cawkwell 2005: 142–143; Hornblower 1991–2008 on 2.7.1, 2.67, and 4.50.

56. Moles 1996.

57. Which is all that Moles claims: "Somewhere beyond the last pages of the *Histories* Nemesis awaits the Athenians, as she did Croesus" (1996: 277).

58. Dewald 1997: esp. 80–82 = 2013: 398–401; Baragwanath 2008: 107–108 and n. 71.

59. Baragwanath 2008: 1–2. Contrast Fornara 1971a: 60–61: "In a word, Thucydides wrote for the future, Herodotus for his contemporaries. . . . Herodotus directed himself *exclusively* [my italics] to his own generation."

60. A "prospective imperfect," Naiden 1999. Cf. Moles 1996: 278–279; de Jong 2013: 257–258; and Grethlein 2013: 222.

16. WHY INDEED?

1. Momigliano 1966c.
2. Momigliano 1966c: 114–115 (= 1960: 15–16).
3. Momigliano 1966c: 117 (= 1960: 18).
4. Momigliano 1966c: 118–119 (= 1960: 20–21).
5. Momigliano 1966c: 121–122 (= 1960: 22–23).
6. Gould 1989: 114–115.
7. More on this in Pelling 2000: ch. 5; see also above, p. 212.
8. Though this should not be overstated: cf. Gribble 1998, acknowledging that in some senses Herodotus' text is more "open" (45) but also suggesting that Thucydides' explicit interpretative formulations "establish a general scheme which can then be refined in detail" (56–58, cf. above, p. 121) and that readers are left to do much of this work, just as they are free to form their own reactions to characters such as Nicias and Alcibiades. Similarly Morrison 2006: 254.
9. Rood 1999; cf. Liotsakis 2016: esp. 75–82 on Sitalces (Thuc. 2.95–101).
10. Cf. esp. Hornblower 1991–2008: ii. 122–137.
11. For "piggybacking," cf. p. 55 and ch. 3(c).
12. Cf. Dewald, cited in p. 300 n. 58; Grethlein 2013: 221–223.
13. In a lecture of 1868: "Wir wollen durch Erfahrung nicht so wohl klug (für ein andermal), als vielmehr weise (für immer) werden" (Burckhardt 1982: 230)—though Burckhardt's "wisdom" would be of a rather different sort from Herodotus'. Cassirer 1950: 279 sets this formulation in the context of Burckhardt's aesthetic and spiritual thinking.

BIBLIOGRAPHY

Abbreviations normally follow the conventions of *L'Année Philologique*.

Abramenko, A. (2000). "Der Fremde auf dem Thron. Die letzte Verschwörung gegen Alexander d. Gr.," *Klio* 82: 361–378.
Achinstein, P. (1983). *The Nature of Explanation*. Oxford.
Adams, J. (1787). *A Defence of the Constitutions of Government of the United States of America*. London.
Alaux, J. (ed.). (2013). *Hérodote: Formes de Pensée, Figures de Récit*. Rennes.
Allan, W. (2006). "Divine justice and cosmic order in early Greek epic," *JHS* 126: 1–35.
Aly, W. (1921; repr. 1969). *Volksmärchen, Sage und Novelle bei Herodot und seinen Zeitgenossen*. Göttingen (repr. with corrections and an appendix by L. Huber, 1969).
Andrewes, A. (1961). "Thucydides and the Persians," *Hist.* 10: 1–18.
Anscombe, G. E. M. (1971; repr. Sosa and Tooly 1993). *Causality and Determination*. Cambridge. Repr. in E. Sosa (ed.), *Causation and Conditionals* (Oxford, 1975), 63–81, and in Sosa and Tooley 1993: 88–104.
Apfel, L. J. (2011). *The Advent of Pluralism: Diversity and Conflict in the Age of Sophocles*. Oxford.
Arafat, K. (2013). "Marathon in art," in Carey and Edwards 2013: 79–89.
Arrington, N. (2015). *Ashes, Images, and Memories: The Presence of the War Dead in Fifth-century Athens*. Oxford.
Asheri, D. (1993). "Erodoto e Bacide: Considerazioni sulla fede di Erodoto negli oraculi (Hdt. VIII 77)," in M. Sordi (ed.), *La profezia nel mondo antico* (Milano), 63–76.
Asheri, D. (1999). "Erodoto e Bisitun," in E. Gabba (ed.), *Presentazione e Scrittura della Storia: Storiografia, Epigrafi, Monumenti* (Atti del Convegno di Pontignano, aprile 1996: Como), 101–116.
Asheri, D., Lloyd, A. B., and Corcella, A. (2007). *A Commentary on Herodotus Books I–IV* (ed. O. Murray and A. Moreno: Italian originals 1988–2001). Oxford.
Assmann, A. (2011). *Cultural Memory and Western Civilization: Functions, Media, Archives* (German original 1999). Cambridge.
Assmann, J. (2011). *Cultural Memory and Early Civilization: Writing, Remembrance, and Political Imagination* (tr. D. H. Wilson: German original 1992). Cambridge.
Atkinson, R. E. (1978). *Knowledge and Explanation in History: An Introduction to the Philosophy of History*. Ithaca, NY.
Avery, H. C. (1972). "Herodotus' picture of Cyrus," *AJPh* 93: 529–546.
Backhaus, W. (1976). "Der Hellenen-Barbaren-Gegensatz und die Hippokratische Schrift περὶ ἀέρων ὑδάτων τόπων," *Hist.* 25: 170–185.

Badian, E. (1968). *Roman Imperialism in the Late Republic.* Oxford.
Badian, E. (1994). "Herodotus on Alexander I of Macedon: A study in some subtle silences," in Hornblower 1994: 107–130.
Bakker, E. J. (2002). "The making of history: Herodotus' *historiēs apodexis*," in Bakker, de Jong, and van Wees 2002: 3–32.
Bakker, E. J., de Jong, I. J. F., and van Wees, H. (eds.). (2002). *Brill's Companion to Herodotus.* Leiden, Boston, and Köln.
Balcer, J. M. (1987). *Herodotus and Bisitun: Problems in Ancient Persian Historiography* (*Historia* Einzelschr. 49). Stuttgart.
Balot, R. (2014). *Courage in the Democratic Polis: Ideology and Critique in Classical Athens.* Oxford.
Baragwanath, E. (2008). *Motivation and Narrative in Herodotus.* Oxford.
Baragwanath, E. (2012). "The mythic plupast in Herodotus," in J. Grethlein and C. B. Krebs (eds.), *Time and Narrative in Ancient Historiography: The 'Plupast' from Herodotus to Appian* (Cambridge): 35–56.
Baragwanath, E. (forthcoming). "History, ethnography, and aetiology in Herodotus' Libyan *logos*," in Fragoulaki and Constantakopoulou, forthcoming.
Baragwanath, E. and de Bakker, M. (eds.). (2012a). *Myth, Truth, and Narrative in Herodotus.* Oxford.
Baragwanath, E. and de Bakker, M. (2012b). "Introduction: Myth, truth, and narrative in Herodotus' *Histories*," in Baragwanath and de Bakker 2012a: 1–56.
Baragwanath, E. and Foster, E. (eds.) (2017). *Clio and Thalia: Attic Comedy and Historiography* (*Histos* Supplement 6). Newcastle-upon-Tyne.
Barker, E. T. E. (2009). *Entering the Agon: Dissent and Authority in Homer, Historiography and Tragedy.* Oxford.
Barker, E. T. E. and Pelling, C. (2016). "Space-travelling in Herodotus 5," in Barker, Bouzarovski, Pelling, and Isaksen 2016: 225–252.
Barker, E. T. E., Bouzarovski, S., Pelling, C., and Isaksen, L. (2016). *New Worlds out of Old Texts: Developing Techniques for the Spatial Analysis of Ancient Narratives.* Oxford.
Barnes, J. (1982). *The Presocratic Philosophers*, revised ed. (first ed. in two volumes 1979). London.
Barrett, W. S. (1964). *Euripides: "Hippolytos."* Oxford.
Barton, J. (2005). "Hippocratic explanations," in van der Eijk 2005b: 29–47.
Beck, I. (1971). *Die Ringkomposition bei Herodot und ihre Bedeutung für die Beweistechnik.* Hildesheim and New York.
Beebee, H., Hitchcock, C., and Menzies, P. (eds.). (2009). *The Oxford Handbook of Causation.* Oxford.
Beer, G. (2009). *Darwin's Plots: Evolutionary Narrative in Darwin, George Eliot and Nineteenth-Century Fiction* (3rd ed.; first ed. 1983). Cambridge.
Belloni, L. (2000). "Il silenzio della βασίλεια: *POxy* 2382 = *TrGF* II 664; Hdt. I 10–11)," in M. Capasso and S. Pernigotti (eds.), *Studium atque urbanitas: Miscellanea in onore di Sergio Daris* (Galatina), 101–110.
Benardete, S. (1969). *Herodotean Inquiries.* The Hague.
Berlin, I. and Hardy, H. (2002). *Liberty, incorporating "Four Essays on Liberty."* Oxford.
Bertelli, L. (2001). "Hecataeus: From genealogy to historiography," in Luraghi 2001a: 67–94.
Berve, H. (1967). *Die Tyrannis bei den Griechen.* 2 vols. Munich.

Bichler, R. (2018a). "Herodotus the geographer," in Bowie 2018a: 139–155.
Bichler, R. (2018b). "Herodotus' book 2 and the unity of the work," in Harrison and Irwin 2018a: 75–98.
Bischoff, H. (1932; repr. Marg 1965). "Der Warner bei Herodot." Diss. Marburg, partly reprinted in Marg 1965: 302–319.
Blondell, R. (2013). *Helen of Troy: Beauty, Myth, Devastation.* Oxford. See also Whitlock Blundell 1989.
Blösel, W. (2001). "The Herodotean picture of Themistocles: A mirror of fifth-century Athens," in Luraghi 2001a: 179–197.
Blösel, W. (2004). *Themistokles bei Herodot: Spiegel Athens im fünften Jahrhundert* (*Historia* Einzelschr. 183). Stuttgart.
Blösel, W. (2018). "Herodotus' allusions to the Sparta of his day," in Harrison and Irwin 2018a: 243–264.
Blundell, S. (1986). *The Origins of Civilization in Greek and Roman Thought.* London.
Boedeker, D. (1988; repr. Munson 2013). "Protesilaos and the end of Herodotus' *Histories*," *ClAnt* 7: 30–48, repr. in Munson 2013: i. 359–378.
Boedeker, D. (2003). "Pedestrian fatalities: The prosaics of death in Herodotus," in Derow and Parker 2003: 17–36.
Boedeker, D. (2011). "Persian gender relations as historical motives in Herodotus," in Rollinger, Truschnegg, and Bichler 2011: 211–235.
Boedeker, D. (2015). "Two tales of Spartan envoys," in Clark, Foster, and Hallett 2015: 103–115.
Boedeker, D. and Sider, D. (eds.). (2001). *The New Simonides: Contexts of Praise and Desire.* Oxford.
Bornitz, H.-F. (1968). *Herodot–Studien: Beiträge zum Verständnis der Einheit des Geschichtswerkes.* Berlin.
Bowie, A. M. (2007). *Herodotus: Histories Book VIII.* Cambridge.
Bowie, E. L. (1986). "Early Greek elegy, symposium, and public festival," *JHS* 106: 13–35.
Bowie, E. L. (2001). "Ancestors of historiography in early Greek elegiac and iambic poetry," in Luraghi 2001a: 45–66.
Bowie, E. L. (2010). "Marathon in fifth-century epigram," in K. Buraselis and K. Meidani (eds.), *Marathon: The Battle and the Deme* (Athens), 203–219.
Bowie, E. L. (ed.). (2018a). *Herodotus: Narrator, Scientist, Historian* (*Trends in Classics* 59). Berlin and Boston.
Bowie, E. L. (2018b). "The lesson of book 2," in Harrison and Irwin 2018a: 53–74.
Brand, M. (1980). "Simultaneous causation," in P. van Inwagen (ed.), *Time and Cause: Essays Presented to Richard Taylor* (Dordrecht, Boston, and London), 137–153.
Briant, P. (2002). *From Cyrus to Alexander* (tr. P. Daniels; French original 1996). Winona Lake, IN.
Bridges, E. (2015). *Imagining Xerxes: Ancient Perspectives on a Persian King.* London, New Delhi, New York, and Sydney.
Brock, R. (2013). *Greek Political Imagery from Homer to Aristotle.* London, New Delhi, New York, and Sydney.
Brooks, P. and Gewirtz, P. (eds.). (1996). *Law's Stories: Narrative and Rhetoric in the Law.* New Haven, CT.
Brosius, M. (1996). *Women in Ancient Persia.* Oxford.
Bruzzone, R. (2017). "The unfriendly Corcyraeans," *CQ* 67: 7–18.

Bryan, J. (2014). "*Eikos* in Plato's *Phaedrus*," in Wohl 2014: 30–46.
Buchan, J. (1929). "The causal and the casual in history." Cambridge.
Burckhardt, J. (1982). "Über das Studium der Geschichte," in *Weltgeschichtliche Betrachtungen* (ed. P. Ganz). München.
Burian, P. (2009). *See* Shapiro and Burian 2009.
Buxton, R. F. (2012). "Instructive irony in Herodotus: The Socles scene," *GRBS* 52: 559–586.
Cairns, D. L. (ed.). (2001). *Oxford Readings in Homer's "Iliad."* Oxford.
Cairns, D. L. (2003). "Ethics, ethology, terminology: Iliadic anger and the cross-cultural study of emotion," in S. Braund and G. W. Most (eds.), *Ancient Anger: Perspectives from Homer to Galen* (*YCS* 32, Cambridge), 11–49.
Caizzi, D. (1969). *Antiphontis Tetralogiae*. Milan.
Cambiano, G. (1983). "Pathologie et analogie politique," in Lasserre and Mudry 1983: 441–458.
Camp, J. McK. (2015). "Excavations in the Athenian Agora 2008–2012," *Hesperia* 84: 467–513.
Carey, C. (2013). "Marathon and the construction of the comic past," in Carey and Edwards 2013: 123–142.
Carey, C. (2016). "Homer and epic in Herodotus' book 7," in A. Efstathiou and I. Karamanou (eds.), *Homeric Receptions across Generic and Cultural Contexts. Trends in Classics—Supplementary volumes, 37* (Berlin and Boston), 71–89.
Carey, C. and Edwards, M. (eds.). (2013). *Marathon—2,500 years*: BICS Supp. 124, London.
Cartledge, P. (2002). *The Greeks: A Portrait of Self and Others* (2nd ed.; first ed. 1993). Oxford.
Cartledge, P. (2016). *Democracy: A Life*. Oxford.
Cartledge, P. and Harvey, D. (eds.). (1985). *CRUX: Essays in Greek History Presented to G. E. M. de Ste Croix*. London.
Cassirer, E. (1950). *The Problem of Knowledge: Philosophy, Science, and History since Hegel*. New Haven, CT.
Cataudella, Q. (1957). "Sulla cronologia del cosidetto 'Frammento di Gige,'" in *Studi in onore di A. Calderini e R. Paribeni* (Milan) ii: 103–116.
Cawkwell, G. L. (1975). "Thucydides judgment of Periclean strategy," *YClS* 24: 53–70.
Cawkwell, G. L. (1997). *Thucydides and the Peloponnesian War*. London.
Cawkwell, G. L. (2005). *The Greek Wars: The Failure of Persia*. Oxford.
Ceccarelli, P. (1993). "La fable des poissons de Cyrus (Hérodote I, 141)," *Mètis* 8: 29–57.
Ceccarelli, P. (2016). "Map, catalogue, narrative: Representations of the Aegean space," in Barker, Bouzarovski, Pelling, and Isaksen 2016: 61–80.
Chiasson, C. C. (2001). "Scythian androgyny and environmental determinism in Herodotus and the Hippocratic περὶ ἀέρων ὑδάτων τόπων," *SyllClass* 12: 33–73.
Chiasson, C. C. (2012). "Myth and truth in Herodotus' Cyrus *logos*," in Baragwanath and de Bakker 2012a: 213–231.
Christ, M. R. (1994; repr. Munson 2013). "Herodotean kings and historical inquiry," *ClAnt* 13, 167–202, repr. in Munson 2013: i. 212–250.
Clark, A. (2016). *Surfing Uncertainty: Prediction, Action, and the Embodied Mind*. Oxford.
Clark, C. A., Foster, E., and Hallett, J. P. (eds.). (2015). *Kinesis: The Ancient Depiction of Gesture, Motion, and Emotion: Essays for Donald Lateiner*. Ann Arbor, MI.

Clarke, K. (1999). *Between Geography and History: Hellenistic Constructions of the Roman World.* Oxford.
Clarke, K. (2008). *Making Time for the Past: Local History and the Polis.* Oxford.
Clarke, K. (2018). *Shaping the Geography of Empire: Man and Nature in the "Histories" of Herodotus.* Oxford.
Clarke, M. (2002). "Spartan *atē* at Thermopylae: Semantics and ideology at Herodotus, *Histories* 7.223.4," in Powell and Hodkinson 2002: 63–84.
Clarke, M. J., Currie, B. G. F., and Lyne, R. O. A. M. (eds.). (2006). *Epic Interactions: Perspectives on Homer, Virgil, and the Epic Tradition Presented to Jasper Griffin.* Oxford.
Cobet, J. (1971). *Herodots Excurse und die Frage der Einheit seines Werkes* (Historia Einzelschr. 17). Wiesbaden.
Cobet, J. (1977). "Wann wurde Herodots Darstellung der Perserkriege publiziert?" *Hermes* 105: 2–27.
Cobet, J. (1987). "Philologische Stringenz und die Evidenz fur Herodots Publikationsdatum," *Athen.* 65: 508–511.
Collard, C., Cropp, M. J., and Gibert, J. (2004). *Euripides: Selected Fragmentary Plays* ii. Warminster.
Collingwood, R. G. (1946). *The Idea of History.* Oxford.
Collingwood, R. G. (1998). *An Essay on Metaphysics* (2nd ed.; first ed. 1940). Oxford.
Corcella, A. (1984; repr. Munson 2013). *Erodoto e l'analogia*, partly tr. and repr. in Munson 2013: ii. 45–77. Palermo.
Craik, E. M. (1998). *Hippocrates: Places in Man.* Oxford.
Craik, E. M. (2015). *The "Hippocratic" Corpus: Content and Context.* London and New York.
Crane, G. S. (1996). "The prosperity of tyrants: Bacchylides, Herodotus, and the contest for legitimacy," *Arethusa* 29, 57–85.
Croally, N. (1994). *Euripidean Polemic: The Trojan Women and the Function of Tragedy.* Cambridge.
Cropp, M. J. (2004). *See* Collard, Cropp, and Gibert 2004.
Currie, B. (2012). "Hesiod on human history," in Marincola, Llewellyn-Jones, and Maciver 2012: 37–64.
D'Alessio, G. B. (2004). "Textual fluctuation and cosmic streams: Ocean and Acheloios," *JHS* 124: 16–37.
Davidson, D. (1967; repr. Sosa and Tooley 1993). "Causal relations," *Journal of Philosophy* 64: 691–703, repr. in Sosa and Tooley 1993: 75–87.
Davies, M. (1989). "Sisyphus and the invention of religion ('Critias' *TrGF* 1 (43) F 19 = B 25 DK)," *BICS* 36: 16–32.
Davies, M. and Finglass, P. J. (2014). *Stesichorus: The Poems.* Cambridge.
Dawson, W. R., with notes by Harvey, F. D. (1986). "Herodotus as a medical writer," *BICS* 33: 87–96.
De Bakker, M. (2012). "Herodotus' Proteus: Myth, history, enquiry and story-telling," in Baragwanath and de Bakker 2012a: 107–126.
De Jong, I. J. F. (2004). "Herodotus," in I. J. F. de Jong, R. Nünlist, and A. M. Bowie (eds.), *Narrators, Narratees and Narrative in Ancient Greek Literature* i (Leiden), 101–114.
De Jong, I. J. F. (2012). "The Helen *logos* and Herodotus' fingerprint," in Baragwanath and de Bakker 2012a: 127–142.

De Jong, I. J. F. (2013). "Narratological aspects of the *Histories* of Herodotus," in Munson 2013: i. 253–291: revised and abridged version of French original, *Lalies* 19 (1999), 217–274.
De Romilly, J. (1963). *Thucydides and Athenian Imperialism* (tr. P. Thody: French original 1947). Oxford.
De Sélincourt, A. (1996). *Herodotus: "The Histories,"* revised and annotated by J. Marincola. London.
Deichgräber, K. (1971). *Die Epidemien und das Corpus Hippocraticum* (2nd ed.; first ed. 1933). Berlin.
Demandt, A. (1972). "Die Ohren des falschen Smerdis," *Iranica Antiqua* 9: 94–101.
Demont, P. (1993). "Die Epideixis über die *Techne* im V. und IV. Jhdt.," in W. Kullmann and J. Althoff (eds.), *Vermittlung und Tradierung von Wissen in der gr. Kultur* (Tübingen), 181–209.
Demont, P. (2013). "Le *nomos*-roi: Hérodote, III, 38," in Alaux 2013: 37–45.
Demont, P. (2018). "Herodotus on health and disease," in Bowie 2018: 175–196.
Depuydt, L. (1995). "Murder in Memphis: The story of Cambyses' wounding of the Apis bull (ca. 523 B.C.E.)," *JNES* 54: 119–126.
Derow, P. S. and Parker, R. (eds.). (2003). *Herodotus and His World*. Oxford.
Dershowitz, A. M. (1996). "Life is not a dramatic narrative," in Brooks and Gewirtz 1996: 99–105.
Detienne, M. (1996). *The Masters of Truth in Archaic Greece* (French original 1967, 2nd ed. 1981: tr. J. Lloyd). New York.
Dewald, C. (1981; repr. Munson 2013). "Women and culture in Herodotus' *Histories*," in H. P. Foley (ed.), *Reflections of Women in Antiquity* (New York): 91–125, repr. in Munson 2013: ii. 151–179.
Dewald, C. (1993). "Reading the world: The interpretation of objects in Herodotus' *Histories*," in R. Rosen and J. Farrell (eds.), *Nomodeiktes: Festschrift for Martin Ostwald* (Ann Arbor, MI), 55–70.
Dewald, C. (1997; repr. Munson 2013). "Wanton kings, pickled heroes, and gnomic founding fathers: Strategies of meaning at the end of Herodotus' *Histories*," in Roberts, Dunn, and Fowler 1997: 62–82, repr. in Munson 2013: i. 379–401.
Dewald, C. (1999). "The figured stage: Focalizing the initial narratives of Herodotus and Thucydides," in N. Felson, D. Konstan, and T. Falkner (eds.), *Contextualizing Classics: Ideology, Performance, Dialogue. Essays in Honor of John J. Peradotto* (Lanham, MD), 221–252.
Dewald, C. (2003). "Form and content: The question of tyranny in Herodotus," in K. A. Morgan (ed.), *Popular Tyranny: Sovereignty and Its Discontents in Ancient Greece* (Austin, TX), 25–58.
Dewald, C. (2011). "Happiness in Herodotus," *SO* 85: 18–39.
Dewald, C. (2012). "Myth and legend in Herodotus' first book," in Baragwanath and de Bakker 2012a: 59–85.
Dewald, C. and Kitzinger, R. (2015). "Speaking silences in Herodotus and Sophocles," in Clark, Foster, and Hallett 2015: 86–102.
Dewald, C. and Marincola, J. (eds.). (2006). *The Cambridge Companion to Herodotus*. Cambridge.
Diels, H. (1879). *Doxographi graeci*. Berlin.
Diels, H. (1887). "Herodotos und Hekataios," *Hermes* 22: 411–444.
Dihle, A. (1977). "Das Satyrspiel 'Sisyphos,'" *Hermes* 105: 28–42.

Diller, H. (1932; repr. Diller 1971). ὄψις ἀδήλων τὰ φαινόμενα, *Hermes* 67, 14–42, repr. in Diller 1971: 119–143.
Diller, H. (1934). *Wanderarzt und Aitiologe* (*Phil.* Supplementband 26.3). Leipzig.
Diller, H. (1955; repr. Diller 1971). Review of Weidauer 1954, *Gnom.* 27: 9–14, repr. in Diller 1971: 482–488.
Diller, H. (1956; repr. Diller 1971). "Zwei Erzählungen des Lyders Xanthos," in *Navicula Chiloniensis. Studia Philologica Felici Jacoby . . . oblata* (Leiden), 66–78, repr. in Diller 1971: 451–463.
Diller, H. (1971). *Kleine Schriften zur antiken Literatur*. Munich.
Dillery, J. (2018). "Making *logoi*: Herodotus' book 2 and Hecataeus of Miletus," in Harrison and Irwin 2018a: 17–52.
Dodds, E. R. (1973). "The ancient concept of progress," in E. R. Dodds, *The Ancient Concept of Progress and Other Essays* (Oxford), 1–25.
Dorati, M. (2011). "Travel writing, ethnographical writing, and the representation of the edges of the world in Herodotus," in Rollinger, Truschnegg, and Bichler 2011: 273–312.
Dover, K. J. (1950; repr. 1988). "The chronology of Antiphon's speeches," *CQ* 44: 44–60, repr. in K. J. Dover, *The Greeks and Their Legacy* (Oxford, 1988), 13–35.
Dray, W. H. (1964). *Philosophy of History*. Englewood Cliffs, NJ.
Drews, R. (1973). *The Greek Accounts of Eastern History*. Cambridge, MA.
Drexler, H. (1972). *Herodot-Studien*. Hildesheim.
Drexler, H. (1976). *Thukydides-Studien*. Hildesheim.
Dueck, D. (2005). "The parallelogram and the pinecone: Definition of geographical shapes in Greek and Roman geography on the evidence of Strabo," *AncSoc* 35: 19–57.
Dunn, F. (2005). "*On Ancient Medicine* and its intellectual context," in van der Eijk 2005b: 49–67.
Easterling, P. E. (1973). "Presentation of character in Aeschylus," *G&R* 20: 3–19.
Easterling, P. E. (1985). "Anachronism in Greek tragedy," *JHS* 105: 1–10.
Easterling, P. E. (1997). "Constructing the heroic," in Pelling 1997a: 21–37.
Edwards, M. W. (1991). *The "Iliad": A Commentary. Volume V: Books 17–20*. Cambridge.
Ellis, A. (2016). "Fictional truth and factual truth in Herodotus," in I. Ruffell and L. Hau (eds.), *Truth and History in the Ancient World: Pluralising the Past* (Edinburgh), 104–129.
Erbse, H. (1956). "Das erste Satz im Werke Herodots," in H. Erbse (ed.), *Festschrift Bruno Snell* (Munich): 209–222.
Erbse, H. (1979). *Ausgewählte Schriften zur klassischen Philologie*. Berlin and New York.
Erbse, H. (1992). *Studien zum Verständnis Herodots*. Berlin and New York.
Evans, J. A. S. (1979). "Herodotus' publication date," *Athen.* 57: 145–149.
Evans, J. A. S. (1987). "Herodotus 9.73.3 and the publication date of the *Histories*," *CPh* 82: 226–228.
Evans, J. A. S. (1991). *Herodotus: Explorer of the Past*. Princeton, NJ.
Farrar, C. (1988). *The Origins of Democratic Thinking: The Invention of Politics in Classical Athens*. Cambridge.
Fehling, D. (1989). *Herodotus and His "Sources": Citation, invention, and narrative art* (tr. J. G. Howie; German original 1971). ARCA 21, Leeds.
Ferrini, M. F. (1996). "Τὸ ὅμοιον/τὸ ἐναντίον. Un aspetto del rapporto tra Corpus Hippocraticum e filosofia," in Wittern and Pellegrin 1996: 15–36.
Fish, S. (1967). *Surprised by Sin: The reader in "Paradise Lost."* Berkeley and Los Angeles.

Fisher, N. R. E. (1992). *Hybris: A Study in the Values of Honour and Shame in Ancient Greece*. Warminster.
Flory, S. (1978). "Laughter, tears, and wisdom in Herodotus," *AJPh* 99: 145–153.
Flower, H. I. (1991; repr. Munson 2013). "Herodotus and Delphic traditions about Croesus," in Flower and Toher 1991: 57–77, repr. in Munson 2013: i. 124–153.
Flower, M. A. (2006). "Herodotus and Persia," in Dewald and Marincola 2006: 274–289.
Flower, M. A., and Marincola, J. (2002). *Herodotus, "Histories": Book IX*. Cambridge.
Flower, M. A., and Toher, M. (eds.). (1991). *Georgica: Greek Studies in Honour of George Cawkwell*. BICS Supp. 58. London.
Fludernik, M. (1996). *Towards a "Natural" Narratology*. London and New York.
Focke, F. (1927). *Herodot als Historiker* (Tübinger Beiträge zur Altertumswissenschaft 1). Stuttgart.
Fornara, C. (1971a). *Herodotus: An Interpretative Essay*. Oxford.
Fornara, C. (1971b). "Evidence for the date of Herodotus' publication," *JHS* 91: 25–34.
Fornara, C. (1981). "Herodotus' knowledge of the Archidamian War," *Hermes* 109: 149–156.
Fornara, C. (1983). *Translated Documents of Greece & Rome* i: *Archaic Times to the End of the Peloponnesian War* (2nd ed.), Cambridge, 1983.
Forsdyke, S. (1999). "From aristocratic to democratic ideology and back again: The Thrasybulus anecdote in Herodotus' *Histories* and Aristotle's *Politics*," *CPh* 94: 361–372.
Forsdyke, S. (2001). "Athenian democratic ideology and Herodotus' *Histories*," *AJP* 122: 329–358.
Foster, E. (2010). *Thucydides, Pericles, and Periclean Imperialism*. Cambridge.
Foster, E. and Lateiner, D. (eds.). (2012). *Thucydides and Herodotus*. Oxford.
Fowler, R. L. (1996). "Herodotos and his contemporaries," *JHS* 116: 62–87.
Fowler, R. L. (1998). "Genealogical thinking, Hesiod's *Catalogue*, and the creation of the Hellenes," *PCPS* 44: 1–19.
Fowler, R. L. (2001–2013). *Early Greek Mythography* i–ii (= *EGM*). Oxford.
Fowler, R. L. (2001). "Early *historiē* and literacy," in Luraghi 2001a: 95–115.
Fowler, R. L. (2003). "Herodotus and Athens," in Derow and Parker 2003: 305–318.
Fowler, R. L. (2006). "Herodotus and his prose predecessors," in Dewald and Marincola 2006: 29–45.
Fowler, R. L. (2015). "History," in E. Eidinow and J. Kindt (eds.). *The Oxford Handbook of Ancient Greek Religion* (Oxford), 195–209.
Fraenkel, E. (1950). *Aeschylus: Agamemnon*. Oxford.
Fragoulaki, M. (2013). *Kinship in Thucydides: Intercommunal Ties and Historical Narrative*. Oxford.
Fragoulaki, M. and Constantakopoulou, C. (eds.). (forthcoming). *Shaping Memory: Ancient Greek Historiography, Poetry, and Epigraphy* (*Histos*, Supplementary Volume).
Frede, M. (1987). *Essays in Ancient Philosophy*. Oxford.
Friedman, R. (2006). "Location and dislocation in Herodotus," in Dewald and Marincola 2006: 165–177.
Friedrich, W. H. (1973; repr. 1977). "Der Tod des Tyrannen," *AuA* 18: 97–129. (Repr. in his *Dauer im Wechsel* [Göttingen, 1977], 336–375.)
Frisch, P. (1968). *Die Träume bei Herodot*. Meisenheim.
Gagarin, M. (1997). *Antiphon: The Speeches*. Cambridge.
Gagarin, M. (2002). *Antiphon the Athenian: Oratory, Law, and Justice in the Age of the Sophists*. Austin, TX.

Gagarin, M. (2003). "Telling stories in Athenian law," *TAPA* 133: 197–207.
Gagarin, M. (2008). *Writing Greek Law*. Cambridge.
Gagarin, M. (2014). "*Eikos* arguments in Athenian forensic oratory," in Wohl 2014: 15–29.
Gagné, R. (2013). *Ancestral Fault in Ancient Greece*. Cambridge.
Gallie, W. B. (1968). *Philosophy and the Historical Understanding* (2nd ed.; first ed. 1964). New York.
Garrett, D. (2009). "Hume," in Beebee, Hitchcock, and Menzies 2009: 73–91.
Garvie, A. F. (2009). *Aeschylus: "Persae."* Oxford.
Gera, D. (1993). *Xenophon's "Cyropaedia": Style, Genre, and Literary Technique*. Oxford.
Giangiulio, M. (2001). "Constructing the past: Colonial traditions and the writing of history," in Luraghi 2001a: 116–137.
Gianotti, G. F. (1996). "Hérodote, les fleuves et l'histoire," in M.-L. Desclos (ed.), *Réflexions contemporaines sur l'Antiquité classique* (Grenoble), 157–187.
Gill, C. and Wiseman, T. P. (eds.). (1993). *Lies and Fiction in the Ancient World*. Exeter.
Goldhill, S. (1986). *Reading Greek Tragedy*. Cambridge.
Goldhill, S. (1988). "Battle narrative and politics in Aeschylus' *Persae*," *JHS* 108: 189–193.
Goldhill, S. (2002). *The Invention of Prose* (Greece & Rome New Surveys in the Classics 32). Oxford.
Gomme, A. W., Andrewes, A., and Dover, K. J. (1970 and 1981). *A Historical Commentary on Thucydides* iv–v. Oxford.
Gorman, R. J. and Gorman, V. B. (2014). *Corrupting Luxury in Ancient Greek Literature*. Ann Arbor, MI.
Gould, J. (1985; repr. Gould 2001). "On making sense of Greek religion," in P. E. Easterling and J. V. Muir (eds.), *Greek Religion and Society* (Cambridge), 1–33, repr. in Gould 2001: 203–234.
Gould, J. (1989). *Herodotus*. London.
Gould, J. (1991; repr. Gould 2001). "Give and take in Herodotus" (15th J. L. Myres memorial lecture), repr. in Gould 2001: 283–303. Oxford.
Gould, J. (1994; repr. Gould 2001). "Herodotus and religion," in Hornblower 1994: 91–106, repr. in Gould 2001: 359–377 and in Munson 2013: ii, 183–197.
Gould, J. (2001). *Myth, Ritual, Memory, and Exchange: Essays in Greek Literature and Culture*. Oxford.
Gray, V. J. (1997). "Reading the rise of Peisistratus: Herodotus 1.56–68," *Histos* 1: 128–153: http://research.ncl.ac.uk/histos/Histos_BackIssues1997.html.
Greenblatt, S. (1991). *Marvelous Possessions: The Wonder of the New World*. Oxford.
Greenwood, E. (2018). "Surveying greatness and magnitude in Herodotus," in Harrison and Irwin 2018a: 163–186.
Gregory, A. (2016). *Anaximander: A Re-assessment*. London.
Gregory, J. (1999–2000). "Comic elements in Euripides," *ICS* 24–25: 59–75.
Grensemann, H. (1979). "Das 24. Kapitel von *De aeribus, aquis, locis* und die Einheit der Schrift," *Hermes* 107: 423–441.
Grethlein, J. (2006). "The manifold uses of the epic past: The embassy scene in Herodotus 7.153–63," *AJPh* 127: 485–509.
Grethlein, J. (2008). "Eine Herodoteische Deutung der sizilischen Expedition (Thuc. 7.87.5f)?" *Hermes* 136: 129–142.
Grethlein, J. (2009). "How not to do history: Xerxes in Herodotus' *Histories*," *AJP* 130: 195–218.

Grethlein, J. (2010). *The Greeks and Their Past: Poetry, Oratory and History in the Fifth Century BCE.* Cambridge.
Grethlein, J. (2011). "Herodot und Xerxes: Meta-Historie in den Historien," in Rollinger, Truschnegg, and Bichler 2011: 103–122.
Grethlein, J. (2013). *Experience and Teleology in Ancient Historiography: "Futures Past" from Herodotus to Augustine.* Cambridge.
Gribble, D. (1998). "Narrator interventions in Thucydides," *JHS* 118: 41–67.
Gribble, D. (1999). *Alcibiades and Athens: A Study in Literary Presentation.* Oxford.
Griffin, J. (1977; repr. Cairns 2001). "The epic cycle and the uniqueness of Homer," *JHS* 97: 39–53, partly repr. in Cairns 2001: 365–384.
Griffin, J. (1980). *Homer on Life and Death.* Oxford.
Griffin, J. (1990). "Die Ursprünge der Historien Herodots," in W. Ax (ed.), *Memoria Rerum Veterum: Neue Beiträge zur antiken Historiographie und Alten Geschichte* (Stuttgart, 1990), 51–82, tr. as "The emergence of Herodotus," *Histos* 8 (2014), 1–24.
Griffin, J. (2006). "Herodotus and tragedy," in Dewald and Marincola 2006: 46–59.
Griffith, M. (2008). "Greek middlebrow drama," in M. Revermann and P. Wilson (eds.), *Performance, Iconography, Reception: Studies in Honour of Oliver Taplin* (Oxford), 59–87.
Griffiths, A. (1989). "Was Kleomenes mad?" in A. Powell (ed.), *Classical Sparta: Techniques behind Her Success* (London), 51–78.
Griffiths, A. (1999). "Euenios the negligent nightwatchman (Herodotus 9.92–6)," in R. Buxton (ed.), *From Myth to Reason? Studies in the Development of Greek Thought* (Oxford), 169–182.
Griffiths, A. (2001). "Kissing cousins: Some curious cases of adjacent material in Herodotus," in Luraghi 2001a: 161–178.
Griffiths, J. G. (1966). "Hecataeus and Herodotus on 'a gift of the river,'" *JNES* 25(1): 57–61.
Grmek, M. D. (1989). *Diseases in the Ancient Greek World* (tr. M. Muellner and L. Muellner: French original 1983). Baltimore and London.
Grofman, B. (1993). "The 2500th anniversary of democracy: Lessons of Athenian democracy (editor's introduction)," *PS: Political Science and Politics* 26: 471–474.
Gruen, E. S. (ed.). (2011a). *Cultural Identity in the Ancient Mediterranean.* Los Angeles.
Gruen, E. S. (2011b). "Herodotus and Persia," in Gruen 2011a: 67–85.
Guthrie, W. K. C. (1962–1981). *A History of Greek Philosophy* i–vi. Cambridge.
Hall, E. (1989). *Inventing the Barbarian: Greek Self-definition through Tragedy.* Oxford.
Hall, E. (1996). *Aeschylus: "Persians."* Warminster.
Hankinson, R. J. (2008). "Reason, cause, and explanation in Presocratic philosophy," in P. Curd and D. W. Graham (eds.), *The Oxford Handbook of Presocratic Philosophy* (Oxford), 434–457.
Hansen, M. H. (1989). "Was Athens a democracy? Popular rule, liberty, and equality in ancient and modern political thought," *Royal Danish Academy of Sciences and Letters*, hist.-fil. Meddelelser 59.
Hansen, M. H. (1994). "The 2500th anniversary of Cleisthenes' reforms and the tradition of Athenian democracy," in Osborne and Hornblower 1994: 25–37.
Hansen, W. (1996). "The protagonist on the pyre: Herodotean legend and modern folktale," *Fabula* 37: 272–285.
Harder, R. (1953; repr. Marg 1965). "Herodot 1.8.3," in G. E. Mylonas and D. Raymond (eds.), *Studies Presented to David Moore Robinson on His Seventieth Birthday*

(St. Louis, MO), ii. 446–449, repr. in *Kleine Schriften* (ed. Marg 1960), 208–211 and in Marg 1965: 370–374.
Harris, I. (2013). "Berlin and his critics," in 2013 reprint of Berlin and Hardy 2002: 349–373.
Harrison, E. B. (1972). "The south frieze of the Nike temple and the Marathon painting in the Painted Stoa," *AJArch* 76: 353–378.
Harrison, T. (2000). *Divinity and Herodotus: The Religion of Herodotus*. Oxford.
Harrison, T. (2003). "Upside down and back to front," in R. Matthews and C. Roemer (eds.), *Ancient Perspectives on Egypt* (London), 145–155.
Harrison, T. (2011a). *Writing Ancient Persia*. London and New York.
Harrison, T. (2011b). "The long arm of the king," in Rollinger, Truschnegg, and Bichler 2011: 65–74.
Harrison, T. (2018). "The moral of history," in Harrison and Irwin 2018a: 335–355.
Harrison, T. and Irwin, E. (2018a). *Interpreting Herodotus*. Oxford.
Harrison, T. and Irwin, E. (2018b). "Introduction," in Harrison and Irwin 2018a: 1–16.
Hart, H. L. A. and Honoré, T. (1985). *Causation in the Law* (2nd ed.; first ed. 1959). Oxford.
Hartog, F. (1988). *The Mirror of Herodotus* (tr. J. Lloyd; French original 1980, with a second edition published in 1991). Berkeley and Los Angeles.
Hartog, F. (1989). "Écriture, généalogies, archives, histoire en Grèce ancienne," in A. de Pury (ed.), *Histoire et Conscience Historique dans les Civilisations du Proche-Orient ancient*, Actes du Colloque de Cartigny 1986 (Leuven), 121–132.
Haussker, F. (2017). "The *ekthesis* of Cyrus the Great: A case study of heroicity versus bastardy in classical Athens," *CCJ* 63: 103–117.
Havelock, E. A. (1976). *Origins of Western Literacy*. Toronto.
Havelock, E. A. (1982). *The Literate Revolution in Greece and Its Cultural Context*. Princeton, NJ.
Havelock, E. A. (1986). *The Muse Learns to Write: Reflections on Orality and Literacy from Antiquity to the Present*. New Haven, CT.
Hawes, G. H. (2014). *Rationalizing Myth in Antiquity*. Oxford.
Heinimann, F. (1945). *Nomos und Physis* (Schweizerische Beiträge zur Altertumswissenschaft 1). Basel.
Hellmann, F. (1934). *Herodots Kroisos-logos* (*Neue Philologische Untersuchungen* 9). Berlin.
Henderson, J. (2012). "Old comedy and popular history," in J. Marincola, L. Llewellyn-Jones, and Maciver, C. (eds.), *Greek Notions of the Past in the Archaic and Classical Eras: History without Historians* (Edinburgh), 144–159.
Henry, D. (2015). "Holding for the most part: The demonstrability of moral facts," in D. Henry and K. M. Nielsen (eds.), *Bridging the Gap between Aristotle's Science and Ethics* (Cambridge), 169–189.
Herington, J. (1991). "The closure of Herodotus' *Histories*," *ICS* 16: 149–160.
Heubeck, A. (1980). "Πρόφασις und keine Ende (zu Thuk. 1.23)," *Glotta* 58: 222–236.
Heuss, A. (1973). "Motive von Herodots lydischem Logos," *Hermes* 101: 385–419.
Hobden, F. (2013). *The Symposion in Ancient Greek Society and Thought*. Cambridge.
Hohti, P. (1975). "Über die Notwendigkeit bei Herodot," *Arctos* 9: 31–37.
Hohti, P. (1976). "Die Schuldfrage der Perserkriege in Herodots Geschichtswerk," *Arctos* 10: 37–48.
Hollmann, A. (2011). *Master of Signs: Signs and the Interpretation of Signs in Herodotus' Histories*. Cambridge MA and London.

Holmes, B. (2010). *The Symptom and the Subject: The Emergence of the Physical Body in Ancient Greece*. Princeton, NJ.
Hölscher, U. (1958). "Karl Reinhardt," *Gnom.* 30: 557–560.
Hölscher, U. (1993). "Karl Reinhardt (1886–1958)," *Eikasmos* 4: 295–304.
Homeyer, H. (1962). "Zu den Anfängen der griechischen Biographie," *Philologus* 106: 75–85.
Hommel, H. (1981). "Herodots Einleitungssatz: Ein Schlüssel zur Analyse des Gesamtwerks?" in G. Kurz, D. Müller, and W. Nicolai (eds.), *Gnomosyne: Menschliches Denken und Handeln in der frühgriechischen Literatur. Festschrift für Walter Marg zum 70. Geburtstag* (Munich), 271–287.
Hornblower, S. (1991–2008). *A Commentary on Thucydides* i–iii. Oxford.
Hornblower, S. (ed.). (1994). *Greek Historiography*. Oxford.
Hornblower, S. (2010). "Thucydides' awareness of Herodotus or Herodotus' awareness of Thucydides?" in V. Fromentin, S. Gotteland, and P. Pascal (eds.), *Ombres de Thucydide: La réception de l'historien depuis l'antiquité jusqu'au début du XXe siècle* (Pessac), 27–33.
Hornblower, S. (2013). *Herodotus: "Histories" Book V*. Cambridge.
Hornblower, S. (2015). *Lykophron: Alexandra*. Oxford.
Hornblower, S. and Pelling, C. (2017). *Herodotus: "Histories" Book VI*. Cambridge.
How, W. W. and Wells, J. (1912). *A Commentary on Herodotus* i–ii. Oxford.
Huber, L. (1965). *Religiöse und politische Beweggründe des Handelns in der Geschichtsschreibung des Herodot*. Tübingen.
Hude, C. (1927). *Herodoti Historiae* i–ii (Oxford Classical Text; 3rd ed., first ed. 1908). Oxford.
Huemer, M. and Kovitz, B. (2003). "Causation as simultaneous and continuous," *Philosophical Quarterly* 53: 556–565.
Hume, D. (1739/1740). *A Treatise of Human Nature*. London.
Hume, D. (1762). *History of England* (new ed.; first ed. 1754–1761), London.
Hutchinson, G. O. (2001). *Greek Lyric Poetry: A Commentary on Selected Larger Pieces*. Oxford.
Huxley, G. (1973). "The date of Pherekydes of Athens," *GRBS* 14: 137–143.
Immerwahr, H. R. (1954). "Historical action in Herodotus," *TAPA* 85: 16–45.
Immerwahr, H. R. (1956; repr. Munson 2013). "Aspects of historical causation in Herodotus," *TAPA* 87: 241–280, repr. in Munson 2013: i. 157–193.
Immerwahr, H. R. (1960). "*Ergon*: History as monument in Herodotus," *AJP* 81: 261–290.
Immerwahr, H. R. (1966). *Form and Thought in Herodotus* (APA Monographs 23). Cleveland, OH.
Irwin, E. (2007). "'What's in a name?' and exploring the comparable: Onomastics, ethnography, and *kratos* in Thrace (5.1–2 and 3–10)," in Irwin and Greenwood: 2007: 41–87.
Irwin, E. (2013). "The hybris of Theseus" and the date of the Histories," in Ruffing and Dunsch 2013: 7–93.
Irwin, E. (2014). "Ethnography and empire: Homer and the Hippocratics in Herodotus' Ethiopian *logos*," *Histos* 8: 25–75.
Irwin, E. (2018). "The end of the *Histories* and the end of the Atheno-Peloponnesian wars," in Harrison and Irwin 2018a: 279–334.

Irwin, E. and Greenwood, E. (eds.). (2007). *Reading Herodotus: A Study of the Logoi in Book 5 of Herodotus' "Histories."* Cambridge.
Jacoby, F. (1913; repr. Jacoby 1956). "Herodotos," *R–E* Supplementband ii: 205–520, repr. in Jacoby 1956: 3–164.
Jacoby, F. (1923–). *Fragmente der griechischen Historiker.* Leiden.
Jacoby, F. (1956). *Griechische Historiker.* Stuttgart.
Jones, C. P. (1999). *Kinship Diplomacy in the Ancient World.* Cambridge, MA, and London.
Jouanna, J. (1980). "Politique et médecine. La problématique du changement dans le *Régime des maladies aiguës* et chez Thucydide (livre VI)," in M. Grmek and F. Robert (eds.), *Hippocratica—Actes du Colloque hippocratique de Paris, 4–9 Septembre 1978* (Paris), 299–319, tr. as "Politics and medicine. The problem of change in regimen in acute diseases and Thucydides (Book 6)," in Jouanna 2012: 21–38.
Jouanna, J. (1984). "Rhétorique et médecine dans la *Collection Hippocratique*. Contribution à l'étude de la rhétorique au Ve siècle," *REG* 97: 26–44, tr. as "Rhetoric and medicine in the Hippocratic corpus. A contribution to the history of rhetoric in the fifth century," in Jouanna 2012: 39–53.
Jouanna, J. (1999). *Hippocrates* (tr. M. B. DeBevoise; Fr. original 1992). Baltimore and London.
Jouanna, J. (2005). "Cause and crisis in historians and medical writers of the classical period," in van der Eijk 2005b: 3–27.
Jouanna, J. (2012). *Greek Medicine from Hippocrates to Galen: Selected Papers* (tr. N. Allies). Leiden and Boston.
Kallet, L. (1998). "Accounting for culture in fifth-century Athens," in D. Boedeker and K. A. Raaflaub (eds.), *Democracy, Empire, and the Arts in Fifth-century Athens* (Cambridge, MA, and London), 43–58.
Kannicht, R. (1969). *Euripides: "Helena"* i–ii. Heidelberg.
King, H. (1989). "The daughter of Leonides: Reading the Hippocratic corpus," in A. Cameron (ed.), *History as Text: The Writing of Ancient History* (London), 11–32.
Kingsley, S. (forthcoming). *Herodotus and the Presocratics: Inquiry and Intellectual Culture in the Fifth Century.* Cambridge.
Kinzl, K. H. (1978). Δημοκρατία, *Gymnasium* 85: 11–27 and 312–326.
Kirk, G. S., Raven, J. E., and Schofield, M. (1983). *The Presocratic Philosophers* (2nd ed.; first ed. 1957). Cambridge.
Kistler, M. (2006). *Causation and the Laws of Nature.* London.
Klees, H. (1965). *Die Eigenart des griechischen Glaubens an Orakel und Seher* (Tübinger Beiträge zur Altertumswissenschaft 43). Stuttgart.
Kleinknecht, H. (1940; repr. Marg 1965). "Herodot und Athen: 7.139/8.140–4," *Hermes* 75: 241–264, repr. in Marg 1965: 541–573.
Köhnken, A. (1980; repr. Köhnken 2006). "Herodots falscher Smerdis," *WJb* 6a: 39–50, repr. in Köhnken 2006: 423–435.
Köhnken, A. (1988; repr. Köhnken 2006). "Der dritte Traum des Xerxes bei Herodot," *Hermes* 116: 24–40, repr. in Köhnken 2006: 436–451.
Köhnken, A. (1990; repr. Köhnken 2006). "Der listige Oibares," *Rh.Mus.* 133: 115–137, repr. in Köhnken 2006: 452–471.
Köhnken, A. (2006). *Darstellungsziele und Erzählstrategien in antiken Texten,* ed. A. Bettenworth. Berlin.

Konijnendijk, R. (2016): "Mardonius' senseless Greeks," *CQ* 66: 1–12.
Konstantakos, I. M. (2016). "Cambyses and the sacred bull (Hdt. 3.27–29 and 3.64: History and legend," in Liotsakis and Farrington 2016: 37–72.
Kouloumentas, S. (2014). "The body and the polis: Alcmaeon on health and disease," *British Journal for the History of Philosophy* 22: 867–887.
Kovacs, D. (1998). "Euripides, *Troades* 1050: Was Helen overweight?" *CQ* 48: 553–556.
Kraus, C. S. (ed.). (1999). *The Limits of Historiography: Genre and Narrative in Ancient Historical Texts*. Leiden.
Krischer, T. (1965). "Herodots Prooimion," *Hermes* 93: 159–167.
Kühn, J.-H. (1956). *System- und Methodenprobleme im Corpus Hippocraticum* (*Hermes* Einzelschr. 11). Wiesbaden.
Kuhrt, A. (2007). *The Persian Empire: A Corpus of Sources from the Achaemenid Empire*. London and New York.
Kullmann, W. (2001). "Past and future in the *Iliad*," in D. Cairns (ed.), *Oxford Readings in Homer's "Iliad"* (Oxford), 385–408. First published as "Vergangenheit und Zukunft in der Ilias," *Poetica* 2 (1968), 15–37, and tr. by Leofranc Holford-Strevens.
Kümmel, H. M. (1967). *Ersatzrituale für den hethitischen König*. Wiesbaden.
Kümmel, H. M. (1968). "Ersatzkönig und Sündenbock," *ZATW* 80: 291–318.
Kurke, L. (1991). *The Traffic in Praise: Pindar and the Poetics of Social Economy*. Ithaca, NY, and London.
Kurke, L. (1999). *Coins, Bodies, Games, and Gold*. Princeton, NJ.
Kurke, L. (2011). *Aesopic Conversations: Popular Tradition, Cultural Dialogue, and the Invention of Greek Prose*. Princeton, NJ, and Oxford.
Kurke, L. (2013). "Imagining Chorality: Wonder, Plato's Puppets, and Moving Statues," in A.-E. Peponi (ed.), *Performance and Culture in Plato's "Laws"* (Cambridge), 123–170.
Kurz, G., Müller, D., and Nicolai, W. (1981). *Gnomosyne: Menschliches Denken und Handeln in der frühgriechischen Literatur. Festschrift für Walter Marg zum 70. Geburtstag*. Munich.
Laird, A. (2001). "Ringing the changes on Gyges: Philosophy and the formation of fiction in Plato's *Republic*," *JHS* 121: 12–29.
Lakoff, G. and Johnson, M. (2003). *Metaphors We Live By* (2nd ed.; first ed. 1980). Chicago and London.
Lang, M. L. (1984). *Herodotean Narrative and Discourse*. Cambridge, MA.
Lang, M. L. (1987). "Commentary on Nagy and Boedeker," *Arethusa* 20: 203–207.
Langholf, V. (1990). *Medical Theories in Hippocrates: Early Texts and the "Epidemics."* Berlin and New York.
Larsen, J. A. O. (1948). "Cleisthenes and the development of democracy at Athens," in M. R. Konvitz and A. E. Murphy (eds.), *Essays in Political Theory Presented to George H. Sabine* (Port Washington, NY, and London), 1–16.
Larsen, J. A. O. (1954). "The judgment of antiquity on democracy," *CPh* 49: 1–14.
Larson, S. (2006). "Kandaules' wife, Masistes' wife: Herodotus' narrative strategy in suppressing names of women (Hdt. 1.8–12 and 9.108–113)," *CJ* 101: 225–244.
Laskaris, J. (2002). *The Art Is Long: "On Sacred Disease" and the Scientific Tradition*. Leiden and Boston.
Lasserre, F. and Mudry, P. (eds.). (1983). *Formes de pensée dans la Collection Hippocratique* (Actes du IVe Colloque International hippocratique, 21–26 Septembre 1981). Geneva.

Lateiner, D. (1977). "No laughing matter: A literary tactic in Herodotus," *TAPA* 107: 173–182.
Lateiner, D. (1984; repr. Munson 2013). "Herodotean historiographical patterning: 'The Constitutional Debate,'" *QS* 20: 257–284, repr. in Munson 2013: i: 194–211.
Lateiner, D. (1986). "The empirical element in the methods of early Greek medical writers and Herodotus: A shared epistemological response," *Antichthon* 20: 1–20.
Lateiner, D. (1989). *The Historical Method of Herodotus*. Toronto.
Lateiner, D. (2005). "The pitiers and the pitied in Herodotus and Thucydides," in Sternberg 2005: 67–97.
Lattimore, R. (1939): "The wise adviser in Herodotus," *CPh* 34: 24–35.
Lattimore, R. (1958). "The composition of the 'History' of Herodotus," *CPh* 53: 9–21.
Lenfant, D. (1996). "Ctésias et Hérodote," *REG* 109: 348–380.
Lévy, E. (2005). "Isonomia," in U. Bultrighini (ed.), *Democrazia e antidemocrazia nel mondo greco* (Alexandria), 119–137.
Lewis, B. (1980). *The Sargon Legend* (American Schools of Oriental Research Dissertation Series 4). Cambridge, MA.
Lewis, D. K. (1973a). *Counterfactuals*. Oxford.
Lewis, D. K. (1973b; repr. Sosa and Tooley 1993). "Causation," *Journal of Philosophy* 70: 556–567, repr. in Sosa and Tooley 1993: 193–204 and with extensive Postscript in Lewis 1986: 159–213.
Lewis, D. K. (1986). *Philosophical Papers* ii. Oxford.
Lewis, D. K. (2000). "Causation as influence," *Journal of Philosophy* 97: 182–197.
Lewis, D. M. (1977). *Sparta and Persia*. Leiden.
Lewis, S. (1998). "Pythius the Lydian," *Histos* 2: 185–191.
Liotsakis, V. (2016). "Narrative defects in Thucydides and the development of ancient Greek historiography," in Liotsakis and Farrington 2016: 73–98.
Liotsakis, V. and Farrington, S. (eds.). (2016). *The Art of History: Literary Perspectives on Greek and Roman Historiography*. Berlin and Boston.
Llewellyn-Jones, L. and Robson, J. (2010). *Ctesias' History of Persia: Tales of the Orient*. London and New York.
Lloyd, A. B. (1975–1986). *Herodotus: Book II* i–iii. Leiden.
Lloyd, A. B. (1990). "Herodotus on Egyptians and Libyans," in Nenci and Reverdin 1990: 215–253.
Lloyd, G. E. R. (1966). *Polarity and Analogy: Two Types of Argumentation in early Greek Thought*. Cambridge.
Lloyd, G. E. R. (1975; repr. Lloyd 1991). "Alcmaeon and the early history of dissection," *Sudhoffs Archiv* 59: 113–147, repr. in G. E. R. Lloyd 1991: 164–193.
Lloyd, G. E. R. (1979). *Magic, Reason and Experience*. Cambridge.
Lloyd, G. E. R. (1983). *Science, Folklore and Ideology: Studies in the Life Sciences in Ancient Greece*. Cambridge.
Lloyd, G. E. R. (1991). *Methods and Problems in Greek Science*. Cambridge.
Lloyd, M. (1984). "Croesus' priority: Herodotus 1.5.3," *LCM* 9.1: 11.
Lloyd, M. (1992). *The Agon in Euripides*. Oxford.
Lloyd, S. (1978). *Suez 1956: A Personal Account*. London.
Lloyd-Jones, H. (1971). *The Justice of Zeus*. Berkeley, Los Angeles, and London.
Lo Presti, R. (2010). "'Visible' and 'invisible' as categories of thought in the Hippocratics: *On Regimen, On Ancient Medicine, On the Art*," *Quaderni del Ramo d'Oro* 3: 164–192.

Lohmann, J. (1952). "Das Verhältnis des Abendländischen Menschen zur Sprache," *Lexis* 3: 5–50.

Long, T. (1987). *Repetition and Variation in the Short Stories of Herodotus* (Beiträge zur klassischen Philologie 179). Frankfurt am Main.

Longrigg, J. (1993). *Greek Rational Medicine: Philosophy and Medicine from Alcmaeon to the Alexandrians*. London and New York.

Loraux, N. (1986). *The Invention of Athens* (tr. A. Sheridan; French original 1981). Cambridge, MA, and London.

Luraghi, N. (ed.) (2001a). *The Historian's Craft in the Age of Herodotus*. Oxford.

Luraghi, N. (2001b). "Local knowledge in Herodotus' *Histories*," in Luraghi 2001a: 138–160.

Luraghi, N. (2013). "The stories before the *Histories*: Folktale and traditional narrative in Herodotus," in Munson 2013: i. 88–112 (Italian original in M. Giangulio [ed.], *Erodoto e il "modello erodoteo": Formazione e tramissione delle tradizioni storiche in Grecia* [Trento, 2005], 61–90).

Mackie, J. L. (1974). *The Cement of the Universe: A Study of Causation*. Oxford.

Mackinney, L. (1964). "The concept of isonomia in Greek medicine," in Mau and Schmidt 1964: 79–88.

Macleod, C. W. (1977; repr. Macleod 1983). "Thucydides' Plataean debate," *GRBS* 18: 227–246, repr. in Macleod 1983: 103–122.

Macleod, C. W. (1983). *Collected Essays*. Oxford.

Mann, J. E. (2012). *Hippocrates: "On the Art of Medicine"* (Studies in Ancient Medicine 39). Leiden and Boston.

Mansfeld, J. (2013). "The body politic: Aëtius on Alcmaeon on *isonomia* and *monarchia*," in V. Harte and M. Lane (eds.), *Politeia in Greek and Roman Philosophy* (Cambridge), 78–95.

Marg, W. (1953; repr. Marg 1965). "'Selbstsicherheit' bei Herodot," in G. E. Mylonas and D. Raymond (eds.), *Studies Presented to David Moore Robinson on His Seventieth Birthday* (St. Louis, MO), ii. 1103–1111, repr. in Marg 1965: 290–301.

Marg, W. (ed.). (1965). *Herodot: Eine Auswahl aus der neueren Forschung* (2nd ed.). Munich.

Marincola, J. (1999). "Genre, convention, and innovation in Greco-Roman historiography," in Kraus 1999: 281–324.

Marincola, J. (2006). "Herodotus and the poetry of the past," in Dewald and Marincola 2006: 13–28.

Marincola, J. (2007). "Odysseus and the historians," *SyllClass* 18: 1–70, partly repr. as "Herodotus and Odysseus" in Munson 2013: ii. 109–132.

Marincola, J. (2012). "Introduction: A past without historians," in Marincola, Llewellyn-Jones, and Maciver 2012: 1–13.

Marincola, J. (2015). "Defending the divine: Plutarch on the gods of Herodotus," *Histos* Supp. 4: 41–83.

Marincola, J. (2016a). "Plutarch's source for *Aristides* 11.3–8," *Mnem.* 69: 853–860.

Marincola, J. (2016b). "History without malice: Plutarch rewrites the battle of Plataea," in J. Priestley and V. Zali (eds.), *Brill's Companion to the Reception of Herodotus in Antiquity and Beyond* (Leiden and Boston): 101–119.

Marincola, J. (2018): "Ομηρικώτατος? Battle narratives in Herodotus," in Bowie 2018: 3–24.

Marincola, J., Llewellyn-Jones, L., and Maciver, C. (eds.). (2012). *Greek Notions of the Past in the Archaic and Classical Eras: History without Historians*. Edinburgh.

Martin, R. (1981). *Tacitus*. London.
Mash, M. C. (2017). "Humour, ethnography, and embassy: Herodotus, *Histories* 3.17–25 and Aristophanes, *Acharnians* 61–133," in Baragwanath and Foster 2017: 67–97.
Masson, O. (1950). "A propos d'un rituel hittite pour la lustration d'une armée: Le rite de purification par le passage entre les deux parties d'une victime," *Revue de l'histoire des religions* 137: 5–25.
Mau, J. and Schmidt, E. G. (eds.). (1964). *Isonomia*. Berlin.
McPhee, B. D. (2018). "A mad king in a mad world," *Histos* 12: 71–96.
Meier, M., Patzek, B., Walter, U., and Wiesehöfer, J. (2004). *Deiokes: König der Meder. Eine Herodot-Episode in ihren Kontexten* (Oriens et Occidens 7). Stuttgart.
Meiggs, R. (1982). *Trees and Timber in the Ancient Mediterranean World*. Oxford.
Mikalson, J. (2002). "Religion in Herodotus," in Bakker, de Jong, and van Wees 2002: 187–198.
Mikalson, J. (2003). *Herodotus and Religion in the Persian Wars*. Chapel Hill, NC, and London.
Mill, J. S. (1846). *A System of Logic*. New York.
Mill, J. S. (1859). *On Liberty*. London.
Millender, E. G. (2002a). "Nómos Déspotēs: Spartan obedience and Athenian lawfulness in fifth-century thought," in V. B. Gorman and E. Robinson (eds.), *Oikistes: Studies in Constitutions, Colonies, and Military Power in the Ancient World* (Leiden), 33–59.
Millender, E. G. (2002b). "Herodotus and Spartan despotism," in Powell and Hodkinson 2002: 1–61.
Mink, L. (1987). *Historical Understanding*. Ithaca, NY.
Mitchell, B. M. (1975). "Herodotus and Samos," *JHS* 95: 75–91.
Mitchell, L. G. (1997). *Greeks Bearing Gifts: The Public Use of Private Relationships in the Greek World, 435–323 B.C.* Cambridge.
Moles, J. L. (1993). "Truth and untruth in Herodotus and Thucydides," in Gill and Wiseman 1993: 88–121.
Moles, J. L. (1996). "Herodotus warns the Athenians," *Proceedings of the Liverpool Latin Seminar* 9: 259–284.
Moles, J. L. (2002). "Herodotus and Athens," in Bakker, de Jong, and van Wees 2002: 33–52.
Möller, A. (2001). "The beginning of chronography: Hellanicus' *Hiereiai*," in Luraghi 2001a: 241–262.
Momigliano, A. (1966a). *Studies in Historiography*. London.
Momigliano, A. (1966b). "The place of Herodotus in the history of historiography," in Momigliano 1966a: 127–142; first published in *History* 43 (1958), 1–13; also repr. in his *Secondo contributo alla storia degli studi classici* (Rome, 1960), 29–44, and German tr. in Marg 1965: 137–156.
Momigliano, A. (1966c). "Some observations on causes of war in ancient historiography," in Momigliano 1966a: 112–126; first published in *Acta Congressus Madvigiani* (1958), i. 199–211; also repr. in his *Secondo contributo alla storia degli studi classici* (Rome, 1960), 13–27.
Momigliano, A. (1979). "Persian empire and Greek freedom," in A. Ryan (ed.), *The Idea of Freedom: Essays in Honour of Isaiah Berlin* (Oxford), 139–151, repr. in his *Settimo Contributo alla Storia degli Studi e del Mondo Antico* (Rome, 1984), 61–75.
Momigliano, A. (1993). *The Development of Greek Biography* (2nd ed.). Cambridge, MA, and London.

Montemaggi, V. (2016). *Reading Dante's "Commedia" as Theology.* Oxford.
Morello, R. (2002). "Livy's Alexander digression (9.17–19): Counterfactuals and apologetics," *JRS* 92: 62–83.
Morgan, K. A. (2012). "Plato and the stability of history," in Marincola, Llewellyn-Jones, and Maciver 2012: 227–252.
Morrison, J. V. (2006). "Interaction of speech and narrative in Thucydides," in A. Rengakos and A. Tsakmakis (eds.), *Brill's Companion to Thucydides* (Leiden and Boston), 251–277.
Moyer, I. S. (2002). "Herodotus and an Egyptian mirage: The genealogies of the Theban priests," *JHS* 122: 70–90, revised and expanded version in Munson 2013: ii. 292–320.
Moyer, I. S. (2011). *Egypt and the Limits of Hellenism.* Cambridge.
Müller, C. W. (2006). *Legende–Novelle–Roman: Dreizehn Kapitel zur erzählenden Prosaliteratur in der Antike.* Göttingen.
Müller, D. (1981). "Herodot—Vater des Empirismus?" in Kurz, Müller, and Nicolai 1981: 299–318.
Mumford, S. and Anjum, R. L. (2013). *Causation: A Very Short Introduction.* Oxford.
Munson, R. V. (1988). "Artemisia in Herodotus," *ClAnt* 7: 91–106.
Munson, R. V. (2001). *Telling Wonders: Ethnographic and Political Discourse in the Work of Herodotus.* Ann Arbor, MI.
Munson, R. V. (2009; repr. Munson 2013). "Who are Herodotus' Persians?" *CW* 102: 457–470, repr. in Munson 2013, ii. 321–335.
Munson, R. V. (2013). *Oxford Readings in Herodotus* i–ii. Oxford.
Müri, W. (1947; repr. Müri 1976). "Bemerkungen zur hippokratischen Psychologie," *Festschrift für Edouard Tieche . . . zum 70. Geburtstag* (Bern), 71–85, repr. in Müri 1976: 100–114.
Müri, W. (1950; repr. Müri 1976). "Der Maßgedanke bei griechischen Ärzten," *Gymnasium* 57: 182–201, repr. in Müri 1976: 115–138.
Müri, W. (1976). *Griechische Studien* (ed. E. Vischer: Schweizerische Beiträge zur Altertumswissenschaft 14). Basel.
Murray, D. (2016). "The waters at the end of the world: Herodotus and Mesopotamian cosmic geography," in Barker, Bouzarovski, Pelling, and Isaksen 2016: 47–60.
Murray, O. (1987: repr. Luraghi 2001a). "Herodotus and oral history," in Sancisi-Weerdenburg and Kuhrt 1987: 93–115, repr. in Luraghi 2001a: 16–44.
Myres, J. L. (1953). *Herodotus, Father of History.* Oxford.
Nagy, G. (1987). "Herodotus the Logios," *Arethusa* 20: 175–184.
Nagy, G. (1990). *Pindar's Homer: The Lyric Possession of an Epic Poet.* Baltimore and London.
Nagy, G. (2018). "Herodotus on queens and courtesans of Egypt," in Bowie 2018: 109–122.
Naiden, F. S. (1999). "The prospective imperfect in Herodotus," *HSCP* 99: 135–149.
Neer, R. (2010). *The Emergence of the Classical Style in Greek Sculpture.* Chicago and London.
Nenci, G. and Reverdin, O. (eds.). (1990). *Hérodote et les peuples non grecs* (Entretiens Hardt 35). Vandoeuvres–Geneva.
Nesselrath, H.-G. (2014). "Ancient comedy and historiography: Aristophanes meets Herodotus," in S. D. Olson (ed.), *Ancient Comedy and Reception: Essays in Honor of Jeffrey Henderson* (Berlin and Boston), 51–61.

Nicolai, R. (1997). "*Pater semper incertus*: Appunti su Ecateo," *QUCC* 56: 143–164.
Olson, S. D. (2002). *Aristophanes: "Acharnians."* Oxford.
Osborne, R. and Hornblower, S. (eds.). (1994): *Ritual, Finance, Politics: Athenian Democratic Accounts Presented to David Lewis.* Oxford.
Osmers, M. (2013). *"Wir aber sind damals und jetzt immer die gleichen": Vergangenheitsbezüge in der polisübergreifenden Kommunikation der klassischen Zeit* (Historia Einzelschr. 226). Stuttgart.
Ostwald, M. P. (1969). *Nomos and the Beginnings of the Athenian Democracy.* Oxford.
Pagel, K.-A. (1927). "Die Bedeutung des aitiologischen Momentes für Herodots Geschichtsschreibung." Diss. Berlin.
Papakonstantinou, Z. (2015). *Lawmaking and Adjudication in Archaic Greece.* London.
Papazarkadas, N. (2014): "Two new epigrams from Thebes," in N. Papazarkadas (ed.), *The Epigraphy and History of Boeotia: New Finds, New Prospects* (Leiden and Boston), 233–251.
Parke, H. W. (1984). "Croesus and Delphi," *GRBS* 25, 209–232.
Parker, R. (1983). *Miasma: Pollution and Purification in Early Greek Religion.* Oxford.
Parker, R. (1998). "Pleasing thighs: Reciprocity in Greek religion," in C. Gill, N. Postlethwaite, and R. Seaford (eds.), *Reciprocity in Ancient Greece* (Oxford), 105–125.
Paton, W. R., Walbank, F. W., Habicht, C., and Olson, S. D. (1922–1927, revised 2010–2012). *Polybius* (Loeb Classical Library, 6 volumes). Cambridge, MA.
Patterson, O. (1991). *Freedom in the Making of Western Culture.* London.
Paul, L. A. (2009). "Counterfactual theories," in Beebee, Hitchcock, and Menzies 2009: 158–184.
Pearson, L. (1952). "*Prophasis* and *aitia*," *TAPA* 83: 205–223.
Peirano, I. (2010). "Hellenized Romans and barbarized Greeks: Reading the end of Dionysius of Halicarnassus, *Antiquitates Romanae*," *JRS* 100: 32–53.
Pelliccia, H. (1992). "Sappho 16, Gorgias' *Helen*, and the preface to Herodotus' *Histories*," *YCS* 76: 63–84.
Pelling, C. (ed.). (1990a). *Characterization and Individuality in Greek Literature.* Oxford.
Pelling, C. (1990b). "Childhood and personality in Greek biography," in Pelling 1990a: 213–244.
Pelling, C. (1991). "Thucydides' Archidamus and Herodotus' Artabanus," in Flower and Toher 1991: 120–142.
Pelling, C. (1992; repr. Pelling 2002a). "Plutarch and Thucydides," in P. A. Stadter (ed.), *Plutarch and the Historical Tradition* (London and New York), 10–40, repr. in Pelling 2002a: 117–141.
Pelling, C. (1996). "The urine and the vine: Astyages' dreams (Herodotus 1.107–108)," *CQ* 46: 68–77.
Pelling, C. (ed.). (1997a). *Greek Tragedy and the Historian.* Oxford.
Pelling, C. (1997b). "Aeschylus' *Persae* and history," in Pelling 1997a: 1–19.
Pelling, C. (1997c; repr. Munson 2013). "East is East and West is West—or are they? National stereotypes in Herodotus," *Histos* 1 (http://research.ncl.ac.uk/histos/Histos_BackIssues1997.html), 51–66: repr. in Munson 2013 ii. 360–379.
Pelling, C. (1997d). "Tragical dreamer: Some dreams in the Roman historians," *G&R* 44: 197–213.
Pelling, C. (1997e). "Biographical history? Cassius Dio on the early principate," in M. J. Edwards and S. Swain (eds.), *Portraits: Biographical Representation in the Greek and Latin Literature of the Roman Empire* (Oxford): 117–144.

Pelling, C. (1997f; repr. Pelling 2002a). "Is death the end? Closure in Plutarch's *Lives*," in Roberts, Dunn, and Fowler 1997: 228–250, repr. in Pelling 2002a: 365–386.
Pelling, C. (1999a). "Epilogue," in Kraus 1999: 325–360.
Pelling, C. (1999b). "Modern fantasy and ancient dreams," in C. Sullivan and B. White (eds.), *Writing and Fantasy* (London and New York), 15–31.
Pelling, C. (2000). *Literary Texts and the Greek Historian*. London.
Pelling, C. (2002a). *Plutarch and History*. Swansea.
Pelling, C. (2002b). "Speech and action: Herodotus' debate on the constitutions," *PCPS* 48: 123–158.
Pelling, C. (2006a). "Homer and Herodotus," in Clarke, Currie, and Lyne 2006: 75–104.
Pelling, C. (2006b). "Educating Croesus: Talking and learning in Herodotus' Lydian *Logos*," *ClAnt* 25: 141–173.
Pelling, C. (2006c). "Speech and narrative in the *Histories*," in Dewald and Marincola 2006: 103–121.
Pelling, C. (2007a). "Aristagoras," in Irwin and Greenwood 2007: 179–201.
Pelling, C. (2007b). "Ion's *Epidemiai* and Plutarch's Ion," in V. Jennings and A. Katsaros (eds.), *The World of Ion of Chios* (Leiden and Boston), 75–109.
Pelling, C. (2007c). Review of Meier, Patzek, Walter, and Wiesehöfer 2004, *CR* 57: 29–30.
Pelling, C. (2011). "Herodotus and Samos," *BICS* 54: 1–19.
Pelling, C. (2012a). "Aristotle's *Rhetoric*, the *Rhetorica ad Alexandrum*, and the Speeches in Herodotus and Thucydides," in Foster and Lateiner 2012: 281–315.
Pelling, C. (2012b). "Commentary," in Marincola, Llewellyn-Jones, and Maciver 2012: 359–365.
Pelling, C. (2013a). "Herodotus' Marathon," in Carey and Edwards 2013: 23–34.
Pelling, C. (2013b). "Historical explanation and what didn't happen: The virtues of virtual history," in Powell 2013: 3–24.
Pelling, C. (2015). "The rhetoric of *The Roman Revolution*," *Syllecta Classica* 26: 207–247.
Pelling, C. (2016a). "Herodotus, Polycrates—and maybe Stesimbrotus too?" *JHS* 136: 113–120.
Pelling, C. (2016b). "Herodotus' Persian stories: Narrative shape and historical interpretation," *Syllecta Classica* 27: 65–92.
Pelling, C. (2018). "Causes in competition: Herodotus and Hippocratics," in Bowie 2018a: 199–222.
Pelling, C. (forthcoming a). "Fifth-century preliminaries," in K. de Temmerman (ed.), *The Oxford Companion to Ancient Biography* (Oxford).
Pelling, C. (forthcoming b). "Stereotyping Sparta, stereotyping Athens: Herodotus, Thucydides—and Plutarch," in L. Athanassaki and F. B. Titchener (eds.), *Plutarch's Cities*.
Pelling, C. (forthcoming c). "Waiting for Herodotus: The mindsets of 425 BCE," to appear in J. Baines, T. Rood, S. Chen, and H. van der Blom (eds.), *Historical Consciousness and Historiography* (Sheffield).
Pelling, C. (forthcoming d). "Homer and the question why," in Fragoulaki and Constakopoulou (forthcoming).
Pendrick, G. J. (2002). *Antiphon the Sophist: The Fragments*. Cambridge.
Perry, B. E. (1937). "On the early Greek ability for viewing things separately," *TAPA* 68: 403–427.

Petrovic, A. (2013). "Marathon in pre-Herodotean sources: On Marathon verse-inscriptions (*IG* I³ 503/4; *SEG* LVI 430)," in Carey and Edwards 2013: 45–61.
Pietsch, C. (2001). "Ein Spielwerk in den Händen der Götter? Zur geschichtlichen Kausalität des Menschen bei Herodot am Beispiel der Kriegsentscheidung des Xerxes (Hist. VII.5–19)," *Gymnasium* 108: 205–221.
Pohlenz, M. (1937; repr. 1961). *Herodot, der erste Geschichtschreiber des Abendlandes* (repr. 1961). Leipzig.
Pontier, P. (2013). "Une question de point de vue: Quelques remarques sur Gygès, d'Hérodote à Platon," in Alaux 2013: 117–130.
Popper, K. R. (1960). *The Poverty of Historicism* (2nd ed.; first ed. 1957). London.
Popper, K. R. (2002). *The Logic of Scientific Discovery* (14th ed.; first ed. 1959). London.
Posner, R. A. (1988). *Law and Literature: A Misunderstood Relation.* Cambridge, MA, and London.
Powell, A. (ed.). (2013). *Hindsight in Greek and Roman History.* Swansea.
Powell, A. and Hodkinson, S. (eds.). (2002). *Sparta: Beyond the Mirage.* Swansea and London.
Powell, J. E. (1938; repr. 1977). *A Lexicon to Herodotus.* Cambridge (repr. Hildesheim).
Priestley, J. (2014). *Herodotus and Hellenistic Culture: Literary Studies in the Reception of the Histories.* Oxford.
Provencal, V. R. (2015). *Herodotus' Sophist Kings: Persians as Other in Herodotus.* London and New York.
Purves, A. (2010). *Space and Time in Ancient Greek Narrative.* Cambridge.
Raaflaub, K. A. (1979). "Polis tyrannos: Zur Entstehung einer politischen Metaphor," in G. W. Bowersock, W. Burkert, and M. C. J. Putnam (eds.), *Arktouros: Hellenic Studies Presented to Bernard M. W. Knox on the Occasion of his 65th Birthday* (Berlin and New York), 237–252.
Raaflaub, K. A. (1987). "Herodotus, political thought, and the meaning of history," *Arethusa* 20: 221–248.
Raaflaub, K. A. (1989). "Contemporary perceptions of democracy in fifth-century Athens," *C&M* 40: 33–70.
Raaflaub, K. A. (2002). "Herodot und Thukydides: Persischer Imperialismus im Lichte der athenischen Sizilienpolitik," in N. Ehrhardt and L.-M. Günther (eds.), *Widerstand–Anpassung–Integration: Die griechische Staatenwelt und Rom. Festschrift für Jürgen Deininger* (Stuttgart), 11–40.
Raaflaub, K. A. (2004). *The Discovery of Freedom in Ancient Greece* (tr. R. Franciscono: German original 1985). Chicago.
Raaflaub, K. A. (2009). "Learning from the enemy: Athenian and Persian 'instruments of empire,'" in J. Ma, N. Papazarkadas, and R. Parker (eds.), *Interpreting the Athenian Empire* (London), 89–124.
Raaflaub, K. A. (2011). "Persian army and warfare in the mirror of Herodotus' interpretation," in Rollinger, Truschnegg, and Bichler 2011: 5–37.
Rawlings, H. R. (1975). *A Semantic Study of PROPHASIS to 400 B.C.* (*Hermes* Einzelschr. 33). Wiesbaden.
Redfield, J. M. (1985; repr. Munson 2013). "Herodotus the tourist," *CPh* 80: 97–118, repr. in Munson 2013: ii. 267–291.
Reinhardt, K. (1939; repr. Reinhardt 1960). "Gyges und sein Ring," *Europaische Revue* 15: 384–391; repr. in Reinhardt 1960: 133–174 (page numbers refer to that reprinting).

Reinhardt, K. (1940; repr. Reinhardt 1960 and Marg 1965). "Herodots Persergeschichten," *Geistige Überlieferung. Ein Jahrbuch* (Berlin), 138–184; repr. in Reinhardt 1960: 133–174 (page numbers refer to that reprinting) and in Marg 1965: 320–369.
Reinhardt, K. (1955; repr. Reinhardt 1960). "Akademisches aus zwei Epochen," *Die Neue Rundschau* 66: 37–58; repr. in Reinhardt 1960: 380–401.
Reinhardt, K. (1960). *Vermächtnis der Antike*. Göttingen.
Reinhardt, K. (1979). *Sophocles* (tr. H. Harvey and D. Harvey: 3rd ed. of German original 1947). Oxford.
Rhodes, P. J. (1972). *The Athenian Boule*. Oxford.
Rhodes, P. J. (2003). "Nothing to do with democracy: Athenian drama and the *polis*," *JHS* 123: 104–119.
Rhodes, P. J. (2018). "Herodotus and democracy," in Harrison and Irwin 2018a: 265–277.
Rieks, R. (1975). "Eine tragische Erzählung bei Herodot (*Hist.* 1.34–45)," *Poetica* 7: 23–44.
Roberts, D. H., Dunn, F. M., and Fowler, D. P. (eds.). (1997). *Classical Closure: Reading the End in Greek and Latin Literature*. Princeton, NJ.
Robertson, N. (1976). "The Thessalian expedition of 480 B.C.," *JHS* 96: 100–120.
Roettig, K. (2010). *Die Träume des Xerxes: Zum Handeln der Götter bei Herodot*. Nordhausen.
Roisman, H. M. (2005). "Old men and chirping cicadas in the *Teichoskopia*," in R. J. Rabel (ed.), *Approaches to Homer, Ancient and Modern* (Swansea), 105–118.
Rollinger, R. (2000). "Herodotus and the intellectual heritage of the ancient Near East," in S. Aro and R. M. Whiting (eds.), *The Heirs of Assyria* (Helsinki), 65–83.
Rollinger, R. (2013). "Dareios und Xerxes an den Rändern der Welt und die Inszenierung von Welthersschaft—Altorientalisches bei Herodot," in Ruffing and Dunsch 2013: 95–116.
Rollinger, R. (2018). "Herodotus and the transformation of ancient Near Eastern motifs: Darius I, Oebares, and the neighing horse," in Harrison and Irwin 2018a: 125–148.
Rollinger, R., Truschnegg, B., and Bichler R. (eds.). (2011). *Herodot und das Persische Weltreich / Herodotus and the Persian Empire* (Classica et Orientalia 3). Wiesbaden.
Romm, J. (1992; repr. Munson 2013). *The Edges of the Earth in Ancient Thought*, partly repr. in Munson 2013: ii. 21–43. Princeton, NJ.
Romm, J. (1998). *Herodotus*. New Haven, NJ, and London.
Romm, J. (2006). "Herodotus and the natural world," in Dewald and Marincola 2006: 178–191.
Rood, T. (1998). *Thucydides: Narrative and Interpretation*. Oxford.
Rood, T. (1999). "Thucydides' Persian Wars," in Kraus 1999: 141–168.
Rood, T. (2006). "Herodotus and foreign lands," in Dewald and Marincola 2006: 290–305.
Rood, T. (2010). "Herodotus' proem: Space, time, and the origins of International Relations," Ἀριάδνη 16: 43–74.
Root, M. C. (2011). "Embracing ambiguity in the world of Athens and Persia," in Gruen 2011a: 86–96.
Rosen, R. (2016). "Towards a Hippocratic anthropology: *On Ancient Medicine* and the origins of humans," in L. Dean-Jones and R. Rosen (eds.), *Ancient Concepts of the Hippocratic: Papers presented at the XIIIth International Hippocrates Colloqium, Austin, Texas, August 2008* (Leiden and Boston), 242–257.

Rosenbloom, D. (2006). *Aeschylus: "Persians."* London.
Rosenbloom, D. (2011). "The panhellenism of Athenian tragedy," in D. Carter (ed.), *Why Athens? A Reappraisal of Tragic Politics* (Oxford), 353–381.
Rowe, C. J. (1983). "'Archaic thought' in Hesiod," *JHS* 103: 124–135.
Ruffing, K. (2011). "Herodot und die Wirtschaft des Achaimeniden-Reichs," in Rollinger, Truschnegg, and Bichler 2011: 75–102.
Ruffing, K. (2013). "300," in Ruffing and Dunsch 2013: 200–221.
Ruffing, K. and Dunsch, B. (eds.). (2013). *Source References in Herodotus—Herodotus' Sources: Conference in memoriam Detlev Fehling (Classica et Orientalia 6)*. Wiesbaden.
Rutherford, R. B. (2018). "Herodotean ironies," *Histos* 12: 1–48.
Ryan, M.-L. (1991). *Possible Worlds, Artificial Intelligence, and Narrative Theory*. Bloomington, IN.
Saïd, E. W. (1978). *Orientalism*. London.
Saïd, S. (2002). "Herodotus and tragedy," in Bakker, de Jong, and van Wees 2002: 117–147.
Saïd, S. (2012). "Herodotus and the 'myth' of the Trojan War," in Baragwanath and de Bakker 2012a: 87–105.
Salmon, J. (1984). *Wealthy Corinth: A History of the City to 338 BC*. Oxford.
Sancisi-Weerdenburg, H. (1983; repr. Munson 2013). "Exit Atossa: Images of women in Greek historiography on Persia," in A. Cameron and A. Kuhrt (eds.), *Images of Women in Antiquity* (London and Detroit), 20–33; repr. in Munson 2013: ii. 135–150.
Sancisi-Weerdenburg, H. (1985; repr. Gray 2010). "The death of Cyrus: Xenophon's *Cyropaedia* as a source for Iranian history," *Acta Iranica* 25: 459–471, repr. in V. J. Gray (ed.), *Oxford Readings in Classical Studies; Xenophon* (Oxford, 2010), 439–453.
Sancisi-Weerdenburg, H. (1987). "Decadence in the empire or decadence in the sources?" in H. Sancisi-Weerdenburg (ed.), *Achaemenid History 1: Sources, Structures, and Synthesis* (Leiden), 33–45.
Sancisi-Weerdenburg, H. and Kuhrt, A. (eds.). (1987): *Achaemenid History 2: The Greek Sources*. Leiden.
Sansone, D. (1989). *Plutarch: Lives of Aristeides and Cato*. Liverpool University Press, 1989.
Scaife, R. (1989). "Alexander I in the Histories of Herodotus," *Hermes* 117: 129–137.
Schadewaldt, W. (1938). *Iliasstudien*. Leipzig.
Schiefsky, M. J. (2005). *Hippocrates: "On Ancient Medicine."* Leiden and Boston.
Schlögel, K. (2016). *In Space We Read Time* (tr. G. Jackson; German original 2003). New York.
Schmid, W. and Stählin, O. (1929–1948): *Geschichte der griechischen Literatur*. Munich.
Schoeck, G. (1961). *Ilias und Aithiopis: Kyklische Motive in homerische Brechung*. Zürich.
Schofield, M. (1986; repr. Cairns 2001). "*Euboulia* in the *Iliad*," *CQ* 36: 6–31, repr. in Cairns 2001: 220–259.
Schulte-Aldorneburg, J. (2001). *Geschichtliches Handeln und tragisches Scheitern: Herodots Konzept historiographischer Mimesis (Studien zur klassischen Philologie 131)*. Frankfurt.
Scodel, R. (1980). *The Trojan Trilogy of Euripides* (*Hypomnemata* 60). Göttingen.
Scullion, S. (2006). "Herodotus and Greek religion," in Dewald and Marincola 2006: 192–208.
Sealey, R. (1957). "Thucydides, Herodotos, and the causes of war," *CQ* 7: 1–12.
Seel, O. (1956). "Lydiaka," *WS* 69: 212–236.

Sergueenkova, V. (2016). "Counting the past in Herodotus' *Histories*," *JHS* 136: 121–131.
Sewell-Rutter, N. J. (2007). *Guilt by Descent: Moral Inheritance and Decision Making in Greek Tragedy*. Oxford.
Shapiro, A. and Burian, P. (2009). *Euripides: "Trojan Women."* Oxford.
Shapiro, S. O. (1994). "Learning through suffering: Human wisdom in Herodotus," *CJ* 89: 349–355.
Shapiro, S. O. (1996). "Herodotus and Solon," *ClAnt* 15: 348–364.
Shimron, B. (1975). "πρῶτος τῶν ἡμεῖς ἴδμεν," *Eranos* 71: 45–51.
Shipley, G. (1987). *A History of Samos 800–188 B.C.* Oxford.
Shipley, G. (2011). *Pseudo-Skylax's Periplous: The Circumnavigation of the Inhabited World*. Exeter.
Shipley, G. (2012). "Pseudo-Skylax and the natural philosophers," *JHS* 132: 121–138.
Skinner, J. (2018). "Herodotus and his world," in Harrison and Irwin 2018a: 187–222.
Skinner, J. (forthcoming). "Writing culture: Historiography, hybridity and the shaping of collective memory," in Fragoulaki and Constantakopoulou, forthcoming.
Skinner, Q. (1998). *Liberty before Liberalism*. Cambridge.
Smith, K. F. (1902). "The tale of Gyges and the king of Lydia," *AJP* 23: 261–287, 361–387.
Smolin, N. I. (2018). "Divine vengeance in Herodotus' Histories," forthcoming in *Journal of Ancient History* 6: 2–43.
Solmsen, Fr. (1974; repr. 1982). "Two crucial decisions in Herodotus," *Medelingen der Koninklijke Nederlandse Akademie van Wetenschappen*, Afd. Letterkunde 37/6: 139–170, repr. in his *Kleine Schriften* iii (Hildesheim, 1982), 79–109.
Sommerstein, A. H. (2001). *Aristophanes: "Wealth."* Warminster.
Sosa, E. and Tooley, M. (eds.). (1993). *Causation* (Oxford Readings in Philosophy). Oxford.
Sourdille, C. (1910). *La durée et l'étendue du voyage d'Hérodote en Égypte*. Paris.
Sourvinou-Inwood, C. (1988; repr. 1991). "'Myth' and 'history': On Herodotus III.48 and 50–53," *Opuscula Atheniensia* 17: 11: 167–182, repr. in her *"Reading" Greek Culture: Texts and Images, Rituals and Myth* (Oxford, 1991), 244–284.
Spatharas, D. (2007). "Gorgias and the author of the Hippocratic treatise *De Arte*," *C&M* 58: 159–163.
Spatharas, D. (2009). "Kinky stories from the rostrum: Storytelling in Apollodorus' *Against Neaira*," *Ancient Narrative* 9: 99–120.
Stadter, P. A. (1989). *A Commentary on Plutarch's "Pericles."* Chapel Hill, NC.
Stadter, P. A. (1992, repr. Munson 2013). "Herodotus and the Athenian *arche*," *ASNSP* 22: 781–809, repr. in Munson 2013a: i. 334–356.
Stadter, P. A. (2006). "Herodotus and the cities of mainland Greece," in Dewald and Marincola 2006: 242–256.
Stadter, P. A. (2012a). "Thucydides as 'reader' of Herodotus," in Foster and Lateiner 2012: 39–66.
Stadter, P. A. (2012b). "Speaking to the deaf: Herodotus, his audience, and the Spartans at the beginning of the Peloponnesian War," *Histos* 6: 1–14.
Stahl, H.-P. (1968). "Herodots Gyges–Tragödie," *Hermes* 86: 385–400.
Stahl, H.-P. (1975). "Learning through suffering? Croesus' conversations in the History of Herodotus," *YCS* 24: 1–36.
Stahl, H.-P. (2012). "Herodotus and Thucydides on blind decisions preceding military action," in Foster and Lateiner 2012: 125–153.

Stahl, H.-P. (2015). "Herodotus and Thucydides on not learning from mistakes," in Clark, Foster, and Hallett 2015: 74–85.
Stein, H. (1901–1908). *Herodoti "Historiae"* (6th edition: first published 1869–1871). Berlin.
Stephenson, P. (2016). *The Serpent Column: A Cultural Biography*. New York and Oxford.
Sternberg, R. (ed.). (2005). *Pity and Power in Ancient Athens*. Cambridge.
Stevens, K. (2016). "From Herodotus to a 'Hellenistic' world? The eastern geographies of Aristotle and Theophrastus," in Barker, Bouzarovski, Pelling, and Isaksen 2016: 121–152.
Stoessl, F. (1959). "Herodots Humanität," *Gymnasium* 66: 477–490.
Strasburger, H. (1955; repr. Marg 1965). "Herodot und das perikleische Athen," *Hist.* 4: 1–25; repr. in Marg 1965: 574–608, and translated as "Herodotus and Periclean Athens," in Munson 2013: i. 295–320.
Strasburger, H. (1972). *Homer und die Geschichtsschreibung*. Heidelberg.
Sutton, D. (1981). "Critias and atheism," *CQ* 31: 33–38.
Swift, L. (2010). *The Hidden Chorus*. Oxford.
Syme, R. (1939). *The Roman Revolution*. Oxford.
Syme, R. (1958). *Tacitus* i–ii. Oxford.
Taplin, O. (1992). *Homeric Soundings*. Oxford.
Thomas, R. (1989). *Oral Tradition and Written Record in Classical Athens*. Cambridge.
Thomas, R. (1997). "Ethnography, proof, and argument in Herodotus' *Histories*," *PCPS* 43: 128–148.
Thomas, R. (2000). *Herodotus in Context*. Cambridge.
Thomas, R. (2001a). "Herodotus' *Histories* and the floating gap," in Luraghi 2001a: 198–210.
Thomas, R. (2001b; repr. Munson 2013). "Ethnicity, genealogy, and Hellenism in Herodotus," in I. Malkin (ed.), *Ancient Perceptions of Greek Ethnicity* (Cambridge MA), 213–233, repr. in Munson 2013: ii. 339–359.
Thomas, R. (2006). "The intellectual milieu of Herodotus," in Dewald and Marincola 2006: 60–75.
Thomas, R. (2011). "Herodotus' Persian ethnography," in Rollinger, Truschnegg, and Bichler 2011: 237–254.
Thomas, R. (2012). "Herodotus and eastern myths and *logoi*: Deioces the Mede and Pythius the Lydian," in Baragwanath and de Bakker 2012a: 233–253.
Thonemann, P. (2016). "Croesus and the oracles," *JHS* 136: 152–167.
Todorov, T. (1973). *The Fantastic: A Structural Approach to a Literary Genre* (tr. R. Howard: French original 1970). London.
Toher, M. (1989). "On the use of Nicolaus' historical fragments," *ClAnt* 8: 159–172.
Tordoff, R. (2014). "Counterfactual history and Thucydides," in Wohl 2014: 101–121.
Travis, R. (2000). "The spectation of Gyges in *P. Oxy.* 2382 and Herodotus Book 1," *ClAnt* 19: 330–359.
Trenkner, S. (1958). *The Greek Novella of the Classical Period*. Cambridge.
Treves, P. (1941). "Herodotus, Gelon, and Pericles," *CPh* 36: 321–345.
Tuplin, C. J. (1985). "Imperial tyranny: Some reflections on a classical Greek political metaphor," in Cartledge and Harvey 1985: 348–375.
Tuplin, C. J. (2018). "Dogs that do not (always) bark: Herodotus on Persian Egypt," in Bowie 2018a: 99–123.

Tzanetou, A. (2005). "A generous city: Pity in Athenian oratory and tragedy," in Sternberg 2005: 98–122.
Ubsdell, S. (1983). "Herodotus on Human Nature." Oxford D.Phil. thesis.
Van der Eijk, P. (1990; repr. Van der Eijk 2005a). "The 'Theology' of the Hippocratic Treatise 'On the Sacred Disease,'" *Apeiron* 23, 87–119, repr. with a postscript in van der Eijk 2005a: 45–73.
Van der Eijk, P. (1991). "'Airs, Waters, Places' and 'On the Sacred Disease': Two different religiosities?" *Hermes* 119, 168–176.
Van der Eijk, P. (2005a). *Medicine and Philosophy in Classical Antiquity: Doctors and Philosophers on Nature, Soul, Health and Disease.* Cambridge.
Van der Eijk, P. (ed.). (2005b). *Hippocrates in Context: Papers Read at the XIth International Hippocrates Colloquium, Newcastle-upon-Tyne, 27–31 August 2002.* Leiden and Boston.
Van Wees, H. (2011). "Defeat and destruction: The ethics of ancient Greek warfare," in M. Linder and S. Tausend (eds.), *Boser Krieg: Exzessive Gewalt in der antiken Kriegsführung und Strategien zu deren Vermeidung* (Graz), 69–110.
Vanderpool, E. (1966). "A monument to the battle of Marathon," *Hesperia* 35: 93–106.
Vandiver, E. (2012). "'Strangers are from Zeus': Homeric *xenia* at the courts of Proteus and Croesus," in Baragwanath and de Bakker 2012a: 143–166.
Vannicelli, P. (2001). "Herodotus' Egypt and the foundations of universal history," in Luraghi 2001a: 211–240.
Vansina, J. (1965). *Oral Tradition: A Study in Historical Methodology* (tr. H. M. Wright: French original 1961). Chicago.
Vansina, J. (1985). *Oral Tradition as History.* Madison, WI.
Vegetti, M. (1983). "Metafora politica e immagine del corpo negli scritti hipppocratici," in Lasserre and Mudt 1983: 459–469.
Vernant, J.-P. (1988). "The historical moment of tragedy in Greece: Some of the social and psychological conditions," in J.-P. Vernant and P. Vidal-Naquet, *Myth and Tragedy in Ancient Greece* (tr. J. Lloyd, New York: French original 1972), 23–28.
Versnel, H. S. (2011). *Coping with the Gods: Wayward Readings in Greek Theology.* Leiden and Boston.
Villard, L. (1996). "Les médecins hippocratiques face au hasard, ou le recours alterné à l''archéologie' et l'étymologie," in Wittern and Pellegrin 1996: 395–411.
Visser, E. (2000): "Herodots Kroisos-Logos: Rezeptionssteuerung und Geschichtsphilosophie," *WJb* 24, 5–28.
Vlastos, G. (1947). "Equality and justice in early Greek cosmologies," *CPh* 42: 156–178.
Vlastos, G. (1953). "Isonomia," *AJPh* 64: 337–366.
Vlastos, G. (1964; repr. Vlastos 1973). "Ἰσονομία πολιτική," in. Mau–Schmidt 1964: 1–35, repr. in Vlastos 1973: 164–203.
Vlastos, G. (1973). *Platonic Studies.* Princeton, NJ.
Von Fritz, K. (1965). "Die griechische ἐλευθερία bei Herodot," *WS* 78: 5–31.
Von Fritz, K. (1967). *Die griechische Geschichtsschreibung: Von den Anfängen bis Thukydides.* Berlin.
Von Leyden, W. M. (1949/1950; repr. Marg 1965). "Spatium historicum," *Durham University Journal* 11: 89–104, partially repr. and tr. into German in Marg 1965: 169–181.
Walcot, P. (1978). "Herodotus on rape," *Arethusa* 11: 137–147.
Wardman, A. E. (1961). "Herodotus on the cause of the Graeco-Persian War," *AJP* 82: 133–150.

Warren, J. (2007). *Presocratics.* Cambridge.
Waterfield, R. and Dewald, C. (1998). *Herodotus: The "Histories."* Oxford.
Waters, K. H. (1971). *Herodotus on Tyrants and Despots: A Study in Objectivity* (Historia Einzelschr. 15). Wiesbaden.
Węcowski, M. (2004). "The hedgehog and the fox: Form and meaning in the prologue of Herodotus," *JHS* 124: 143–164.
Weidauer, K. (1954). *Thukydides und die Hippokratischen Schriften.* Heidelberg.
Welser, C. A. (2009). "Two didactic strategies at the end of Herodotus' *Histories* (9.108–122)," *ClAnt* 28: 359–385.
Wenskus, O. (1982). *Ringkomposition, anaphorisch-rekapitulierende Verbindung und anknüpfende Wiederholung in der hippokratischen Corpus.* Diss. Göttingen.
Wenskus, O. (1996). "Die Rolle des Zufalls bei der Gewinnung neuer Erkenntnisse. *De vetere medicina* 12 gegen *de affectionibus* 45," in Wittern and Pellegrin 1996: 413–418.
West, S. R. (1987). "And it came to pass that Pharaoh dreamed: Notes on Herodotus 2.139, 141," *CQ* 37: 262–271.
West, S. R. (1991). "Herodotus' portrait of Hecataeus," *JHS* 111: 144–160.
West, S. R. (2007). "Herodotus lyricorum studiosus," *Palamedes* 2: 1–22.
West, S. R. (2011). "Herodotus' sources of information on Persian matters," in Rollinger, Truschnegg, and Bichler 2011: 255–272.
White, H. (1973). *Metahistory: The Historical Imagination in Nineteenth-century Europe.* Baltimore and London.
White, H. (1987). *The Content of the Form: Narrative Discourse and Historical Representation.* Baltimore and London.
White, H. (1999). *Figural Realism: Studies in the Mimesis Effect.* Baltimore and London.
Whitlock Blundell, M. (1989). *Helping Friends and Harming Enemies: A Study in Sophocles and Greek Ethics.* Cambridge. See also Blondell 2013.
Whitmarsh, T. (2016). *Battling the Gods: Atheism in the Ancient World.* London.
Williams, B. (1993). *Shame and Necessity.* Berkeley, Los Angeles, and Oxford.
Willink, C. W. (1986). *Euripides: "Orestes."* Oxford.
Wilson, N. G. (2015a). *Herodotea.* Oxford.
Wilson, N. G. (2015b). *Herodoti "Historiae"* i–ii (Oxford Classical Text). Oxford.
Wittern, R. and Pellegrin, P. (eds.). (1996). *Hippokratische Medizin und antike Philosophie: Verhandlungen des VIII. Internationalen Hippokrates-Kolloqium in Kloster Banz/Staffelstein von 23. bis 28 September 1993.* Hildesheim and Zürich.
Wohl, V. (ed.). (2014). *Probabilities, Hypotheticals, and Counterfactuals in Ancient Greek Thought.* Cambridge.
Wolbergs, T. (2012). "ὄψις ἀδήλων τὰ φθεγγόμενα," *RhM* 155: 113–127.
Wolff, E. (1964; repr. Marg 1965). "Das Weib des Masistes," *Hermes* 92: 51–58, repr. with alterations in Marg 1965: 668–678.
Wood, C. (2016). "'I am going to say . . .': A sign on the road of Herodotus' *logos,*" *CQ* 66: 13–31.
Woodman, A. J. (1988). *Rhetoric in Classical Historiography.* London and Sydney.
Zali, V. (2014). *The Shape of Herodotean Rhetoric: A Study of the Speeches in Herodotus' "Histories," with special attention to Books 5–9.* Leiden and Boston.
Zali, V. (2018). "Herodotus mapping out his genre: The interaction of myth and geography in the Libyan logos," in Bowie 2018a: 125–138.
Zhmud, L. (2012). *Pythagoras and the Early Pythagoreans.* Oxford.

PASSAGES IN HERODOTUS

Passages are included when they are discussed, but not when they are quoted in a list of parallels. Bold type indicates that the passages are quoted or discussed at length.

Proem: 1–2, **22–25**, 133, 162

1.1–5: **25–30**, 35, 37, 107–109
1.1.1: 14, 24, 244 n. 13
1.1.3–2.1: 107
1.2.1: 26, 107
1.2.2–3: 107
1.3.1–2: 107
1.4.2: 36
1.4.4: 26, **27**, 37, 65, 110
1.5.1: 14, 26
1.5.2: 28
1.5.3–4: **28–30**, 31, 66, 76, 90, 106
1.5.3: 8, 14, 38, 114, 176
1.5.4: 231
1.6.2–3: 106, 176, 218
1.8–13: 32, **106–110**, 129, 130
1.8.1: 107, 116
1.8.2: 24, 33, 107–108, 146
1.12.1: 32, 109, 110
1.13.2: 108–109, 112, 142, 146
1.14.4: 106
1.15: 106
1.16–18: 106
1.16–25: 115
1.24–25: 149
1.26–28: 115, 116
1.26.1: 137
1.26.3: **7–8**, 32, 110, 112, 114, 117, 120, 136, 176
1.27: 12, 114, 117, 137
1.29–33: 12, 49, **110–112**, 138, 156

1.29.1: 9
1.30.1: 9
1.30.2: 30, 76, 114
1.30.4–5: 120
1.32: 111, 118
1.32.9: 214
1.34.1: 112, 152, 155
1.34.3–35.1: 152
1.37.2–3: 140–141, 152
1.45.2: 70
1.46.1: 91, 93, 103, 110, 112, **116**, 139, 213
1.49: 269 n. 28
1.51.5: 270 n.40
1.52: 269 n. 28
1.53.2: 111
1.55.1: 116
1.59–68: 115
1.59.5: 191
1.59.6: 286 n. 16
1.60.3: **191**, 205, 208, 218
1.62.1: 179
1.66.1: 136
1.69–70: 124, 212
1.71–85: 115
1.71: 12, **91–92**, 137, 170
1.72: 117
1.73.1: **103**, 110, 112, 114, 116
1.74: 115
1.75: 117
1.75.1: 8
1.75.3: **117**
1.75.6: 117

1.76.2: 112, 117, 239 n. 30
1.77: 118
1.78.1: 118
1.79.1: 118, 271 n. 16, 276 n. 21
1.86–91: **111–113**, 153, 156
1.86.3: 111
1.86.5: 111
1.87.1–2: 140, 146
1.87.3: 112
1.90.2: 111, 112, 166
1.90.4: 111, 112
1.91.1: 112, 114, 142, 146, 268 n. 19
1.91.2: 112
1.91.3: 146, 148, 269–270 n. 30
1.91.5–6: 152
1.91.6: 146, 148
1.92.2–4: 113, 117
1.95.1: 149–150, 275–276 n. 21
1.95.2: 175, 211
1.96–101: **17**, 78, 143–144, 211
1.99.2: 150
1.102.1: 136
1.106.1: 124, 176
1.107–130: 143–144, **149–153**, 280 n. 25, 280 n. 30
1.107.2: 152, 280 n. 30
1.108–113: 129
1.108: 67
1.108.4–5: 151
1.110.1: 150
1.111.1: 151
1.112.1: 151
1.113.1: 151
1.114–119: 129, **151**
1.114.3: 117–118, 151, 288 n. 27
1.119–20: 57, **151**
1.119: 114
1.120.5–6: 151, 175
1.120.6–121.1: 280 n. 30
1.122.3: **150**
1.123.2: 153
1.124.1: 151–152
1.124.3: 152, 153
1.125–130: 129
1.126: 18, 93, 175
1.126.6: 151–152
1.127.1: 175
1.127.2: 152

1.127.3: 280–281 n. 34
1.128.2: 153
1.129: 175, 177
1.130.1–2: **153**, 179
1.136.1: 243 n. 3
1.155–156: 18
1.155.3: 239 n. 26
1.155.4: **91–92**
1.156–160: 67
1.159.4: 155
1.170.2: 186
1.174.5: 157
1.177.1: 117
1.178.1: 136
1.179: 216
1.189: 117, 157
1.204.2: **102**, 116, **119**, 139, 152, 272 n. 23
1.207: 92, 138, 139, **141–142**, 277 n. 46
1.208: 139
1.210.2: 175
1.212: 92

2.1.2–2.1: 243 n. 5
2.2.5: **63**
2.3.2: 98, 148
2.5.1: **62**
2.10.3: 300 n. 52
2.11.4: 3, 43
2.13.2–14.1: 229
2.15–17: 65
2.20–27: **2–3**, **41–42**, 53
2.20.1: 64
2.20.2–3: 2, 6, 228
2.21: 64
2.22: 2
2.23: 2, 41, **64–65**
2.24–27: 2, 41, 77
2.26.2: 3, 43
2.30.2–3: 7
2.33.2: 2, 81
2.35.2: 18, 38, 90
2.43–45: 60
2.45.2: 39
2.52.3–53: 60
2.57.1: 11
2.77.3: 18
2.84: 80
2.91.1: 38, 90

2.99.1: 148
2.100.3: 7
2.102.5: 177
2.104: 3, 237 n. 7
2.112–120: **36–38**
2.113.1: 37, 38
2.113.2: 38
2.113.3: 36
2.114–5: 38
2.115.3–5: 36
2.116.1: 38
2.118.1: 38
2.118.3: 37
2.119: 37, 38
2.120: 44
2.120.1: 38
2.120.5, 36, 37–38, 126–127, **146–147**, 148
2.121: 207
2.122.2: 102
2.134.1: 254 n. 45
2.139.2: 240 n. 34
2.143: 62
2.161.3–4: **9**, 146
2.173.2: 150

3.1–38: 129
3.1: 34, 119, 121, 131
3.1.1: 80
3.3: 131
3.4: 121
3.12.2–5: 239 n. 25
3.12.4: **218**, 220
3.15.3: **218**
3.16.6–7: 150
3.17–21: 277 n. 52
3.17: 136
3.19.3: 139
3.21.2: 176, 286 n. 14
3.27–29: 277 n. 53
3.30.1: 159
3.33: 80, 105, 159
3.34.4–5: 138
3.35.5: 7
3.36.3: 9, 10
3.38: 78, **142–143**
3.39–60: 115, 133
3.40–43: 111, 144
3.40.2–3: 268 n. 24
3.42.4: 146

3.47–49: 124, 136–137
3.49.1: 3, **44–46**, 50, 56, 226
3.50–53: 144
3.52.7: 7
3.61–79: 67, 207
3.64: 159
3.66: 129
3.67–88: 129
3.69.2: 131
3.69.5: 131
3.73.2: 131
3.74.1: 10–11
3.80.5: 113
3.80.6: 193, 194
3.81.1: 193
3.81.2: 191, 200
3.82: 278 n. 63
3.82.3: 187
3.82.4: 193, 290 n. 56
3.82.5: **175–176**, 211
3.83.1: 193
3.83.3: 291 n. 6
3.84.2: 130
3.85–87: 207, 211
3.93.2: 117
3.106.1: 18–19, 86
3.108–109: 2, 20, 86
3.108.2: 19
3.118–119: 129
3.118.1–2: 130–131
3.120–121: **34**, 124
3.122.1: 34
3.126–128: 124
3.129–138: 80
3.131.3: 80
3.132–134: 121, 274 n. 57
3.134: 108, 121, 129, 136, **140**
3.134.5: 115
3.139–147: 124, **179–180**
3.139.1: 8, 137
3.142: 179, 191, 193, 194
3.142.1: 196
3.142.5: 125
3.143.2: 125, **179–180**, 191, 197, 211, 287 n. 23
3.144.5: 179
3.145: 125
3.146–147: 124–125
3.147: 179

PASSAGES IN HERODOTUS 331

3.149: 124
3.150–160: 207, 211
3.160.2: **218**

4.1.1: 119, 124, 139
4.8.2: 237 n. 8
4.13.1: 237 n. 8
4.29: 53
4.30.1: 2
4.36.2: 254 n. 45
4.43.2: 7
4.42.4: 237 n. 4
4.44.1: 219
4.43.6: 6, **218–219**
4.50.3–4: 41
4.76.1: 240 n. 33
4.76.2: 76
4.79.1: 146
4.80.1: 240 n. 33
4.80.5: 240 n. 33
4.83: 119, 137
4.84.2: 119
4.93: 178
4.97–98: 139
4.97.2: 138
4.99.4–5: 249 n. 21
4.101: 64
4.118: 119
4.119: 176–177
4.119.4: 119
4.135.2: 8
4.137–138: 208
4.137.2: **194**, 225
4.142: 177
4.143: 274 n. 57
4.145–205: **125–128**
4.145.1: **126**
4.148.4: **219**
4.159.3–4: 9
4.164.1: 127
4.164.4: 126
4.165.2: 126
4.165.3: 126
4.166–167: 134
4.166.2: 126, 239 n. 30
4.167.1–2: 125, 127, 274 n. 58
4.167.3: **10**, 103, 125, 240 n. 35
4.186.1: 11
4.187: 2

4.187.3: 102
4.197.1: 127
4.198–199: 125
4.200.1: 7, 126
4.201: 207
4.202–203.1: 127
4.202.1: 7
4.203: 127–128, 134, 274 n. 58
4.203.2: 294 n. 31
4.204: 117, 274 nn. 58–59
4.205: **126–127**, 128, 146, 156

5.1.1: 136
5.2.1: 175
5.3.1: 182
5.11.2: 143
5.12–13: 121
5.14.1: 117
5.17–20: 180
5.21: 180
5.22: 180
5.28.1: 14, 219, 223
5.30–31: 219
5.30.3: 143
5.32: 143, 210, **219**
5.33.1: 8
5.36: 62
5.37.2: 193, 194, 225, 290 n. 3
5.42–48: 209
5.49: 205
5.49.1: 290 n. 3
5.49.2: 196
5.49.3–4: **92, 165**, 169, 263 n. 44
5.51: 169, 284 n. 14
5.64–65: 209
5.65.1: 44
5.66.1: 195
5.66.2: 196, 294 n. 33
5.69–70: 193
5.69.2: 196, 294 n. 33
5.70.1: 7
5.70.2: 7
5.71.2: 7
5.73.3: 7, 192
5.74.1: 137, 191, 209
5.75.1: 286 n. 15
5.78: 19, 138, **164**, 179, 185–186, 191, 193–195, 199, 211
5.83.1: 178

5.91–93: 137, 224
5.91: 137, 209
5.91.1: **185**, 195, 212–213, 283 n. 3
5.91.2: 191, 193, 194, 196
5.92: 190, 196
5.92α.1: 193, 196
5.92ζ: 206
5.92η.5: 196
5.93: 196
5.93.1: 226
5.96.2: 192
5.97–102: 67
5.97: 124. **191–192**, 209, 228
5.97.1: 289 n. 46
5.97.3: 105, 192
5.103.1: 192
5.105: 9, 31, 104, 119, 129, 134
5.109.2–3: 175, 190
5.113: 290 n. 3
5.124.1: 182
5.125–126: 62
5.125: 65

6.3.1: 34
6.5.1: 143
6.9.3: 240 n. 35
6.10: 50. 178
6.11.3: 166
6.12: 172, 179
6.13.1: 9
6.14.1: 172, 179
6.15–16: 161
6.15.1: 178–179
6.21.2: 197
6.23.2: 192
6.27: 161
6.30.1: 44, 46
6.32: 176
6.35.3: 196
6.37.1: 137
6.39–41: 135
6.39.2: 208
6.42.1: 286 n. 16
6.43.3: 193, 286 n. 16
6.44.1: **104**
6.49.2: 10, 209
6.50.1: 6
6.53.1: 255 n. 45

6.61–70: 108–109, 135, 143–144, 160
6.61.1: 178, 188, 209
6.61.3–4: 280 n. 25
6.62–63: 207
6.64.1: 146
6.66: 207
6.67.3: 266 n. 32
6.69: 280 n. 25
6.70: 209
6.72: 169, 209, **219**, 284 n. 14
6.74.3: 20
6.75: 20, **159–160**, 172, 209
6.76–80: 160, 209
6.84: 20–21, 80, **160**, 209, 254 n. 27, 269 n. 25
6.84.3: **160**
6.85.1: 135
6.86: 219, 224, 230, 281 n. 42
6.86.1: 8
6.87–93: 187
6.89: 226
6.91.1: **219**, 298 n. 22
6.94.1: 9, 10, 31, 187
6.94.2: 176
6.97: 224–225, 286 n. 16
6.98.2: **187**, **216**, 219, 223
6.99.2: 178
6.100: 178
6.102: 168
6.103.3: 196
6.104: 189, 192
6.104.2: 196, 197
6.105: 147–148
6.106: 178
6.108: 135, 195, 209, 227
6.109–110: 135, 196
6.109: **185–186**, 197
6.109.2: 294 n. 33
6.109.3: 293–294 n. 31
6.109.5: 166, 172, **188**
6.111.3: 135
6.112.1: 182
6.112.2: 172–173
6.112.3: **92, 170**
6.113.2–114: 202, 295 n. 14
6.117: 147–148
6.118.1: 224–225, 286 n. 16
6.118.3: 219

6.119: 117, 176
6.120: 178
6.121–124: 197
6.124.1: 197
6.124.2: 189
6.126–131: 57
6.131: 193, 196, **219–220**
6.132: 205
6.133.1: **10**
6.135: 280 n. 25
6.135.1: 205
6.136: 189, 196, 197, 206
6.137.2: 64, 137
6.139–140: 208
6.140: 206

7.2–3: 129
7.3.4: **103**
7.5: 121
7.5.1: 136
7.6.1–2: **103**, 121
7.6.4: 150
7.7: **220**
7.8–11: **121–123**, 129, 284 n. 10, 299 n. 48
7.8α.1: **123**, 139–140, 141
7.8α.2: 121
7.8β: 104
7.8γ.3: 117, 120
7.8δ.2: **121–122**
7.9: 121
7.9.1–2: 104
7.9α.2: 121, 136
7.9β.1: 272 n. 35
7.10: 137, 138
7.10.1: 121, 122
7.10ε: 156–157
7.10θ.3: 122
7.11: 119, 138
7.11.1: 122
7.11.2–3: 117, 213
7.11.4: **122**
7.12–19: 129, 137, **153–156**, 284 n. 10
7.12.1: 139, 140, 153
7.12.2: 140, **153–155**
7.13.3: 122, 153
7.14: **153–154**, 155
7.16: 154
7.16β: 140

7.17: 140
7.17.2: **154**
7.18.3: 154
7.19.1: 154–155
7.22–24: 117, 158, 159
7.22.1: 288 n. 27
7.27–28: 92
7.34–35: 117, 158, 159
7.35: 181
7.37.2: 272 n. 24
7.39: 119–120, 272 n. 24
7.39.1: 176
7.43.1: 157
7.44–52: 111, 123, 129–130
7.46.3–4: 268 n. 24
7.47: 249 n. 18
7.49: **157**
7.50.1–3: **141**, 200
7.51.2: 177
7.54.3: 181
7.56.1: 288 n. 27
7.58.3: 157
7.83.2: 92
7.96.2: 286 n. 10
7.101–104: **165**, **181–182**, 199, 204, 284 n. 9
7.101.3: 138, 182
7.102.1: 121, **165**, 169
7.102.2: 166, 172, 204–205, 211
7.103.3–4: 128, **181–182**, 188, 200
7.104: 138
7.104.1: 172, 182
7.104.2: 166
7.104.4–5: **165**, 172, 182, 205
7.106: **220**, 223
7.107: **220**
7.108–109: 157
7.114.2: **220**
7.118–120: 157
7.118: 117
7.125: 2
7.127.2: 157
7.132: 177
7.133–137: 102
7.133.2: **102**
7.135–137: **143**, 224
7.135.3: **163–164**, 175–176
7.137.2–3: 147, 216, **220**, 224

7.138.1: **104**
7.138.2: 177–8, 287 n. 19
7.139: 3, **42–43**, 45, 81, 164, 170, 178, 195, 220, 221, 223
7.139.5: 43, 156, 169
7.142–143: 208
7.143: 135, 192
7.144: **188**, 192, 208, 225
7.144.1: 290 n. 57
7.145.1: 178
7.145.2: 290 n. 56
7.148–152: 102
7.149.3: 179
7.151: **220–221**
7.156.2: 7, 239 n. 29
7.157–162: 187, 299 n. 48
7.157.1: **10**, 103–104
7.158.1: 289 n. 39
7.158.2: 190
7.161: 289 n. 43
7.162–163: **225**, 299 n. 44
7.162.1: 187
7.163–164: 45
7.164.1: 196
7.168: 45, 46, 226
7.170.3: **221**
7.172.1: 177
7.173.3: 287 n. 24
7.174: 177–178, 287 n. 19
7.175: 165
7.178.1: 158, 159, 161
7.188–189: 158, 168
7.189.3: **158**
7.190: 92
7.194.1: 7
7.196: 157
7.203.2: 111
7.208.3–209.1: **165–166**
7.209.2: 166
7.213.3: 7, 102
7.214.3: 7
7.219.2: 171–172, 283 n. 5
7.220–222: 283 n. 5
7.220.2: **203**
7.220.4: **203**, 295 n. 20
7.223: 181, 285 n. 21
7.223.4: 285 n. 24
7.225.1: 203

7.225.2: 81, 203
7.226–227: 172
7.226.2: 204, 295 n. 19
7.229: 204
7.229.2: 249 n. 22
7.231: 204
7.233.2: **221**, 227
7.235: 217

8.3: 184, 187, 210, **221**, 223, 240 n. 35
8.4.1–5.1: 169, 221
8.4.1: 182, 221
8.5: 169, 284 n. 14
8.10.1: 173
8.12–13: 158
8.13: **158–159**, 161, **166**
8.17: 172
8.18: 182
8.19: 205
8.22.2: 177
8.23.1: 182
8.26.2–3: **166**, 169, 281 n. 40
8.30.2: 3, **44–46**, 50, 56, 186
8.37: 148
8.38–39: **147–148**, 156, 168
8.39.2: 148
8.53.2: 161
8.55: 154
8.56–64: 165
8.57.2: 171
8.58.2: 171
8.59–64: 138, 143, **183–185**, 224, 283 n. 5
8.59: 183, 289 n. 39
8.60.1: 171, 182, 184
8.60α–β: **170–171**
8.60γ: 161
8.61.1: 183, 289 n. 40
8.61.2: 183
8.62: 285 n. 20
8.62.1: 185
8.62.2: 171, 183, 185
8.63–64.1: 183–184, 283 n. 5
8.64.1: 184
8.64.2: 161
8.65: 146
8.67–69: 138, **182–183**
8.68α.1: 243 n. 3, 288 n. 37
8.68γ: 286 n. 10, 288 n. 37

PASSAGES IN HERODOTUS 335

8.69.2: 128, 182
8.70.1: 171
8.70.2: 184
8.72: 178
8.73.3: 178
8.74–76: 143, 171
8.74: 165, 184
8.75: 182
8.77.2: **149**
8.78: 184, 203
8.79.2: 135, 196
8.80.2: 182
8.84.2: 147, 174
8.86: 170, 171, 172, 182
8.88–90: 130
8.89.2: 81, 171
8.94–95: 184
8.94: 177
8.97.1: 182
8.100.1: 182
8.100.3–4: 138
8.101.2: 7, 276 n. 40
8.102.2: 176
8.109: 208–209
8.109.3: 161
8.109.5: 206, **221–222**, 223
8.110.1: 209
8.110.2–3: 285 n. 23
8.111–112: 221–222
8.111: 205
8.112: 169
8.115: 158
8.118–119: 44, 130
8.123: 172, 184
8.124: 184, 206–207, 222, 281 n. 40
8.125: 207, 210
8.126–128: 299–300 n. 48
8.129: 6, 158, 239 n. 25
8.136.1: 287 n. 24
8.140: 182, 288 n. 34
8.140β.1: 287 n. 24
8.143–144: **168**, **180**, 182, 195
8.143.1–2: 161, **167**, 168, **180**, 288 n. 34
8.144.2–3: **168**, 180

9.2: 92, 169, 289 n. 38
9.3.1: 169, 178, 207–208
9.4.2: 50, 178

9.5: 168
9.5.1: 293 n. 27
9.6–8: 168
9.6: 181
9.8.2: **6**, 50, 164, 170
9.9–10: 168
9.9: 170
9.11.1: 181
9.16: 183, 213
9.17.1: 177
9.22.2: 92, 284 n. 17
9.26–28.1: 184
9.26.1: 184, 203
9.27.4: 227
9.27.6: 184, 223
9.35.2: **222**
9.37.4–38.1: **222**
9.41.2–3: 92, 169
9.41.4: 103
9.42.1: 183
9.42.3: 102
9.44–45: 180, 287 n. 24
9.45.2: 103, 180
9.49.1: 289 n. 38
9.51: 165
9.51.1: 283 n. 5
9.53.2: 172, 181, 205
9.54.1: 172
9.55.1–2: 172
9.57: 173
9.58: 173, 182
9.59.1–2: 173
9.62.3: 173
9.63.2: 81, 128, 170, 173
9.64.2: **222**
9.65.2: **148**, 156, 168
9.71–73: 172
9.71.3: 204
9.73.3: **216–217**, 222, 224, 298 n. 18
9.75: 222
9.76–78: 210
9.80–82: 92
9.82: 92, **170**, 210, 223
9.85.3: 177, 222
9.86–88: 177
9.87: 239 n. 26
9.88: 7, 177, 210
9.89: 207

9.93: 246 n. 51
9.93.4: 6
9.100: 149
9.102.3: 170
9.104: 11
9.105: 222

9.108–113: **32–34**, 108, 129, 222, 268 n. 15
9.109.2: 33, 146
9.109.3: 92
9.110: 7, 32, 34
9.120: 214–215
9.122: 18, **92–93**, 169, 186, 214, 215

PASSAGES IN OTHER AUTHORS

Passages are included when they are discussed, but not when they are quoted in a list of parallels. Bold type indicates that the passages are quoted or discussed at length.

ACUSILAUS (*FGRH* 2)

F 39: 256 n. 69

AESCHINES

(3) *Against Ctesiphon* 21: 288 n. 31

AESCHYLUS

Oresteia: 31, 38
  Agamemnon: 15–16, 90
  Choephori: 527–539: 281 n. 45
  Eumenides: 31
Persians: 91, 120, 202, 263 n. 41, 268 n. 15,
    282 n. 52
  176–199: 281 n. 45
  391–407: **174–175**
Suppliant Women: 291 n. 6, 292 n. 16

[AESCHYLUS]

Prometheus
436–506: 16, 79

ALCIDAMAS

fr. 3: 78

ALCMAEON (DK 24)

A 3: 75–76, 85
B 4: 4, **84–85**, 262 n. 23

ANAXAGORAS (DK 59)

B 21a: 2, 5

ANAXIMANDER (DK 12)

B 1: 4

ANDOCIDES

(1) *On the Mysteries*
1–5: 69
52–53: 73
57–59: 73
68: 73
137–139: 69
(2) *On His Return*
11–12: 74
(3) *On the Peace with Sparta* 54
2–12: 54, 251 n. 49

ANTHOLOGIA PALATINA

11.130: **297 n. 12**

ANTIPHON

(1) *On the Murder of Herodes*
21–22: 239 n. 31
21–28: 68
26: 239 n. 31
41–45: 68
52–56: 68

ANTIPHON (continued)
63: 68
68–70: 68
(2–4) Tetralogies: **69–72**, 95
  First Tetralogy
  α 4: 69
  β 3: 257 n. 79
  β 5–6: 69
  β 9: 69
  γ 2: 69
  γ 6: 69
  δ 4–5: 69
  Second Tetralogy
  β 4: 70
  β 5: 70
  β 7: 70
  β 8: 70
  γ 3: 70
  γ 6: 70
  γ 7: 70
  γ 8: 70
  γ 10: 70
  δ 4: 70
  Third Tetralogy: 26
  α 3–4: 70
  β 1–2: 71
  β 3–4: 71
  β 6: 71
  γ 2: 71
  γ 4: 71
  δ 2: 71
  δ 6: 71
  δ 8: 71

ANTIPHON (DK 87)

B 44b: **77–78**
B 61: 242 n. 62

ARISTOPHANES

Acharnians
62–125: 230
65–90: 91
496–556: 31, 215–216
630: 192
632: 192
634–640: 192

Birds
1124–1131: 216
Clouds: 72
Wasps: 294 n. 34
Wealth
908: 273 n. 37

ARISTOTLE

Metaphysics
Γ 1000b12–13: 259 n. 116
Nicomachean Ethics
3.1110b9–17: 258 n. 92
3.1111a21–b3: 258 n. 92
Physics 2.196a11–b9: 49
Poetics
9.1451b17–19: 56
25.1461b15: 49
Politics
1.1252b6–9: 78
1.1254a17–55b15: 78
5.1311b37–39: 33
6.1317a40–43: 190
Rhetoric
1.1365a31–33: 225
2.1402a: 257 n. 79
3.1411a2–4: 225
3.1411a9–11: 196
3.1411a15: 226

CICERO

de Finibus 5.50: 76
de Oratore 2.53: 66

CHARON OF LAMPSACUS (*FGRH* 262)

F 9: 67
F 10: 67
F 14: 67

CHRYSIPPUS

fr. 361: 292 n. 21

(?) CRITIAS

Sisyphus (*TGrF* 43)
F 19: 16, 78

PASSAGES IN OTHER AUTHORS 339

CTESIAS (*FGRH* 388)

F 13.32: 33

CYPRIA

fr. 1: 246 n. 50

DEMOCRITUS (DK 68)

A 13: 76
A 37: 4
A 111: 2

DEMOSTHENES

(18) *On the Crown*
136: 289 n. 39
203: 289 n. 39
(19) *On the False Embassy*
303: 196
(21) *Against Meidias*: **54–55**
73–76: 54–55
128: 55
143–150: 55
199: 55
209: 55
(24) *Against Timocrates*
170–171: 192

[DEMOSTHENES]

(59) *Against Neaera*: 54

DICAEARCHUS

fr. 113 W: 65

DIOCLES OF CARYSTUS

fr. 176: 260 n. 3

DIODORUS SICULUS

1.37.3–4: 256 n. 65
1.38.11–12: 248 n. 6
11.69: 33

DIONYSIUS OF HALICARNASSUS

On Thucydides 5: 23, 58, 63, 66–67

DIONYSIUS OF MILETUS (*FGRH* 687)

T 1: 66
F 2: 67

DISSOI LOGOI: 72

EMPEDOCLES (DK 31)

B 103: 49
B 128: 16
B 130: 16

EPHORUS (*FGRH* 70)

F 180: 67

EURIPIDES

Helen
1676–1679: 246 n. 52
Hippolytus: 15
Orestes
1374: 288 n. 31
Phoenician Women
528–585: 194
Suppliant Women
195–215: 16
417–425: 291 n. 9
433–441: 138, 191, 273 n. 37
481–485: 291 n. 9
Trojan Women: 36
764: 39
860–1060: **73–75**
891–893: 75
915–965: 73–74
948: 74
998: 258 n. 95
1049: 75
1050: 74–75
1054–1055: 75

GALEN

Commentary on Epidemics 1
XVII p. 52 K: 82

GORGIAS

Helen: 35–36, **72–73**, 95
7: 70
13: 260 n. 12
21: 72
On Not-Being: 72
Palamedes: 73–74
3: 73
12–21: 73

HECATAEUS (*FGRH* 1)

T 17a: 63
T 20: 63–64
T 4 Fo.: 62
T 5 Fo.: 62
T 12a Fo.: 64
T 60 Fo.: 62
F 1: 59, **62–63**
F 15: 64
F 18: 64
F 19: 63
F 27: 63
F 30: 64
F 127: 64
FF 140–143: 65
F 197: 64
F 301: 62, 64
F 302: 64

HELLANICUS (*FGRH* 4)

F 170: 67

HERACLITUS (DK 22)

B 94: 4

HESIOD

Works and Days
106–201: 16, 79, 242 nn. 59–60

HIPPOCRATIC CORPUS

Airs, Waters, Places: 18, 88, **89**, **98–99**
4 I p. 76 J = II p. 20 L: 82, 97, 98
5 I pp. 78–80 J = II pp. 22–24 L: 97
6 I p. 82 J = II p. 24 L: 82
7 II pp. 82–88 J = II pp. 26–32 L: **97**
8 I p. 88 J = II p. 30 L: 97
8 I p. 90 J = II p. 34 L: 57
9 I p. 94 J = II p. 38 L: 4
12 I p. 104 J = II p. 52 L: 89
12–13 I pp. 104–108 J = II pp. 52–58 L: 265 n. 19
12 I p. 106 J = II p. 54 L: 4
13 I p. 108 J = II p. 56 L: 97
14 I p. 110 J = II pp. 58–60 L: **99**
15 I p. 112 J = II p. 62 L: 97
16 I pp. 114–116 J = II pp. 62–66 L: **19–20**, 65, 77, 81, 91, 96, 169, 175, 199, 210
19 I p. 122 J = II p. 72 L: 97
22 I p. 126 J = II p. 76 L: 260 n. 3
22 I pp. 126–130 J = II pp. 76–82 L: 97–98, **100–101**
22 I p. 128 J = II pp. 78–80 L: 42
23 I p. 132 J = II p. 82 L: 97
24 I pp. 132–134 J = II p. 86 L: 97
24 I p. 134 J = II p. 90 L: 97
24 I p. 136 J = II p. 90 L: **100**
Aphorisms
1 IV p. 99 J = IV p 458 L: 261 n. 14
Epidemics
1.10 I p. 162 J = 1.4 II p. 630 L: 51
1.19 I p. 174 J = 1.9 II p. 658 L: 251 n. 47
1.20 I p. 176 J = 1.9 II p. 660 L: 51
2.2.24 VII p. 42 S = V pp. 96–98 L: 53
3.15 I pp. 254–256 J = III pp. 98–100 L: 86
4.1.25 VII p. 118 S = V p. 168 L: **52**
6.2.5 VII p. 226 S = V pp. 278–280 L: **52–53**, 118, 120, 227
6.3.7 VII p. 238 S = V p. 296 L: **52**
6.3.12 VII pp. 238–240 S = V p. 298 L: **51**, 52
6.5.1 VII p. 254 S. = V p. 314 L: 86
6.7.1 VII p. 272 S = V p. 336 L: 51
6.8.26 VII p. 286 S = V pp. 352–354 L: 52
In the Surgery
III p. 58 W = III p. 272 L: 51
On Ancient Medicine: 16, 88, 97
2 I p. 16 J = I pp. 572–574 L: 57
10–11 I pp. 30–32 J = I pp. 592–594 L: 52

11 I p. 30 J = I p. 594 L: 261 n. 18
13 I p. 34 J = I p. 598 L: 262 n. 26
14 I p. 38 J = I p. 602 L: 85
16 I p. 42 J = I p. 606 L: 261 n. 18
17–19 I pp. 42–52 J = I pp. 612–620 L: **52**, 96
19 I p. 48 J = I pp. 616–618 L: 250–251 n. 40
18 I p. 46 J = I p. 614 L: 57
20 I p. 52 J = I p. 620 L: 87
20 pp. 52–54 J = I pp. 620–622 L: 87–88
21 I p. 56 J = I p. 624 L: 82
22 I p. 56 J = I p. 626 L: 97
22 I pp. 56–58 J = I p. 626 L: 57
On Breaths: **88–89**, 100
1 II p. 228 J = VI p. 92 L: 85
3 II p. 230 J = VI p. 94 L: 81, **89**, 260 n. 12
14 II pp. 248–252 J = VI pp. 110–114 L: 89
14 II p. 248 J = VI p. 110 L: 251 n. 40
15 II p. 252 J = VI p. 114. L: 89, **100**
On Crises
16 IX p. 282 P = p. 282 L: 251 n. 40
On Female Diseases
2.29 XI pp. 348–349 = 2.138 VIII pp. 310–312 L: 83
On Fractures
26 III p. 156 W = III p. 504 L: 82
On Regimen 1: 4, 85, 88
On Regimen 3
70 IV p. 384 J = VI p. 606 L: 250 n. 38
On Regimen 4: 264 n. 11
88 IV pp. 422–424 J = VI p. 642 L: 281 n. 35
On Sevens: 4
On the Nature of Man: 88
1–2 IV pp. 2–8 J = VI pp. 32–36 L: 96
4 IV pp. 10–12 J = VI pp. 38–40 L: 86
7 IV p. 18 J = VI pp. 46–48 L: 57
9 IV pp. 24–26 J = VI pp. 52–54 L: **50–51**, 83, 96
9 IV p. 26 J = VI p. 54 L: 82
12 IV p. 36 J = VI 12 p. 64 L: 86
On the Places in Man
42 VIII p. 84 P = VI p. 334 L: 85
On the Sacred Disease: 18, 88, **97–99**, 100, 161

2 II p. 142 J = VI p. 356 L: 241 n. 45
5 II pp. 150–152 J = 2 VI pp. 364–366 L: 42
7 II p. 154 J = 4 VI p. 368 L: 57
13 II pp. 164–168 J = 10 VI pp. 378–380 L: 98–99
14 II p. 168 J = 11 VI p. 382 L: 96
15 II p. 171 J = 12 VI p. 382 L: 96, 98
Prognostikon
1 II p. 6 J = II p. 110 L: 229
Prorrhetikon
2.16 VIII p. 256 P = IX p. 42 L: 83
2.24 VIII p. 272 P = IX p. 56 L: 83
The Art
4–8 II pp. 194–204 J = VI pp. 6–14 L: 81, 260 nn. 9–10
6 II p. 198 J = VI p. 10 L: **80**
11 II p. 208 J = VI p. 20 L: 81
11 II p. 210 J = VI p. 20 L: 82

HOMER

Iliad
1.1–7: 24
1.4–5: 122
1.8: 24, 89, 108
2.225–242: 35
2.701–702: 215
3.1–9: 145, 174
3.10–37: 145
3.38–57: 34
3.164–165: 35, 70
3.171–180: 35
3.380–382: 281 n. 45
3.453–454: 35
4.158–168: 35
4.234–239: 35
4.269–271: 35
5.62–63: 105, 192, 228
6.208: 201
6.280–285: 35
6.344–359: 35
6.357–358: 203–204
6.525: 35
7.127–128: 241 n. 53
7.351–353: 35
7.385–397: 35
9.189: 23

HOMER (continued)
9.515–523: 35
9.624–642: 202
9. 650–653: 202
11.186–194: 271 n. 6
11.284–309: 271 n. 6
11.654: 35
11.784: 201
13.108–113: 35
13.624–625: 35
15.716–717: 202, 295 n. 14
16.273–274: 35
Books 17–18: 203
17.434–435: 203
18.97–126: 35, 201–202
18.607–608: 64, 255 n. 51
19.181–182: 35
19.302: 240 n. 36
20.325–329: 281 n. 45
21.194–198: 64
21.275–278: 35
22.104: 35
22.305: 203–204
22.322–325: 284 n. 17
22.410–411: 175
24.468–676: 145, 156
24.525–533: **21**, 89–90, 145, 213
24.768–775: 35
Odyssey
1.3: 29, 76
1.5: 202
1.7–9: 205
2.47: 202
2.234: 202
Book 4: 75
4.561–569: 246 n. 52
5.12: 202
5.262–493: 149
12.260–425: 205
22.351–353: 177
22.356: 177

ISOCRATES

(4) *Panegyric*
85–99: 278 n. 61
(11) *Busiris*
28: 76

JUSTIN

3.1: 33

LIVY

9.17–19: 200–201, 294 n. 3

[LONGINUS]

On the Sublime
27.2: 63–64

MIMNERMUS

frr. 13–13a W^2: 59

NICOLAUS OF DAMASCUS (*FGRH* 90)

F 47.1–11: 108, 267 n. 9

OLD TESTAMENT

Esther 2: 131

PARMENIDES (DK 28)

A 37: 4
B 8.14: 4

PAUSANIAS

1.27.5: 217

PHERECYDES (*FGRH* 3)

F 2: 256–257 n. 71

PINDAR

Pythian 1: 291 n. 4

PLATO

Gorgias
452d: 186
470c–471d: 144
Laws
10.889b–c: 49

Menexenus
244e: 192
Phaedo
97b8–c2: 61
Protagoras
320c–8d: 16, 78
Republic: 90, 187
2.358b-361d: 16–17, 78
2.359c–360b: 107, 267 nn. 5–6 and 12
8.558b: 292 n. 20
8.561e: 291 n. 8, 292 n. 20
8.563b: 291 n. 8
Symposium
182a–d: 76–77
186d-187c: 84
188a: 84
208c: 295 n. 17

PLUTARCH

Alcibiades
10.1–2: 206
Aristeides: 135, 279 n. 7
10.4–6: 293 n. 27
11: 169
Cimon
6.4–5: 296 n. 43
Coriolanus
6: 238 n. 20
Pericles 36.5: 69–70, 295–296 n. 30
Themistocles: 279 n. 7
18.2: 294–295 n. 5
18.8: 294–295 n. 5
24: 275 n. 7
Apophthegmata Laconica
225c: 295 n. 19
God's slowness to punish
10 555c: 296 n. 43
On Herodotus' Malice: 279 n. 7
12 857a–b: 247 n. 58
On the Pythian Oracles
16 401e–f: 270 n.40

POLYBIUS

3.6.1: 105
3.8.8–11: 257 n. 77
5.106.5: 186

PROTAGORAS

Antilogiai: 72

PYTHAGORAS (DK 14)

A 4: 76

PS.-SCYLAX

105.1: 65, 256 n. 55

SIMONIDES

Plataea: 15, 59, 202
fr. 11.30 W²: 284 n. 13
Salamis: 59

SOPHOCLES

Antigone
332–375: 16
904–920: 129
Oedipus Coloneus
538–540: 70
Oedipus Tyrannus: 15–16, 280 n. 25
Philoctetes: 38

STESICHORUS

Palinodes: 37, 247 n. 57

STESIMBROTUS OF THASOS

On Themistocles, Thucydides, and Pericles: 134–135

STRABO

14.1.16: 76

TACITUS

Annals 1.1: 150

THALES (DK 11)

A 11: 76

THUCYDIDES

1.1–19: 46
1.2.5–6: 93
1.6.2: 237 n. 7
1.9.1: 104
1.20.3: 62
1.22.3–4: 212, 231
1.23.6: 40, 121, 232, 261–262 n. 22
1.24–55: 56
1.31–44: 226
1.32.3–4: 226
1.36.3: 299 n. 47
1.37.2–4: 226
1.40.5: 299 n. 47
1.41.2: 299 n. 47
1.55–65: 299–300 n. 48
1.69.1: 74
1.70: 212
1.70.2: 205
1.75.4: 231
1.76.1–2: 212
1.78.1: 49
1.84.4: 49
1.86.2: 227
1.88.1: 104
1.99.3: 124
1.104: 218
1.109–110: 218
1.108.5: 217
1.111.1: 56
1.112.3: 218
1.126–127: 239 n. 27
1.128.1–135.1: 209, 210, 212
1.132.2–3: 210
1.135.2–138: 206, 210, 212, 275 n. 7
1.140.1: 49
1.144.1: 87
2.1–6: 227
2.1.1: 105
2.7.1: 230
2.8.4: 189
2.9.1: 56
2.11.4: 49
2.17.4: 56
2.22.2: 56
2.23.2: 56
2.25: 56

2.27: 217, **219**, 226
2.30: 56
2.36.5–46: 164
2.37.1: 291 n. 7
2.38.2: 93
2.39.1: 93
2.49.2: 83
2.56: 56, 217
2.63.2: 231
2.64.3: 231
2.65.4: 192
2.65.7: 231
2.65.9: 86–87
2.65.11: 40, 104
2.65.13: 231
2.67.1: 230
2.70: 299–300 n. 48
3.26.3: 217, 298 n. 19
3.36.6: 209
3.38: 192
3.52–68: 68, 72
3.55.1: 74
3.57.1: 74
3.62.3–4: 291 n. 7
3.67.2: 227
3.67.6: 74
3.68.4: 75
3.68.5: 192, 227, 293 n. 29
3.82.2: 212
3.82.8: 194, 291 n. 8
3.86: 299 n. 48
3.93.2: 56
3.101.2: 56
4.1–41: 56
4.22.2: 289 n. 39
4.50: 230
4.53–57: 217
4.57: 217
4.57.4: 226
4.61.5: 212
4.62.4: 49
4.78.2–3: 291 n. 7
4.97–98: 225
4.108.7: 206
5.1: 230
5.72.2: 230
5.105.2: 212
6.18.3: 141

6.18.6: 86
6.20–23: 144
6.35.2: 209
6.38.5: 291 n. 8
7.2.4: 50
7.18: 230, 286 n. 12
7.57.1: 104
7.87.6: 279 n. 6
8.48.5: 190
8.96.5: 212, 262 n. 29
8.97.2: 86

XANTHUS OF LYDIA (*FGRH* 765)

FF 12–13a: 67
F 30: 67
F 32: 67

XENOPHANES (DK 21)

B 15–16: 76
B 18: 16

XENOPHON

Cyropaedia: 132, 144
1.3.10: 292 n. 21
7.2.15–17: 269 n. 28
8.8: 91
Hellenica
7.1.38: 91
Memorabilia
4.2.14: 286 n. 14
4.4.19–20: 76

PS.-XENOPHON ('THE OLD OLIGARCH'),
ATH. POL.

1.8: 186
1.12: 292 n. 21

ZENO

fr. 288: 292 n. 21

GENERAL INDEX

Bold type indicates that the subjects are quoted or discussed at length.

Abydus, 12, 111, 123, 130, 141, 157, 200
Achaemenes (son of Darius), 218, 220
Acheloüs, 300 n. 52
Achilles: and Agamemnon, 24, 35, 59, 89; armor of, 284 n. 17; choice of, 278 n. 64; community of, 201–202; greatness and destruction of, 18, 189, 228; and Priam, 21, 145, 156, 213; in Simonides, 15, 202, 284 n. 13; singing of, 23; wrath of, 35, 202, 204
Acropolis, Athenian, 93, 154, 161, 281 n. 40
Acusilaus, 22, 256 n. 69
Adams, John, 294 n. 1
Adeimantus of Corinth, 183–184, 208
Admetus (king of the Molossians), 275 n. 7
Adrastus, 70, 152
Aeacidae, 161
Aegina/Aeginetans, 171, 178, 222; and Athens, 8, 10, 134, 136, 137, 187, 188, 208, 217, 225, 226, 228; and Cleomenes, 6, 178, 188, 209, 290 n. 58; expulsion of, in 424 BCE, 217, 219, 224, 298 n. 22
Aeimnestus, 222
Aeneas, 256 n. 69, 281 n. 45
Aeolia, 7, 106
Aeschines of Eretria, 178
Aeschylus, 149, *Oresteia* 15–16, 31; *Persians* 91, 120, 132, 174–175, 202, 268 n. 15, 282 n. 15, 285 n. 2; *Suppliant Women* 291 n. 6, 292 n. 16. See also Index 2, "Passages in Other Authors"
Aesop, 59

Aëtius, 84
Africa, 60, 218, 247 n. 53, 274 n. 59; circumnavigation of, 6, 218–219
Agamemnon: in Aeschylus, 15–16, 90, 268 n. 20; at Aulis, 39; in Euripides, 73; in Homer, 24, 35, 59, 89, 204
Agariste, 57, 219
Agatharchides, 248 n. 6
Agbatana, 159
aitiē: in Herodotus, **5–8**, 24–26, 32, 34, 49, 90, 102, 109, 110, 119, 126, 127, 234, 239 nn. 25 and 29, 276 n. 40; in Hippocratics, 50–51, **81–84**, 89, 99–100, 158, 250–251 n. 40, 261 nn. 17–18; in other authors, 49, 69–71, 186, 260 n. 3, 261–262 n. 22
Ajax, 202
Alcibiades, 55, 86, 141, 200, 206, 262 n. 31, 300 n. 8
Alcidamas, 78
Alcmaeonids, 7, 189, 197
Alcmaeon of Croton, 4, 80, **84–85**, 238 n. 12, 262 n. 23
Aleuadae, 103, 121, 287 n. 24
Alexander of Macedon, 6, 103, **180–182**, 287 n. 24, 288 n. 34
Alexander the Great, 218–219, 272 n. 19, 275 n. 16, 294 n. 3
Alyattes, 106, 115
Amasis (king of Egypt), 34, 119, 121, 131, 268 n. 24, 282 n. 49
Amasis (Persian general), 126, 127, 207, 274 n. 58
Amestris, 7, 32–34, 108, 220

Ammon, 136
Amompharetus, 172, 181, 205
Amphiaraus, 269 n. 28
Amyrtaeus, 218
Anacharsis, 76
Anaxagoras, 2, 61, 256 n. 65
Anaximander, 4, 237 n. 5, 238–239 n. 21
Andocides, 54, 67, 69, 73–74, 254 n. 28
Andromache, 39, 73
Andros, 205, 208, 221
Antigone, 18, 189. *See also* Sophocles
Antiochus (Arcadian), 91
Antiphon (orator), 26, 68, **69–72**, 95, 239 n. 31, 292 n. 16
Antiphon (sophist), 77, 242 n. 62; possibly same as Antiphon the orator, 77
Aphidnae, 207
Aphrodite, 72–74, 160, 256 n. 69, 281 n. 45
Apis, 105, 159, 277 n. 53
Apollo: and Croesus, 111–113, 114, 146, 153, 156, 268 n. 19, 269 n. 25, 269–270 n. 30; in Homer, 169; protects his shrines, 147–148, 156, 168
Apollodorus ([Dem.] 59), 54
Apollonia, 6
Apries, 9, 119, 131, 146
Apsinthians, 137
Araxes, 141–142
Arcadia, 136, 178, 222
Arcesilaus, 10, 125–127, 270 n. 42, 273 n. 53
archē, 13–14, 26, 105, 192
Archidamus (king of Sparta), 49
Ardys, 106
Areopagus, 67
Arginusae, 74, 278 n. 58
Argo, 25, 27
Argos, 20, 25, 102, 136, 160, 179, 209, 212, 220, 222, 273 n. 47
Arimnestus, 222
Arion, 149, 274 n. 5
Aristagoras of Miletus: at Athens, 124, 192, 209, 289 n. 46; cause of troubles of, 14, 199, 223; "gives up tyranny," 193–194, 225, 290 n. 3, 292 n. 15; in Ionia, 105, 121, 143, 219; runs away, 182; at Sparta, 92, 169, 196, 205; tyrannical aspirations of, 143, 219

Aristeas of Corinth, 220
Aristeides, 135, 196, 197, 279 n. 7, 293 n. 27
Aristodemus of Sparta, 204, 224, 249 n. 22
Aristodicus of Cumae, 155
Aristogeiton, 194
Ariston (king of Sparta), 109, 207
Aristophanes, 144, 292 n. 16; *Acharnians*, 31, 91, 215–216, 230; *Birds*, 216; *Clouds*, 72 *See also* Index 2, "Passages in Other Authors"
Aristotle, 4, 49, 56, 76, 78, 190, 248 n. 12, 258 n. 92, 259 n. 116, 268 n. 23. *See also* Index 2, "Passages in Other Authors"
Artabanus (commander of Xerxes' bodyguard), 33, 246 n. 44
Artabanus (Xerxes' uncle): at Abydus, 12, 111, 123, 141, 157, 177, 200, 249 n. 18, 268 n. 24; advising Darius against Scythian expedition, 119, 137; advising Xerxes against Greek expedition, 119, **122–123**, 137–138, 139–140, **153–154**, 156–158, 181, 281 n. 38
Artabazus, 183
Artaphrenes, 44, 219
Artaxerxes (son of Xerxes), 33, 220
Artaxerxes I, 187, 216, 219
Artaÿctes, 214–215
Artaÿnte, 32–33, 129, 146
Artembares, 92
Artemisia, 1, 138, 183, 243 n. 2, 286 n.10, 288 n. 37
Artemisium, 158, 166, 173, 288 n. 3, 296 n. 33
Aryandes, 10, 125–128, 270 n. 42, 273 n. 51, 274 n. 58
Asia and Europe, 19–21, 25–26, 89, 91, 96, 214, 244 n. 21, 245 n. 25; dividing point between, 26–27, 65, 122, 158, 214. *See also* East and West, contrasts and similarities between; Hellespont
Asopus, 173
Assyria, 118, 136, 175
Astyages: dream of, 67; fall of, 8, 34, 92, 103, 116, 143–144, **151–153**; and Harpagus, 57, 114, 151, 177, 277 n. 50, 280 n. 30; harshness of rule of, 153, 179; and young Cyrus, 129

GENERAL INDEX

Athena, 74, 93, 191, 208
Athenades, 102
Athenagoras of Syracuse, 209
Athens/Athenians: and Aegina, 8, 10, 134, 136–137, 187–188, 208, 217, 224–228, 276 n. 35, 298 n. 22; democracy, impact of, 19, 164, 185, 191, 193–198, 207–209, 212–213; difficulty of handling great men, 206–207, 209–210; and Egypt, 163, 218; empire, 106, 124, 185, 186, 198, **ch. 15**; after 479 BCE, 117, 185, 220–223; from 480–479 BCE, 6, 154, 156, 167–168, 172–173, 178, 181–189, 192; freedom, inspired by, 164, 179–181, 193–195, 199; ideology of, 202, 283 n. 3, 284 n. 9, 285 n. 1, 289 n. 50, 293 nn. 24–25; and Ionian Revolt, 67, 121, 124, 192, 205–206; and Marathon campaign, 147, 169–170, 172–173, 176, 178, 185–186, 188–189; national characteristics of, 192, **ch. 14(d)–(e)**, 224, 288 n. 37; before Peloponnesian War, 84, 185, 217, 219–20, 225, 226, 299 n. 47; in Peloponnesian War, 56, 212, **ch. 15**; and Plataea, 72, 74, 192, 195, 226–227; as saviors of Greece, 42, 178, 220, 227; as target of Darius' and Xerxes' vengeance, 9, 10, 31, 103–104, 119, 134; as tyrant city, 86–87, 93, 144, 189, 235–236, 278 n. 59, 286 n. 14; under tyranny, 115, 191, 286 n. 16; unpopularity of, with other Greeks, 43, 178, 195, 225; and Xerxes' heralds, 101–102, 143, 220, 224. *See also* democracy
Atossa, 80, 103, 108, 115, 121, 129, 131, 136, 140, 174
Atreus, 15–16, 114, 277 n. 43
Attaginus, 177
Atys, 112, 140–141, 152
audiences, different, 17–18, 60–61, 73, 75, 84, 86, 195, 196, 198, 215, 216, 226, 231, 236, 254 n. 31, 285 n. 1
Aulis, 16, 39
Autonous, 147

Babylon/Babylonia, 76, 118, 163, 107, 216, 218

Bacis, 149
Bacon, Francis, 41
Bactria, 32, 33, 240 n. 35
Badian, Ernst, 137
Badres, 127
balancing/blending, 18–19, 20–21, 36, 82–83, **84–88**, 98, 189, 233, 234, 262 n. 29. *See also* harmony
Baragwanath, Emily, 11
Barce, 125–128, 207
Battiadae, 127, 273 n. 56
Beer, Gillian, 4
Behistun, 130, 134, 200, 275 n. 9
Berlin, Isaiah, 289–290 n. 51, 294 n. 2
Bias of Priene, 12, 114, 117, 118, 137, 142, 186, 270
binary thinking, **ch. 4(c)**, 98–99
biography and "biostructuring," **ch. 9(b)**, 200
Biton, 120
Black Sea, 64
blame/blamers, 5–8, 13–14, **ch. 2**, 68–75, 82, 102, 109, 117, 119, **ch. 8(c)**, 184, 239 nn. 26–30, 250 n. 38, 258 n. 84, 261–262 n. 22, 276 n. 40
blending. *See* balancing/blending
Boeotia, 54, 77, 78, 209
Boges, 220, 223
Boreas, 158, 168
Bosporus, 119, 122, 194
Boulis, 220
Bovary, Emma, 131
Branchidae, 155
Brasidas, 206, 212, 230
Brentesion, 249 n. 21
Buchan, John, 48
Burckhardt, Jacob, 236
"but-for" thinking, 46–47, 55

Cadmus of Cos, 196
Cadmus of Miletus, 66, 67, 256 n. 65, 257 n. 73
Callias, 220
Callimachus (Athenian polemarch), 135, 185–186, 188, 196, 197, 202, 293–294 n. 31
Cambyses: and attack on Ethiopia, 136, 176; death of, 159; Herodotus' treat-

ment and characterization of, 133, 277 nn. 53–54; like and unlike other Persian kings, 116, 119, 121, 139; madness of, 12, 80, 105, 129, 139, 159–160; reasons of, for attacking Egypt, 34, 80, 119, **131**; treatment of courtiers and subjects by, 7, 9, 10–11, 138, 143, 159. *See also* Cleomenes
Candaules and his unnamed wife, 27, 32, 33, 36, **ch. 7(a)**, 116, 129, 130, 146, 246 n. 44, 267 n. 11
cap-badges, Greek army, 203
Carneia, 178
Carthage, 136, 139, 219, 221, 257 n. 77
Carystus, 178, 205, 208, 222
Casablanca, 47
Cassandane, 131
Cassandra, 73
Catherine of Aragon, 47
Cephisodotus, 196
Ceyx, 64
chance, 47, **48–49**, 81, 83, 242 n. 12, 250 n. 28, 260 n. 9, 271 n. 18
Chaos, 67
Charon of Lampsacus, 66, 67, 253 n. 16, 257 n. 72
Chersonese, 134, 135, 137, 194, 208. *See also* Miltiades
Chileos of Tegea, 170
Chios, 161, 179, 283 n. 64. *See also* Ion of Chios
chronological scaffolding, 60, 66
Cicero, 14, 28, 66
Cilicia, 138, 286 n. 10
Cimmerians, 106
Cimon, 67, 220, 223
Cleidemus, 284 n. 13
Cleobis, 120
Cleomenes: and Aegina, 6, 178, 188, 209, 219, 290 n. 58; and Athens, 7; and Delphi, 20, 159–160, 207, 283 n. 60; and Demaratus, 20, 108–109, 135, 207; Herodotus' treatment and characterization of, 135, 204, 205, 209, 296 n.31; madness of, and similarity to Cambyses, 80, **159–160**, 172, 211, 269 n. 25, 270 n. 3, 277–278 n. 55; self-mutilation and death of, 20–21, 172; succeeded by Leonidas, 135; tempted by Aristagoras' approach, 169, 192
Cleon, 56, 192, 209, 278 n. 59, 289 n. 39
Cleopatra, 47
Clytemnestra, 54, 281 n. 45
Cnidus, 157
Coes, 138, 139
Colchis/Colchians, 3, 25, 27, 237 n. 7
Colophon, 106
Corax, 69, 257 n. 79
Corcyra, 45–46, 104, 206, 226, 249 n. 20, 261–262 n. 22, 299 n. 47; animosity of, with Corinth, 3, 44, 46, 50, 56, 226
Corinth: and attack on Samos, 44, 136–137; in 480 BCE, 178, 183–184, 289 n. 40; supports Athens in 440 BCE, 299 n. 47; in run-up to Peloponnesian War, 40, 74, 124, 185, 226, 261–262 n. 22; and oligarchy, 190; and tyranny, 198. *See also* Adeimantus of Corinth; Corcyra: animosity of, with Corinth; Periander; Soclees of Corinth
corroborative argument, **88–93**, 97
counterfactual thinking, 3, **43–46**, 47, 50, 54–55, 68–75, 164, 204, 233, 248 nn. 11–15, 249 nn. 18, 21–22, and 26, 257 n. 77
court dynamics, 33–34, **ch. 9**
Crete, 25–28, 74, 242 n. 55
Croesus, **chs. 7, 8(a)**; attacks Greeks, 7–8, 14, 27, 29, 31, 90, 106, 110, 114–115, 136–137, 176, 218, 239 n. 30, 266 n. 28, 266–267 n. 3; and Atys, 70, 140, 152; between East and West, 25, 114; and Cambyses, 9, 10, 138; and Cyrus, 91–92, 93, 103, **114–118**, 137, 138, 139, **141–142**, 213, 239 n. 26, 271 n. 16; intellectual curiosity of, 12, 114–116; prefigures later kings, 8, 31, 114–117, 120, 129, 155, 270 n. 42; on pyre, **111–113**, 140, 146, 149, 152–153, 166; reasons for fall of, 32, 49–50, **109–113**, 142, 268 n. 20; and Solon, 30, 49, **110–113**, 138, 166; tests oracles, 111, 269 n. 20
Croton, 80. *See also* Alcmaeon of Croton; Democedes
Ctesias, 132, 246 n. 44. 275 nn. 8 and 13, 277 n. 53
Cyaxares, 115, 116

Cylon, 7
Cyno, 150–151
Cypria, 246 n. 50
Cyprus, 138, 175, 190, 286 n. 10, 295 n. 19
Cyrene, 9, 80, 125, 127–128
Cyrus, **chs. 7(b), 8(b)**; and Assyrians, 118, 136; and Astyages, 8, 34, 73, 114, 129, 151–153, 175; as boy, 117–118, 129, 149–151, 288 n. 27, 292 n. 21; and Croesus campaign, 93, 103, 114–116, 118, 133, 139, 266 n. 28, 271 n. 26; and Croesus on pyre, 111–113; cylinder, 134, 200; like and unlike other kings, 12, 116–117, 119, 138, 157, 207; and Lydians, 18, 91–93, 175, 239 n. 26; and Massagetae, 92, 102, 119, 137–138, 139, **141–142**; mindset of, 102, 116, 118, 119, 139; in other authors, 91, 133–134, 144, 150, 200, 275 n. 20, 278 n. 62; retrospective of, at end of *Histories*, 18, **92–93**, 214–215
Cythera, 217, 226, 230

Danaus, 63
Dante Alighieri, 270 n. 36
Danube. *See* Nile: symmetry of, with Danube
Darius (son of Xerxes), 32–33, 246 n. 44
Darius I: against Greece, 6, 9, 80, 108, 115, 121, 129, 136, 273–274 n. 57; against Libya, 125–128; against Perinthians, 136; against Samos, 8, 124–125, 137; against Scythia, 8, 12, 119, 137, 139, 176–177, 194, 272 n. 25; campaigns of, against Getae, 178; desire of, for vengeance, 9, 10, 31, 104, 119, 134; gains throne and speech in constitutions debate, 129, 130, 175, 187, 193, 207, 211, 225, 278 n. 63; Herodotus' treatment and characterization of, 12, 131, 133–134, 200, 207; and Histiaeus, 34, 44, 46; insight of, into cultural diversity, 78, 142–143, 277 n. 54; like or unlike predecessors and successor, 12, 116–122, 139, 154–155; treatment of subjects by, 7, 8, 138
Darwin, Charles, 4

Datis, 134, 224–225, 286 n. 16
Decelea, 216–217, 222, 223, 224, 227, 228, 298 n. 18
Deioces, 17, 78, 143–144, 150, 211, 278 n. 66
delay, narrative, 115, 135, 271 n. 6, 276 n. 31
Delium, 219, 224–225, 227
Delos, 219, 286 n. 16, 296 n. 51
Delphi: Apollo's protection of, 147–148, 156, 168–169; and Cleomenes' bribery, 20, 159–160, 207, 283 n. 60; Croesus' dealings with, 103, **111–116**, 146, 148, 156, 269 n. 29, 270 n. 40; Mardonius spares, 102; oracles, 42, 102, 108, 112, 156, 157, 158, 160, 281 n. 42; and Pausanias' victory epigram, 210
Demaratus: and Cleomenes and Leutychidas, 20, 108–109, 135, 160, 207, 209, 219, 266 n. 32, 283 n. 60; at Persian court, 103; with Xerxes, 121, 138, **165–166**, 169, 172, 181–182, 188, 199, 200, 203–205, 211, 217, 226, 230, 284 n. 9
Demeter, 148, 156, 168
Democedes, 80, 121
Democritus, 2, 4, 49, 76, 256 n. 65
democracy, 79, 87, **ch. 13**, 212, 219, 291 n. 9; avoidance of (the word), 193–194; best explored under stress, 88; and connection with individuality, 199, 207–208, 234; in constitutions debate, 175, 179, 193, 278 n. 63, 290 n. 56; and "democratic courage," 164; as easily misled, 191; felt by Sparta as threat, 137, 212; and freedom, 164, 190–191, 195–198, 199, 283 n. 4, 291 n. 6, 293 n. 26, 294 n. 2; influence of "democratic ideology," 284 n. 9, 285 n. 1, 293 nn. 24 and 28–29, 294 n. 31; as inspiring, 164, 191, 230; not always emphasized, 195–197, 207–209, 292 nn. 16 and 20; prospects of, for future, 228, **230–231**, 236; slogans about, 138, 179, 191, **194–195**, 273 n. 37, 291 n. 8; and texture of democratic debate, 121–122, 164, 283 n. 5; and tyranny, 78, 86–87, 93, 144, 164, 184, 189, **191–198**, 206, 234–236,

278 n. 59, 286 n. 14, 294 n. 34. *See also* Athens/Athenians: as tyrant city
Demosthenes (fifth-century general), 56, 262 n. 32
Demosthenes (fourth-century orator), 54–55, 251 n. 50. *See also* Index 2, "Passages in Other Authors"
determinism: climatic, 18, 242 n. 68, 242–243 n. 70; historical, 48, 118, 167–168, 235–236, 248 n. 12
Deucalion, 64
Dicaearchus, 65
Dicaeopolis, 215
Dieneces, 204
dikē, 4, 20, 26
Dinon, 132
Diocles of Carystus, 260 n. 3
Diodorus Siculus, 248 n. 6, 256 n. 65
Diodotus, 186
Dionysius of Halicarnassus, 23, 58, 63, 66–67, 241 n. 53
Dionysius of Miletus, 66, 67, 253 n. 16, 257 n. 74
Dionysius of Phocaea, 166, 179
Dionysus, 160
Dioscuri, 284 n. 13
Dissoi Logoi, 72
Dodona, 11
Dorians, 106
Dorieus, 209
Doriscus, 220
dreams, 67, 73, 140, 152, **153–156**, 181, 219–220, 240 n. 34, 249 n. 18, 281 nn. 35–40 and 44–45

East and West, contrasts and similarities between, 19–20, 27, 38–39, 54, 65, 77–78, 132–133, 169, 175, 179, 199, 211, 225, 228, 234. *See also* Asia and Europe
Echetlus, 202
Eden, Sir Anthony, 218
Edonians, 222
Egypt/Egyptians: culture and customs of, 11, 18, 38–39, 80, 102; desert or revolt, 7, 9; Greek campaign in, 218; Greeks learning from, 60, 76, 90; Helen in, **35–38**, 143; and Herodotus' presentation, 23, 35–39, 63, 90, 98, 148; and memory, stretching back further there than elsewhere, 38, 246–247 n. 53; other authors on, 22–23, 67, 216; Persian invasions of, 34, 80, 119, 121, **131**, 136, 165, 218, 220, 243 n. 5; sources from, for Herodotus?, 247 n. 57, 254 n. 36. *See also* Amasis, king of Egypt; Apries; Hecataeus of Miletus; Nile; Proteus; Psammetichus; Sesostris
eikos reasoning, 68–69, 71, 74, 257 n. 79
Eion, 220
Electra, 54
Eleusis, 20, 146, 148, 160
Elis, 2, 77, 78, 178, 219, 222
Elizabeth I, 159
Empedocles, 16, 49, 61, 82, 84, 259 n. 116
Ennea Hodoi, 220
envy, divine, 156–157, 161, 268 n. 24, 282 n. 49
Ephesus, 137
Ephialtes (Greek traitor at Thermopylae), 7, 102
Ephorus, 67
epic cycle, 67, 216, 267 n. 8, 297 n. 12
Epidaurus, 178
Epimetheus, 262 n. 27
epinician odes, 59, 206
Epizelus, 147, 148
Erbse, Hartmut, 146
Eretria, 31, 104, 119, 134, 176, 178, 287 n. 20
erga, 23–24, 28–30
erōs, 67, 72, 78, 84
Eryximachus, 84
Esther, 131
Eteocles, 194
Ethiopia, 31, 76, 136, 176, 286 n. 14
Euaion, 54–55
Euboea, 158. 204–205, 221
Euesperides, 274 n. 58
Euripides, 144, 242 n. 61; *Hippolytus*, 15; *Phoenician Women*, 194; *Suppliant Women*, 16, 191; *Telephus*, 216, 275 n. 27; *Trojan Women*, 36, 39, **72–75**. *See also* Index 2, "Passages in Other Authors"
Europa, 25, 107
Europe and Asia. *See* Asia and Europe

352 GENERAL INDEX

Eurybiades, 169, 171, 183–184, 185, 208, 221, 283 n. 5
Eurymachus, 221
Eurystheus, 63
Eurytus, 204

Fabius Pictor, 257 n. 77
familiar experience, appeals to, 5, 56–57, 64, 88–89, 229, 241 n. 46, 252 n. 60
Fish, Stanley, 113
Fludernik, Monika, 241 n. 46
Focke, Friedrich, 146, 161
Fornara, Charles, 120, 217, 272 n. 30
Fowler, Robert, 66, 68, 239 n. 23, 255 n. 41
freedom, **chs. 12 and 13(a)**; from Athens, 225, 229; and democracy, 164, **190–191**, 195–198, 199, 283 n. 4, 291 n. 6, 293 n. 26, 294 n. 2; downsides of as well as upsides, 43, 87, 143, 170, **181–184, 188–189**, 197–198, 234; in East as well as West, 169, 175–176, 211, 213, 228, 285 n. 4; freedom from and freedom to, 176, **184–189**, 289 nn. 50–51; as inspirational, 19–20, 164, **174–181**, 185–186, 199; internal and external threats to, 190, 291 n. 5; "not wanting to be free," 125, 178–180, 211, 287 n. 23; reflected in narrative shape, 135–136, 187–188; and slavery, 176–177; of speech, 122, 125, 138, 178, 182–184, 191, 288 n. 32; at stake in Persian wars, 15, 42, 167, 174–181; and tyranny, 163–164, 191, **194–196**, 231, 293 n. 26
French Revolution, 47
future, **ch. 15(c)**, 235–236

Gaia, 67
Galen, 82–83
Gelon of Syracuse: arguments of ambassadors to, 10, 103–104, 190, 266 n. 30, 289 n. 40, 299–300 n. 48; response of to ambassadors, 187, 225, 289 n. 39; strategy of, 45, 221, 249 n. 19; and treatment of Megara Hyblaea, 239 n. 29
genealogies, 15, 60, 66, 67, 241 n. 53, 254 n. 36. *See also* Hecataeus of Miletus
genres, 17–18, 58–59, 79, 101
geography and history, 3, 15, 58, **65–66**, 67, 297 n. 10
Getae, 178
Glaucon, 78
Glaucus, 281 n. 42
Gorgias, 35–36, 70, **72–73**, 74, 78, 95, 186, 258 nn. 91–95
Gould, John, 30–31, 232, 241 n. 49
"Great Man" and "Great Woman" theories, 47, 199–200, cf. 206, 209–210
Greenblatt, Stephen, 132
Gyges, 32, 59, **106–109**, 112, 142, 146, 267 nn. 5–9, 270 n. 32, 275 n. 6
Gylippus, 212
Gyndes, 117, 157

habrotēs. *See* softness
Halicarnassus, 1, 60, 130, 242 n. 55
Halys, 117
Handel, George Frideric, 130
harems, 129–131, 176
Harmodius, 194
harmony, 14, 18, **84–88**, 97, 233, 262 n. 25, 264 n.10. *See also* balance
Harpagus (general of Darius), 44
Harpagus (rebel): and campaign against Cnidians, 157; rebellion of, 8, **151–153**, 177, 280 n. 30, 280–281 n. 34; and "Thyestean banquet," 57, 114, **151**
Hart, H. L. A., and Tony Honoré, 14, 95, 241 n. 49, 264 n. 2
Hecataeus of Miletus, 14–15, 23, 29, **58–66**, 137, 256 n. 65. *See also* Nile: Hecataeus on
Hector, 35, 73, 175, 202–204, 228, 284 n. 17
Hecuba, 36, 73–75, 258 n. 100
Hegesistratus, 222
Helen: in Euripides, 36, **73–75**, 246 n. 52; in Gorgias, 35–36, 70, **72–73**, 95, 258 n. 95, 260 n. 12; in Herodotus, 25–28, 31, **36–39**, 44, 57, 108, 143, 146–147, 216, 245 n. 40, 280 n. 25; in Homer,

35, 70, 74, 105, 124, 192, 203–204, 246 n. 52; in Stesichorus, 38
Hellanicus of Lesbos, 67, 256 n. 65
Hellespont, 8, 189, 206, 208, 214, 220, 285 n. 23; as dividing point of continents, 27, 122, 158, 214; Xerxes' crossing and maltreatment of, 10, 117, 119, 122, 158–159, 181, 288 n. 27
Helms, Mary, 238 n. 19
Hera, 1, 73–74
Heracles, 63, 202
Heraclidae, 64, 109, 112
Heraclitus, 4
Hermion, 178
Hermocrates of Syracuse, 49
Hermolycus, 222
Herodes (murder victim), 68–69, 239 n. 31
Hesiod, 16, 61, 63, 79, 101, 241 n. 53, 242 n. 59. *See also* Index 2, "Passages in Other Authors"
Hippias (tyrant of Athens), 185, 226. *See also* Peisistratids
Hippias of Elis, 76, 253 n. 4
Hippocratic Corpus, 14, 16, 18–20, 39, 41–42, **50–54**, 56–57, 61, **chs. 5–6**, 227, 229, 233–234. *See also* Index 2, "Passages in Other Authors"
Hippodameia, 57
Histiaeus of Miletus, 14, 34, 44, 46, 121, 194, 199–200, 225, 276 n. 22
historical consciousness, **15–17**, 78–79, 202, 228
historiē, 23
Hobbes, Thomas, 16, 116
Holmes, Brooke, 87
Homer: blame and blaming in, 35; and capacity for invention, 2; debt of historiography to, 2, 5, 12, 21, 61; echoes of, in Herodotus' first chapters, 22–23, 29, 107; episodes in Herodotus that echo or remold, 57, 122, 192, **202–204**, 213, 215, 234; and gods, 149; individualism in, 201–202; and orality, 61; revision in stride, 89–90, 108, 145 *See also* Index 2, "Passages in Other Authors"
Homeyer, Helene, 133

homoia kai anomoia. *See* similarities and dissimilarities
Honoré, Tony. *See* Hart, H. L. A., and Tony Honoré
Huber, Ludwig, 115
Hume, David, **40–41**, 46, 52, 56, 94, 247–248 n. 4
Hydarnes, 163, 175, 176
Hystaspes, 175, 187, 216

Idaeus, 35
ideology, 164, 181, 195, 202, 283 n. 3, 284 n. 9, 285 n. 1, 286 n. 10, 293 nn. 24–25
Inaros, 218, 220, 298 n. 28
India, 22, 78, 118, 142–143, 182
individuality and individualism, **ch. 14**
Intaphernes and his wife, 129, 130, 131
intertextuality, 57, 213, 215, **ch. 15(b)**, 234–235. *See also* Homer
Io, 25–28, 107
Ionia/Ionians: attacked and defeated by Croesus, 7, 106; at Bosporus, 139, 194; conquered and administered by Persia, 186, 193, 243 n. 73; in 480–479 BCE, 104, 177, 208, 286 n. 13; intellectual contributions of, 65, 237 n. 5; source of troubles of, 14, 219, 223. *See also* Ionian revolt
Ionian revolt: Aristagoras' role in, 92, 105, 121, 193; Athenian involvement in, 67, 121, 124, 192, 205–206; and Ionian decisions and debates, 34, 62, 65, 178, 190; and Ionian lack of resolve, 9, 177, 287 n. 17, 293 n. 24; Persian handling of, 193, 240 n. 35; Persian victory in, 117, 118, 163, 172, 176; and start of evils, 105, 219, 223
Ion of Chios, 59, 135
Irwin, Elizabeth, 217, 298 n. 17
Isagoras, 7, 196
isēgoriē/-ia, 138, 164, 184, 191, 193–194, 211, 285 n. 1, 292 n. 21
Isocrates, 280 n. 23
isokratiē, 193–194, 292 n. 16
isonomiē/-ia, 4, 84, 125, 179, 191, 193–194,

isonomiē̆l-ia (continued)
 196, 225, 238 n. 12, 285 n. 1, 291 n. 8,
 292 nn. 14, 16, 20, and 22
Istanbul, 210
Isthmus wall, 6, 42, 50, 56, 157, 170–171,
 221
Ithaca, 205

Jocasta, 194
Johnson, Mark. *See* Lakoff, George, and
 Mark Johnson
Jouanna, Jacques, 97

Kant, Immanuel, 52, 251 n. 41
King, Helen, 53–54
kinship, 15, 46
kleos, 22–23, 203–204
krisis, 81, 261 n. 15

Lade, 167, 172, 178–179, 182, 189,
 256 n. 56, 287 n. 17
Laius, 15
Lakoff, George, and Mark Johnson, 4
Lampon, 210
Lampsacus, 137. *See also* Charon
"league-table thinking," 95, 100–102,
 104, 105, 120
Lemnos, 206, 208
Leonidas, 135, **202–204**, 205, 210, 213,
 224, 228, 230, 234, 283 n. 5, 295 n. 19
Leontiades, 221
Leros, 65
Leutychidas, 108–109, 169, 207, 224, 230,
 266 n. 32
Lewis, David K., 248 n. 12, 252 n. 54
Libya/Libyans: culture of, 11, 77, 102; geography of, 65, 219, 248 n. 6; health of, 2, 18, 102; other writers on, 22, 65; Persian invasions of, 9–10, 31, 103, 104, **125–128**, 134, 163, 218
lieux de mémoire, 66
life-is-like-that explanations, 5, 21, 30, 46, 105, 228, 234
literacy. *See* writing
Livy, 200–201, 290 n.1, 294 n. 3
Lloyd, G. E. R., 88
Lloyd, Selwyn, 298 n. 24
"Longinus," 63–64

Lucretius, 61
luxury, 18, 74, 91–93, 170, 263 n. 47,
 296 n. 44. *See also* softness
Lycidas, 168
Lycophron (son of Periander), 144,
 278 n. 57
Lydia, 25, 91–93, 213, 239 n. 26, 271 n. 12,
 279 n. 5. *See also* Candaules and his
 unnamed wife; Croesus; Gyges; Xanthus of Lydia
Lysagoras, 10

Maeandrius of Samos, **124–125**, 179–180,
 191, 193–194, 196, 197, 211, 292 n. 14
Magi, 67, 257 n. 74
Magnesia, 158
Mantinea, 230
Mardonius: campaign of, 493–492 BCE,
 121, 134, 193; in 480 BCE, 138, 166, 167,
 180, 182; monarchic traits of, 135, 183,
 200, 289 n. 38; and Plataea battle, 173,
 210, 222; and preliminaries of Plataea campaign, 92, 102, 103, 169, 178,
 180, 207–208, 211; urges Xerxes to invade, 103, 104, 121–122, 136, 272 n. 35,
 276 n. 40
Marathon, battle of, 92, 167, 169–170,
 172–173, 182, 202–203, 206, 225; campaign of, 10, 134, 135, 147, 178, 188, 192,
 219; commemoration of, 15, 144, 202;
 divine phenomena at, 147, 168; Miltiades' speech before, 135, 166, 172, 185–
 186, 188–189, 196
Mascames of Doriscus, 220
Masistes and Masistes' unnamed wife,
 32–34, 108, 129, 222, 268 n. 15
Massagetae, 31, 92, 119, 137, 139, 141, 142,
 163
Mastyes, 121
Medea, 25–26, 107, 108
Medes: empire of, passes to Persians, 123,
 150–153, 175, 186, 280–281 n. 34; fight
 of, for freedom, 175, 211; invaded by
 Scythians, 119, 176–177; terrifying,
 92, 93, 170. *See also* Astyages; Deioces;
 Medizing; Phraortes
Mediterranean, 3, 65
Medizing, 3, 6, 42–44, 126–127, **177–178**,

186, 189, 206, 209, 239 n. 26, 287 n. 19 and 20
Megabates, 8, 210, 219
Megabyxus (son of Zopyrus), 218
Megabyxus (speaker in constitutions debate), 191, 193, 200, 291 n. 9
Megacles, 191, 219,
Megara, 40, 171
Megara Hyblaea, 239 n. 29
Meidias, 54–55, 251 n. 50
memory, collective and social, 59–61
Memphis, 63
Menelaus, 36–39, 73–75, 145, 246 n. 52
Menenius Agrippa, 238 n. 20
Messenia, 78, 222, 223
metaphor, 4–5, 184, 187, 189, 284 n. 17
Miletus: attacked by Lydian kings, 106; in Ionian revolt, 14, 143, 192, 193, 194, 219, 223, 290 n. 3, 292 n. 15; in Mycale campaign, 11; Phrynichus' *Fall of Miletus*, 197. *See also* Cadmus of Cos; Dionysius of Miletus; Hecataeus of Miletus; Histiaeus of Miletus; Thales of Miletus
Mill, John Stuart, **94–95**, 199, 201, 252 n. 52, 264 n. 1, 294 nn. 1–2
Miltiades: attacks Paros, 10, 205; and Herodotus' presentational strategy, 133, 135, 199, 206, 208, 210, 228, 296 n. 31; at Marathon, 135, 166, 172, 185, 188, 189, 196, 197, 202, 293–294 n. 31; trials of, 192, 196, 197, 206; as tyrant of Chersonese, 135, 135, 194, 208
Milton, John, and *Paradise Lost*, 113
mimesis, 11, 112–113, 155–156, 181, 232–233, 270 n. 37, 282 n. 52
Mimnermus, 59
Minyans, 219
Mitradates, 150
Mitrobates, 124–125
Mnesiphilus, 171
"modeling," historical, **16–17**, 78–79, 144, 242 n. 62
modus tollendo tollens, 41–44, 69, 74, 81, 233, 248 n. 6, 257 n. 77
Moles, John, 231
Momigliano, Arnaldo, 58, 67, 133–134, 232–236

motive-statements, 11
Mt. Athos, 117, 158–159, 288 n. 27
Munson, Rosaria 24
Mycale, 11, 134, 149, 170, 222, 296 n. 33
Mycene, 242 n. 55
Myres, John, 1, 24
Myrmidons, 35, 201–202
myth: echoing or remolding of, 57, 267 n. 11, 272 n. 20; making sense of present, 16, 67, 225, 278 n. 57; rationalizing of, 28, 38, 63–64, 107, 150, 255 n. 41, 267 n. 5; *spatium mythicum*?, 38, 246–247 n. 53

"narrative codes," 47–55
narrative shape, **ch. 9(a)–(b)**, **ch. 14(b)**, 187–188, 233
Nasser, General Abdel, 218
nature, humans against, 117, 122–123, 157–158, 282 n. 50
Naxos, 8, 14, 132, 143, 219, 221
Nazism, 55
Neaera, 54
Neoptolemus, 38
Nicias, 144, 217, 226, 262 n. 31, 298 n. 20, 300 n. 8
Nicolaus of Damascus, 108, 267 n. 9
Nile: flooding of, 2, 6, 41, 43, 46, 53, 228; Hecataeus on, 2, 41, 62, 64, 65; other writers on, 66, 67, 256 n. 65; silting up of, 24, 46, 229; symmetry of, with Danube, 2, 3, 20, 43, 45–46, 77, 237 n. 6
Nitetis, 131
nomos, 78, 99, 123, 165, 172, 228, 242 n. 68, 265 n. 17, 277 n. 54, 284 n. 9. *See also physis*
"novella," 129–133, 144

obscurum per obscurius, 65
Ocean, 2, 41, 64–65, 237 n. 8
Odysseus, 29, 35, 149, 201–202, 204–205, 297 n. 2; in Gorgias, 73; in Hellanicus, 67; in Sophocles, 38
Oebares, 207, 211, 275 n. 9
Oedipus, 18, 70. *See also* Sophocles
Oeobazus, 119, 272 n. 24

356   GENERAL INDEX

"Old Oligarch" (ps.-Xenophon, *Ath. pol.*), 186, 291 n. 9, 292 nn. 16 and 21
Olympia/Olympic games, 166, 178, 180, 281 n. 40
Onomacritus, 121
opera, 130, 275 n. 6
oracles, Herodotus' treatment of, 149, 161, 162, 280 n. 22. *See also* Branchidae; Delphi; Dodona
oral tradition, 59–61, 130, 134, 235, 251 n. 49, 253 nn. 16–19, 254 nn. 27–29, 276 n. 23, 284 n. 13
Orchomenus, 183
Oreithyia, 158
Orestheus, 64
Oroetes, 34, 124–125
Otanes, 124–125, 131, 179, **193–194**, 290 n. 56

Pactyes, 67, 239 n. 26
Paeonia, 121
Palamedes, 73–74
Pan, 147, 148, 168
Pandarus, 35
Panyassis, 58
Paris: in Euripides, 73–4; in Gorgias, 72; in Herodotus, 25–26, 31, 36–38, 107; in Homer, 35, 105, 145, 281 n. 45
Parmenides, 4
Parnassus, 148
Paros, 10, 205, 208, 221
parrhesia, 138
Patroclus, 35, 201, 203, 240 n. 36, 284 n. 17
Pausanias (character in Plato's *Symposium*), 76
Pausanias (regent of Sparta), 133, 135, 179, 210; later aspirations and disgrace of, 143, 207, **209–210**, 219, 221; in Plataea campaign, 172–173, 177, 200; in Thucydides, 209, 212; unimpressed by Spartan food, 92, **170**, 210, 211, 223
payback, 7–8, **ch. 2(c)**, 105, 109, 114–115, 124–125, 142, 146, 147, 224, 246 n. 51. *See also tisis*
Peisistratids, 44, 103, 121, 185, 194, 196, 197, 226. *See also* Hippias
Peisistratus, 179, 191–192, 205, 208, 286 n. 16

Pelasgians, 60, 64, 137, 206
Peloponnese, 42, 43, 56, 171, 178, 182, 186, 217, 230, 290 n. 53
Pelops, 57, 122
Periander, 7, 115, 133, 144, 206, 270 n. 2, 278 n. 57
Pericles, 40, 69–70, 192, 193, 200, 219–220, 225, 226; in Thucydides, 49, 86–87, 93, 164, 231, 263 n. 48, 278 nn. 59 and 61, 286 n. 41
Perinthos, 136, 175
Perry, Ben, 101
Phaedra, 15
Phaedymië, 131, 275 n. 12
Phanes, 121
Phano, 54
Pheidippides, 147, 148
Pherecydes of Athens, 22, 66, 67, 256 n. 69, 257 n. 71
Pheretime, **125–128**, 146, 147, 156
Phlious, 178
Phocis, 3, 44–46, 50, 56, 177, 186
Phoenicians, 24–28, 138, 139
Phoenix, 35
Phraortes, 136
Phrygia, 63, 122, 288 n. 31
Phrynichus (Athenian politician), 190
Phrynichus (playwright), 197
Phye, 191, 208
Phylacus, 147
physis, 27, 76, 77–78, 81, 99, 228, 237 n. 8, 265 n. 17. *See also nomos*
Pigres, 121
Pindar, 206
Piraeus, 226
Pittacus, 12, 114, 117, 118, 137, 142, 270
Plataea: aftermath of battle of, 92, 149, 170, 177, 204, 209–210, 223; Athenian alliance with, 135, 226–227, 293 n. 29; battle of, 92, 103, 128, 165, 167, 170, 200, 222; divine aspects of, 148, 169, 280 n. 19, 284 n. 13; preliminaries of campaign in, 180, 184, 227, 283 n. 5, 287 n. 24; in Simonides, 59, 202; and Spartan indiscipline, 172, 181, 182; in Thucydides, 68, 72, 74, 75, 105, 192, 195, 221, 227, 228, 230
platitudes, value of, 14, 39, 46, 241 n. 49
Plato, 4, 76–77, 78, 84, 90, 187, 242 n. 62,

244 n. 11, 253 n. 11, 262 n. 25, 278 n. 63. *See also* Index 2, "Passages in Other Authors"
Player, Gary, 260 n. 10
Plutarch, 135, 169, 206, 247 n. 58, 251 n. 44, 279 n. 7, 280 n. 19, 284 n. 13, 293 n. 27, 294–295 n. 5, 295 nn. 19 and 30. *See also* Index 2, "Passages in Other Authors"
pollution and purification, 69, 70–71, 239 n. 27, 272 n. 24
Polybius, 13, 14, 104–105, 162, 186, 232, 257 n. 77, 289 n. 50, 290 n. 53. *See also* Index 2, "Passages in Other Authors"
Polycrates of Samos: fall of, **34**, 124, 179; and the story of the ring, 12, 111, 144, 146, 268 n. 24, 274 n. 5; tyranny, 115, 282 n. 49
polyphony, 16, 101, 233
Popper, Karl, 53, 237–238 n. 10, 250 n. 27, 251 n. 45, 252 n. 54
Poseidon, 35, 239 n. 25, 281 n. 45
Potidaea, 6, 104, 158, 239 n. 25, 262 n. 22, 299–300 n. 48
predictability and explicability, 15, 32, **48–50**, 53, 81, 118, 123, 162, 167–168, 189, 198, 229–231, 235–236, 237–238 n. 10, 241 n. 52, 250 nn. 27–32
predisposition and trigger, 9–10, 82–84, 94–99, 104–105, 128, 159–160, 240 nn. 33 and 36, 264 n. 2
preemptive strikes, 103, 116, 118
Prexaspes, 10–11
Priam: and Achilles, 21, 145, 156, 213; and Helen, 35, 70; and the infant Paris, 73
Priene, 106. *See also* Bias of Priene
"prisoners of history?," 123, 140–142, 143, 200
prisoners of war, 286 n. 15
Procles, 7
progressive correction. *See* revision in stride
Prometheus, 79
Pronoia, temple of, 148
prophasis: in Herodotus, **8–10**, 11, 13, 126, 240 nn. 32–36, 255 n. 48; in Hippocratics, 51, 64, **82–83**, 95, 98–99, 261 nn. 18–22; in other authors, 239 n. 31, 241 n. 45

proschema, 8, **9–10**, 13, 103–104, 125, 240 n. 35
Protagoras, 16, 69–70, 72, 78
Protesilaus, 215
Proteus, 36–39, 143
provisionality of explanations, 4, 11, **52–54**, 89, 113, 152, 229, 231, 233–234, 238 n. 19, 251 n. 45. *See also* revision in stride
Psammetichus, 63
Pteria, 117, 118
"publication" date, **215–218**
purification, see pollution
Pylos, 56, 230
Pythagoras, 76
Pythius, 119–20, 176, 272 n. 24

Raaflaub, Kurt, 175, 191, 285 n. 2, 291 n. 6
rationalization. *See* myth
reciprocity. *See* payback
Reinhardt, Karl, 130, 132, 133, 141, 145, 151, 159, 274 n. 1, 280 n. 25
religion and religious explanations, 16, 78, 97–98, 107–108, **ch. 10**, 168–169, 230, 239 n. 27, 257 n. 82, 264 n. 13, 265 nn. 15–16, 277 n. 50, 279 nn. 6 and 14, 282 n. 52, 286 n. 12
remembrancers, 15, 242 n. 55
revision in stride, 24, 26, **ch. 5(c)**, 106, 107, 108, 120–121, 211–212, 234–235, 266–267 n. 3, 299 n. 41
Rhampsinitus, 207
Rhegium, 221, 223
ring composition, 29, 115, 265 n. 19, 271 n. 7
river boundaries, 117, 141
Rousseau, Jean-Jacques, 16
Rowe, Christopher, 101

Sabacos, 240 n. 34
Sadyattes, 106, 267 n. 9
Saguntum, 105
Saïd, Edward, 132, 143
Salamis, battle of, 170, 172, 173, 177–178; in Aeschylus, 174–175; Greek debate before, 138, 143, 161, 170–171, **183–185**, 224, 283 n. 5; Persian debate before, 138, 143, **182–183**; preliminaries of, 135, 146, 147, 167, 208; responses to, 138,

Salamis, battle of (*continued*)
167, 208, 223; in Simonides, 59; tactics at, 165, 170–171; Xerxes' viewing of, 130
Sallust, 290 n.1
Samos: and Corinth, 44, 56, 226, 299 n. 47; in Ionian Revolt, 9; Maeandrius and experiment with freedom in, **124–125**, **179–180**, 189, 191, 193–194, 196, 197, 211, 287 n. 23, 292 n. 14; Persian conquest of, 8, 124–125, 136–137; revolt of, from Athens, 217, 299 nn. 44 and 47. *See also* Polycrates of Samos
Sancisi-Weerdenburg, Heleen, 132, 133
Sandanis, 12, 91–92, 103, 137, 142, 170, 266 n. 28
Sardinia, 186
Sardis, 31, 118, 129, 207, 239 n. 26, 271 n. 16
Satan, 113
Sataspes, 219
scientific and historical explanations, 3, 14–15, 26, 41, **ch. 3(b)**, 56–57, 58, 66, **chs. 5–6**, 229, 237–238 n. 10, 238 n. 15, 249 n. 25, 250 nn. 27 and 30, 251 n. 50, 265 n. 22
Scylax, Ps.-, 65
Scyles, 146, 240 n. 33
Scythia/Scythians: Cleomenes perhaps learned hard drinking from, 160; contempt of, for Ionians, 177, 287 n. 17; Darius' campaign against, 8, 12, **118–119**, 123, 137, 139, 163, 176–177, 194; and empire, 176–177, 288 n. 28; ethnography of, 31, 53, 77, 240 n. 33, 243 n. 74, 259 n. 109, 295–296 n. 5; geography of, 64, 249 n. 21, 255 n. 52; other writers on, 42, 64, **97–98**, 100, 255 n. 52
Selbstsicherheit. *See* self-certainty
self-certainty, 116, **ch. 9(d)**
Sesostris, 177
Sestos, 214
Shakespeare, William: *Coriolanus*, 238 n. 20; *King Lear*, 47
Sicily, 40, 50, 69, 134, 235, 249 n. 19, 299 n. 48. *See also* Gelon of Syracuse
Sicinnus, 171, 180
Sicyon, 178

similarities and dissimilarities (*homoia kai anomoia*), 51–55, 68, **ch. 4(e)**, 82, 120, 227, 232, 234. *See also* East and West, contrasts and similarities between
Simonides, 15, 59, 202, 284 n. 13
Siris, 171, 183, 185
"situational irony," 218, 277 n. 52
Smerdis, 11, 130, 207
Smyrna, 59, 106
Soclees of Corinth, 137, 185, 190, 193, 194, 196, 226, 289 n. 48
Socrates, 61, 76, 292 n. 20
softness, 11, 18, 91–93, 165, 170, 173, 179, 199, 211, 234, 263 n. 41, 284 n. 18. *See also* luxury
Solon: meeting of, with Croesus, 30, 49, **110–111**, 114, 118, 138, 166, 214, 245 n. 38, 268 n. 22, 270 n. 2; travels of, 9, 30, 76, 245 n. 38; wisdom of, recalled in later narrative, 12, **111–113**, 120, 142, 153, 156, 268 n. 24, 269 n. 26, 282 n. 49
Sophanes, 216, 222, 298 n. 16
Sophocles: *Antigone*, 16, 129; *Oedipus at Colonus*, 70; *Oedipus Rex*, 15–16, 280 n. 25; *Philoctetes*, 38. *See also* Index 2, "Passages in Other Authors"
source material affecting Herodotus' narrative, 38, 68, 130, 132–134, 247 n. 57, 254 nn. 27 and 36, 276 n. 23
Spako, 150–151
Spanish Armada, 159
Sparta: and Argos, 159–160, 179; court intrigue and dispute over succession in, 20, 108–109, 135, 144, 160, 197, 198, 207, 209; after 479 BCE, 187, 209–210, **ch. 15**; and Ionian revolt, 169, 192, 205; and Marathon, 178; and Messenia, 78, 222–223; in mid-sixth century, 115; national characteristics of, 166, 172–173, 205, **ch. 14(e)**, 223–224, 230, 277–278 n. 55, 284 nn. 9, 14, and 18, 285 n. 24, 288 n. 35; before Peloponnesian War, 40, 232; in Peloponnesian War, 56, 189, 206, 212, **ch. 15**, 286 n. 12; and Plataea, 74, 227–228; and Plataea campaign, 168, 170, 172–

173, 181, 182, 184, 200; role of, in removing Peisistratids, 44, 209; and Salamis campaign, 50, 170, 178–179, 184, 187, 207, 217; and Samos, 137; temptation in, to restore Peisistratids, 137, 185, 191, 193–196, 212; and Thermopylae, 166, **203–204**, 249 n. 22; and Xerxes' heralds, 101–102, 143, 147, 163–164, 175, 176, 220, 224. See also Cleomenes; Demaratus; Leonidas; Leutychidas; Pausanias

spatium historicum?, 246–247 n. 53
Sperthies, 220
Stesichorus, 38, 247 n. 57
Stesimbrotus of Thasos, 59, 134
Sthenelaidas, 227
Stoa Poikile, 15, 59, **202**, 295 n. 10
Stobaeus, 84
Strymon, 158, 159
Suez Canal, 218
Susa, 44, 159, 220, 222
Syloson, 8, 124, 125, 298–299 n. 31
Syme, Ronald, 56
Syracuse, 50
Syria, 117, 239 n. 30

Tacitus, 28, 150, 232, 298 n. 31
Taenarum, 63
Tanagra, 222, 223
Taras, 221, 223, 249 n. 21
Tegea, 184, 219, 222. See also Chileos of Tegea
Teisamenus, 222
Teisias, 69, 257 n. 79
Telesarchus of Samos, 179
Telmessus, 118
Thales of Miletus, 76, 117, 256 n. 65, 259 n. 116, 270 n. 2
Thebes, Boeotian, 169, 183, 210, 213, 269 n. 28; Medism of, 177, 210, 239 n. 26; in Peloponnesian War and in Thucydides, 72, 74–75, 221, 225, 227, 230, 286 n. 12
Thebes, Egyptian, 62
Themistocles: and Athens and democracy, 205–206, 208–209, 211–212; before Artemisium, 169, 177, 221; before Salamis, 143, **170–171**, 173, **183–185**, 208; "biostructuring"?, 133–136; and gods, 161, 279 n. 7, 281 n. 63; as "Great Man," 199, 210, 228; like Odysseus, 204–205, 211; persuades Athenians to spend money on ships, 188, 192, 208, 276 n. 35, 290 n. 57; response of, to Salamis, 161, 208–209, 221–222; rivalry of, with Aristeides before 480, 135, 196, 197; subsequent career of, 205–207, 210, 221, 223, 275 n. 7

Thermopylae: Demaratus' remarks prepare for, 166, 203–205; and Ephialtes shows Xerxes the path, 7, 102; Greek tactics and heroism at, 165, 172, 202–205, 285 n. 21 and 24, 289 n. 42; Herodotus' presentation on battle of, **202–4**, 221, 222, 225, 230, 234, 285 n. 21; lasting memories of, 203–204; and Persian whips, 181; preliminaries to, 165, 172; sequel to, at Sparta, 204, 224, 249 n. 22; Xerxes' response to, 166

Thersites, 35
Theseus, 191, 202, 216, 255 n. 41, 273 n. 37
Thessaly/Thessalians, 2, 3, 44, 50, 56, 103, 121, 134, 177, 186, 207, 219
Thomas, Rosalind, 2, 42
Thonis, 38
Thrace, 76, 178, 182, 220, 222, 223
Thrasybulus (tyrant of Miletus), 206
Thucydides: alluding to Herodotus?, 62, 141, 234–235; on Athens, 18, 86, 144, 164, 189, 190, 205–206, 211–212; on balancing and blending, 86–88; on blaming, 124, 286 nn. 12–13; on causes of war, 40, 104–105, 232, 234–235; on democracy, 194, 209; on empire, 186, 286 n. 14; on human nature, 145, 212, 231; on national characteristics, 210–211; on Pausanias and Themistocles, 206, 210; on Persia, 230; and Plataean debate, 68, 72–75, 227; on predictability, 49, 231; and revision in stride, 90, 120–121, 211–212, 235; on sea-power, 46; and underdetermined events, 50; vocabulary of, for explanation, 83, 261 n. 22; writing for posterity, 231, 236. See also Index 2, "Passages in Other Authors"

Thyestes, 114, 277 nn. 50, 62
Timegenides, 239 n. 26
Timodemus of Aphidnae, 207, 210
Tiryns, 242 n. 55
tisis, 4, 20, 30, 31–32, 36, 86, 160, 219, 243 n. 75. *See also* payback
Tomyris, 119, 141
trigger. *See* predisposition and trigger
Tritantaichmes, 166, 169, 281 n. 40
Troezen, 178
Trojan War, 3, 14, 15, 25–26, **35–38**, 72–75, 109, 146–149, 175, 202, 215, 246 n. 50. *See also* Homer
Twain, Mark, 12
tyranny: best explored under stress, 88; and democracy, 78, 86–87, 93, 144, 164, 184, 189, **191–198**, 206, 234–236, 278 n. 59, 286 n. 14, 294 n. 34; as "despotic template?," 53–54, 109–110, 112, 113, 116, 123, 139, 143–144, 157, 282 n. 50; and difficulty of talking, 110–111, 137–138; effect of, on subjects' character, 19–20, 77–78, 81, 164, 169, 177, 185; and freedom, 191, **194–196**, 231; Herodotus' readiness to give credit to, 177, 286 nn. 15–16; as model of extreme, 144, 197–198, 231, 278 n. 57; sexual transgression as typical of, 32, 107, 116
Tyre, 25

unifocal models, 18, 31, 33, 38, 83–84, 85, 90, 116, 128, 169, 170, 233

Vansina, Jan, 60, 247 n. 53, 254 nn. 27–30
Vernant, Jean-Pierre, 79
Versailles, Treaty of, 47
Versnel, Henk, 268–269 n. 25
"virtual history." *See* counterfactual thinking
vocabulary for causation and explanation: in Herodotus, 5–11; in Hippocratics, 82–83. *See also* *aitiē*; *prophasis*; *proschēma*
"voiceprint," 5, 68, 298 n. 26

Wall Street crash, 55
West and East. *See* East and West, contrasts and similarities between
whips, 117–118, **181–182**, 183, 211, 288 nn. 27–28
White, Hayden, 249 n. 25
William the Conqueror, 40–41, 46
writing, 59–61

Xanthippus, 196, 214
Xanthus of Lydia, 66, 67, 108, 253 n. 16, 267 n. 9
Xenophanes, 16, 61, 76
Xenophon, 76, 91, 132, 144, 278 n. 62. *See also* Index 2, "Passages in Other Authors"
Xerxes: blaming or not blaming individuals, 7, 45–46, 218–219; conspiracy against, 33; and conversations and debates, 12, 165–166, **181–183**, 249 n. 18, 288 n. 37; and court, ch. 9; and destruction of shrines, 168–169; dream of, and second thoughts about invasion, 137, 139–140, **153–156**, 281 n. 38; and invasion of Greece, 3, 12, 102, 104, **121–123**, 157–158 and *passim*; like or unlike predecessors, 12, 116–117, 119–122; magnanimity of, 220, 224; and Masistes' wife, **32–34**, 108, 129, 222; moments of insight of, 128, 141, 181–182, 188, 199, 200; succession of, to throne, 103, 129

Zeus, 28, 74, 108, 141, 157, 271 n. 6; Zeus Eleutherios at Samos, 179, 191, 196, 287 n. 22
Zopyrus (father of Megabyxus), 207, 211, 218
Zopyrus (son of Megabyxus), 218

www.ingramcontent.com/pod-product-compliance
Lightning Source LLC
Chambersburg PA
CBHW032012300426
44117CB00008B/997